Microsoft Office™
2010
PRODUCTIVITY STRATEGIES FOR TODAY AND TOMORROW

Jean Kotsiovos, MA
Carolyne Faddis, MS
Loralyn Duley, MS

JONES & BARTLETT
LEARNING

World Headquarters
Jones & Bartlett Learning
5 Wall Street
Burlington, MA 01803
978-443-5000
info@jblearning.com
www.jblearning.com

Jones & Bartlett Learning books and products are available through most bookstores and online booksellers. To contact Jones & Bartlett Learning directly, call 800-832-0034, fax 978-443-8000, or visit our website, www.jblearning.com.

Substantial discounts on bulk quantities of Jones & Bartlett Learning publications are available to corporations, professional associations, and other qualified organizations. For details and specific discount information, contact the special sales department at Jones & Bartlett Learning via the above contact information or send an email to specialsales@jblearning.com.

Production Credits
Executive Publisher: Kevin Sullivan
Senior Developmental Editor: Amy Bloom
Director of Production: Amy Rose
Production Editor: Keith Henry
Marketing Manager: Lindsay White
V.P., Manufacturing and Inventory Control: Therese Connell
Composition: Aptara®, Inc.
Cover and Title Page Design: Michael O'Donnell
Rights & Photo Research Assistant: Miranda Rivers
Cover Image: © Ljupco Smokovski/Dreamstime.com
Printing and Binding: Courier Companies
Cover Printing: Courier Companies

To order this product, use ISBN: 978-1-4496-9821-8

Library of Congress Cataloging-in-Publication Data
Kotsiovos, Jean.
  Microsoft Office 2010 : productivity strategies for today and tomorrow / Jean Kotsiovos, Carolyne Faddis, Loralyn Duley.
    p. cm.
  Includes index.
  ISBN 978-1-4496-7944-6
  1. Microsoft Office 2. Business—Computer programs. I. Faddis, Carolyne. II. Duley, Loralyn. III. Title.
  HF5548.4.M525K7297 2014
  005.5—dc23
                                                                          2012029908

6048

Printed in the United States of America
17 16 15 14 13   10 9 8 7 6 5 4 3 2 1

Dedication

We respectfully dedicate this book to everyone tuning in to the digital world. This book is for all of you! However, for those of you who are nervous about computers, please know that you are foremost in our hearts and minds. We won't leave you behind.

We also gratefully acknowledge our teaching and writing community. To our fellow professionals—both those who came before us and those who will take our places—we sincerely appreciate your generous efforts to promote the art and science of teaching in its ever-changing incarnations.

Table of Contents

2 Create Documents Using Microsoft Word 2010 55

3 Enhance a Microsoft Word 2010 Document 129

4 Create Presentations Using Microsoft PowerPoint 2010 195

5 Modify Presentations Using Microsoft PowerPoint 2010 247

6 Create Workbooks Using Microsoft Excel 2010 321

7 Create Formulas, Charts, and Tables . . . 373

8 Create Databases Using Microsoft Access 2010 435

9 Create Forms, Queries, and Reports . . . 485

Preface

We are so excited to release this first edition of *Microsoft Office 2010: Productivity Strategies for Today and Tomorrow*. This textbook is designed for use in an introductory course on Microsoft Office applications. By reading the textbook and completing the hands-on exercises and activities that are included in each chapter, you will become proficient in multiple Microsoft Office 2010 applications.

Our long-term record of success introducing diverse learners to computers compelled us to write this book. We understand the areas that challenge learners and recognize the frustration that unclear directions and the assumption of familiarity can cause. This book is based on the comments and recommendations of the thousands of students we have encountered during our teaching careers.

Our strategy in this book is to divide each objective into targeted, small activities designed to simplify the learning process and allow you to complete the exercises at your own pace. The chapters provide step-by-step instructions along with plenty of screenshots to help you complete the exercises. The steps are clearly formatted so that you can easily refer back to the text for help while creating your own projects. Once you have mastered the techniques in these pages, this text will be a valuable strategic and systematic resource for your desk.

With decades of experience explaining technical subjects to nontechnical readers in a myriad of online and classroom situations, we know that it is best to teach students to craft usable materials that will inspire them to create projects of their own. Furthermore, your finished projects will be an impressive portfolio that will demonstrate to prospective employers your knowledge and experience. You will craft an effective cover letter, promote your organization, create a budget that you can actually use, and much more. And with Microsoft Office 2010, you will be able to complete this work quickly and easily.

Start simply and take it one step at a time. With that philosophy, anyone can succeed.

Key Features

Microsoft Office 2010: Productivity Strategies for Today and Tomorrow:

- Easily adapts to both campus and online learning environments by providing explicit details that students will need to complete each task, whether or not they are in an actual classroom
- Includes full-color screenshots that provide visual assistance in completing all hands-on exercises
- Asks readers to complete relevant real world projects within chapters and as end-of-chapter exercises
- Teaches skills that are widely used in businesses and at home, which enable students to create useful reports, documents, spreadsheets, and presentations
- Reinforces chapter objectives through multiple-choice questions and projects at the end of each chapter
- Includes definitions of key terms in chapter margins for easy reference, as well as a comprehensive glossary at the end of the text
- Provides additional online resources for students and instructors that help to reinforce key topics from the text

Summary of Chapters

Chapter 1 Microsoft Office Fundamentals

Chapter 1 presents the common elements, commands, and features of Microsoft Office 2010 applications. You will learn how to create, save, print, and open a document, as well as how to navigate within the application window. We discuss these commonalities in detail so you can hit the ground running.

Chapter 2 Create Documents Using Microsoft Word 2010

Microsoft Word 2010 is a word processing application used to create professional-looking documents, including letters, memos, newsletters, brochures, flyers, and resumes. Chapter 2 begins with a discussion of the basic commands. You will learn how to create a cover letter and format the document to give it a professional appearance. You will also create a memo from a template.

Chapter 3 Enhance a Microsoft Word 2010 Document

Chapter 3 goes deeper and describes how to enhance a Microsoft Word 2010 document by adding visual objects to engage the reader and communicate information more effectively. In this chapter, you will learn to insert and modify visual objects such as pictures, clip art, and WordArt; create a marketing brochure for an innovative recreational facility; insert and modify tables; add headers and footers; insert hyperlinks; and apply page layout commands such as margins, tabs, and page breaks.

Chapter 4 Create Presentations Using Microsoft PowerPoint 2010

Microsoft PowerPoint 2010 is used to create presentations that are shared with an audience in the form of a slide show. Chapter 4 walks you through how to create presentations in just a few minutes. In this chapter, you will create a presentation that includes clip art, tables, WordArt, and a theme; insert and format text and paragraphs; modify slide layouts; and navigate between slides. You will also learn how to print handouts of a presentation and how to navigate a slide show.

Chapter 5 Modify Presentations Using Microsoft PowerPoint 2010

A presentation would not be complete without the addition of visual effects. In Chapter 5, you will learn how to create a presentation that includes images and illustrations such as clip art, pictures, SmartArt, text boxes, and shapes; insert backgrounds; add slide transitions and animation effects to enhance the presentation; delete and organize slides; insert hyperlinks; insert audio clips; and insert headers and footers.

Chapter 6 Create Workbooks Using Microsoft Excel 2010

Microsoft Excel 2010 is a spreadsheet application used to organize, manipulate, and chart data. It can be used to track income and expenses, perform mathematical calculations, and analyze data to make informed decisions. In Chapter 6, you will create a household budget while learning to navigate within a workbook, enter and modify data, modify column and row settings, and calculate totals. You will also format your workbook to give it a professional appearance.

Chapter 7 Create Formulas, Charts, and Tables

Chapter 7 explores how to create formulas to perform mathematical calculations in Microsoft Excel 2010. In this chapter, you will create formulas, use functions, create and modify charts, and format cells as a table. You will also create a sales commissions report and manipulate the data in order to make effective business decisions, learn about sorting and filtering data, and learn how to apply conditional formatting.

Chapter 8 Create Databases Using Microsoft Access 2010

Microsoft Access 2010 is a database management system used to store and maintain large amounts of data. Chapter 8 explains how to locate and retrieve data in a matter of seconds. In this chapter, you will learn how to create a database, create a table, add records to a table, and navigate between the records in a table. In the real-world example presented in this chapter, you will design and use a database for a medical center.

Chapter 9 Create Forms, Queries, and Reports

Chapter 9 describes how to create forms, queries, and reports with Microsoft Access 2010. You will be introduced to wizards that can be used to create database objects. You will also learn how to create relationships between tables as well as how to manipulate data using sorting and filtering commands.

Chapter 10 Integrate Projects Using Microsoft Office 2010 Applications

In Chapter 10 you will use all the knowledge you've attained about the individual applications and pull it all together. A benefit of using Microsoft Office 2010 applications is that data can be shared between applications through the Object Linking and Embedding (OLE) technology. In this chapter, you will learn how to embed and link data.

Additional Resources

Every new copy of the text includes access to the companion website *Microsoft Office 2010: Productivity Strategies for Today and Tomorrow*. The website, available at <u>go.jblearning.com/ MSOffice2010</u>, provides audio/visual tutorials, web links, practice quizzes, and additional resources to reinforce understanding of key topics presented in the text.

The companion website also includes the **student data files** required to complete the hands-on-exercises and projects included in the text. You can download and save the student data files to your computer or an external device. We recommend that you create a separate folder to store these files. Make certain to note where the files are saved.

PowerPoint lecture outlines, answers to end-of-chapter questions and projects, and a test bank are available for free instructor download. To request access, please visit www.jblearning.com or contact your account representative.

Acknowledgments

The Authors would like to acknowledge the family, friends, and coworkers who have graciously supported them.

I would like to thank my family for their encouragement and support while I was working on this project. To my parents, Angelos and Vasiliki Changas, who taught me the meaning of hard work and the importance of attaining my goals. To my husband, Chris Kotsiovos, and my children, Georgia and Peter, who have encouraged me in the writing of this textbook and have always motivated me to do my best. And a special thanks to Georgia, who reviewed the textbook, created various resources, and provided valuable feedback.

Jean Kotsiovos

I would like to thank my husband, Jack, who listened to my concerns and offered his advice; my sister, Marolyne, who encouraged me while I worked on the project, and my three sons, Michael, John, and Christopher, who mean the world to me.

Carolyne Faddis

For my parents, Flora and Clarence Duley, who worked so hard so that I could have so much. To my brother, Jeff Duley, whose faith in me made me believe that all of this was possible. Finally, for my late husband, Ron Browne, who thought being a computer teacher was pretty cool.

Lora Duley

About the Authors

Jean Kotsiovos is the Executive Director of Curriculum for Kaplan University. Jean is currently pursuing her PhD in Business Administration with a concentration in Applied Computer Science. She earned a master's degree in Education and a bachelor's degree in Business Administration—Information and Decision Sciences.

Jean began her career as a computer programmer/analyst. She decided to share her passion for computers as an evening adjunct instructor, teaching software applications, programming, and web design courses, and it was then that she realized that education was her passion. Since then, Jean has worked in various positions in higher education as an instructor, program coordinator, department chair, and assistant dean. Jean has served as an author, contributing author, and technical editor on various textbooks and has extensive experience in curriculum development, instructional design, and teaching. A resident of Illinois, she enjoys traveling and spending time with her husband, her two children, and her dog.

Carolyne Faddis is an Assistant Professor at Northwestern College. She earned a master's degree in Education and a bachelor's degree in Business Education. Carolyne began her teaching career at the high school level where she taught business courses. She retired from teaching to raise a family, but during that time she managed her husband's law office; it was there that her interest in computer technology began. When her oldest son entered college, she returned to higher education as an instructor at Northwestern College, where she has held various positions as a program coordinator, online instructor, and, currently, as an assistant instructor. Carolyne resides in Illinois with her husband. She enjoys spending time with her family, including three sons and four young grandchildren, who fortunately live nearby.

Loralyn Duley is the Curriculum Manager for the School of Information Technology at Kaplan University. She earned a master's degree in Higher Education with an emphasis on teaching and learning. She also holds a bachelor of science degree in Speech Communications. Lora began her teaching career as an adjunct instructor for computer classes.

The urge for adventure and a giving spirit led Lora to Juneau, Alaska, to work as an AmeriCorps Vista volunteer, where one of her responsibilities was managing the organization's website. In order to fulfill those tasks she studied web design at the University of Alaska, which sparked and cultivated her interest in design and adult-learning theory. Lora has extensive experience in teaching, instructional design, and curriculum development. Lora now lives in Illinois, where she enjoys volunteering and traveling.

Microsoft Office Fundamentals

Chapter Objectives

After completing this chapter, you will be able to do the following:

- Launch Microsoft Office 2010 applications.
- Identify parts of an application window.
- Open an existing document.
- Navigate within an application window.
- Identify common features available in Microsoft Office 2010 applications.
- Select text.
- Save a document.
- Print a document.
- Work with multiple applications.
- Close a document.
- Exit an application.

Microsoft Office 2010 contains various applications, which are commonly referred to as programs. **Applications** are software **programs** that help users perform specific tasks to increase their productivity.

This textbook will provide you with the skills to become knowledgeable with four of the Microsoft Office 2010 applications (**Table 1.1**). These applications are widely used in businesses and for personal use to create various reports, documents, spreadsheets, databases, and presentations.

Applications: Software programs that help users perform specific tasks.

Programs: Software applications that help users perform specific tasks.

Microsoft Access 2010: Application used to create databases to track and report information.

Microsoft Excel 2010: Application used to create spreadsheets that consist primarily of numbers that can be manipulated to help make decisions. Charts can be created based on the data in the spreadsheet.

Microsoft PowerPoint 2010: Application used to create presentations to engage the audience.

Microsoft Word 2010: Application used to create professional-looking documents that consist primarily of text and graphics.

Graphical user interface (GUI): Allows the user to communicate and interact with the application through the use of graphical elements such as icons, buttons, and menus.

Start menu: Displays a list of commonly used programs installed on the computer.

Start button: A button located at the bottom-left corner of the desktop that opens the Start menu.

Table 1.1 Microsoft Office 2010 Applications	
Application	Description
Microsoft Access 2010	Create databases to track and report information.
Microsoft Excel 2010	Create spreadsheets that consist primarily of numbers that can be manipulated to help make decisions.
	Create charts based on the data in the spreadsheet.
Microsoft PowerPoint 2010	Create presentations to engage the audience.
Microsoft Word 2010	Create professional-looking documents that consist primarily of text and graphics.

Microsoft Office 2010 has a graphical user interface (GUI), which allows the user to communicate and interact with the application through the use of graphical elements such as icons, buttons, and menus.

The GUI provides a consistent design and layout within the Microsoft Office 2010 applications. For example, the save command uses the same button and is located in the same location in all Microsoft Office 2010 applications. Once you learn one application, you can apply many of the skills you learned to the other applications. This is a benefit of using Microsoft Office 2010 applications.

In this chapter, you will learn about the common elements contained in Microsoft Office 2010 applications and the graphical user interface. You will become familiar with terms used to identify various parts and features of the applications.

Launch a Microsoft Office 2010 Application

Microsoft Office 2010 applications can be launched (opened) from the Start menu, which is accessed by clicking the **Start** button located at the bottom-left corner of the desktop.

Use these steps to launch an application:

- Click the Start button on the desktop (**Figure 1.1**) *or* press the **Windows logo** key ⊞ on the keyboard. The Start menu displays a list of commonly used programs installed on the computer (**Figure 1.2**).

Figure 1.1 Start Button on Desktop

Figure 1.2 Start Menu

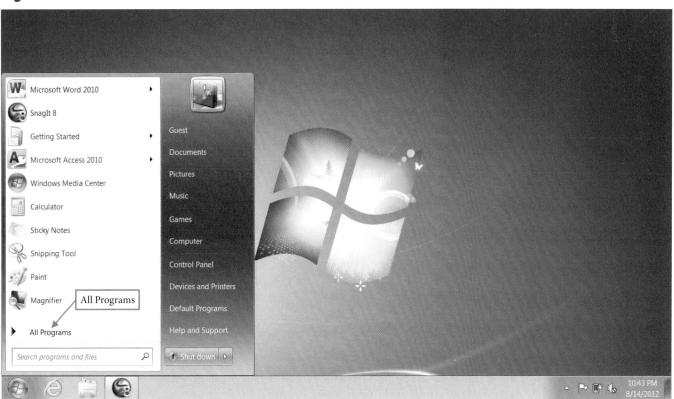

- Click the desired application to open it.
  - If the application does not display in the list in the Start menu, click **All Programs** (Figure 1.2) to view all programs installed on the computer.
  - Click the **Microsoft Office** folder to display a list of the Microsoft Office 2010 applications installed on the computer (**Figure 1.3**). You may need to scroll through the Start menu to locate the folder.
  - Click the application to open it.

Figure 1.3 Microsoft Office Folder

Hands-On Exercise: Launch Microsoft Word 2010

(1) Click the Start button (Figure 1.1) on the desktop, and the Start menu displays (Figure 1.2).

(2) Click All Programs (Figure 1.2), and a list of all programs installed on your computer displays.

(3) Click the Microsoft Office folder (Figure 1.3). You may need to scroll through the Start menu to locate the folder.

(4) Click Microsoft Word 2010 (**Figure 1.4**), and the application opens in a new window.

Figure 1.4 Microsoft Word 2010

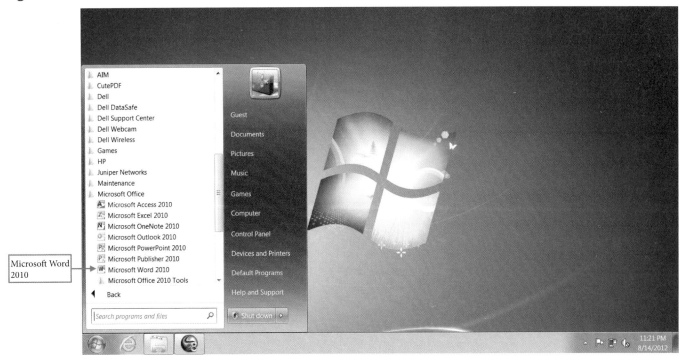

Identify Parts of the Graphical User Interface

When an application is launched, it displays a blank file and the application icon displays on the taskbar on the desktop. The taskbar is a bar, usually located at the bottom of the desktop, which displays the icons of open applications (**Figure 1.5**). For example, if you launch Microsoft Word 2010, it displays a new blank document and the Microsoft Word application icon displays on the taskbar (Figure 1.5).

Title Bar

The top bar on the application window is called the title bar. The title bar displays the name of the file that is currently open and the name of the application. In the middle of the title bar of a new Microsoft Word 2010 document, *Document1—Microsoft Word* displays (Figure 1.5). *Document1* is the default document name. A default is a setting that is automatically set by the application. The default document name will remain on the title bar until you save the document with a new name. The application being used to create the document is listed after the document name. In this example, *Microsoft Word* displays after the document name, indicating that Microsoft Word is the application being used to create the document (Figure 1.5).

Minimize, Maximize (Restore Down), and Close Buttons

There are three buttons located at the far-right corner of the title bar (**Figure 1.6**), which are used to manipulate the application window. The second button is a toggle button. A toggle button switches back and forth to a different state when clicked. **Table 1.2** describes the various buttons located on the far-right corner of the title bar.

Taskbar: A bar, usually located at the bottom of the desktop, which displays the icons of open applications.

Title bar: The top bar on the application window, which displays the name of the file that is currently open and the name of the application.

Default: A setting that is automatically set by the application.

Close button: Closes a document.

Toggle button: A button that switches back and forth to a different state when clicked.

Figure 1.5 New Blank Document

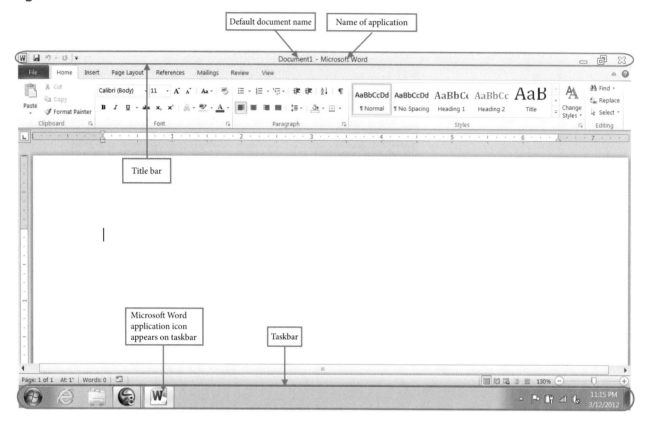

Figure 1.6 Minimize, Restore Down, and Close Buttons

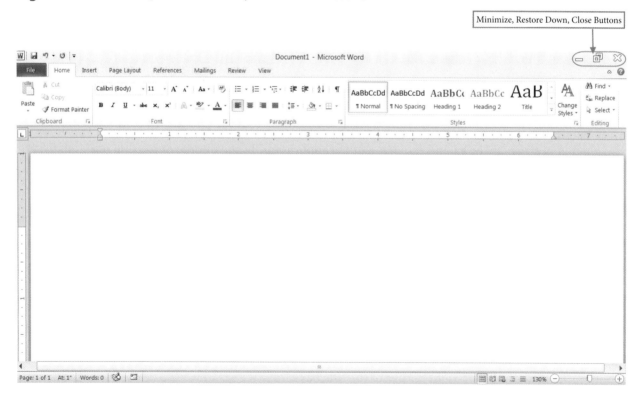

Table 1.2 Buttons on Title Bar

Button Name	Icon	Description
Minimize button	▭	Collapses a window to an icon on the taskbar. Click the application icon on the taskbar to restore the window.
Maximize button	▫	Enlarges a window to fill up the entire screen. Once clicked, it toggles to the Restore Down button.
Restore Down button	⧉	Changes a window to its original size. While in this mode, you can move or resize the window. Once clicked, it toggles to the Maximize button: • Drag the title bar to move the window. • Point to a window border and drag the two-headed arrow to change the size of the window.
Close button	✕	Closes a document.

Minimize button: Collapses a window to an icon on the taskbar.

Maximize button: Enlarges a window to fill up the entire screen.

Restore Down button: Changes a window to its original size.

Hands-On Exercise: Use Minimize, Maximize (Restore Down), and Close Buttons

① Click the Minimize button, and the application window disappears from the screen. The window collapses to an icon on the taskbar (**Figure 1.7**).

② Click the Microsoft Word application icon on the taskbar to reopen the window (Figure 1.7).

③ Click the Restore Down button if the window is maximized. The window becomes smaller, and the Restore Down button changes to a Maximize button (**Figure 1.8**).

④ Click the Maximize button. The window becomes enlarged and fills the entire screen. The Maximize button changes to the Restore Down button.

⑤ Click the Close button, and the Microsoft Word 2010 application closes. The application is no longer displayed on the screen or taskbar.

⑥ Reopen Microsoft Word 2010.

Figure 1.7 Window Collapses

Microsoft Word application icon

Figure 1.8 Window Becomes Smaller

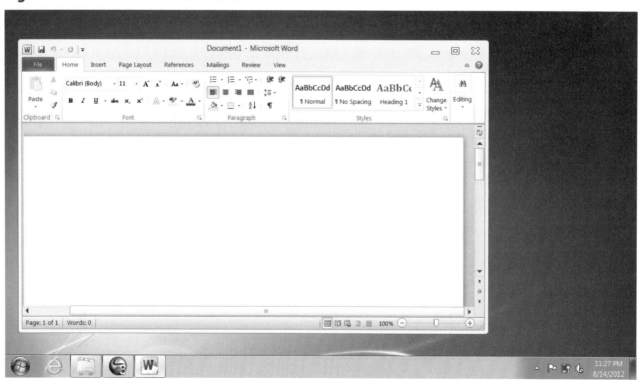

ToolTip

A **ToolTip**, also known as a **ScreenTip**, displays when the mouse hovers over a command. **Hover** refers to positioning the mouse on an object without clicking it. A **command** is a button or text that performs an action or task. The ToolTip lists the name of the command and sometimes includes a brief description of the command. It may also display **keyboard shortcuts**, which you can use to access the command using the keyboard. For example, Ctrl + U is a keyboard shortcut to underline text. Hold the Ctrl key while pressing the letter U to activate the command. You do not need to worry about capitalizing the letter U. You need only to press the letter on the keyboard.

ToolTip (ScreenTip): Displays when the mouse hovers over a command. It lists the name of the command and sometimes includes a brief description of the command, along with the keyboard shortcut to access the command.

Hover: Refers to positioning the mouse on an object.

Command: A button or text that performs an action or task.

Keyboard shortcut: Keys you can use to access a command.

Hands-On Exercise: Display ToolTip

① Hover over the Minimize button, and a ToolTip displays that states *Minimize* (**Figure 1.9**).

Figure 1.9 ToolTip Displayed

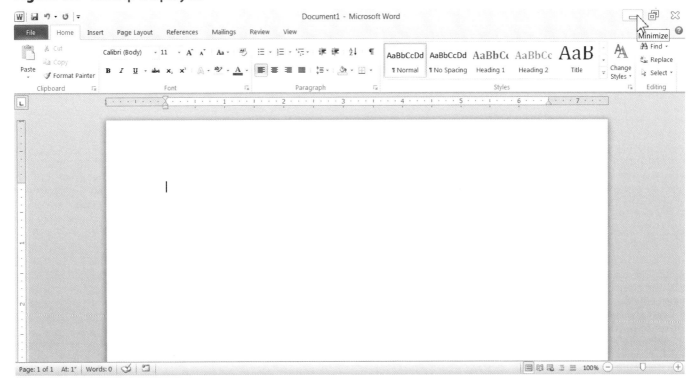

Shortcut Menu

A **shortcut menu** displays when you right-click on an object or area of the window (**Figure 1.10**). The shortcut menu contains a list of commands related to the object that was right-clicked. Press the **Esc** key on the keyboard or click in the document window to close the shortcut menu.

Shortcut menu: Contains a list of commands related to the object that was right-clicked. Displays when you right-click on an object or area of a window.

Figure 1.10 Shortcut Menu

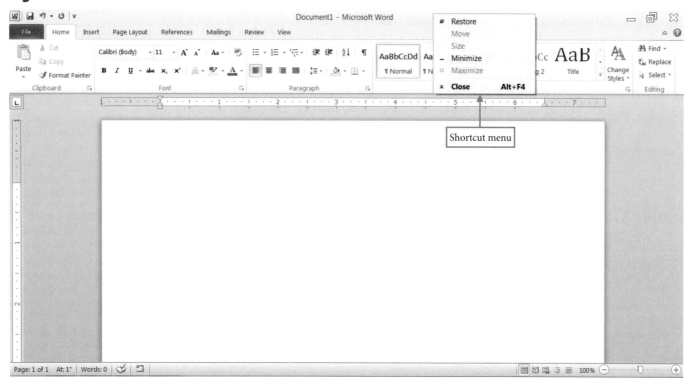

Shortcut menu

Hands-On Exercise: Display Shortcut Menu

(1) Right-click the title bar , and the shortcut menu displays (Figure 1.10).

(2) Press Esc on the keyboard to close the shortcut menu.

Quick Access Toolbar: A toolbar that provides quick access to the most frequently used commands. By default, it is located in the left-hand corner of the title bar.

Customize Quick Access Toolbar: The last button on the Quick Access Toolbar, which allows you to customize the toolbar.

Quick Access Toolbar

In the left-hand corner of the title bar is the Quick Access Toolbar (**Figure 1.11**). This toolbar provides access to the most frequently used commands. The Customize Quick Access Toolbar button is the last button on the toolbar (**Figure 1.12**). The commands that are currently displayed on the Quick Access Toolbar contain a check mark before the command name (Figure 1.12). Commands can be added to or removed from the Quick Access Toolbar.

Figure 1.11 Quick Access Toolbar

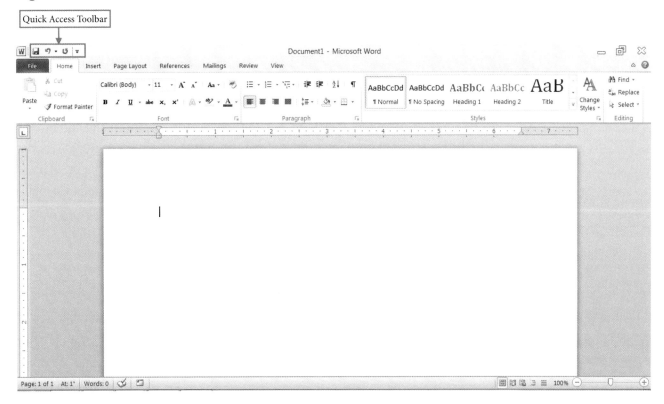

Figure 1.12 Customize Quick Access Toolbar

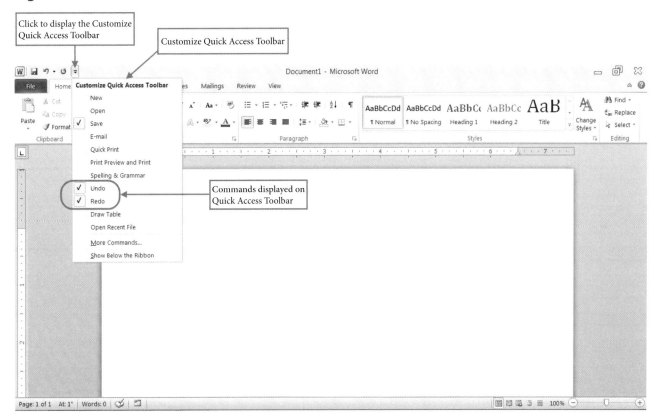

Table 1.3 indicates how to add or remove commands from the Quick Access Toolbar.

Table 1.3 Add or Remove Commands from the Quick Access Toolbar

Task	Steps
Add a command to the Quick Access Toolbar	• Click the **Customize Quick Access Toolbar** button located at the end of the Quick Access Toolbar to open the Customize Quick Access Toolbar (Figure 1.12). • Click the command to add.
Remove a command from the Quick Access Toolbar	• Click the **Customize Quick Access Toolbar** button located at the end of the Quick Access Toolbar to open the Customize Quick Access Toolbar (Figure 1.12). ▪ The commands that are available on the Quick Access Toolbar contain a check mark before the command name (Figure 1.12). • Click the command you wish to remove from the Quick Access Toolbar.
Add a command to the Quick Access Toolbar using the shortcut menu	• Right-click a command and the shortcut menu displays (**Figure 1.13**). • Click **Add to Quick Access Toolbar** on the shortcut menu (Figure 1.13).

Figure 1.13 Add Commands to the Quick Access Toolbar Using the Shortcut Menu

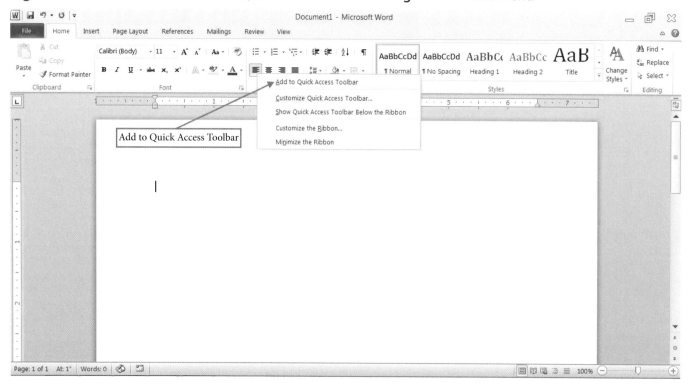

Hands-On Exercise: Customize Quick Access Toolbar

① Click the Customize Quick Access Toolbar button to open the Customize Quick Access Toolbar (**Figure 1.14**).

② Click Quick Print to add the command to the Quick Access Toolbar. The Quick Print button now displays on the Quick Access Toolbar (Figure 1.14).

③ Click the Customize Quick Access Toolbar button.

④ Click the Quick Print command to remove the command from the Quick Access Toolbar.

⑤ Click the Customize Quick Access Toolbar button.

⑥ Click the Quick Print command to add the command back to the Quick Access Toolbar.

⑦ Next you will add a command to the Quick Access Toolbar using the shortcut menu. Right-click the Format Painter button, and the shortcut menu displays (**Figure 1.15**).

⑧ Click Add to Quick Access Toolbar , and the Format Painter command displays in the Quick Access Toolbar.

⑨ Next you will remove the Format Painter button from the Quick Access Toolbar. Right-click the Format Painter button in the Quick Access Toolbar, and the shortcut menu displays (**Figure 1.16**).

⑩ Click Remove from Quick Access Toolbar (Figure 1.16), and the command is removed.

Figure 1.14 Quick Print Button Added to the Quick Access Toolbar

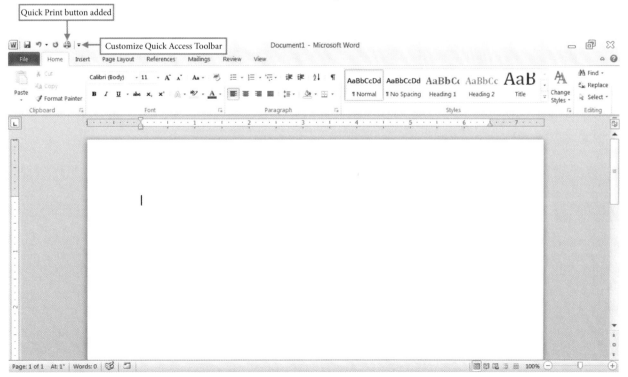

Figure 1.15 Right-Click the Format Painter Button

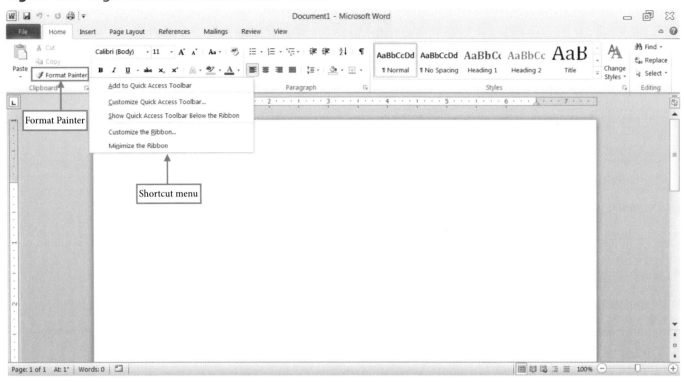

Figure 1.16 Remove a Command from the Quick Access Toolbar

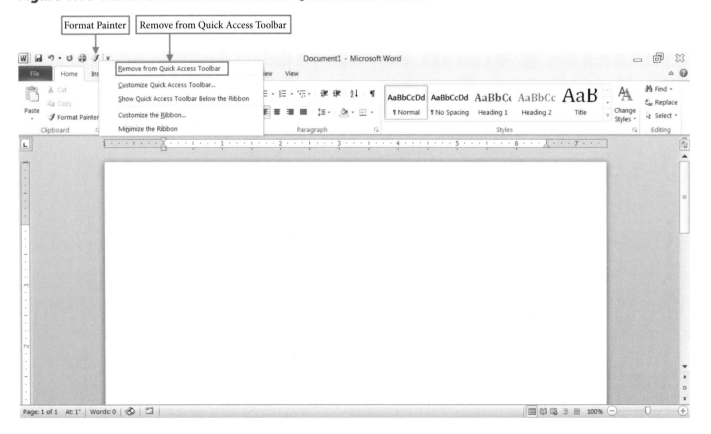

Backstage View

The **Backstage view** contains commands to manage your files. It is available when you click the File tab in the upper-left corner of the window below the Quick Access Toolbar. The Backstage view contains the commands to create new documents, open, save, print, and share documents. **Table 1.4** illustrates how to open and exit the Backstage view and how to open a recently viewed document.

> **Backstage view:** A view that displays when the File tab is selected. It contains commands to manage your files.

Table 1.4 Backstage View Commands	
Task	**Steps**
Open the Backstage view	• Click the **File** tab, and the Backstage view displays. (**Figure 1.17**).
Open a recent document	• Click the **File** tab, and the Backstage view displays (Figure 1.17).
	• Click **Recent**, and a list of recently opened documents displays (**Figure 1.18**).
	• Click the file to open.
Exit the Backstage view	• Press the **Esc** key or click the **File** tab to exit the Backstage view.

Figure 1.17 Backstage View

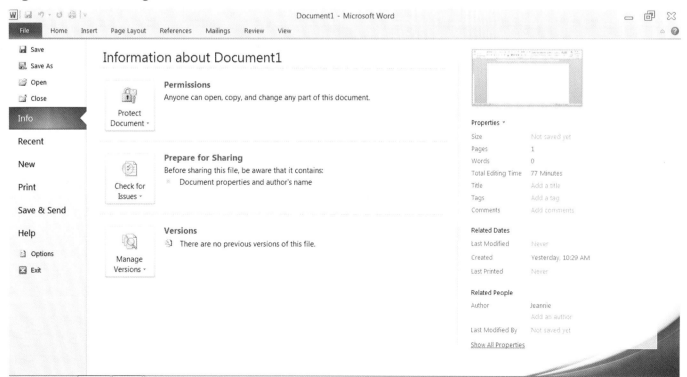

Figure 1.18 Recent Documents

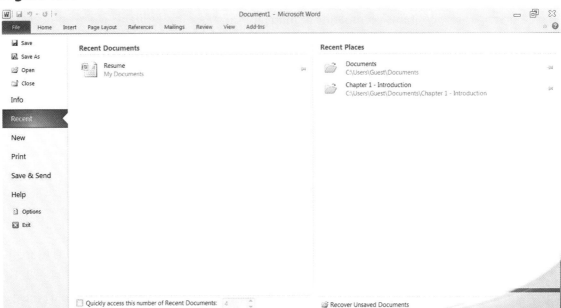

Ribbon: Contains all the commands needed to create a document. The Ribbon is located below the title bar and contains tabs that are organized by groups of related commands.

Ribbon

Below the title bar is the Ribbon (**Figure 1.19**). The Ribbon contains all the commands you need to create your document. Seven tabs display by default at the top of the Ribbon, starting with the Home tab. The File tab is not part of the Ribbon. The File tab is used to open the Backstage view. The Backstage view provides features that are not available on the Ribbon.

Figure 1.19 Ribbon

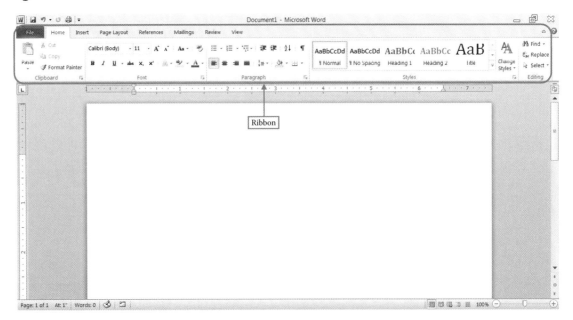

Each **tab** on the Ribbon contains a set of commands related to specific tasks. Click a button within a tab to execute a command. The buttons are arranged in **groups** of related tasks. The group names display at the bottom of the Ribbon (**Figure 1.20**). The Ribbon on your computer may look different than the screenshots in this book because the appearance of the Ribbon and window depends on the monitor size and settings. The buttons may be compressed or rearranged to accommodate smaller monitor sizes. Buttons may also be compressed or rearranged when the window is not maximized.

Tab: Located on the Ribbon and contains a set of commands related to specific tasks.

Group: Buttons arranged by related tasks on the Ribbon. Group name displays at the bottom of the Ribbon.

Figure 1.20 Group Names and the Minimize the Ribbon Button

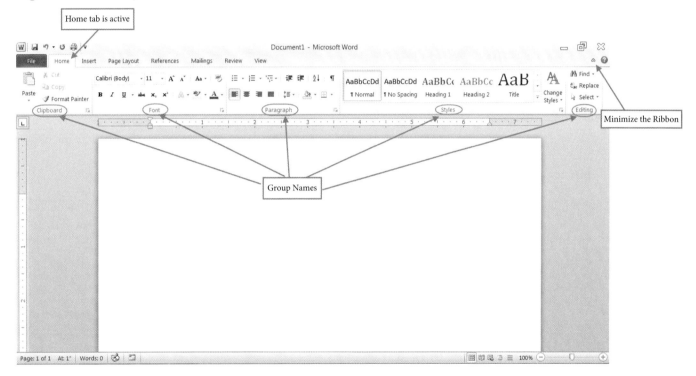

When you launch an application, the Home tab is automatically active (Figure 1.20). The Home tab contains commands for formatting the document. Many of the same commands on the Home tab are available in other Microsoft Office 2010 applications. At times, additional tabs display on the Ribbon when you create or select a particular object such as a picture or table. These tabs are called **contextual tabs** and contain commands that pertain to the object that is selected. For example, if you add a graphic to a document, a contextual tab displays when the graphic is selected with tools related to the graphic.

Contextual tab: A tab that displays when a particular object is created or selected. It contains commands that pertain to that object.

The Ribbon can be expanded or collapsed. When the Ribbon is collapsed, only the tab names display on the Ribbon. The buttons are no longer visible. When the Ribbon is expanded, all the buttons are displayed within the tabs. **Table 1.5** illustrates how to collapse and expand the Ribbon.

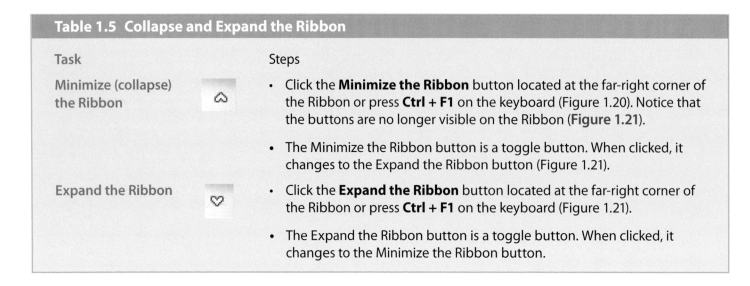

Table 1.5 Collapse and Expand the Ribbon

Task		Steps
Minimize (collapse) the Ribbon		• Click the **Minimize the Ribbon** button located at the far-right corner of the Ribbon or press **Ctrl + F1** on the keyboard (Figure 1.20). Notice that the buttons are no longer visible on the Ribbon (**Figure 1.21**). • The Minimize the Ribbon button is a toggle button. When clicked, it changes to the Expand the Ribbon button (Figure 1.21).
Expand the Ribbon		• Click the **Expand the Ribbon** button located at the far-right corner of the Ribbon or press **Ctrl + F1** on the keyboard (Figure 1.21). • The Expand the Ribbon button is a toggle button. When clicked, it changes to the Minimize the Ribbon button.

Figure 1.21 Expand the Ribbon Button

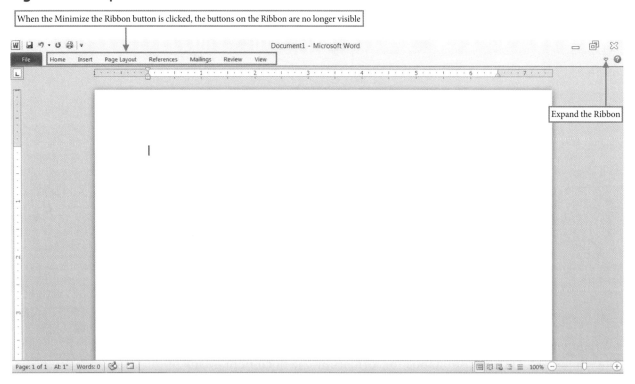

Key Tip: A shortcut for accessing the commands on the Ribbon and Quick Access Toolbar. The Key Tips are displayed when the Alt key is pressed.

To access commands on the Ribbon or Quick Access Toolbar without using your mouse, press **Alt** on your keyboard, and the Key Tips will display. A **Key Tip** is a shortcut to access the commands on the Ribbon and Quick Access Toolbar. The Key Tips display when the Alt key is pressed and indicate which key to press to access the tabs on the Ribbon and the commands on the Quick Access Toolbar (**Figure 1.22**). Press the letter indicated under the tab to open the tab. Press the number indicated under the command on the Quick Access Toolbar to launch the command (**Figure 1.23**). You may press the Alt key, the Esc key, the spacebar *or* click in the document window to remove the Key Tips from the window. If you use the Esc key, you may need to press Esc more than once to remove the Key Tips from the window.

Figure 1.22 Key Tips Displayed on the Tabs and the Quick Access Toolbar

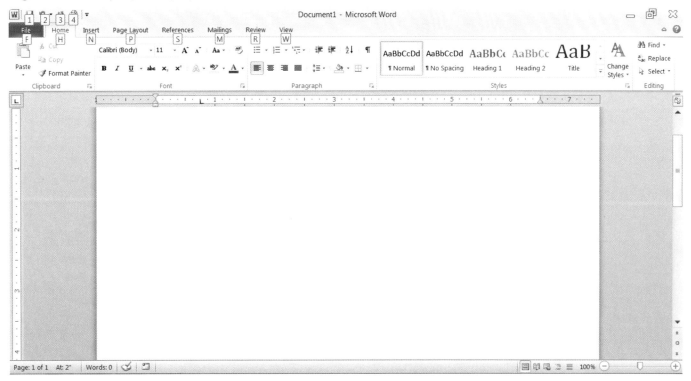

Figure 1.23 Key Tips to Access Commands on the Home Ribbon

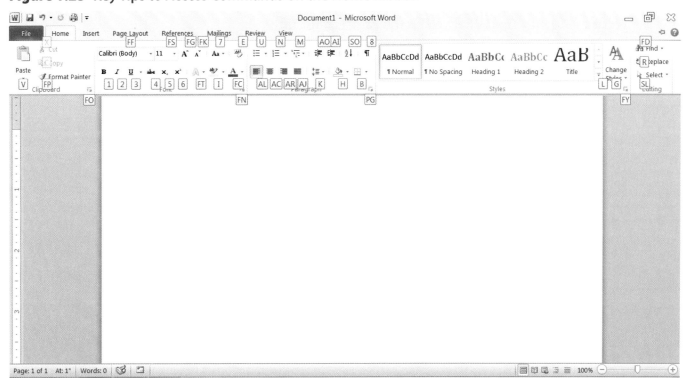

Hands-On Exercise: Minimize and Expand the Ribbon, and Display Key Tips

① Click the Insert tab on the Ribbon. View the various buttons that display. There are seven groups in the Insert tab: the Pages, Tables, Illustrations, Links, Header & Footer, Text, and Symbols groups.

② Point to the Clip Art button in the Illustrations group, and a ToolTip displays.

③ Click the Home tab on the Ribbon.

④ Click the Minimize the Ribbon button to display only the tab names on the Ribbon. The button changes to the Expand the Ribbon button, and the buttons are no longer visible on the Ribbon.

⑤ Click the Expand the Ribbon button to display the commands.

⑥ Press the Alt key on your keyboard. The Key Tips display, indicating which key to press to access the Ribbon tabs.

⑦ Press the letter P on the keyboard (for the Page Layout tab). The Page Layout tab becomes active. The Ribbon displays the Key Tips to access commands on the Page Layout tab (**Figure 1.24**).

⑧ Press the Alt key to remove the Key Tips from the Ribbon.

⑨ Click the Home tab to make the Home tab active.

Figure 1.24 Key Tips Displayed on the Page Layout Tab

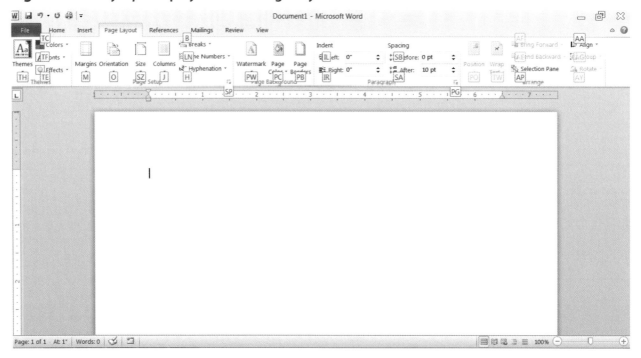

Document Window

The **document window** is an area in the application in which you create and edit a document. The document window is located below the Ribbon (**Figure 1.25**).

Insertion Point

The vertical blinking line in the application is called the **insertion point** (Figure 1.25). The insertion point indicates where text is inserted when you type.

Ruler Bar

The **ruler bar** is used to align text, graphics, and other elements in a document. The horizontal ruler displays below the Ribbon and the vertical ruler displays to the left of the document window (Figure 1.25). If the rulers are not displaying, click the **View** tab and click the **Ruler** check box. This feature is not available in all applications.

Figure 1.25 Document Window, Insertion Point, and Ruler Bars

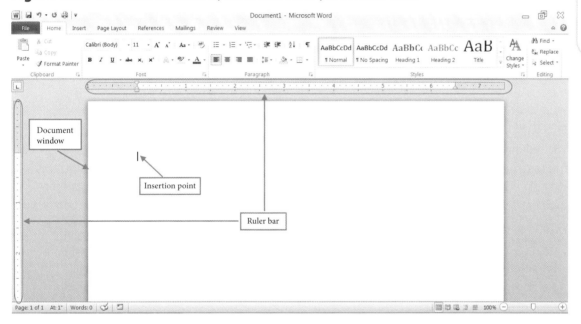

Document window: An area in the application in which you create and edit a document. The document window is located below the Ribbon.

Insertion point: The vertical blinking line in the application, which indicates where text is inserted when you type.

Ruler bar: Used to align text, graphics, and other elements in a document. The horizontal ruler displays below the Ribbon and the vertical ruler displays to the left of the document window.

Open File

You can open an existing file to view, print, or edit the file. When you open a file, a dialog box displays. A **dialog box** is a window that allows a user to perform commands or apply settings. Use these steps to open a file:

- Click the **File** tab and the Backstage view displays.
- Click **Open** and the Open dialog box displays (**Figure 1.26**).
- Select the location in which the file is stored.
- Select the file.
- Click the **Open** button (Figure 1.26) and the file opens.

Dialog box: A window that displays and allows a user to perform commands or apply settings.

Figure 1.26 Open Dialog Box

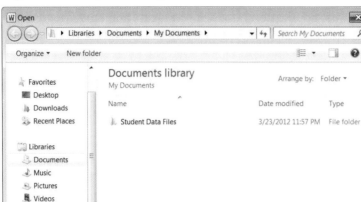

Hands-On Exercise: Open a File

You will open the file named *applications*, which is one of the student data files provided with the textbook. If you have not downloaded the files yet, please do so before beginning this exercise. The instructions for downloading the student data files are located in the preface.

① Click the File tab.

② Click Open , and the Open dialog box displays.

③ If you have downloaded the student data files to a USB flash drive:

- Click the USB flash drive , which is located in the left pane (navigation pane) of the Open dialog box (**Figure 1.27**). The drive may display as drive D, E, or F depending on your computer.

④ If you have downloaded the student data files to the Documents library:

- Click the Documents library, which is located in the left pane (navigation pane) of the Open dialog box (Figure 1.27).

⑤ The Student Data Files folder should display in the file list located on the right pane of the Open dialog box (Figure 1.27). Double-click the Student Data Files folder (Figure 1.27) to open the contents of the folder.

⑥ Double-click the file named applications (**Figure 1.28**), and the document opens. The document resembles **Figure 1.29**.

Figure 1.27 Select the Location of the Document

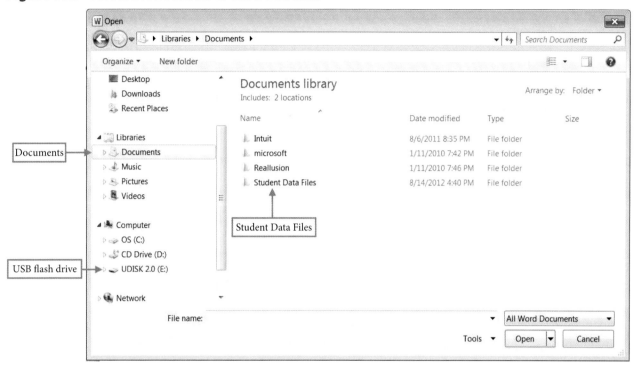

Figure 1.28 Select a File to Open

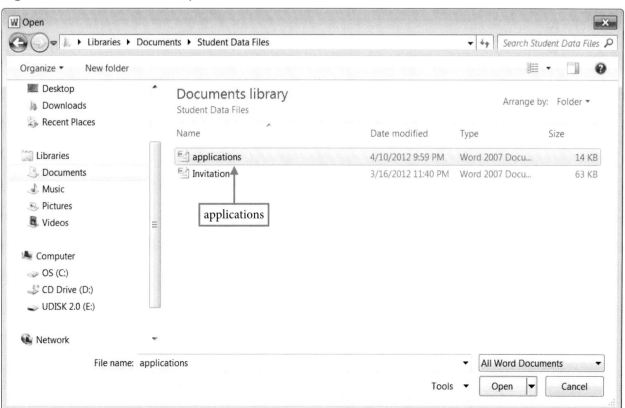

Figure 1.29 Document Opened

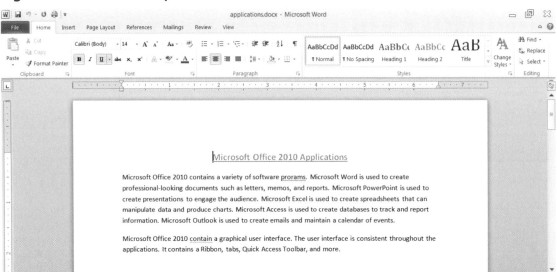

Status Bar

The **status bar** provides information about the status of your document and contains the View buttons and Zoom controls. The status bar is located at the bottom of the application window (**Figure 1.30**).

View Buttons

The **View buttons** provide options for viewing the document. The View buttons are located on the right side of the status bar (Figure 1.30). The Print Layout view is the default view. The **Print Layout view** depicts how the document will look when the document is printed. You can tell which view is currently selected because the active view has a gold outline surrounding the button. The View buttons vary, depending on the application you have open. There may be some content that is inaccessible when you select certain views. **Draft view** is used to edit and format text quickly. Some elements, such as headers and footers, page breaks, backgrounds, and some pictures, do not display in Draft view.

Zoom Controls

The **Zoom controls** allow the user to zoom in and out of specific areas in the document. This feature controls the magnification of the document. The Zoom controls are located at the far right of the status bar (Figure 1.30). For example, if you need to magnify parts of the text, you may want to zoom in to that area. However, if you want to print the document, it does not print using the zoom settings. It prints based on the font settings of your document. **Table 1.6** illustrates the various Zoom controls.

Figure 1.30 View Buttons and Zoom Controls on the Status Bar

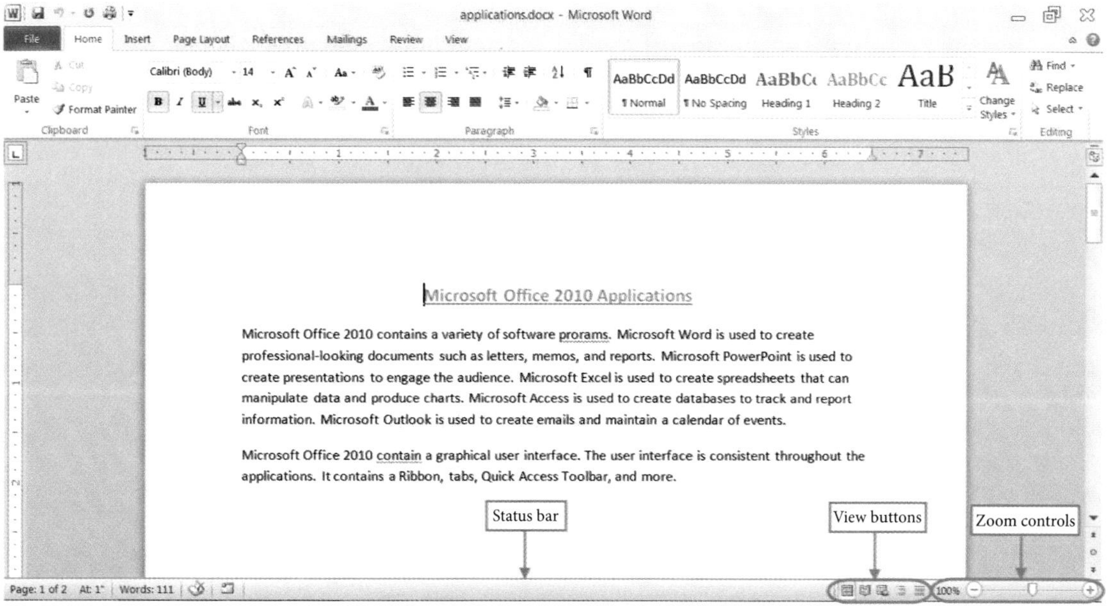

Table 1.6 Zoom Controls		
Button Name	**Button**	**Button Description**
Zoom Level	100%	Opens the Zoom dialog box.
Zoom Out	⊖	Decreases the magnification of the document.
Zoom		Increases or decreases the magnification of the document as you drag the Zoom button. This button is commonly referred to as the *Zoom slider*.
Zoom In	⊕	Increases the magnification of the document.

Hands-On Exercise: Use View Buttons and Zoom Controls

1. At the far left of the status bar, the current page number and the total number of pages display (**Figure 1.31**).

2. Click the Draft button in the View controls (Figure 1.31). The view changes and resembles **Figure 1.32**.

3. Click the Print Layout button in the View controls (Figure 1.32). (Be careful not to click the Page Layout tab in the Ribbon.) The gold outline around the Print Layout button indicates that it is the active view.

4. Click the Zoom In button to magnify the text in the document (Figure 1.31).

5. Click the Zoom Out button a few times to decrease the magnification of the text in the document (Figure 1.31).

⑥ Drag the Zoom button to the right to magnify the text (Figure 1.31).

⑦ Drag the Zoom button to the left to reduce the magnification of the text.

⑧ Click the Zoom level button (Figure 1.31) to open the Zoom dialog box (**Figure 1.33**).

⑨ Click the 100% option (Figure 1.33). This is the default zoom level.

⑩ Click OK.

Figure 1.31 Buttons on the Status Bar

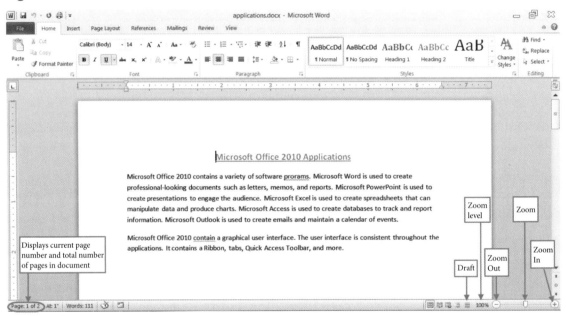

Figure 1.32 Draft View

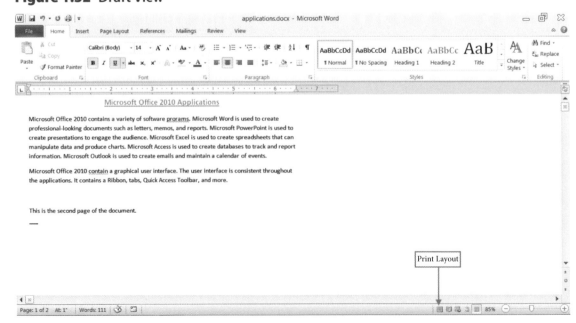

Figure 1.33 Zoom Dialog Box

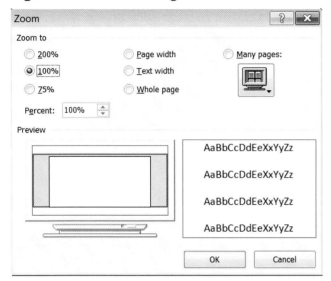

Navigation Techniques

You can navigate to different parts of the document by using the Page Up, Page Down, and arrow keys. Additional ways to navigate a document are shown in **Table 1.7**.

Table 1.7 Navigation Techniques	
Key(s)	Description
Ctrl + Home	Navigates to the beginning of a document.
Ctrl + End	Navigates to the end of a document.
Home	Navigates to the beginning of a line.
End	Navigates to the end of a line.

Hands-On Exercise: Navigate a Document

① Press Ctrl + End to navigate to the end of the document. Notice that the status bar states *Page: 2 of 2*, and the insertion point is positioned at the end of the sentence in the document (**Figure 1.34**).

② Press Home to navigate to the beginning of the line.

③ Press End to navigate to the end of the line.

④ Press Ctrl + Home to navigate to the top of the document.

Figure 1.34 Press Ctrl + End to Navigate to the End of the Document

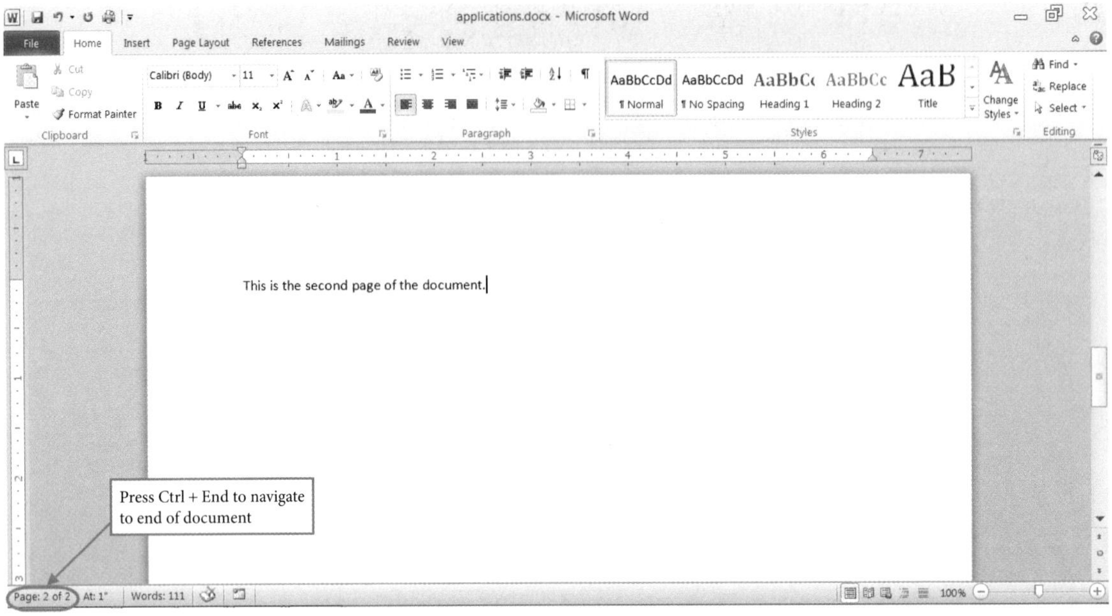

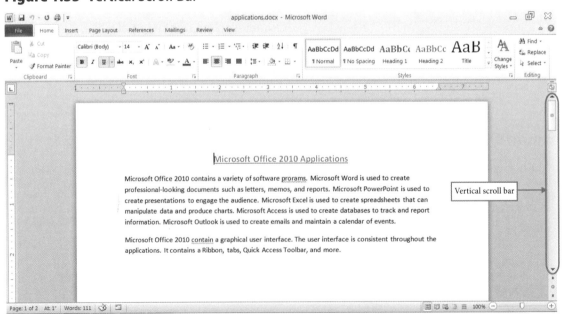

Scroll Bars

Scroll bar: Allows the user to navigate either up and down or left and right to view all the information in a document.

Scroll bars allow you to navigate either up and down or left and right to view all the information in a document. The vertical scroll bar displays on the right side of the window and is used to scroll up and down in a document (**Figure 1.35**). The horizontal scroll bar is positioned at the bottom of the window and scrolls left or right through a document. The horizontal scroll bar may display when the Restore Down button is selected or when the text in the document is wider than the application window and you need to scroll to view all the text.

Figure 1.35 Vertical Scroll Bar

The scroll bar contains a scroll box and arrows (**Figure 1.36**). The position of the scroll box indicates your current position within the document. The scroll box in Figure 1.36 displays at the top of the scroll bar, which indicates that you are at the top of the document. You can drag the scroll box to navigate the document *or* you can click the arrows to scroll in the document.

Figure 1.36 Scroll Bar Elements

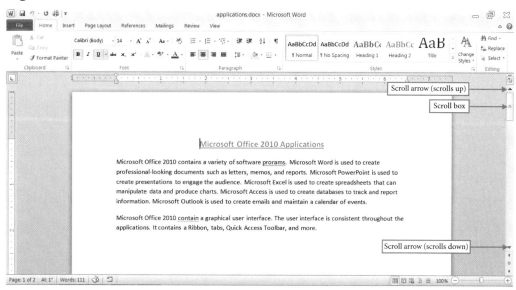

Hands-On Exercise: Use the Scroll Bar

(1) Drag the scroll box until Page 2 displays as a ToolTip. The status bar will also state *Page: 2 of 2* (**Figure 1.37**).

(2) Navigate to the first page of the document by clicking the up scroll arrow on the vertical scroll bar. Keep clicking until *Page 1* displays.

Figure 1.37 Drag Scroll Box

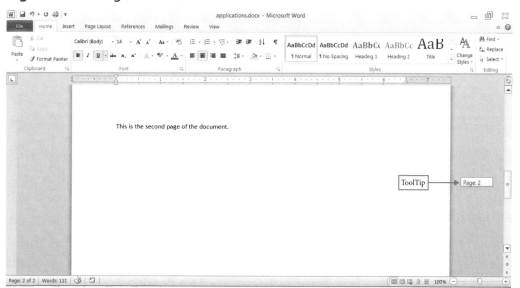

Common Features

There are many common features that are used in the Microsoft Office 2010 applications. This section describes some of those features.

Gallery: A collection of visual options that display when the More button is clicked.

Gallery

A **gallery** is a collection of visual options that display. A gallery will display when you click the More button, . As you point to various items in a gallery, a preview of the effect will display in the document.

Hands-On Exercise: Display a Gallery

① Click the Home tab if the tab is not currently active.

② Press Ctrl + Home to navigate to the top of the document.

③ The Styles group displays various styles you can apply to text in the document. Not all the styles are displayed. To display all the styles, click the More button in the Styles group on the Home tab, and a gallery of styles displays (**Figure 1.38**).

④ Point to the Title style in the gallery to view the effects of the style to the first line of the document (**Figure 1.39**). You have two options. You can click the style if you want to apply that style to the text or press Esc to exit the gallery.

⑤ Press the Esc key to exit the gallery.

Figure 1.38 More Button in Styles Group

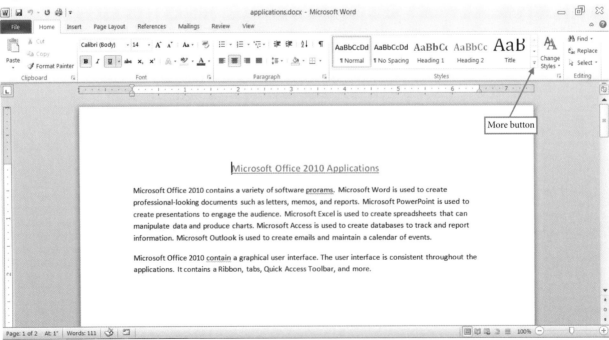

Figure 1.39 Title Style Previewed in Document

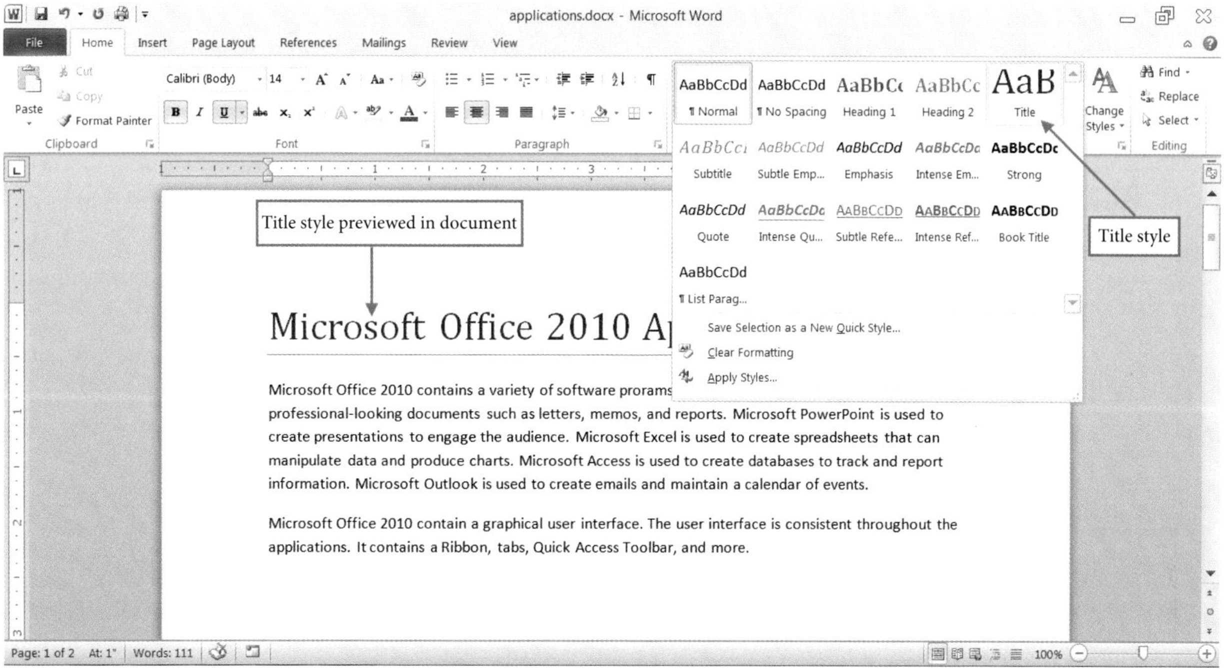

Selection Techniques

You need to select text in order to perform certain tasks. **Table 1.8** displays various selection techniques that work in all Microsoft Office 2010 applications.

Table 1.8 Selection Techniques	
Task	Step
Select a word	Double-click the word.
Select a paragraph	Triple-click in the paragraph.
Select the entire document	Press Ctrl + A.

Hands-On Exercise: Select Text in a Document

1. Double-click the word software in the first sentence in the paragraph. The word is selected (**Figure 1.40**).

2. Triple-click anywhere in the second paragraph, and the entire paragraph is selected.

3. Press Ctrl + A and the entire document is selected.

4. Click the white area of the document window to deselect the text.

Figure 1.40 Text Selected

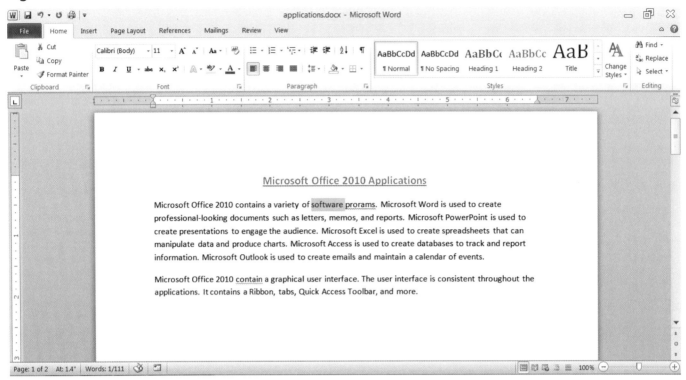

Mini Toolbar

Mini Toolbar:
Contains formatting commands that can be applied to the selected text.

The **Mini Toolbar** displays when text is selected. The Mini Toolbar contains formatting commands that can be applied to the selected text. When text is selected, the Mini Toolbar will display at the top right of the selected text and will appear faded or dimmed (**Figure 1.41**). When the insertion point is positioned on the Mini Toolbar, it becomes solid and active. Press **Esc** *or* move the insertion point away from the selected text to close the Mini Toolbar.

Hands-On Exercise: Display Mini Toolbar

① Double-click the word PowerPoint in the first paragraph to select the word. The Mini Toolbar will display at the top right of the selected text and appears faded or dimmed.

② Move the insertion point on the Mini Toolbar, and it becomes active (Figure 1.41).

③ Press Esc to close the Mini Toolbar.

④ Press Ctrl + Home to navigate to the top of the document. Notice the word *PowerPoint* is no longer selected.

Figure 1.41 Mini Toolbar

Dialog Box

A dialog box is a window that allows a user to perform commands, apply settings, or provides the users with additional information. A dialog box displays when the dialog box launcher is clicked. A **dialog box launcher** is a button that resembles a diagonal arrow, which appears to the right of the group names on the Ribbon (**Figure 1.42**).

dialog box launcher: A button that resembles a diagonal arrow, which appears to the right of the group names on the Ribbon.

Figure 1.42 Dialog Box Launcher

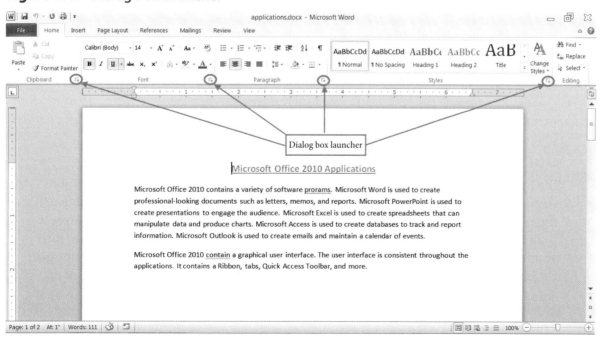

Hands-On Exercise: Use Dialog Box Launcher

① Double-click the word emails in the first paragraph of the document to select the text.

② Click the Font dialog box launcher located in the Font group, and the Font dialog box displays (**Figure 1.43**). The dialog box contains a variety of font options that you can select and apply to your text.

③ Click Bold in the Font style list to make the text bold. A preview of the text displays in the Preview section (Figure 1.43).

④ Click OK to apply the settings.

Figure 1.43 Font Dialog Box

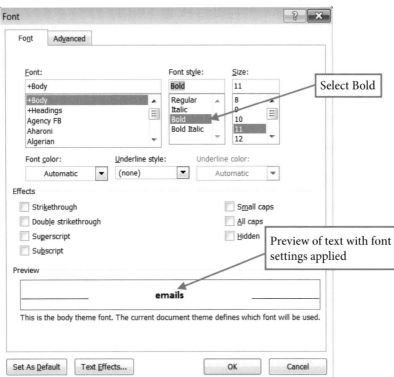

Undo, Redo, and Repeat Commands

Undo button: A command that will undo (or remove) the last action performed as well as previous actions. The Undo button is located on the Quick Access Toolbar and can be accessed by using the shortcut keys Ctrl + Z.

Repeat button: Repeats the last action performed.

Redo button: Redoes an action that was undone.

The Undo, Redo, and Repeat commands are available on the Quick Access Toolbar (**Figure 1.44**). The **Undo button** will undo (or remove) the last action performed as well as previous actions. You can undo multiple actions at a time by clicking the Undo arrow on the Quick Access Toolbar and selecting the actions to undo. There are some actions you cannot undo, such as printing or saving the document. The **Repeat button** will repeat the last action performed. The **Redo button** will redo an action that was undone. The Repeat and Redo buttons are toggle buttons. By default, the Repeat button displays. Once the Undo button is clicked, the Redo button displays on the Quick Access Toolbar. **Table 1.9** illustrates the Undo, Redo, and Repeat buttons.

Table 1.9 Undo, Redo, and Repeat Buttons	
Command	Button
Undo	↰
Redo	↱
Repeat	↻

You can access the Undo button by using the shortcut keys Ctrl + Z. When using the shortcut keys Ctrl + Z, hold down **Ctrl**, press **Z** on the keyboard, and then release both keys. You do not need to worry about capitalizing the letter *Z*. You need only to press the letter on the keyboard.

Hands-On Exercise: Use Undo and Redo Buttons

① Click the Undo button on the Quick Access Toolbar to remove the bold formatting from the text (Figure 1.44).

② Click the Redo button on the Quick Access Toolbar to reapply the bold formatting to the text (Table 1.9).

③ Press Ctrl + Z to remove the bold formatting from the text.

④ Press Ctrl + Home to navigate to the top of the document.

Figure 1.44 Undo and Repeat Buttons on the Quick Access Toolbar

AutoCorrect

AutoCorrect: This feature automatically checks commonly misspelled or mistyped words and corrects the word with a word from the main dictionary.

The AutoCorrect feature is a tool that saves you time and effort as you type in a document. The **AutoCorrect** feature automatically checks commonly misspelled or mistyped words after you insert a space or a punctuation mark and replaces the word with a word from the main dictionary. For example, if you type *teh* and press the spacebar, the AutoCorrect feature automatically replaces the misspelled word with the word *the*.

AutoComplete

AutoComplete: This feature automatically completes words that you are typing such as the days of the week and the months. Type the first four characters of the word and a ToolTip displays asking you if you want to insert the completed word.

The **AutoComplete** feature automatically completes words that you are typing, such as the days of the week or names of months. If you type the first four characters of the word, a ToolTip displays asking if you want to insert the completed word. For example, if you type *Augu*, a ToolTip displays asking if you want to insert the word *August*. If you press **Enter**, the word is inserted into the document.

Spelling and Grammar

The Spelling and Grammar feature checks spelling and grammar as you type. By default, this feature is automatically active. A wavy colored line under the text indicates that there is a potential error in the document. If potential errors are found, the Proofing Errors button on the status bar displays with a red *x* (**Figure 1.45**). If no errors are found, the Proofing Errors button displays on the status bar with a blue check mark.

Figure 1.45 Proofing Errors Button on Status Bar

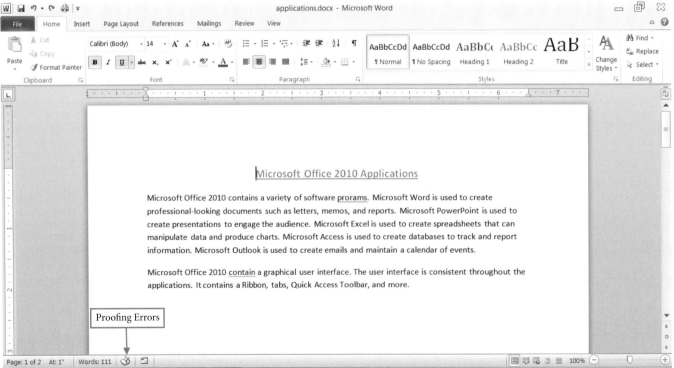

Table 1.10 illustrates the various types of spelling and grammar errors that are identified.

Table 1.10 Spelling and Grammar Errors	
Error	Description
Wavy red line under text	Indicates a potential spelling error.
Wavy green line under text	Indicates a potential grammar error.
Wavy blue line under text	Indicates a potential contextual spelling error.

If a wavy red line displays under text, it indicates a potential spelling error. Use these steps to correct the spelling:

- Right-click the misspelled word, and alternative spellings will display (**Figure 1.46**).
- Select the correct spelling from the list, and it will change in the document. Some proper names may not be included in the dictionary and may display as a potential spelling error. In this case, click **Ignore All** to indicate that the word is spelled correctly *or* click **Add to Dictionary** to store it in the dictionary (Figure 1.46).

If a green wavy line displays under a word or a phrase, it indicates a potential grammar error. Use these steps to correct the error in grammar:

- Right-click the word(s), and possible grammar suggestions will display.
- Accept or ignore the suggestion.

If a blue wavy line displays under a word or a phrase, it indicates a potential contextual spelling grammar. This may display if you use a word incorrectly—for example, using the word *to* instead of *too*. Use these steps to correct a contextual grammar error:

- Right-click the word(s), and possible suggestions will display.
- Accept or ignore the suggestion.

Please note that suggestions are not infallible, so it is imperative that you proofread all work.

The Spelling & Grammar command is available on the Review tab. This feature checks the entire document at once for errors and displays the errors in a dialog box.

The Proofing Errors button (Figure 1.45) on the status bar contains a red *x*, which means there are errors in the document. You will correct those errors in this exercise.

> Spelling & Grammar: A command that checks the entire document at once for errors and displays the errors in a dialog box.

Hands-On Exercise: Correct Spelling and Grammar Errors Using Shortcut Menu

1. Notice the red wavy line under the word *prorams* in the first paragraph. This indicates a potential spelling error. Right-click the word, and the shortcut menu displays (Figure 1.46).

2. Click the correct spelling, programs , and the word is corrected in the document.

③ There is a green wavy line under the word contain in the second paragraph. This indicates a potential grammar error. Right-click the word *contain*, and the shortcut menu displays.

④ The correct word should be *contains*. Click the word contains , and the word will be corrected in the document.

⑤ All errors have been corrected. The Proofing Errors button changed to a blue check mark, indicating that no errors are found.

Figure 1.46 Shortcut Menu Displays to Correct Spelling Errors

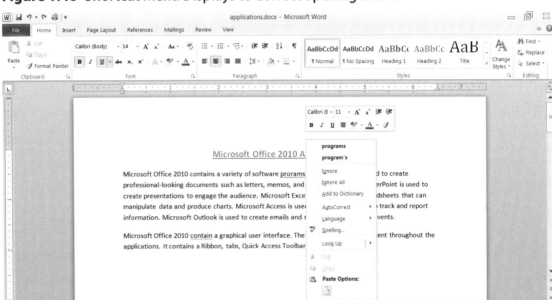

Perhaps your friend asked you to proofread a paper. Instead of correcting errors as you type, you want to check all the spelling and grammar at once. You can use the Spelling & Grammar command in the Review tab.

Hands-On Exercise: Use Spelling & Grammar Button

① Press Ctrl + End to navigate to the end of the document.

② Press Enter to navigate to the next line.

③ You will misspell a word. Type I love compters .

④ Press Enter . A red way line displays under the word *compters*.

⑤ Click the Review tab on the Ribbon (**Figure 1.47**).

⑥ Click the Spelling & Grammar button located in the Proofing group (Figure 1.47), and the Spelling and Grammar dialog box displays (**Figure 1.48**). This command checks the spelling and grammar of all the text in the document and displays the errors one by one in the dialog box.

⑦ The dialog box displays the misspelled word in red in the Not in Dictionary box. In the Suggestions box, it displays suggestions on how to correct the misspelled word. Click the correct spelling, computers (Figure 1.48).

⑧ Click Change (Figure 1.48).

⑨ When the spelling and grammar check is completed, a dialog box displays indicating it is completed (**Figure 1.49**). Click OK.

⑩ Click the Home tab to make it the active tab.

Figure 1.47 Spelling & Grammar Button on the Review Tab

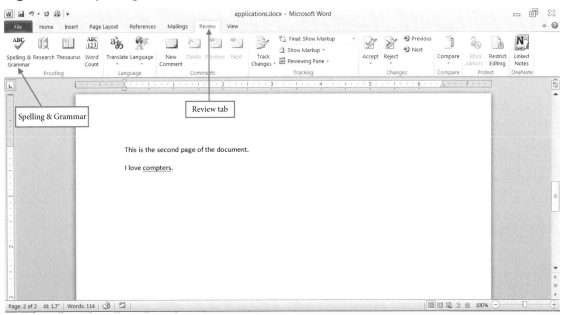

Figure 1.48 Spelling and Grammar Dialog Box

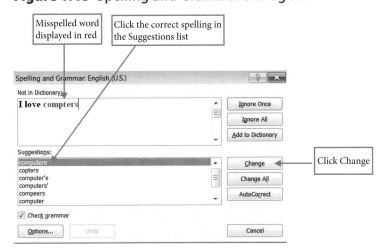

Figure 1.49 Spelling and Grammar Check Completed

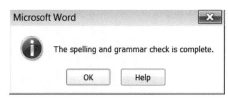

Help Button

You can use the Help feature if you need help with a task. The Help feature is accessed by clicking the Help button, which is located on the far right-hand corner of the Ribbon (**Figure 1.50**). The Help feature is also available on the File tab or by pressing F1 on the keyboard. The search results display as a hyperlink with blue text. A **hyperlink**, when clicked, links to another place in the current document or a different document.

> **Hyperlink:** Links to another place in the current document or a different document.

Figure 1.50 Help Button

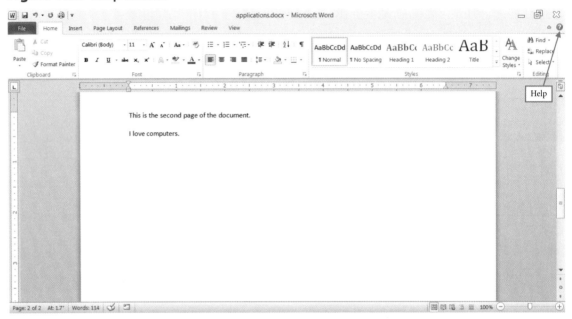

Follow these steps to use Help (**Figure 1.51**):

- Click the **Help** button or press **F1** on the keyboard, and the Word Help dialog box displays.
- Type the topic/feature you need help with in the Search box.
- Click **OK**, and a list of search results displays. These search results are articles or links that will illustrate how to complete the task.
- Click the link of the search result you want to view.
- Click the **Print** button in the Word Help dialog box to print the help information.
- Click the **Close** button on the Word Help title bar when you are done.

Hands-On Exercise: Use Help

① Click the Help button, *or* press F1 , and the Word Help dialog box displays.

② Type **print** in the Search box (Figure 1.51), and press Enter. Search results display in the Word Help dialog box.

③ The search results display as a hyperlink with blue text (Figure 1.51). A hyperlink, when clicked, links to another place in the current document or a different document. When you click the blue text, it will hyperlink to the search results.

④ Click the first search result, and it displays the instructions on how to print a document.

⑤ Click the Close button on the Word Help dialog box to exit the Help window (Figure 1.51).

⑥ Press Ctrl + Home to navigate to the top of the document.

Figure 1.51 Word Help Dialog Box

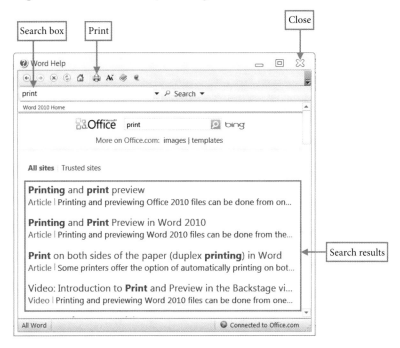

Save Commands

When you save a file, you need to specify the name of the file, the file type (such as Microsoft Word 2010), and the location to which you want to save the file. You should save your files often to avoid losing your data.

There are two commands you can use to save files:

- **Save command**: automatically saves the file with the current file name.
  - Use this when you are making changes to a document and want to save the document with the same name, type, and location.
- **Save As command**: saves the file with a new file name, type, or location.
  - Use this when you want to make changes to a document and save it as a different file name, keeping the original file intact.
  - This command opens the Save As dialog box, which allows you to specify the file name and the location in which the file will be stored.
  - Click the **Save as type** arrow in the Save As dialog box to select a different format in which to save the document. The document can be saved as a Microsoft Word 97–2003 document. This is helpful if you need to send the document to an individual who has an older version of Microsoft Word. You can also save the document in other formats such as PDF, Web Page, rich text format, or plain text.

Save command: Saves the file with the current settings.

Save As command: Saves the file with a new file name, type, or location.

If you are saving the document for the first time, it does not matter whether you select the Save or Save As command because the file has not yet been saved. By default, the Save As command opens. Use any of these methods to save your files:

- Press **Ctrl + S** on the keyboard.
- Click the **Save** button on the Quick Access Toolbar (**Figure 1.52**).
- Click the **File** tab and select **Save** or **Save As**.

Figure 1.52 Save Button

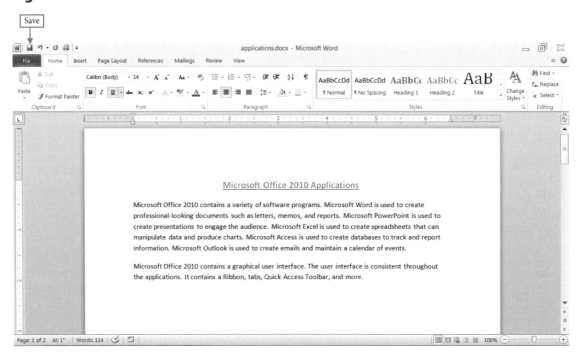

The file name may contain up to 255 characters, including the drive letter, folder name, and filename extension. The file name may include letters, spaces, hyphens, and underlines. However, shorter file names are preferred. File names cannot contain special characters such as these < > ? : " | \ /.

A file name contains a **filename extension** following the file name and a period. A filename extension consists of a three- to five-letter suffix that identifies the application used to create the file. For example, the file name called resume.docx has the filename extension docx, which represents a Microsoft Word 2010 document.

A list of the Microsoft Office 2010 filename extensions is given in **Table 1.11**.

> **Filename extension:** A three- to five-letter suffix that identifies the application used to create the file. The file-name extension follows the file name and a dot.

Table 1.11 Filename Extensions	
Application	Filename Extension
Microsoft Word 2010	docx
Microsoft PowerPoint 2010	pptx
Microsoft Excel 2010	xlsx
Microsoft Access 2010	accdb

Hands-On Exercise: Save a Document in the Documents Library

Complete this exercise only if the student data files are located in the Documents library on the hard drive (Drive C). You will save the document with a new name in the Student Data Files folder in the Documents library on the hard drive.

① Click the File tab.

② Click Save As (**Figure 1.53**), and the Save As dialog box displays (**Figure 1.54**).

③ The address bar indicates where the file will be stored, which includes the drive and folder information (Figure 1.54). The Student Data Files folder should already be opened, as indicated in the address bar (Figure 1.54). If the Student Data Files folder is not open:

a. Click Documents under Libraries (Figure 1.54).

b. Double-click the Student Data Files folder to open the folder.

④ Type **applications_lastname** in the File name box to save the document (Figure 1.54). If your last name is Doe, the file name would be *applications_Doe*.

⑤ Click the Save button.

⑥ The title bar displays as *applications_lastname*.

Figure 1.53 Save As Button

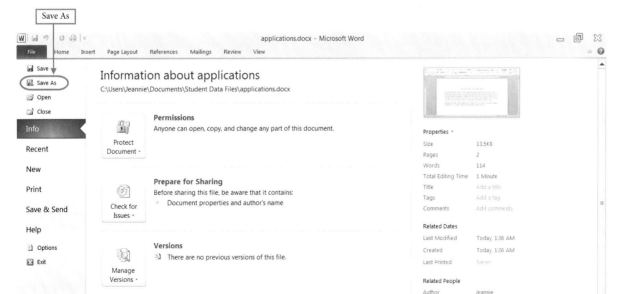

Figure 1.54 Save As Dialog Box

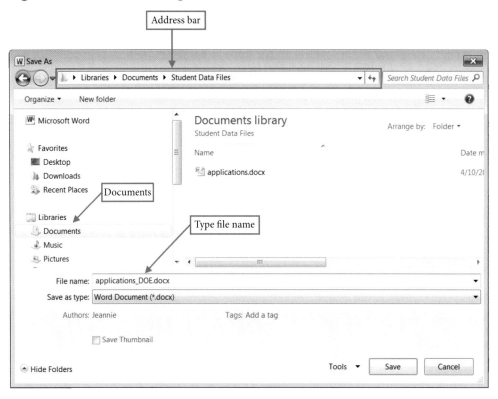

Hands-On Exercise: Save a Document on the USB Flash Drive

 DOWNLOAD

Complete this exercise only if the student data files are located in the Student Data Files folder on the USB flash drive. You will save the document with a new name in the Student Data Files folder on the USB flash drive.

① Click the File tab.

② Click Save As (Figure 1.53), and the Save As dialog box displays (**Figure 1.55**).

③ The address bar indicates where the file will be stored which includes the drive and folder information (Figure 1.55). The Student Data Files folder should already be opened, as indicated in the address bar. If the Student Data Files folder is not open:

   a. Click the USB flash drive from the list (Figure 1.55). It may display as drive D, E, or F, depending on your computer.

   b. Double-click the Student Data Files folder to open the folder.

④ Type **applications_*lastname*** in the File name box to save the document (Figure 1.55). If your last name is Doe, the file name would be *applications_Doe*.

⑤ Click the Save button. The title bar displays as *applications_lastname*.

Figure 1.55 Save on the USB Flash Drive

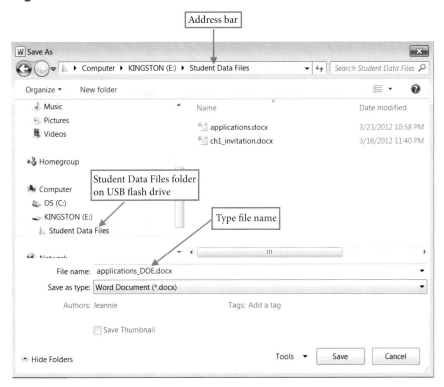

Print Command

To print the entire document, click the **Quick Print** button in the Quick Access Toolbar (**Figure 1.56**).

Figure 1.56 Quick Print Button

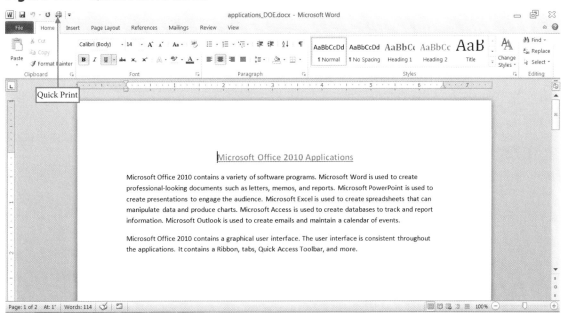

To select the following print options, you must use the Print command on the File tab, *or* you can press **Ctrl + P**, which are the shortcut keys to access the print command. The following options are available with the print command:

- Number of copies to print.
- Select printer.
- Select pages to print.
- Select page orientation (portrait or landscape). **Portrait orientation** is when the page orientation prints on a vertical page, which means that the page is taller than it is wide (8½″ × 11″). **Landscape orientation** is when the page orientation prints on a horizontal page which means that the page is wider than it is taller (11″ × 8½″).
- Select paper size.
- Select margins.

Use these steps to print a document:

- Click the **File** tab.
- Click **Print**, and a preview of the document will display on the right-hand side (**Figure 1.57**).
- Adjust the print settings as needed:
  - To print in landscape mode:
    - Click the **Portrait Orientation** arrow (Figure 1.57);
    - Click **Landscape Orientation**.
  - To print specific pages that are in a sequential range:
    - Type the page range in the Pages box starting with the first page number followed by a hyphen followed by the ending page number (for example, to print pages 1 through 4, you would enter 1-4).

Figure 1.57 Print Settings

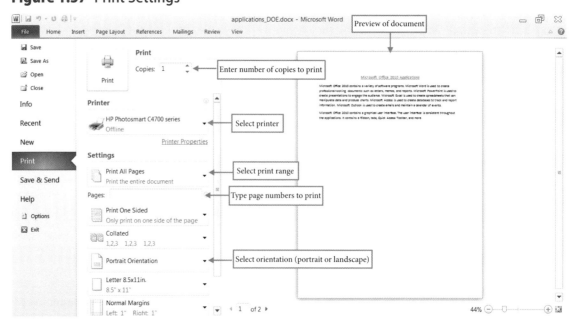

- To print certain pages of the document that are not in a sequential range:
  - Type the page numbers in the Pages box followed by a comma (for example, to print pages 1 and 4, you would enter 1,4).
- A preview of the document displays on the right-hand side.
- Click the **Print** button once the settings have been selected, and the document will be printed.

Use these steps to print a selected portion of a document:

- Select the content to be printed.
- Click the **File** tab.
- Click **Print**.
- Click the **Print All Pages** arrow in the Settings section (Figure 1.57).
- Click **Print Selection**.
- Click the **Print** button.

Hands-On Exercise: Print a Document

① Click the File tab.

② Click Print .

③ Click the Print button.

Using Multiple Applications

You can have multiple applications or multiple files opened at the same time. Each application that is open will have the application icon displayed on the taskbar. **Table 1.12** illustrates the various application icons for the Microsoft Office 2010 applications. You can navigate to the open applications by clicking on the icon on the taskbar. If more than one file is open in an application, click the **application icon** and a listing of open files display. Click the file you want to open.

Table 1.12 Microsoft Office Application Icons	
Application	Application Icon
Microsoft Access 2010	![Access icon]
Microsoft Excel 2010	![Excel icon]
Microsoft PowerPoint 2010	![PowerPoint icon]
Microsoft Word 2010	![Word icon]

Hands-On Exercise: Use Multiple Applications

① Open Microsoft Excel 2010. Click the Start button on the taskbar and the Start menu displays.

② Click Microsoft Excel 2010 .

    a. If Microsoft Excel 2010 does not display in the Start menu, click All Programs , and a list of all programs installed on your computer will display.

    b. Click the Microsoft Office folder.

    c. Click Microsoft Excel 2010 , and the application opens in a new window. The Microsoft Excel application icon displays on the taskbar (**Figure 1.58**).

    d. Click the Microsoft Word application icon on the taskbar to navigate back to Microsoft Word.

Figure 1.58 Multiple Applications Open

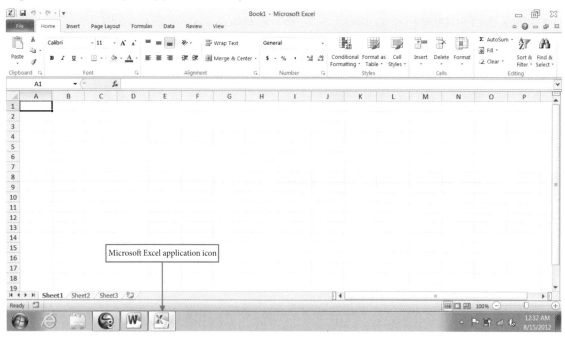

Close Command

You should close a file when you are finished working with it. When you close a file, it will ask you to save the file if you haven't done so already. It does not close the application; it closes only the file. Follow these steps to close a file:

- Click the **File** tab.
- Click **Close**.
- If the file is not saved, it will prompt you to save the file at that time.

You can also close a file by double-clicking the application icon located to the left of the Quick Access Toolbar (Figure 1.59). If only one document is open, it will close the document and exit the application.

Hands-On Exercise: Close a Document

(1) Click the File tab.

(2) Click Close (**Figure 1.59**).

(3) The document closes, but the application remains open.

Figure 1.59 Close Command

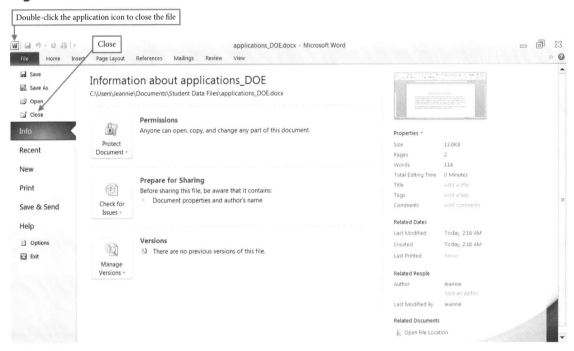

Exit Application

Use the **Exit command** to exit (or quit) the application. The Exit command is located on the File tab. Use any of these methods to exit the application:

Exit command: Exits (or quits) the application.

- Click the **Close** button on the title bar (**Figure 1.60**).
  - This works only if one document is open within the application. If multiple documents are open, the Close button will close the current document and leave the other documents open within the application.
- Click the **File** tab and then click **Exit** (**Figure 1.61**).
- Press **Alt + F4**, which are the shortcut keys to exit the application
- Double-click the **application icon** located to the left of the Quick Access Toolbar.
  - This works only if one document is open within the application.

Hands-On Exercise: Exit Application

① Click the Close button on the title bar, and the application closes (Figure 1.60).

② Click the Microsoft Excel application icon on the taskbar.

③ Click the File tab.

④ Click Exit (Figure 1.61) and the application closes.

Figure 1.60 Close Button

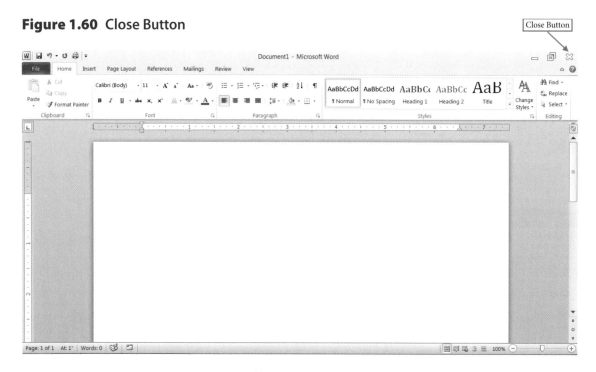

Figure 1.61 Exit Command

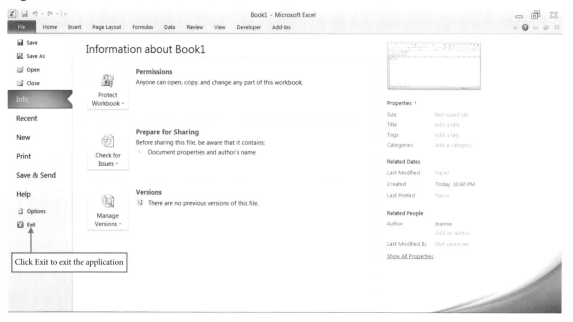

Multiple-Choice Questions

1. What is displayed on the title bar?
   a. Backstage view
   b. The name of the file that is currently open, along with the name of the application used to create file
   c. The status of the document
   d. The Ribbon

2. A _____ displays when the mouse hovers over a command.
   a. ToolTip
   b. ScreenTip
   c. File name
   d. Both A and B

3. What displays when you right-click an object or area of the window?
   a. Title bar
   b. Ribbon
   c. Shortcut menu
   d. Gallery

4. How is the Help command accessed?
   a. Click the Review tab
   b. Press F1 on the keyboard
   c. Click on the title bar
   d. Open a dialog box

5. The _____ provides quick access to the most frequently used commands.
   a. Quick Access Toolbar
   b. ToolTip
   c. Insertion point
   d. View buttons

6. The _____ contains commands to manage your files.
   a. Gallery
   b. Mini Toolbar
   c. Backstage view
   d. Undo button

7. A _____ is a collection of visual options.
   a. Zoom Control
   b. Quick Access Toolbar
   c. Scroll bar
   d. Gallery

8. Which tab on the Ribbon is automatically active when you launch an application?

   a. Home tab

   b. View tab

   c. File tab

   d. Review tab

9. The _____ command is used when you want to make changes to a document and save it with a different file name, keeping the original file intact.

   a. Save As

   b. Save

   c. New

   d. Close

10. When you click the Close button in the File tab, it closes the _____.

   a. Application

   b. Ribbon

   c. Dialog box

   d. Document

Project #1: Use the Help Feature, and Create a Screenshot of Result

In this exercise you will launch Microsoft Word 2010, use the Help feature, create a screenshot of the search results, and save the document.

① Launch Microsoft Word 2010.

② Use the Help feature to search for help on how to save a document.

③ Once you find the Help information, you will take a screenshot of the information and place it in your document using the Screenshot command. Screenshot is a command used to capture a snapshot (take a picture) of an open window. Follow these instructions to take a screenshot of the Help dialog box:

Screenshot: A command used to capture a snapshot (take a picture) of an open window.

   a. Click in the document window.

   b. Click the **Insert** tab on the Ribbon.

   c. Click **Screenshot** in the Illustrations group, and a gallery displays the various windows that are open (**Figure 1.62**).

   d. Point to the choices in the gallery, and a ToolTip displays.

   e. Click the **Word Help** window in the gallery (Figure 1.62).

   f. The screenshot is inserted into the document.

Figure 1.62 Screenshot Command

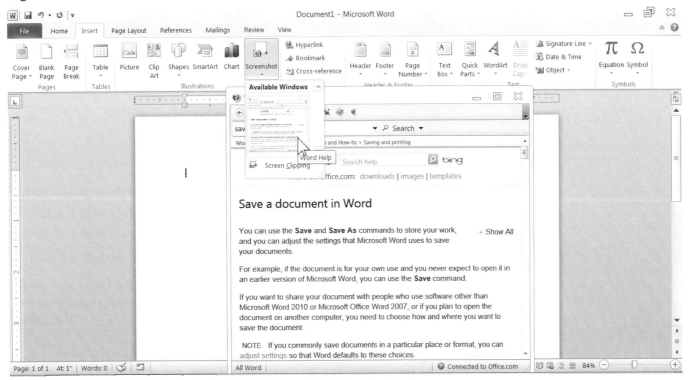

④ Close the Word Help dialog box.

⑤ Save the document as **Help Project**.

⑥ Print the document.

⑦ Close the document.

⑧ Exit the application.

Project #2: Open a Document and Correct Spelling and Grammar Errors

In this exercise you will open a document and use the Spelling & Grammar feature to correct spelling and grammar errors.

① Open the Invitation document.

② Correct all spelling errors.

③ Save the document as **Invitation Revised**.

④ Print the document.

⑤ Close the document.

⑥ Exit the application.

Project #3: Customize the Quick Access Toolbar, and Minimize and Expand the Ribbon

In this exercise you work with various commands on the Quick Access Toolbar.

1. Launch Microsoft Word 2010.

2. Add the Spelling & Grammar command to the Quick Access Toolbar.

3. Minimize the Ribbon.

4. Press the **Print Screen** key on the keyboard to capture the current screen in memory.

    a. The Print Screen key may be labeled Prnt Scrn, Prtsc, Prtscn, or something similar. Some keyboards may require the use of the Fn (Function) key along with the Print Screen key or may use other keyboard combinations, such as Fn + Insert, to take a capture of the screen. Refer to your computer manual if the Print Screen key does not exist on your keyboard.

    b. You cannot use the Screenshot command that was used in a previous exercise because the Ribbon is minimized.

5. Press **Ctrl + V**, which are the shortcut keys for the Paste command, to paste the screenshot into the document.

6. Press **Ctrl + Enter** to navigate to the second page of the document.

7. Expand the Ribbon.

8. Remove the Spelling & Grammar command from the Quick Access Toolbar.

9. Press the **Print Screen** key on your keyboard to capture the current screen in memory.

10. Press **Ctrl + V** to paste the screenshot into the document.

11. Save the document as **Toolbar Project**.

12. Print the document.

13. Close the document.

14. Exit the application.

Create Documents Using Microsoft Word 2010

Chapter Objectives

After completing this chapter, you will be able to do the following:

- Identify Microsoft Word 2010 components.
- Create a document.
- Insert, modify, and delete text.
- Navigate a document.
- Select text.
- Cut, copy, and paste text.
- Format text and paragraphs.
- Find and replace text.
- Check spelling and grammar.
- Save a document.
- Print a document.
- Use templates.

Microsoft Word 2010 is a word processing application used to create professional-looking documents, including letters, memos, newsletters, brochures, flyers, resumes, and other documents. It is used to create documents for both personal and work-related tasks. Microsoft Word 2010 contains many tools for formatting text in the document.

In this chapter, you will become acquainted with various features and elements of Microsoft Word 2010. You will create a letter and format the document to give it a professional appearance. You will also get an introduction to working with templates.

Launch Microsoft Word 2010

You will open Microsoft Word 2010 and get acquainted with its components.

Hands-On Exercise: Launch Microsoft Word 2010

1. Click the Start button.
2. Click All Programs .
3. Click Microsoft Office . You may need to scroll through the Start menu to locate the folder.
4. Click Microsoft Word 2010 .
5. A new blank Microsoft Word 2010 document displays (**Figure 2.1**).

Identify Microsoft Word 2010 Components

Backstage view: Commands to manage your files such as creating, opening, saving, and printing a document. Click the File tab to open the Backstage view.

Command: A button or text that performs an action or task.

Dialog box: A window that allows a user to perform commands or apply settings.

Dialog box launcher: A button that resembles a diagonal arrow, which displays to the right of a group name on the Ribbon.

Mini Toolbar: Contains formatting commands that can be applied to the selected text. The Mini Toolbar displays at the top right of the selected text and will appear faded or dimmed.

Quick Access Toolbar: A toolbar that provides access to the most frequently used commands. By default, the Quick Access Toolbar is located at the left corner of the title bar.

Table 2.1 illustrates many common elements and key terms used in Microsoft Office applications.

Table 2.1 Common Microsoft Office 2010 Elements and Terms	
Common Element	**Description**
Backstage View	The Backstage view contains commands to manage your files such as creating, opening, saving, and printing a document. Click the **File tab** to open the Backstage view.
Command	A command is a button or text that performs an action or task.
Dialog Box	A dialog box is a window that allows a user to perform commands or apply settings. A dialog box displays when the dialog box launcher is clicked. A dialog box launcher is a button that resembles a diagonal arrow, which displays to the right of a group name on the Ribbon (Figure 2.1).
Mini Toolbar	The Mini Toolbar displays when text is selected and contains formatting commands that can be applied to the selected text. The Mini Toolbar displays at the top right of the selected text and will appear faded or dimmed.
Quick Access Toolbar	The Quick Access Toolbar provides access to the most frequently used commands. By default, the Quick Access Toolbar is located at the left corner of the title bar (Figure 2.1).

Table 2.1 *continued*

Ribbon	The Ribbon contains all the commands a user needs to create and edit a document. The Ribbon is located below the title bar and contains tabs that are organized by groups of related commands (Figure 2.1). Seven tabs display by default at the top of the Ribbon, starting with the Home tab. (The File tab is not considered part of the Ribbon.)
Ruler bar	The ruler bar is used to align text, graphics, and other elements in a document. The horizontal ruler displays below the Ribbon and the vertical ruler displays to the left of the document window (Figure 2.1). The white area of the ruler bar indicates the area of the document in which text and objects can be inserted. The gray area represents the margin. If the rulers are not displaying, click the **View** tab and click the **Ruler** box in the Show group *or* click the **View Ruler** button (Figure 2.1) at the top of the vertical scroll bar.
Scroll bar	A scroll bar allows the user to navigate either up and down or left and right to view the information in a document (Figure 2.1).
Shortcut menu	A shortcut menu displays when the user right-clicks an object or area of the window. It contains a list of commands related to the object.
Status bar	The status bar provides information about the status of the document. The status bar is located at the bottom of the application window (Figure 2.1).
Title bar	The title bar displays the name of the file that is currently open and the name of the application. The title bar is the top bar on the application window (Figure 2.1).
ToolTip (ScreenTip)	A ToolTip (ScreenTip) lists the name of the command and sometimes includes a brief description of the command. A ToolTip displays when the mouse points, or hovers, over a command. It may also display keyboard shortcuts that can be used to initiate the command using the keyboard.
View buttons	The View buttons provide options for viewing the document. The View buttons are located on the right side of the status bar (Figure 2.1). By default, the document opens in Print Layout view.
Zoom controls	The Zoom controls allow the user to zoom in and out of specific areas in the document. This feature controls the magnification of the document. The Zoom controls are displayed on the right side of the status bar (Figure 2.1).

Ribbon: Contains all the commands a user needs to create and edit a document. The Ribbon is located below the title bar and contains tabs that are organized by groups of related commands.

Ruler bar: Used to align text, graphics, and other elements in a document. The *horizontal ruler* displays below the Ribbon, and the *vertical ruler* displays to the left of the document window.

Scroll bar: Allows the user to navigate either up and down or left and right to view the information in a document.

Shortcut menu: Displays when the user right-clicks an object or area of the window. It contains a list of commands related to the object.

Status bar: Provides information about the status of the document. The status bar is located at the bottom of the application window.

Title bar: Displays the name of the file that is currently open and the name of the application. The title bar is the top bar on the application window.

ToolTip (ScreenTip): Lists the name of the command and sometimes includes a brief description of the command. A ToolTip displays when the mouse points, or hovers, over a command. It may also display keyboard shortcuts that can be used to initiate the command using the keyboard.

View buttons: Provide options for viewing the document. The View buttons are located on the right side of the status bar.

Zoom controls: Allow the user to zoom in and out of specific areas in the document. This feature controls the magnification of the document. The Zoom controls are displayed on the right side of the status bar.

Figure 2.1 A New Microsoft Word 2010 Document

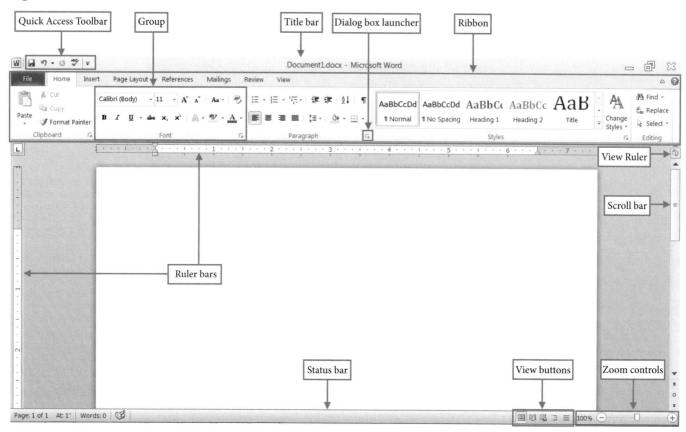

Insert Text

When you open a new blank document, a blinking insertion point displays. Click in the location where you want to insert the text and start typing. As you type a line of text and reach the end of the line, the insertion point and text automatically wrap to the next line. You do not need to press Enter at the end of each line in a paragraph. This is called word wrap. Press Enter only if you want to begin a new paragraph. If you enter a few words and press Enter, that is considered a paragraph, because a paragraph comprises the entire text entered before you press the Enter key.

> **Word wrap:** As the user types a line of text and reaches the end of the line, the insertion point and text automatically wrap to the next line.

Use these steps to insert text into a document:

- Position the insertion point at the place in the document where you want to insert text.
- Type the text to insert it.

When you press Enter after a paragraph, there is additional spacing between the paragraphs, which makes the text appear to be double-spaced. You will learn how to change the spacing after the paragraphs later in the chapter.

Hands-On Exercise: Insert Text

① You are going to create a cover letter. If the ruler is not displaying, click the View Ruler button above the vertical scroll bar to display the rulers.

② Type the following into the document (**Figure 2.2**):

a. Type **Chris Watson** and press Enter .

b. Type **1223 Main Street** and press Enter .

c. Type **Riverdale, GA 61365** and press Enter twice.

d. Next you will type **September 1, 2014**. As you type the first four letters of the word September, *Sept,* the AutoComplete tip displays above the text `September (Press ENTER to Insert)` `Sept` Press Enter to insert the word September and then type the rest of the date. Press Enter three times.

e. Type **Mr. Howard Jackson** and press Enter .

f. Type **TEC Corporation** and press Enter .

g. Type **8901 Randall Road** and press Enter .

h. Type **Atlanta, GA 64307** and press Enter .

i. Type **Dear Mr. Jacson** and press Enter . Notice that the name *Jacson* was deliberately misspelled. You will correct the spelling later in the chapter.

j. Type the following paragraph.

I am writing in response to the job opening listed in the Atlanta Times for a sales manager. I am a conscientious and thorough worker. I am passionate about the opportunity to grow and further the development of my skills. I am confident that my business experience, communication skills, and technical skills are a perfect match for this position.

k. Press Enter .

l. Type **I have the following qualifications that I feel would benefit your organization:** and press Enter .

m. Type **Three years of sales experience** and press Enter .

n. Type **Excellent communication and customer service skills** and press Enter .

o. Type **Proficient in Microsoft Office applications** and press Enter .

p. Type the following paragraph.

I believe my experience and skills will be an asset for your organization and would welcome the opportunity to speak with you further about this job opportunity. I have enclosed my resume for your review. I am available for an interview at your convenience and may be reached at (783) 450-0926. I look forward to hearing from you soon.

q. Press Enter .

r. Type **Sincerely** and press Enter .

s. Type **Chris Watson** and press Enter . The document should resemble Figure 2.2.

Figure 2.2 Document Created

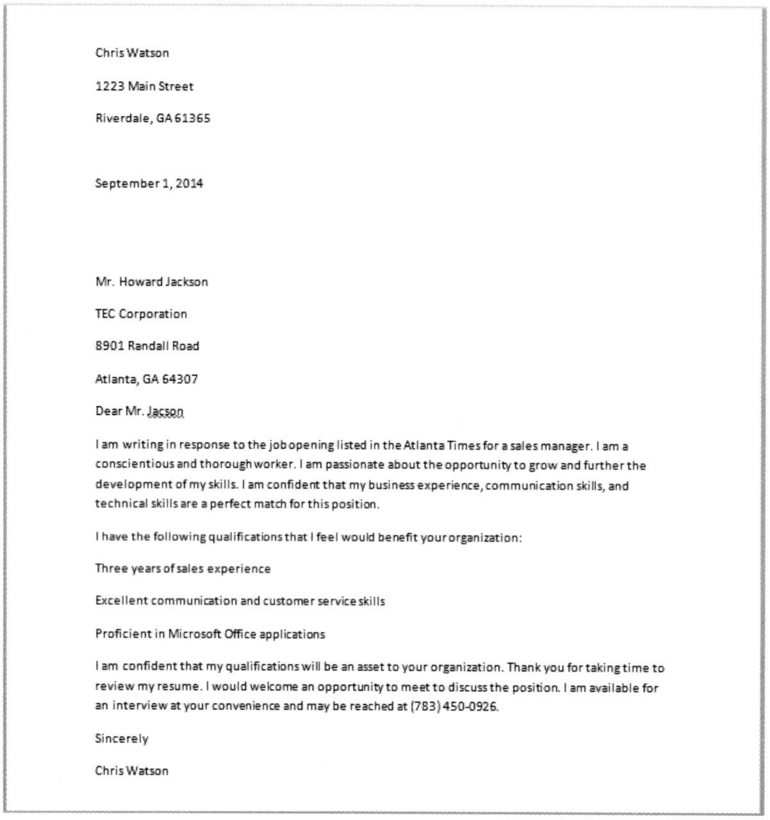

Chris Watson

1223 Main Street

Riverdale, GA 61365

September 1, 2014

Mr. Howard Jackson

TEC Corporation

8901 Randall Road

Atlanta, GA 64307

Dear Mr. Jacson

I am writing in response to the job opening listed in the Atlanta Times for a sales manager. I am a conscientious and thorough worker. I am passionate about the opportunity to grow and further the development of my skills. I am confident that my business experience, communication skills, and technical skills are a perfect match for this position.

I have the following qualifications that I feel would benefit your organization:

Three years of sales experience

Excellent communication and customer service skills

Proficient in Microsoft Office applications

I am confident that my qualifications will be an asset to your organization. Thank you for taking time to review my resume. I would welcome an opportunity to meet to discuss the position. I am available for an interview at your convenience and may be reached at (783) 450-0926.

Sincerely

Chris Watson

Navigation Techniques

There are several ways to navigate within a document. **Table 2.2** displays various navigation techniques.

Table 2.2 Navigation Techniques	
Key	Navigation
Home	Moves to the beginning of a line.
End	Moves to the end of a line.
Ctrl + Home	Moves to the beginning of the document.
Ctrl + End	Moves to the end of the document.
Arrows	Moves up, down, right, and left.
Page Up	Moves up one screen of the document.
Page Down	Moves down one screen of the document.

Hands-On Exercise: Navigate a Document

1. Press Ctrl + Home to navigate to the beginning of the document.
2. Press End to navigate to the end of the line.
3. Press Home to navigate to the beginning of the line.
4. Press Ctrl + End to navigate to the end of the document.
5. Press Page Up on the keyboard to move up one screen in the document.
6. Press the Down arrow on the keyboard to move down one line in the document.
7. Press Ctrl + Home to navigate to the beginning of the document.

Selection Techniques

You may need to select text in order to perform certain tasks. **Table 2.3** displays various selection techniques.

Table 2.3 Selection Techniques	
Task	Steps
Select text	Drag the mouse over text.
Select a word	Double-click the word.
Select a line	Place the mouse pointer at the left margin of the line, and an arrow displays. Click once, and the entire line is selected.
Select a paragraph	Triple-click anywhere in the paragraph.
Select a sentence	Hold the **Ctrl** key and click anywhere in the sentence.
Select entire document	Press **Ctrl + A**.

When text is selected, the selection may include the spacing or line break after the text. If you want to select only the text without the spacing or line break, drag the mouse over the text backward, meaning drag the mouse from the end of the word to the left until the entire word or text is selected.

Hands-On Exercise: Select Text in a Document

1. Double-click the word *Watson* in the first paragraph. The word is selected.
2. Click anywhere in the document window to deselect the word.
3. Triple-click in the paragraph that starts with *I am writing in response,* and the entire paragraph is selected.

→

④ Click anywhere in the document window to deselect the paragraph.

⑤ Hold the Ctrl key and click anywhere in the sentence that starts with *I am writing in response,* and the entire sentence is selected.

⑥ Press Ctrl + A to select the entire document.

⑦ Press Ctrl + Home to navigate to the beginning of the document.

⑧ Place the mouse pointer at the left margin of the first line in the document, and an arrow displays (**Figure 2.3**).

⑨ Click once and the entire line is selected.

Figure 2.3 Selection Techniques

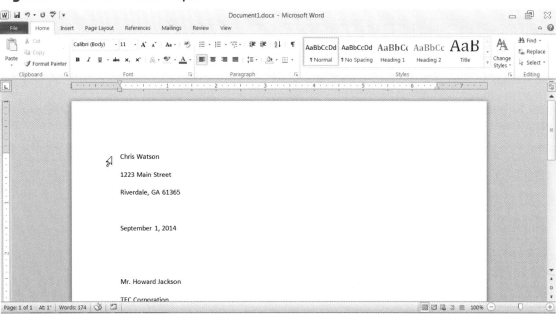

Edit and Delete Text

You can edit text by selecting the text to edit and retyping the correct information. You can delete text by using the Backspace or Delete keys. **Table 2.4** describes ways to delete text using the Backspace and Delete keys. If text is selected and you press Delete or Backspace, it will delete the entire selection.

Table 2.4 Delete Text

Key(s)	Description
Backspace	Deletes the character to the left of the insertion point.
Delete	Deletes the character to the right of the insertion point.
Ctrl + Backspace	Deletes the word to the left of the insertion point.
Ctrl + Delete	Deletes the word to the right of the insertion point.

Hands-On Exercise: Edit and Delete Text

1. Double-click the word *September*. The word is selected.

2. Type **October**. The word *September* is deleted and *October* is inserted in its place.

3. Click before the *W* in *Watson* in the first line of the document. You will insert the middle initial.

4. Type **J.** and press the space bar to add a space after the middle initial.

5. The address should be 223 Main Street. You will delete the number *1* in the address. Position the insertion point to the right of the number *1* in the address.

6. Press Backspace , and the number *1* is deleted.

7. Click the Undo button on the Quick Access Toolbar to undo the deletion (**Figure 2.4**). You will delete the number *1* again using the Delete key.

8. Position the insertion point to the left of the number *1* in the address.

9. Press Delete and the number *1* is deleted. The document should resemble Figure 2.4.

Figure 2.4 Text Modified

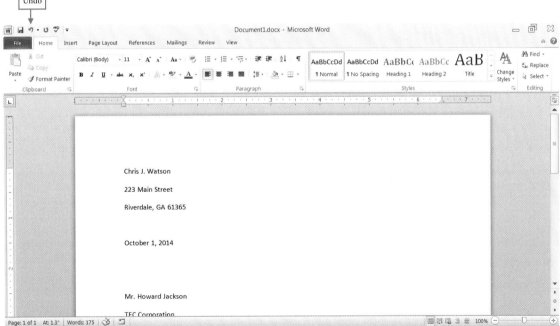

Chris J. Watson

223 Main Street

Riverdale, GA 61365

October 1, 2014

Mr. Howard Jackson

TEC Corporation

Show/Hide Command

The **Show/Hide button**, when clicked, displays paragraph marks and other hidden formatting symbols in the document. This option remains active until you click the button again. These marks and symbols will not display when printing the document. **Table 2.5** displays common formatting marks and what they represent.

Show/Hide button: A command that displays paragraph marks and other hidden formatting symbols in the document.

Table 2.5 Common Formatting Marks		
Format	Marks/Symbols	Description
Space	•	A dot indicates when the space bar was used. If words seem too far apart or sentences too close together, check for the correct number of dots.
End of Paragraph	¶	Displays when you press the Enter key.
Tab	→	Displays tabs that are inserted in the document.

Hands-On Exercise: Use Show/Hide Button

① Click the Show/Hide button (**Figure 2.5**) in the Paragraph group on the Home tab. The formatting marks and symbols display. The document should resemble **Figure 2.6**.

② Make any changes to the document to ensure it matches Figure 2.6. Missing paragraph marks mean that you did not press the Enter key at the appropriate places. If you have extra paragraph marks, delete them by clicking before the paragraph mark and pressing the Delete key.

③ Click the Show/Hide button a second time, and the formatting marks and symbols are hidden.

Figure 2.5 Show/Hide Button

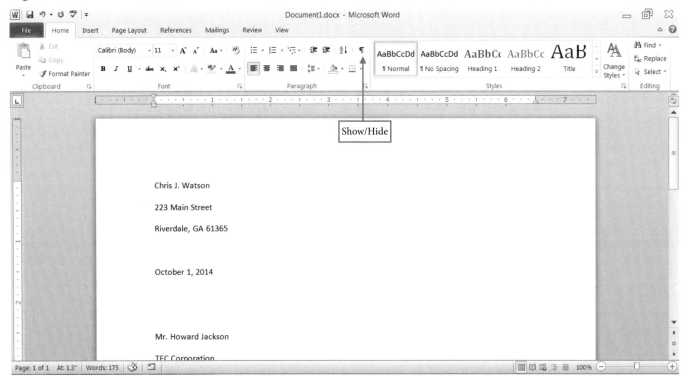

Figure 2.6 Formatting Marks and Symbols Displayed in Document

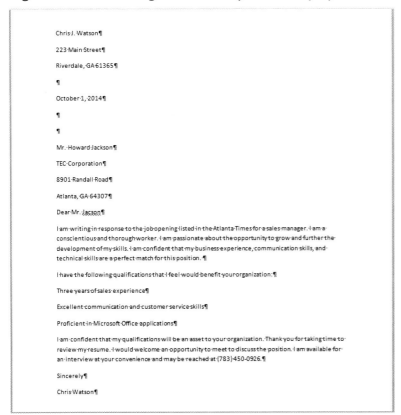

Cut, Copy, and Paste Text

You can cut, copy, and paste text and objects to other locations in the document or to other documents. When you cut or copy text or objects, they are stored on the Clipboard. The **Clipboard** holds up to 24 items that have been cut or copied. The commands to cut, copy, and paste are located on the Clipboard group on the Home tab (**Figure 2.7**). **Table 2.6** describes the cut, copy, and paste commands.

Clipboard: Holds up to 24 items that have been cut or copied.

Table 2.6 Clipboard Commands

Command	Shortcut Key	Description
Cut	Ctrl + X	The **Cut** command removes selected text and objects from the document and places them on the Clipboard so you can paste it to another location.
		Cut is not the same as delete. When you delete text, it is removed from the document. You cannot paste it to another location.
Copy	Ctrl + C	The **Copy** command copies selected text and objects and places it on the Clipboard.
Paste	Ctrl + V	The **Paste** command allows you to paste items from the Clipboard. Click the Paste arrow to display additional paste options.

Cut: A command that removes selected text and objects from the document and places them on the Clipboard.

Copy: A command that copies selected text and objects and places it on the Clipboard.

Paste: A command that allows you to paste items from the Clipboard.

Figure 2.8 Office Clipboard Task Pane

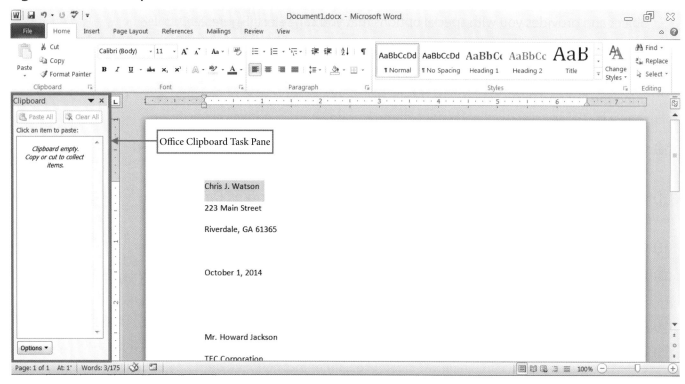

Figure 2.9 Text Pasted into the Document and Paste Options Button

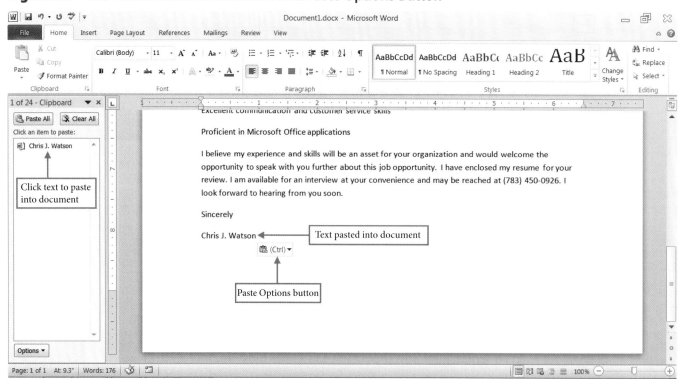

Figure 2.10 Paragraph Cut and Pasted into the Document

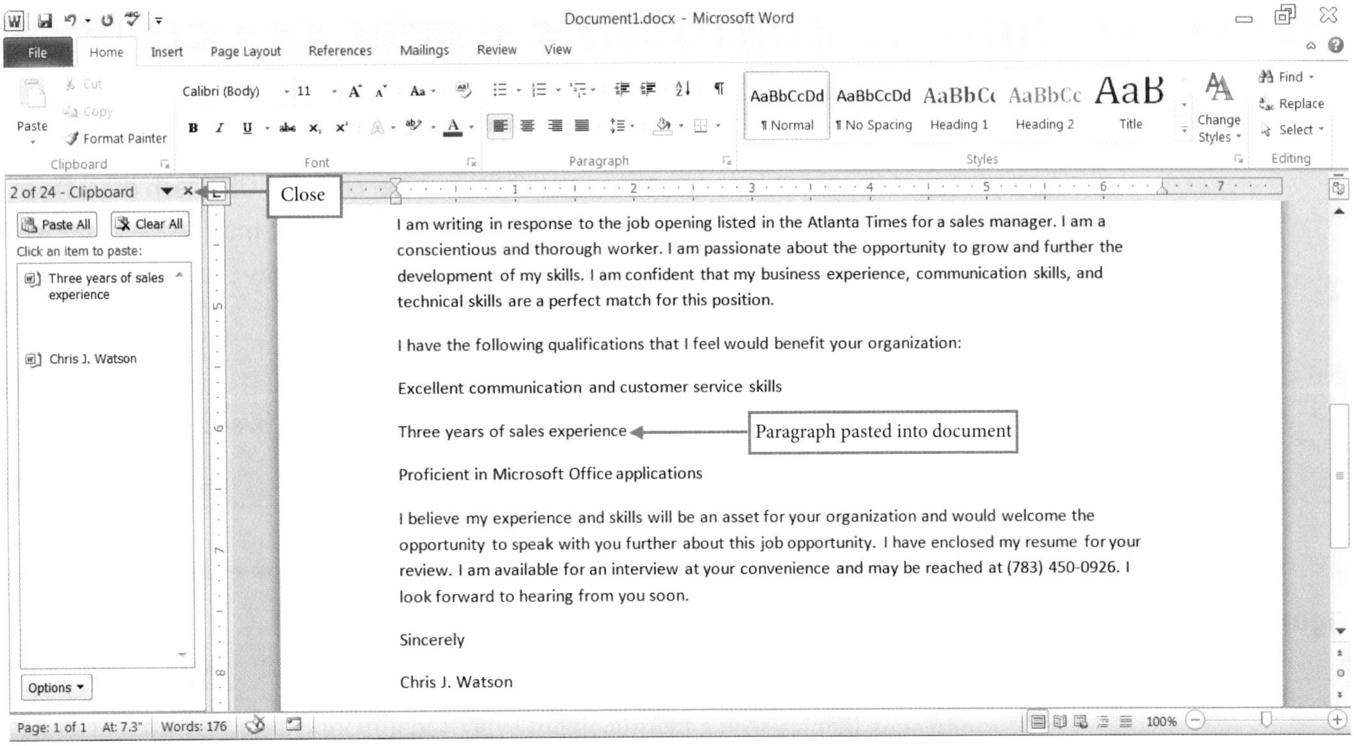

Save a Document

You should save your document often to avoid losing the data in your document. The file name can contain up to 255 characters including the drive letter, folder name, and extension but cannot contain special characters such as these: <> ? : " | \ / . Microsoft Word 2010 documents contain a filename extension of docx.

Use any of these methods to save the document:

- Press **Ctrl + S** on the keyboard.
- Click the **Save** button on the Quick Access Toolbar (**Figure 2.11**).
- Click the **File** tab and select **Save** or **Save As**.

When you save the document for the first time or when you use the Save As command, you can select the location where you want to save the document and name the document. The new name of the document displays in the title bar.

Hands-On Exercise: Save a Document

① Click the Save button on the Quick Access Toolbar (Figure 2.11). The Save As dialog box displays (**Figure 2.12**).

An easy way to format text is to select the text and click a command from the Font group on the Home tab. Many of the commands on the Ribbon contain arrows that you can click to view additional choices.

Use these steps to format text:

- Select the text you want to format.
- Select the format command you want to apply to the text by clicking the command in the Font group on the Home tab. If the command contains a down arrow, that means there are several options. Once a command has been applied, a gold background displays in the button, indicating that the command is applied to the selected text.

Some of the formatting commands, such as the Bold, Italic, and Underline commands, are toggle buttons. If you click the button, it applies the format to the text. Click the button again, and it removes the format from the text.

The Mini Toolbar can also be used to format text. The Mini Toolbar displays when text is selected. It displays at the top right of the selected text and will appear faded or dimmed. When the insertion point is positioned on the Mini Toolbar, it becomes solid and active.

Table 2.7 contains a list of the commands in the Font group.

Table 2.7 Commands in Font Group

Command	Button	Description
Font	Calibri	Changes the font.
Font Size	11	Changes the font size. You can select the font size from the list or type the font size in the box.
Grow Font	A˘	Increases the font size.
Shrink Font	A�‘	Decreases the font size.
Change Case	Aa	Changes the case of the selected text.
Clear Formatting		Clears the formatting.
Bold	B	Bolds the selected text.
Italic	I	Italicizes the selected text.
Underline	U	Underlines the selected text.
Strikethrough	abc	Inserts a line in the middle of the selected text.
Subscript	x₂	Creates small letters below text level.
Superscript	x²	Creates small letters above text level.
Text Effects	A	Applies a visual effect to the selected text.
Text Highlight Color		Makes the selected text appear that it was marked with a high-lighter pen.
Font Color	A	Changes the font color.

Figure 2.10 Paragraph Cut and Pasted into the Document

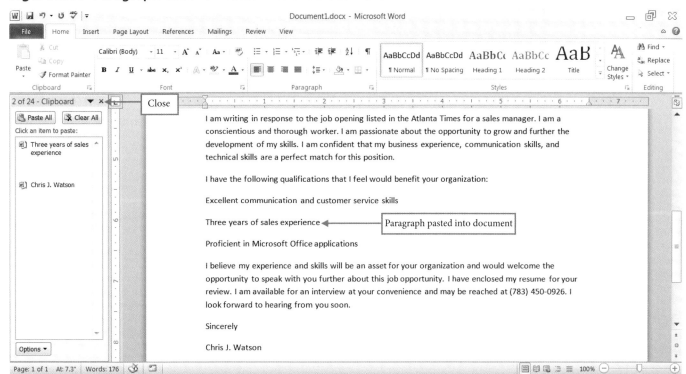

Save a Document

You should save your document often to avoid losing the data in your document. The file name can contain up to 255 characters including the drive letter, folder name, and extension but cannot contain special characters such as these: <> ? : " | \ / . Microsoft Word 2010 documents contain a filename extension of docx.

Use any of these methods to save the document:

- Press **Ctrl + S** on the keyboard.
- Click the **Save** button on the Quick Access Toolbar (**Figure 2.11**).
- Click the **File** tab and select **Save** or **Save As**.

When you save the document for the first time or when you use the Save As command, you can select the location where you want to save the document and name the document. The new name of the document displays in the title bar.

Hands-On Exercise: Save a Document

① Click the Save button on the Quick Access Toolbar (Figure 2.11). The Save As dialog box displays (**Figure 2.12**).

② Select the location where you want to save the document.

   a. Click Documents under Libraries to save the document on your computer (Figure 2.12). You can then double-click the folder in the Documents Library where you want to store the document.

   b. If you want to save the document to a USB flash drive, click the USB flash drive from the list in the left pane in the Computer section (Figure 2.12). It may display as drive D, E, F, or G, depending on your computer. You can then double-click a folder in the USB flash drive where you want to store the document.

③ Type **Cover Letter** in the *File name* box (Figure 2.12).

④ Click the Save button (Figure 2.12). The name of the document, *Cover Letter,* displays in the title bar.

Figure 2.11 Save a Document

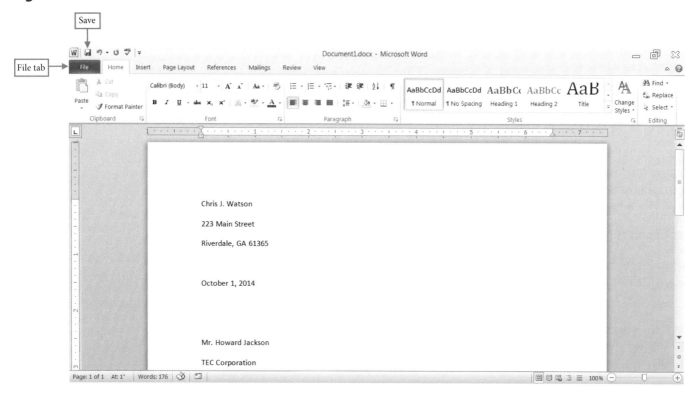

Figure 2.12 Save As Dialog Box

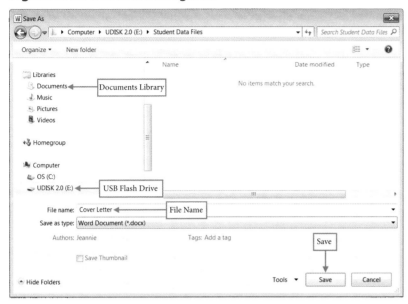

Format Text

You can format the text in the document to give the document a professional appearance. The commands to format the text are located in the Font group on the Home tab (**Figure 2.13**). A **font** is a character set of a single size and style of a typeface. Changing the font changes how the letters look. When you create a new blank document, the default font is Calibri and the font size is 11 pt. One inch has 72 points. Points are measurements used in the printing industry to measure font size. A font size of 11 points is 11/72 inch. The higher the point size, the larger the font size.

> **Font:** A character set of a single size and style of a typeface.

Figure 2.13 Font Commands

An easy way to format text is to select the text and click a command from the Font group on the Home tab. Many of the commands on the Ribbon contain arrows that you can click to view additional choices.

Use these steps to format text:

- Select the text you want to format.
- Select the format command you want to apply to the text by clicking the command in the Font group on the Home tab. If the command contains a down arrow, that means there are several options. Once a command has been applied, a gold background displays in the button, indicating that the command is applied to the selected text.

Some of the formatting commands, such as the Bold, Italic, and Underline commands, are toggle buttons. If you click the button, it applies the format to the text. Click the button again, and it removes the format from the text.

The Mini Toolbar can also be used to format text. The Mini Toolbar displays when text is selected. It displays at the top right of the selected text and will appear faded or dimmed. When the insertion point is positioned on the Mini Toolbar, it becomes solid and active.

Table 2.7 contains a list of the commands in the Font group.

Table 2.7 Commands in Font Group

Command	Button	Description
Font	Calibri	Changes the font.
Font Size	11	Changes the font size. You can select the font size from the list or type the font size in the box.
Grow Font	A˄	Increases the font size.
Shrink Font	A˅	Decreases the font size.
Change Case	Aa ˅	Changes the case of the selected text.
Clear Formatting		Clears the formatting.
Bold	B	Bolds the selected text.
Italic	I	Italicizes the selected text.
Underline	U ˅	Underlines the selected text.
Strikethrough	abc	Inserts a line in the middle of the selected text.
Subscript	x₂	Creates small letters below text level.
Superscript	x²	Creates small letters above text level.
Text Effects	A ˅	Applies a visual effect to the selected text.
Text Highlight Color	ab ˅	Makes the selected text appear that it was marked with a high-lighter pen.
Font Color	A ˅	Changes the font color.

Hands-On Exercise: Format Text

1. Triple-click *Chris J. Watson* in the first line in the document to select the entire paragraph. You will apply the following commands to the selected text:

   a. Click the Bold button to bold the selected text (**Figure 2.14**). A gold background displays in the Bold button, indicating that the command was applied to the selected text.

   b. Click the Font Size arrow and select 18 (Figure 2.14). The font size becomes larger.

   c. Click the Shrink Font button twice to decrease the size of the font (**Figure 2.15**). The font size becomes 14.

   d. Click the Grow Font button twice to increase the size of the font size to 18.

   e. Click the Clear Formatting button to clear the formatting from the selected text (Figure 2.15). Notice the text remains in the document, but all the formatting is removed.

   f. Click the Undo button to undo the clear formatting command. The document should resemble Figure 2.15.

   g. Click the Font Color arrow, and a gallery of colors displays (**Figure 2.16**).

   h. Click Blue in the Standard Colors group. In the Font Color gallery, you can point to the color, and the name of the color displays as a ToolTip (Figure 2.16).

2. Press Ctrl + A to select the entire document.

3. Click the Font arrow and select Times New Roman from the list (**Figure 2.17**). You can scroll through the list to find the font or type the first few letters of the font name, and a listing of fonts that match the letters will display in the list. Click Times New Roman and the font is changed throughout the document.

4. Click anywhere in the document window to deselect the text.

5. Drag the mouse across the text *Atlanta Times* to select the text.

6. The Mini Toolbar displays at the top right of the selected text and appears faded or dimmed. Move the insertion point on the Mini Toolbar, and it becomes active (**Figure 2.18**).

7. Click the Italic button on the Mini Toolbar to italicize the text (Figure 2.18).

8. Press the Home key to navigate to the beginning of the line. The text is deselected.

9. Click the Save button.

Figure 2.14 Apply Bold and Change Font Size of Selected Text

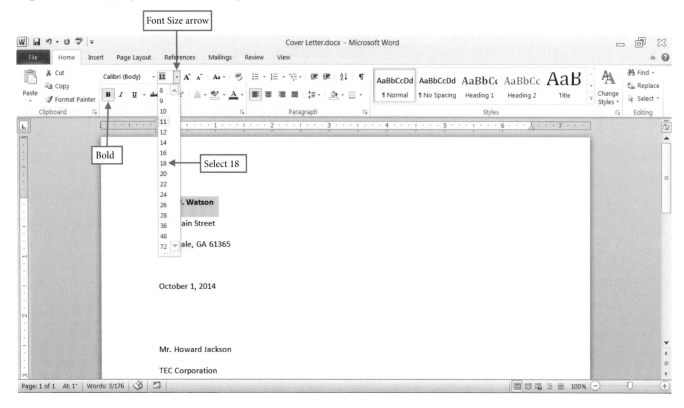

Figure 2.15 Grow Font, Shrink Font, and Clear Formatting Commands

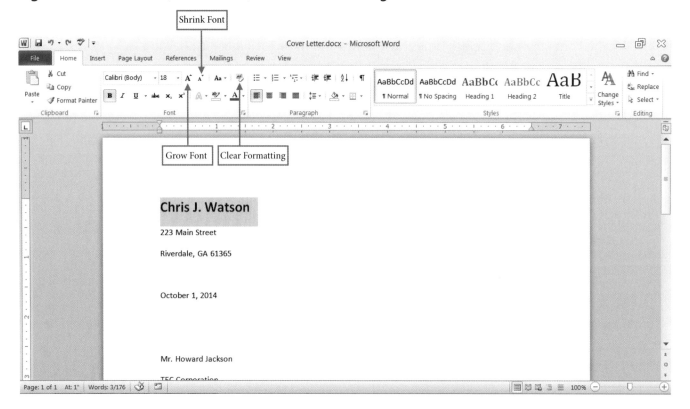

Figure 2.16 Change Font Color

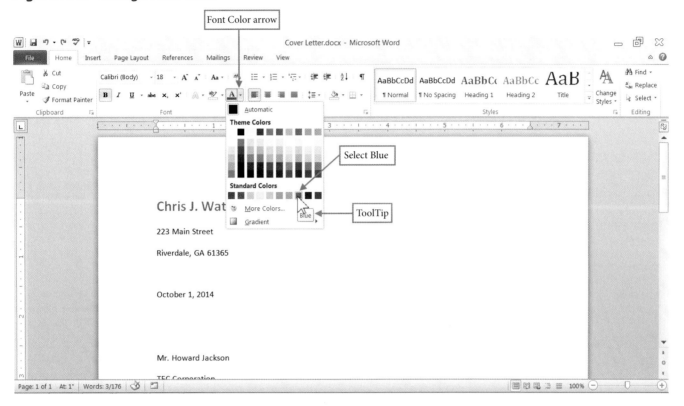

Figure 2.17 Change Font of the Entire Document

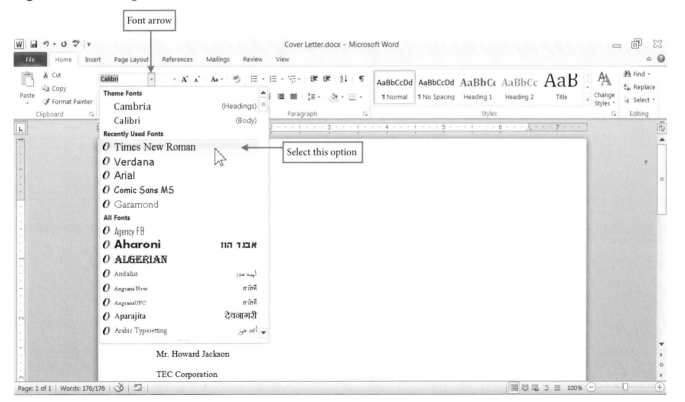

Figure 2.18 Italicize Text

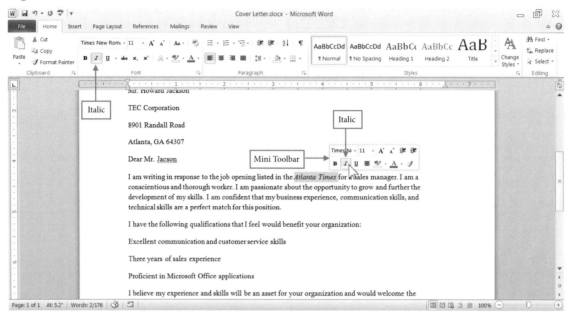

Use the Font Dialog Box

In addition to using the commands in the Font group to change the formatting of text, you can click the Font dialog box launcher to open the Font dialog box (**Figure 2.19**). You can add many font commands at once using the Font dialog box.

Hands-On Exercise: Format Text Using the Font Dialog Box

1. Press Ctrl + Home to navigate to the top of the document.
2. Triple-click in the second paragraph in the document that contains the address *223 Main Street*.
3. Click the Font dialog box launcher to open the Font dialog box (Figure 2.19).
4. Click Bold in the *Font Style* list (Figure 2.19).
5. Scroll in the *Size* list and select 12 (Figure 2.19).
6. Click OK to close the Font dialog box.
7. Select the text from the date *October 1, 2014* to the end of the document by dragging the mouse across the text. You will change the font size to 12 for the selected text.
8. Click the Font dialog box launcher to open the Font dialog box.
9. Scroll in the *Size* list and select 12.
10. Click OK to close the Font dialog box.
11. Press Ctrl + Home to navigate to the beginning of the document. The text is dese-lected. The document should resemble **Figure 2.20**.

Figure 2.19 Font Dialog Box

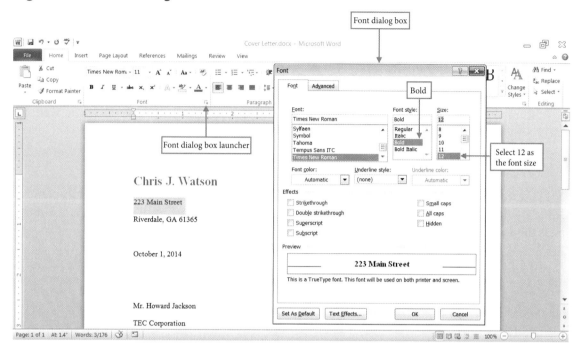

Figure 2.20 Font Changes Made to Document

Format Painter Command

The Format Painter command copies the formatting of the selected text and applies that formatting to other text in the document.

Use these steps to copy formatting:

- Click in the text that has the formatting you want to copy.
- Click the **Format Painter** button in the Clipboard group on the Home tab if you want to copy the format to one selection.
- Drag the mouse pointer, which has changed to a brush, over the text to which you want to copy the format.

If you want to use the Format Painter to format text throughout the document multiple times, double-click the **Format Painter** button. It will remain active until you click it again or press the **Esc** key.

Hands-On Exercise: Use Format Painter Button

① You will copy the format of the address line and apply the formatting to the next line, which contains the city, state, and zip code. Position the insertion point anywhere in the text *223 Main Street,* which contains the formatting you want to copy (**Figure 2.21**).

② Click the Format Painter button in the Clipboard group on the Home tab (Figure 2.21). The mouse pointer displays as a brush (Figure 2.21).

③ Drag the mouse pointer (which has become a brush) over the words *Riverdale, GA 61365* in the third line of the document (Figure 2.21).

④ Press Home to navigate to the beginning of the line. The text is deselected. The document should resemble **Figure 2.22**.

Figure 2.21 Format Painter

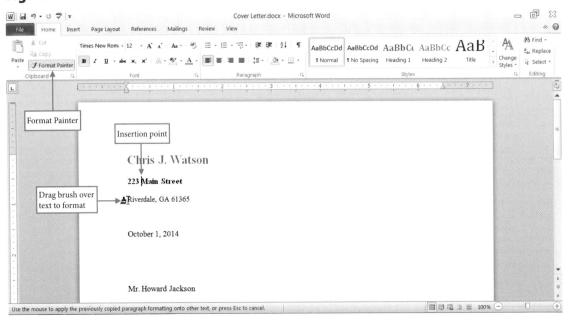

Figure 2.22 Text Formatted Using the Format Painter Button

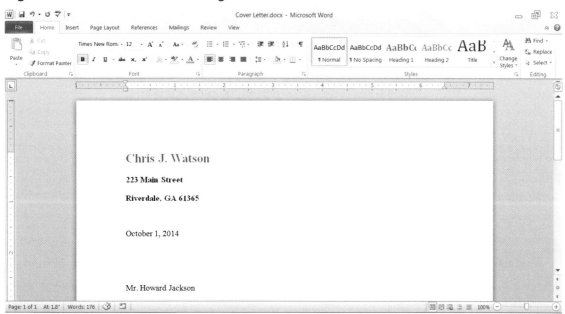

Format Paragraph

You can apply formatting to paragraphs. You can modify the alignment and line spacing. You can also insert bullets, line numbering, indents, borders, and shading.

Table 2.8 describes various formatting commands located in the Paragraph group on the Home tab.

Table 2.8 Format Paragraph Commands

Command	Button	Description
Bullets		Starts a bulleted list. Click the arrow to select a different bullet style.
Numbering		Starts a numbered list. Click the arrow to select a different numbering format.
Multilevel List		Starts a multilevel list.
Decrease Indent		Decreases the indent level of the paragraph.
Increase Indent		Increases the indent level of the paragraph.
Sort		Alphabetizes the selected text or sorts numeric data.
Show/Hide		Shows paragraph marks and other hidden formatting symbols.
Align Text Left		Aligns text to the left margin.
Center		Centers text.
Align Text Right		Aligns text to the right margin.
Justify		Aligns text to both the left and right margins.

Table 2.8 *continued*		
Line and paragraph spacing		Changes the spacing between lines of text.
Shading		Colors the background behind the selected text or paragraph.
Border		Customizes the border of the selected text.

Create a Bulleted List

Bullets are commonly used in documents to create lists. The arrow next to the Bullets button opens the Bullet Library. The Bullet Library contains a variety of bullet styles.

Use these steps to create a new bulleted list:

- Click the **Bullets** button to insert the default bullet style or click the **Bullets** arrow and select a bullet style from the Bullet Library.
- Type the text and press **Enter**. Another bullet displays. Repeat this step until you create the entire bulleted list.

Use these steps to apply bullets to existing text in a document:

- Select the text to which you want to apply the bullets.
- Click the **Bullets** button to insert the default bullet style *or* click the **Bullets** arrow and select a bullet style from the Bullet Library. A bullet will display at the beginning of each paragraph.

You can also press the * (Asterisk key) and then the space bar to start a bulleted list.

Use any of these methods to remove a bullet:

- Position the insertion point to the right of the bullet you want to remove.
- Perform any of the steps:
  a. Press the **Backspace** key.
  b. Click the **Bullets** button to turn off the Bullets command.
  c. Click the **Bullets** arrow and select **None**.

Hands-On Exercise: Create a Bulleted List

1. Select the following three lines of text by dragging the mouse across the text:

   Excellent communication and customer service skills
   Three years of sales experience
   Proficient in Microsoft Office applications

2. Click the Bullets button in the Paragraph group on the Home tab to insert the default bullet style to the selected text. The document should resemble **Figure 2.23**.

3. You will change the style of the bullets. Click the Bullets arrow, and the Bullet Library displays (**Figure 2.24**).

4. Click the checkmark arrow as shown in Figure 2.24.

5. Click anywhere in the document window to deselect the text. The document should resemble **Figure 2.25**.

Figure 2.23 Bullets Button

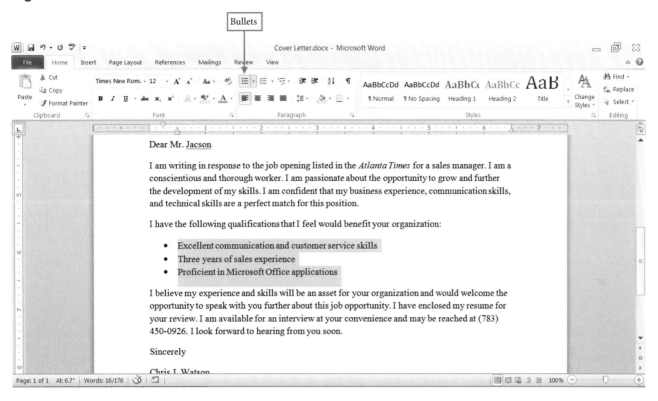

Figure 2.24 Bullet Library

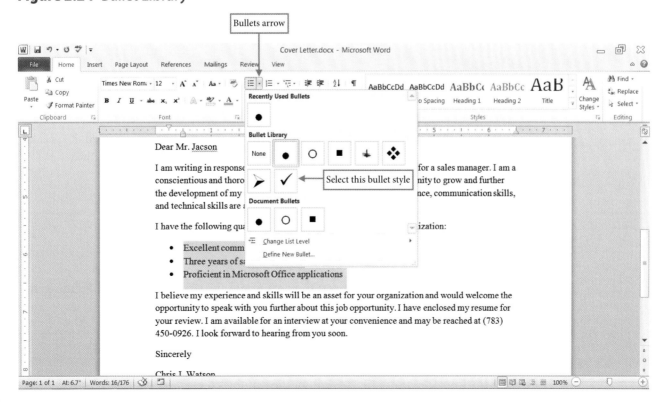

Figure 2.25 Bullets Added to Document

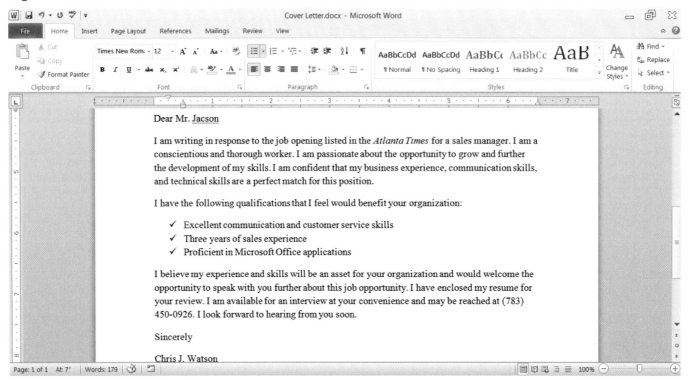

Create a Numbered List

You can create a numbered list in the document. Click the **Numbering** button in the Paragraph group to begin a numbered list (**Figure 2.26**). Click the **Numbering** arrow to select a different numbering format.

Use these steps to create a new numbered list:

- Position the insertion point in the location where you want to start the numbered list.
- Click the **Numbering** button to insert the default numbered list style *or* click the **Numbering** arrow and select a different style from the Numbering Library (Figure 2.26).
- Type the text and press **Enter**. The next number displays. Repeat this step until you create the entire numbered list.

Use these steps to apply a numbered list to existing text in a document:

- Select the text to which you want to apply a numbered list.
- Click the **Numbering** button to insert the default numbered list *or* click the **Numbering** arrow and select a numbered list style from the Numbering Library.

You can also type 1. and then press **Tab** to start a numbered list.

Use any of these methods to remove a numbered list:

- Position the insertion point to the right of the numbered list you want to remove.

- Perform any of the steps:
  a. Press the **Backspace** key.
  b. Click the **Numbering** button to turn off the command.
  c. Click the **Numbering** arrow and select **None**.

Hands-On Exercise: Create a Numbered List

① Select the following three lines of text by dragging the mouse across the text:

Excellent communication and customer service skills
Three years of sales experience
Proficient in Microsoft Office applications

② You will change the three lines to a numbered list. Click the Numbering button and the default numbered list displays (Figure 2.26).

③ Click the Numbering arrow and the Numbering Library displays (**Figure 2.27**).

④ Click the Number alignment: Left option as shown in (Figure 2.27).

⑤ Click anywhere in the document window to deselect the text. The document should resemble **Figure 2.28**.

Figure 2.26 **Numbering Button**

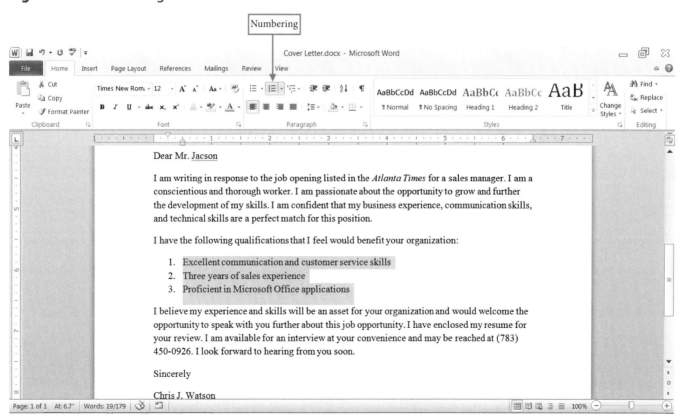

Figure 2.27 Numbering Library

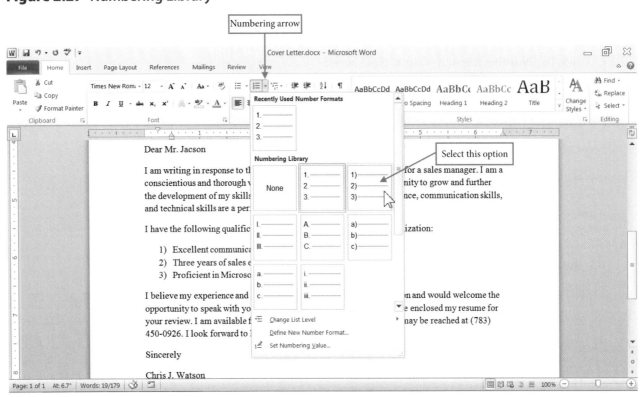

Figure 2.28 Numbered List Created

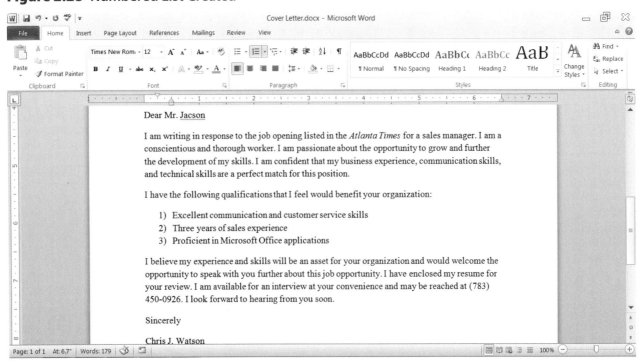

Increase and Decrease Indents

You can increase the indent level of a paragraph using the **Increase Indent** button (**Figure 2.29**). This button increases the indent level by ½ inch. When applied to numbers, this button increases the indent level by ¼ inch. When an indent is applied to a bulleted or numbered list, it changes the style of the list.

You can decrease the indent level of the paragraph using the **Decrease Indent** button. This button decreases the indent level by ½ inch (**Figure 2.30**).

Use these steps to increase the indent of a paragraph:

- Click in the paragraph in which you want to increase the indent.
- Click the **Increase Indent** button in the Paragraph group on the Home tab (Figure 2.29). The entire paragraph is indented.

Use these steps to decrease the indent of a paragraph:

- Click in the paragraph in which you want to decrease the indent.
- Click the **Decrease Indent** button in the Paragraph group on the Home tab (Figure 2.30).

Hands-On Exercise: Increase and Decrease Indents

① Triple-click in the following paragraph to select the entire paragraph:

I am writing in response to the job opening listed in the Atlanta Times for a sales manager. I am a conscientious and thorough worker. I am passionate about the opportunity to grow and further the development of my skills. I am confident that my business experience, communication skills, and technical skills are a perfect match for this position.

② Click the Increase Indent button (Figure 2.29). The entire paragraph is indented ½ inch to the right.

③ Click the Increase Indent button again. The entire paragraph is indented another ½ inch to the right.

④ Click the Decrease Indent button twice to decrease the indent and move the paragraph back to its original position (Figure 2.30).

⑤ Triple-click the second numbered list to select the entire paragraph:

2) Three years of sales experience

⑥ Click the Increase Indent button. The text indents to the right and the numbered list changes to a bullet (**Figure 2.31**).

⑦ Click the Undo button on the Quick Access Toolbar to undo the change.

⑧ Click the Save button in the Quick Access Toolbar.

Figure 2.29 Increase Indent

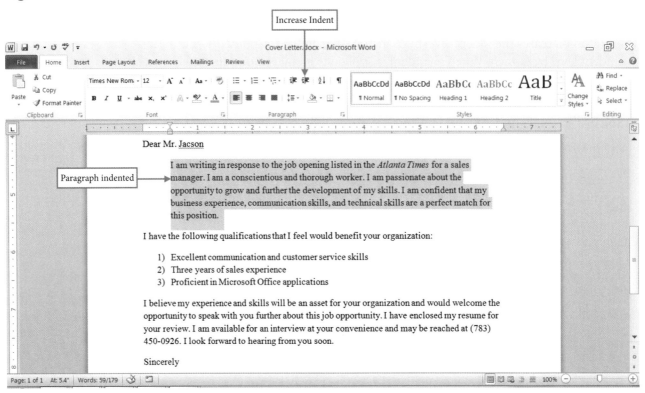

Figure 2.30 Decrease Indent

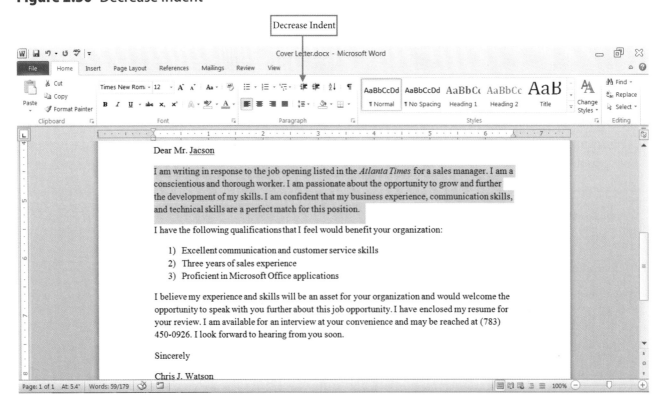

Figure 2.31 Numbered List Indented

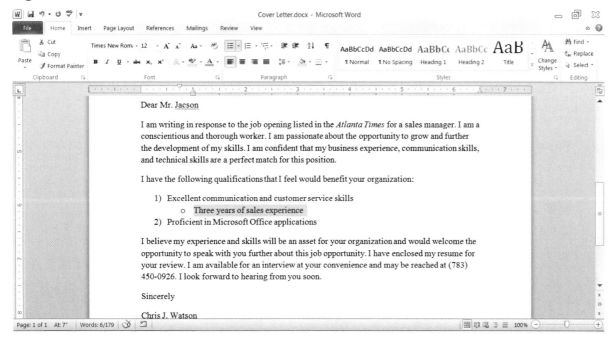

Sort Paragraphs

You can alphabetize selected text in ascending or descending order. You can also sort numerical data. The Sort command is available in the Paragraph group on the Home tab.

Use these steps to sort text:

- Select the text to be sorted.
- Click the **Sort** button in the Paragraph group on the Home tab (**Figure 2.32**). The Sort Text dialog box displays (Figure 2.32).
- Make a selection from the Sort by list. Select **Paragraphs** to sort the selected text by paragraphs.
- Make a selection from the Type list. Select whether the selection contains text, numbers, or a date.
- Select the **Ascending** or **Descending** option. Ascending will sort the selection from A to Z. Descending will sort the selection from Z to A.

Hands-On Exercise: Sort Paragraphs

① Select the following three lines of text, which contain the numbered list:

Excellent communication and customer service skills

Three years of sales experience

Proficient in Microsoft Office applications

② Click the Sort button (Figure 2.32). The Sort Text dialog box displays (Figure 2.32).

③ Select Paragraphs in the Sort by list if it is not already selected, because the selected text are paragraphs.

④ Select Text from the Type list if it is not already selected, because you are sorting text.

⑤ Select the Ascending option if it is not already selected. Ascending will sort the text from A to Z.

⑥ Click OK. The list is sorted in alphabetical order. The document should resemble (**Figure 2.33**).

Figure 2.32 Sort Button and Sort Text Dialog Box

Figure 2.33 Paragraph Sorted

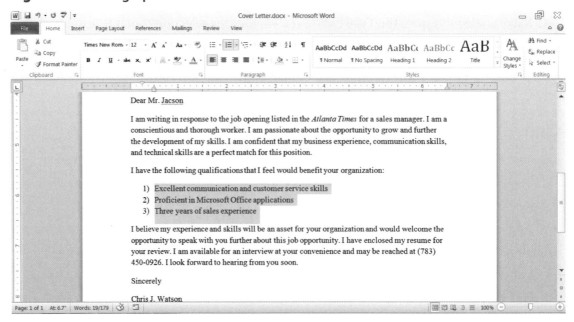

Align Text

By default, the text in a document is left aligned. The alignment buttons in the Paragraph group allow you to change the alignment of text and objects. **Table 2.9** explains the various ways to align text.

Table 2.9 Alignment Buttons		
Command	Button	Description
Align Text Left	≣	Aligns text with the left margin.
Center	≣	Centers the text between the left and right margins.
Align Text Right	≣	Aligns text with the right margin.
Justify	≣	Aligns text with both the left and right margins, adding extra space between the words as necessary.

Use these steps to align text:

- Click in the paragraph that you want to align.
- Click one of the Alignment buttons in the Paragraph group.

Hands-On Exercise: Align Text

1. Press Ctrl + Home to navigate to the top of the document.
2. Select the following text by dragging the mouse across the text:

   Chris J. Watson
   223 Main Street
   Riverdale, GA 61365

3. Click the Center button in the Paragraph group on the Home tab (**Figure 2.34**). The selected text is centered.
4. Triple-click in the following paragraph to select the entire paragraph:

   I believe my experience and skills will be an asset for your organization and would welcome the opportunity to speak with you further about this job opportunity. I have enclosed my resume for your review. I am available for an interview at your convenience and may be reached at (783) 450-0926. I look forward to hearing from you soon.

5. Click the Align Text Right button (**Figure 2.35**). The paragraph is aligned with the right margin.
6. Click the Justify button (**Figure 2.36**). The left and right margins are aligned. Extra spaces are added between the words as necessary. The document should resemble Figure 2.36.
7. Click the Align Text Left button (**Figure 2.37**). The paragraph is aligned with the left margin.

Figure 2.34 Center Text

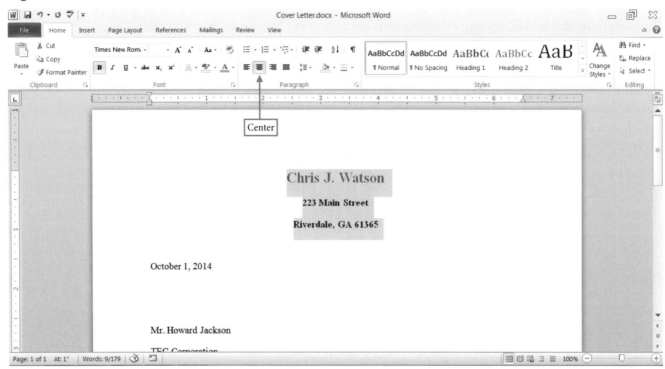

Figure 2.35 Paragraph Aligned on the Right

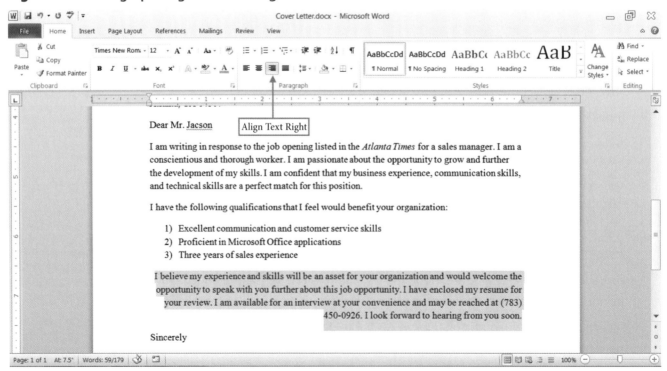

Figure 2.36 Paragraph Justified

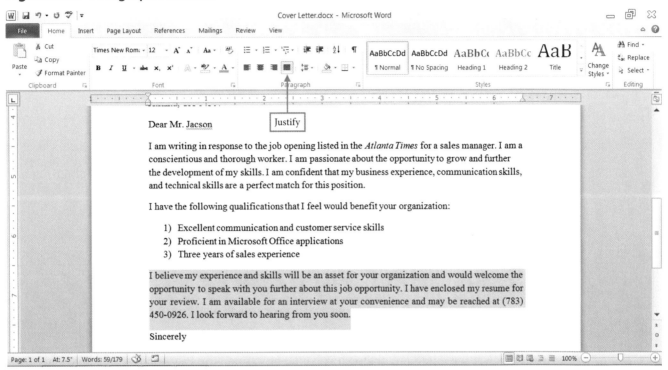

Figure 2.37 Paragraph Aligned on the Left

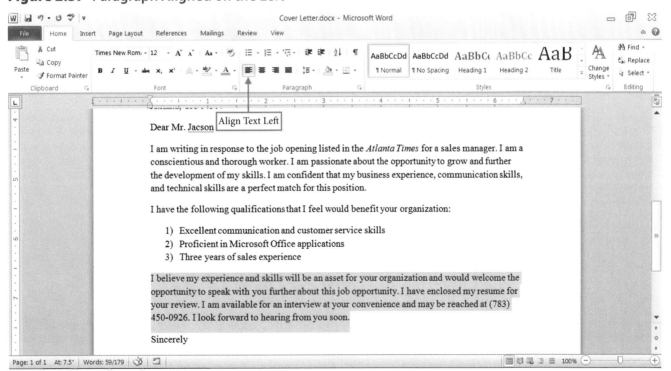

Apply Line and Paragraph Spacing

You can change the spacing between lines of text. You can also change the amount of space that displays before and after paragraphs. By default, a Microsoft Word 2010 document has a line spacing of 1.15. There is no spacing before paragraphs but a 10-point spacing after paragraphs. The paragraph spacing commands are used instead of using the Enter key to increase the spacing between paragraphs.

Use these steps to change the line spacing of text in the document:

- Select the lines of text for which you want to change the line spacing.
- Click the **Line and Paragraph Spacing** button (**Figure 2.38**) in the Paragraph group on the Home tab and select one of the options.

Use these steps to change the spacing before or after a paragraph:

- Select the lines of text that you want to change.
- Click the **Line and Paragraph Spacing** button in the Paragraph group on the Home tab (Figure 2.38).
  - Click **Add Space Before Paragraph** to add space before a paragraph.
  - Click **Remove Space After Paragraph** to remove space after a paragraph.

You can click the Paragraph dialog box launcher to open the Paragraph dialog box. This dialog box contains commands that you can apply to a paragraph. You can change the spacing before and after a paragraph in the Spacing Before and Spacing After boxes. A 0-point indicates that there is no space. Increase the point size to add additional space between paragraphs.

You can also click the **Line and Paragraph Spacing** button and select **Line Spacing Options** to open the Paragraph dialog box. Additionally, the Spacing Before and Spacing After commands are located in the Paragraph group on the Page Layout tab.

Hands-On Exercise: Apply Line and Paragraph Spacing

(1) Press Ctrl + Home to navigate to the top of the document.

(2) Select the following text located at the top of the document:

Chris J. Watson
223 Main Street
Riverdale, GA 61365

(3) Click the Line and Paragraph Spacing button (Figure 2.38).

(4) Click Remove Space After Paragraph (**Figure 2.39**).

(5) Select the text from *October 1, 2014* through *8901 Randall Road,* as shown in **Figure 2.40.**

(6) You will remove the space after the paragraph using the Paragraph dialog box. Click the Paragraph dialog box launcher (Figure 2.40).

⑦ The Paragraph dialog box displays. Type **0** in the *Spacing After* box to remove the spacing after the paragraphs (**Figure 2.41**).

⑧ Click OK. The document should resemble **Figure 2.42**.

⑨ Triple-click anywhere in the following paragraph to select it:

I believe my experience and skills will be an asset for your organization and would welcome the opportunity to speak with you further about this job opportunity. I have enclosed my resume for your review. I am available for an interview at your convenience and may be reached at (783) 450-0926. I look forward to hearing from you soon.

⑩ Click the Line and Paragraph Spacing button.

⑪ Click 2.0 , and the paragraph is double-spaced. Notice that the spacing between the lines increases.

⑫ With the paragraph still selected, click the Line and Paragraph Spacing button.

⑬ Click 1.15 to apply the default line spacing back to the document.

⑭ Click Save on the Quick Access Toolbar. The document should resemble **Figure 2.43**.

Figure 2.38 Line and Paragraph Spacing Button

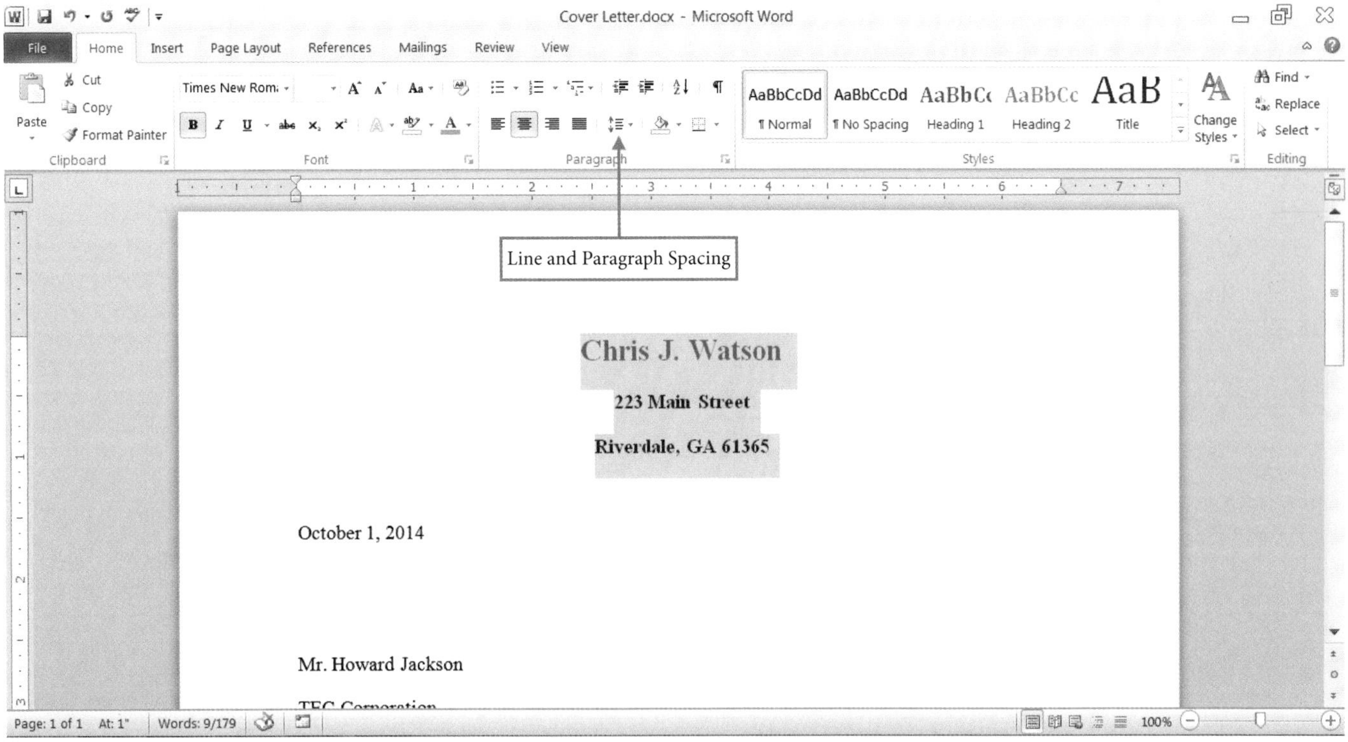

Figure 2.39 Remove Space after Paragraph

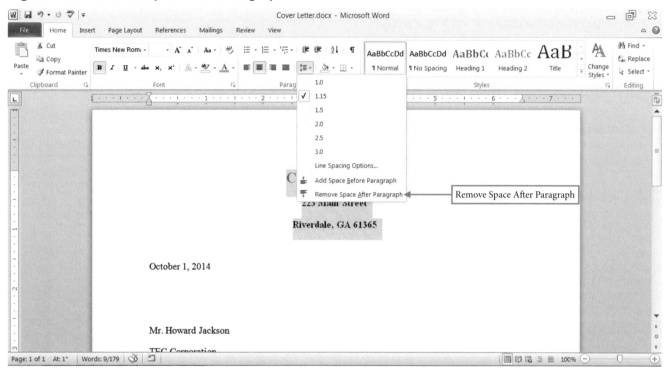

Figure 2.40 Paragraph Dialog Box Launcher

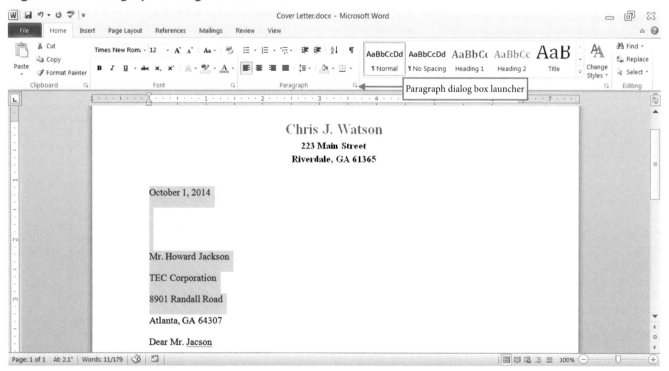

Figure 2.41 Paragraph Dialog Box

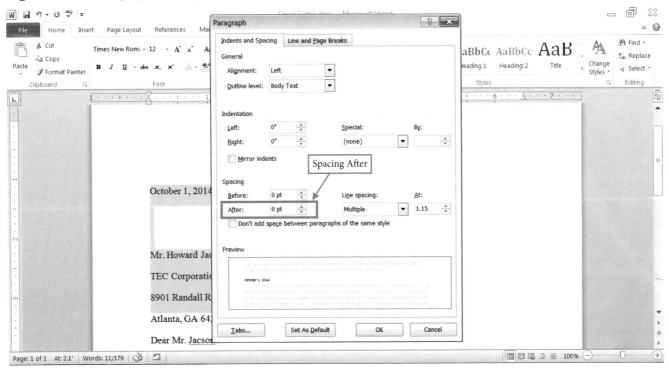

Figure 2.42 Spaces Removed after Paragraph

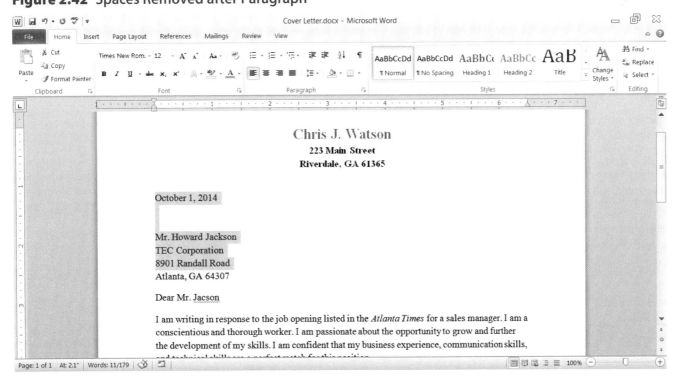

Figure 2.43 Line Spacing Changed to 1.15

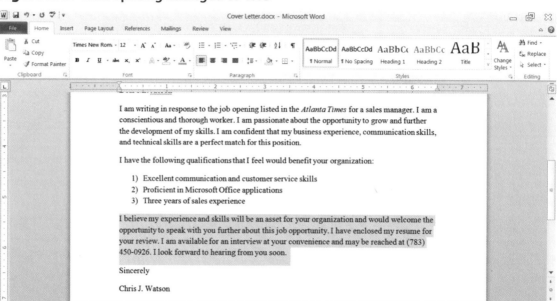

Insert Borders

You can insert a border around text or objects. The Borders button is located in the Paragraph group on the Home tab.

Use these steps to insert a border:

- Click in the paragraph to which you want to add a border.
- Click the **Borders** button in the Paragraph group on the Home tab to insert the default border *or* click the **Borders** arrow and a list of border options displays (**Figure 2.44**).
- Click the border you want to insert.

Use these steps to delete a border:

- Click in the paragraph to which you want to delete a border.
- Click the **Borders** arrow.
- Click **No Border** from the list *or* click the **Border** option you want to remove.

Hands-On Exercise: Insert Borders

① Position the insertion point in the following paragraph:

Riverdale, GA 61365

② Click the Borders button in the Paragraph group on the Home tab to insert the default border (Figure 2.44).

③ Click the Undo button to remove the border.

④ Click the Borders arrow.

(5) Click Bottom Border from the list (**Figure 2.45**). The document should resemble Figure 2.46.

(6) Next, you will remove the border. Be certain that the insertion point is positioned in the text *Riverdale, GA 61365*. Click the Borders arrow.

(7) Click No Border, and the border is removed.

Figure 2.44 Borders Button

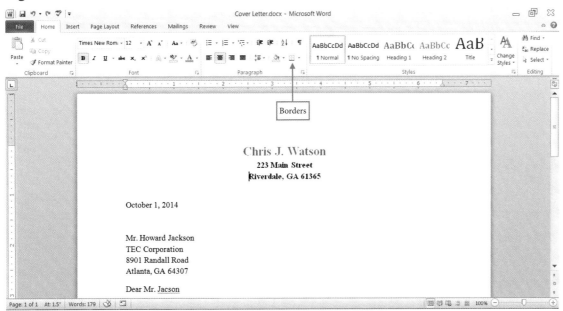

Figure 2.45 Select Bottom Border from the List

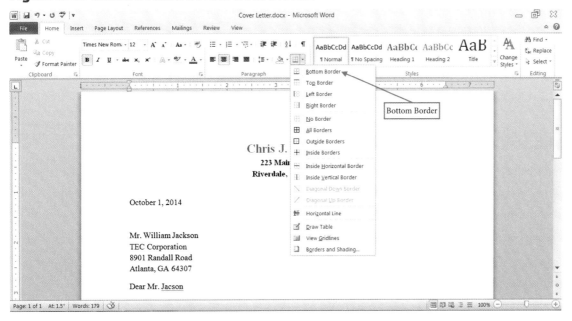

Figure 2.46 Bottom Border Inserted

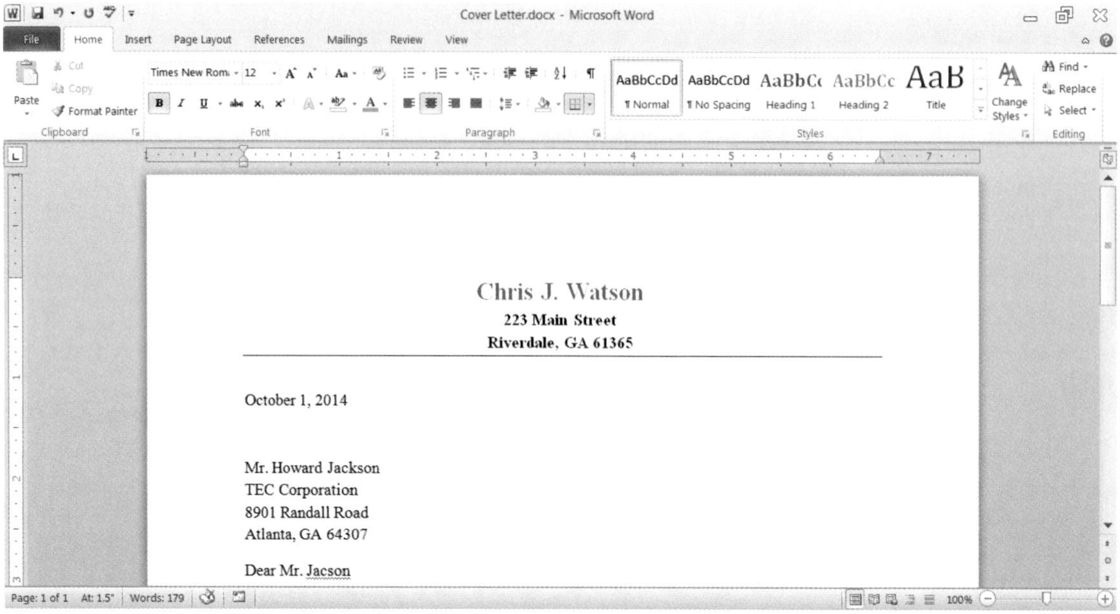

Apply Shading to Text

Shading: A command that colors the background of selected text.

The Shading command colors the background of selected text. When you click the Shading arrow, a gallery of colors displays (**Figure 2.47**).

Use these steps to apply shading to text:

- Select the text you want to shade.
- Click the **Shading** arrow in the Paragraph group on the Home tab.
- Select a color from the gallery.

If you click the Shading button instead of the Shadow arrow, the default shading color is applied to the selected text. When you first create a document, the shading color by default is set to No Color. If you select a color from the Shading button, it stores that color as the default.

Use these steps to delete shading from text:

- Select the text from which you want to remove the shading.
- Click the **Shading** arrow in the Paragraph group on the Home tab.
- Click **No Color**.

Hands-On Exercise: Apply Shading to Text

① Select the first three lines of the document, as shown in Figure 2.47.

② Click the Shading arrow in the Paragraph group on the Home tab (Figure 2.47). A gallery displays.

③ Click White, Background 1, Darker 15% in the gallery (**Figure 2.48**).

④ Press Home to navigate to the beginning of the line. The text is deselected. The document should resemble **Figure 2.49**.

Figure 2.47 Shading Button

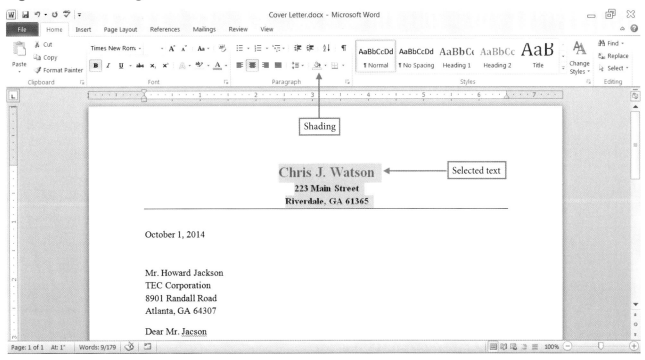

Figure 2.48 Select a Shading Color from the Gallery

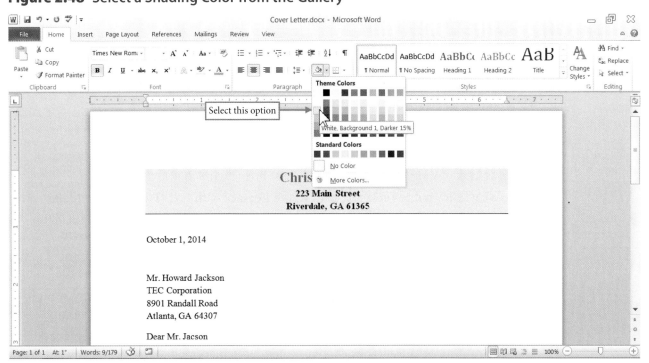

Figure 2.49 Shading Applied to the Text

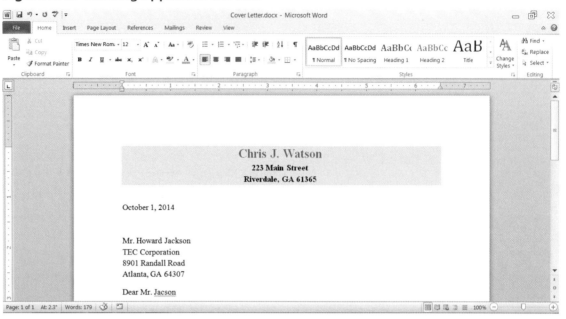

Find and Replace Text

You may want to find or replace certain text in the document. An easy way to do this is to use the Find and Replace commands, which are located in the Editing group on the Home tab.

The Find button allows you to locate text or other content in the document.

Use these steps to find text:

- Click the **Find** button in the Editing group on the Home tab (**Figure 2.50**).
- The Navigation pane displays on the left side of the document (Figure 2.50).
- Type the text for which you are searching in the Search Document box (Figure 2.50). Matches will be listed in the Navigation pane and highlighted in yellow in the document.
- Click a result in the list to view it in the document, *or* click the **Previous Search Result** or **Next Search Result** buttons to browse through the results (Figure 2.50).

Use these steps to replace text:

- Click the **Replace** button in the Editing group on the Home tab (**Figure 2.51**).
- The Find and Replace dialog box displays (**Figure 2.52**).
- Type what you want to find in the Find what box (Figure 2.52).
- Type what you want to replace it with in the Replace with box (Figure 2.52). Make certain to type it correctly. If you add a space unintentionally after you type the word in the Replace with box, the word and the space will be entered as the replacement.
- Click the **Replace**, **Replace All**, or **Find Next** button as you proceed through the document (Figure 2.52).
  - Replace will take you to the first word that is found in the document. If you want to replace the text, click **Replace**. If you want to skip that word, click **Find Next**.
  - **Replace All** will replace all words that are found in the document. Use Replace All with caution because it may cause unintended replacements.

Hands-On Exercise: Find and Replace Text

① Click Ctrl + Home to go to the top of the document.

② Click the Find button in the Editing group on the Home tab (Figure 2.50). The Navigation Pane displays on the left side of the document window (Figure 2.50).

③ Type **communication** in the Search Document box. The document highlights all occurrences of the word *communication* in yellow.

④ Click the Close button in the Navigation Pane (Figure 2.50).

⑤ Next you will replace the word *Howard* with *William* throughout the document. Click the Replace button in the Editing group on the Home tab (Figure 2.51). The Find and Replace dialog box displays (Figure 2.52).

⑥ Type **Howard** in the Find what box (Figure 2.52).

⑦ Type **William** in the Replace with box (Figure 2.52).

⑧ Click the Replace All button (Figure 2.52). A Microsoft Word dialog box displays that states, *Word has completed its search of the document and has made 1 replacement.*

⑨ Click OK to close the Microsoft Word dialog box.

⑩ Click the Close button on the Find and Replace dialog box. The document should resemble **Figure 2.53**.

Figure 2.50 Find Text

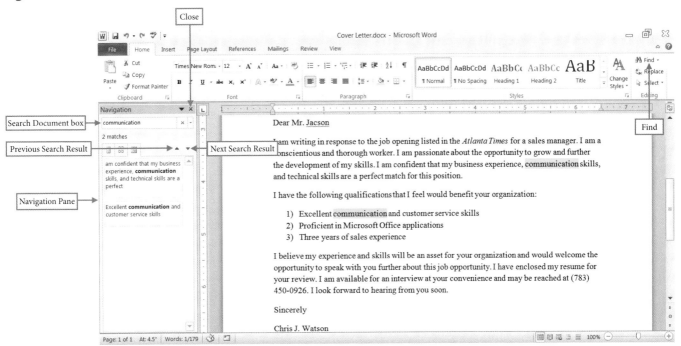

Figure 2.51 Replace Text

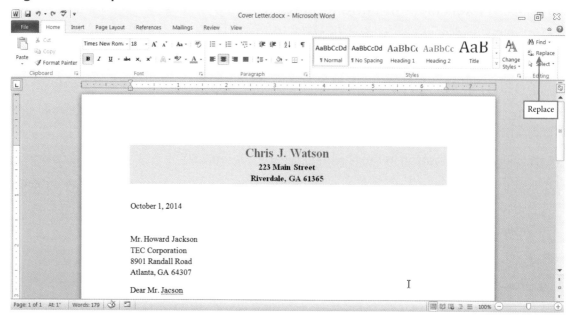

Figure 2.52 Find and Replace Dialog Box

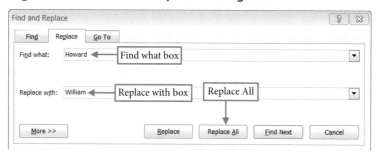

Figure 2.53 Text Replaced in a Document

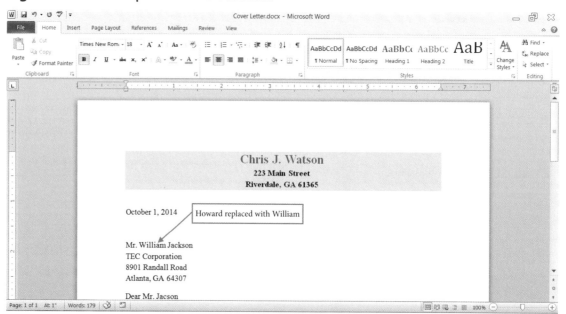

Correct Spelling and Grammar Errors

Make certain to correct spelling and grammar errors before the document is printed. Always proofread your work for content and additional word errors.

The Spelling & Grammar command checks spelling and grammar as you type. The Spelling & Grammar button is located in the Review tab in the Proofing group (**Figure 2.54**). Microsoft Word 2010 notifies you of possible errors by placing colored wavy lines under the text of potential errors (**Table 2.10**).

Table 2.10 Spelling and Grammar Errors	
Error	Description
Wavy red line under text	Indicates a potential spelling error.
Wavy green line under text	Indicates a potential grammar error.
Wavy blue line under text	Indicates a potential contextual spelling error.

Use these steps to check and correct spelling errors or add words to the dictionary:

- Click the **Review** tab.
- Click the **Spelling & Grammar button** in the Proofing group, and the Spelling and Grammar dialog box displays. Correct all errors.
- Some proper names may not be included in the dictionary and may display as potential spelling errors. In this case, click **Ignore All** to indicate that the word is spelled correctly, *or* click **Add to Dictionary** to store it in the dictionary.

If a wavy line displays under a word, right-click the word, and a shortcut menu displays with suggestions about spelling the word or makes grammar suggestions.

The Proofing Errors button on the status bar contains a blue check mark when no errors are found in the document. The Proofing Errors button contains a red *x* when there are errors in the document. Please keep in mind that the application can miss errors, so proofing a document is highly recommended. You can double-click the Proofing Errors button on the status bar to open the Spelling and Grammar dialog box.

The AutoCorrect feature is a great tool that helps correct spelling errors. The AutoCorrect feature automatically corrects commonly misspelled words as you type the text in the document. Have you ever typed *hte* instead of *the*? If so, the AutoCorrect feature would automatically change the word to the correct spelling. Many commonly misspelled words are in the dictionary and will automatically change to the correct spelling if you type them incorrectly.

> **AutoCorrect:** Automatically corrects common misspelled words as you type the text in the document.

Hands-On Exercise: Correct Spelling and Grammar Errors

① This document contains a spelling error. You can tell that an error may exist because the Proofing Errors button contains a red *x*. There is also a red wavy line under the word *Jacson* in the document. Click the Review tab (Figure 2.54).

② Click the Spelling & Grammar button in the Proofing group (Figure 2.54).

③ Click the word *Jackson* in the Suggestions list (**Figure 2.55**).

④ Click Change (Figure 2.55).

⑤ A dialog box displays, indicating that the spelling and grammar check is complete. Click OK .

⑥ Click the Undo button. You will correct the spelling error using the shortcut menu.

⑦ Right-click the word *Jacson* in the document. A shortcut menu displays with a list of spelling suggestions.

⑧ Click *Jackson*, and it is replaced in the document.

⑨ Place the insertion point after the word *Jackson* that you corrected and press the space bar . You will type in a word incorrectly and AutoCorrect will automatically correct it for you.

⑩ Type **hte**.

⑪ Press the space bar and the word automatically changes to the correct spelling.

⑫ Double-click the word *the*.

⑬ Press Delete .

⑭ Click the Save button in the Quick Access Toolbar. The document should resemble **Figure 2.56**. The Proofing Error contains a blue check mark, indicating that no errors exist.

Figure 2.54 Spelling & Grammar Button

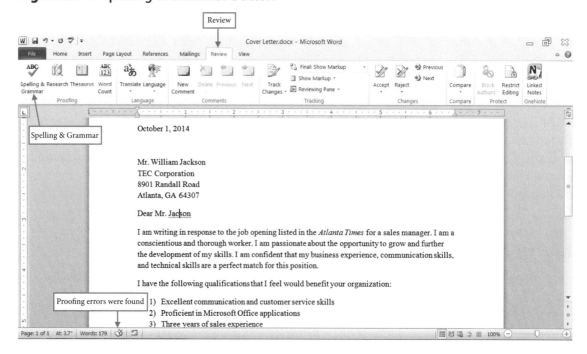

Figure 2.55 Spelling and Grammar Dialog Box

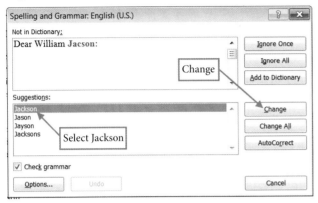

Figure 2.56 Spelling Errors Corrected

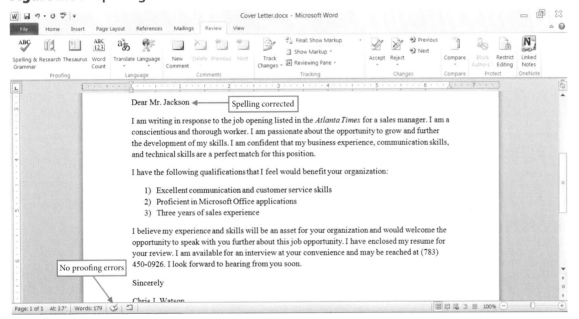

Word Count

Microsoft Word 2010 automatically counts the number of pages and words in the document and displays the information on the left side of the status bar. The Word Count command displays additional information, such as the number of paragraphs and lines in the document.

Use these steps to view word count:

- Click the **Word Count** button in the status bar, *or* click the **Word Count** button in the Proofing group on the Review tab (**Figure 2.57**). The Word Count dialog box displays. It contains information about the number of pages, words, characters, paragraphs, and lines in the document.
- Click the **Close** button when completed.

You can also select text in the document and then double-click the **Word Count** button to view the word count of the selected text.

Hands-On Exercise: Use Word Count Button

1. Click the Review tab.

2. Click the Word Count button in the Proofing group, and the Word Count dialog box displays (Figure 2.57). It states that 179 words are in the document.

3. Click the Close button in the Word Count dialog box.

4. Triple-click in the following paragraph:

I am writing in response to the job opening listed in the Atlanta Times for a sales manager. I am a conscientious and thorough worker. I am passionate about the opportunity to grow and further the development of my skills. I am confident that my business experience, communication skills, and technical skills are a perfect match for this position.

5. Double-click the Word Count button in the status bar (Figure 2.57) and the Word Count dialog box displays (**Figure 2.58**). The Word Count in the status bar states *Words: 59/179*, which means there are 59 words selected and 179 words in the document (Figure 2.58).

6. Click the Close button in the Word Count dialog box.

Figure 2.57 Word Count

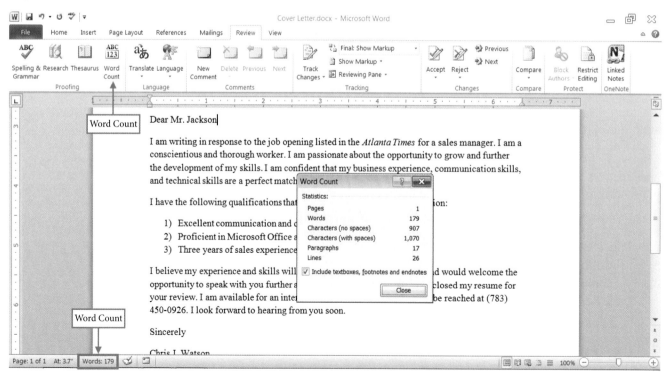

Figure 2.58 Word Count of Selected Text

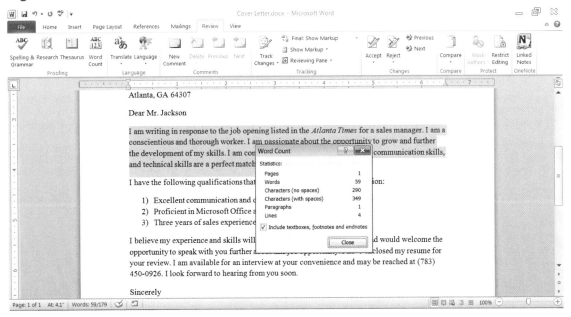

Thesaurus

A **thesaurus** is used to find a synonym or antonym of a word. A **synonym** is a word with the same meaning. An **antonym** is a word with the opposite meaning.

Use any of these methods to open the thesaurus:

- Right-click the word and click **Synonyms** on the shortcut menu (**Figure 2.59**). Select a synonym from the list.
- Click the word *or* double-click it. Click the **Thesaurus** button in the Proofing group of the Review tab, and the Research task pane displays on the right side of the document window (**Figure 2.60**).
- Press **Shift + F7** and the Research task pane displays on the right side of the document window.

Use these steps to use the thesaurus in the Research task pane:

- Type the word for which you are searching in the Search for box, and press **Enter**. If you selected a word, the word displays in the Search for box.
- A list of synonyms displays in the Research task pane. Point to a word and an arrow displays. Click the **arrow** next to the word and click **Insert**. The document replaces the word with the synonym.
- Click the **Close** button to close the Research task pane.

> **Thesaurus:** Used to find synonyms and antonyms of words.
>
> **Synonym:** Words with the same meaning.
>
> **Antonym:** Words with opposite meanings.

Hands-On Exercise: Use Thesaurus

① Right-click the word *skills* in the following paragraph.

I believe my experience and skills will be an asset for your organization and would welcome the opportunity to speak with you further about this job opportunity. I have enclosed my resume for

➡

your review. I am available for an interview at your convenience and may be reached at (783) 450-0926. I look forward to hearing from you soon.

② A shortcut menu displays. Point to or click Synonyms (Figure 2.59) and a list of synonyms displays.

③ Click *abilities* (Figure 2.59). The word *skills* is replaced with *abilities* in the paragraph.

④ Now you will use the Thesaurus to find a synonym for *abilities*. Double-click or click in the word *abilities* in the document.

⑤ Click the Review tab.

⑥ Click Thesaurus in the Proofing group and the Research task pane displays (Figure 2.60).

⑦ Point to the word *skills* (**Figure 2.61**). An arrow displays.

⑧ Click the arrow next to the word *skills*.

⑨ Click Insert from the list. *Skills* replaces *abilities* in the document.

⑩ Click Save on the Quick Access Toolbar.

⑪ Click the Close button on the Research task pane. The document should resemble Figure 2.62.

Figure 2.59 Synonyms

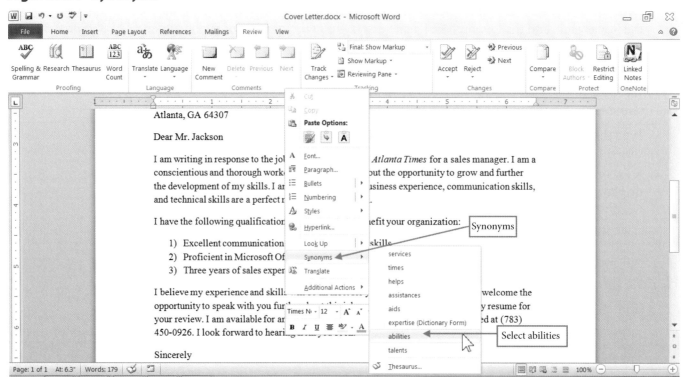

Figure 2.60 Thesaurus Button and Research Task Pane

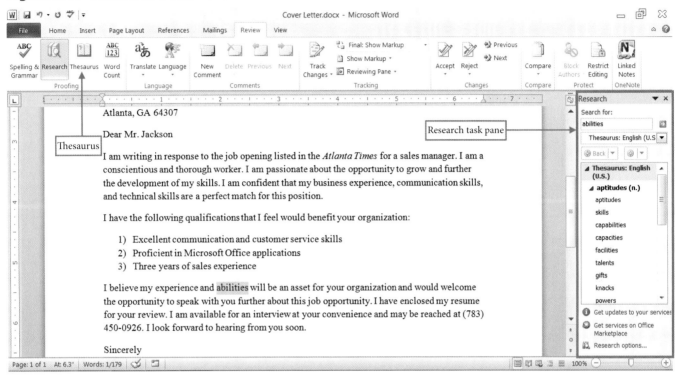

Figure 2.61 Research Task Pane

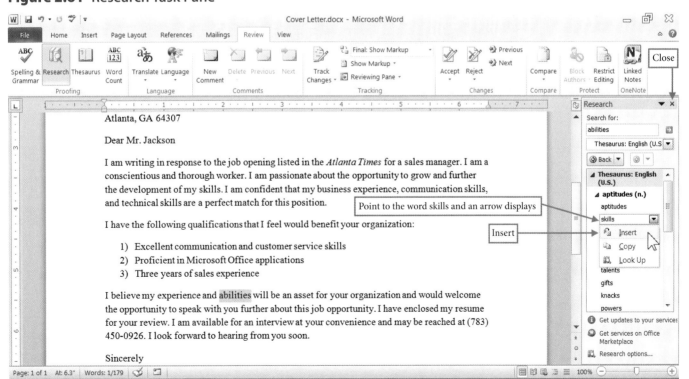

Figure 2.62 Words Replaced Using Thesaurus

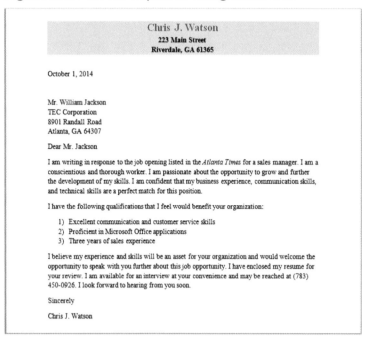

Print a Document

You can use the Print command on the File tab, *or* you can press **Ctrl + P** to access the print command.

Use these steps to print the document:

- Click the **File** tab.
- Click **Print**, and a preview of the document will display on the right side of the window (**Figure 2.63**).
  - If you notice any errors or changes that need to be made to the document, exit the Print window by pressing **Esc** *or* by clicking a tab on the Ribbon to return to the document.
- Adjust the print settings as needed.
- Click the **Print** button once the settings have been selected, and the document is printed (Figure 2.63).

Hands-On Exercise: Print a Document

① Click the File tab.

② Click Print (Figure 2.63). A preview of the document displays on the right side of the window (Figure 2.63).

③ Notice that there is not enough spacing between the last two lines of the document. You will return to the document to correct it before printing.

④ Press Esc to exit the print window and to return to the document.

⑤ Press Ctrl + End to navigate to the end of the document.

⑥ Position the insertion point at the beginning of the last line in the document that states *Chris J. Watson*.

⑦ Press Enter , and a blank line is inserted. The text *Chris J. Watson* moves down one line. The document should resemble Figure 2.64.

⑧ Click Save on the Quick Access Toolbar.

⑨ Click the File tab.

⑩ Click Print under the File tab.

⑪ Click the Print button.

⑫ Next, you will close the document. Microsoft Word 2010 remains open. Click the File tab.

⑬ Click Close . The application window should resemble Figure 2.65.

Figure 2.63 Print Command

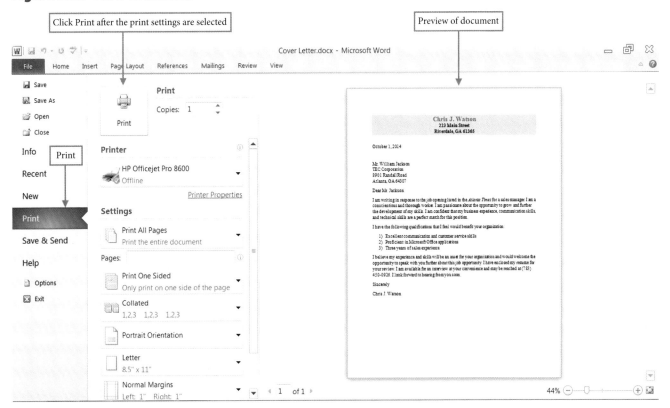

Figure 2.64 Completed Document

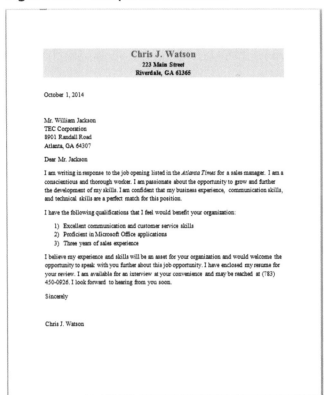

Figure 2.65 Close Document

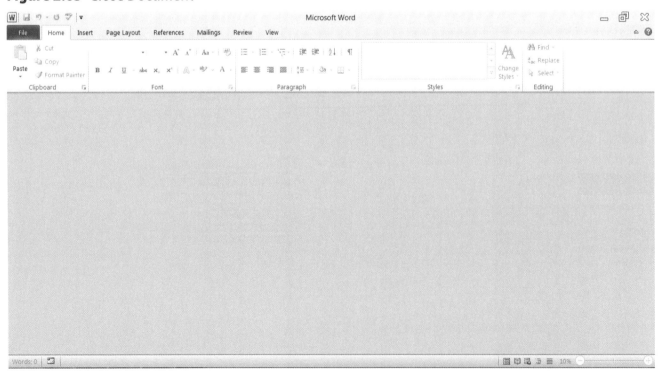

Templates

If you want to create a document quickly, you can use a template. Microsoft Office has many built-in templates available for your use. A **template** is a prebuilt document that contains formatting and standard text that can be modified to fit your specifications. Templates are available for creating letters, resume, memos, and many other documents. You can also access additional Microsoft Word 2010 templates online.

Many of the templates contain placeholders as well as text in the document. **Placeholders** indicate where you need to supply information. Placeholders are commonly displayed in brackets or appear as bold text. When you click the placeholder, you can replace the text or delete the placeholder.

Use these steps to insert a template:

- Click the **File** tab on the Ribbon.
- Click **New**.
- Select the template you want to use in the Available Templates category and click **Create** (**Figure 2.66**). You can also download a template from the Office.com Templates category. You must have an Internet connection to access the templates in the Office.com Templates category. If you do not have an Internet connection, you will be able to access only the templates in the Sample templates section in the Available Templates category. Click on **template** in the Office.com Templates category and click **Download** (**Figure 2.67**)
- The document displays in the document window.
- Type information in the placeholders (**Figure 2.68**) and in the document. Delete unwanted placeholders and text.

> **Template:** A prebuilt document that contains formatting and standard text that can be modified to fit your specifications.
>
> **Placeholders:** Indicate where you need to supply information. Commonly found in templates and display in brackets or appear as bold text.

Hands-On Exercise: Use a Template

① Click the File tab.

② Click New .

③ Click Memos from *Office.com Templates* (Figure 2.66). You may need to scroll down to find this option.

④ Click Memo (Professional Design) (Figure 2.67). A preview displays on the right side of the window (Figure 2.67).

⑤ Click Download (Figure 2.67). The document displays in the document window (Figure 2.68). The placeholders display in brackets (Figure 2.68).

⑥ Triple-click in *Company Name Here* paragraph at the top of the document.

⑦ Type **Beverly Distributors**.

⑧ Click in the placeholders and type the following:

To:	**All Employees**
From:	**John Schmitz, President**
CC:	**Dana Alexander, Vice President**
Re:	**Mandatory Meeting**

→

⑨ Drag the mouse to select the entire date in the Date placeholder. Type **8/5/2014**.

⑩ Triple-click in the *How to Use This Memo Template* paragraph.

⑪ Press Delete to delete the paragraph.

⑫ Triple-click in the last paragraph in the document. Instead of deleting the text using the Delete key, you will just start typing and the text will be replaced.

⑬ Type the following:

There will be a mandatory meeting for all employees on Friday morning at 8:00 a.m. in Conference Room A. The staff from the Human Resources department will be discussing the new health insurance policy for the staff.

⑭ The document should resemble **Figure 2.69**. Click Save on the Quick Access Toolbar. The Save As dialog box displays.

⑮ Type **Meeting Memo** in the File name box.

⑯ Click the Save button.

⑰ A message may display stating to save the file in a newer format (**Figure 2.70**). Click OK .

Figure 2.66 Templates

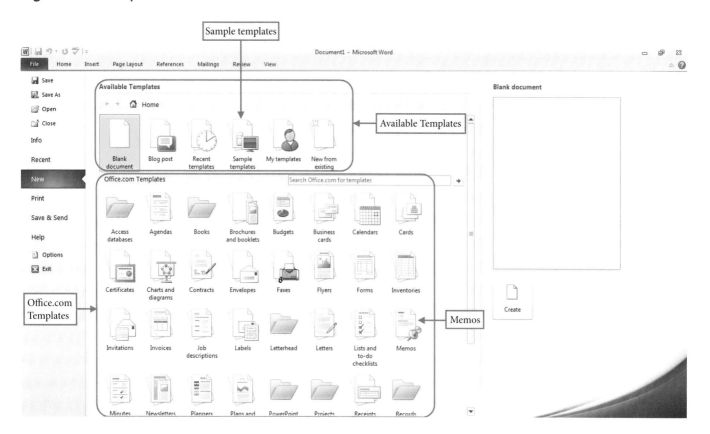

Figure 2.67 Memo (Professional design) Template

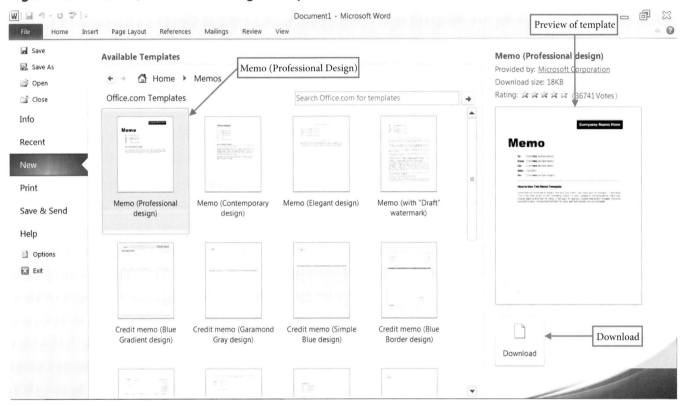

Figure 2.68 Placeholders

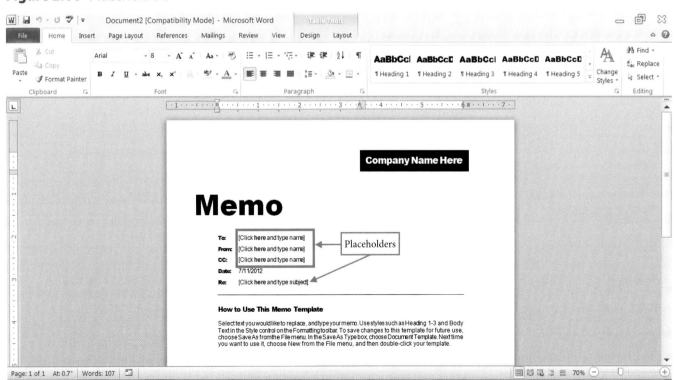

Figure 2.69 Memo Created

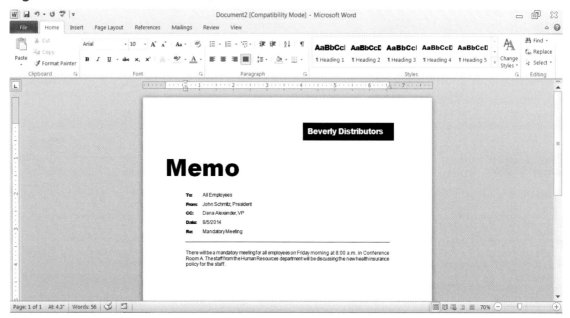

Figure 2.70 Message when Saving Memo

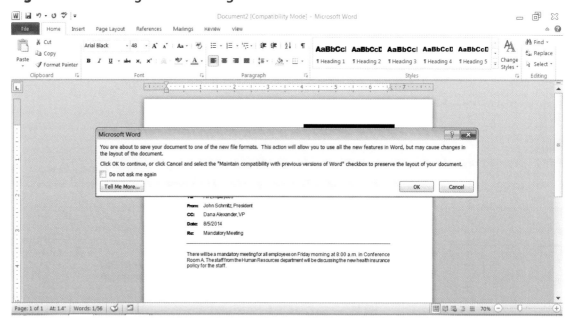

Apply Styles

Style: A set of formatting characteristics, such as font, size, color, paragraph spacing, and alignment.

Microsoft Word 2010 has predesigned styles to apply to text. A **style** is a set of formatting characteristics, such as font, size, color, paragraph spacing, and alignment. Applying a style to text in the document can give it a professional look.

Assume you have paragraph headings throughout the document. You can apply the same heading style each time you type a paragraph heading instead of applying your own formatting. This will give the document a cohesive appearance.

The Styles group contains various formatted styles to apply to titles, subtitles, headings, captions, and so on. Once a style is applied, it can be modified by using the Font and Paragraph commands.

Use these steps to apply a style:

- Click in the text to which you want to apply a style.
- Click the **More** button in the Styles group (**Figure 2.71**) and a gallery of styles displays (**Figure 2.72**).
- As the mouse hovers over the different styles, the change can be previewed in the document. As you click the different styles, the spacing, font and font size, and color change.
- Click a style, and it is applied to the text.

Use these steps to remove a style:

- Click in the text to which you want to delete the style.
- Click **Normal** *or* **Clear Formatting** in the Styles group.

Hands-On Exercise: Apply Styles

① Double-click the word *Memo* (Figure 2.71).

② Click the More button in the Styles group (Figure 2.71). A gallery of styles displays (Figure 2.72).

③ Click Intense Emphasis (Figure 2.72), and the style is applied to the text.

④ Click anywhere in the document window to deselect the text. The document should resemble **Figure 2.73**.

⑤ Click Save on the Quick Access Toolbar.

Figure 2.71 More Button in the Styles Group

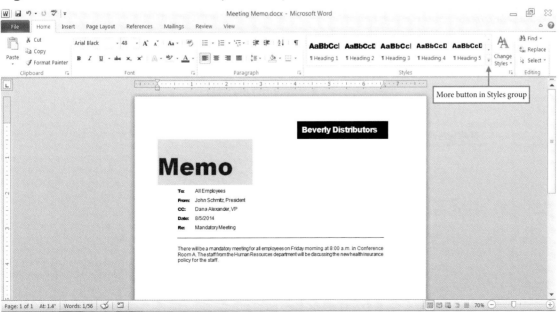

Figure 2.72 Gallery of Styles

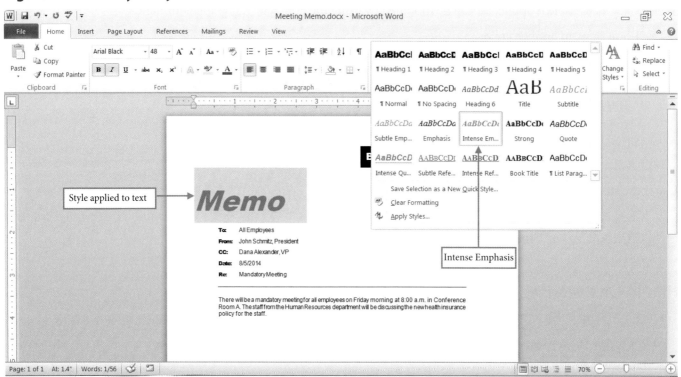

Figure 2.73 Style Applied to Text

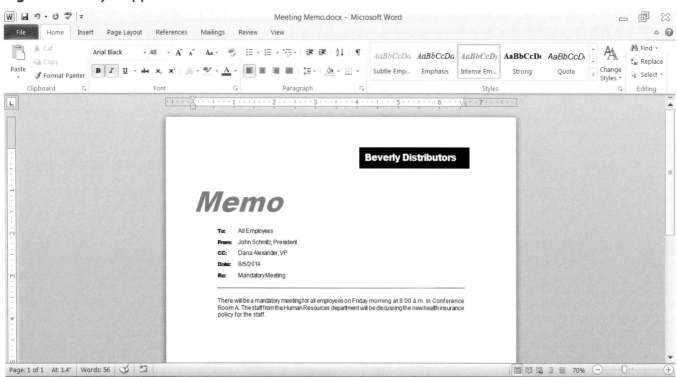

Hands-On Exercise: Check Spelling and Grammar, Print, and Exit Application

① Click the Review tab.

② Click the Spelling & Grammar button in the Proofing group.

③ Correct any errors.

④ Click the Save button on the Quick Access Toolbar.

⑤ Click the File tab.

⑥ Click Print under the File tab.

⑦ Click the Print button.

⑧ Click the File tab.

⑨ Click Exit .

Multiple-Choice Questions

1. Microsoft Word 2010 is a _____ application.
   a. Presentation
   b. Spreadsheet
   c. Datasheet
   d. Word processing

2. The _____ button displays paragraph marks and other hidden formatting symbols in the document.
   a. Editing
   b. Show/Hide
   c. Find
   d. Paragraph

3. Which key(s) erases the character to the left of the insertion point?
   a. Ctrl + Delete
   b. Delete
   c. Ctrl + Backspace
   d. Backspace

4. The Borders button is found in what group on the Home tab?
   a. Paragraph
   b. Font
   c. Clipboard
   d. Styles

5. The _____ command aligns text with both the left and right margins.
   a. Align Text Left
   b. Align Text Right
   c. Justify
   d. Center

6. The Format Painter command _____ .
   a. Copies formatting of text
   b. Copies text
   c. Is located in the Font group on the Home tab
   d. Clears the formatting of text

7. What are the default font settings for Microsoft Word 2010?
   a. Arial 12 points
   b. Verdana 11 points
   c. Calibri 11 points
   d. Times New Roman 12 points

8. What is the default alignment of text?
   a. Left
   b. Centered
   c. Right
   d. Justified

9. The Clipboard can store up to _____ items that have been cut or copied.
   a. 24
   b. 10
   c. 2
   d. 100

10. The _____ command displays the number of paragraphs in the document.
    a. Thesaurus
    b. Spelling & Grammar
    c. Word Count
    d. Line and Paragraph Spacing

Project #1: Create an Agenda for a School Board Meeting

1. Open Microsoft Word 2010.

2. Type the following document (**Figure 2.74**):

   a. Type **Glen Lakes School Board Meeting Agenda** and press **Enter**.

   b. Type **September 8, 2014** and press **Enter**.

   c. Type **7:00 p.m.** and press **Enter** twice.

   d. Type **Roll Call** and press **Enter**.

   e. Type **Approval of August 2014 Meeting Minutes** and press **Enter**.

   f. Type **Welcome and Introductions from School Board President (Janet Hopkins)** and press **Enter**.

   g. Type **New Teachers** and press **Enter**.

   h. Type **New Staff** and press **Enter**.

   i. Type **Treasurer's Report** and press **Enter**.

   j. Type **Results of 2013 Audit** and press **Enter**.

   k. Type **2014 - 2015 Proposed Budget** and press **Enter**.

Figure 2.74 Create Document

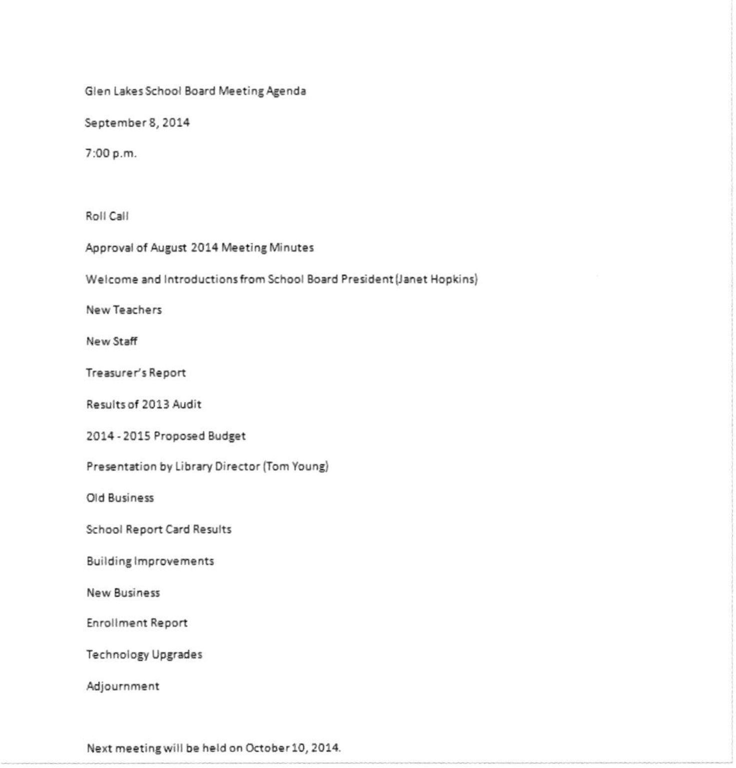

Glen Lakes School Board Meeting Agenda

September 8, 2014

7:00 p.m.

Roll Call

Approval of August 2014 Meeting Minutes

Welcome and Introductions from School Board President (Janet Hopkins)

New Teachers

New Staff

Treasurer's Report

Results of 2013 Audit

2014 - 2015 Proposed Budget

Presentation by Library Director (Tom Young)

Old Business

School Report Card Results

Building Improvements

New Business

Enrollment Report

Technology Upgrades

Adjournment

Next meeting will be held on October 10, 2014.

    l. Type **Presentation by Library Director (Tom Young)** and press **Enter**.

    m. Type **Old Business** and press **Enter**.

    n. Type **School Report Card Results** and press **Enter**.

    o. Type **Building Improvements** and press **Enter**.

    p. Type **New Business** and press **Enter**.

    q. Type **Enrollment Report** and press **Enter**.

    r. Type **Technology Upgrades** and press **Enter**.

    s. Type **Adjournment** and press **Enter** twice.

    t. Type **Next meeting will be held on October 10, 2014.**

③ Select the entire document.

④ Change the font to Arial.

⑤ Change the font size to 12 points.

⑥ Select the first three lines in the document, which contain the following text:

Glen Lakes School Board Meeting Agenda
September 8, 2014
7:00 p.m.

⑦ Apply the following formats to the selected text:

    a. Center the text.

    b. Bold the text.

    c. Set the font color to Blue.

    d. Set the spacing before and after paragraphs to 0 points.

    e. Apply Dark Blue, Text 2, Lighter 80% shading.

    f. Add a top border.

    g. Add a bottom border.

⑧ Change the font size of the first line in the document to 18 points.

⑨ Change the font size of the second and third line in the document to 16 points.

⑩ Select all the text from Roll Call to Adjournment and apply the following formats:

    a. Insert a numbered list.

    b. Double-space the text.

⑪ Indent the following lines of text:

New Teachers
New Staff
Results of 2013 Audit
2014 - 2015 Proposed Budget

School Report Card Results
Building Improvements
Enrollment Report
Technology Upgrades

(12) Select the last line in the document and apply the following formats:

   a. Center the text.

   b. Underline the text.

(13) Correct all spelling errors.

(14) Save the document as Glen Lakes Agenda. The completed document should resemble **Figure** 2.75.

(15) Print the document.

Figure 2.75 Completed Document for Project #1

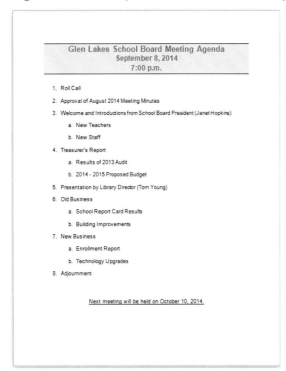

Project #2: Create a Flyer

As a volunteer at the Chicago Science Museum, you have been asked to create a flyer announcing the yearly fundraising event.

(1) Create a new document with the following text:

   a. Type **Chicago Museum of Science** and press **Enter**.

   b. Type **Presents...** and press **Enter**.

c. Type **A Weekend in Space** and press **Enter**.

d. Type **9 a.m. - 6 p.m.** and press **Enter**.

e. Type **December 2 and 3, 2014** and press **Enter**.

f. Type **A hands-on community forum for understanding the cosmos! Join your neighbors in our planiterium for an exciting weekend of exploring the wonders of space**. Press **Enter**.

g. Type **Travel through the tail of a comet**. Press **Enter**.

h. Type **Research a solar eclipse**. Press **Enter**.

i. Type **Monitor the Earth's environment from the International Space Station.** Press **Enter**.

j. Type **Watch a sunset become a star-laced sky**. Press **Enter**.

k. Type **Zip to the outer reaches of the known universe in a breathless minute.** Press **Enter**.

l. Type **A donation of $5.00 per person is requested**. Press **Enter**.

m. Type **For more information call 1-800-555-1324**. Press **Enter**.

2. Save the document with the name **Museum Flyer**. The document should resemble Figure 2.76.

Figure 2.76 Museum Flyer

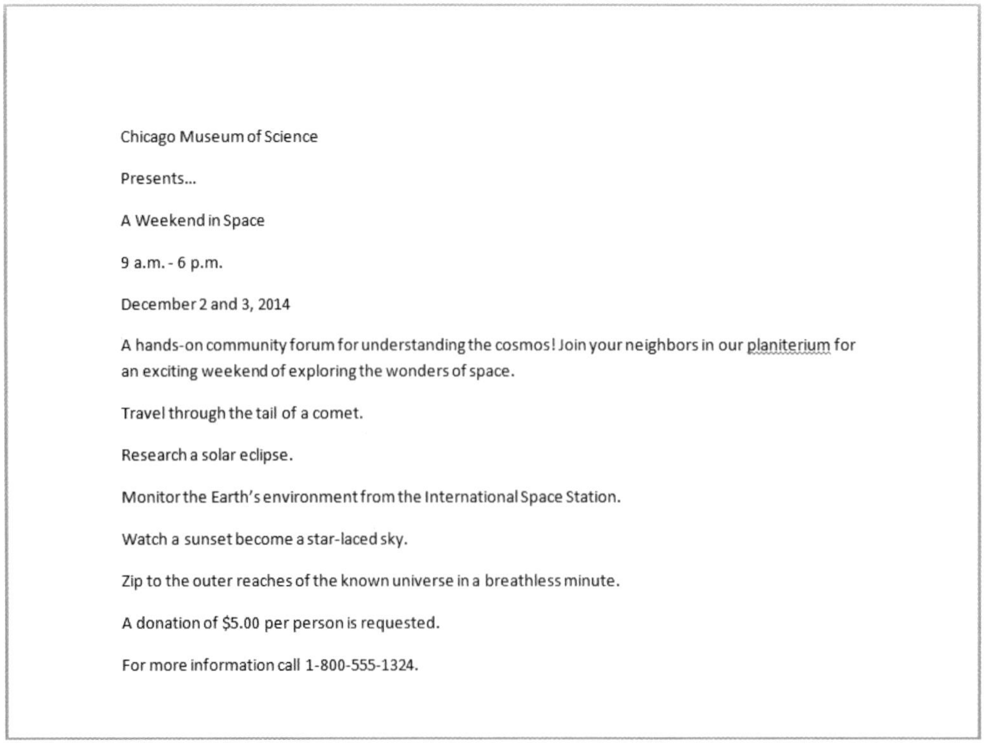

Chicago Museum of Science

Presents...

A Weekend in Space

9 a.m. - 6 p.m.

December 2 and 3, 2014

A hands-on community forum for understanding the cosmos! Join your neighbors in our planiterium for an exciting weekend of exploring the wonders of space.

Travel through the tail of a comet.

Research a solar eclipse.

Monitor the Earth's environment from the International Space Station.

Watch a sunset become a star-laced sky.

Zip to the outer reaches of the known universe in a breathless minute.

A donation of $5.00 per person is requested.

For more information call 1-800-555-1324.

③ Apply the following formatting to the first line of the document, which contains the text *Chicago Museum of Science.*

   a. Set the style to Title.

   b. Center the text.

   c. Bold the text.

④ Select all the text except for the first line and apply the following formatting:

   a. Set the line spacing to 2.

   b. Change the font to Cambria.

   c. Change the font size to 14.

⑤ Apply the following formatting to the second line of the document, which contains the text *Presents….*

   a. Change the font color to Aqua, Accent 5 (first row, ninth column).

   b. Change the font size to 22.

   c. Bold the text.

   d. Set the spacing after the paragraph to 0 points.

⑥ Copy the formatting of the text in the second line which contains the text *Presents…,* to the third line, which contains the text *A Weekend in Space.*

⑦ Cut the fifth line, which contains the text *December 2 and 3, 2014* and paste it at the end of the document.

⑧ Apply the following formatting to the fourth line, which contains the text *9 a.m. - 6 p.m.*:

   a. Change the font color to dark blue from the Standard Colors group.

   b. Bold the text.

   c. Center the text.

   d. Set the shading to Aqua, Accent 5, Lighter 80% (second row, ninth column).

   e. Insert an outside border.

⑨ Use the Format Painter and copy the formats from the text in the fourth line, which contains the text *9 a.m. - 6 p.m.,* to the last line in the document, which contains the text *December 2 and 3, 2014.*

⑩ Italicize the following paragraph:

   A hands-on community forum for understanding the cosmos! Join your neighbors in our planiterium for an exciting weekend of exploring the wonders of space.

⑪ Correct the spelling mistake on the word *planiterium.*

⑫ Insert square bullets to the paragraphs beginning with *Travel through the tail of a comet* and ending with the sentence *Zip to the outer reaches of the known universe in a breathless minute.*

⑬ Correct all spelling and grammar errors.

⑭ Save the document.

⑮ Print the document.

Your project should resemble **Figure 2.77**.

Figure 2.77 Completed Project #2

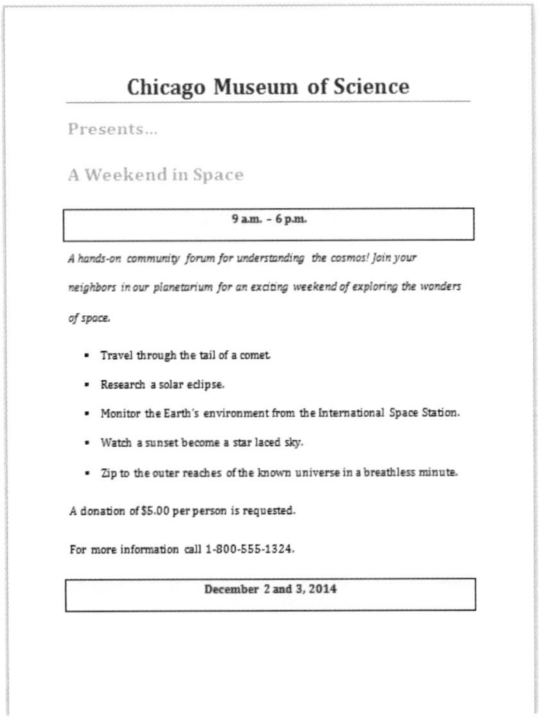

Project #3: Create a Thank You Letter Using a Template

You just completed an interview and want to send a thank you letter to the interviewer. You will use a template to create the letter.

① Open the template called *Thank you for interview*. It is located in the Office.com Templates in the Letters, Employment and resignation letters, Interview letter folder. The document should resemble **Figure 2.78**.

② Save the document as **Thank You Letter**. Click OK if a message displays stating to save the file in a newer format.

③ Type **John Patla** in the [Your Name] placeholders. This placeholder displays in the document twice. Make certain to replace both placeholders with the new text.

④ Type **4596 West 57th Street** in the first [Street Address] placeholder.

⑤ Type **Boulder, CO 55555** in the [City, ST ZIP Code] placeholder

(6) Type **Ron Browne** in the [Recipient Name] placeholders. This placeholder displays in the document twice. Make certain to replace both placeholders with the new text.

(7) Type **President** in the [Title] placeholder.

(8) Type **Browne and Associates** in the [Company Name] placeholders. This placeholder displays in the document in four locations. Make certain to replace all four placeholders with the new text.

(9) Type **5760 West Centennial Drive** in the [Street Address] placeholder.

(10) Type **Wicker Park, CO 99999** in the [City, ST ZIP Code] placeholder.

(11) Type **Legal Assistant** in the [job title] placeholder.

(12) Delete the text *on [date],* which will delete the word *on* and the date placeholder from the document.

(13) Type **555-304-9384** in the [phone] placeholder.

(14) Select the entire document and make the following formatting changes:

a. Change the font to Calibri.

b. Change the font size to 11.

(15) Select the first three lines of the document and make the following formatting changes:

a. Change the font color to Light Blue.

b. Change the font size to 14.

c. Right align the text.

d. Bold the text.

e. Add a bottom border.

(16) Correct all grammatical and spelling errors.

(17) Save the document. The document should resemble **Figure 2.79**.

(18) Print the document.

(19) Make the following changes to the document:

a. Using the Replace command, replace all occurrences of *Browne and Associates* with **Browne Legal Associates**.

b. Replace the word *impressed* with another synonym.

(20) Save the document as **Thank You Letter Revised**. The document should resemble **Figure 2.80**.

(21) Print the document.

Figure 2.78 Template

[Your Name]
[Street Address]
[City, ST ZIP Code]
July 17, 2014

[Recipient Name]
[Title]
[Company Name]
[Street Address]
[City, ST ZIP Code]

Dear [Recipient Name]:

Thank you for the opportunity to discuss your opening for a **[job title]**. It was a pleasure meeting you on **[date]** and learning more about the position and **[Company Name]**. I was impressed with the projects that **[Company Name]** is developing and with your plans for the company's growth.

I am enthusiastic about the possibility of working for you at **[Company Name]**. The position sounds like a perfect match for my skills and experience. Please contact me at **[phone number]** if you have any questions. I look forward to hearing from you soon.

Sincerely,

[Your Name]

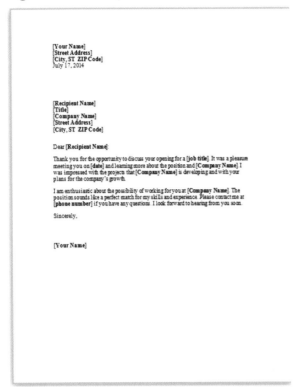

Figure 2.79 Thank You Letter Document Completed

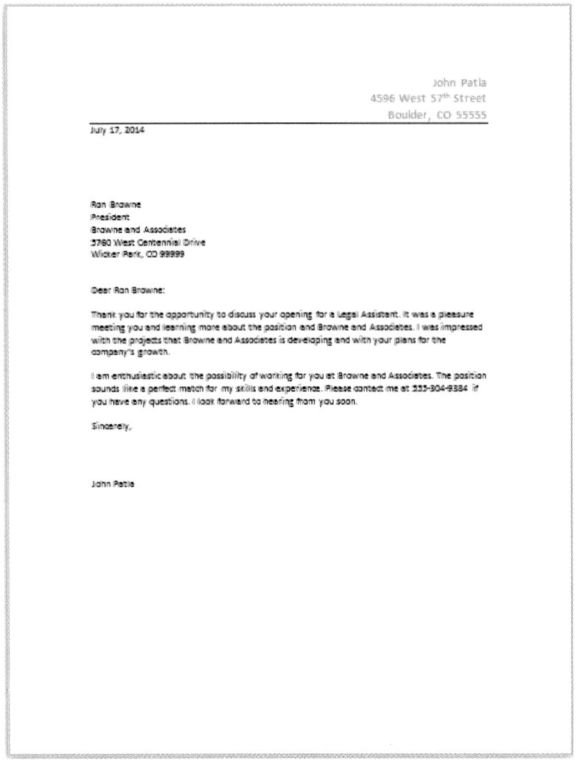

John Patla
4596 West 57th Street
Boulder, CO 55555

July 17, 2014

Ron Browne
President
Browne and Associates
3760 West Centennial Drive
Wicker Park, CO 99999

Dear Ron Browne:

Thank you for the opportunity to discuss your opening for a Legal Assistant. It was a pleasure meeting you and learning more about the position and Browne and Associates. I was impressed with the projects that Browne and Associates is developing and with your plans for the company's growth.

I am enthusiastic about the possibility of working for you at Browne and Associates. The position sounds like a perfect match for my skills and experience. Please contact me at 555-304-9384 if you have any questions. I look forward to hearing from you soon.

Sincerely,

John Patla

Figure 2.80 Thank You Letter Revised Document

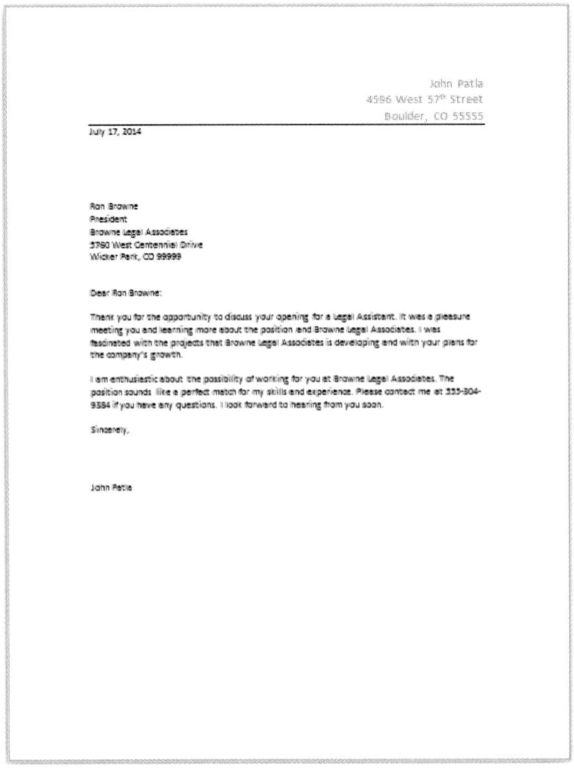

John Patla
4596 West 57th Street
Boulder, CO 55555

July 17, 2014

Ron Browne
President
Browne Legal Associates
3760 West Centennial Drive
Wicker Park, CO 99999

Dear Ron Browne:

Thank you for the opportunity to discuss your opening for a Legal Assistant. It was a pleasure meeting you and learning more about the position and Browne Legal Associates. I was fascinated with the projects that Browne Legal Associates is developing and with your plans for the company's growth.

I am enthusiastic about the possibility of working for you at Browne Legal Associates. The position sounds like a perfect match for my skills and experience. Please contact me at 555-304-9384 if you have any questions. I look forward to hearing from you soon.

Sincerely,

John Patla

Enhance a Microsoft Word 2010 Document

3

Chapter Objectives

After completing this chapter, you will be able to do the following:

- Set page margins.
- Set tabs.
- Create and format tables.
- Insert and format clip art and pictures.
- Insert WordArt.
- Insert a hyperlink.
- Insert a page break.
- Insert a header and footer.
- Insert a symbol.

Now that you have learned the basics of Microsoft Word 2010, you are going to learn how to enhance documents by adding visual objects to the document, such as inserting pictures, clip art, and WordArt. Inserting visual objects engages the reader and communicates the information more effectively.

This chapter illustrates how to apply page layout commands such as setting page margins, tabs, and inserting page breaks. You will also create and format tables, insert headers and footers, and insert hyperlinks.

You will open Microsoft Word and create a brochure for Lakeview Recreation.

Hands-On Exercise: Launch Microsoft Word 2010

1. Open a blank document.
2. Click the Start button.
3. Click All Programs .
4. Click Microsoft Office .
5. Click Microsoft Word 2010 . A blank document displays.

Set Page Margins

Page margins: The blank spaces at the top, bottom, and left and right sides of the document between the text and the edge of the paper.

Page margins are the blank spaces at the top, bottom, and left and right sides of the document between the text and the edge of the paper (**Figure 3.1**). The page margins are outside of the printing area of a page.

By default, Microsoft Word 2010 creates a new document with 1-inch top, bottom, left, and right margins. The text and graphics display differently on the page when you change the page margins. You can select margins from the gallery or create your own margins.

Use these steps to set page margins:

- Click the **Page Layout** tab on the Ribbon (**Figure 3.2**).
- Click **Margins** in the Page Setup group. A list of predefined margin setting display in the gallery (Figure 3.2).
- Click a margin setting from the Margins gallery, *or* click **Custom Margins** to create your own margin settings (Figure 3.2).
- If you select the Custom Margins option, the Page Setup dialog box displays. Type the margin settings for the top, bottom, left, and right margins (**Figure 3.3**).
- Click **OK** and the margins are set.

Figure 3.1 Page Margins

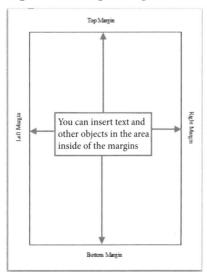

Hands-On Exercise: Set Page Margins

①　Click the Page Layout tab (Figure 3.2).

②　Click the Margins button in the Page Setup group (Figure 3.2).

③　Click Custom Margins (Figure 3.2). The Page Setup dialog box displays (Figure 3.3). The Margins tab should be selected (Figure 3.3). If not, click the Margins tab.

④　Type **.5** in the *Top* box in the Margins group (Figure 3.3).

⑤　Type **.5** in the *Bottom* box in the Margins group (Figure 3.3)

⑥　Click OK .

Figure 3.2 Margins Command

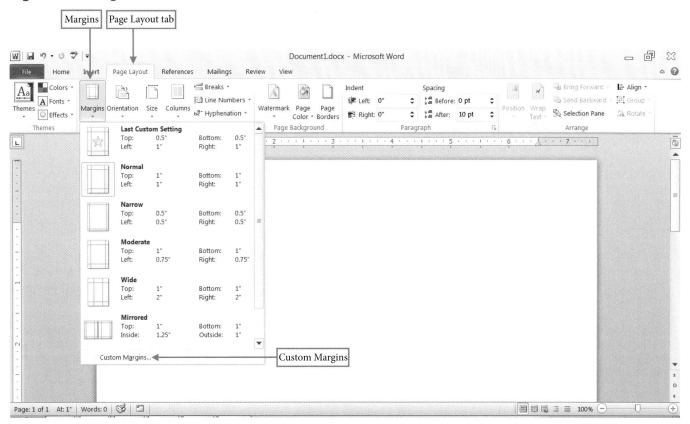

Figure 3.3 Create Custom Margins Using Page Setup Dialog Box

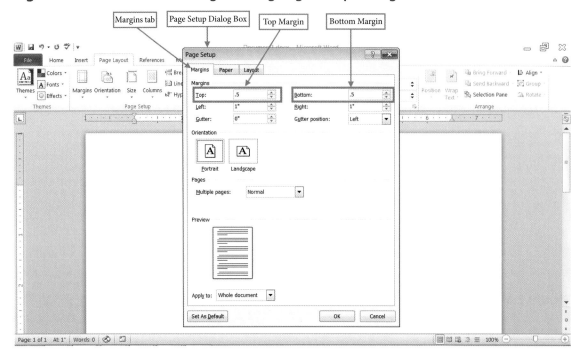

Hands-On Exercise: Create and Format a Document

① You will change the font and font size of the text. Click the Home tab to make it active. The Home tab contains the formatting commands.

② Click the Font arrow in the Font group and select Cambria (**Figure 3.4**).

③ Click the Font Size arrow in the Font group and select 12 (Figure 3.4).

④ Type **Lakeview Recreation** and press Enter .

⑤ Type the following paragraph. Press the spacebar once after each sentence. Do not press Enter until you complete the paragraph because Microsoft Word automatically word wraps to the next line.

Whether you want to stay fit or just have fun, Lakeview Recreation is the place to be this summer. Lakeview Recreation is a state-of-the-art facility that offers both indoor fitness and water recreation activities. Exciting new additions to the schedule this summer include kickboxing and Jet-Skiing lessons.

⑥ Press Enter .

⑦ Type the following paragraph.

The new summer classes and water park will be open to our members starting June 1. We look forward to seeing you in our facilities. Reserve your spot today because classes fill up quickly.

⑧ Press Enter .

⑨ Triple-click the text *Lakeview Recreation* to select it.

⑩ Make the following format changes to the selected text using the commands from the Home tab (Figure 3.4):

   a. Click the Bold button in the Font group.

   b. Click the Font Size arrow and select 18 .

   c. Click the Font Color arrow and select Blue from Standard Colors.

   d. Click the Center button in the Paragraph group.

⑪ Press Ctrl + End to navigate to the end of the document. The document should resemble Figure 3.4.

Figure 3.4 **Text Inserted and Formatted in Document**

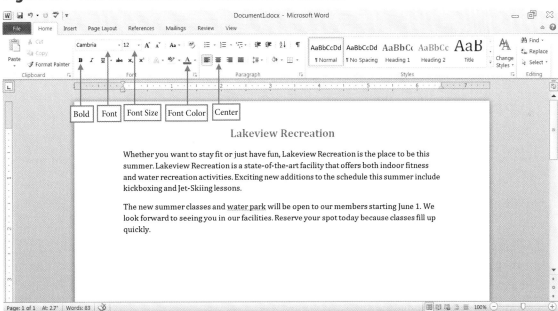

Set Tabs

You can set tab stops on the ruler to better organize the text for easier reading. **Tabs** align text to a specific place in the document. By default, tab stops are set every ½ inch when you open a new blank document. These tab stops do not display on the ruler. Press the Tab key and the insertion point moves ½ inch to the right.

To the far left of the horizontal ruler is the **tab selector** (**Figure 3.5**). By default, a Left Tab displays in the tab selector ⌊L⌋. Click the tab selector to view other types of tabs. **Table 3.1** displays the various types of tabs that are available.

Tabs: Align text to a specific place in the document.

Tab Selector: Located to the far left of the horizontal ruler and used to select various tabs.

Table 3.1 Types of Tabs

Type of Tab	Icon	Description
Left Tab	⌊L⌋	The text is left-aligned with the tab stop.
Center Tab	⌊⊥⌋	The text is centered with the tab stop.
Right Tab	⌊⌋	The text is right-aligned with the tab stop.
Decimal Tab	⌊⊥⌋	This tab is used for numbers that contain decimals. The decimal point of the number is aligned with the tab stop.
Bar Tab	⌊l⌋	This tab is used to insert a vertical line (or bar) at the tab stop.

You can set tabs by using the horizontal ruler bar.

Use these steps to set a tab using the ruler:

- If the horizontal ruler is not showing at the top of the document, click the **View Ruler** button at the top of the vertical scroll bar (Figure 3.5).
- Click the **tab selector** until you locate the type of tab you want to create (Figure 3.5).
- Click the position on the ruler where you want the tab stop to be set.

To change the location of a tab using the ruler:

- Drag the tab to another position on the ruler.

To delete a tab using the ruler:

- Drag the tab up or down to remove it from the ruler.

You can also create, modify, and delete tabs by using the Tabs dialog box.

Use these steps to set tabs using the Tabs dialog box:

- Click the **Paragraph dialog box launcher** in the Paragraph group (Figure 3.5), and the Paragraph dialog box displays (**Figure 3.6**). The Indents and Spacing tab should be selected (Figure 3.6). If not, click the **Indents and Spacing** tab.
- Click the **Tabs** button (Figure 3.6), and the Tabs dialog box displays (**Figure 3.7**).
- Enter the tab settings (Figure 3.7):
  - Type the tab stop position in the Tab stop position box.
  - Select an alignment option (left, center, right, decimal, bar).
  - Select a leader option (none, dots, dashed lines, solid lines). A leader will insert dots, dashed lines, or solid lines from the text to the tab stop.
  - Click **Set**.
  - Click **OK**.

Use these steps to delete tabs using the Tabs dialog box:

- Click the **Paragraph dialog box launcher** in the Paragraph group (Figure 3.5), and the Paragraph dialog box displays (Figure 3.6). The Indents and Spacing tab should be selected (Figure 3.6). If not, click the **Indents and Spacing** tab.

- Click the **Tabs** button (Figure 3.6), and the Tabs dialog box displays (Figure 3.7).
- Select the tab position you want to delete in the Tab stop position list.
- Click **Clear** to delete the tab, *or* click **Clear All** to delete all the tab stops.
- Click **OK**.

Double-clicking a tab on the ruler will also open the Tabs dialog box.

Hands-On Exercise: Create, Move, and Delete Tabs

1. Type **Hours of Operation** and press Enter .

2. Next you will set a 3-inch right tab. Click the Paragraph dialog box launcher in the Paragraph group (Figure 3.5), and the Paragraph dialog box displays (Figure 3.6). The Indents and Spacing tab should be selected (Figure 3.6). If not, click the Indents and Spacing tab.

3. Click the Tabs button (Figure 3.6) and the Tabs dialog box displays (Figure 3.7).

4. Type **3** in the Tab stop position box (Figure 3.7).

5. Click Right in the Alignment option (Figure 3.7).

6. Click 2…….. in the Leader option (Figure 3.7).

7. Click Set . A 3-inch right tab is created and is listed in the Tab stop position list (**Figure 3.8**).

8. Next, you will create a left tab at the 5-inch mark on the ruler. Type **5** in the Tab stop position box.

9. Click Left in the Alignment option.

10. Click Set .

11. Click OK to close the dialog box. The tabs display on the ruler (**Figure 3.9**).

12. Next you will move the tab from the 5-inch mark to the 6-inch mark on the ruler.

    a. Drag the left tab from the 5-inch mark on the ruler to the 6-inch mark on the ruler. If you make a mistake, click Undo and try it again.

13. Next, you will delete the tab from the 6-inch mark on the ruler.

    a. Drag the 6" left tab stop down to remove it from the ruler.

14. Click Undo to undo the deletion. The left tab is back on the 6-inch mark on the ruler.

15. You will delete the tab using the Tabs dialog box. Double-click the 6" left tab stop , and the Tabs dialog box displays.

16. Select the 6" tab stop in the Tab stop position list (**Figure 3.10**).

17. Click Clear .

18. Click OK and the tab stop is deleted.

Figure 3.5 Tab Selector, Paragraph Dialog Box Launcher, and View Ruler Button

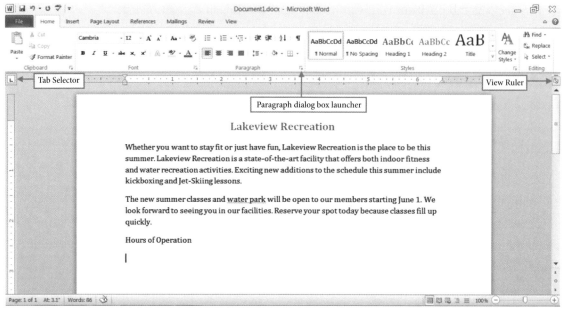

Figure 3.6 Paragraph Dialog Box

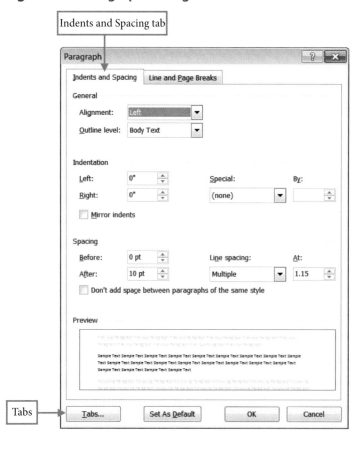

Figure 3.7 Tabs Dialog Box

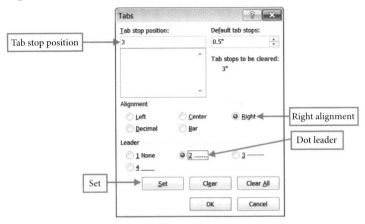

Figure 3.8 Right Tab Created

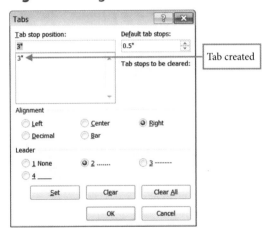

Figure 3.9 Tabs Display on Ruler Bar

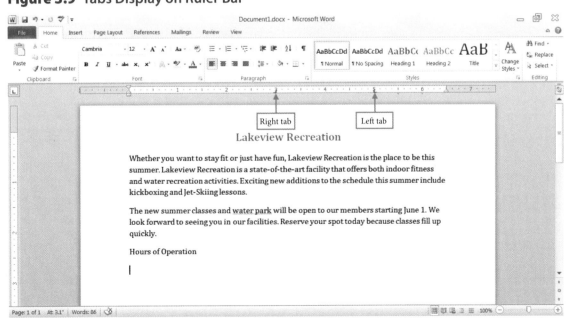

Figure 3.10 Remove Tab Stop

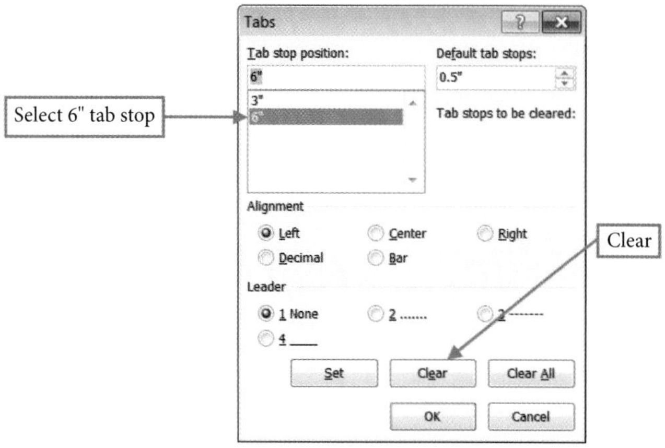

Select 6" tab stop →

Clear

Hands-On Exercise: Insert Text Using Tabs

1. Type **Days** and press Tab . The dot leaders display from the text to the tab stop.
2. Type **Times** and press Enter .
3. Type **Sunday** and press Tab .
4. Type **9 a.m. to 7 p.m.** and press Enter .
5. Type **Monday–Friday** and press Tab .
6. Type **9 a.m. to 10 p.m.** and press Enter .
7. Type **Saturday** and press Tab .
8. Type **8 a.m. to 10 p.m.** and press Enter twice.
9. Next you will format the text. Triple-click the *Hours of Operation* text.
10. Click Heading 2 style in the Styles group (**Figure 3.11**).
11. You will remove the spacing from the paragraphs you just typed. Drag the mouse to select the following paragraphs:

    Days .... Times
    Sunday .... 9 a.m. to 7 p.m.
    Monday–Friday............. 9 a.m. to 10 p.m.
    Saturday .... 8 a.m. to 10 p.m.

12. Click the Page Layout tab.
13. Type **0** in the Spacing After box in the Paragraph group (**Figure 3.12**). Press Enter , and the spacing after the paragraphs is removed.
14. Press Ctrl + End to navigate to the end of the document.
15. Click the Save button on the Quick Access Toolbar.
16. Save the document as **Lakeview Recreation**. The document should resemble **Figure 3.13**.

Figure 3.11 Heading 2 Style Applied to Selected Text

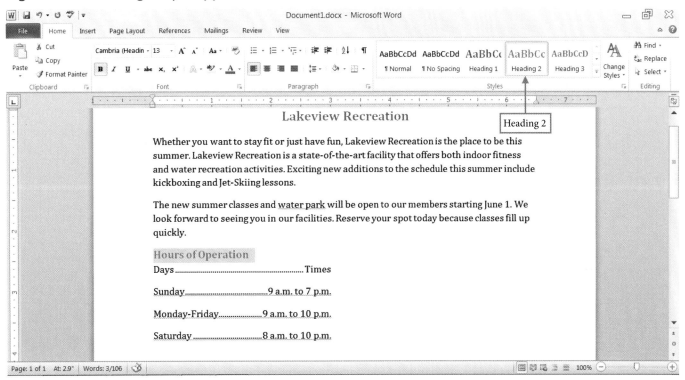

Figure 3.12 Spacing After button

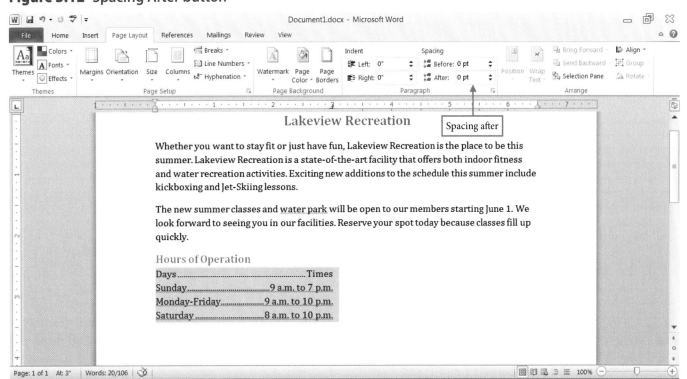

Figure 3.13 Spacing After Paragraphs Removed

Create a Table

Table: Displays information that is organized by rows and columns.

A **table** displays information that is organized by rows and columns. The intersection of a row and column is called a **cell**. The columns of the table are created equal in size. Once the table is created, you can insert text into the table and format the table. There are several ways to create tables.

Cell: The intersection of a row and column in a table.

Use these steps to create a table using the grid:

- Click the **Insert** tab (**Figure 3.14**).
- Click **Table** in the Tables group (Figure 3.14).
- Move the mouse over the grid to select the number of rows and columns in the table (Figure 3.14).
- Click to create the table.

Use these steps to create a table using the Insert Table command:

- Click the **Insert** tab (Figure 3.14).
- Click **Table** in the Tables group (Figure 3.14).
- Click **Insert Table**, and the Insert Table dialog box displays.
- Type the number of columns you want to create in the Number of columns box.
- Type the number of rows you want to create in the Number of rows box.
- Click **OK**.

Table move handle: Displays at the top left corner of the table and is used to select and/or move the table.

Once the table is inserted in the document, the insertion point is located in the first cell of the table. The **table move handle** displays at the top left corner of the table when the mouse pointer is located in the table (**Figure 3.15**). You can click the table move handle to select and/or move the table.

Use these steps to move a table:

- Click the **table move handle**.
- Drag the **table move handle** to another location in the document.

The Table Tools contextual tab displays at the top of the Ribbon, which contains the Design and Layout tabs (Figure 3.15). These commands are used to format the table. The insertion point must be inside the table to activate the Table Tools tab.

Once you type the information in a cell in a table, you can press Tab or the right arrow to advance to the next cell. Do not press the Enter key because this inserts an additional line within the cell. When you are in the last cell in the table, do not press Tab because that inserts a new row in the table. To exit the table, simply click outside the table.

Hands-On Exercise: Create a Table Using the Grid

(1) You will create a 4 × 8 table, which contains four columns and eight rows, using the grid. Click the Insert tab (Figure 3.14).

(2) Click the Table button in the Tables group (Figure 3.14).

(3) Move the insertion point over the grid and highlight four columns and eight rows, as shown in Figure 3.14. *4 × 8 Table* displays above the grid.

(4) Click and the table displays in the document.

(5) Type the following text into the table (**Table 3.2**). Press the Tab or right arrow keys to navigate to the next cell. When you type the text for the last cell, do not press Tab because that will insert a new row into the table.

(6) Click the Save button in the Quick Access Toolbar. The document should resemble Figure 3.15. Notice that the Table Tools contextual tab displays on the Ribbon and the table move handle displays at the top left corner of the table. This indicates that the table is active.

Table 3.2 Text Entered into Table

Summer Class Schedule			
Class	Day	Time	Age
Fitness Boot Camp	M/W/F	8–9 a.m.	18 and over
Jet-Skiing Lessons	Saturday	1–3 p.m.	16 and over
Kickboxing	T/TH	5–6 p.m.	13 and over
Morning Aerobics	T/W/TH	10–11 a.m.	13 and over
Sports Camp	M/F	9–11 a.m.	13 and under
Swimming Lessons	Daily	9–11 a.m.	All ages

Figure 3.14 Create Table Using Grid

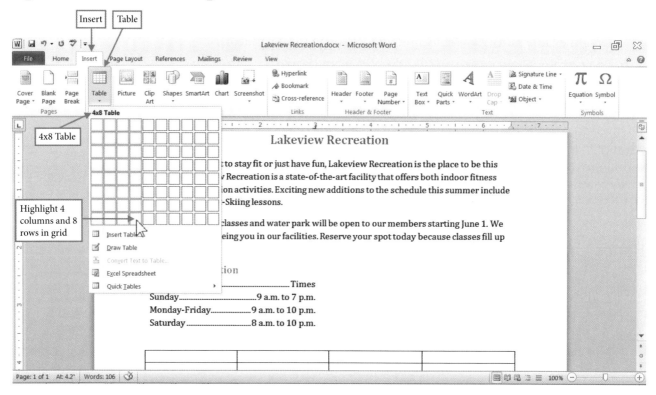

Figure 3.15 Text Inserted into Table

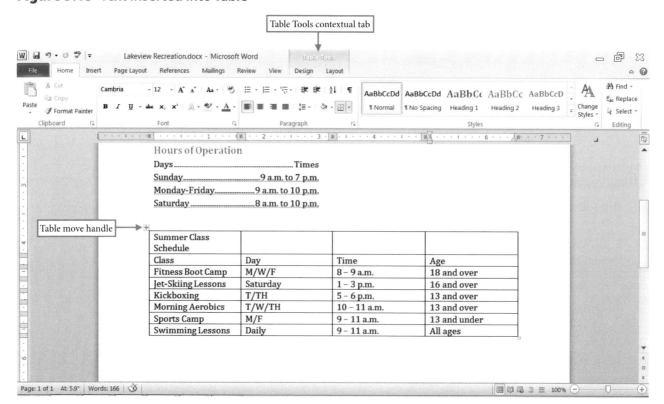

Modify a Table Layout

You can modify the table layout using the commands in the Layout tab in the Table Tools contextual tab. You can add or delete rows or columns. You can **merge cells** which combines two or more cells into one cell. This is frequently used to create headings. You can also **split cells**, which will split the selected cells into multiple new cells. You can use the **AutoFit Contents** command to automatically adjust the column widths to fit the contents of the text in the cells.

Table 3.3 contains various table layout commands you can apply to a table. These commands are available when the insertion point is located in the table. You can also apply many of these commands by right-clicking in a row or column in a table and selecting the command from the shortcut menu.

> **Merge cells:** A command that combines two or more cells in a table into one cell.
>
> **Split cells:** A command that splits the selected cells into multiple new cells.
>
> **AutoFit Contents:** A command that automatically adjusts the column widths in a table to fit the contents of the text in the cells.

Table 3.3 Table Layout Commands

Task	Steps
Select a cell, column, row, or table	• Position the insertion point in the table, row, or column you want to select. • Click the **Layout** tab in the Table Tools tab. • Click the **Select** button in the Table group. • Select Cell, Column, Row, or Table.
Insert a row	• Click in the row where you want to insert a new row. • Click the **Layout** tab in the Table Tools tab. • Click **Insert Above** in the Rows & Columns group to insert a row above the active row, *or* click **Insert Below** to insert a row below the active row. You can also insert a row by clicking in the last cell of the table and pressing the **Tab** key.
Insert a column	• Click in the column where you want to insert a new column. • Click the **Layout tab** in the Table Tools tab. • Click **Insert Left** in the Rows & Columns group to insert a column to the left of the active column, *or* click **Insert Right** to insert a column to the right of the active column.
Delete a row	• Click anywhere in the row you want to delete. • Click the **Layout** tab in the Table Tools tab. • Click the **Delete** button in the Rows & Columns group. • Click **Delete Rows**.
Delete a column	• Click anywhere in the column you want to delete. • Click the **Layout** tab in the Table Tools tab. • Click the **Delete** button in the Rows & Columns group. • Click **Delete Columns**.
Delete entire table	• Click anywhere in the table. • Click the **Layout** tab in the Table Tools tab. • Click the **Delete** button in the Rows & Columns group. • Click **Delete Table**.

Table 3.3 *continued*

Merge cells	• Select the cells you want to merge. • Click the **Layout** tab in the Table Tools tab. • Click the **Merge Cells** button in the Merge group.
Split cells	• Select the cells you want to split. • Click the **Layout** tab in the Table Tools tab. • Click the **Split Cells** button in the Merge group and the Split Cells dialog box displays. • Type the **number of columns** to create in the Number of columns box. • Type the **number of rows** to create in the Number of rows box. • Click **OK**.
Automatically resize column widths	• Click in the table. • Click the **Layout** tab in the Table Tools tab. • Click the **AutoFit** button in the Cell Size group. • Click **AutoFit Contents**.

Hands-On Exercise: Modify the Layout of the Table

1. Click in the first row in the table.
2. Click the Layout tab in the Table Tools tab (**Figure 3.16**).
3. Click the Select button in the Table group (Figure 3.16).
4. Click Select Row from the list (Figure 3.16) and the row is selected.
5. Click Merge Cells in the Merge group (**Figure 3.17**). The cells are merged into one cell (**Figure 3.18**).
6. Next you will split the cell in row 1 into two columns. Click the Split Cells button in the Merge group and the Split Cells dialog box displays (**Figure 3.19**).
7. Type **2** in the Number of columns box (Figure 3.19).
8. Click OK . The cell is split into two columns.
9. Next you will merge the cells again. Click the Merge Cells button to merge the cells in row 1.
10. Next you will insert a new row. Click in row 2.
11. Click the Layout tab if it is not selected.
12. Click the Insert Above button in the Rows & Columns group and the row is inserted (**Figure 3.20**).
13. Next, you will delete row 2. Row 2 is already selected. Click the Delete button in the Rows & Columns group (**Figure 3.21**).
14. Click Delete Rows and the row is deleted (Figure 3.21).
15. Click the Save button. The document should resemble **Figure 3.22**.

Figure 3.16 Select Button in Layout Tab

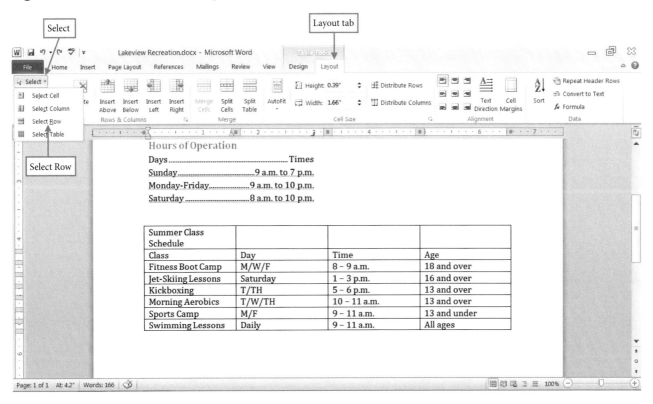

Figure 3.17 Merge Cells Button

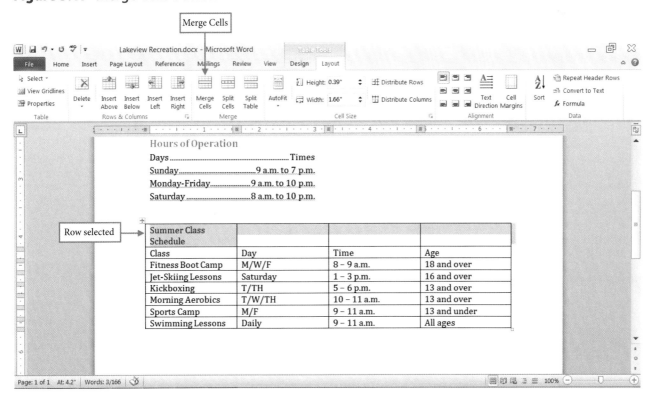

Figure 3.18 First Row Merged into One Cell

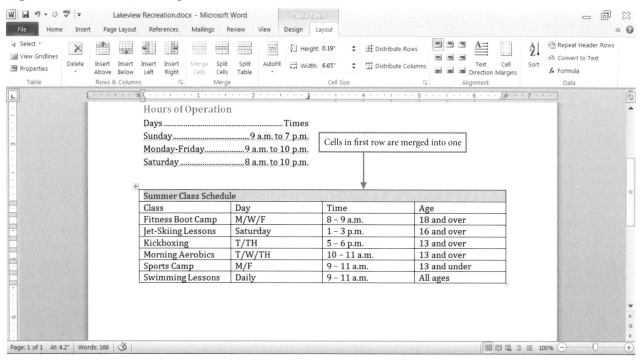

Figure 3.19 Split Cells

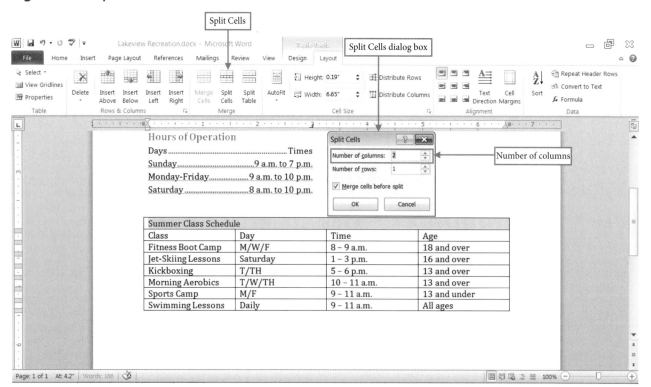

Figure 3.20 Insert Row

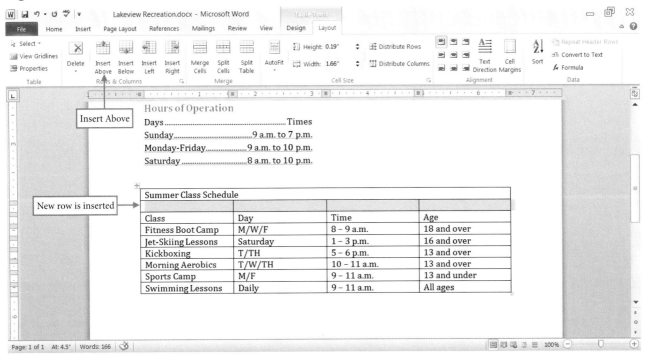

Figure 3.21 Delete Command

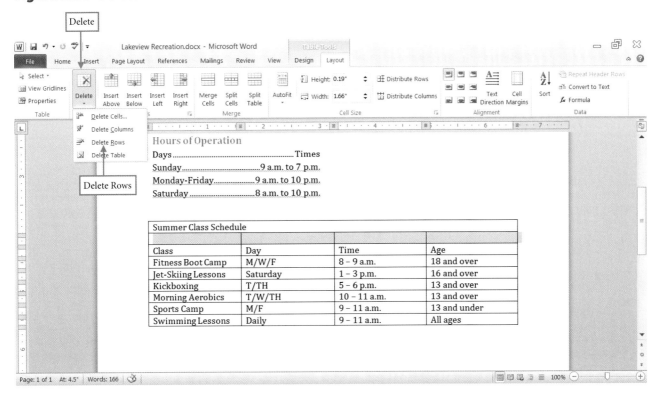

Figure 3.22 Table Created

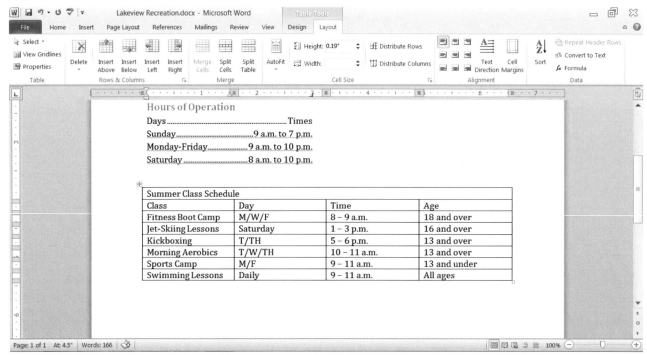

Modify a Table Style

Microsoft Word 2010 has predefined table styles that can be applied to a table to give the table a consistent, professional look. A style applies borders, shading, alignment, and text-formatting options to a table.

Use these steps to apply a table style:

- Click in the table.
- Click **Design** in the Table Tools tab (**Figure 3.23**).
- Click the **More** button in the Table Styles group (Figure 3.23).
- Click a table style from the gallery.

Hands-On Exercise: Modify a Table Style

1. Click in the table.

2. Click Design in the Table Tools tab (Figure 3.23).

3. Click the More button in the Table Styles group (Figure 3.23). The gallery displays.

4. Click Medium Grid 3—Accent 1 from the gallery (**Figure 3.24**). You will need to scroll down to find this option.

5. Click the Save button on the Quick Access Toolbar. The document should resemble **Figure 3.25**.

Figure 3.23 More Button in Table Styles Group

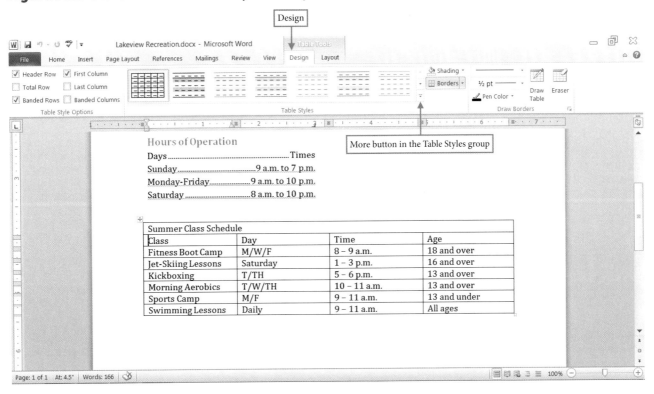

Figure 3.24 Select Medium Grid 3—Accent 1 from the Table Styles Gallery

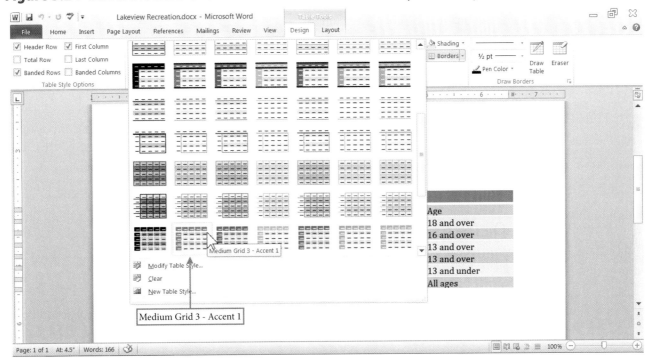

Figure 3.25 Style Applied to Table

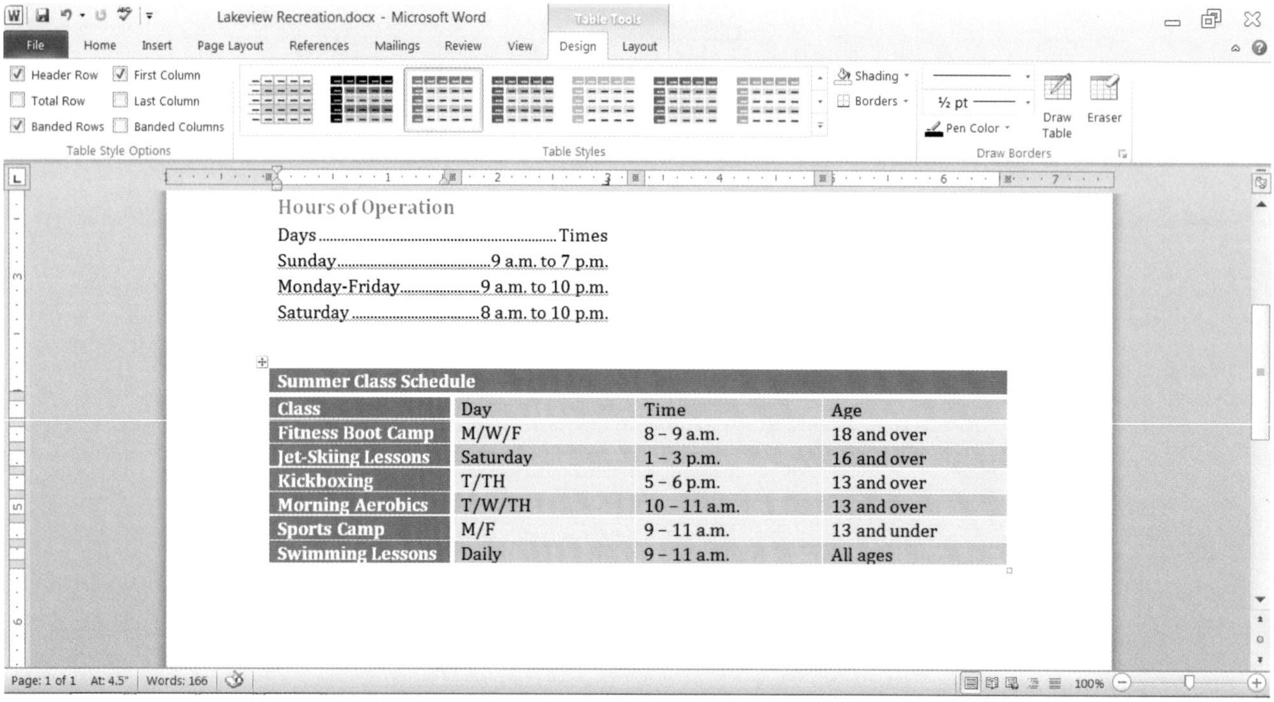

Change Row Height and Column Width of Cells in a Table

Use these steps to change the row height and/or column width of cells in a table:

- Select the cells you want to change in the table.
- Click **Layout** in the Table Tools tab.
- Type the height in the Table Row Height box in the Cell Size group (**Figure 3.26**) and press **Enter**.
- Type the width in the Table Column Width box in the Cell Size group (Figure 3.26) and press **Enter**.

You can also drag the column boundary or row boundary to change the size of a column or row. The **column boundary** is the vertical line that separates the columns in a table (Figure 3.26). The **row boundary** is the horizontal line that separates the rows in a table (Figure 3.26)

Column boundary: The vertical line that separates the columns in a table.

Row boundary: The horizontal line that separates the rows in a table.

Hands-On Exercise: Change Row Height of Table

① Click the table move handle to select the entire table.

② Click Layout in the Table Tools tab.

③ Type **.4** in the Table Row Height box in the Cell Size group and press Enter (Figure 3.26). This will change the height of every row in the table because the entire table is selected.

④ Click inside the table to deselect the entire table. The document should resemble Figure 3.26.

⑤ Next, you will change the size of a column using the column boundary. Point to the column boundary of the column that contains the time (Figure 3.26). When the resize pointer displays, ‖, drag the column boundary to the left. The column width becomes smaller.

⑥ Click Undo .

Figure 3.26 Change Table Row Height and Resize Column

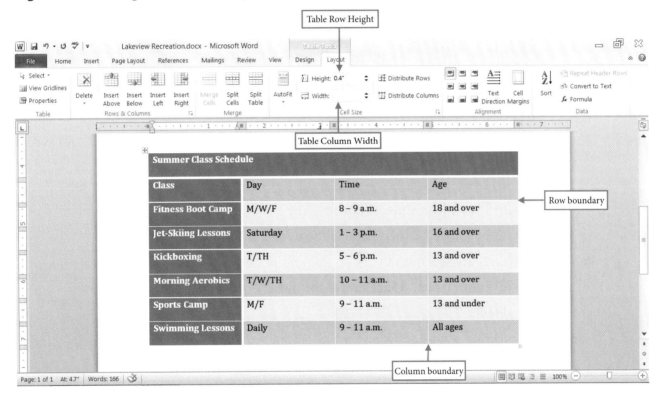

Insert Hyperlink

A **hyperlink** creates a link to another location, such as a webpage, picture, place in the current document, another document, an email address, or a program. A hyperlink is automatically created in a document if you type a URL or email address. The hyperlinked text in the document changes colors and is underlined, indicating that it is a hyperlink. Clicking on the hyperlink will take you to the link.

Use these steps to create a hyperlink to a webpage:

- Select the text or object that you want to display as the hyperlink.
- Click the **Insert** tab.
- Click **Hyperlink** in the Links group (**Figure 3.27**). The Insert Hyperlink dialog box displays (**Figure 3.28**).

> **Hyperlink:** A link to another location, such as a webpage, picture, place in the current document, another document, an email address, or a program.

- Click **Existing File or Web Page** in the Link to section (Figure 3.28).
- Type the address of the file or webpage in the Address box (Figure 3.28).

Use this steps to hyperlink to a webpage:

- Hold the **Ctrl** key and click the **hyperlink**, or right-click the **hyperlink** and click **Open Hyperlink** from the Shortcut Menu.

Use these steps to remove a hyperlink:

- Right-click the text or object that contains the hyperlink.
- Click **Remove Hyperlink** from the shortcut menu.

Use these steps to hyperlink to an email address:

- Select the text or object that you want to display as the hyperlink.
- Click the **Insert** tab.
- Click **Hyperlink** in the Links group (Figure 3.27). The Insert Hyperlink dialog box displays (Figure 3.28).
- Click **E-mail Address** in the Link to section.
- Type the **email address** in the E-mail Address box.
- Click **OK**.

Hands-On Exercise: Insert Hyperlink

1. Press Ctrl + End to go to the end of the document.
2. Press Enter three times.
3. Type **Visit our website for more information.**
4. Press Enter .
5. You will create a hyperlink on the word *website* that links to the Lakeview Recreation website. Double-click the word *website* to select it.
6. Click the Insert tab.
7. Click the Hyperlink button in the Links group (Figure 3.27).
8. The word *website* displays in the Text to display box because the word was selected as the hyperlink to the website.
9. Click the Existing File or Web Page option in the Link to section (Figure 3.28).
10. Type **https://sites.google.com/site/lakeviewrecreation/home** in the Address box (Figure 3.28).
11. Click OK . The word *website* is now linked to the webpage. The text in the document has changed colors and is underlined, which indicates that it is a hyperlink (**Figure 3.29**).
12. Point to the word *website,* and a ToolTip displays with instructions on how to hyper-link to the website.

⑬ Hold the Ctrl key and click the hyperlink. The website opens in a new window (**Figure 3.30**).

⑭ Close the browser window and navigate to the document.

⑮ Triple-click the paragraph Visit our <u>website</u> for more information .

⑯ Click the Home tab.

⑰ Click the Center button.

⑱ Click the Font Size button and select 18 .

⑲ Click Save in the Quick Access Toolbar. The document should resemble **Figure 3.31**.

Figure 3.27 Hyperlink Button

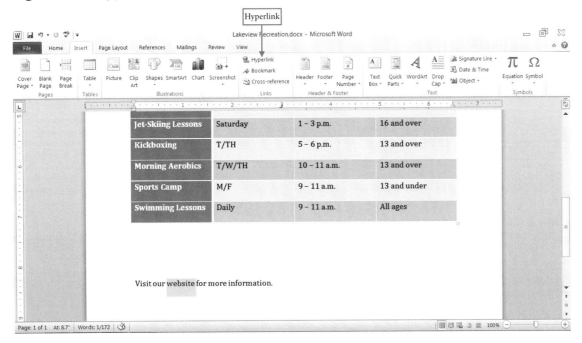

Figure 3.28 Insert Hyperlink Dialog Box

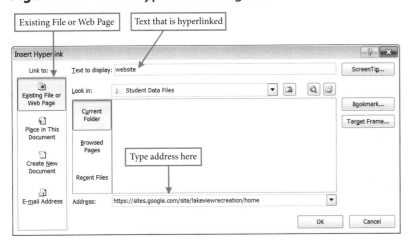

Figure 3.29 Hyperlink Created

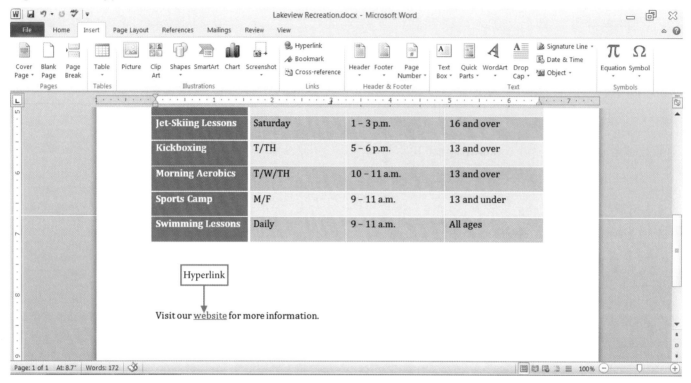

Figure 3.30 Hyperlink to Lakeview Recreation Website

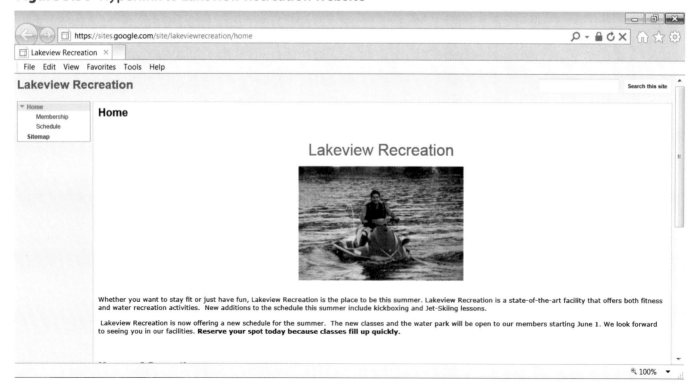

Figure 3.31 Text Formatted

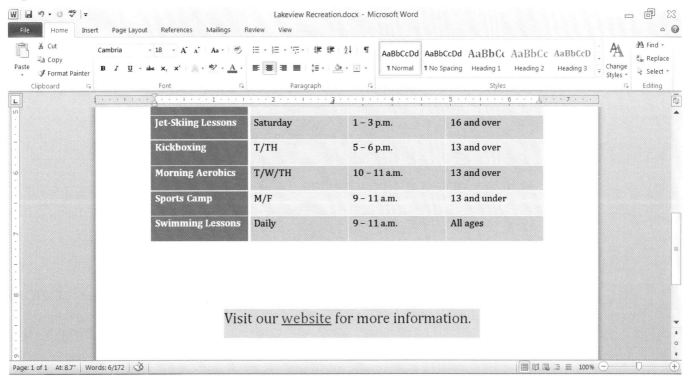

Insert Page Break

A page break inserts a new page at the location of the insertion point. Microsoft Word 2010 automatically inserts a page break when you reach the end of a page. If you are in the middle of a page and you want to begin typing on a new page, you can insert a manual page break to insert a new page. **Ctrl + Enter** is the keyboard shortcut to insert a manual page break.

> **Page break:** A command that inserts a new page at the location of the insertion point.

Use these steps to insert a page break using the Ribbon:

- Click the location in the document where you want to insert the page break.
- Click the **Insert** tab.
- Click the **Page Break** button in the Pages group (**Figure 3.32**). A new blank page displays in the document. The page number will display in the status bar (Figure 3.32).

The Page Break command is also available by clicking the **Breaks** button in the Page Setup group on the Page Layout tab and selecting **Page**.

Use these steps to delete a page break:

- Click the **Show/Hide** button in the Paragraph group on the Home tab.
- Find the formatting symbol for the page break: ————Page Break————¶
- Double-click the **page break symbol** to select it.
- Press **Delete**.

Hands-On Exercise: Insert and Delete Page Breaks

① Press Ctrl + End to navigate to the end of the document.

② Click the Insert tab.

③ Click the Page Break button in the Pages group (Figure 3.32). A new blank page displays. You now have two pages, and the status bar states *Page: 2 of 2.*

④ You will remove the page break and create it using the keyboard shortcut. Click the Show/Hide button in the Paragraph group on the Home tab.

⑤ Scroll up to page 1 and locate the page break symbol.

⑥ Double-click the page break symbol to select it (**Figure 3.33**).

⑦ Press Delete and the second page is deleted. The status bar now states *Page: 1 of 1.*

⑧ Click the Show/Hide button to turn off the feature.

⑨ Press Ctrl + Enter and a page break is inserted. The insertion point is located at the top of page 2.

⑩ Click Save on the Quick Access Toolbar.

Figure 3.32 Page Break

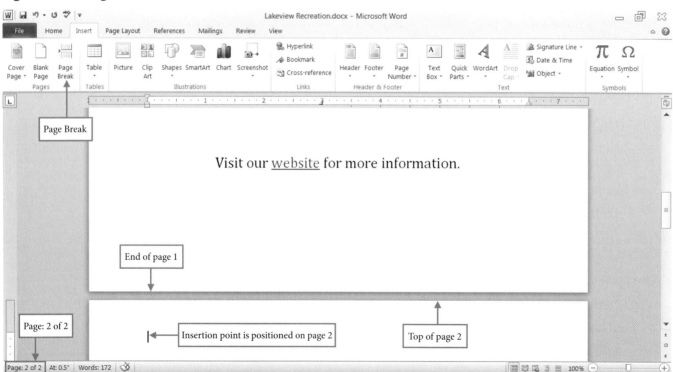

Figure 3.33 Select Page Break Symbol

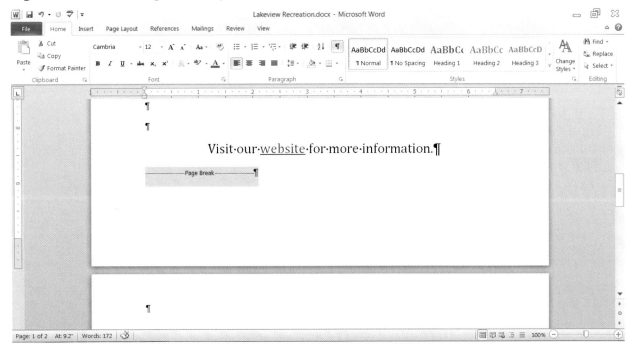

Insert Picture

You can insert pictures to enhance the appearance of a document. A picture can provide visual appeal or support the content of the document.

Use these steps to insert a picture from a file on a computer:

- Position the insertion point where you want the picture to be inserted.
- Click the **Insert** tab.
- Click **Picture** in the Illustrations group (**Figure 3.34**). The Insert Picture dialog box displays (Figure 3.34).
- Select the location in which the picture is stored.
- Select the picture.
- Click the **Insert** button and the picture is inserted into the document.

Once a picture is inserted or selected, the Picture Tools contextual tab displays on the Ribbon (**Figure 3.35**). It contains a Format tab that contains commands to format the picture.

Hands-On Exercise: Insert a Picture

You will insert a picture from the student data files provided with the textbook. If you have not downloaded the files, do so before beginning this exercise. The instructions for downloading the student data files are located in the preface.

1. Click the Insert tab.
2. Click Picture in the Illustrations group and the Insert Picture dialog box displays (Figure 3.34).

③ Select the drive and folder where the student data files are located.

④ Double-click the kickboxing picture to insert it into the document (Figure 3.34). Scroll down as needed so you can view the entire picture. The Picture Tools contextual tab displays on the Ribbon. The document should resemble Figure 3.35.

Figure 3.34 Insert Picture Dialog Box

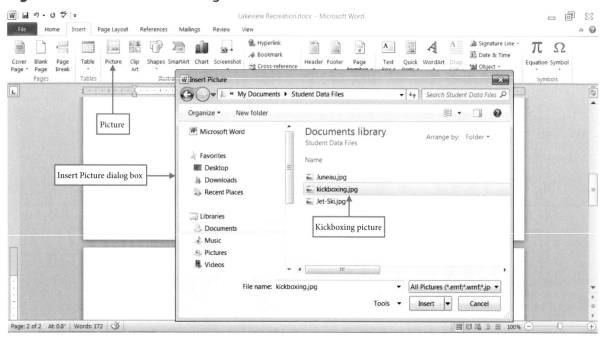

Figure 3.35 Picture Inserted

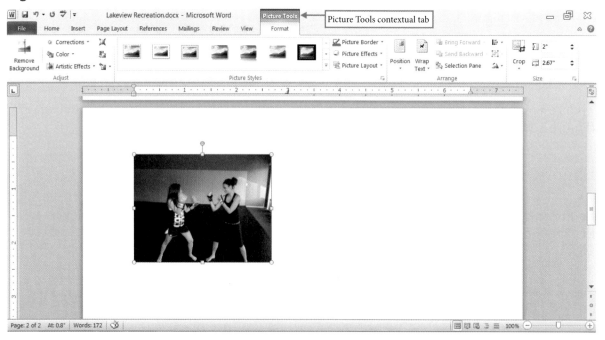

Apply Picture Style

You can enhance a picture by adding a style to it.

Use the steps to add a style:

- Click the picture to select it.
- Click the **Format** tab in the Picture Tools tab.
- Select a style from the Picture Styles group or click the **More** button in the Picture Styles group to view the gallery (**Figure 3.36**). Choose a style from the gallery.

Hands-On Exercise: Apply a Picture Style

(1) Click the picture if not selected.

(2) Click the More button in the Picture Styles group on the Format tab (Figure 3.36).

(3) Click the Metal Rounded Rectangle style from the Picture Styles gallery (**Figure 3.37**).

(4) Click the Home tab.

(5) Click the Center button to center the picture.

(6) Press End to position the insertion point after the picture.

(7) Press Enter to navigate to the next line. The insertion point is centered on the next line.

Figure 3.36 More Button in Picture Styles Group

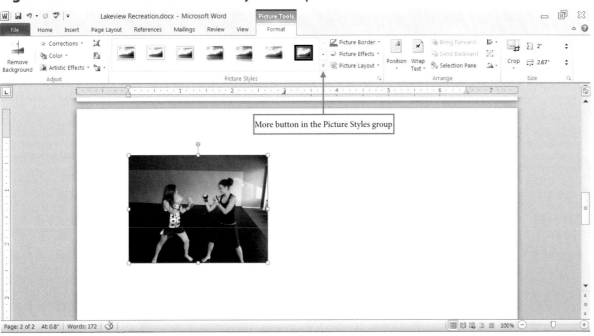

Figure 3.37 Picture Styles Gallery

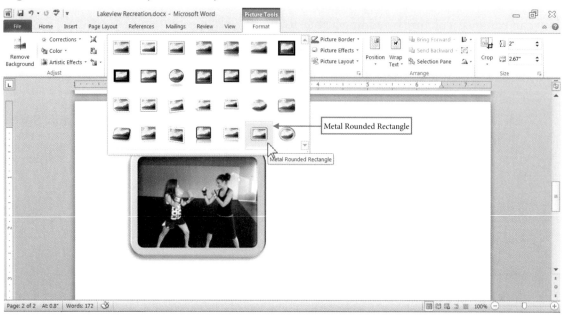

Modify Picture Size

When a picture is inserted in a document, it might need to be resized. When the picture is selected, it has a border around it with sizing handles in the corners for adjusting the size, handles in the middle to adjust the width, and a green rotation handle at the top of the object to rotate the picture (**Figure 3.38**).

Use these steps to change the size of a picture using the sizing handles:

- Click the **picture** if it is not selected.
- Hold the mouse over a sizing handle until a two-headed arrow displays. Using the corner sizing handles will keep the object in proportion as you change the size.
- Drag the arrow to change the size of the picture.

Use these steps to change the size of a picture using the commands on the Ribbon:

- Click the **picture** if it is not selected.
- Click the **Format** tab in the Picture Tools tab.
- Type the height of the picture in the Shape Height box in the Size group (**Figure 3.39**).
- Type the width of the picture in the Shape Width box in the Size group (Figure 3.39).

Hands-On Exercise: Insert a Picture and Modify Picture Size

(1) Click the Insert tab.

(2) Click Picture in the Illustrations group. The Insert Picture dialog box displays.

(3) Click the drive and folder where the student data files are located.

④ Double-click the Jet-Ski picture to insert it into the document. The document should resemble Figure 3.38. The Picture Tools contextual tab displays on the Ribbon.

⑤ Click the Format tab.

⑥ Type **1.4** in the Shape Height box in the Size group and press Enter (Figure 3.39). The Shape Width box automatically changes to 2.1 (Figure 3.39). The picture should resemble Figure 3.39.

Figure 3.38 Picture Inserted

Figure 3.39 Shape Height and Shape Width Commands

Wrap Text Command

Wrap Text: A command that changes the way the text wraps around an object, such as a picture or clip art.

Inline object: An object that is inserted like text in a document and moves along with the text around it.

Floating object: An object that keeps its position relative to the page.

The **Wrap Text** command is used to change the way the text wraps around an object, such as a picture or clip art. When an object is inserted into a document, it is an inline object. An **inline object** is inserted like text in a document and moves along with the text around it. You can change an inline object to a floating object. For example, if you have an inline object and you add a paragraph before the object, the object will be positioned after the paragraph. A **floating object** keeps its position relative to the page. If you have a floating object in the middle of the page and you insert a new paragraph in the middle of the page, the object will remain in the same location and the text will flow around the object.

Use these steps to wrap text around an object:

- Click the object to select it.
- Click the **Format** tab in the Picture Tools tab.
- Click the **Wrap Text** button in the Arrange group (**Figure 3.40**).
- Click **In Line with Text** to make the object an inline object. Click any of the other options to make the object a floating object. Some of the common floating object options are as follows:
  - *Square* option: you can move the object anywhere in the document, and the text will wrap around the border of the object.
  - *Tight* option: you can move the object anywhere in the document, and the text will wrap around the object's edges. There will be little white space between the text and object.

Hands-On Exercise: Wrap Text Around a Picture

① Click the Jet-Ski picture to select it (Figure 3.40).

② Click the Wrap Text button in the Arrange group in the Format tab (Figure 3.40).

③ Click Tight from the list (Figure 3.40).

Figure 3.40 Wrap Text Command

Move a Picture

A picture can be moved to another location in a document.

Use these steps to move a picture to a new location:

- Position the mouse pointer over the picture until a four-headed arrow displays.
- Drag the **picture** to a new location. If the picture does not move, you will need to make it a floating object using the Wrap Text command.

Hands-On Exercise: Move a Picture

In this exercise, you are going to move the Jet-Ski picture next to the tabbed text on the first page.

1. You will change the zoom level to 50% so you can view both pages in the document on the screen. Drag the Zoom button on the status bar to the left until the Zoom Level button states 50% (**Figure 3.41**).

2. Position the mouse pointer over the Jet-Ski picture until a four-headed arrow displays.

3. Drag the picture next to the tabbed text on page 1 as shown in **Figure 3.42**.

4. Drag the Zoom button to the right until the Zoom Level button states 100%.

5. Press Ctrl + End to navigate to the end of the document. The insertion point is centered on the line below the picture. You will change the alignment to left.

6. Click the Home tab.

7. Click the Align Text Left button.

8. Click the Save button on the Quick Access Toolbar.

Figure 3.41 Zoom Level 50%

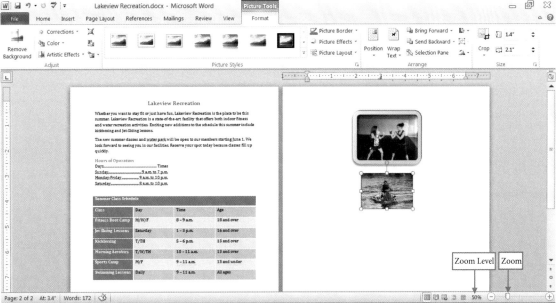

Figure 3.42 Jet-Ski Picture Moved to First Page

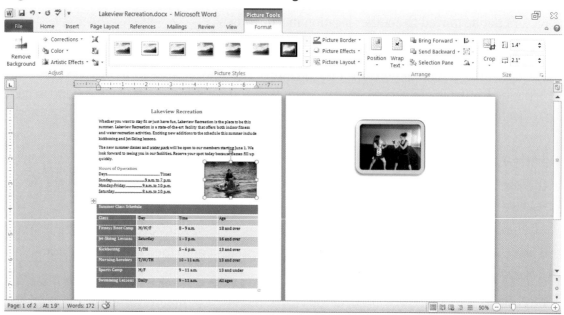

Create a Table Using the Insert Table Command

To create a table using the Insert Table command:

- Click the **Insert** tab.
- Click **Table** in the Tables group (**Figure 3.43**).
- Click **Insert Table** and the Insert Table dialog box displays (Figure 3.43).
- Type the number of columns you want to create in the Number of columns box (**Figure 3.44**).
- Type the number of rows you want to create in the Number of rows box (Figure 3.44).
- Click **OK**.

Hands-On Exercise: Create a Table Using the Insert Table Command

You will create a 3 × 6 table (three columns, six rows) that contains the yearly membership rates.

1. Click the Insert tab.

2. Click Table in the Tables group (Figure 3.43).

3. Click Insert Table (Figure 3.43) and the Insert Table dialog box displays (Figure 3.44).

4. Type **3** in the Number of columns box (Figure 3.44).

5. Type **6** in the Number of rows box (Figure 3.44).

6. Click OK .

7. Type the following text into the table (**Table 3.4**). Use the Tab or right arrow keys to navigate to the next cell in of the table.

Table 3.4 Text Entered into Table

Yearly Membership Rates		
Membership Type	Ages	Cost
Child	Under 18	$200
Adult	19–64	$300
Senior	65 and over	$250
Family	All	$500

Figure 3.43 Insert Table Command

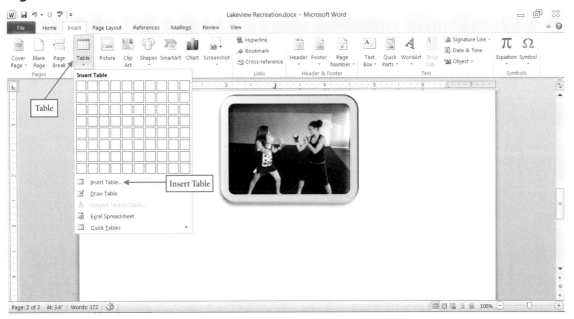

Figure 3.44 Insert Table Dialog Box

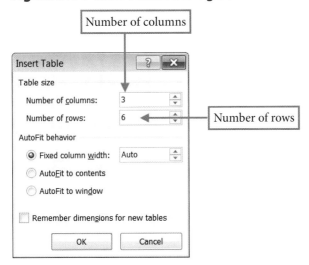

Apply the AutoFit Command

You can use the AutoFit command to automatically adjust the table width or column widths of a table. **Table 3.5** displays the AutoFit commands.

Table 3.5 AutoFit Commands	
Command	Description
AutoFit Contents	Automatically adjusts the column widths to fit the contents of the text in the cells.
AutoFit Window	Automatically adjusts the table width based on the window size. The table displays between the left and right margins.
Fixed Column Width	Does not automatically adjust the table width or column widths. Converts the table back to a fixed column width.

To change the table width or column widths of a table using the AutoFit command:

- Click in the table.
- Click the **Layout** tab in the Table Tools tab.
- Click the **AutoFit** button in the Cell Size group.
- Select an **option** from the list.

Hands-On Exercise: Format a Table and Apply the AutoFit Command

1. You will merge the cells in row 1. Click in the first row in the table.
2. Click Layout in the Table Tools tab.
3. Click the Select button in the Table group.
4. Click Select Row and the first row is selected.
5. Click Merge Cells in the Merge group. The cells in row 1 are merged into one cell.
6. Next, you will apply a table style to the table. Click the Design tab.
7. Click the More button in the Table Styles group. The gallery displays.
8. Click Light Shading—Accent 1 from the gallery (first row, second column).
9. Click the table move handle at the top left corner of the table to select the entire table.
10. Click the Home tab.

⑪ Type **14** in the Font Size box.

⑫ Triple-click on the text *Yearly Membership Rates*.

⑬ Click the Center button in the Paragraph group.

⑭ Next, you will autofit the contents of the table to automatically increase the column widths to fit the contents of the text in the cells. Click Layout in the Table Tools tab.

⑮ Click the AutoFit button in the Cell Size group (**Figure 3.45**).

⑯ Click AutoFit Contents (Figure 3.45). The table is automatically resized to fit the text in the table (**Figure 3.46**). You prefer the table to be larger so you will modify the size of the table using the AutoFit command.

⑰ Click the AutoFit button.

⑱ Click AutoFit Window . This command enlarges the table so that it displays between the left and right margins.

⑲ Click the Save button in the Quick Access Toolbar.

Figure 3.45 AutoFit Command

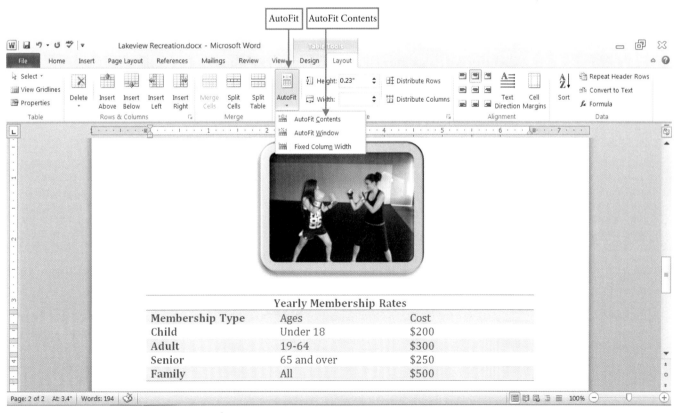

Figure 3.46 Table Resized Using AutoFit Command

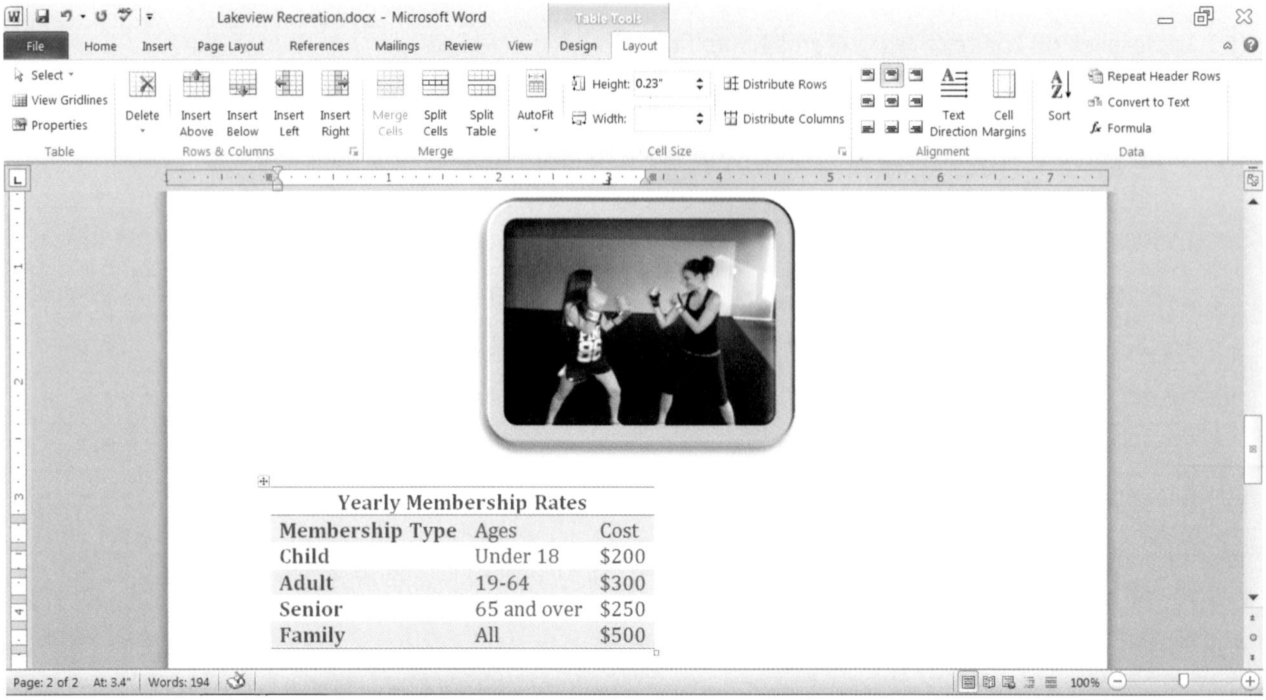

Insert WordArt

WordArt: Inserts decorative text in a document.

WordArt is another great feature that can be used to enhance a document. **WordArt** inserts decorative text in a document.

Use these steps to insert WordArt:

- Click the **Insert** tab.
- Click the **WordArt** button in the Text group (**Figure 3.47**). A gallery displays.
- Select an option and the WordArt object displays in the document. The Drawing Tools contextual tab displays on the Ribbon (**Figure 3.48**). It contains a Format tab that contains commands to format the WordArt.
- Type the text in the WordArt object (Figure 3.48).
- Click outside the WordArt object to exit the WordArt.

Use these steps to move a WordArt object:

- Click the WordArt.
- Point to the the border of the WordArt.
- When the four-headed arrow displays, drag the WordArt to a new location.

Hands-On Exercise: Insert, Format, and Move a WordArt Object

1. Press Ctrl + End to navigate to the end of the document.
2. Press Enter twice to navigate down two lines.
3. Click the Insert tab.

④ Click the WordArt button in the Text group and the gallery displays (Figure 3.47).

⑤ Click Fill—Blue, Transparent Accent 1, Outline—Accent1 (second row, first column) (Figure 3.47). The WordArt object displays in the document and the Drawing Tools contextual tab displays (Figure 3.48). This tab contains commands to format the WordArt.

⑥ Type **Come in and try our facilities!** in place of *Your text here*.

⑦ Triple-click the text to select it.

⑧ Click the Home tab.

⑨ Click the Font Size arrow and select 26 .

⑩ Point to the the border of the WordArt. When the four-headed arrow displays, drag the WordArt to the right so it is centered (**Figure 3.49**).

⑪ Press Ctrl + End to navigate to the end of the document. The WordArt is no longer selected.

⑫ Press Enter three times.

⑬ Click the Save button on the Quick Access Toolbar.

Figure 3.47 WordArt Gallery

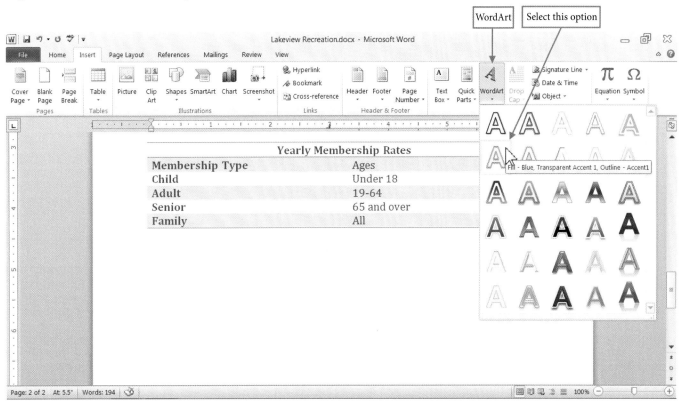

Figure 3.48 WordArt Inserted

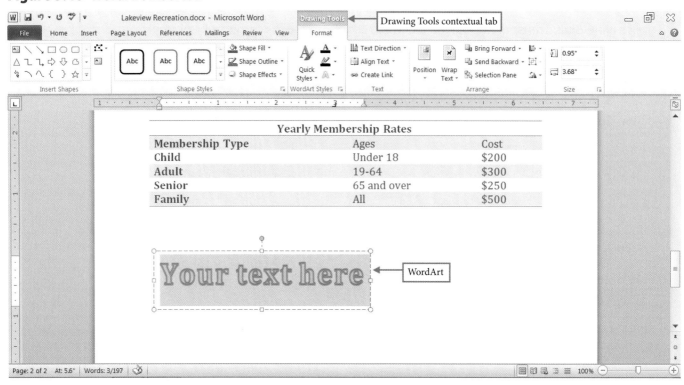

Figure 3.49 WordArt Formatted and Moved to the Right

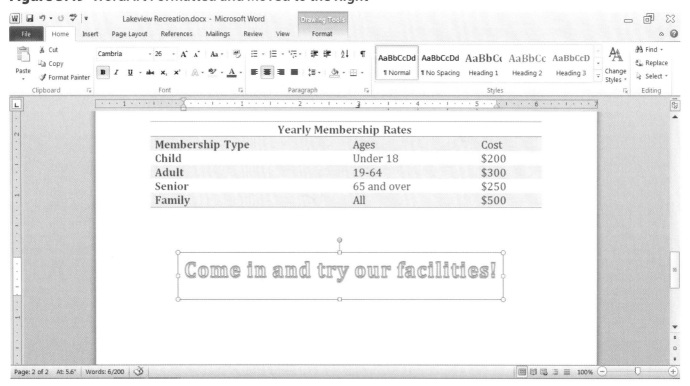

Insert Clip Art

Clip art is a multimedia item such as an illustration, photograph, video, or audio clip that can be inserted in a document. Microsoft Word 2010 has many built-in clip art images that you can insert into your document. Once clip art is inserted or selected, the Picture Tools contextual tab displays in the Ribbon, which contains a Format tab. The Format tab contains commands to format the clip art. Clip art images and pictures are formatted the same way using the commands from the Picture Tools contextual tab. Make certain to select the clip art before formatting it.

> **Clip art:** A multimedia item such as an illustration, photograph, video, or audio clip that can be inserted into a document.

Use these steps to insert clip art:

- Click the **Insert** tab.
- Click the **Clip Art** button in the Illustrations group (**Figure 3.50**). The Clip Art task pane opens on the right side of the document window (Figure 3.50).
- Type a word or phrase describing the clip art image for which you are searching in the Search for box (Figure 3.50).
- Click the **Results should be** box or arrow (Figure 3.50) to select the media types for which you are searching. The media types include illustrations, photographs, videos, and audio. By default, all media types are selected and contain a check mark before the media type. Click the **checkbox** next to the media types for which you are searching, *or* click **All media file types** to select all options. You may need to press **Esc** to exit the selection.
- Click the **Include Office.com content** checkbox to insert a check mark, if it does not already contain one (Figure 3.50). This will expand the search to include clip art images that are available online.
- Click **Go**, and a listing of clip art images displays at the bottom of the Clip Art task pane. Click the scroll box on the right to scroll through the images.
- Click a **Clip Art** image, and it is inserted in the document.
- Click the **Close** button on the Clip Art task pane to close the Clip Art task pane.

Hands-On Exercise: Insert and Format Clip Art

1. Click the Insert tab.
2. Click the Clip Art button in the Illustrations group (Figure 3.50). The Clip Art task pane opens on the right side of the document window (Figure 3.50).
3. Type **water park** in the Search for box (Figure 3.50).
4. Click the Results should be box or arrow (Figure 3.50).
5. Click All media file types if it is not already selected. You may need to press Esc to exit the list.
6. Click the Include Office.com content checkbox to insert a check mark, if it does not already contain one (Figure 3.50), to search for clip art images that are available online at Office.com.
7. Click Go , and clip art images that match the search term display in the Clip Art task pane.

→

⑧ Click the image shown in Figure 3.50. If you cannot find the image, choose a similar one. The clip art is inserted on the third page.

⑨ Click the Close button on the Clip Art task pane.

⑩ Click the clip art if it is not already selected. The Picture Tools contextual tab displays on the Ribbon. The sizing handles display around the border of the clip art. You will change the size of the clip art so that it fits on the second page.

⑪ Type **3** in the Shape Height box in the Size group of the Format tab and press Enter. The Shape Width box automatically changes to 2 to keep the clip art in proportion. Scroll up to view the entire clip art image. The document should resemble **Figure 3.51**.

⑫ Drag the Zoom button to the left until the Zoom Level reaches 40%. This allows you to view the entire document.

⑬ Click the Wrap Text button in the Arrange group on the Format tab.

⑭ Click Tight .

⑮ Drag the water park clip art image to the right to resemble **Figure 3.52**.

⑯ Click Save on the Quick Access Toolbar.

⑰ Drag the Zoom button to the right until the Zoom Level reaches 100%.

Figure 3.50 Clip Art Task Pane

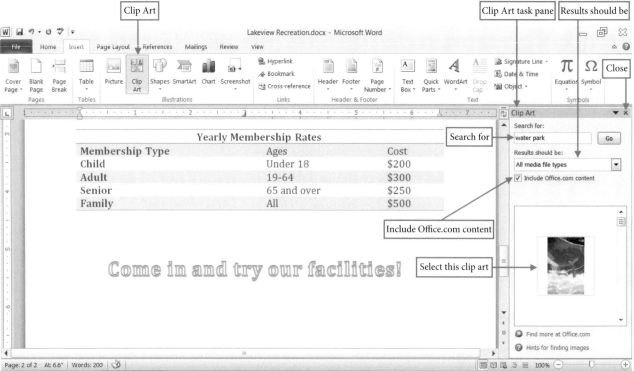

Figure 3.51 Resized Clip Art

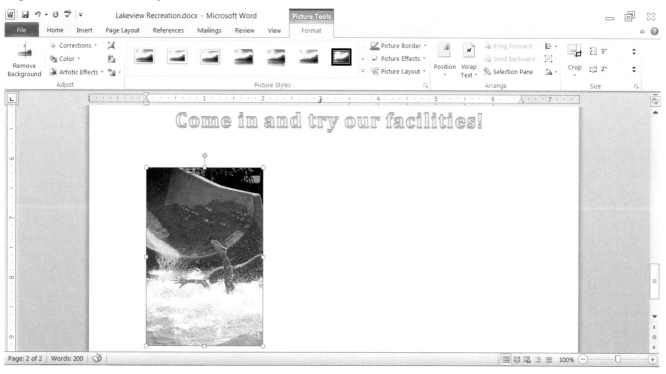

Figure 3.52 Clip Art Moved

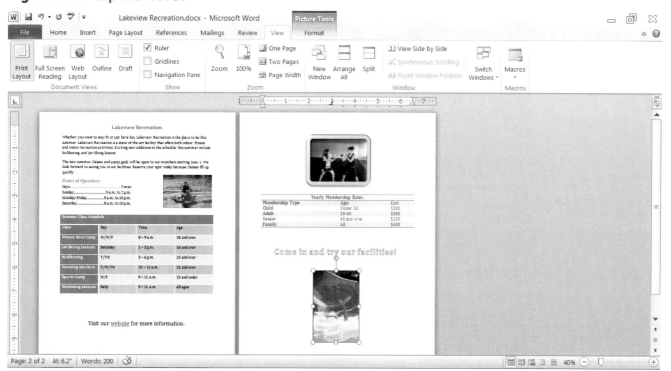

Insert Header, Footer, and Page Number

Header: Text that displays in the top margin of each page in a document.

Footer: Text that displays in the bottom margin of each page in a document.

Headers, footers, and page numbers can be inserted in a document. A **header** is text that displays in the top margin of each page in a document. A **footer** is text that displays in the bottom margin of each page in a document. The header and footer are divided into three sections (left, center, and right). You can insert the date and time, page number, and text in the header and footer.

There are three commands in the Header & Footer group on the Insert tab, which include Header, Footer, and Page Number. If you want just a page number to display, you should select the Page Number command instead of using the Header or Footer command.

When you insert a header or footer, the appearance of the page changes. The Header & Footer Tools contextual tab displays. The document becomes dim except for the header and footer sections. Placeholders may display in the header or footer in which you can type or delete information. When you close the Header & Footer Tools tab, the document displays the header or footer, which will appear dimmed.

Use these steps to insert a header or footer:

- Click the **Insert** tab.
- Click **Header** or **Footer** in the Header & Footer group (**Figure 3.53**). A gallery options displays.
- Click an option from the gallery (**Figure 3.54**).
- Type the text in the placeholders (**Figure 3.55**).
- Click the **Close Header and Footer** button on the Close group in the Design tab of the Header & Footer Tools contextual tab.

Use these steps to insert a page number:

- Click the **Insert** tab.
- Click **Page Number** in the Header & Footer group (Figure 3.53).
- Select a location for the page number from the list.
- Select a format for the page number from the list.
- Click the **Close Header and Footer** button on the Close group in the Design tab of the Header & Footer Tools contextual tab.

Hands-On Exercise: Insert and Format Header and Footer

1. Press Ctrl + Home to navigate to the top of the document.
2. Click the Insert tab.
3. Click Header in the Header & Footer group (Figure 3.53). A gallery displays.
4. Click Blank (Three Columns) from the gallery (Figure 3.54). The header displays with the placeholders (Figure 3.55).
5. Click the left placeholder . Press Delete .
6. Click the center placeholder . Press Delete .

⑦ Click in the right placeholder and type **Lakeview Recreation-Summer Schedule**.

⑧ Triple-click the header text to select it.

⑨ Click the Home tab.

⑩ Click the Font arrow and select Cambria .

⑪ Press End to go to end of the text and the text is deselected.

⑫ Click the Design tab in the Header & Footer Tools contextual tab. The header should resemble **Figure 3.56**.

⑬ Click the Go to Footer button in the Navigation group to navigate to the footer (Figure 3.56).

⑭ Click the Page Number button in the Header & Footer group (**Figure 3.57**).

⑮ Point to Bottom of Page (Figure 3.57).

⑯ Click Plain Number 2 (Figure 3.57). The page number displays in the footer.

⑰ Double-click the page number in the footer to select it.

⑱ Click the Home tab.

⑲ Click the Font arrow and select Cambria .

⑳ Press End to go to end of the text, and the text is deselected.

㉑ Click the Design tab.

㉒ Click Close Header and Footer in the Close group (**Figure 3.58**).

㉓ Click the Save button on the Quick Access Toolbar.

Figure 3.53 Commands in the Header & Footer Group

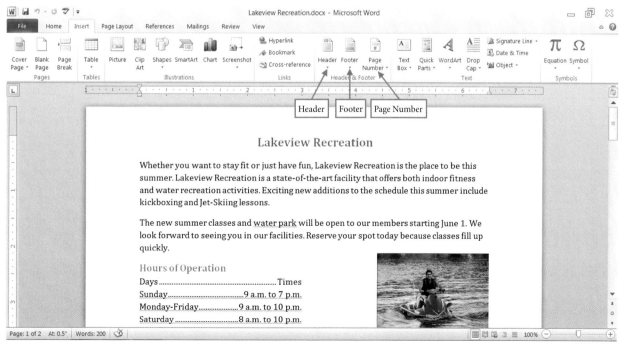

Figure 3.54 Blank (Three Columns) Header

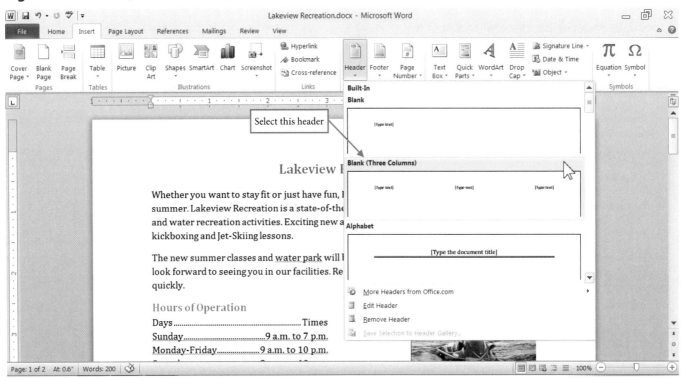

Figure 3.55 Placeholders in Header

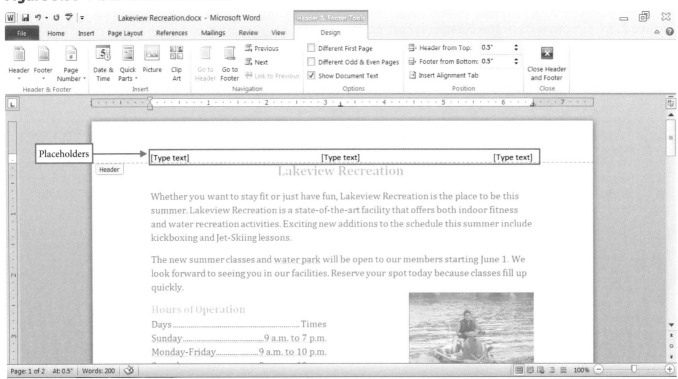

Figure 3.56 Header Created and Formatted

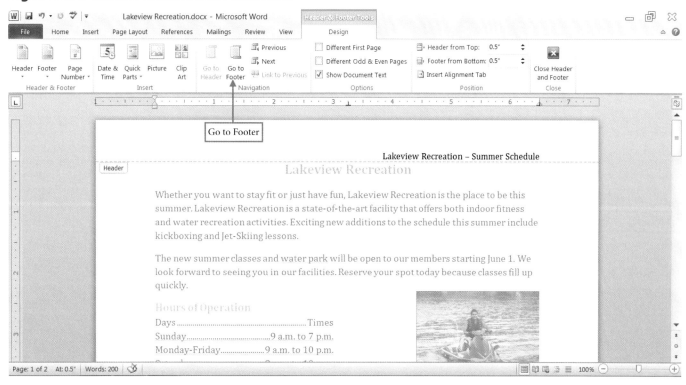

Figure 3.57 Insert Page Number in Footer

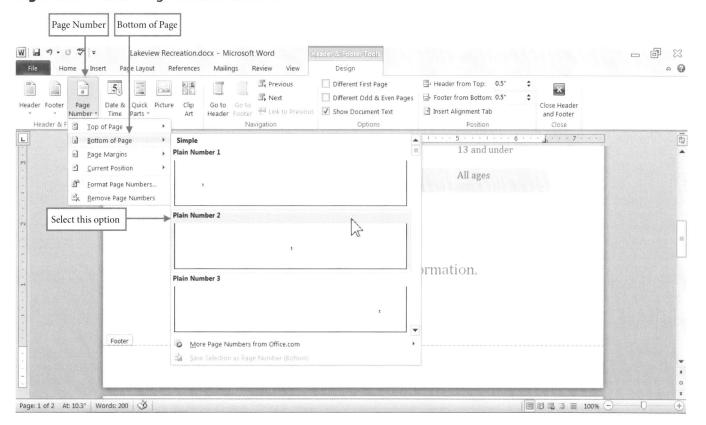

Figure 3.58 Footer Created and Formatted

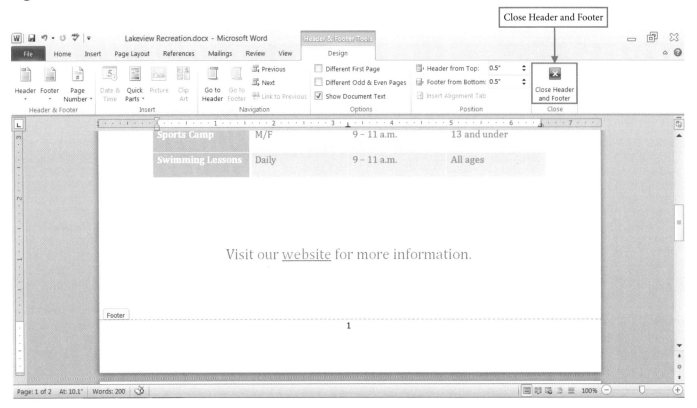

Change Page Orientation

When you open a Microsoft Word 2010 document, by default the document opens in portrait orientation. In **portrait orientation**, the page orientation prints on a vertical page, which
means that the page is taller than it is wide (8.5 × 11 inches).

You can change the orientation of the document to landscape orientation. In **landscape orientation**, the page orientation prints on a horizontal page, which means that the page is wider
than it is tall (11 × 8.5 inches).

Use these steps to change page orientation:

- Click the **Page Layout** tab.
- Click the **Orientation** button in the Page Setup group (**Figure 3.59**).
- Click **Portrait** or **Landscape**.

Hands-On Exercise: Change Page Orientation

① Click the Page Layout tab.

② Click Orientation in the Page Setup group (Figure 3.59).

③ Click Landscape (Figure 3.59). Notice how the layout changes (Figure 3.60).

④ Click the Undo button on the Quick Access Toolbar to set the orientation back to portrait.

Figure 3.59 Orientation Button

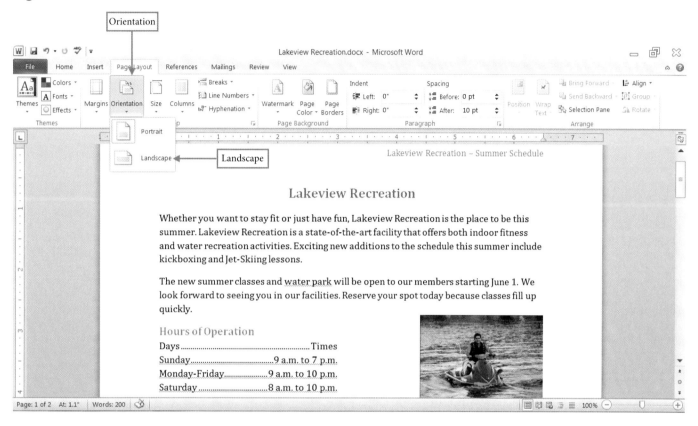

Figure 3.60 Landscape Orientation

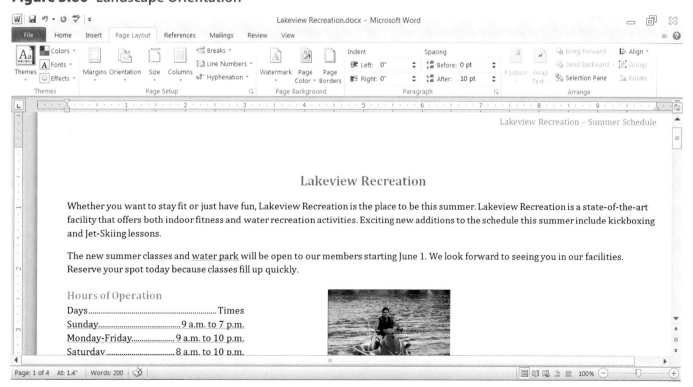

Insert a Symbol

Symbol: A special character that does not appear on the keyboard.

A **symbol** is a special character that does not appear on the keyboard. Examples of symbols include the copyright ©, trademark ™, and check mark symbols. **Table 3.6** displays keyboard shortcuts for the commonly used symbols that can be inserted in a document.

Table 3.6 Keyboard Shortcuts for Commonly Used Symbols	
Symbol	Keyboard shortcut
©	(c)
®	(r)
™	(tm)

Use these steps to insert a symbol:

- Click the **Insert** tab.
- Click the **Symbol** button in the Symbols group (**Figure 3.61**).
- Select a symbol from the gallery or click **More Symbols** to open the Symbol dialog box, which contains additional symbols (**Figure 3.62**).
- To view additional special characters, click the **Font** arrow and select **Wingdings**.
- Select a symbol from the gallery and click **Insert**.
- Click **Close**.

Hands-On Exercise: Insert a Symbol

1. Position the mouse pointer after the text *Hours of Operation* on the first page.
2. Press the space bar .
3. You will insert a symbol of a clock. Click the Insert tab.
4. Click the Symbol button in the Symbols group (Figure 3.61).
5. Click More Symbols to open the Symbol dialog box (Figure 3.61).
6. Click the Font arrow and select Wingdings (Figure 3.62).
7. Scroll through the list and click the clock symbol that resembles ☒ (Figure 3.62).
8. Click Insert (Figure 3.62).
9. Click Close . The document should resemble **Figure 3.63**.

Figure 3.61 Symbol Button

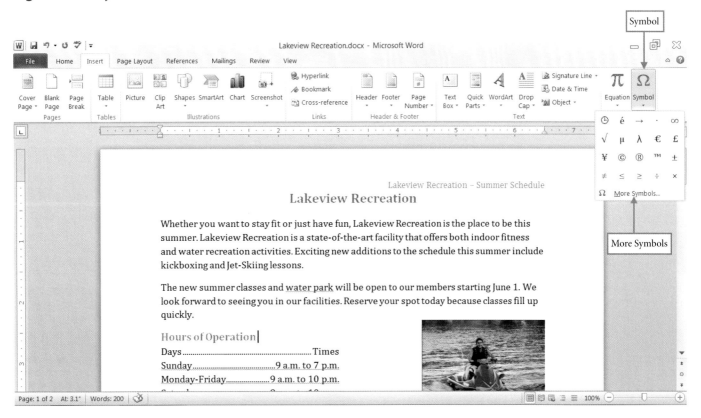

Figure 3.62 Symbol Dialog Box

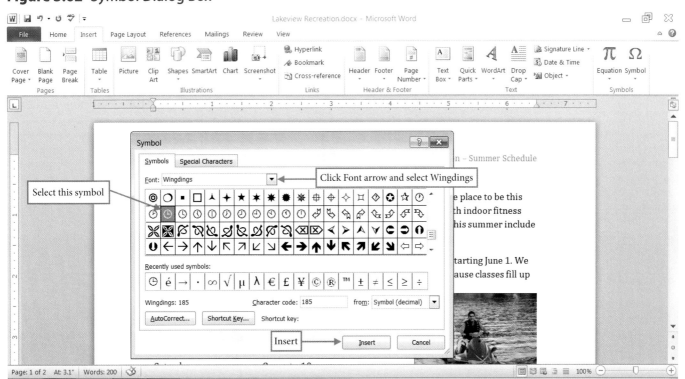

Figure 3.63 Symbol Inserted into Document

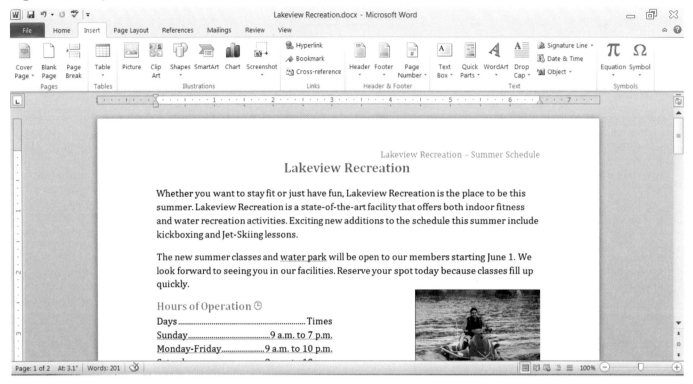

Review, Proof, and Finalize Document

Before you print a document, you should check the document for spelling and grammar errors and make any changes to the formatting of the document as needed. When the document contains tables, clip art, or pictures, check those objects to ensure the size, position, spacing, and formatting look appropriate.

In this exercise you will check the document for spelling and grammar errors. You will preview the document and make changes to the formatting. You will print the document and exit Microsoft Word 2010.

Hands-On Exercise: Review, Proof, and Finalize Document

1. Click the Review tab.

2. Click the Spelling & Grammar button. Correct any errors.

3. Click the File tab.

4. Click Print . A preview of the document displays on the right side of the window. Notice that the header and the text *Lakeview Recreation* appear close to each other on the first page (**Figure 3.64**).

⑤ Click the Next Page arrow to view second page (Figure 3.64). The table displays too close to the kickboxing picture. You will modify the document to enhance the layout.

⑥ Click Esc to exit the Print window.

⑦ First, you will modify the margins so the header and text have more space between them. Click the Page Layout tab.

⑧ Click the Margins button.

⑨ Click Normal .

⑩ Next, you will add some line spacing after the kickboxing picture. Position the insertion point after the kickboxing picture. If you are having trouble, click on the kickboxing picture and then press End to navigate to the end of the line.

⑪ Press Enter and a new blank line displays. The table moves down one line.

⑫ Click Save on the Quick Access Toolbar to save the changes.

⑬ Click the File tab.

⑭ Click Print . Change any print settings as appropriate.

⑮ Click the Print button. The first page of the document should resemble **Figure 3.65**. The second page of the document should resemble **Figure 3.66**.

⑯ Click Exit .

Figure 3.64 Preview Document

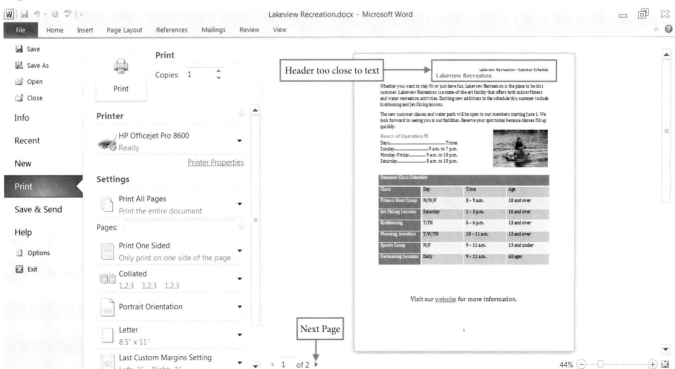

Figure 3.65 Completed First Page

Figure 3.66 Completed Second Page

Multiple-Choice Questions

1. The Clip Art task pane allows you to insert _____.
   a. Illustrations
   b. Photographs
   c. Audio and videos
   d. All of the above

2. You can find the WordArt command on the _____ tab.
   a. Home
   b. Insert
   c. Page Layout
   d. Picture Tools

3. A _____ creates a link to another location, such as a webpage, picture, place in the current document, another document, an email address, or a program.
   a. Tab
   b. Footer
   c. Hyperlink
   d. Page break

4. To keep an object in proportion while resizing it, drag the _____.

   a. Middle sizing handle

   b. Rotation handle

   c. Corner sizing handle

   d. Proportional handle

5. Use the shortcut keys _____ to insert a manual page break.

   a. Ctrl + Enter

   b. Tab + Enter

   c. Shift + Enter

   d. Alt + Enter

6. The _____ contextual tab displays at the top of the Ribbon when you insert clip art or a picture.

   a. Drawing Tools

   b. Picture Tools

   c. Table Tools

   d. Clip Art Tools

7. To move a table, drag the table move handle, which is located _____.

   a. Near the top-left corner of the table

   b. Near the top right corner of the table

   c. Near the last cell of the table

   d. In the first cell of the table

8. The default margin settings are _____.

   a. 0.5 inch on the top, bottom, left, and right margins

   b. 1 inch on the top, bottom, left, and right margins

   c. 0.5 inch on the top and bottom margins and 1 inch on the left and right margins

   d. 1 inch on the top and bottom margins and 0.5 inch on the left and right margins

9. Tabs display on the _____.

   a. Status bar

   b. Scroll bar

   c. Ruler bar

   d. None of the above

10. The _____ displays in the top margin of each page in a document.

   a. Page break

   b. Footer

   c. Border

   d. Header

Project #1: Create a Flyer

You work for a real estate agency. You want to create a flyer to advertise a house that is for sale.

① Open a new blank document.

② Change top and bottom margin to 0.75".

③ Set the font to Verdana.

④ Set the font size to 14.

⑤ Insert WordArt.

    a. Select Fill—Blue, Accent 1, Metal Bevel, Reflection as the style (the last option in gallery).

    b. Type **HOUSE FOR SALE**.

    c. Center the WordArt horizontally on the page.

    d. Set the Wrap Text option to Square.

⑥ Press **Ctrl + End** to navigate to the end of the document.

⑦ Press **Enter** three times.

⑧ Save the document as **House For Sale**.

⑨ Insert clip art of a house.

    a. Insert the clip art named *exterior of a house* (**Figure 3.67**).

    b. Set the shape height to 2 inches.

    c. Select the Metal Rounded Rectangle picture style (fourth row, sixth column).

    d. Center the clip art horizontally on the page.

⑩ Press **End** to navigate to the end of the clip art.

⑪ Press **Enter** twice.

⑫ Set the alignment to Align Text Left.

⑬ Type the following:

OPEN HOUSE
Sunday, July 1
1 p.m. to 4 p.m.
248 6th Avenue
Westport, MA 89701

⑭ Press **Enter** twice.

⑮ Type **Asking Price: $419,000**.

⑯ Press **Enter** twice.

⑰ Set left tabs at 1 inch and 4 inches.

⑱ Type the following using the tab stops:

Four bedrooms	**New appliances**
Three full bathrooms	**Vaulted ceilings**
Two fireplaces	**Fresh paint**
Granite countertops	**3,500 square feet**
Hardwood floors	**Great location**

⑲ Press **Enter** twice.

⑳ Type **For further information, contact Jack Johnson**.

㉑ Make the following changes to the text *For further information, contact Jack Johnson.*

   a. Set the font size to 16.

   b. Bold the text.

   c. Center the text.

   d. Create a hyperlink on the text *Jack Johnson* and link it to the email address **jjohnson@johnsonrealtors.com**.

㉒ Select the text *OPEN HOUSE* and apply the following formats:

   a. Bold the text.

   b. Center the text.

   c. Change the font size to 18.

   d. Set the font color to Blue in Standard Colors.

   e. Set the spacing after the paragraph to 0.

㉓ Select the following four lines and apply the following formats:

Sunday, July 1
1 p.m. to 4 p.m.
248 6th Avenue
Westport, MA 89701

   a. Center the selected text.

   b. Change the font size to 16.

   c. Set the spacing after the paragraph to 0.

㉔ Make the following formatting changes to the text *Asking Price: $419,000.*

   a. Bold the text.

   b. Underline the text.

   c. Set the font color to Blue in Standard Colors.

   d. Set the font size to 16.

㉕ Make the following change to the tabbed text.

Set the spacing after the paragraph to 0.

㉖ Insert a footer that contains the text **Johnson Realtors** in the center section of the footer.

㉗ Correct all spelling and grammar errors.

㉘ Save the document.

㉙ Print the document. The document should resemble **Figure 3.68**.

Figure 3.67 Clip Art of House

Figure 3.68 Completed Document

Project #2: Create a Workshop Evaluation Form

You have been asked to create an evaluation form for the workshop your company is conducting for its employees.

① Open a new document.

② Insert a header with the text **Your Name** in the left section and the text **Evaluation Form** in the right section of the header.

③ Insert a footer with the page number in the center section.

④ Set the left and right margins to 1.5.

⑤ Type the text **Workshop Evaluation Form**.

⑥ Select the text *Workshop Evaluation Form* and apply the following formatting changes:

a. Apply the Title style.

b. Set the font color to Dark Blue, Text 2, Lighter 60% (third row, fourth column).

   c. Bold the text.

   d. Change the font size to 24.

   e. Center the text.

⑦ Press **Ctrl + End** to navigate to the end of the document.

⑧ Press **Enter**.

⑨ Insert clip art.

   a. Type **evaluation** in the Search for box.

   b. Select the **Checkmark on clipboard** option (**Figure 3.69**). You may substitute with
      another clip art if this clip art is not available on your computer.

   c. Set the shape height to 0.64 inch.

   d. Set the Wrap Text option to square.

   e. Move the clip art to the right of the text.

⑩ Press **Ctrl + End** to navigate to the end of the document.

⑪ Change the line spacing of the document to 2.0.

⑫ Type the following text: **On a scale of 4 to 1 with 4 being the highest score,
   rate each item by placing a ✓ in the appropriate box.** The ✓ is inserted
   by using the Symbol command. The checkmark symbol can be found in the
   Wingdings font.

⑬ Press **Enter**.

⑭ Insert a table with 5 columns and 14 rows.

⑮ Type the following in the first row:

   a. First column: **Workshop overall:**

   b. Second column: **4**

   c. Third column: **3**

   d. Fourth column: **2**

   e. Fifth column: **1**

⑯ In the second row, first column, type **The workshop materials were appropriate**.

⑰ Set the AutoFit command to AutoFit Contents.

⑱ Type the following in first column of the remaining rows:

   The workshop covered the topics in sufficient detail.
   The room was comfortable and conducive to learning.
   I would recommend this workshop to others.
   Overall rating of the workshop.

   (Leave a blank row)

Instructor:
The instructor was available to assist with the learning of materials.
The instructor responded appropriately to questions.
The instructor was well prepared.
The instructor was knowledgeable of the subject matter.
The instructor presented the materials in an effective manner.
Overall rating of the instructor.

(19) Set the AutoFit command to AutoFit Window.

(20) Select columns 2 through 5 in the first row.

(21) Bold the selected text.

(22) Copy the selected text to row 8, columns 2, 3, 4, and 5.

(23) Select the cells with the number 4 (first row, second column and eighth row, second column). Apply red shading to the cells.

(24) Select the cells with the number 3 (first row, third column and eighth row, third column). Apply yellow shading to the cells.

(25) Select the cells with the number 2 (first row, fourth column and eighth row, fourth column). Apply light blue shading to the cells.

(26) Select the cells with the number 1 (first row, fifth column and eighth row, fifth column). Apply light green shading to the cells.

(27) Select row 7 and merge the cells.

(28) Remove the left and right borders in row 7.

(29) Press **Ctrl + End** to navigate to the end of the document.

(30) Insert a manual page break.

(31) Type **What did you like about the workshop?** and press **Enter**.

(32) Insert a table with one column and four rows.

(33) Select the entire table.

(34) Remove the left and right borders.

(35) Press **Ctrl + End** to navigate to the end of the document.

(36) Press **Enter**.

(37) Type **What did you dislike about the workshop?** and press **Enter**.

(38) Copy the table from the top of page 2 and paste it below the text **What did you dislike about the workshop?**

(39) Press **Ctrl + End** to navigate to the end of the document.

(40) Press **Enter**.

(41) Type **Suggestions to improve the workshop:** and press **Enter**.

㊷ Paste the copied table.

㊸ Correct all spelling and grammar errors.

㊹ Save the document as **Workshop Evaluation Form**. The document should resemble Figure 3.70 and Figure 3.71.

Figure 3.69 Clip Art

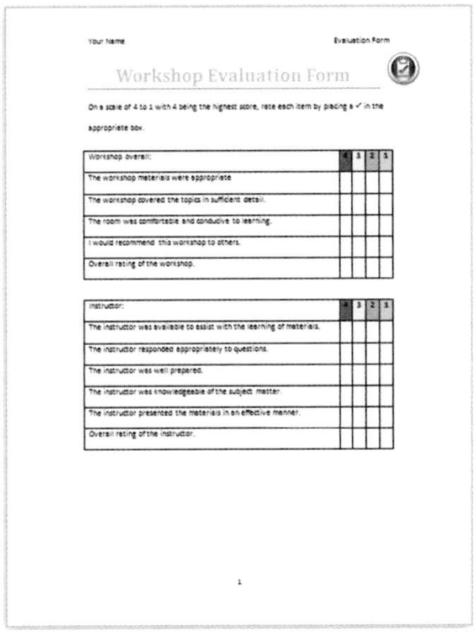

Figure 3.70 Completed First Page

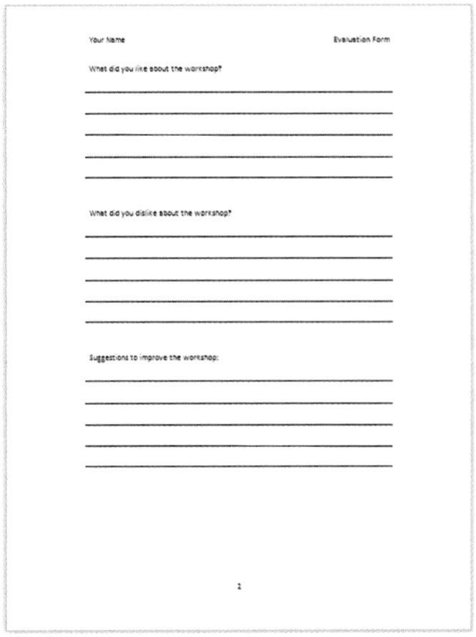

Figure 3.71 Completed Second Page

Project #3: Create an Agenda for the New Orientation

① Open a new document.

② Set the orientation as landscape.

③ Set the top and bottom margins to 0.5 inch.

④ Set the line spacing as 1.5.

⑤ Type the following text. Press **Enter** after each line.

FRANKFORT HOSPITAL
NEW EMPLOYEE ORIENTATION
MONDAY, NOVEMBER 1

⑥ Press **Enter** twice after the text **MONDAY, NOVEMBER 1**.

⑦ Insert a table with 2 columns and 10 rows.

⑧ Type the following text in the table (**Table 3.7**).

Table 3.7 Enter Text into Table	
New Employee Orientation Agenda	
Time	Topic
8:30 a.m. - 9:00 a.m.	Breakfast buffet
9:00 a.m. - 9:30 a.m.	Welcome and introductions by Philip Morgan, CEO of Frankfort Hospital
9:30 a.m. - 10:30 a.m.	Photo IDs taken and parking passes distributed
10:30 a.m. - 12:00 p.m.	Presentation by Human Resources regarding payroll system and employee benefits
12:00 p.m. - 1:00 p.m.	Lunch
1:00 p.m. - 2:00 p.m.	Presentation by IT department
2:00 p.m. - 4:00 p.m.	Departmental breakout meetings
4:00 p.m. - 4:30 p.m.	Wrap up session

⑨ Select the entire table and make the following changes:

   a. Set the AutoFit command to AutoFit Contents.

   b. Set the table row height to 0.3.

   c. Center the table.

⑩ Make the following formatting changes to the first row of the table:

   a. Select the first row and merge the cells.

   b. Change the shading to light blue.

   c. Change the font color to White—Background 1.

   d. Bold the text.

   e. Center the text.

   f. Change the font size to 18.

⑪ Make the following formatting changes to the second row of the table:

   a. Change the shading to White, Background 1, Darker 15%.

   b. Bold the text.

⑫ Make the following formatting changes to the first three lines of the document:

   a. Bold the text.

   b. Center the text.

   c. Change the font size to 18.

   d. Set the spacing after the paragraph to 0.

⑬ Insert clip art of a hospital above the table (**Figure 3.72**). The clip art is called "ambulance driving on the road towards the hospital." You may substitute with another clip art if this clip art is not available on your computer.

⑭ Make the following formatting changes to the clip art:

   a. Set the shape height to 1.7.

   b. Set the picture style to Rounded Diagonal Corner, White (second row, seventh column).

   c. Center the clip art.

⑮ Correct all spelling and grammar errors.

⑯ Save the document as **New Employee Orientation**. The completed document should resemble **Figure 3.73**.

⑰ Print the document.

Figure 3.72 Clip Art of Hospital

Figure 3.73 Completed Document

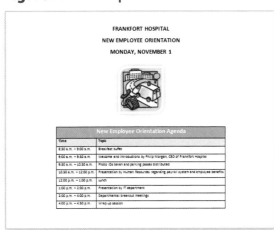

Create Presentations Using Microsoft PowerPoint 2010

Chapter Objectives

After completing this chapter, you will be able to do the following:

- Identify Microsoft PowerPoint 2010 components.
- Create a presentation.
- Insert and format text and paragraphs.
- Insert a theme.
- Insert and modify clip art and WordArt.
- Insert and modify a table.
- Modify slide layouts.
- Navigate between slides.
- Run and navigate a slide show.
- Save, close, and print a presentation.

Microsoft PowerPoint 2010 is an application used to create presentations that are shared with an audience in the form of a slide show. Text, graphics, animations, and other media elements can be inserted into the presentation.

In this chapter, you will become acquainted with various components of Microsoft PowerPoint 2010. You will learn how to create a presentation that includes various elements such as clip art, tables, WordArt, and themes. Additionally, you will learn how to print handouts of the presentation and run the slide show.

Identify Microsoft PowerPoint 2010 Components

You will open Microsoft PowerPoint 2010 and get acquainted with its components.

Hands-On Exercise: Launch Microsoft PowerPoint 2010

① Click the Start button on the taskbar.

② Click All Programs .

③ Click Microsoft Office . You may need to scroll through the Start menu to locate the folder.

④ Click Microsoft PowerPoint 2010 .

⑤ A new blank presentation displays (**Figure 4.1**).

Table 4.1 illustrates many common elements and key terms used in Microsoft Office applications.

Table 4.1 Common Microsoft Office Elements and Key Terms	
Common Element	Description
Backstage view	The Backstage view contains commands to manage your files such as creating, opening, saving, and printing a presentation. Click the **File tab** to open the Backstage view.
Commands	A command is a button or text that performs an action or task.
Dialog box	A dialog box is a window that allows a user to perform commands or apply settings. A dialog box displays when the dialog box launcher is clicked. A dialog box launcher is a button that resembles a diagonal arrow, which displays to the right of a group name on the Ribbon (Figure 4.1).
Mini Toolbar	The Mini Toolbar displays when text is selected and contains formatting commands that can be applied to the selected text. The Mini Toolbar displays at the top right of the selected text and will appear faded or dimmed.
Quick Access Toolbar	The Quick Access Toolbar provides access to the most frequently used commands. By default, the Quick Access Toolbar is located at the left corner of the title bar (Figure 4.1).
Ribbon	The Ribbon contains all the commands needed to create and edit a presentation. The Ribbon is located below the title bar and contains tabs that are organized by groups of related commands (Figure 4.1). Eight tabs display by default at the top of the Ribbon, starting with the Home tab. The File tab is not considered part of the Ribbon.

Microsoft PowerPoint 2010: An application used to create presentations that are shared with an audience in the form of a slide show.

Backstage view: Commands for managing files, such as creating, opening, saving, and printing a presentation.

Command: A button or text that performs an action or task.

Dialog box: A window that allows a user to perform commands or apply settings. A dialog box displays when the dialog box launcher is clicked.

Dialog box launcher: A button that resembles a diagonal arrow, which displays to the right of a group name on the Ribbon.

Mini Toolbar: Contains formatting commands that can be applied to the selected text. The Mini Toolbar displays at the top right of the selected text and will appear faded or dimmed.

Quick Access Toolbar: A toolbar that provides access to the most frequently used commands. By default, the Quick Access Toolbar is located at the left corner of the title bar.

Ribbon: Contains the commands you need to create and edit a presentation. The Ribbon is located below the title bar and contains tabs that are organized by groups of related commands.

Table 4.1 *continued*

Ruler	The **ruler** is used to align objects in a presentation. If the rulers are not displayed, click the **View** tab and click the **Ruler** box in the Show group.
Scroll bar	A **scroll bar** allows the user to navigate either up and down or left and right to view the information in a presentation.
Shortcut menu	A **shortcut menu** displays when the user right-clicks an object or area of the window. It contains a list of commands related to the object.
Status bar	The **status bar** provides information about the status of a presentation. The status bar is located at the bottom of the application window.
Title bar	The **title bar** displays the name of the file that is currently open and the name of the application. The title bar is the top bar on the application window.
ToolTip (ScreenTip)	A **ToolTip (ScreenTip)** lists the name of the command and sometimes includes a brief description of the command. A ToolTip displays when the mouse hovers over, or points to, a command. It may also display keyboard shortcuts that can be used to initiate the command using the keyboard.
View buttons	The **View buttons** provide options for viewing the presentation. The View buttons are located on the right side of the status bar (Figure 4.1). By default, the presentation opens in Normal view.
Zoom controls	The **Zoom controls** allow the user to zoom in and out of specific areas in the presentation. This feature controls the magnification of the presentation. The Zoom controls are displayed on the right side of the status bar (Figure 4.1).

Figure 4.1 New Presentation

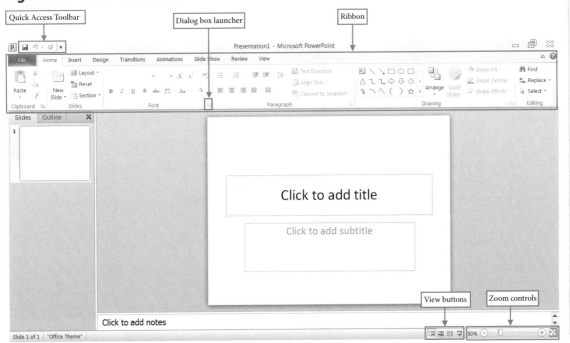

Ruler: Used to align objects in a presentation.

Scroll bars: Allows the user to navigate either up and down or left and right to view the information in a presentation.

Shortcut menu: A menu that displays when the user right-clicks an object or area of the window. It contains a list of commands related to the object.

Status bar: A bar that provides information about the status of a presentation. The status bar is located at the bottom of the application window.

Title bar: A bar that displays the name of the file that is currently open and the name of the application. The title bar is the top bar on the application window.

ToolTip (ScreenTip): Lists the name of a command and, sometimes, includes a brief description of the command. A ToolTip displays when the mouse hovers over, or points to, a command.

View buttons: Provides options for viewing the presentation. The View buttons are located on the right side of the status bar.

Zoom controls: Allow the user to zoom in and out of specific areas in the presentation. This feature controls the magnification of the presentation. The Zoom controls are displayed on the right side of the status bar.

Normal view: A view that allows the user to enter text and graphics directly on the slide. Normal view has four working areas: Slide pane, Notes pane, Slides tab, and Outline tab.

Slide pane: An area in Normal view where the presentation is created and edited. The Slide pane displays one slide at a time.

Notes pane: An area in Normal view used to add speaker notes for each slide. The Notes pane is located under the Slide pane.

Slides tab: A tab in Normal view that displays a thumbnail (miniature picture) of the slides.

Outline tab: A tab in Normal view that displays the text on each slide in an outline format. Graphics and multimedia elements are not displayed in the Outline tab.

Thumbnail: A miniature picture.

Title Slide: A slide that contains the title and subtitle for the presentation and is by default the first slide of a new presentation.

Slide layout (layout): Contains a variety of formatting, positioning, and placeholder options for the content that displays on a slide.

A Microsoft PowerPoint 2010 presentation consists of one or more slides. A slide can contain text, pictures, graphics, animations, and other multimedia elements. When Microsoft PowerPoint 2010 is launched, Normal view displays by default (**Figure 4.2**). Normal view allows you to enter text and graphics directly on the slide. Normal view has four working areas, the Slide pane, Notes pane, Slides tab, and Outline tab (Figure 4.2). The status bar displays the current slide number, the number of slides in the presentation, and the theme used in the presentation.

The Slide pane is an area in Normal view where the presentation is created and edited (Figure 4.2). The Slide pane displays one slide at a time.

The Notes pane is an area in Normal view used to add speaker notes for each slide (Figure 4.2). This is like your "script." The audience cannot view the information in the Notes pane. You can print the notes and use them as you present the information to the audience. The Notes pane is located under the Slide pane.

The Slides tab displays a thumbnail (miniature picture) of the slides. The Slides tab can be used to rearrange the order of the slides, to select slides, or to delete slides.

The Outline tab displays the text on each slide in an outline format (Figure 4.2). Graphics and multimedia elements are not displayed in the Outline tab.

A slide layout, or layout, contains a variety of formatting, positioning, and placeholder options for the content that displays on a slide. A Title Slide is one of the layouts you can select. The Title Slide, by default, is the first slide of a new presentation (Figure 4.2). A Title Slide contains the title and subtitle for the presentation. The subtitle usually contains the presenter's name and title. A layout can easily be changed by clicking the **Layout** button in the Slides group on the Home tab. There are nine layouts available in Microsoft PowerPoint 2010.

When Microsoft PowerPoint 2010 is launched, the Home tab is automatically active. The Home tab contains commands to insert new slides, select a slide layout, as well as commands to format the text and paragraphs on the slide.

Figure 4.2 The Slide in Normal View

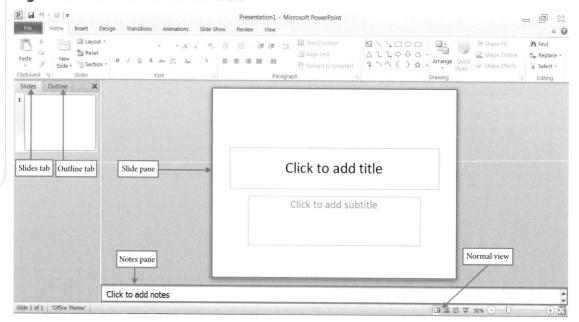

Insert and Format Text

A **placeholder** is a box with a dotted border that allows you to insert text or objects such as charts, tables, and pictures (**Figure 4.3**).

Use these steps to add text to a placeholder:

- Click the placeholder.
- Type the text.

Placeholder: A box with a dotted border that allows you to insert text or objects such as charts, tables, and pictures.

Figure 4.3 Placeholders

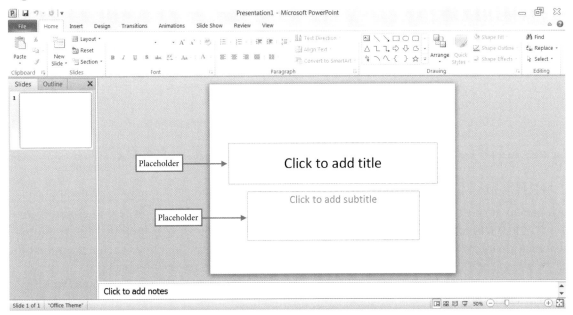

Hands-On Exercise: Insert and Format Text in Placeholders

1. Click the top placeholder, which states *Click to add title*.
2. Type **All About Me** (do not press the Enter key).
3. Select the text *All About Me* (triple-click anywhere in the text and the entire text is selected).
4. Click the Bold button in the Font group on the Home tab to bold the text (**Figure 4.4**).
5. Click the bottom placeholder that states *Click to add subtitle*.
6. Type **Presented By: Your Name** (type your first and last name—for example, John Student).
7. Triple-click anywhere in the text to select it.
8. Click the Italic button in the Font group on the Home tab to italicize the text (Figure 4.4). The slide should resemble Figure 4.4. Notice that a slide thumbnail displays in the Slides tab.

Figure 4.4 First Slide

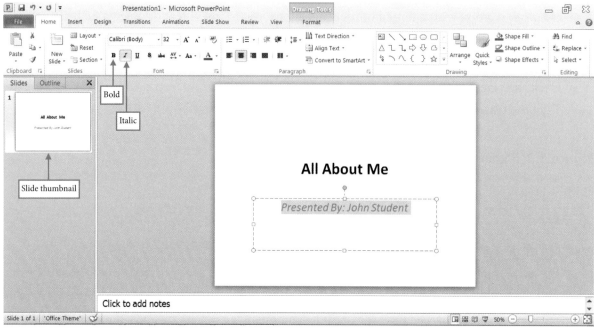

Design Theme

Theme: A design that contains a set of predefined colors, fonts, and backgrounds that are applied to slides to create professional-looking presentations.

All presentations contain a theme. A **theme** is a design that contains a set of predefined colors, fonts, and backgrounds that are applied to slides to create professional-looking presentations. Themes are located in the Design tab on the Ribbon. By default, the Office theme is applied to all new presentations. The Office theme is a plain theme that uses a white background, black font color, and the Calibri font. The theme name is displayed on the left side of the status bar (**Figure 4.5**). When a theme is selected, it is applied to all slides in the presentation.

Use these steps to apply a theme:

- Click the **Design** tab (Figure 4.5).
- Some themes display in the Themes group, but not all of them do. Click the **More** button in the Themes group (Figure 4.5) and a gallery of themes displays.
- Point to a theme in the gallery and a preview of the theme displays on the slide. The name of the theme displays as a ToolTip when you point to a theme.
- Click a theme to apply it to the entire presentation.

Hands-On Exercise: Apply a Theme

1. Click the Design tab (Figure 4.5).

2. Click the More button in the Themes group (Figure 4.5) and a gallery of themes displays.

3. When you point to each theme in the gallery, a ToolTip displays with the name of the theme. Locate the *Austin* theme (**Figure 4.6**).

4. Click the Austin theme. The theme is applied to the slide and the name of the theme displays on the status bar (**Figure 4.7**).

Figure 4.5 Themes Group on Design Tab

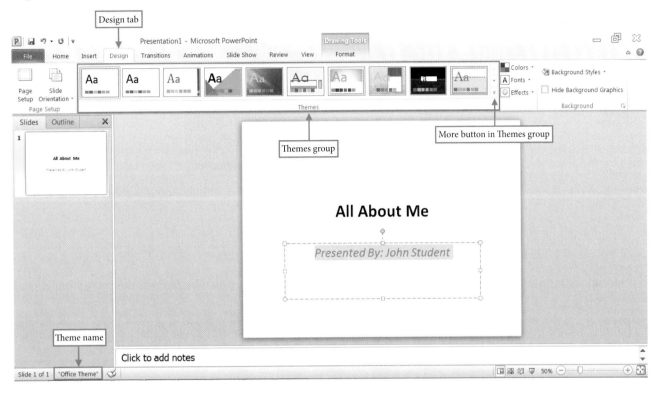

Figure 4.6 Austin Theme

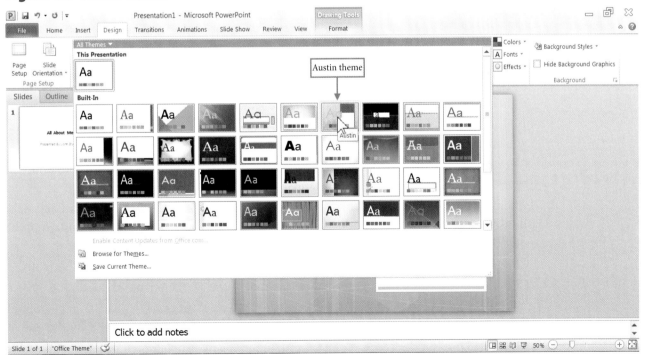

Figure 4.7 Austin Theme Applied to Presentation

Insert Clip Art

> **Clip art:** A multi-media item such as an illustration, photograph, video, or audio clip that can be inserted into a presentation.

Clip art is a multimedia item such as an illustration, photograph, video, or audio clip that can be inserted into a presentation. Microsoft PowerPoint 2010 has many built-in clip art images from which to choose.

Use the following steps to insert clip art on a slide:

- Click the **Insert** tab (**Figure 4.8**).
- Click the **Clip Art** button in the Images group and the Clip Art task pane opens on the right side of the application window (Figure 4.8).
- Type a word or phrase in the Search for box that describes the clip art image for which you are searching (Figure 4.8).
- Click the **Results should be** box (Figure 4.8) to select the media types. The media types include illustrations, photographs, videos, and audio.
- Click the **check box** next to the media types for which you are searching, *or* click **All media types** to select all options. Press **Esc** or click the **Results should be** box to exit the list.
- Click the check box to search for clip art images that are available online at Office.com.
- Click **Go** and a listing of clip art images that match the search term displays at the bottom of the Clip Art task pane.
- Click the clip art image to insert it in the middle of the slide.
- Click the **Close** button on the Clip Art task pane to close the pane.

Hands-On Exercise: Insert Clip Art

1. Click the Insert tab (Figure 4.8).

2. Click the Clip Art button in the Images group, and the Clip Art task pane opens on the right side of the application window (Figure 4.8).

3. Type **home** in the Search for box (Figure 4.8).

4. Click the Results should be button (Figure 4.8).

5. Click All media types if it is not already selected (**Figure 4.9**).

6. Press Esc to exit the list.

7. Click the Include Office.com content check box if it is not already selected (Figure 4.8).

8. Click Go , and a listing of clip art images displays at the bottom of the Clip Art task pane.

9. Click the first clip art image, and it is inserted in the middle of the slide (**Figure 4.10**). If the clip art image is not available on your computer, select a different image.

10. Click the Close button on the Clip Art task pane to close the pane (Figure 4.10).

Figure 4.8 Clip Art Task Pane

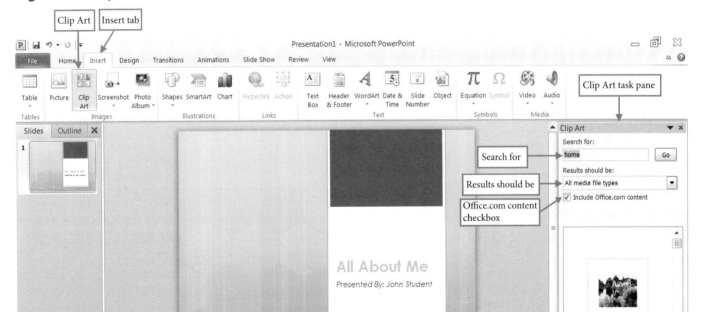

Figure 4.9 Select All Media Types

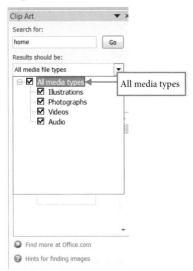

Figure 4.10 Clip Art Inserted

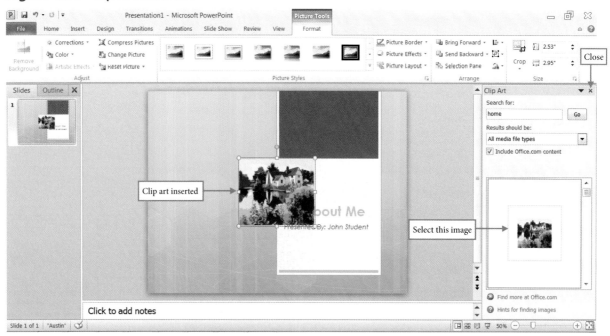

Move an Object

> **Object:** An item that can be inserted into a presentation such as a table, image (clip art, picture), illustration WordArt, text box, placeholder, and media elements.

An **object** is an item that can be inserted into a presentation such as a table, image (clip art, picture), illustration, WordArt, text box, placeholder, and media clips. You can move, delete, and change the size of an object on a slide.

To move an object:

- Click the object to select it.
- Hover over the object until a four-headed arrow displays.
- Drag the object to another location.

An object must be selected before it can be modified, resized, or deleted. Click the object to select it. When selected, a border displays around the object, with circles positioned on each corner and squares positioned on each side of the border that are used to resize the object.

Hands-On Exercise: Move a Clip Art Image

① Select the clip art if it is not already selected.

② Hover over the clip art until a four-headed arrow displays. Drag the clip art into the brown box at the top right of the slide. The slide should resemble **Figure 4.11**.

Figure 4.11 Clip Art Image Moved

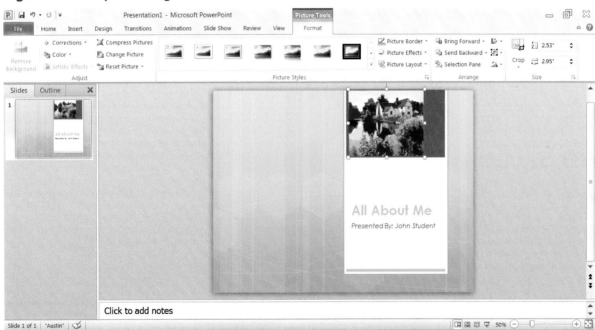

Modify the Size of an Object

When an object is inserted in a presentation, it might need to be resized. To change the size of an object, select the object by clicking it. When a picture or clip art image is selected, the Picture Tools contextual tab displays, which contains the Format tab. The Format tab contains commands to format the object.

When the object is selected, it has a border around it that contains sizing handles in the corners for adjusting the size, handles in the middle to adjust the width, and a green rotation handle at the top to rotate it.

To change the size of the object using the sizing handles:

- Click the object if it is not selected.
- Hold the mouse over a sizing handle until a two-headed arrow displays. Use the corner sizing handles to keep the object in proportion as you change the size.
- Drag the arrow to change the size of the object.

To change the size of an object using the commands on the Ribbon:

- Click the object if it is not selected.
- Click the **Format** tab in the Picture Tools tab (**Figure 4.12**).
- Type the height of the object in the **Shape Height** box in the Size group (Figure 4.12).
- Type the width of the object in the **Shape Width** box in the Size group (Figure 4.12).

Hands-On Exercise: Modify the Size of the Clip Art

① Select the clip art if it is not selected.

② Point to the square in the middle of the right border of the selected clip art, and a two-headed arrow displays. Drag it to the right to make the clip art wider.

③ The clip art should resemble Figure 4.12.

Figure 4.12 Clip Art Image Resized

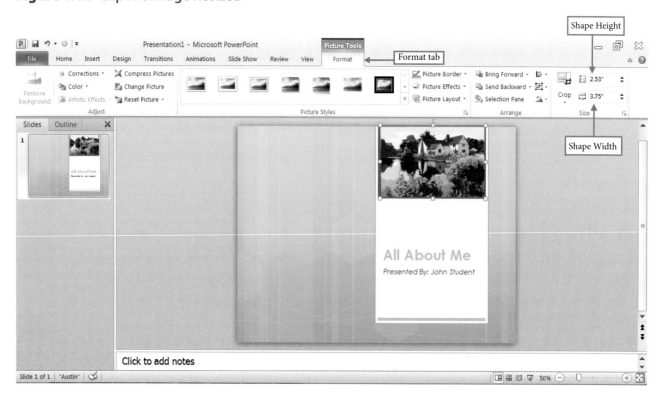

Save Presentation

Microsoft PowerPoint 2010 presentations contain a file-name extension *pptx*. When you save a Microsoft PowerPoint 2010 presentation, the file name displays in the title bar. By default, the filename extension displays in the title bar.

Use any of these methods to save a presentation:

- Click the **Save** button on the Quick Access Toolbar.
- Click the **File** tab and then click **Save** or **Save As**.
- Press **Ctrl + S**.

Hands-On Exercise: Save a Presentation

You have completed the first slide of the presentation. You will now save the presentation.

1. Click the File tab.

2. Click Save .

3. Select the location where you want to store the presentation.

4. Type **All About Me** in the File name box (**Figure 4.13**).

5. Click Save . The file name displays on the title bar.

Figure 4.13 Save As Dialog Box

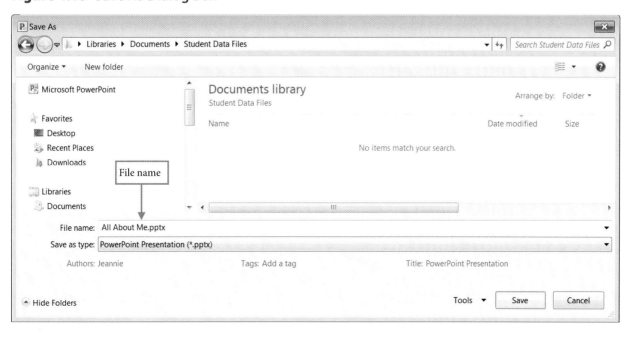

Insert New Slide

When you insert a new slide into the presentation after the title slide, the layout of the slide defaults to the Title and Content layout. A **Title and Content layout** allows you to enter a title for the slide and insert content such as text, bulleted list, table, chart, SmartArt graphic, picture, clip art, or media clip.

> **Title and Content layout:** A layout that allows the user to enter a title for the slide and insert content such as text or a table, chart, SmartArt graphic, picture, clip art, or media clip.

Use any of these methods to insert a new slide with the default layout:

- Click the **New Slide** button in the Slides group on the Home tab (**Figure 4.14**).
- Right-click the current slide in the Slides tab. A shortcut menu displays with options.
- Click **New Slide.**
- Press **Ctrl + M.**

Use these steps to insert a new slide with a different layout:

- Click the **New Slide arrow** in the Slides group on the Home tab and a gallery of slide layouts displays (**Figure 4.15**).
- Click the layout to insert (Figure 4.15).

When a new slide is inserted and the Slide pane is active, you do not need to click a placeholder to start typing. You can start typing, and the text displays in the title placeholder on the slide.

Hands-On Exercise: Insert New Slide

1. Click the Home tab.

2. Click the New Slide button and a new slide displays (Figure 4.14).

3. Type **My Favorite Activities** and it is inserted in the first placeholder. You do not need to click in the placeholder.

4. Click the second placeholder labeled Click to add text .

5. Type **Hockey** and press Enter. Another bullet displays.

6. Type **Tennis** and press Enter .

7. Type **Reading** and press Enter .

8. Type **Traveling** (do not press Enter). The slide should resemble Figure 4.14. If you accidentally press Enter and another bullet displays, the bullet can be removed by pressing the Backspace key or clicking the Bullets button in the Paragraph group on the Home tab.

Figure 4.14 New Slide Button

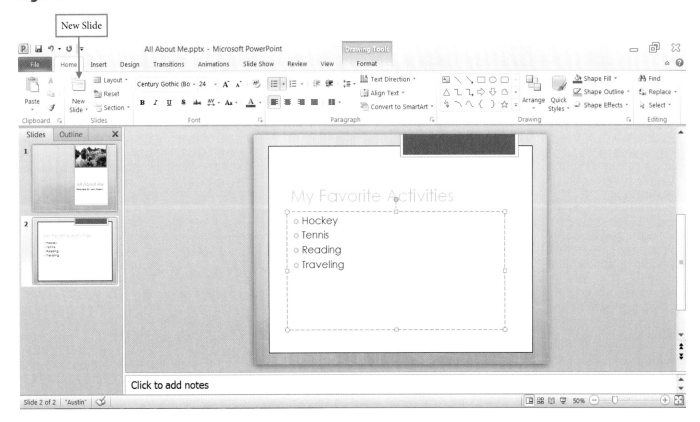

Figure 4.15 Gallery of Slide Layouts

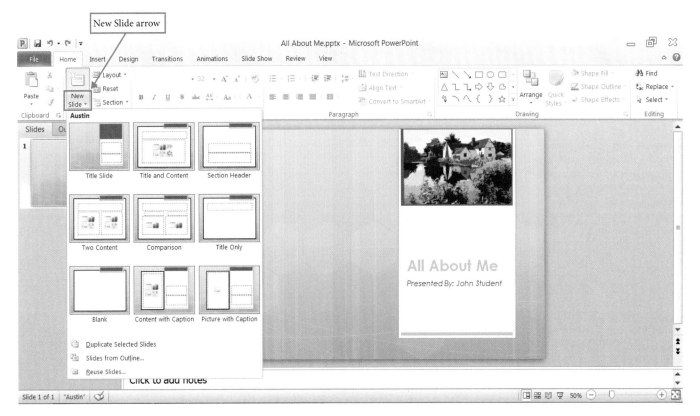

Edit and Delete Text

You can edit and delete text on a slide. First you should select the text you want to edit or delete. You can select text by dragging the mouse over the text. You can also double-click a word to select the word or triple-click in a paragraph to select the entire paragraph.

Use these steps to edit text:

- Select the text to edit.
- Type the new text.

Use these steps to delete text:

- Select the text to delete.
- Press the **Delete** or **Backspace** key.

Hands-On Exercise: Edit and Delete Text

(1) Select the text labeled *Hockey* by double-clicking the word.

(2) Type **Sports**.

(3) Select the text labeled *Tennis* by double-clicking the word.

(4) Press the Delete key to remove the text.

(5) Press the Delete key again to remove the bullet.

(6) Navigate to the end of the bulleted list after the word *Traveling*.

(7) Press Enter and another bullet displays.

(8) Type **Exercising** (do not press Enter). The slide should resemble **Figure 4.16**.

Figure 4.16 Edit and Delete Text on Second Slide

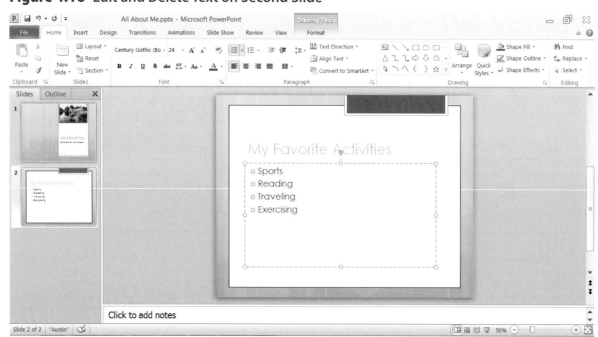

Hands-On Exercise: Insert Clip Art

You will add a clip art image of a volleyball to the slide.

① Click the Insert tab.

② Click the Clip Art button and the Clip Art task pane opens on the right side of the application window.

③ Type **volleyball** in the Search for box.

④ Click Go .

⑤ Click the clip art shown in **Figure 4.17**. If the clip art image is not available on your computer, select a different image. The clip art image is inserted in the middle of the slide.

⑥ Click the Close button on the Clip Art task pane.

⑦ Drag the clip art to the bottom-right corner of the slide so it resembles Figure 4.17.

Figure 4.17 Clip Art Inserted

Change Slide Layout

When a new slide is added to a presentation, it has the same layout as the previous slide. The only exception is when a new slide is inserted after the first slide that contains the Title Slide layout. In that case, the layout defaults to the Title and Content layout.

Use any of these methods to apply a layout:

- Click the **Layout** button in the Slides group on the Home tab. A gallery of layouts displays. Click the layout to apply it to the slide.
- Right-click the slide (do not right-click in a placeholder). Point to the **Layout** command on the shortcut menu, and a gallery of layouts displays. Click the layout to apply it to the slide.
- Right-click the slide thumbnail in the Slides tab. Point to the **Layout** command on the shortcut menu, and a gallery of layouts displays. Click the layout to apply it to the slide.

Use these steps to add a new slide with a different layout:

- Click the **New Slide arrow** in the Slides group on the Home tab.
- Select the layout from the gallery.

Hands-On Exercise: Insert a New Slide and Change Slide Layout

1. Click the Home tab.
2. Click the New Slide button and a new slide displays as a Title and Content layout.
3. Click the Layout button in the Slides group and a gallery of layouts displays (**Figure 4.18**).
4. Click the Two Content layout (Figure 4.18). The slide should resemble **Figure 4.19**.

Figure 4.18 Layout Button

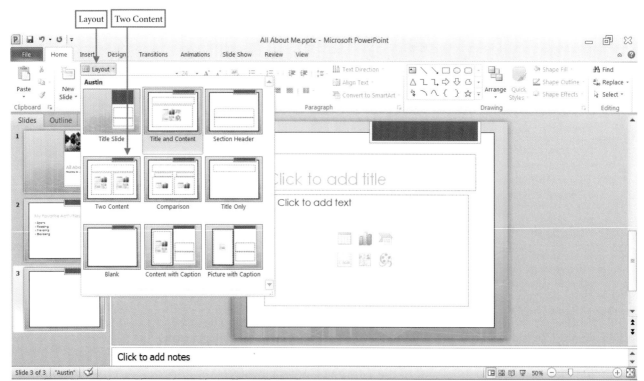

Figure 4.19 Two Content Layout

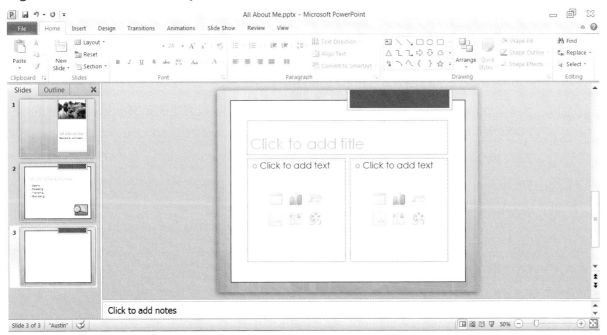

Increase and Decrease the List Level

Two types of lists can be inserted in a slide: a bulleted list and a numbered list. A list can be indented to the left or right. The Increase List Level button increases the indent level of a list (**Figure 4.20**). The Decrease List Level button decreases the indent level of a list (Figure 4.20). These commands are available in the Paragraph group on the Home tab. Depending on the layout and bullets used in the list, the bullets may change shape or size when you increase and decrease list levels. The Tab key can also be used to increase the indent level of bulleted and numbered lists. Be certain to position the insertion point at the beginning of the bulleted or numbered list you want to indent before pressing the Tab key.

> **Increase List Level button:** A button that increases the indent level of a paragraph.
>
> **Decrease List Level button:** A button that decreases the indent level of a paragraph.

Use these steps to increase and decrease list levels:

- Position the insertion point in the paragraph of the list you want to indent.
- Click the **Increase List Level** or **Decrease List Level** button on the Paragraph group on the Home tab.

Hands-On Exercise: Increase and Decrease List Levels

1. Click the top placeholder labeled Click to add title to enter the title of the slide.
2. Type **My Goals** (do not press Enter).
3. Click the Click to add text placeholder on the left-hand side of the slide.
4. Type **Educational Goals** and press Enter .
5. Click the Increase List Level button in the Paragraph group on the Home tab (Figure 4.20) and the bullet indents to the right.

⑥ Type **Obtain college degree** and press Enter .

⑦ Click the Increase List Level button.

⑧ Type **Major: Accounting** and press Enter .

⑨ Type **Minor: Finance** (do not press Enter).

⑩ Next, you will add the information in the placeholders on the right side of the slide. Click the Click to add text placeholder on the right-hand side of the slide.

⑪ Type **Personal Goals** and press Enter .

⑫ Click the Increase List Level button.

⑬ Type **Healthy lifestyle** and press Enter .

⑭ Click the Increase List Level button.

⑮ Type **Exercise** and press Enter .

⑯ Type **Diet** and press Enter .

⑰ Click the Decrease List Level button to decrease the indent (Figure 4.20).

⑱ Type **Save money** (do not press Enter).

⑲ Click the Save button in the Quick Access Toolbar (Figure 4.20). The completed slide should resemble Figure 4.20.

Figure 4.20 Completed Third Slide

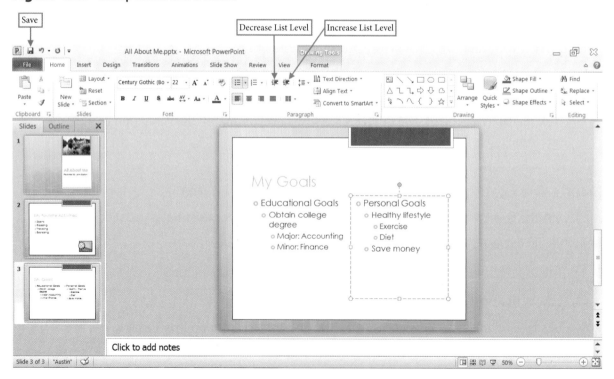

Insert Table

A **table** displays information that is organized by rows and columns. The intersection of a row and column is called a **cell**. Once the table is created, you can insert text into the table and format the table. Additionally, you can add or delete rows and columns to the table.

Use either of these methods to insert a table in a slide:

- Click the **Insert Table** icon in the middle of the slide (**Figure 4.21**).
- Click the **Insert** tab on the Ribbon and then click the **Table** button in the Tables group.

The Insert Table dialog box displays. You will specify the number of columns and rows needed in the table.

> **Table:** Displays information that is organized by rows and columns.
>
> **Cell:** The intersection of a row and column in a table.

Hands-On Exercise: Insert a Table

1. Click the New Slide arrow .
2. Click Title and Content.
3. Type **Professional Skills** and it displays in the top placeholder.
4. Click the Insert Table icon in the middle of the slide (Figure 4.21). The Insert Table dialog box displays.
5. Type **2** in the Number of columns box (**Figure 4.22**).
6. Type **4** in the Number of rows box (Figure 4.22).
7. Click **OK**. The table is created and displays on the slide. The slide should resemble **Figure 4.23**.

Figure 4.21 Insert Table Icon

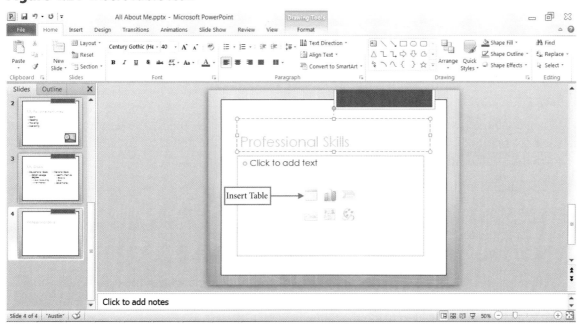

Figure 4.22 Insert Table Dialog Box

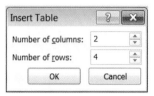

Figure 4.23 Table Created

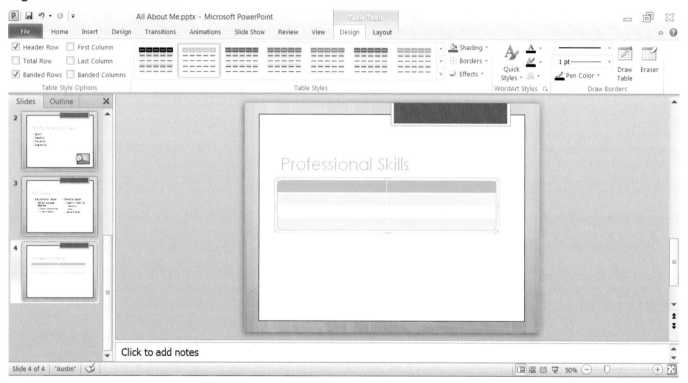

Insert Text in Table

When a table is inserted, it is automatically formatted based on the theme that was selected for the presentation. Titles or headings are usually inserted in the first row. The first row is usually formatted differently from the rest of the rows in the table.

Use these steps to insert text in a table:

- Position the insertion point in the cell you want to insert text.
- Type the text.
- Press **Tab** or the **right arrow** key to advance to the next cell.

If you press the Enter key in a cell it inserts an additional line within the cell. When you are on the last cell in the table, do not press Tab because that inserts a new row in the table. To exit the table, simply click outside the table.

Hands-On Exercise: Insert Text in Table

① The insertion point is located in the first cell in the table. Type **Skill** and press the Tab key.

② Type **Level** and press Tab. The insertion point navigates to the next row in the table.

③ Type **Presentation Skills** and press Tab.

④ Type **Beginner** and press Tab.

⑤ Type **Word Processing Skills** and press Tab.

⑥ Type **Intermediate** and press Tab.

⑦ Type **Database Skills** and press Tab.

⑧ Type **Beginner** (do not press Tab).

⑨ The slide should resemble **Figure 4.24**.

Figure 4.24 Text Inserted in Table

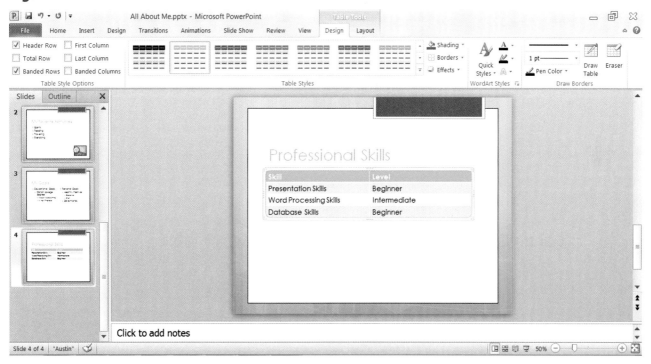

Modify Table Layout

You can insert or delete rows or columns in a table. Additionally, you can sort the table in ascending or descending order. When the insertion point is located in a table, the Table Tools contextual tab displays on the Ribbon and contains the Design and Layout tabs. **Table 4.2** contains commands that are used to modify the layout of a table. You can also apply many of these commands by right-clicking in the row or column in the table and selecting the command from the shortcut menu.

Table 4.2 Table Commands	
Task	**Steps**
To insert a row	• Click in the row where you want to insert the new row. • Click the **Layout** tab in the Table Tools tab. • Click **Insert Above** in the Rows & Columns group to insert a row above the row that is currently selected, *or* click **Insert Below** to insert a row below the row that is currently selected.
To insert a column	• Click in the column where you want to insert a new column. • Click the **Layout tab** in the Table Tools tab. • Click **Insert Left** in the Rows & Columns group to insert a column to the left of the column that is currently selected. Click **Insert Right** to insert a column to the right of the column that is currently selected.
To delete a row	• Click in the row you want to delete. • Click the **Layout** tab in the Table Tools tab. • Click the **Delete** button in the Rows & Columns group. • Click **Delete Rows**.
To delete a column	• Click in the column you want to delete. • Click the **Layout** tab in the Table Tools tab. • Click the **Delete** button in the Rows & Columns group. • Click **Delete Columns**.
To delete table	• Click anywhere in the table. • Click the **Layout** tab in the Table Tools tab. • Click the **Delete** button in the Rows & Columns group. • Click **Delete Table.**

Hands-On Exercise: Insert and Delete Rows in Table

① Click in the second row, which contains the text *Presentation Skills*.

② Click the Layout tab in the Table Tools tab (**Figure 4.25**).

③ Click Insert Below to insert a row below row 2 (Figure 4.25).

④ Click in the first cell of the new row.

⑤ Type **Spreadsheet Skills** and press Tab .

⑥ Type **Advanced**.

⑦ Click in the last row in the table, which contains the text *Database Skills*.

⑧ Click the Delete button in the Rows & Columns group.

⑨ Click Delete Rows , and the row is deleted.

⑩ Press Ctrl + Z to undo the deletion. The slide should resemble Figure 4.25.

Figure 4.25 Insert and Delete Rows in Table

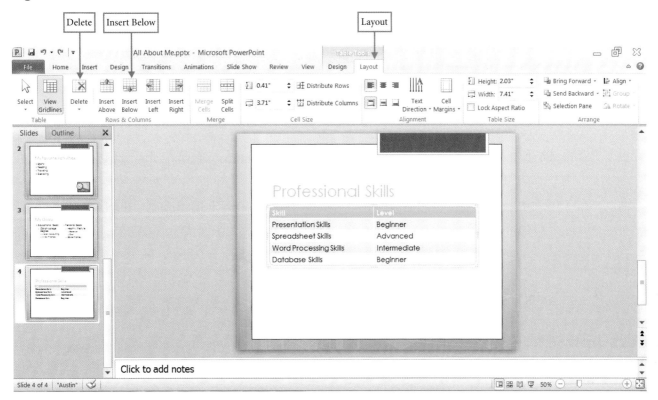

Insert WordArt

WordArt is decorative text, such as shadowed or mirrored text, that can be inserted into a presentation. Microsoft PowerPoint 2010 contains a gallery of WordArt styles from which to choose. You can insert WordArt or apply WordArt to existing text on a slide. **Table 4.3** illustrates various WordArt commands.

> **WordArt:** Decorative text, such as shadowed or mirrored text, that can be inserted into a presentation.

Table 4.3 WordArt Commands	
Task	**Steps**
To insert WordArt	• Click the **Insert** tab. • Click **WordArt** in the Text group and a gallery displays. • Select a WordArt style from the gallery.
To apply WordArt to existing text	• Select the text in which you want to apply WordArt. The Drawing Tools contextual tab displays on the Ribbon (**Figure 4.26**). • Click the **Format** tab (Figure 4.26). • Click the **More** button in the WordArt Styles group and a gallery displays (Figure 4.26). • Select a WordArt style from the gallery.

Hands-On Exercise: Insert WordArt

1. Triple-click the title Professional Skills to select the text. The Drawing Tools contextual tab displays on the Ribbon (Figure 4.26).

2. Click the Format tab (Figure 4.26).

3. Click the More button in the WordArt Styles group (Figure 4.26) and a gallery displays.

4. Click the Fill-Green, Accent 1, Metal Bevel, Reflection , which is the last style in the gallery (Figure 4.27).

5. Click anywhere on the slide to deselect the text. The slide should resemble Figure 4.28.

6. Click the Save button on the Quick Access Toolbar.

Figure 4.26 Drawing Tools Contextual Tab

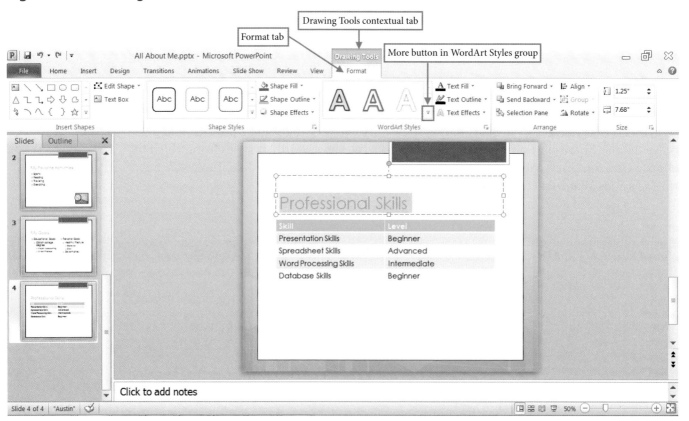

Figure 4.27 WordArt Gallery

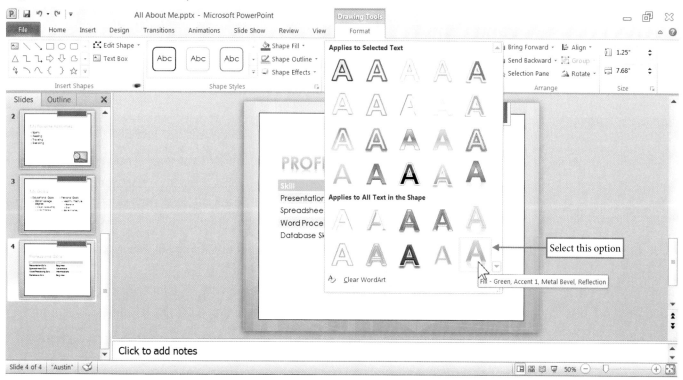

Figure 4.28 WordArt Applied to Text

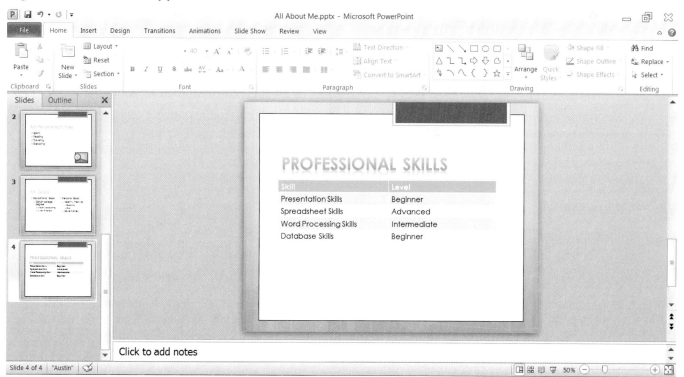

Use Keyboard Shortcuts

So far you have been using the mouse to navigate and select placeholders and to insert new slides. **Table 4.4** illustrates various keyboard shortcuts that can be used Microsoft PowerPoint 2010.

Table 4.4 Keyboard Shortcuts

Key	Description
Ctrl + Enter	These keys navigate to the next placeholder on a slide. If the insertion point is located on the last placeholder on the slide, pressing **Ctrl + Enter** creates a new slide.
Ctrl + M	These keys insert a new slide after the current slide.
Enter	Pressing the **Enter** key in a placeholder inserts a new paragraph on the next line in a placeholder. If positioned in a bulleted list, pressing **Enter** causes a new bullet to display on a new line.
Shift + Enter	These keys insert a new line in a placeholder.
Esc	Click in a placeholder and press the **Esc** key. The border of the placeholder becomes a solid line, indicating that the entire placeholder is selected. You can move, delete, or format the text in the placeholder once it is selected. Pressing the Delete key deletes the text in the placeholder. If the placeholder does not contain any text, pressing the Delete key deletes the placeholder.

Selection Techniques

You may need to select text or slides in order to perform certain tasks. **Table 4.5** displays various selection techniques that can be used.

Table 4.5 Selection Techniques

Task	Steps
Select a word	Double-click the **word**.
Select a paragraph	Triple-click in the **paragraph**.
Select entire text in placeholder	Click the **placeholder** and then press **Ctrl + A**.
Select placeholder	Click the **placeholder** and then click the **border** of the placeholder.
Select all objects on slide	Click in an open area of the slide that does not contain an object, and then press **Ctrl + A**.
Select all slides in presentation	Click a **thumbnail** in the Slides tab and a gold background displays around the thumbnail indicating that the slide is selected. Press **Ctrl + A** to select all slides in the presentation.

Hands-On Exercise: Select Text and Slides

1. Double-click the word Spreadsheet in the table. The word is selected.

2. Press Ctrl + A and the entire text in the table is selected.

3. Click the thumbnail for Slide 3 in the Slides tab and a gold background displays around the thumbnail indicating that the slide is selected.

4. Press Ctrl + A to select all the slides in the presentation. A gold background displays around the thumbnails for all slides indicating that they are all selected.

5. Click the thumbnail for Slide 4 in the Slides tab.

6. Triple-click the paragraph Professional Skills in the Slide pane and the entire paragraph is selected.

Format Text

You can format text using the font commands, which are located in the Font group on the Home tab. If a command in the Font group contains an arrow, that indicates there are other options from which to choose. **Table 4.6** illustrates the various font commands.

Make certain to select the text before applying the command, *or* you can select the placeholder and apply the command to the entire placeholder.

In addition to using the commands in the Font group to format text, you can click the Font dialog box launcher (Figure 4.29) to open the Font dialog box. You can apply many font commands at once using the Font dialog box.

Table 4.6 Font Commands

Command	Button	Description
Font	Century Gothic (He ▾	Changes the font face. The name of the font displays in the Font box. The default font for new presentations is Calibri. If you change the theme of a presentation, the font may change. *Century Gothic* currently displays in the Font box which is the font used in the Austin theme. To change the font, click the **Font arrow** and select a font from the list.
Font Size	40 ▾	Changes the font size. The font size displays in the Font Size box. To change the font size, click the **Font Size arrow** and select a font size from the list, *or* type the font size in the Font Size box and press **Enter**.
Increase Font Size	A˙	Increases the font size.
Decrease Font Size	A˙	Decreases the font size.
Clear All Formatting		Clears all formatting from the text.

Table 4.6 *continued*

Bold	B	Makes the text bold.
Italic	I	Makes the text italic.
Underline	U	Underlines the text.
Text Shadow	S	Adds a shadow behind the text.
Strikethrough	abc	Inserts a line through the middle of the text.
Character Spacing	AV	Adjusts the spacing between characters.
Change Case	Aa	Changes the case of the text.
Font Color	A	Changes the text color.

Hands-On Exercise: Format Text

1. Press Ctrl + M to insert a new slide.
2. Type **My Family**.
3. Press Ctrl + Enter to navigate to the next placeholder.
4. Type **Parents born in London, England** and press Enter .
5. Type **Two siblings named Tom and Mary** and press Enter .
6. Type **Engaged to Samantha** and press Enter .
7. Type **Dog named Sparky** (do not press Enter).
8. Triple-click the title of the slide labeled *My Family*.
9. Click the Font Size arrow (**Figure 4.29**).
10. Click 48 .
11. Click the Bold button to bold the selected text (Figure 4.29).
12. Double-click the word Samantha in the third bulleted list.
13. Click the Underline button (Figure 4.29).
14. Double-click the word Sparky in the last bulleted list.
15. Click the Font Color arrow (Figure 4.29).
16. Click the Light Green option in the Standard Colors group.
17. Click the Bold button.
18. Click Esc and the entire placeholder is selected (solid border around placeholder).
19. Click the Increase Font Size button to increase the font size of all the text in the place-holder (Figure 4.29). The font size becomes 28. The slide should resemble Figure 4.29.

Figure 4.29 Font Commands Applied to a Slide

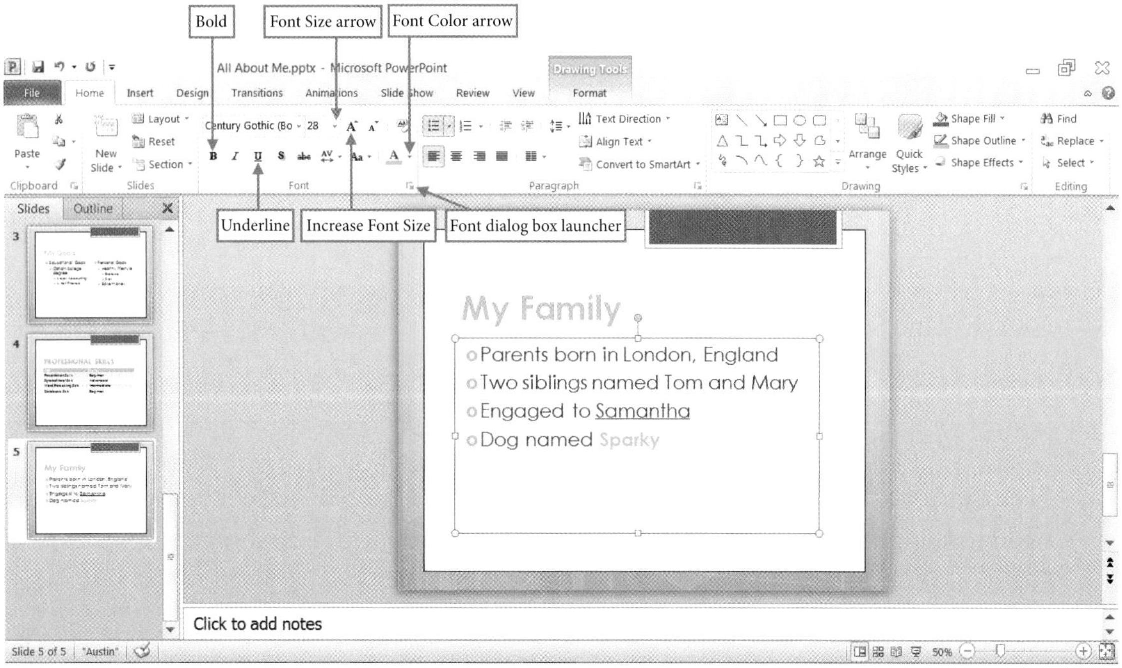

Format a Paragraph

You can insert bullets and numbers, align text, and change the line spacing of a paragraph. The commands to format a paragraph are located in the Paragraph group on the Home tab. If a command in the Paragraph group contains an arrow, that indicates there are additional options from which to choose. **Table 4.7** illustrates various commands to format a paragraph.

Table 4.7 Commands to Format a Paragraph

Command	Icon	Description
Bullets	☰ ▾	Inserts a bulleted list.
Numbering	☷ ▾	Inserts a numbered list.
Line Spacing	↕☰ ▾	Selects the line spacing.
Align Text Left	☰	Aligns text to the left.
Center	☰	Centers text.
Align Text Right	☰	Aligns text to the right.
Justify	☰	Aligns text to both the left and right margins.
Text Direction	⏐⏐ᴬ Text Direction ▾	Changes the orientation of the text.
Align Text	⊟ Align Text ▾	Changes the alignment of text

Hands-On Exercise: Format a Paragraph

1. Click in the bulleted list.

2. Press Esc to select the entire placeholder.

3. Click the Bullets arrow and a gallery of bullets displays (**Figure 4.30**).

4. Click the Arrow Bullets , which is the first bullet option in the third row (Figure 4.30). The bullet shapes change.

5. Click the Line Spacing button (**Figure 4.31**).

6. Click 2.0 .

7. Click in the top placeholder labeled *My Family*.

8. Click the Center button to center the paragraph (Figure 4.31). Notice that you did not need to select the text before applying this command. The slide should resemble Figure 4.31.

Figure 4.30 Bullets Gallery

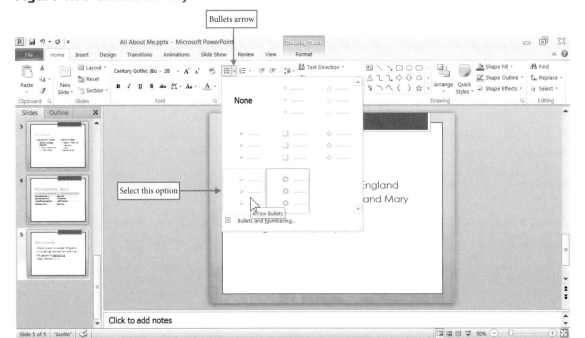

Figure 4.31 Paragraph Commands Applied to Slide

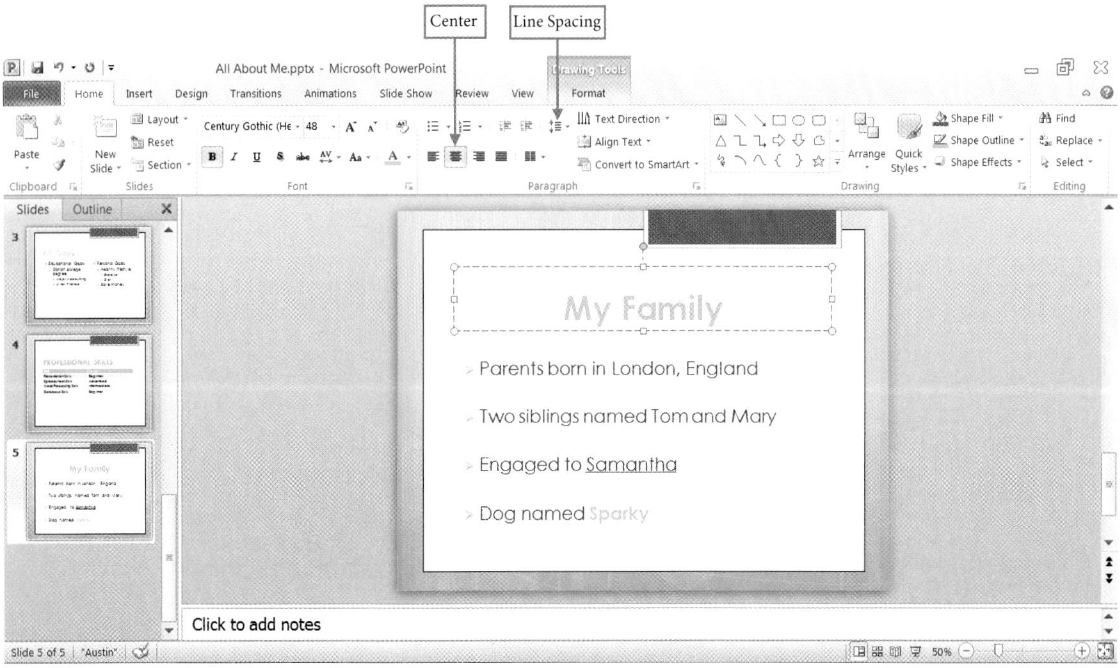

Navigate a Presentation

There are many ways to navigate to different slides in the presentation. Click in an area of the slide that does not contain an object before using any of the following navigation tips:

- Press **Home** *or* **Ctrl + Home** to navigate to the first slide in the presentation.
- Press **End** *or* **Ctrl + End** to navigate to the last slide in the presentation.
- Drag the scroll box to navigate throughout the slides (**Figure 4.32**). When you drag the scroll box, a ToolTip displays indicating the slide number.
- Click the **Previous Slide** button on the vertical scroll bar to navigate to the previous slide (Figure 4.32).
- Click the **Next Slide** button on the vertical scroll bar to navigate to the next slide (Figure 4.32).
- Click the **thumbnail** in the Slides tab to navigate to a specific slide.

You can also use the Page Up and Page Down keys to navigate through the slides. Remember to look at the status bar. It provides details about the presentation, such as the current slide number, the number of slides in the presentation, and the theme used in the presentation.

Hands-On Exercise: Navigate a Presentation

1. Click in an area of the slide that does not contain an object.
2. Press Ctrl + Home to navigate to the first slide.
3. Click the Next Slide button on the vertical scroll bar to navigate to Slide 2 (Figure 4.32).

④ Click the Previous Slide button on the vertical scroll bar to navigate to Slide 1 (Figure 4.32).

⑤ Drag the scroll box down to navigate to Slide 3 (Figure 4.32).

⑥ Click the Slide 4 thumbnail in the Slides tab to navigate to Slide 4 (Figure 4.32).

⑦ Click Save on the Quick Access Toolbar.

Figure 4.32 Navigating Slides

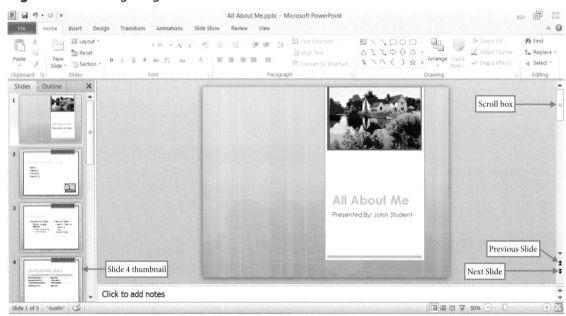

Delete a Slide

You can delete one or more slides in a presentation. You can also undo the deletion of a slide in case you accidently delete it.

Use any of these methods to delete a slide in Normal view:

- Click the **slide thumbnail** in the Slides tab and press **Delete**.
- Right-click the **slide thumbnail** in the Slides tab, and then click **Delete Slide** from the shortcut menu.

Hands-On Exercise: Delete a Slide

① Right-click the Slide 5 thumbnail in the Slides tab and the shortcut menu displays (**Figure 4.33**). A scroll bar displays to the right of the slide thumbnails on the Slides tab. You may need to scroll down to locate the Slide 5 thumbnail.

② Click Delete Slide from the shortcut menu (Figure 4.33).

③ Click the Undo button on the Quick Access Toolbar to undo the deletion (Figure 4.33).

Figure 4.33 Delete Slide Command

Check Spelling

Now that you have completed the presentation, you should check the document for spelling errors. The Spelling button is located on the Review tab in the Proofing group (**Figure 4.34**). If a wavy red line displays under text, it indicates a potential spelling error. If potential errors are found in the presentation, the Proofing Errors button on the status bar displays with a red X (Figure 4.34).

Use any of these methods to correct spelling errors:

- Right-click the misspelled word, and alternative spellings display. Select the correct spelling from the list. Some proper names may not be included in the dictionary and may display as a potential spelling error. In this case, click **Ignore All** to indicate that the word is spelled correctly, *or* click **Add to Dictionary** to store it in the dictionary.
- Click the **Proofing Errors** button on the status bar, and the Spelling dialog box displays. This feature checks the entire presentation at once for errors and displays the errors in the dialog box.
- Click the **Spelling** button in the Proofing group on the Review tab and the Spelling dialog box displays. This feature checks the entire document at once for errors and displays the errors in the dialog box.

Hands-On Exercise: Check Spelling

You will make a spelling error in the presentation. Then you will use the Spelling command to correct the spelling error.

(1) Select the word *Engaged* on Slide 5 by double-clicking on the word.

(2) Press Delete .

(3) Type **Engeged** and press the space bar.

(4) Click anywhere on the slide. Notice that a wavy red line appears beneath the word *Engeged* indicating that it is a potential spelling error. The Proofing Errors button displays with a red X.

(5) Click the Review tab on the Ribbon (Figure 4.34).

(6) Click the Spelling button in the Proofing group (Figure 4.34), and the Spelling dialog box displays (**Figure** 4.35).

(7) *Engeged* displays in the Not in Dictionary box indicating it is a potential spelling error. Click the correct spelling **Engaged** in the Suggestions list (Figure 4.35).

(8) Click Change to accept the suggestion.

(9) Correct any other spelling errors in the presentation.

(10) Click OK to exit the spelling dialog box when completed.

(11) Click the Save button in the Quick Access Toolbar.

Figure 4.34 Spelling Command

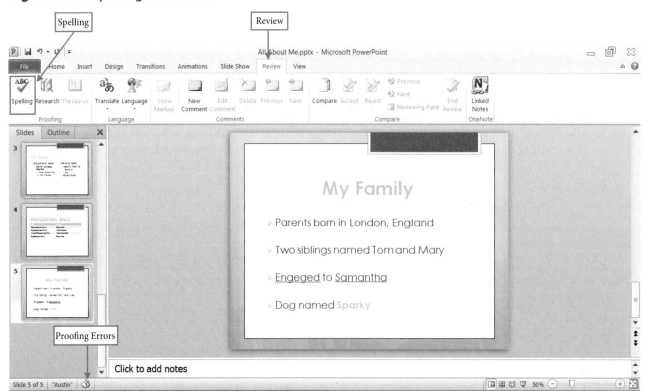

Figure 4.35 Spelling Dialog Box

| Spelling | ? | X |

Not in Dictionary: Engeged

Change to: Engaged   Ignore   Ignore All

Suggestions: Engaged

Change   Change All

Add   Suggest

Options...   AutoCorrect   Close

Run and Navigate a Slide Show

The presentation is completed, and it is time to run the slide show. The slide show displays the entire presentation to the audience one slide at a time.

> Slide show: A display of the entire presentation to the audience, one slide at a time.

Use any of these methods to run the slide show:

- Press **F5** to start the slide show from the beginning of the presentation.
- Click the **Slide Show** button on the status bar (**Figure 4.36**).
  - Before you run the slide show, make certain to select the first slide in the presentation; otherwise, the slide show presentation starts from the current slide.
- Click the **Slide Show** tab on the Ribbon (Figure 4.36).
  - Click **From Beginning** in the Start Slide Show group to start the slide show from the beginning of the presentation (Figure 4.36).
  - Click **From Current Slide** in the Start Slide Show group to start the slide show from the current slide (Figure 4.36).

Table 4.8 illustrates how to navigate during the slide show.

Table 4.8 Navigate Slide Show

Task	Steps
Navigate to next slide	Use any of these methods to navigate to the next slide: • Press **Enter**. • Press the **space bar**. • Press the letter **N**, which stands for next slide. • Press the **right arrow**. • Press the **down arrow**. • Press **Page Down**.
Navigate to previous slide	Use any of these methods to navigate to the previous slide: • Press the letter **P**, which stands for previous slide. • Press the **up arrow**. • Press the **left arrow**. • Press **Page Up**. • Press **Backspace**.

Table 4.8 *continued*

Exit the presentation	Press **Esc**.
Go to a specific slide	Type the slide number and press **Enter**.
Navigate presentation using the navigation buttons located at the lower-left corner of the slide	These buttons appear dimmed until you point on the buttons. Previous Slide button ⬅ —Navigates to the previous slide. Pointer Options button ✎ —Allows you to annotate (write or draw) on the slides during the presentation to emphasize information. You can: • Select the pen to annotate the slide. • Select the highlighter to annotate the slide. • Select an ink color. • Select the eraser to delete the annotations. Slide button ▤ —Allows you to select the slide in which to navigate. Next Slide button ⮕ —Navigates to the next slide.
Navigate presentation using the shortcut menu	Right-click in a slide and the shortcut menu displays with options to navigate and annotate the presentation.

Hands-On Exercise: Run and Navigate Slide Show

(1) Click Slide 1 in the Slides tab.

(2) Click the Slide Show button on the status bar (Figure 4.36).

(3) The slide show opens. The slide is maximized and takes up the entire screen. Press Enter and the next slide displays.

(4) Press the letter *P* on the keyboard to navigate to the previous slide.

(5) Click the Next Slide button on the lower-left corner of the slide (**Figure 4.37**).

(6) Right-click the slide and the shortcut menu displays.

(7) Point to the Go to Slide command.

(8) Click 4 Professional Skills to navigate to Slide 4.

(9) Next, you will select the highlighter so you can annotate the slide using blue ink. Click the Pointer Options button on the lower-left corner of the slide (**Figure 4.38**).

(10) Click Highlighter .

⑪ Click the Pointer Options button.

⑫ Point to Ink Color and click Blue from Standard Colors. The mouse pointer displays as a blue highlighter.

⑬ Hold down the mouse and drag it through the text *Spreadsheet Skills*.

⑭ Next you will erase the annotation. Right-click the slide.

⑮ Point to Pointer Options and click Erase All Ink on Slide .

⑯ Right-click the slide.

⑰ Point to Pointer Options and click Arrow to turn off the highlighter.

⑱ Press *N* to navigate to the next slide.

⑲ Press Enter and the presentation is completed. A message displays at the top of the screen stating that the slide show has ended. Press the Esc key to go back to Normal view.

⑳ Click Slide 1 in the Slides tab.

㉑ Click Save on the Quick Access Toolbar.

Figure 4.36 Slide Show

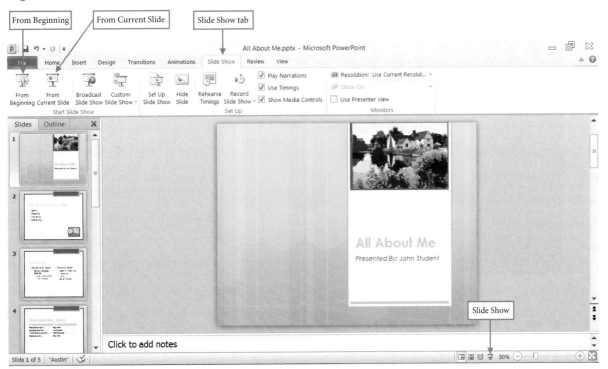

Figure 4.37 Next Slide Button in Slide Show

Figure 4.38 Pointer Options Button in Slide Show

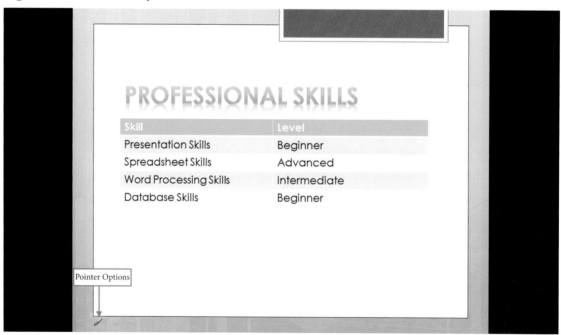

Print a Presentation

You can print a presentation using the Print command on the File tab or by pressing **Ctrl + P**.
Table 4.9 displays various print settings that you can apply to a presentation.

Table 4.9 Print Settings	
Task	**Steps**

Select slides to print	• Click the **File** tab.
	• Click **Print**.
	• Click **Print All Slides** in the Settings group and then select one of the following options:
	  ◦ **Print All Slides**.
	  ◦ **Print Selection**.
	  ◦ **Print Current Slide**.
	  ◦ **Custom Range**.
	    ▪ To print specific slides that are in a sequential range:
	      • Type the first slide number followed by a hyphen followed by the ending slide number in the Slides box. For example, to print slides 1 through 4 you would enter 1-4.
	    ▪ To print certain slides that are not in a sequential range:
	      • Type the slide numbers in the Slides box followed by a comma. For example, to print slides 1 and 4 you would enter 1,4.

Select print layout	• Click **Full Pages Slides**. • Select a layout from the Print Layout group, or select a handout type from the Handouts group. The choices in the Handouts group allows you to select the number of slides to print on a page along with how you want them to appear on the slide (horizontally or vertically).

To print the presentation:

- Click the **File** tab.
- Click **Print** and a preview of the presentation displays on the right side of the window (**Figure 4.39**).
- Adjust the print settings as needed.
- Click the **Print** button once the settings have been selected and the presentation is printed.

Hands-On Exercise: Print a Presentation

1. Click the File tab.

2. Click Print .

3. Click Print All Slides (Figure 4.39). You have the option to print all slides, print selection, print current slide, or custom range.

4. Click Print All Slides .

5. Click Full Page Slides (Figure 4.39), and a variety of choices display.

6. Select 3 Slides in the Handouts group. This option prints three slides on one page. The handouts contain lines that the audience members can use to write notes during the presentation.

7. Click the Print button and the presentation prints.

8. Click the Save button on the Quick Access Toolbar.

Figure 4.39 Print Options

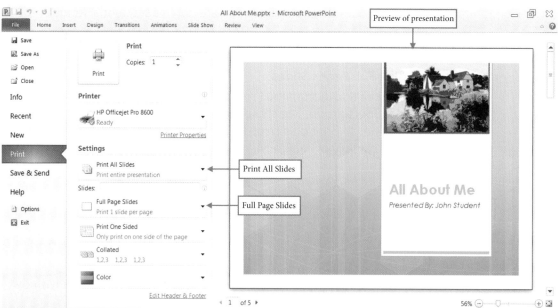

Help Button

You can use the Help feature if you need assistance with a task. The Help feature is accessed by clicking the Help button, which is located on the far-right corner of the Ribbon (**Figure 4.40**). It can also be accessed from the File tab *or* by pressing **F1** on the keyboard.

Hands-On Exercise: Use Help

① Click the Help button and the PowerPoint Help dialog box displays (Figure 4.40).

② Type **print presentation** in the Search box (Figure 4.40) and press Enter . Search results display in the PowerPoint Help dialog box.

③ Click a link to review the information on printing the presentation.

④ Click the Close button on the PowerPoint Help dialog box to close the window (Figure 4.40).

Figure 4.40 PowerPoint Help Dialog Box

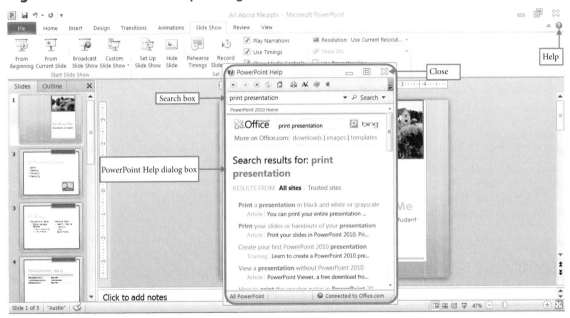

Close a Presentation

You should close a presentation when you are finished working with it. When you close a presentation, it will ask you to save the presentation it you have not done so already. This command does not close the application; it only closes the presentation.

To close a presentation:

- Click the **File** tab.
- Click **Close**. If the presentation has not been saved, it will prompt you to save the presentation.

If only one presentation is open in Microsoft PowerPoint 2010, you can close the presentation and exit the application at once by clicking the **Close** button on the title bar, pressing Alt+F4, or double-clicking the **Microsoft PowerPoint 2010 application icon** (**Figure 4.41**). The

Microsoft PowerPoint 2010 application icon is located at the upper-left corner of the window, to the left of the Quick Access Toolbar.

If multiple presentations are open, these commands will close the active presentation.

Figure 4.41 Close Commands

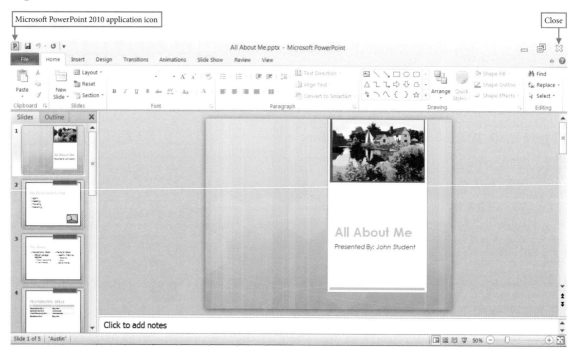

Hands-On Exercise: Close a Presentation

① Click the File tab.

② Click Close . The presentation closes but the application remains open.

Exit Application

Use the Exit command to exit (or quit) the application. The Exit command is located on the File tab.

Hands-On Exercise: Exit Application

① Click the File tab.

② Click Exit and the application closes.

Multiple-Choice Questions

1. A slide may contain _____.
   a. Text
   b. Clip Art
   c. Tables
   d. All of the above

2. Microsoft PowerPoint 2010 defaults to _____.
   a. PowerPoint View
   b. Notes View
   c. Normal View
   d. Slide Show View

3. By default, the first slide of the presentation is the _____.
   a. Title slide
   b. Header slide
   c. Notes view
   d. Bulleted slide

4. You create the slides in the _____.
   a. Notes pane
   b. Slide pane
   c. Slide show
   d. Design theme

5. Normal view has _____ working area(s).
   a. One
   b. Two
   c. Three
   d. Four

6. _____ is decorative text, such as shadowed or mirrored text, that can be inserted into a presentation.
   a. Clip Art
   b. Theme
   c. WordArt
   d. Layout

7. Themes are located in the _____ on the Ribbon.
   a. Home tab
   b. Design tab
   c. Insert tab
   d. Animations tab

8. The Slide Show button is located on the _____.

   a. Home tab

   b. Slide tab

   c. Slide pane

   d. Status bar

9. There are _____ layouts available in Microsoft PowerPoint 2010.

   a. Four

   b. Five

   c. Nine

   d. Ten

10. You can advance to the next slide during the Slide Show by using any of these methods except _____.

   a. Tab

   b. Enter

   c. *N*

   d. Page Down

Project #1: Create a Presentation of Employment Opportunities for an Organization

You will create a presentation that lists the employment opportunities available at JK Global Enterprises.

① Open Microsoft PowerPoint 2010.

② Type **Employment Opportunities** in the title placeholder**.**

③ In the second placeholder, type **JK Global Enterprises**.

④ Apply the **Opulent** theme to the presentation.

⑤ Insert a new Title and Content slide that resembles **Figure 4.42**. Make certain to increase and decrease list levels as indicated in the slide.

Figure 4.42 Second Slide

ACCOUNTANT
- Duties:
  - Prepare financial records
  - Prepare tax returns
- Education:
  - B.S. in Accounting
- Salary:
  - $55,000

⑥ Insert a new Title and Content slide that resembles **Figure 4.43**. Make certain to increase and decrease list levels as indicated in the slide.

Figure 4.43 Third Slide

⑦ Insert a new Title and Content slide that resembles **Figure 4.44**. Make certain to increase and decrease list levels as indicated in the slide.

Figure 4.44 Fourth Slide

⑧ Correct any spelling errors.

⑨ Save the presentation as **Employment Opportunities**.

⑩ Run the slide show.

⑪ Print handouts of the presentation and select the 4 Slides Horizontal option. The printed presentation should resemble **Figure 4.45**.

⑫ Close the presentation.

⑬ Exit the application.

Figure 4.45 Printed Presentation

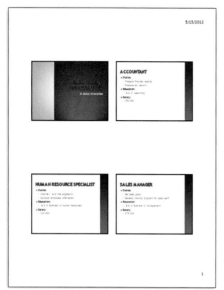

Project #2: Create a Presentation for a Family Reunion

You will create a presentation to show at your family reunion.

1. Open Microsoft PowerPoint 2010.

2. Apply the **Flow** theme to the presentation.

3. Type **Family Reunion** in the title placeholder**.**

4. Center the text in the title placeholder labeled *Family Reunion*.

5. In the second placeholder, type **Created by Name** (replace *Name* with your first and last names).

6. Insert a new Title and Content slide.

7. Type **Welcome Family Members** in the title placeholder.

8. Create a bulleted list in the second placeholder with the following text:

   Aunt Martha from California
   Cousin Antoinette from Paris
   Uncle Chris from Florida

9. Change the font color of the words *California*, *Paris*, and *Florida* to Light Blue in the Standard Colors group.

10. Underline the words *California*, *Paris*, and *Florida*.

11. Search for a clip art image of a *family* and insert it on slide 2.

12. Move the clip art image to the lower-left corner of the slide. Resize the clip art image as needed.

⑬ Insert a new Title and Content slide.

⑭ Type **Reunion Schedule** in the title placeholder.

⑮ Apply the **Gradient Fill—Blue, Accent 1** WordArt style to the Reunion Schedule text. This option is located in the third row, fourth column.

⑯ Insert a table with two columns and six rows.

⑰ Type the following information in the table.

Day	Event
Friday Night	Hayride
Saturday Morning	Brunch
Saturday Afternoon	Volleyball
Saturday Evening	Karaoke
Sunday	Pool Party

⑱ Correct any spelling errors.

⑲ Save the presentation as **Family Reunion**.

⑳ Run the slide show.

㉑ Print handouts of the presentation and select the 3 Slides option. The printed presentation should resemble **Figure 4.46**.

㉒ Close the presentation.

㉓ Exit the application.

Figure 4.46 Printed Presentation

Project #3: Create a Presentation of a Vacation Package for a Travel Agency

You work for a travel agency and have a special vacation package available for a summer cruise. You will create a presentation to advertise the vacation package.

1. Open Microsoft PowerPoint 2010.

2. Type **Mediterranean Cruise** in the title placeholder.

3. In the second placeholder, type **Sponsored by Vacation Enterprises.**

4. Apply the **Concourse** theme to the presentation.

5. Insert a new Title and Content slide that resembles **Figure** 4.47. Make certain to increase and decrease list levels as indicated in the slide.

Figure 4.47 Second Slide

6. Search for a clip art image of a *ship* and insert it on slide 2.

7. Move the clip art image to the lower-right corner of the slide. Resize the clip art image as needed.

8. Insert a new Title and Content slide that contains a table with two columns and four rows that resembles **Figure** 4.48.

Figure 4.48 Third Slide

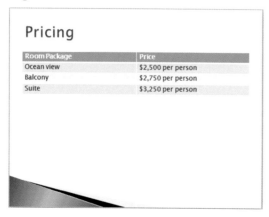

9. Insert a new Title and Content slide that contains a bulleted list that resembles **Figure 4.49**.

10. Search for a clip art image of a *pool* and insert it on slide 4.

11. Move the clip art image to the lower-right corner of the slide. Resize the clip art image as needed.

12. Correct any spelling errors.

13. Save the presentation as **Mediterranean Cruise**.

14. Run the slide show.

15. Print handouts of the presentation and select the 4 Slides Horizontal option. The printed presentation should resemble **Figure 4.50**.

16. Delete slide 4.

17. Save the presentation as **Mediterranean Cruise Revised**.

18. Print handouts of the presentation and select the 3 Slides option. The printed presentation should resemble **Figure 4.51**.

19. Close the presentation.

20. Exit the application.

Figure 4.49 Fourth Slide

Figure 4.50 Mediterranean Cruise Presentation

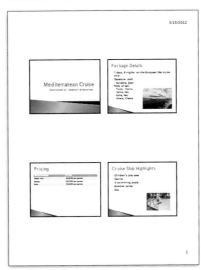

Figure 4.51 Mediterranean Cruise Revised Presentation

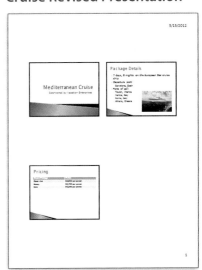

Modify Presentations Using Microsoft PowerPoint 2010 5

Chapter Objectives

After completing this chapter, you should be able to do the following:

- Modify the colors and fonts of a theme.
- Insert and format images and illustrations.
- Modify a slide using the Outline tab.
- Modify the layout and design of a table.
- Duplicate, select, delete, and reorder slides.
- Insert and format a text box.
- Insert a hyperlink.
- Insert a background.
- Apply slide transitions and animation effects.
- Insert audio clips.
- Add notes to the Notes pane.
- Insert headers and footers.

Now that you have learned the basics of Microsoft PowerPoint 2010, you will learn how to insert and format images and illustrations such as clip art, pictures, SmartArt, and shapes. You will learn how to insert a background onto a slide and insert audio clips to enhance the presentation. Additionally, you will apply slide transitions and animation effects to the slides.

You will open Microsoft PowerPoint 2010 and create a presentation.

Hands-On Exercise: Launch Microsoft PowerPoint 2010, Create First Slide, and Apply Theme

① Click the Start button.

② Click All Programs .

③ Click Microsoft Office . You may need to scroll through the Start menu to locate the folder.

④ Click Microsoft PowerPoint 2010 . A new blank presentation displays with a Title Slide layout. You will create the first slide.

⑤ Click the top placeholder that states *Click to add title*.

⑥ Type **Indulgent Organics**.

⑦ Click the second placeholder that states *Click to add subtitle*.

⑧ Type **Jane Van Gogh**.

⑨ You will apply a theme to the presentation. Click the Design tab on the Ribbon.

⑩ Click the Civic theme in the Themes group.

⑪ If the Civic theme does not display in the Themes group, click the More button in the Themes group (**Figure 5.1**) and a gallery of themes displays (**Figure 5.2**). Click the Civic theme from the gallery (Figure 5.2).

Figure 5.1 More Button in Themes Group

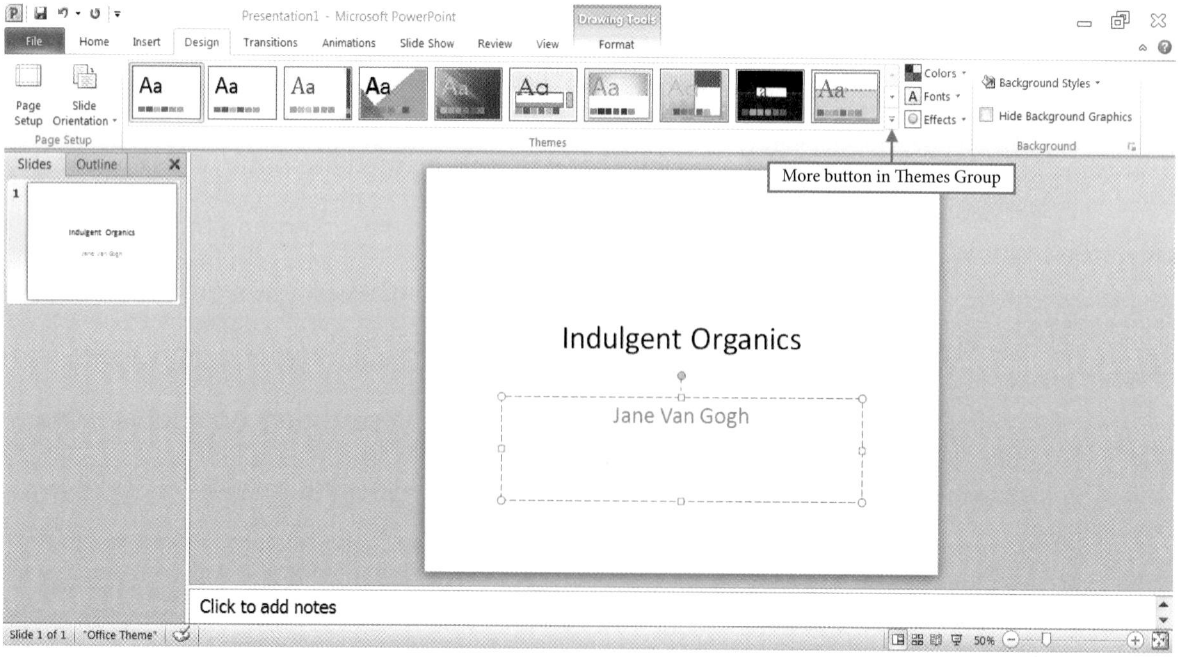

Figure 5.2 Gallery of Themes

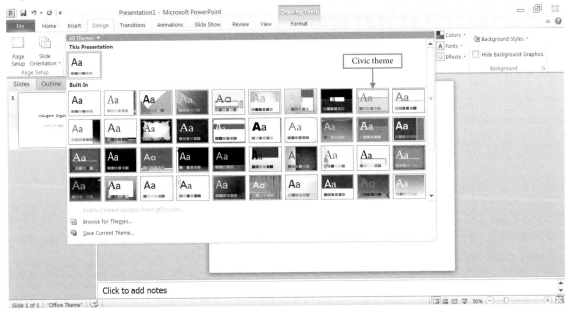

Modify the Colors and Fonts of a Theme

You can change the fonts and colors of a theme to change the look and feel of the presentation.

The Theme Colors gallery gives you choices of complementary color schemes that can be selected for a presentation. Theme colors contain 12 colors that include colors for the text, background, accent colors, and hyperlinks. The first four colors in the scheme are text and background colors. If the background contains a dark color, the text will be lighter, or vice versa, for easier reading.

Use these steps to change the theme colors:

- Click the **Design** tab.
- Click the **Colors** button in the Themes group and a gallery of colors displays (**Figure 5.3**).
- Select a color scheme from the list.

The Theme Fonts gallery is used to change the fonts used in a theme. A Theme Font has two font types. The first font is used for the headings and the second font is used for the body text.

Use these steps to change the theme fonts:

- Click the **Design** tab.
- Click the **Fonts** button in the Themes group and a gallery of fonts displays (**Figure 5.4**).
- Select a font from the list.

Hands-On Exercise: Modify the Colors and Fonts of a Theme

(1) Click the Colors button in the Themes group on the Design tab (Figure 5.3).

(2) Click Grid (Figure 5.3).

→

③ Click the Fonts button in the Themes group on the Design tab (Figure 5.4).

④ Click Adjacency (Figure 5.4).

⑤ Click Save on the Quick Access Toolbar. The Save As dialog box displays.

⑥ Select the location where you want to save the presentation.

⑦ Type **Indulgent Organics** in the File name box.

⑧ Click Save .

Figure 5.3 Modify Theme Colors

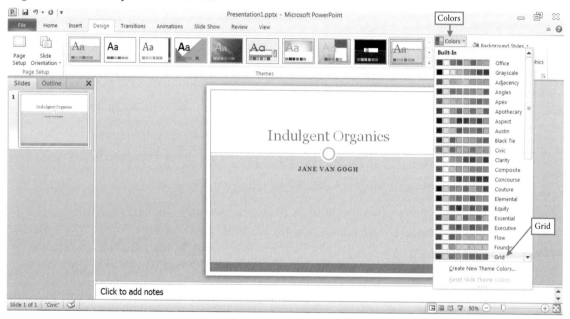

Figure 5.4 Modify Theme Fonts

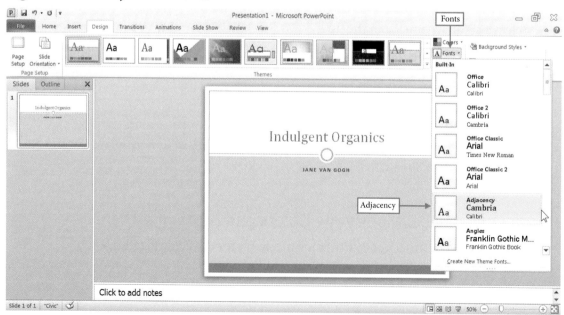

Hands-On Exercise: Insert a Two Content Slide

In this exercise you will create the second slide.

① Click the Home tab.

② Click the New Slide arrow in the Slides group.

③ Click Two Content .

④ Type **We Make It Easy** in the title placeholder. Type the following bullet points in the left placeholder (**Figure 5.5**):

- **Order online**
- **Fast free delivery**
- **Catering** (Do not press Enter after this bulleted item.)

Figure 5.5 Insert Two Content Side with Bulleted List

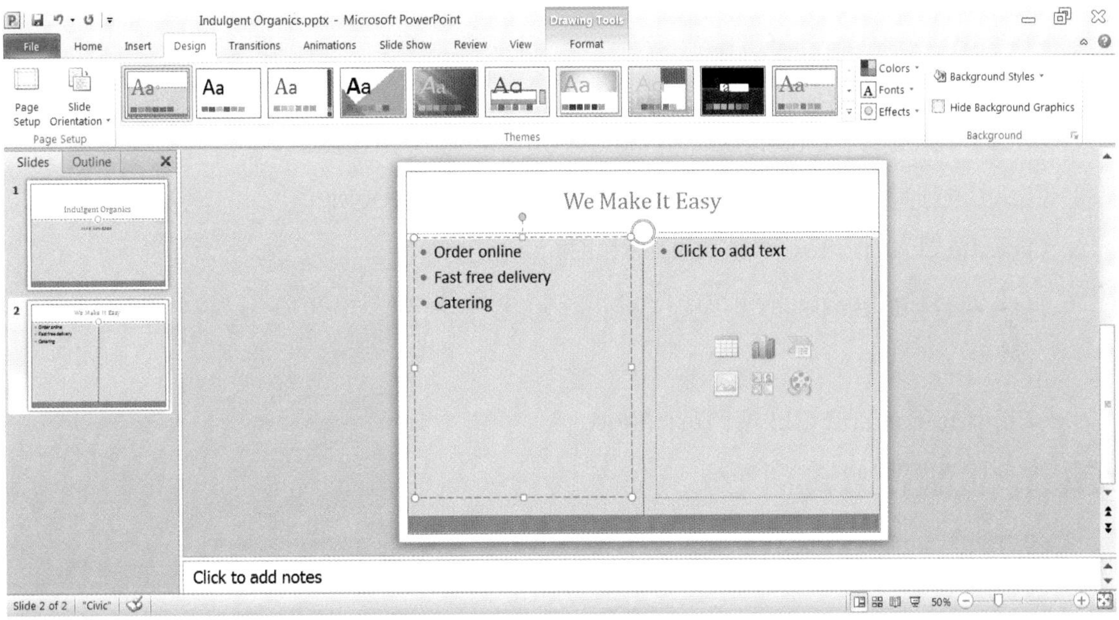

Insert Pictures and Clip Art

Pictures and clip art can be inserted on a slide. The difference between a picture and clip art is that a picture is inserted on the slide from a file that is stored on your computer or external device such as a CD or USB flash drive; whereas a clip art image is a premade image that is available with Microsoft Office. A clip art image can be an illustration, photograph, video, or audio clip.

Use these steps to insert a picture:

- Click the **Picture** button in the Images group on the Insert tab, or click the **Insert Picture from File** icon (**Figure 5.6**) on the slide.
- The Insert Picture dialog box displays. Locate the picture you want to insert and double-click the **picture**, *or* click the **picture** and click **Insert**.

A clip art image is inserted by clicking the **Clip Art** button in the Images group on the Insert tab or by clicking the **Clip Art** icon on the slide (Figure 5.6).

Hands-On Exercise: Insert Clip Art

You will search for a clip art image of take-out food. Instead of searching all clip art images, you will limit the search to pictures.

① Click the Clip Art icon in the right placeholder and the Clip Art task pane displays on the right side of the application window (Figure 5.6).

② Type **food take out** in the Search for box (Figure 5.6).

③ Click the Results should be: arrow (Figure 5.6).

④ You want to find clip art images that are photographs. If there is a check mark next to All media types or to any of the other options, click to deselect.

⑤ Click the Photographs option and a check mark displays (**Figure 5.7**).

⑥ Click Go and a listing of clip art images displays.

⑦ Scroll down to the picture entitled *Take-out containers and cutlery* (**Figure 5.8**). If you do not have the picture, you can choose an appropriate one.

⑧ Click the clip art image, and it is inserted into the placeholder.

⑨ Click the Close button in the Clip Art task pane.

⑩ Click Save on the Quick Access Toolbar. The slide should resemble **Figure 5.9**.

Figure 5.6 Clip Art Icon and Clip Art Task Pane

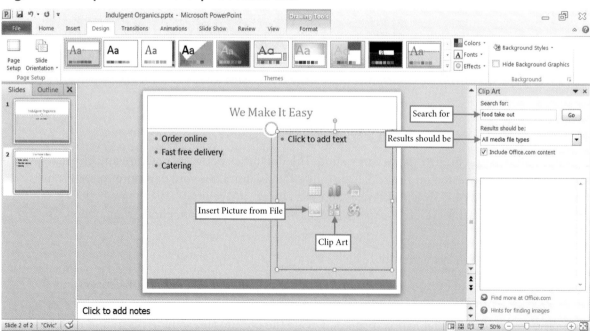

Figure 5.7 Select Media File Type—Photographs

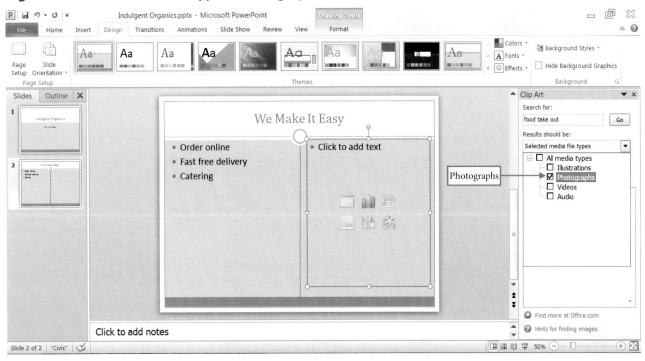

Figure 5.8 Select a Clip Art Image

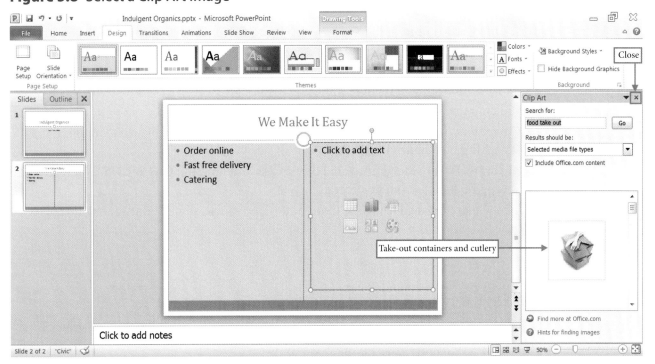

Figure 5.9 Clip Art Inserted

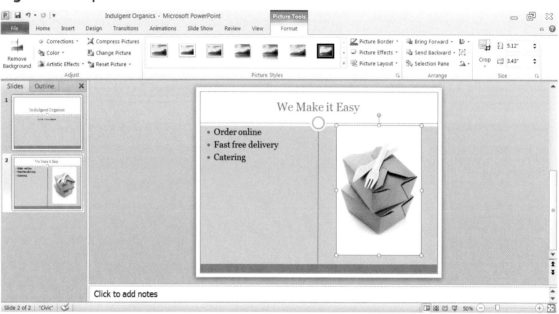

Crop an Image

When an image is selected, such as clip art or a picture, the Picture Tools contextual tab displays on the Ribbon. The Picture Tools tab contains a Format tab, which has commands to format the image. The **Crop** command is used to delete part of the image you do not want or need.

Crop: A command that is used to delete part of the image you do not want or need.

Use these steps to crop an image:

- Click the **image**. The Picture Tools tab displays on the Ribbon.
- Click the **Format** tab.
- Click the **Crop** button in the Size group (**Figure 5.10**). Cropping handles display around the selected image (Figure 5.10).
  - When the mouse hovers over the image, the mouse pointer changes to a four-headed arrow. You can drag the image outside the border to crop a section of the image.
  - To crop one side of the image, drag the center cropping handle of the side border.
  - To crop two sides at the same time, press and hold the **Ctrl** key while dragging the cropping handle from the side.
  - To crop all four sides at the same time, press and hold the **Ctrl** key while dragging the cropping handle from any corner.
- When you are finished, click the **Crop** button, press **Esc**, or click outside the image to deselect.

Hands-On Exercise: Crop an Image

① Click the image if not already selected. The Picture Tools contextual tab displays.

② Click the Format tab if not already selected.

③ Click the Crop button in the Size group (Figure 5.10). The cropping handles display around the image.

④ Press and hold the Ctrl key while dragging the top center cropping handle down to crop (remove) some of the white space from the top and bottom of the image (**Figure 5.11**).

⑤ Press the Esc key when completed and the dark area of the image will be deleted.

⑥ Type **3.82** in the Shape Height box and press Enter . The image should resemble **Figure 5.12**.

Figure 5.10 Crop Button and Cropping Handles

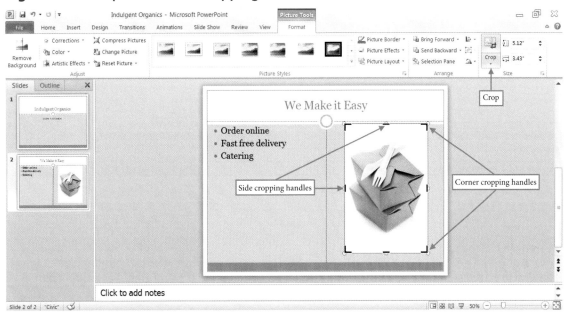

Figure 5.11 Image Cropped

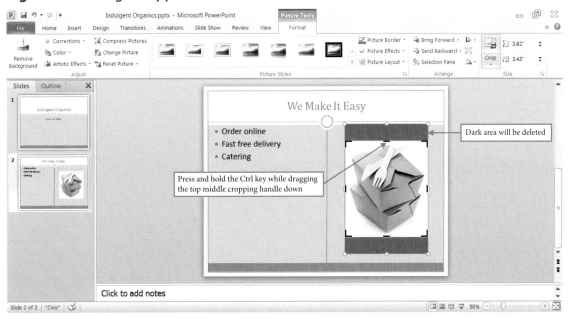

Figure 5.12 Modify Shape Height

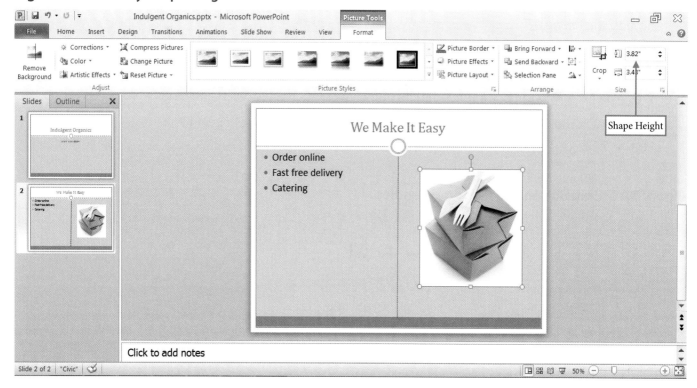

Apply Picture Style

The Picture Styles command allows you to select a visual style for an image, which contains various border and shape options.

Use these steps to apply a picture style:

- Click the **image** to select it.
- Click the **Format** tab.
- Click the **More** button in the Picture Styles group to view a gallery of picture styles (**Figure 5.13**).
- Select a picture style from the gallery.

Hands-On Exercise: Apply Picture Style

1. Click the image if not selected.
2. Click the More button in the Picture Styles group on the Format tab (Figure 5.13).
3. Click Rotated, White (third row, third column) as shown in **Figure 5.14**.
4. Click outside the image to deselect. The slide should resemble **Figure 5.15**.

Figure 5.13 The More Button in Picture Styles Group

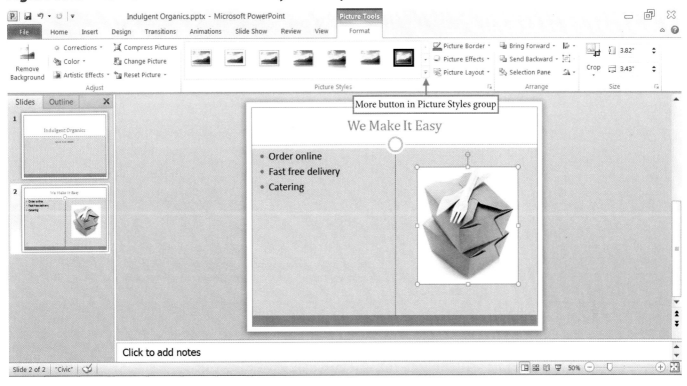

Figure 5.14 Picture Styles Gallery

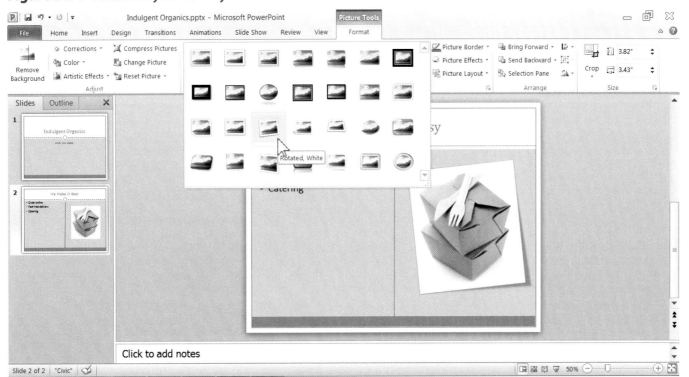

Figure 5.15 Picture Style Applied to Clip Art

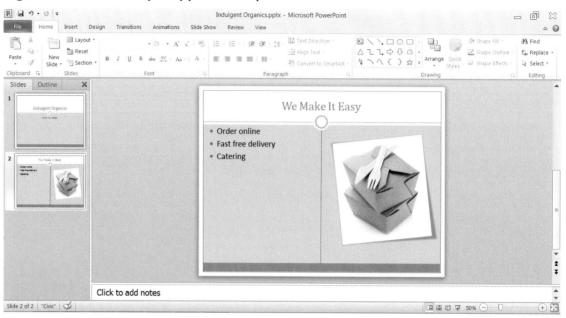

Hands-On Exercise: Change Size of Placeholder

(1) You are going to change the size of the left placeholder to make room for a shape under the bulleted list. Click anywhere in the bulleted list and the placeholder displays.

(2) Drag the sizing handle on the bottom border of the placeholder up so it resembles Figure 5.16.

Figure 5.16 Modify the Size of the Placeholder

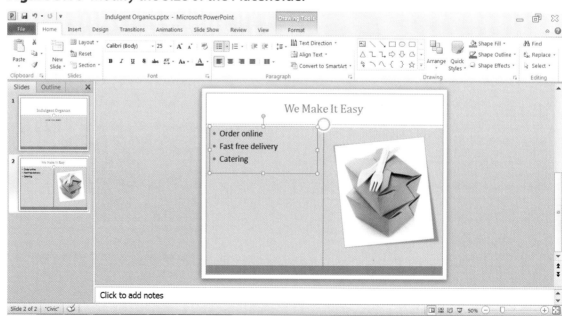

Insert and Format a Shape

You can insert shapes in the presentation. There are an assortment of shapes from which to choose, including lines, rectangles, circles, triangles, block arrows, equation shapes, flow-chart shapes, and stars and banners. When a shape is inserted or selected, the Drawing Tools contextual tab displays on the Ribbon. It contains a Format tab with commands to format the shape.

Use these steps to insert a shape:

- Click the **Insert** tab.
- Click the **Shapes** button in the Illustrations group (**Figure 5.17**).
- Click a **shape**. The mouse pointer changes to a plus shape.
- Click the location of the slide where you want to place the shape or drag to create the shape.

Use these steps to delete a shape:

- Click the **shape**.
- Press the **Delete** key.

Use these steps to change the size of a shape:

- Click the **shape**.
- Drag the sizing handles to change the size of the shape, *or* specify the exact size of the shape:
  - Click the **Format** tab on the Drawing Tools tab.
  - Type the height of the shape in the Shape Height box in the Size group (**Figure 5.18**).
  - Type the width of the shape in the Shape Width box in the Size group (Figure 5.18)

Hands-On Exercise: Insert and Format a Shape

1. Click the Insert tab.
2. Click the Shapes button in the Illustrations group, and the gallery displays (Figure 5.17).
3. Click the first shape in the Block Arrows category called Right Arrow (Figure 5.17).
4. Click in the bottom left side of the slide to create the shape.
5. Click the Format tab.
6. Type **2** in the Shape Height box in the Size group (Figure 5.18).
7. Type **4.5** in the Shape Width box in the Size group (Figure 5.18).
8. Press Enter .
9. Point to the shape and a four-headed arrow displays.
10. Drag the shape to the location as shown in Figure 5.18.

Figure 5.17 Shapes Button and Gallery

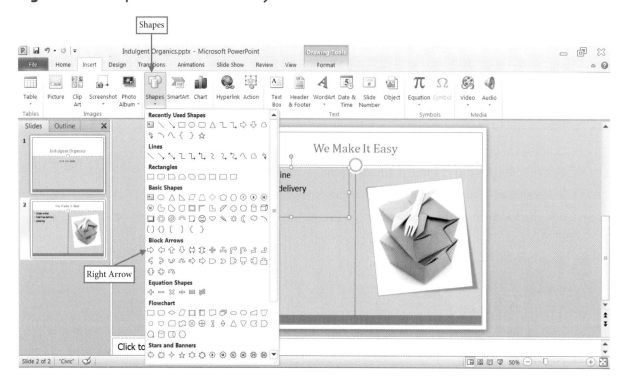

Figure 5.18 Modify the Size of the Shape

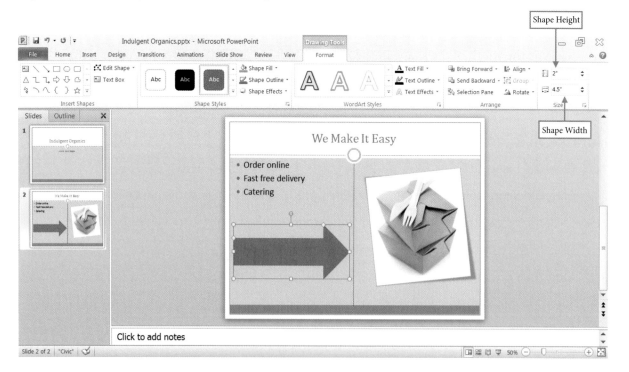

Insert Text in a Shape

You can add text to many shapes. Simply click the shape and then type.

Hands-On Exercise: Insert Text in a Shape

① Click the shape if it is not already selected.

② Type **Earth Friendly Packaging!**

③ Triple-click the text Earth Friendly Packaging! The Mini Toolbar displays at the top right of the selected text and appears faded or dimmed.

④ Move the mouse pointer on the Mini Toolbar, and it becomes active.

⑤ Click the Font Size arrow and select 28 (**Figure 5.19**).

⑥ Click the Save button on the Quick Access Toolbar.

Figure 5.19 Shape with Text Inserted and Formatted

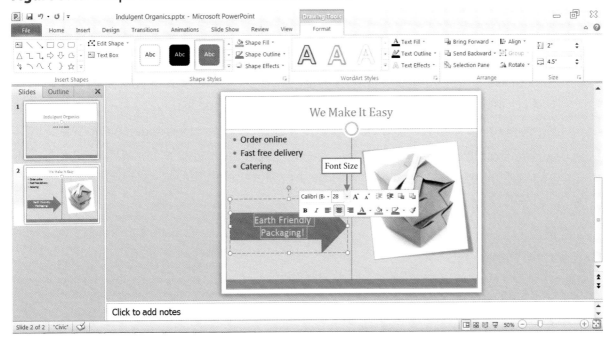

Modify a Slide Using the Outline Tab

The **Outline tab** displays the text of each slide in an outline format (**Figure 5.20**). Graphics and multimedia elements are not displayed in the Outline tab. Additionally, it does not display the text typed in a shape. You can use the Outline tab to view the text in the presentation or to insert or modify text on a slide.

> **Outline tab:**
> Displays the text on each slide in an outline format without graphics and multimedia elements.

Hands-On Exercise: Modify a Slide Using the Outline Tab

① Click in the bulleted list .

② Click the Outline tab (Figure 5.20). Notice that the shape and clip art image on Slide 2 do not display in the Outline tab.

③ Triple-click the paragraph Order online in the Outline tab.

④ Type **Online or phone**. As you edit in the Outline tab, the slide is also modified.

⑤ Press Enter and a bullet displays.

⑥ Press the Tab key to indent the bullet.

⑦ Type **Same great service!**

⑧ Click after the word *delivery* in the next bulleted item.

⑨ Press Enter and a bullet displays.

⑩ Press Tab to indent the bullet.

⑪ Type **Home or office**.

⑫ Click after the word *Catering* in the next bulleted item and press Enter .

⑬ Press the Tab key.

⑭ Type **Any size event!** As you type, the text will get smaller on the slide to fit in the placeholder (**Figure 5.21**).

⑮ Click the Slides tab (**Figure 5.22**).

⑯ Click in the left placeholder which contains the bulleted list.

⑰ Point to the sizing handle on the bottom border of the placeholder. A two-headed arrow displays.

⑱ Drag the arrow downward to enlarge the placeholder. The slide should resemble Figure 5.22.

Figure 5.20 Outline Tab

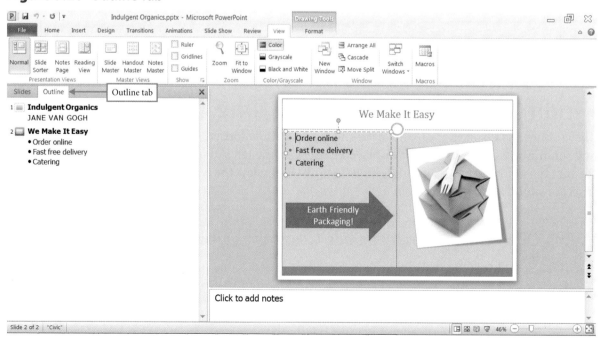

Figure 5.21 Modify Slide in the Outline Tab

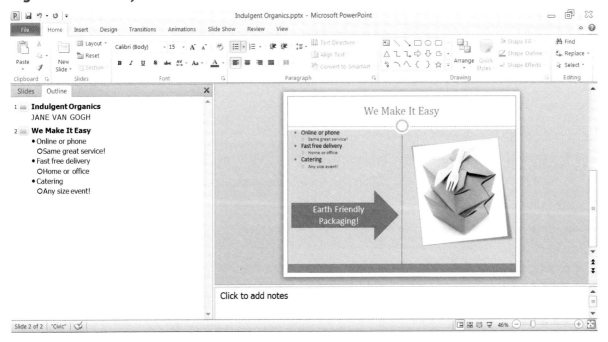

Figure 5.22 Resized Placeholder

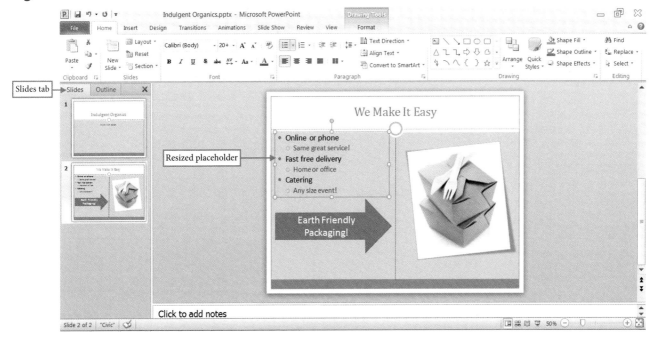

Hands-On Exercise: Insert New Slide with Table

① Click the New Slide arrow in the Slides group on the Home tab to insert the third slide.

② Click the Title and Content layout. A new slide displays.

③ Type **Why Go Organic?** in the title placeholder.

④ Click the Insert Table icon on the slide (**Figure 5.23**), and the Insert Table dialog box displays (**Figure 5.24**).

⑤ Type **2** in the Number of columns box (Figure 5.24).

⑥ Type **4** in the Number of rows box (Figure 5.24).

⑦ Click OK . The table displays on the slide.

⑧ You will enter the text (**Table 5.1**) into the table. Press Tab, Enter , *or* use the arrow keys to navigate to the next cell in the table. The slide should resemble **Figure 5.25**.

Table 5.1 Table Information	
What our Customers Say…	
Better for the planet	Grown without pesticides
Supports the community	Money reinvested in the community
Cuts down on greenhouse gases	Produce does not travel far

Figure 5.23 Insert Table Icon

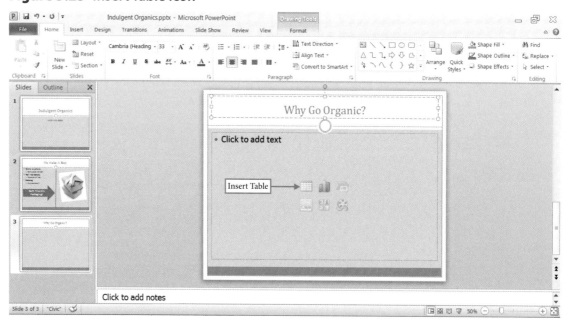

Figure 5.24 Insert Table Dialog Box

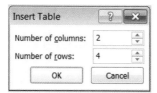

Figure 5.25 Table with Text Inserted

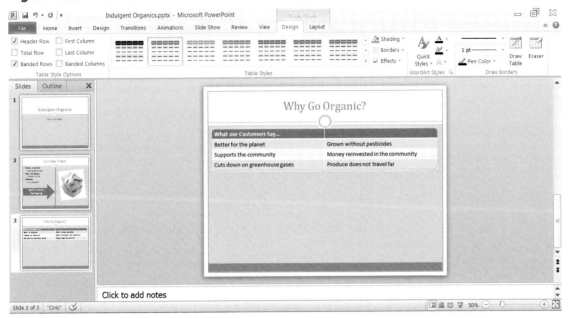

Modify Table Layout

The Table Tools contextual tab displays on the Ribbon when a table is created or selected. The Table Tools tab contains the Design and Layout tabs, which contain commands to modify the table.

The Layout tab contains commands for inserting and deleting columns and rows, changing the alignment of the text in the table, and changing the size of the cells and the table.

The **Select** command in the Layout tab is used to select a table, row, or column (**Figure 5.26**).

Use these steps to select a table, row, or column:

- Click inside the table or in the row or column you want to select.
- Click the **Layout** tab in the Table Tools tab.
- Click the **Select** button in the Table group (Figure 5.26).
- Click **Select Table**, **Select Column**, or **Select Row**.

The **Merge Cells** command is used to combine two or more cells into one cell (**Figure 5.27**).

Use these steps to merge cells:

- Select the cells you want to merge.
- Click the **Layout** tab.
- Click the **Merge Cells** button in the Merge group (Figure 5.27).

The commands in the Alignment group are used to modify the alignment of text in a cell (**Table 5.2**).

Select: A command that is used to select a table, row, or column.

Merge Cells: A command used to combine two or more cells into one cell.

Table 5.2 Alignment Group Commands

Command	Button	Description
Align Text Left		Aligns text to the left.
Center		Centers the text.
Align Text Right		Aligns text to the right.
Align Top		Aligns text at the top of the cell.
Center Vertically		Centers the text vertically in the cell.
Align Bottom		Aligns text at the bottom of the cell.
Text Direction	Text Direction	Changes the orientation of the text in a cell to vertical, stacked, or rotated.
Cell Margins	Cell Margins	Changes the margins of the cell.

Hands-On Exercise: Select and Format Table, Merge Cells, Align Text in Cell

1. Click anywhere in the table.
2. Click the Layout tab.
3. Click the Select button in the Table group (Figure 5.26).
4. Click Select Table .
5. Click the Home tab.
6. Click the Font Size arrow.
7. Click 24 .
8. Click the Layout tab.
9. Click in the first row of the table.
10. Click the Select button.
11. Click Select Row .
12. Click the Merge Cells button in the Merge group (Figure 5.27).
13. Click the Center button in the Alignment group to center the text (**Figure 5.28**).
14. Click outside the table to deselect the table.

Figure 5.26 Select Button

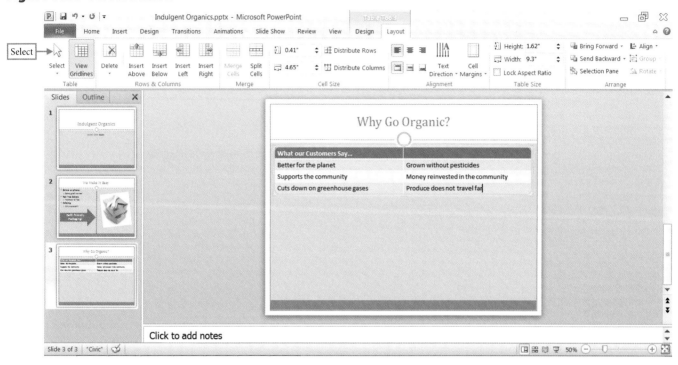

Figure 5.27 Merge Cells Button

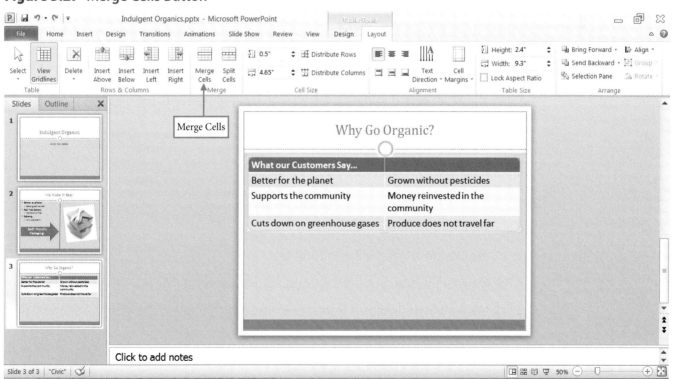

Figure 5.28 Center Button

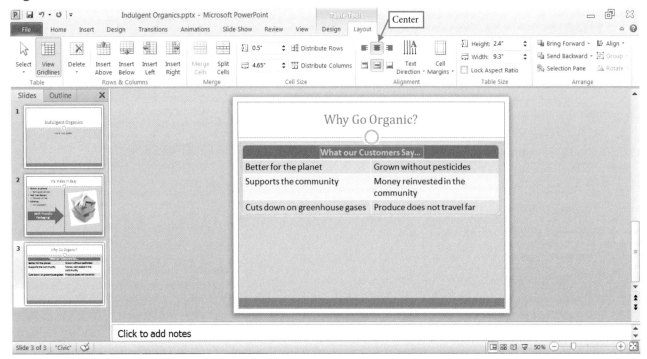

Apply a Table Style

You can modify the table design by applying a style to the table. The Table Styles gallery contains various formatting options, including a color scheme and border options, which can be applied to a table.

Use these steps to apply a table style:

- Click in the table.
- Click the **Design** tab in the Table Tools tab.
- Click the **More** button in the Table Styles group (**Figure 5.29**) and a gallery of table styles displays.
- Select a table style from the gallery.

Hands-On Exercise: Apply a Table Style

1. Click anywhere in the table.
2. Click the Design tab in the Table Tools tab.
3. Click the More button in the Table Styles group (Figure 5.29).
4. Click Medium Style 1-Accent 6, (first row, seventh column) in the Medium section of the gallery (**Figure 5.30**).
5. Click outside the table to deselect the table. The slide should resemble **Figure 5.31**.

Figure 5.29 More Button in Table Styles Group

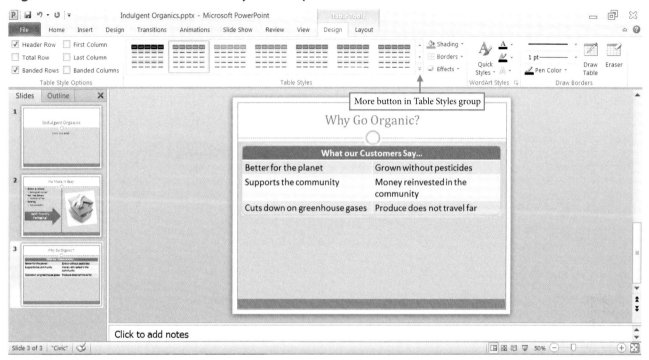

Figure 5.30 Table Styles Gallery

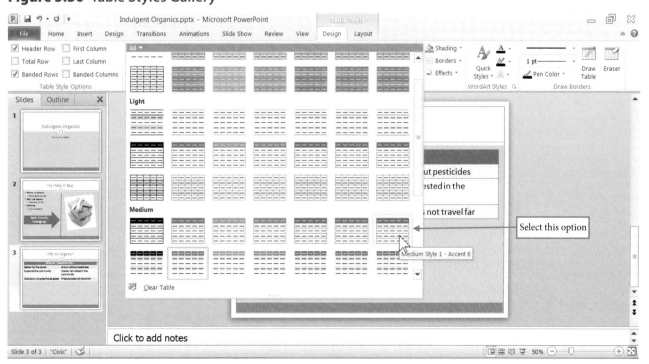

Figure 5.31 Table Style Applied

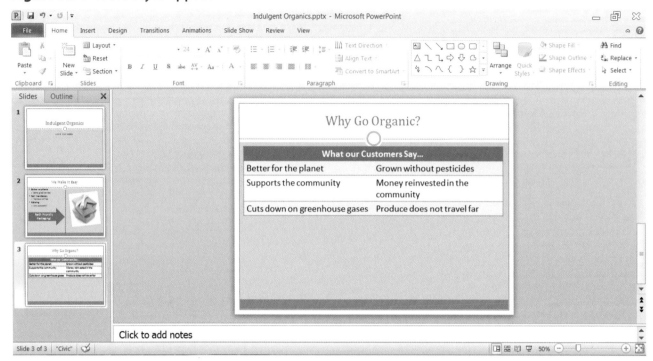

Select Slides

You may need to select a slide in order to delete it, copy it, or change the order of the slides in the presentation. You can select slides using the Slides tab in Normal view or the Slide Sorter view. A gold background displays around the slide thumbnails indicating that the slide is selected. **Table 5.3** displays the methods for selecting slides.

Table 5.3 Select Slides	
Task	Steps
Select one slide	• Click the slide.
Select adjacent slides	• Select the first slide. • Press and hold the **Shift** key and click on last slide.
Select multiple nonadjacent slides	• Select the first slide. • Press and hold the **Ctrl** key and click the other slides.

Hands-On Exercise: Selecting Slides

① You will select Slides 1 and 3. Click Slide 1 in the Slides tab.

② Press and hold the Ctrl key and click Slide 3 . Both slides are selected and contain a gold background around the slide thumbnails.

③ Next you will select Slides 1, 2, and 3 using the Slide Sorter view. Click the Slide Sorter button on the status bar (**Figure 5.32**).

④ Click Slide 1 .

⑤ Press and hold the Shift key and click Slide 3 . All three slides are selected (Figure 5.32).

⑥ Double-click Slide 3 , and it displays in Normal view.

Figure 5.32 Slides Selected in Slide Sorter View

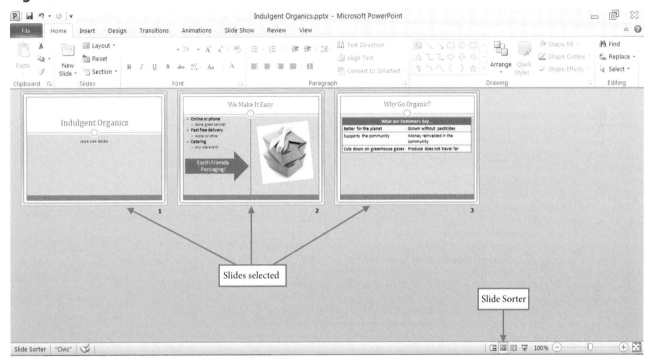

Duplicate Slides

If you need two similar slides in the presentation, you can use the **Duplicate Slide** command to make a copy of a slide instead of creating two separate slides. You can duplicate slides in either Slide Sorter view or from the Slides tab in Normal view (**Table 5.4**).

Duplicate Slide:
A command that makes a copy of a slide.

Table 5.4 Duplicate Slides	
Task	**Steps**
Duplicate a slide using the Slides tab	• Right-click the slide you want to duplicate in the Slides tab.
	• Click **Duplicate Slide** from the shortcut menu. The new slide displays below the original.

Table 5.4 *continued*

Task	Steps
Duplicate slides from the Slide Sorter view using Copy and Paste commands	• Click the **Slide Sorter** button on the status bar to navigate to the Slide Sorter view. • Click the slide to duplicate. ◦ To duplicate multiple slides, hold down the **Ctrl** key while clicking the slides to duplicate. • Click the **Copy** button on the Clipboard group on the Home tab. • Navigate to the location where you want the duplicate slide to display. • Click the **Paste** button on the Clipboard group on the Home tab.
Duplicate slides from the New Slide button	• Select the slide or slides you want to duplicate. • Click the **New Slide** arrow in the Slides group on the Home tab. • Click **Duplicate Selected Slides.**

Hands-On Exercise: Duplicate Slides

(1) You will duplicate Slides 2 and 3. Click Slide 2 in the Slides tab.

(2) Press and hold the Shift key and click Slide 3 . Both slides are selected (**Figure 5.33**).

(3) Right-click one of the selected slides and click Duplicate Slide on the shortcut menu (**Figure 5.34**).

(4) The slides are duplicated and are pasted at the end of Slide 3 (**Figure 5.35**).

(5) Click Slide 4 in the Slides tab. The slide is a duplicate of Slide 2.

(6) Click Slide 5 in the Slides tab. The slide is a duplicate of Slide 3.

Figure 5.33 Slides Selected

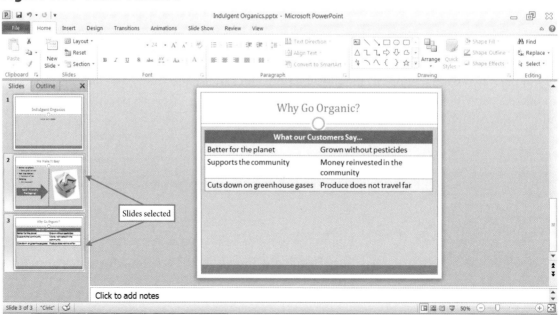

Use these steps to move a slide by cutting and pasting the slide to another location using the Slides tab or Slide Sorter view:

- Click the slide you want to move.
- Click the **Cut** command in the Clipboard group on the Home tab, *or* press **Ctrl + X**.
- Click the location where you want the slide pasted.
- Click the **Paste** button in the Clipboard group on the Home tab, *or* press **Ctrl + V**.

Hands-On Exercise: Reorder Slides

① Click Slide 3 from the Slides tab.

② Press Ctrl + X to cut the slide.

③ Click between the first and second slides, and a blinking line displays (**Figure 5.37**).

④ Click Ctrl + V to paste the slide. The slide displays as Slide 2.

⑤ Now, you will move the slide back. Click Slide 2 .

⑥ Drag the slide until the horizontal line displays below Slide 3. The screen should resemble **Figure 5.38**.

⑦ Click Save on the Quick Access Toolbar.

Figure 5.37 Blinking Line Indicates Where Slide Will Paste

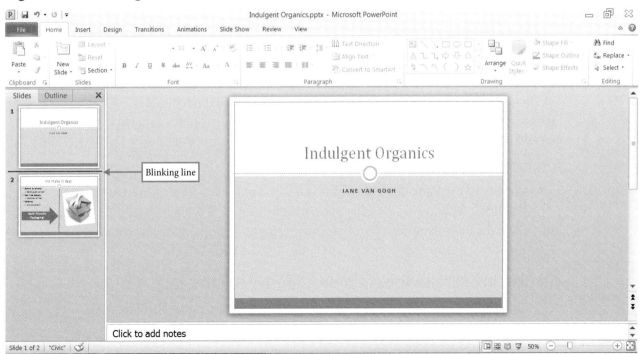

Figure 5.38 Slides Reordered

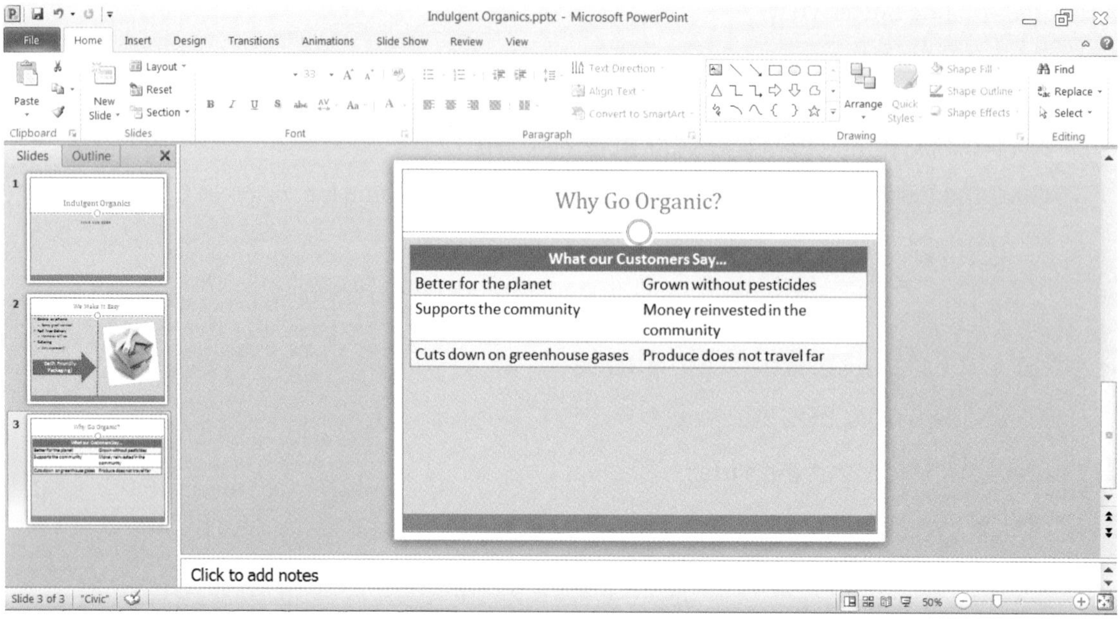

Insert SmartArt Graphic

> **SmartArt:** A graphic that enables you to visually display and communicate information. SmartArt graphics can display graphical lists, processes, and various diagrams.

SmartArt is a graphic that enables you to visually display and communicate information. SmartArt graphics can display graphical lists, processes, and various diagrams. You can insert text into the SmartArt graphic and change the colors of the SmartArt graphic.

Use these steps to insert SmartArt:

- Click the **Insert SmartArt Graphic** icon on the slide if you are using a layout with that option (**Figure 5.39**), *or* click the **Insert** tab and click **SmartArt** in the Illustrations group. The Choose a SmartArt Graphic dialog box displays (**Figure 5.40**).
- Choose the desired SmartArt.
- Click **OK**.
- Click in each placeholder to enter text.

When you insert SmartArt, the SmartArt Tools contextual tab displays, which contains a Design and Format tab. The Text Pane displays the entire text in the SmartArt graphic. You can add, modify, and delete text in the Text Pane.

Use any of these methods to open the Text Pane:

- Click the **Text Pane control**, which is located to the left of the SmartArt graphic (**Figure 5.41**).
- Click the **Text Pane** button in the Create Graphic group on the Design tab.

Hands-On Exercise: Insert New Slide with SmartArt

1. Click the Home tab. You will insert the fourth slide that contains SmartArt.
2. Click the New Slide arrow.

③ Click the Title and Content layout.

④ Type **Extras** in the top placeholder.

⑤ Click the Insert SmartArt Graphic icon on the slide (Figure 5.39). The Choose a SmartArt Graphic dialog box displays (Figure 5.40).

⑥ Click Cycle in the left pane (Figure 5.40).

⑦ Click Radial Cycle in the right pane (third row, second column), as shown in Figure 5.40.

⑧ Click OK .

⑨ The SmartArt displays on the slide with text placeholders. You will click in the place-holders to enter the text.

   a. The center placeholder is selected. Type **Indulge!**

   b. Type **Easy Ordering** in the top placeholder.

   c. Type **Cooking Classes** in the right placeholder.

   d. Type **Special Events** in the bottom placeholder.

   e. Type **Recipe Ideas** in the left placeholder.

⑩ Click the Text Pane control or the Text Pane button in the Create Graphic group on the Design tab (Figure 5.41). The entire text in the SmartArt displays in the Text Pane (**Figure 5.42**). You can add, modify, and delete text from the Text Pane.

⑪ Click the Close button in the Text Pane to remove the Text Pane from the slide (Figure 5.42).

⑫ Click outside the SmartArt graphic to deselect it.

Figure 5.39 Insert SmartArt Graphic

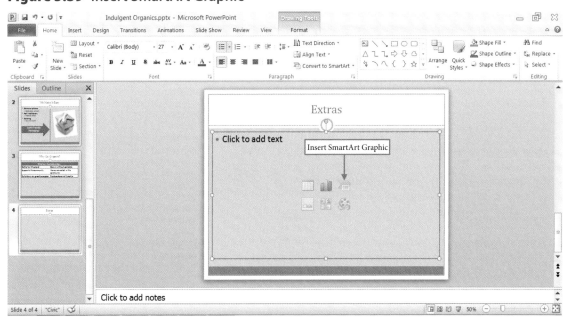

Figure 5.40 Choose a SmartArt Graphic Dialog Box

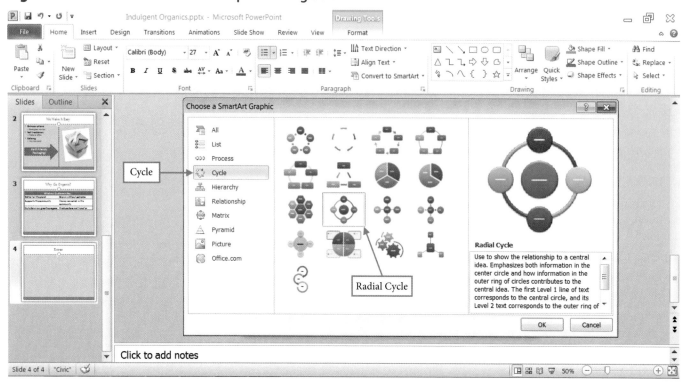

Figure 5.41 Text Pane Control and Text Pane Button

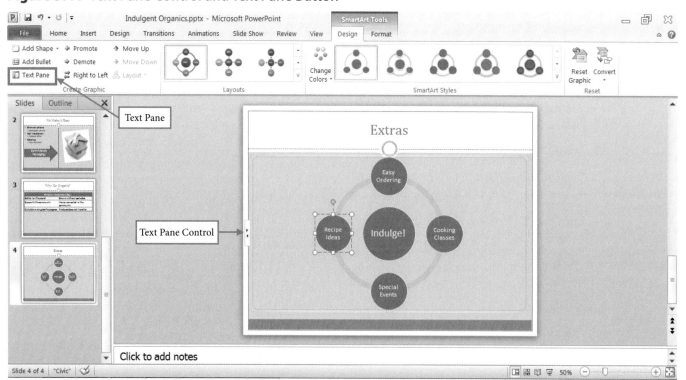

Figure 5.42 Text Pane Open

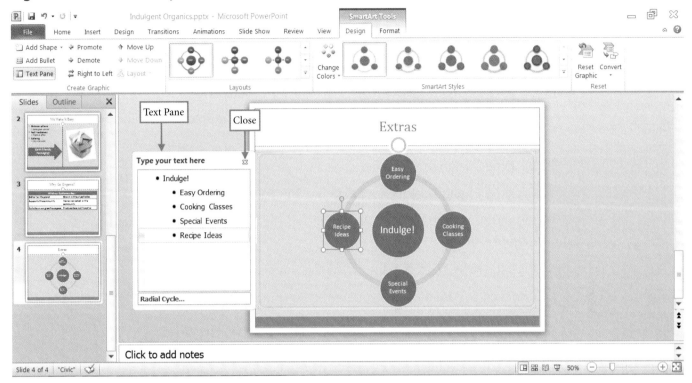

Modify a SmartArt Graphic

The SmartArt graphic must be selected before it can be modified. When you click a SmartArt graphic, it may select a shape in the SmartArt graphic or the entire SmartArt graphic. Click the border of the SmartArt graphic to select the entire graphic. You can change the color, layout, or style of the SmartArt graphic.

Use these steps to change the colors of a SmartArt graphic:

- Click the **SmartArt graphic**, and the SmartArt Tools contextual tab displays on the Ribbon. If the entire SmartArt graphic is not selected, click the **border** to select it.
- Click the **Design** tab.
- Click the **Change Colors** button in the SmartArt Styles group (**Figure 5.43**).
- Select a color from the gallery.

Use these steps to change the layout of a SmartArt graphic:

- Click the **SmartArt graphic**, and the SmartArt Tools contextual tab displays on the Ribbon. If the entire SmartArt graphic is not selected, click the **border** to select it.
- Click the **Design** tab.
- Click the **More** button in the Layouts group (**Figure 5.44**).
- Choose a layout.

Use these steps to change the style of the SmartArt graphic:

- Click the **SmartArt graphic**, and the SmartArt Tools contextual tab displays on the Ribbon. If the entire SmartArt graphic is not selected, click the **border** to select it.

- Click the **Design** tab.
- Click the **More** button in the **SmartArt Styles** group (**Figure 5.46**).
- Choose a style.

Hands-On Exercise: Modify a SmartArt Graphic

① Click the SmartArt graphic . If the entire SmartArt graphic is not selected, click the border to select it.

② Click the Design tab.

③ Click the Change Colors button in the SmartArt Styles group (Figure 5.43).

④ Click the Colorful-Accent Colors , which is the first option in the Colorful group (Figure 5.43).

⑤ Click the More button in the Layouts group (Figure 5.44).

⑥ Choose the Basic Radial layout, which is located in the third row, third column (**Figure 5.45**).

⑦ Click the More button in the SmartArt Styles group (Figure 5.46).

⑧ Click Polished , which is the first option in the 3-D group (**Figure 5.47**).

Figure 5.43 Change Colors of SmartArt Graphic

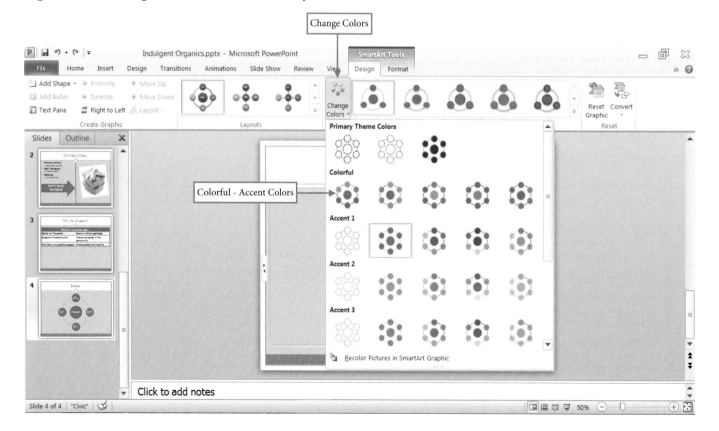

Figure 5.44 More Button in Layouts Group

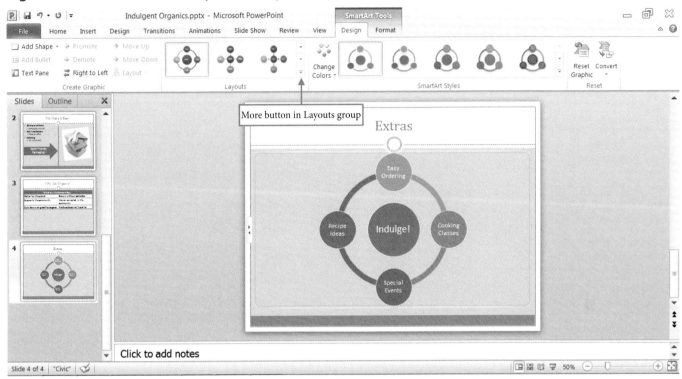

Figure 5.45 Basic Radial Layout

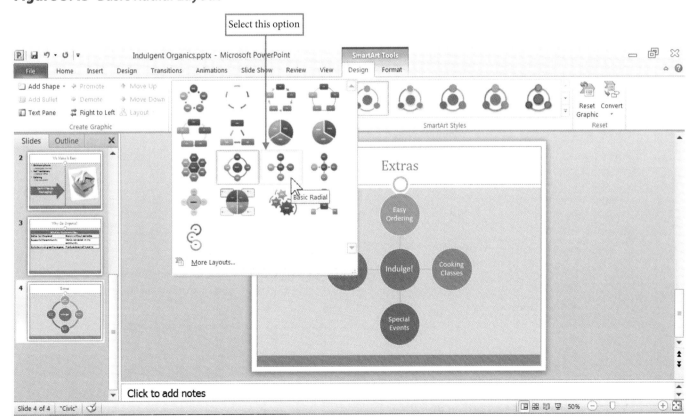

Figure 5.46 More Button in SmartArt Styles Group

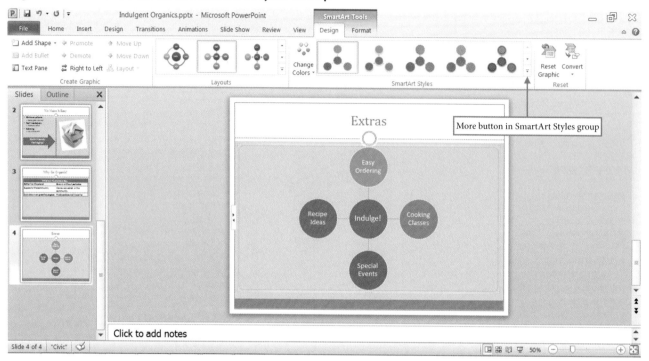

Figure 5.47 Polished SmartArt Style

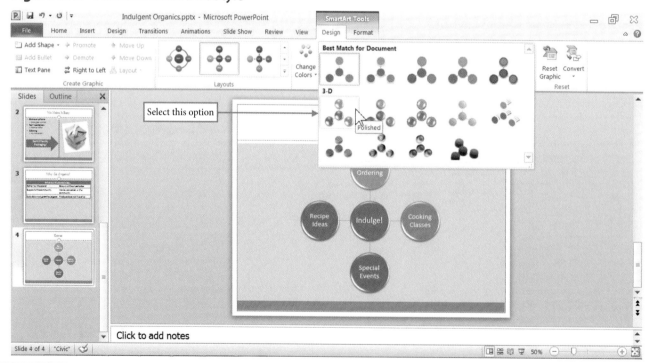

Text Box: A command that inserts a box on a slide, in which you can add text.

Insert Text Box

The Text Box command inserts a box on a slide, in which you can add text. You can move or resize the text box on the slide.

Use these steps to insert a text box:

- Click the **Insert** tab.
- Click the **Text Box** button in the Text group (**Figure 5.48**).
- Click the mouse in the slide and a text box displays, *or* drag the mouse on the slide to draw the text box.
- The insertion point displays in the text box. Type the text in the text box.

Hands-On Exercise: Insert a Text Box

You will insert a blank slide in the presentation and insert text boxes.

1. Click the Home tab.
2. Click the New Slide arrow.
3. Click Blank. The slide contains a white background with no objects.
4. Click the Insert tab.
5. Click the Text Box button in the Text group (Figure 5.48).
6. Click in the top section of the slide and a text box displays. The Home tab is now active.
7. Type **Indulgent Organics—The Path to a Healthier YOU!** (Figure 5.49).
8. Drag the border of the text box to move the text box to the location shown in Figure 5.49.

Figure 5.48 Text Box Button

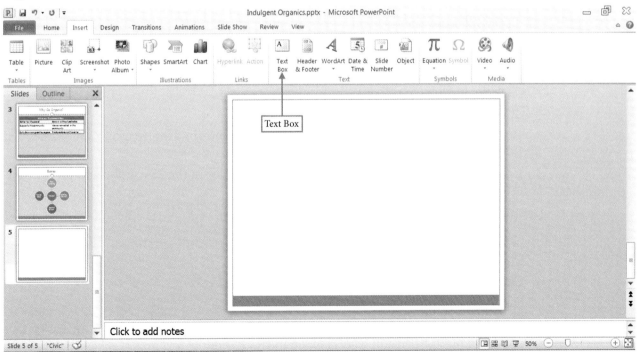

Figure 5.49 Text Box Inserted

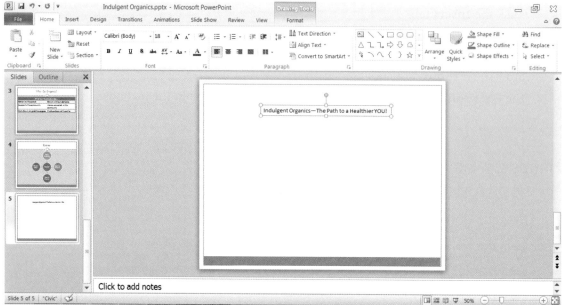

Modify the Format of a Text Box

When a text box is inserted or selected, the Drawing Tools contextual tab, which contains a Format tab, displays. The Format tab contains commands to format the text box, such as applying a style and changing the size and alignment of the text box.

Use these steps to apply a style to the text box:

- Click the **text box** to select it.
- Click the **Format** tab (**Figure 5.50**).
- Click the **More** button in the Shape Styles group (Figure 5.50) and a gallery of styles displays (**Figure 5.51**).
- Select a style from the gallery.

Use these steps to change the size of the text box:

- Click the **text box** to select it.
- Click the **Format** tab (Figure 5.50).
- Type the height of the text box in the Shape Height box in the Size group and press **Enter** (**Figure 5.52**).
- Type the width of the text box in the Shape Width box in the Size group and press **Enter** (Figure 5.52).

Use these steps to change the alignment of the text box:

- Click the **text box** to select it.
- Click the **Format** tab (Figure 5.50).
- Click the **Align** button in the Arrange group (Figure 5.52).
- Select an alignment option from the list.

If you want to format all the text in the text box by applying commands from the Home tab, you must select the entire text box by clicking the border of the text box. Conversely, if you are applying commands from the Drawing Tools contextual tab, the text box must be active. The insertion point can be located in the text box or the entire text box can be selected by clicking the border of the text box.

Hands-On Exercise: Format a Text Box

1. Click the text box if not already selected.
2. Click the Format tab (Figure 5.50).
3. Click the More button in the Shape Styles group (Figure 5.50).
4. Click the Colored Outline—Black Dark, 1 option from the gallery (Figure 5.51).
5. Triple-click in the text to select all the text in the text box.
6. The Mini Toolbar displays. Click the Font Size arrow in the Mini Toolbar and select 36 .
7. Position the insertion point before the word *to*.
8. Press Enter , and the rest of the sentence moves to the next line.
9. Click the border of the text box to select it.
10. Click the Home tab.
11. Click the Center button to center the text.
12. Click the Format tab.
13. Type **1.5** in the Shape Height box in the Size group (Figure 5.52).
14. Type **7.5** in the Shape Width box in the Size group (Figure 5.52).
15. Click the Align button in the Arrange group (Figure 5.52).
16. Click Align Center to center the text box on the slide.
17. If necessary, drag the text box to the location as shown in **Figure 5.53**.
18. Click anywhere outside of the text box to deselect it.

Figure 5.50 More Button in Shape Styles Group

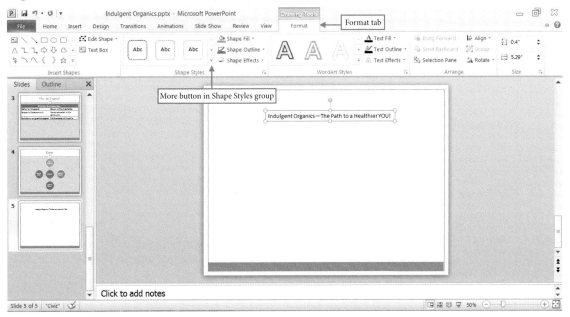

Figure 5.51 Shape Styles Gallery

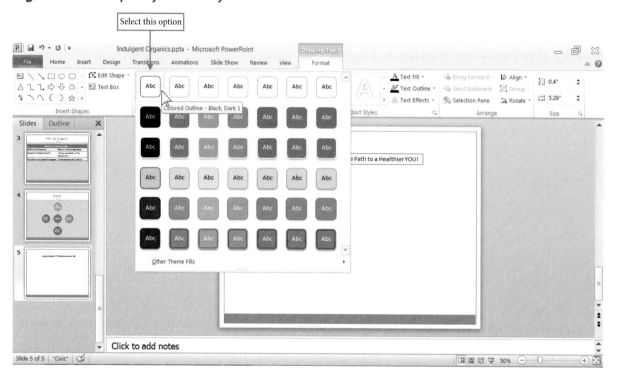

Figure 5.52 Modify Size and Alignment of a Text Box

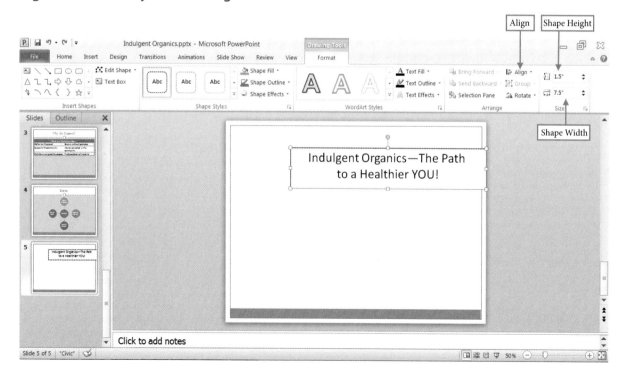

Figure 5.53 Text Box Aligned

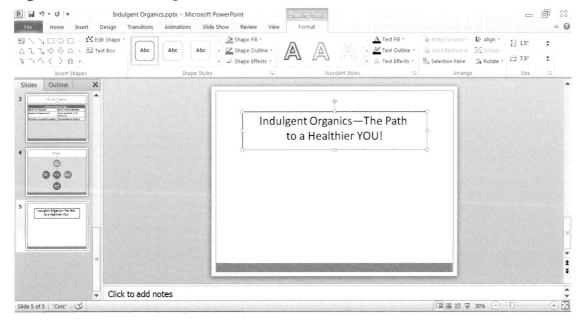

Insert a Hyperlink

A hyperlink, also known as a link, is an object that when clicked, navigates to another location. You can navigate to a file, a webpage, a place in the current presentation, or an email.

> Hyperlink (link): An object that, when clicked, navigates to another location.

Hyperlinks are active only when running a slide show. If the presentation contains a hyperlink to a webpage or to an email, the hyperlink will work only if you are connected to the Internet. A hyperlink to a webpage or email opens in a new window. Exit the window to return to the presentation or click the Microsoft PowerPoint 2010 icon in the taskbar.

If you link to another document, that link will work only if the document is located on the computer or network where the presentation is stored. Make certain to check your links before you present a slide show to an audience.

Use these steps to link to a webpage:

- Select the object or text that you want to link.
- Click the **Insert** tab.
- Click the **Hyperlink** button in the Links group, and the Insert Hyperlink dialog box displays (**Figure 5.54**).
- Click **Existing File or Web Page** from the Link to options.
- Type the URL in the Address box (Figure 5.54).
- Click **OK**.

Hands-On Exercise: Insert a Hyperlink

You will insert a text box of the slide that contains a hyperlink to a website.

1. Click the Insert tab.

2. Click Text Box .

③ Drag to create the text box in the right side of the slide.

④ Type **For more information**.

⑤ Triple-click on the words *For more information*.

⑥ Click the Font Size arrow from the Mini Toolbar and select 28 .

⑦ Click the Format tab in the Drawing Tools tab.

⑧ Type **1** in the Shape Height box.

⑨ Type **3** in the Shape Width box and press Enter .

⑩ Position the insertion point before the word *information* in the text box and press Enter . The word *information* is positioned on the next line.

⑪ Select the text *For more information* by dragging the mouse through the text.

⑫ Click the Insert tab.

⑬ Click Hyperlink in the Links group (Figure 5.54).

⑭ Click Existing File or Web Page in the Link to section (Figure 5.54).

⑮ Type **https://sites.google.com/site/indulgentorganics/** in the Address box (Figure 5.54).

⑯ Click OK .

⑰ If necessary, drag the text box to the location shown in **Figure 5.55**.

⑱ Click anywhere outside of the text box to deselect it.

Figure 5.54 Insert Hyperlink

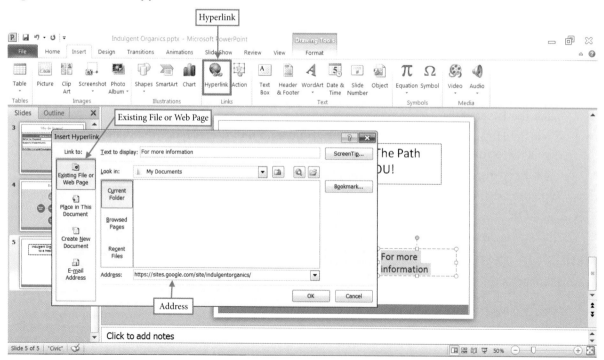

Figure 5.55 Hyperlink Inserted

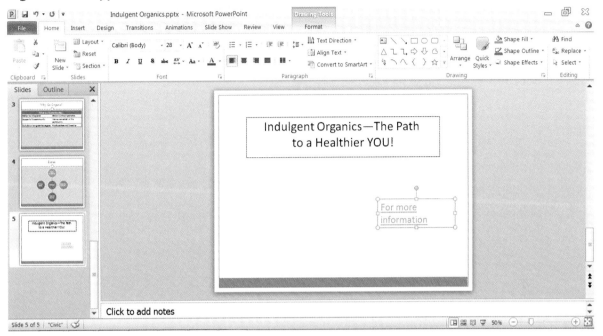

Link to a Slide in a Presentation

You can insert a hyperlink to navigate to a specific slide in a presentation.

Use these steps to link to a specific slide:

- Select the object or text that you want to link.
- Click the **Insert** tab.
- Click the **Hyperlink** button in the Links group, and the Insert Hyperlink dialog box displays.
- Click **Place in This Document** in the Link to section (**Figure 5.56**).
- Select the slide to which you want to hyperlink from the Select a place in this document list.
- Click **OK**.

Hands-On Exercise: Link to a Slide in a Presentation

① Click the Insert tab.

② Click Text Box .

③ Drag the mouse to create a text box in the lower right side of the slide under the For more information text box.

④ Type **Restart presentation**.

⑤ Position the insertion point before the word *presentation* and press Enter . The word *presentation* is positioned on the next line.

⑥ Select the text *Restart presentation*.

⑦ Click the Font Size arrow on the Mini Toolbar and select 28 .

⑧ Click the Format tab.

⑨ Type **1** in the Shape Height box.

⑩ Type **3** in the Shape Width box and press Enter .

⑪ Click the Insert tab.

⑫ Click Hyperlink .

⑬ Click Place in This Document in the Link to section.

⑭ Click First Slide in the Select a place in this document list (Figure 5.56).

⑮ Click OK .

Figure 5.56 Link to First Slide in Presentation

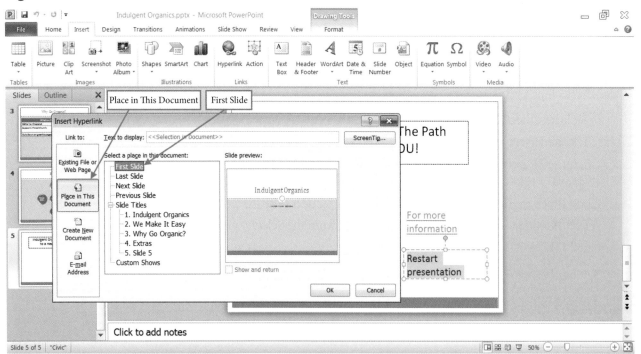

Hands-On Exercise: Format the Text Boxes

① Click the text box that reads *Restart presentation*.

② Hold the Shift key, and click the text box that reads *For more information*.

③ Click the Format tab.

④ Click the More button in the Shape Styles group and a gallery displays.

⑤ Click the Colored Outline—Black, Dark 1 option, which is the first option in the gallery.

⑥ Click anywhere outside of the text boxes to deselect them.

⑦ If necessary, drag the text boxes to the location shown in **Figure 5.57.**

Figure 5.57 Text Boxes Formatted

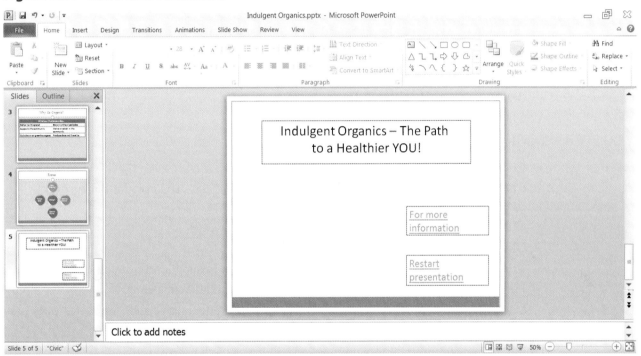

Hands-On Exercise: Open Hyperlinks in Slide Show

① Click the Slide Show tab.

② Click From Current Slide .

③ When the slide displays, click the first link, *For more information.* The webpage displays.

④ Click the Close button in the top right of the window to close the webpage.

⑤ Navigate back to the slide show.

⑥ Click the second link, *Restart presentation,* and the first slide displays.

⑦ Press Esc to exit the presentation.

Insert a Background

You can insert a background on a slide or apply it to the entire presentation. Adding a background is a great way to create a custom look for the presentation. You can insert a picture as a background, or you can insert a color, texture, or pattern as the background of a slide.

The Background Styles command allows you to select from various background styles for the theme.

Use these steps to insert a background style to the current slide:

- Click the **Design** tab.
- Click the **Background Styles** button in the Background group (**Figure 5.58**).
- Select a background style from the list.

Use these steps to insert a background style to the entire presentation:

- Click the **Design** tab.
- Click the **Background Styles** button in the Background group (Figure 5.58).
- Right-click a background style from the list.
- Click **Apply to All Slides**.

Use these steps to insert a picture as the background:

- Click the **Design** tab.
- Click the **Background dialog box launcher** (Figure 5.58). The Format Background dialog box displays.
- Click **Fill** in the left pane.
- Click **Picture or texture fill** in the right pane.
- Click the **File** button in the Insert from section. The Insert Picture dialog box displays.
- Locate the picture you want to use as the background and click **Insert**.
- Click **Close** to apply the picture as the background to the active slide, *or* click **Apply to All** to apply the picture as the background to all the slides.

Use these steps to insert a color, texture, or pattern as the background:

- Click the **Design** tab.
- Click the **Background dialog box launcher** (Figure 5.58). The Format Background dialog box displays.
- Click **Fill** in the left pane.
- Select any of these options in the right pane:
  - Click **Solid fill**, and then click the **Color** arrow to select a color for the background.
  - Click **Picture or texture fill**, and click the **Texture** arrow to select a texture for the background.
  - Click **Pattern fill**, and then select a pattern from the list. You can also select a foreground and background color for the slide.
- Click **Close** to apply the background to the active slide, or click **Apply to All** to apply the background to all the slides.

Use these steps to remove a background:

- Select the slides that contain the background you want to remove.
- Click the **Design** tab.

- Click the **Background Styles** button.
- Click **Style 1**, which is the first option in the gallery.

Hands-On Exercise: Insert a Background

You will open the picture called *Juneau,* which is one of the student data files provided with the textbook. The instructions for downloading the student data files are located in the preface of the textbook.

① Click the Design tab.

② Click the Background dialog box launcher (Figure 5.58). The Format Background dialog box displays.

③ Click Fill in the left pane, if it is not already selected (Figure 5.58).

④ Click the Picture or Texture fill option in the right pane (Figure 5.58).

⑤ Click the File button in the Insert from section (Figure 5.58). The Insert Picture dialog box displays (**Figure 5.59**).

⑥ Select the drive and folder where the student data files are located.

⑦ Click the picture titled *Juneau,* which is one of the student data files provided with the textbook (Figure 5.59).

⑧ Click Insert (Figure 5.59).

⑨ Click Close to apply the picture as the background to the active slide. The slide should resemble **Figure 5.60**.

⑩ Click the Save button on the Quick Access Toolbar.

Figure 5.58 Background Dialog Box Launcher

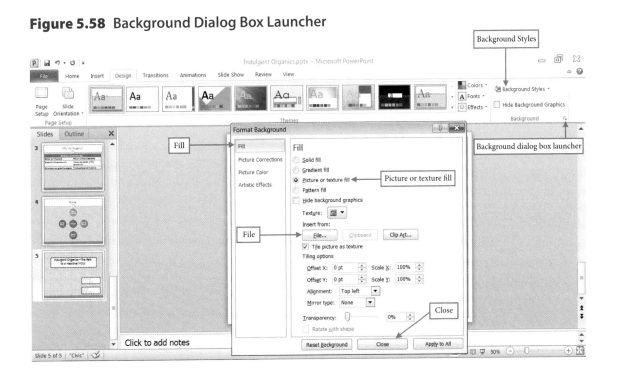

Figure 5.59 Insert Picture Dialog Box

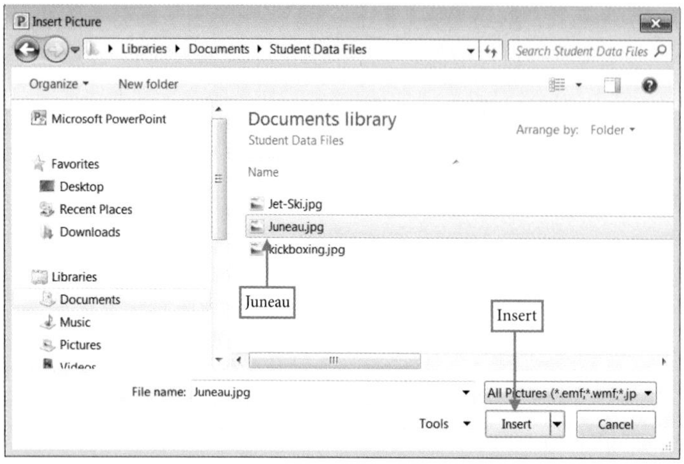

Figure 5.60 Picture Background Inserted on Slide

Apply a Slide Transition

> **Slide transition:** A motion effect that is applied when you navigate to another slide in a presentation.

A **slide transition** is a motion effect that is applied when you navigate to another slide in a presentation. Keep transitions simple and consistent throughout the presentation. When you apply a transition, a transition icon displays to the left of the slide in the Slides tab and at the bottom left of the slide in Slide Sorter view.

Use these steps to apply a slide transition:

- Select the slide(s) to which you want to apply a transition.
- Click the **Transitions** tab (**Figure 5.61**).
- Click the **More** button in the Transition to This Slide group (Figure 5.61). A gallery of transitions displays.
- Select a transition from the gallery.
- Click **Apply To All** in the Timing group to apply the transition to the entire presentation (Figure 5.61).

Use these steps to preview a slide transition:

- Navigate to the slide in which you want to preview the transition.
- Click the **Transitions** tab.
- Click **Preview** in the Preview group (Figure 5.61).

Use these steps to delete a slide transition:

- Select the slide(s) from which you want to delete a transition.
- Click the **Transitions** tab (Figure 5.61).
- Click the **None** option in the Transition to This Slide group.

Hands-On Exercise: Apply a Slide Transition

1. Click the Transitions tab (Figure 5.61).

2. Click the Fade option in the Transition to This Slide group (Figure 5.61). If the option is not displayed, click the More button in the Transitions to This Slide group to display the gallery, and select Fade .

3. Click Apply to All in the Timing group to apply the transition to the entire presentation (Figure 5.61). A transition icon displays to the left of the slide thumbnail in the Slides tab, which indicates that a transition has been applied (Figure 5.61).

4. Click the Preview button in the Preview group to preview the slide transition.

5. You want a more revealing transition so you will select a different option. Click the Split option in the Transitions to This Slide group.

6. Click the Preview button.

7. Click Apply to All .

Figure 5.61 Apply Slide Transition

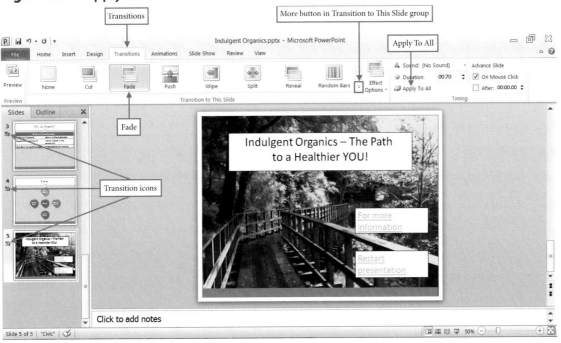

Apply Animation Effects

Animation effect:
The movement of objects on a slide, which displays during a slide show.

An **animation effect** is the movement of objects on a slide, which displays during a slide show. You can apply animation effects to text and objects, including pictures, clip art, shapes and text boxes. You use an animation effect to add interest or to emphasize an object on the slide. Animations can be set to play automatically when a slide displays or when the mouse is clicked.

When you apply an animation effect, a number displays next to the object, indicating that an animation has been applied. If you have two animations on one slide, the numbers represent the order in which the animations will display.

Use these steps to add an animation effect to an object:

- Select the object to animate.
- Click the **Animations** tab (**Figure 5.62**).
- Choose the desired animation effect in the Animation group, *or* click the **More** button in the Animation group to view the gallery and then select an animation effect from the gallery.

Use these steps to delete an animation effect:

- Select the object that contains the animation effect you want to delete.
- Click the **Animations** tab (Figure 5.62).
- Choose **None** from the Animation group.

Use these steps to preview the animation on a slide:

- Navigate to the slide that contains the animation you want to preview.
- Click the **Animations** tab.
- Click the **Preview** button in the Preview group.

Hands-On Exercise: Apply an Animation Effect

You will add animation effects to the SmartArt graphic and the Arrow shape.

1. Click Slide 4 in the Slides tab.
2. Click the SmartArt and the border is displayed.
3. Click the border of the SmartArt to select the entire object.
4. Click the Animations tab (Figure 5.62).
5. Click the More button in the Animation group (Figure 5.62).
6. Click Grow and Turn in the Entrance group (**Figure 5.63**). A number displays next to the SmartArt, indicating that animation has been applied to it (**Figure 5.64**).
7. If you want to preview the animation again, click the Preview button in the Preview group on the Animations tab (Figure 5.64).
8. Click Slide 2 in the Slides tab.
9. Click the arrow shape to display the border.
10. Click the arrow border to select the entire shape.

⑪ Click the More button in the Animation group.

⑫ Click Float in from the Entrance group. The number 1 displays to the left of the shape indicating that an animation effect was applied.

⑬ Click the Save button in the Quick Access Toolbar.

Figure 5.62 Animations Tab

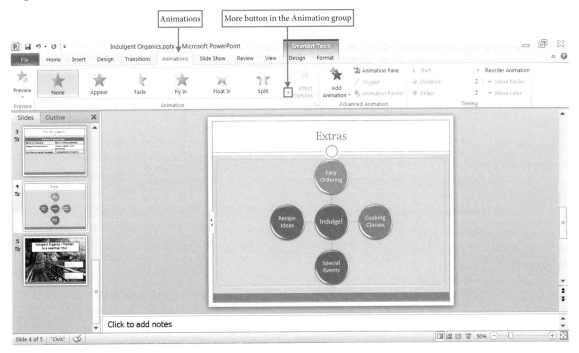

Figure 5.63 Animation Gallery

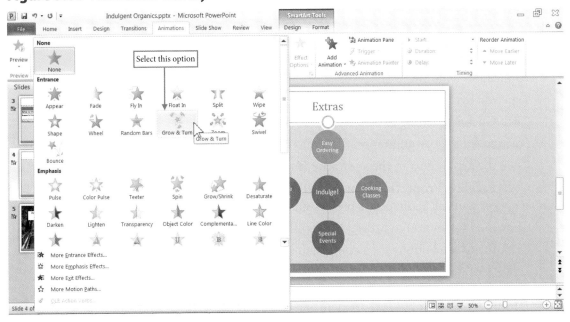

Figure 5.64 Preview Animation Effect

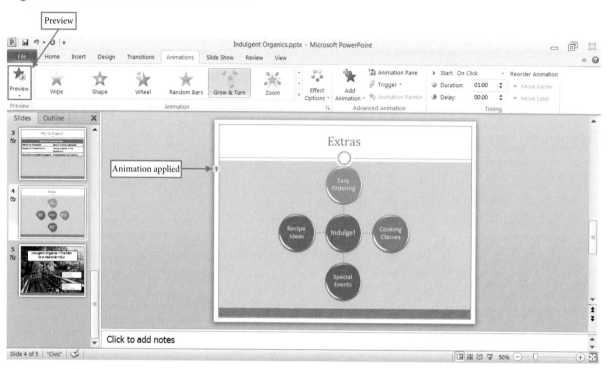

Insert Audio

You can insert audio clips to enhance the presentation. You can insert audio on one slide or on all slides. Be certain that the speakers are turned on if you are using audio in a presentation. You can insert an audio clip from a file or from the Clip Art audio files. You can also record an audio clip.

Use these steps to insert a Clip Art audio file:

- Navigate to the slide where you want to insert the audio file.
- Click the **Insert** tab.
- Click the **Audio** arrow in the Media group (**Figure 5.65**).
- Click **Clip Art Audio**, and the Clip Art task pane displays on the right side of the application window.
- Type what you are searching for in the Search for box.
- Click **Go**, and a listing of Clip Art audio files displays.
- Position the mouse pointer on the audio clip you want to insert into the presentation.
- Click the **arrow** next to the audio clip (Figure 5.65).
- Click **Preview/Properties** from the list (**Figure 5.66**). The Preview/Properties dialog box displays, and the audio clip is previewed (**Figure 5.67**).
- Click the **Play** button to preview the audio clip (Figure 5.67).
- Click the **Close** button when completed to close the Preview/Properties dialog box (Figure 5.67).
- Click the audio clip to insert it in the slide. A picture of a speaker displays in the slide (**Figure 5.68**). This indicates that an audio file has been added to the slide.

Hands-On Exercise: Insert an Audio Clip

① Click Slide 5 to make it the active slide.

② Click the Insert tab.

③ Click the Audio arrow in the Media group (Figure 5.65).

④ Click Clip Art Audio , and the Clip Art task pane displays.

⑤ Type **birds singing** in the Search for box.

⑥ Click Go .

⑦ Position the mouse pointer on the *Birdie Chirps* audio clip and an arrow displays to the right of the audio clip (Figure 5.65).

⑧ Click the arrow and select Preview/Properties from the list (Figure 5.66). The Preview/ Properties dialog box displays, and the audio clip is previewed (Figure 5.67).

⑨ If you cannot hear the audio clip, make certain your speakers are turned on. Click the Play button to preview the audio clip (Figure 5.67).

⑩ Click the Close button to close the Preview/Properties dialog box (Figure 5.67).

⑪ Click the audio file called Birdie Chirps to insert it in the slide.

⑫ Close the Clip Art task pane. The audio clip icon, which resembles a picture of a speaker, displays on the slide (**Figure 5.68**).

Figure 5.65 Insert Audio

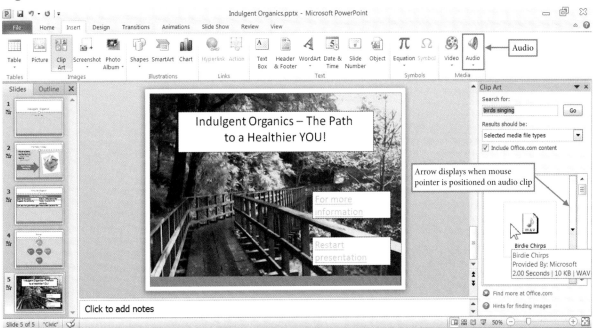

Figure 5.66 Preview/Properties

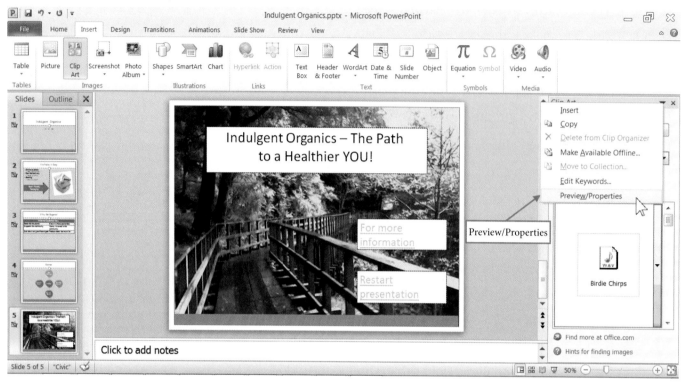

Figure 5.67 Preview/Properties Dialog Box

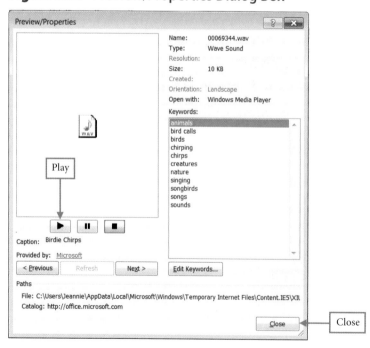

Figure 5.68 Audio File Inserted

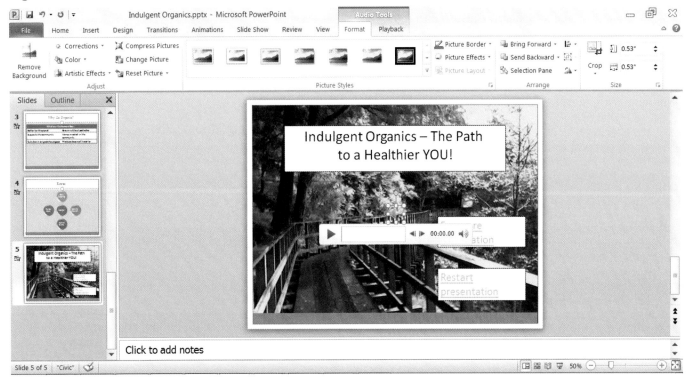

Apply Audio Options

When you insert audio or when an audio clip is selected, the Audio Tools contextual tab displays, which contain commands to modify the settings of the audio clip. There are several options you can select to play an audio clip:

- *Automatically* plays the audio clip automatically when a slide is displayed.
- *On Click* plays the audio clip when you click the mouse.
- *Play across slides* plays the audio clip throughout the presentation.

Use these steps to set an audio clip to start automatically:

- Click the **audio clip icon** (**Figure 5.69**).
- Click the **Playback** tab in the Audio Tools tab (Figure 5.69).
- Click the **Start** arrow, and choose **Automatically** (Figure 5.69).

Use these steps to hide an audio clip icon during the slide show:

- Click the **audio clip icon**.
- Click the **Playback** tab (Figure 5.69).
- Click the **Hide During Show** checkbox (Figure 5.69).

Use these steps to preview an audio clip on the slide:

- Click the **audio clip icon**.
- Click the **Play** button beneath the audio clip icon, *or* click the **Play** button in the Preview group on the Playback tab (Figure 5.69).

Use these steps to delete an audio clip on the slide:

- Click the **audio clip icon**.
- Press **Delete**.

Hands-On Exercise: Apply Audio Options

① Click the audio clip icon if it is not already selected (Figure 5.69).

② Click the Playback tab (Figure 5.69).

③ Click the Start arrow and choose Automatically (Figure 5.69).

④ Click the Hide During Show checkbox (Figure 5.69).

⑤ Click the Play button in the Preview group to preview the audio file (Figure 5.69).

Figure 5.69 Audio Options

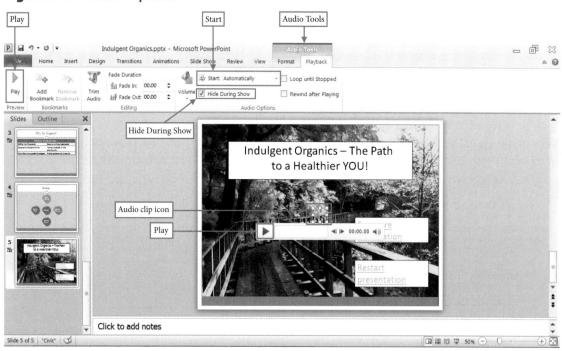

Add Notes to the Notes Pane

Notes pane: An area in Normal view used to add speaker notes to each slide.

The Notes pane is an area in Normal view used to add speaker notes to each slide (**Figure 5.70**). You can print the notes so you can use them during your presentation. The notes do not display when the presentation is running.

Use these steps to insert notes on a slide:

- Click the **Notes pane** at the bottom of the slide in Normal view and type your notes (Figure 5.70).

Hands-On Exercise: Add Notes to the Notes Pane

① Click Slide 1 in the Slides tab.

② Point to the border between the slide and notes pane. The sizing arrow displays (Figure 5.70). Drag up slightly to view more of the Notes pane.

③ Type the following in the Notes pane (Figure 5.70):

Welcome the audience and introduce yourself.

④ Click Slide 2 .

⑤ Type the following in the Notes pane:

We make customer service a priority. We also pride ourselves on our small carbon footprint. All of our packaging is 100% recyclable.

⑥ Click Slide 3 .

⑦ Type the following in the Notes pane:

Here are just a few reasons our customers prefer Indulgent Organics.

⑧ Click Slide 4 .

⑨ Type the following in the Notes pane:

If you are new to the organic craze, we have everything you need!

⑩ Click Slide 5 .

⑪ Type the following in the Notes pane:

Mention this presentation at our store and receive a free sample of fresh-squeezed orange juice.

Figure 5.70 Insert Notes in Notes Pane

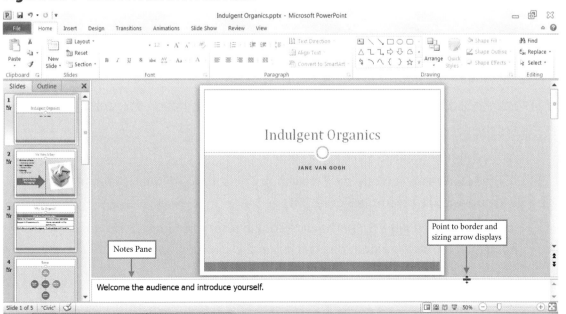

Headers and Footers

Header: Text that displays in the top margin of a slide or printed page.

Footer: Text that displays in the bottom margin of a slide or printed page.

Headers and footers can be inserted into a presentation. A **header** is text that displays in the top margin of a slide or printed page. A **footer** is text that displays in the bottom margin of a slide or printed page. A header and/or footer can be inserted to the notes or handouts. Only a footer can be inserted on a slide.

Use these steps to insert a footer on a slide:

- Click the **Insert** tab.
- Click **Header & Footer** in the Text group, and the Header & Footer dialog box displays (**Figure 5.71**).
- Click the **Slide** tab.
- Select the footer options (Figure 5.71):
  - Click the **Date and Time** checkbox to insert the date and time in the footer.
  - Click the **Slide number** checkbox to insert the slide number in the footer.
  - Click the **Footer** checkbox, and type the text you want to display in the footer, in the Footer box.
  - Click the **Don't show on title slide** checkbox to remove the footer from the title slide.
- Click **Apply to All** to apply the footer to the entire presentation, *or* click **Apply** to apply the footer on the current slide only.

Hands-On Exercise: Insert Footer on Slides

① Click Slide 2 .

② Click the Insert tab.

③ Click Header & Footer in the Text group and the Header and Footer dialog box displays (Figure 5.71).

④ Click the Slide tab if it is not already selected.

⑤ Click the Date and Time checkbox.

⑥ Click Update Automatically if it is not already selected. This automatically inserts the current date and time to the slides.

⑦ Click the Slide number checkbox to insert the slide number on the footer.

⑧ Click the Footer checkbox.

⑨ Type **Indulgent Organics** in the Footer box.

⑩ Click the Don't show on title slide checkbox. The settings in the Header and Footer dialog box should resemble Figure 5.71.

⑪ Click Apply to All (Figure 5.71). The slide should resemble **Figure 5.72**. Notice in this Theme that the slide number displays in the circle at the top of the slide and the footer displays at the bottom of the slide.

⑫ Click Slide 1 . Notice that the footer does not display.

Figure 5.71 Header and Footer Dialog Box

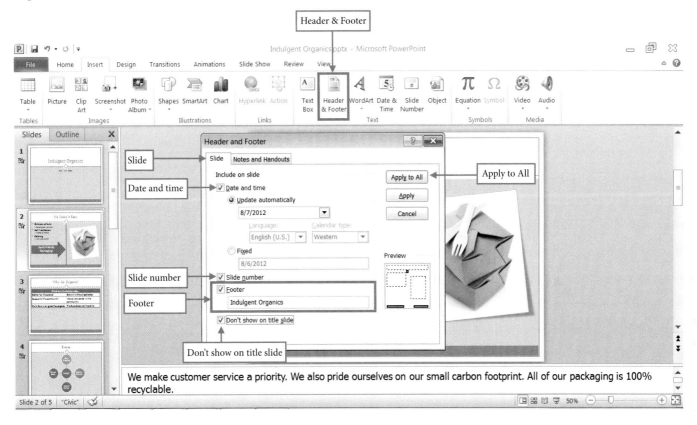

Figure 5.72 Footer Inserted

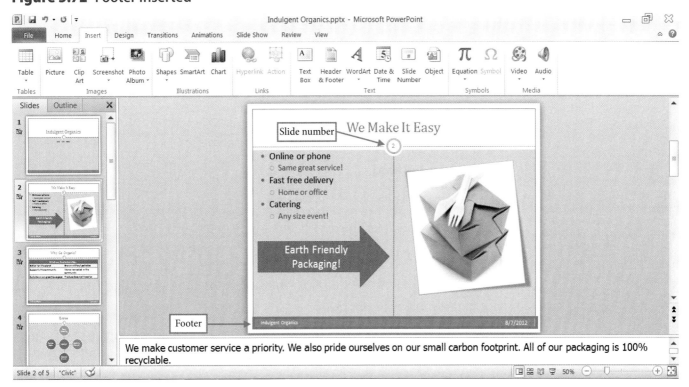

Use these steps to insert a header or footer on the notes pages or handouts:

- Click the **Insert** tab.
- Click **Header & Footer** in the Text group, and the Header and Footer dialog box displays (**Figure 5.73**).
- Click the **Notes and Handouts** tab (Figure 5.73).
- Select the header and footer options (Figure 5.73):
  - Click the **Date and time** checkbox to insert the date and time.
  - Click the **Header** checkbox and type the text you want to display in the header, in the Header box.
  - Click the **Page number** checkbox to insert the page number.
  - Click the **Footer** checkbox and type the text you want to display in the footer, in the Footer box.
- Click **Apply to All** to apply the header and footer to all the notes pages and handouts.

Hands-On Exercise: Insert Header and Footer on the Notes Pages and Handouts

1. Click the Insert tab.
2. Click Header & Footer in the Text group.
3. Click the Notes and Handouts tab (Figure 5.73).
4. Click the Date and time checkbox.
5. Click the Update automatically option, if it is not already selected. This will automatically insert the current date and time on the printed pages.
6. Click the Header checkbox.
7. Type **Indulgent Organics** in the Header box.
8. Click the Page number checkbox, if not already selected.
9. Click the Footer checkbox.
10. Type **Jane Van Gogh** in the Footer box. The settings in the Header and Footer dialog box should resemble Figure 5.73.
11. Click Apply to All . The header and footer will display when you print the notes pages or handouts.

Figure 5.73 Insert Header and Footer on Notes and Handouts

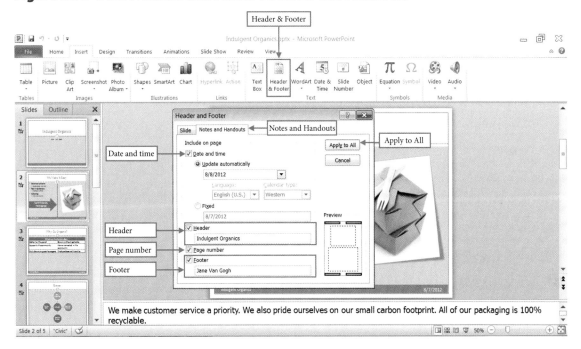

Review, Proof, and Finalize Presentation

Once you finished creating the presentation, you should review the text, objects, and formatting of each slide to ensure they are correct and appropriate. Check the size, position, and format of all text and objects on the slide such as clip art, pictures, shapes, SmartArt, WordArt, text boxes, etc.

Besides checking the spelling of the presentation, you should review the text carefully to ensure the formatting, capitalization and grammar of the text is correct and appropriate. Microsoft PowerPoint 2010 does not check for grammar errors so you must carefully review the presentation and correct all errors that you find.

Hands-On Exercise: Check Spelling Review and Proof Presentation, and Run Slide Show

Now that the presentation has been completed, you will check the presentation for errors and then run the slide show.

1. Click the Review tab.

2. Click the Spelling button in the Proofing group, and the Spelling dialog box displays. Make any corrections needed.

3. Review each slide and correct any grammar, capitalization, or formatting errors that you find.

4. Click Slide 2 .

5. There should be a hyphen between the text *Earth* and *Friendly* in the shape. Position the insertion point before the word Friendly.

⑥ Press Backspace .

⑦ Type - to insert a hyphen.

⑧ Click Slide 3 .

⑨ The first letter of the word *our* in the first row of the table should be capitalized. Position the insertion point before the letter o in the word our.

⑩ Press Delete .

⑪ Type O .

⑫ Click Save on the Quick Access Toolbar.

⑬ Click the Slide Show tab.

⑭ Click the From Beginning button.

⑮ Click through the presentation. Be certain to click the hyperlinks on the last slide.

⑯ Press Esc to exit the slide show when completed.

⑰ Navigate to Slide 1.

Print Presentation

In this exercise, you will print the handouts. You can select the numbers of slides to print on each page of the handouts.

Hands-On Exercise: Print Handouts

① Click the File tab.

② Click Print .

③ Click the Full Page Slides button, which is the third option under Settings.

④ Click 2 Slides in the Handouts group (**Figure 5.74**). A preview of the handouts displays on the right. The header and footer also displays in the preview.

⑤ Click Print .

Print in Grayscale

Grayscale: A series of shades of black and white used to display the text and graphics in the presentation.

You can print your presentation in grayscale. **Grayscale** is a series of shades of black and white used to display the text and graphics in the presentation. Use the grayscale option if you are printing the presentation on a black-and-white printer or if you are making transparencies.

Use these steps to print in grayscale:

- Click the **File** tab.
- Click **Print**.
- Click the **Color** button in the Print settings.
- Click **Grayscale** (**Figure 5.75**).

Figure 5.74 Print Handouts

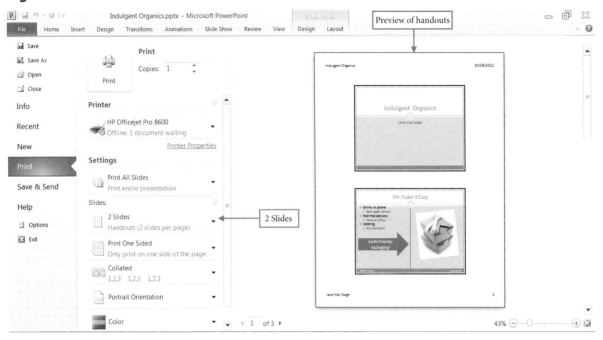

Figure 5.75 Print Grayscale

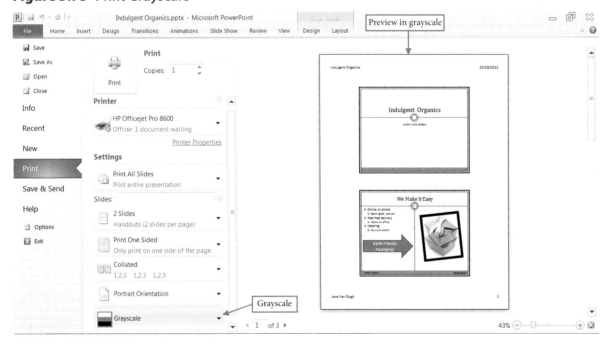

Print Notes Pages

Finally, you will print the notes pages, to which you can refer during your presentation. Notes pages print one slide per page, with the notes below each slide.

Hands-On Exercise: Print Notes Pages

① Click the File tab.

② Click Print .

③ Click the 2 Slides button.

④ Click Notes Pages (**Figure 5.76**).

⑤ Click Print .

Figure 5.76 Print Notes Pages

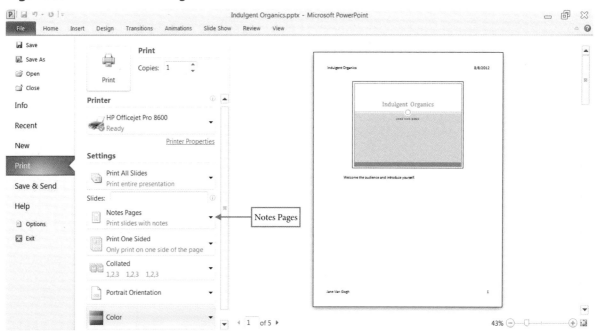

Hands-On Exercise: Exit Application

① Click the **Save** button on the Quick Access Toolbar.

② Click the File tab.

③ Click Exit to exit Microsoft PowerPoint 2010.

Multiple-Choice Questions

1. You can modify theme _____.

    a. Colors

    b. Fonts

    c. Names

    d. A and B

2. You can search clip art by all the following media types *except* _____.
   a. Illustrations
   b. Photographs
   c. Shapes
   d. Audio

3. When you crop a picture, you _____.
   a. Remove parts of the picture
   b. Add a color scheme to the picture
   c. Increase the size of the picture
   d. Change the location of the picture

4. To crop all four sides of a picture at the same time, you _____.
   a. Press and hold the Ctrl key while dragging the cropping handle from any side of the border
   b. Press and hold the Ctrl key while dragging the cropping handle from any corner
   c. Press and hold the Shift key while dragging the cropping handle from any corner
   d. Press and hold the Shift key while dragging the cropping handle from any side of the border

5. A _____ is a graphic that displays lists, processes, and diagrams.
   a. Text Box
   b. Shape
   c. SmartArt
   d. WordArt

6. A _____is a motion effect that is applied when you navigate to another slide in a presentation.
   a. Slide transition
   b. Animation effect
   c. Slide Show
   d. Grayscale

7. To select multiple nonadjacent slides, select the first slide; then hold the _____ key and click the other slides.
   a. Shift
   b. Ctrl
   c. Alt
   d. Esc

8. A hyperlink can _____.
   a. Link to a webpage
   b. Link to another slide in the presentation
   c. Link to an email address
   d. All of the above

9. The Outline pane displays _____ on each slide.
   a. Text, backgrounds, and graphics
   b. Graphics only
   c. Text only
   d. Text and graphics

10. Animation effects display in which view?
   a. Slide Show view
   b. Outline view
   c. Slide Sorter view
   d. Normal view

Project #1: Create a Presentation for an Animal Shelter

You will create a presentation for the Tender Care Animal Shelter. You will insert the picture called *dog1*, which is one of the student data files provided with the textbook. The instructions for downloading the student data files are given in the preface of the textbook.

① Open Microsoft PowerPoint 2010.

② Type **Tender Care Animal Shelter** in the title placeholder.

③ Delete the subtitle placeholder.

④ Select Style 7 as the background style.

⑤ Insert the picture called *dog1*, which is one of the student data files provided with the textbook.

⑥ Change the height of the picture to 2.5.

⑦ Move the picture so it is located under the title placeholder and is centered.

⑧ Insert a Clip Art audio clip of a dog barking. Select the *Yappy Dog* audio clip. Hide the audio clip icon during the slide show. Set the audio clip to start automatically.

⑨ Apply the Fly In animation effect to the *dog1* picture.

⑩ Save your presentation as **Tender Care Animal Shelter**.

⑪ Insert a new slide with a Title and Content layout.

⑫ Type **Who We Are** in the title placeholder.

⑬ Type the following in the bulleted list:
   • **Provide shelter and care for homeless animals**
   • **Provide homes for animals through our adoption program**

⑭ Insert the clip art of a dog, named *Portrait of two terrier dogs*. If you are unable to find this clip art, you can select a different one.

⑮ Change the height of the clip art to 2.5.

⑯ Move the clip art to the lower center of the slide under the bullets.

⑰ Apply the Fly In animation effect to the clip art.

⑱ Insert a new slide with a Title and Content layout.

⑲ Type **Pet Adoption Fees** in the title placeholder.

⑳ Insert a table with two columns and seven rows.

㉑ Type the following text in the table:

Animal	Adoption Fee
Birds	$40
Cats	$75
Dogs	$100
Ferret	$75
Hamster	$80
Guinea Pig	$15

㉒ Apply the Medium Style 1-Accent 1 style as the table style.

㉓ Insert a new slide with a Two-Content layout.

㉔ Type **Adoption Process** as the title placeholder.

㉕ Type the following text in the left pane:

- **Complete adoption application**
- **Adoption fees include:**
- **Neutering/spay surgery**
- **Rabies shot**
- **Collar**
- **Leash**
- **Tag**
- **Microchip**

㉖ Indent the bullets from Neutering/spay surgery through Microchip.

㉗ Insert a clip art of a dog, named *Couple walking dog in park*, in the right placeholder. If you are unable to find this clip art, you can select a different one.

㉘ Apply the Bevel Rectangle picture style.

㉙ Apply the Fly In animation effect to the clip art.

㉚ Insert a new slide with a Title and Content layout.

㉛ Type **Donations Needed** in the title placeholder.

③② Type the following text in the bullets:

- **Animal shampoo**
- **Blankets and towels**
- **Food**
- **Grooming brushes**
- **Leashes**
- **Litter boxes**
- **Nail clippers**
- **Toys**
- **Treats**

③③ Insert a 7-Point Star (sixth option in the Stars and Banners group) on the right side of the slide.

③④ Type **Thank you!** in the shape.

③⑤ Change the height and width of the shape to 4.

③⑥ Change the shape style to Subtle Effect-Black, Dark 1.

③⑦ Change the font size of the text to 28.

③⑧ Bold the text.

③⑨ Change the font color to Blue in Standard Colors.

④⓪ Move the shape so it resembles **Figure 5.77**.

④① Insert a new slide with a Title and Content layout.

④② Type **Volunteers Needed** in the title placeholder.

④③ Insert a Vertical Box List SmartArt graphic on the slide. This option is in the List group.

④④ Type the following in the placeholders in the SmartArt graphic.

Dog Walkers

Groomers

Feed and Play with Animals

④⑤ Change the colors of the SmartArt graphic to Colorful Range-Accent Colors 5 to 6 from the Colorful group.

④⑥ Add a footer to the handouts with the text **Tender Care Animal Shelter** and include the page number in the footer.

④⑦ Add a Split transition to all slides in the presentation.

④⑧ Check the spelling of the presentation.

④⑨ Save the presentation. The presentation should resemble Figure 5.77.

⑤⓪ Run the slide show.

⑤① Print the handouts as 4 Slides Horizontal.

Figure 5.77 Completed Presentation

Project #2: Create a Presentation for a Student Orientation

You will create a student orientation presentation for Deerfield Community College.

① Open Microsoft PowerPoint 2010.

② Type **Deerfield Community College** in the title placeholder.

③ Type **Student Orientation** in the subtitle placeholder.

④ Select Pushpin as the theme.

⑤ Save your presentation as **Deerfield Community College**.

⑥ Insert a new slide with a Title and Content layout.

⑦ Type **Mission Statement** in the title placeholder.

⑧ Type the following text in the bulleted list:

- **Provide students with the knowledge and skills needed to be successful in their career and lives**
- **Promote lifelong learning**
- **Provide academic excellence**

⑨ Insert the clip art of a student, named *Young adult students in class*. If you are unable to find this clip art, you can select a different one.

⑩ Change the height of the picture to 2.

⑪ Apply the Wheel animation effect to the clip art.

⑫ Move the clip art to the lower-right corner of the slide.

⑬ Insert a new slide with a Title and Content layout.

⑭ Type **Orientation Agenda** in the title placeholder.

⑮ Insert a table with two columns and eight rows.

⑯ Type the following text in the table:

Time	Description
8:30 a.m. – 9:00 a.m.	Welcome by the President
9:00 a.m. – 9:30 a.m.	Presentation by academic advising staff
9:30 a.m. – 10:00 a.m.	Presentation by financial aid staff
10:00 a.m. – 10:30 a.m.	Presentation by library staff
10:30 a.m. – 12:00 p.m.	Pick up schedule, purchase textbooks, take photo ID
12:00 p.m. – 1:00 p.m.	Lunch
1:00 p.m. – 3:00 p.m.	Tour of the college

⑰ Apply the Medium Style 3-Accent 6 style to the table.

⑱ Insert a new slide with a Two Content layout.

⑲ Type **College Facts** in the title placeholder.

⑳ Type the following in the left placeholder:

- **20,000 students**
- **8,000 full-time students**
- **12,000 part-time students**
- **375 faculty members**
- **50 degree programs**
- **Day, evening, weekend, and online classes**

㉑ Indent the second and third bullets to the right.

㉒ Insert the clip art of a college, named *University campus in Wismar*, in the right place-holder. If you are unable to find this clip art, you can select a different one.

㉓ Add the Swivel animation effect to the clip art.

㉔ Insert a new slide with a Title and Content layout.

㉕ Type **Departments** in the title placeholder.

㉖ Insert a Block Cycle SmartArt graphic on the slide. This option is in the Cycle group.

㉗ Type the following in the placeholders in the SmartArt graphic:

Academic Advising

Admissions

Bookstore

Library

Career Services

㉘ Change the colors of the SmartArt to Colorful Range-Accent Colors 4 to 5 from the Colorful group.

㉙ Insert a new slide with a Blank layout.

㉚ Insert WordArt with the Fill-Ice Blue, Text 2, Outline-Background 2 style which is the first option in the gallery.

㉛ Type **Stay focused** and press **Enter**.

㉜ Type **on your goal!** on the next line.

㉝ Move the WordArt to the upper center part of the slide, as shown in **Figure 5.78**.

㉞ Insert the clip art of a graduation cap, named *Graduation cap and blue rays*. If you are unable to find this clip art, you can select a different one.

㉟ Change the height of the Clip Art to 3.

㊱ Move the clip art to the bottom center of the slide.

㊲ Add the Grow & Turn animation effect to the clip art.

㊳ Insert a Clip Art audio clip of a clapping sound. Select the *Claps and Cheers* audio clip. Hide the audio clip icon during the slide show. Set the audio clip to start automatically.

㊴ Add a footer to the slides with the text **Deerfield Community College**, and include the slide number in the footer. Do not show the footer on the title slide. Apply the footer to all the slides.

㊵ Apply the Dissolve transition to all slides in the presentation.

㊶ Check the spelling of the presentation.

Figure 5.78 Completed Presentation

㊷ Save the presentation. The presentation should resemble Figure 5.78.

㊸ Run the slide show.

㊹ Print the presentation as Full Page Slides.

Project #3: Create a Presentation for a Bank

JCK Bank & Trust is opening a new branch. You will create a presentation about the bank for prospective customers, which will be presented on their opening day.

① Open Microsoft PowerPoint 2010.

② Select Apothecary as the theme.

③ Type **JCK BANK & TRUST** in the title placeholder.

④ Type **PAUL DIAMOND, CEO** in the subtitle placeholder.

⑤ Save your presentation as **JCK Bank**.

⑥ Insert a new slide with a Title and Content layout.

⑦ Type **ABOUT US** in the title placeholder.

⑧ Type the following text in the bulleted list:

- **Founded in 1971**
- **Full-service financial institution**
- **Locations throughout Illinois**

⑨ Insert the clip art of a bank building, named *banking, banking industry, banks*. If you are unable to find this clip art, you can select a different one.

⑩ Change the height of the picture to 3.

⑪ Apply the Appear animation effect to the clip art.

⑫ Move the clip art to the bottom center of the slide.

⑬ Add the following notes to the slide:

JCK Bank & Trust was founded in 1971. It started as a small bank in Chicago, IL, and has expanded into a full-service financial institution.

⑭ Insert a new slide with a Two-Content layout.

⑮ Type **SERVICES** in the title placeholder.

⑯ Type the following in the left placeholder and indent the bullets as shown below:

- **Bank Accounts**
  - **Checking**
  - **Savings**
  - **Money Market**

- **Certificate of Deposit**
- **Loans**
  - ◦ **Home**
  - ◦ **Commercial**
  - ◦ **Line of Credit**
- **Financial Advisors**
- **Safety Deposit Box Rentals**

⑰ Insert the clip art of a bank teller, named *bank tellers, banking, banks*, in the right place-holder. If you are unable to find this clip art, you can select a different one.

⑱ Add the Bounce animation effect to the clip art.

⑲ Add the following note to the slide:

We provide a variety of services to our customers. We have also expanded our services for our commercial customers.

⑳ Insert a new slide with a Title and Content layout.

㉑ Type **LOCATIONS** in the title placeholder.

㉒ Insert a Vertical Curved List SmartArt graphic to the slide. This option is in the List group.

㉓ Type the following in the placeholders in the SmartArt graphic:

Chicago, IL

Lemont, IL

Palos Park, IL

㉔ Change the colors of the SmartArt to Colorful Range-Accent Colors 5 to 6 from the Colorful group.

㉕ Add the following note to the slide:

We have three locations throughout Illinois, with Chicago being our main branch.
We are going to expand to other locations in the southwest suburbs in the next year.

㉖ Insert a new slide with a Title and Content layout.

㉗ Type **INTEREST RATES** in the title placeholder.

㉘ Insert a table with two columns and five rows.

㉙ Type the following text in the table:

Loan Type	Interest Rate
15-year home loan	3.00%
30-year home loan	4.00%
Commercial loan	4.50%
Line of credit	2.25%

30. Apply the Medium Style 2-Accent 5 table style to the table.

31. Add the following note to the slide:

    We have competitive interest rates on our loans. Please speak to a loan officer for more information about our loans.

32. Insert a new slide with a Blank layout.

33. Insert the wave shape from the Stars and Banners group.

34. Type **We are here to serve your banking needs!**

35. Change the font size of the text to 28.

36. Bold the text.

37. Change the height of the shape to 2 and the width to 6.

38. Apply the Light 1 Outline, Colored Fill-Gray–50%, Accent 1 shape style.

39. Move the WordArt to the center of the slide, as shown in **Figure 5.79**.

40. Navigate to Slide 3.

41. Create a hyperlink on the word *Loans* that navigates to Slide 5.

42. Insert a header on the notes and handouts with the text **JCK Bank & Trust**.

43. Apply the Ripple transition to all slides in the presentation.

44. Check the spelling of the presentation.

45. Save the presentation. The presentation should resemble Figure 5.79.

46. Run the slide show.

47. Print the note pages.

Figure 5.79 Completed Presentation

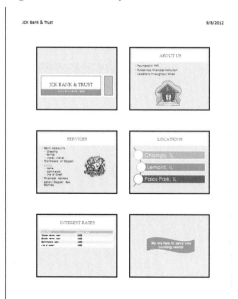

Create Workbooks Using Microsoft Excel 2010

6

Chapter Objectives

After completing this chapter, you will be able to do the following:

- Identify Microsoft Excel 2010 components.
- Enter and modify data in a worksheet.
- Navigate within a worksheet.
- Copy, cut, paste, and move cells.
- Modify column and row settings.
- Calculate totals.
- Apply formatting to cells.
- Display formulas.
- Save and print a workbook.

Microsoft Excel 2010 is a spreadsheet application used to organize, manipulate, and chart data. Microsoft Excel 2010 can be used to track income and expenses, perform mathematical calculations, and analyze data to make informed decisions.

In this chapter, you will become acquainted with various components of Microsoft Excel 2010. You will create a workbook, modify column and row settings, and calculate totals. Additionally, you will format the workbook to give it a professional appearance.

Identify Microsoft Excel 2010 Components

You will open Microsoft Excel 2010 and get acquainted with its components.

Hands-On Exercise: Launch Microsoft Excel 2010

(1) Click the Start button.

(2) Click All Programs .

(3) Click Microsoft Office . You may need to scroll through the Start menu to locate the folder.

(4) Click Microsoft Excel 2010 .

(5) A new blank workbook displays (**Figure 6.1**).

Figure 6.1 Microsoft Excel 2010 Workbook

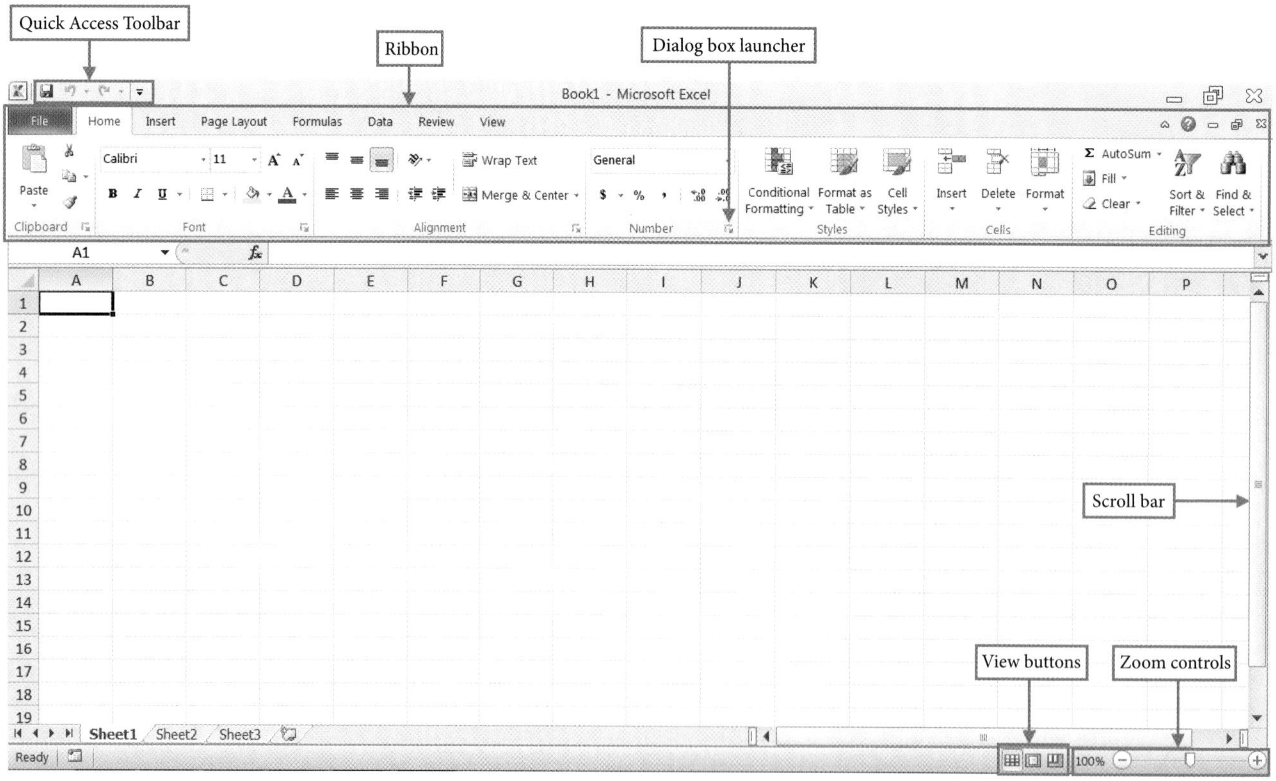

Table 6.1 illustrates many common elements and key terms used in Microsoft Office 2010 applications.

Table 6.1 Common Microsoft Office 2010 Elements and Key Terms

Common Element	Description
Backstage view	The Backstage view contains commands to manage your workbooks such as creating, opening, saving, and printing. Click the **File tab** to open the Backstage view.
Command	A command is a button or text that performs an action or task.
Dialog Box	A dialog box is a window that allows a user to perform commands or apply settings. A dialog box displays when the dialog box launcher is clicked. A dialog box launcher is a button that resembles a diagonal arrow, which displays to the right of a group name on the Ribbon (Figure 6.1).
Mini Toolbar	The Mini Toolbar displays when text is selected and contains formatting commands that can be applied to the selected text. The Mini Toolbar displays at the top right of the selected text and appears faded or dimmed.
Quick Access Toolbar	The Quick Access Toolbar provides access to the most frequently used commands. By default, the Quick Access Toolbar is located at the left corner of the title bar (Figure 6.1).
Ribbon	The Ribbon contains all the commands needed to create and edit a workbook. The Ribbon is located below the title bar and contains tabs that are organized by groups of related commands (Figure 6.1). Seven tabs display by default at the top of the Ribbon, starting with the Home tab. The File tab is not considered part of the Ribbon.
Scroll bar	A scroll bar allows the user to navigate either up and down or left and right to view the information in a worksheet.
Shortcut menu	A shortcut menu displays when the user right-clicks an object or area of the window. It contains a list of commands related to the object.
Status bar	The status bar provides information about the status of the workbook. The status bar is located at the bottom of the application window.
Title bar	The title bar displays the name of the file that is currently open and the name of the application. The title bar is the top bar on the application window.
ToolTip (ScreenTip)	A ToolTip (ScreenTip) lists the name of the command and sometimes includes a brief description of the command. A ToolTip displays when the mouse hovers, or points to, a command. It may also display *keyboard shortcuts* that can be used to initiate the command using the keyboard.
View buttons	The View buttons provide options for viewing the workbook. The View buttons are located on the right side of the status bar (Figure 6.1). By default, the workbook opens in Normal view.
Zoom controls	The Zoom controls control the magnification of the workbook. It allows the user to zoom in and out of specific areas in the workbook. The Zoom controls are located on the right side of the status bar (Figure 6.1).

Backstage view: Contains commands to manage your workbooks such as creating, opening, saving, and printing.

Command: A button or text that performs an action or task.

Dialog box: A window that allows a user to perform commands or apply settings. A dialog box displays when the dialog box launcher is clicked.

Dialog box launcher: A button that resembles a diagonal arrow, which displays to the right of a group name on the Ribbon.

Mini Toolbar: Contains formatting commands that can be applied to the selected text. The Mini Toolbar displays at the top right of the selected text and appears faded or dimmed.

Quick Access Toolbar: Provides access to the most frequently used commands. By default, the Quick Access Toolbar is located at the left corner of the title bar.

Ribbon: Contains all the commands needed to create and edit a workbook. The Ribbon is located below the title bar and contains tabs that are organized by groups of related commands.

Scroll bar: Allows a user to navigate either up and down or left and right to view the information in a worksheet.

Shortcut menu: A menu that displays when the user right-clicks an object or area of the window. It contains a list of commands related to the object.

Status bar: Provides information about the status of the workbook. The status bar is located at the bottom of the application window.

Title bar: Displays the name of the file that is currently open and the name of the application. The title bar is the top bar on the application window.

ToolTip (ScreenTip): Lists the name of the command and sometimes includes a brief description of the command. A ToolTip displays when the mouse hovers, or points to, a command.

View buttons: Provides options for viewing the workbook. The View buttons are located on the right side of the status bar.

Zoom controls: Controls the magnification of the workbook. It allows the user to zoom in and out of specific areas in the workbook. The Zoom controls are located on the right side of the status bar.

Workbook: Contains a collection of worksheets used to organize information.

Worksheet: A page in a workbook.

Sheet: A page in a workbook.

Formula Bar: A horizontal bar located below the Ribbon. It displays the contents of the active cell.

Column headings: Identify the columns in the worksheet.

Row headings: Identify the rows in the worksheet. The row headings are numbered sequentially and start with row 1.

Cell: The intersection of a row and column.

Active cell: The cell that has a black border around it. When you enter data in the worksheet, the data is placed in the active cell.

When you open Microsoft Excel 2010, an empty workbook displays. A **workbook** contains a collection of **worksheets**, or **sheets**, used to organize information. A worksheet contains rows and columns that resembles a ledger. Although workbooks and spreadsheets are sometimes used interchangeably, a spreadsheet is actually the type of software program used to create a Microsoft Excel 2010 workbook. A workbook is similar to a notebook that has many pages. Each page in a workbook is called a *worksheet,* or *sheet.* Three sheets are shown by default in a workbook (**Figure 6.2**). Additional sheets can be inserted into a workbook and sheets can be deleted.

The **Formula Bar** is the horizontal bar located below the Ribbon (Figure 6.2). Below the Formula Bar are the column headings. The **column headings** identify the columns in the worksheet (Figure 6.2). The column headings contain the alphabet. The first column is column A, the second column is B, the third column is C, continuing through column Z. After column Z, the column headings are labeled with two letters of the alphabet, starting with AA, AB, and so on. After column ZZ, the column headings are labeled with three letters of the alphabet, starting with AAA. The last column is XFD. The **row headings** identify the rows in the worksheet (Figure 6.2). The row headings are numbered sequentially and start with row 1. There are a maximum of 1,048,576 rows on a worksheet.

The intersection of a row and column is called a **cell**. Notice below column A, the cell has a black border around it (**Figure 6.3**). This is called the **active cell**. When you enter data in the worksheet, the data is placed in the active cell. You can insert text, numbers, or formulas

Figure 6.2 Microsoft Excel 2010 Components

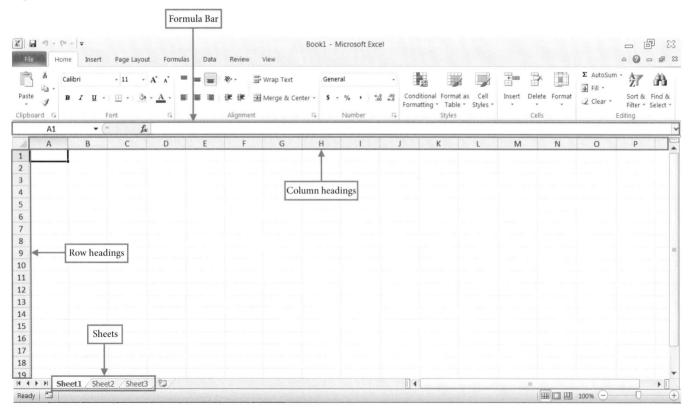

Figure 6.3 Active Cell

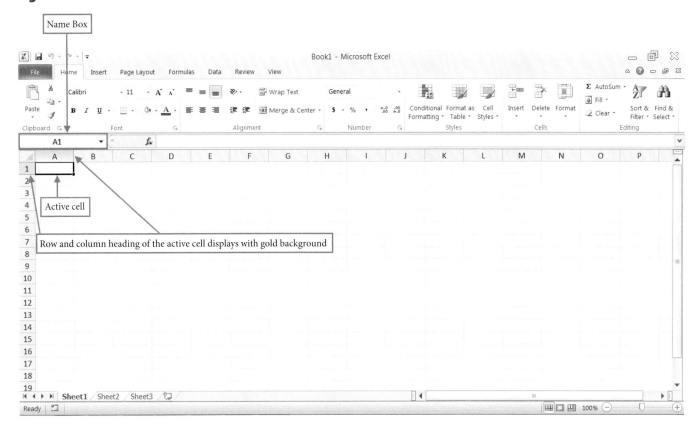

into a cell. If you navigate to another cell, that cell becomes the active cell. You can tell which column and row contains the active cell because the column and row headings display with a gold background (Figure 6.3).

Each cell has a **cell address**, which is also called a **cell reference**. The cell address indicates the location of the cell in the worksheet. It is the column letter followed by the row number of the cell. When referencing the cell address, you can use either uppercase or lowercase letters to identify the column. The name of the active cell in Figure 6.3 is A1 or a1.

The cell address of the active cell displays in the **Name Box** on the Formula Bar (Figure 6.3). To navigate to a cell in the worksheet, type the cell address in the Name Box and press **Enter**. The cell address in the Name Box becomes the active cell.

Navigation Techniques

You can use the mouse or keyboard to navigate within the worksheet. Clicking in a cell will make it the active cell. Press **Enter** to move down to the next row in the current column. Press **Tab** to move to the right of the active cell.

When you navigate a worksheet using the mouse, the mouse pointer may change shape and size, depending on your position within the workbook. When you move around in the cells of a worksheet, the mouse pointer displays as a block plus sign. The mouse pointer displays as an arrow when pointing to the commands on the Ribbon. **Table 6.2** displays various ways to navigate within a worksheet.

Cell address (cell reference): Indicates the location of the cell in the worksheet. The cell address is the column letter followed by the row number of the cell.

Cell reference (cell address): Indicates the location of the cell in the worksheet. The cell reference is the column letter followed by the row number of the cell.

Name Box: The area on the Formula Bar that contains the cell address of the active cell.

Table 6.2 Navigation Techniques

Key	Navigation
Home	Navigates to column A of the current row.
Ctrl + Home	Navigates to the beginning of the worksheet.
Ctrl + End	Navigates to the last cell in worksheet that contains data.
Arrows	Navigates up, down, right, and left.
Tab	Navigates to the cell to the right of the active cell.
Shift + Enter	Navigates to the cell above the active cell.
Enter	Navigates to the cell below the active cell.
Page Up	Navigates up one screen of the worksheet.
Page Down	Navigates down one screen of the worksheet.

Hands-On Exercise: Navigate the Worksheet

1. Press Enter and the active cell is A2 as displayed in the Name Box (**Figure 6.4**).
2. Click cell F6 to make it the active cell. *F6* displays in the Name Box.
3. Press Home , and the active cell is A6.
4. Type **D3** in the Name Box and press Enter . The active cell is D3.
5. Press Ctrl + Home , and the active cell is A1.

Figure 6.4 Navigating the Worksheet

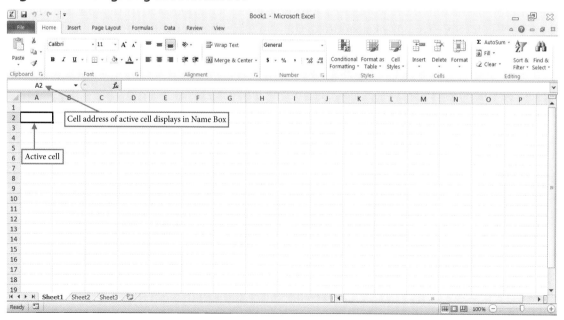

Enter Text in a Worksheet

When you enter text in a cell, the text is automatically left-aligned. The text displays in the Formula Bar and in the cell while you are typing. The Formula Bar contains the Name Box, Cancel button, Enter button, Insert Function button, and displays the contents of the active cell. The Cancel and Enter buttons are available on the Formula Bar only when entering or editing data in a cell. The Cancel button clears the contents from the cell (**Figure 6.5**). This is useful if you make a mistake while typing. The Enter button stores the data in a cell (**Figure 6.5**). The Insert Function button will be discussed in another chapter.

Use these steps to enter text in a cell:

- Click the cell to make it the active cell.
- Type the text.
- Press the **Enter** key on the keyboard or click the **Enter** button on the Formula Bar (Figure 6.5).
  - If you press the Enter key, the cell one row down becomes the active cell.
  - If you press the Enter button on the Formula Bar, the current cell remains as the active cell.
  - Example: If you are in cell A1 and you enter text and then press the Enter key, A2 becomes the active cell. If you were to click the Enter button instead, A1 would remain as the active cell.

After you enter text in a cell, you can also use the arrow keys to navigate to another cell. If you are entering data in a cell and want to cancel the entry, you can click the **Cancel** button on the Formula Bar.

Cancel button: Clears the contents from the cell. The button is located on the Formula Bar and is available only if data is being entered or modified in a cell.

Enter button: Stores the data in a cell. The button is located on the Formula Bar and is available only if data is being entered or modified in a cell.

Hands-On Exercise: Enter Text in a Worksheet

1. Click cell A1 if it is not the active cell.

2. Type **My Household Budget** and press Enter . The text displays in cell A1 but overlaps through cells B1 and C1. You can tell if text overlaps to other cells because the cell borders do not display around the entire cell. Notice that you cannot see the cell borders of cells B1 and C1. This overlapping occurred because cell A1 is not wide enough to display all the text so it had to wrap to the adjacent cells.

3. Click cell A3 .

4. Type **Expenses** (do not press Enter). Notice that the text displays in the cell and in the Formula Bar (Figure 6.5).

5. Click the Cancel button on the Formula Bar, and the text is removed from the cell (Figure 6.5).

6. Type **Expenses** in cell A3 (do not press Enter).

7. Click the Enter button on the Formula Bar (Figure 6.5). Cell A3 is still the active cell.   →

⑧ Type the following text into the cells: (**Figure 6.6**)

a. Cell A4: **Electric**   e. Cell A8: **Insurance**

b. Cell A5: **Gas**   f. Cell A9: **Cable**

c. Cell A6: **Phone**   g. Cell A10: **Total**

d. Cell A7: **Rent**   h. Cell B3: **January**

Figure 6.5 Formula Bar

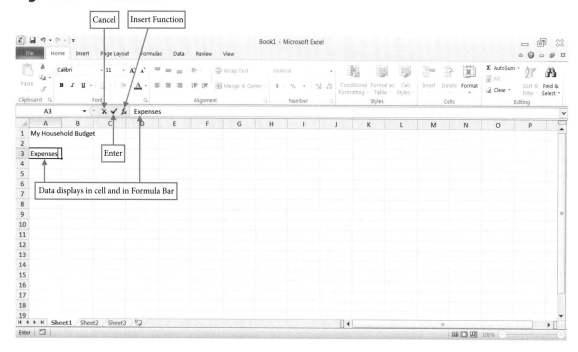

Figure 6.6 Text Entered in Worksheet

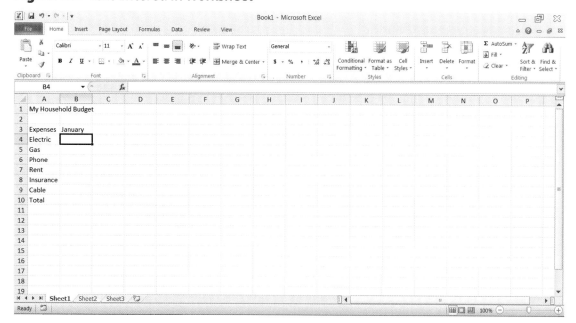

Enter Numbers in a Worksheet

When you enter numbers into a cell, the numbers are automatically right-aligned. When you enter numbers in a worksheet, do not include dollar signs or commas. Do not include a decimal point or decimal places if the decimals are zero. If you want the cell to contain $1,000.00, you should enter 1000 in the cell. If you want the cell to contain $50.10, you should type 50.10 in the cell. Microsoft Excel 2010 contains various formatting options that you can apply to numbers and formulas. This is discussed later in the chapter.

Hands-On Exercise: Enter Numbers in a Worksheet

You will enter the expense amounts for January.

(1) Type **100** in cell B4 and press Enter .

(2) Type **50** in cell B5 and press Enter .

(3) Enter the remaining expenses in the following cells. The worksheet should resemble **Figure 6.7**.

    a. Cell B6: **75.50**

       • The cell displays as *75.5*. Microsoft Excel 2010 automatically deletes trailing zeros. You can format the cells to display a specific number of decimal places. (This is discussed later in this chapter.)

    b. Cell B7: **800**

    c. Cell B8: **40.25**

    d. Cell B9: **80**

Figure 6.7 January Expenses

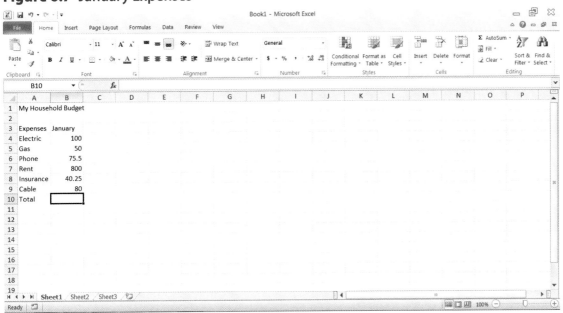

Edit and Delete Cell Contents

There are several ways to edit data in cells.

Use any of the following methods to edit data in a cell:

- Click the cell to edit. Retype the correct information, and press **Enter** on the keyboard.
- Click the cell to edit. Retype the correct information, and click the **Enter** button on the Formula Bar.
- Click the cell to edit. Press **F2**. The insertion point is positioned at the end of the data in the cell. The word *Edit* displays on the status bar indicating you can edit the cell. Make any corrections to the cell contents and press **Enter** *or* click the **Enter** button on the Formula Bar.
- Click the cell to edit. The cell contents display in the Formula Bar. Click in the Formula Bar, make the corrections, and press **Enter** *or* click the **Enter** button on the Formula Bar.
- Double-click the cell to edit. The insertion point displays in the cell. Make the necessary corrections, and press **Enter**.

Use any of the following methods to delete data from a cell:

- To delete the entire contents of a cell:
  - Click the cell and press the **Delete** key.
- To delete part of the contents of a cell:
  - Click the cell.
  - Position the insertion point to the left or right of the character(s) you want to delete.
  - Press the **Delete** or **Backspace** key.
    - Delete: deletes the character to the right of the insertion point.
    - Backspace: deletes the character to the left of the insertion point.

Do not use these methods to delete an entire row or column from a worksheet. That is discussed later in the chapter.

Hands-On Exercise: Edit and Delete Cell Contents

1. Click cell A6 .

2. Press F2 , and the insertion point displays at the end of the cell.

3. Type **s** at the end of the word *Phone*.

4. Move the insertion point to the beginning of the cell by pressing the Home key, clicking before the letter *P*, or using the left arrow key.

5. Type **Tele**.

6. Next you need to delete the capital letter *P* and replace it with a lowercase *p*. Make certain the insertion point is located before the letter *P*. Press Delete to remove the capital letter *P*.

⑦ Type **p**.

⑧ Press Enter . You cannot view the entire text, *Telephones*, in the cell. This happened because the column width is too small to fit the entire text. It cannot overlap to the next cell (cell B6) because data is already in that cell. You will learn how to adjust the column size later in the chapter.

⑨ You will change the text in cell A7. Type **Mortgage** in cell A7 and press the right arrow to navigate to cell B7.

⑩ The contents of cell B7 displays in the Formula Bar. Click in the Formula Bar and change the number to **825**. Press Enter .

⑪ Double-click cell B9 . The insertion point is in the cell.

⑫ Change the number to **85**. Press Enter .

⑬ Click cell A1 .

⑭ Press the Delete key. The content in cell A1 is deleted.

⑮ Click the Undo button on the Quick Access Toolbar to undo the deletion (**Figure 6.8**). The worksheet should resemble Figure 6.8.

Figure 6.8 Modified Cell Contents

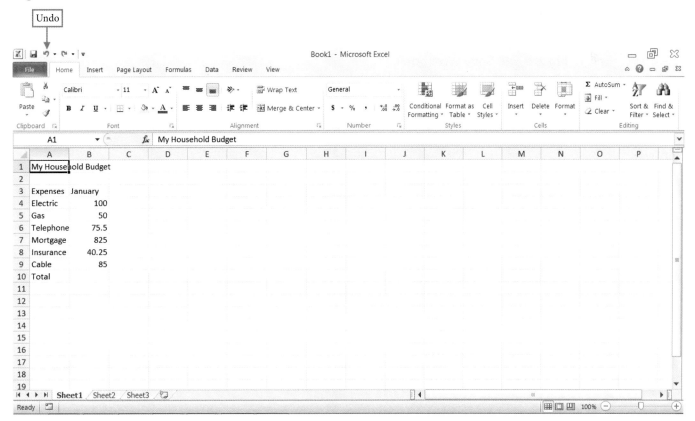

Save a Workbook

The name of the workbook displays on the title bar. It currently displays as *Book1—Microsoft Excel*. Once you save the workbook, *Book1* will be replaced with the new file name. The file extension *xlsx* will automatically be inserted at the end of the file name. The file extension may or may not display on the title bar. It depends on your computer settings.

Use any of these methods to save a workbook:

- Click the **Save** icon on the Quick Access Toolbar (**Figure 6.9**).
- Click the **File** tab and then click **Save** or **Save As**.
- Press **Ctrl + S**.

Remember to save your workbook periodically so you do not lose your work.

Hands-On Exercise: Save a Workbook

1. Click the Save icon on the Quick Access Toolbar and the Save As dialog box displays (Figure 6.9)

2. Select the location where you want to save the workbook in the left pane.

3. Type **Household Budget** in the File name box (Figure 6.9).

4. Click Save . The title bar states *Household Budget .xlsx - Microsoft Excel*.

Figure 6.9 Save Workbook

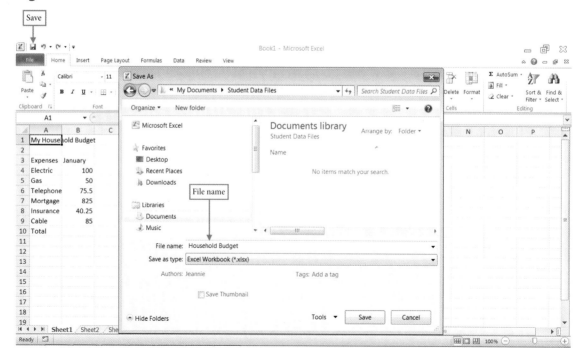

Select Cells

You may need to select cells in a worksheet in order to apply formatting, apply a command, or to move or copy cells. Two or more adjacent cells in a worksheet are considered a **range**. A range is identified by the starting cell, followed by a colon, followed by the ending cell. If you want to select the cells B1, B2, B3, the range would be written as B1:B3. The cell before the colon (B1) indicates the first cell in the range and the cell after the colon (B3) indicates the last cell in the range. **Table 6.3** illustrates how to select various cells on a worksheet. When selected, a black border will appear around the range of cells.

Range: Two or more adjacent cells in a worksheet. A range is identified by the starting cell, followed by a colon, followed by the ending cell.

Table 6.3 Selection Techniques

Task	Steps
Select a cell	• Click the cell.
Select a range of cells	• Position the mouse pointer in the middle of the first cell and a block plus sign displays. • Drag the mouse across the entire range.
Select a large range of cells	• Click the first cell in the range. • Press and hold the **Shift** key and click the last cell in the range.
Select the row	• Click the row heading.
Select the column	• Click the column heading.
Select the entire worksheet	• Press **Ctrl + A** *or* click the **Select All** button, which is located above row heading 1 and to the left of column heading A (**Figure 6.10**).
Select multiple adjacent rows or columns	• Drag the mouse through the column or row headings you want to select.
Select multiple nonadjacent rows or columns	• Press and hold the **CTRL** key while you click the row or column headings.

Hands-On Exercise: Select Cells

① Click the Select All button to select the entire worksheet.

② You will select the cells from B3 through B9, which is the range B3:B9. Click cell B3 .

③ Position the mouse pointer in the middle of the cell, and a block plus sign displays (Figure 6.10).

④ Drag the mouse all the way to cell B9 to select all the January expenses (**Figure 6.11**). Notice that there is a black border around the range that is selected.

⑤ Click cell A1 .

⑥ You will use the Name Box to select the range of cells from A3 through A9. Type
A3:A9 in the Name Box (**Figure 6.12**).

⑦ Press Enter and the cells in the range are selected. A black border is displayed around
the cells.

⑧ Press Ctrl + Home to navigate to cell A1.

Figure 6.10 Select All Button and Block Plus Sign

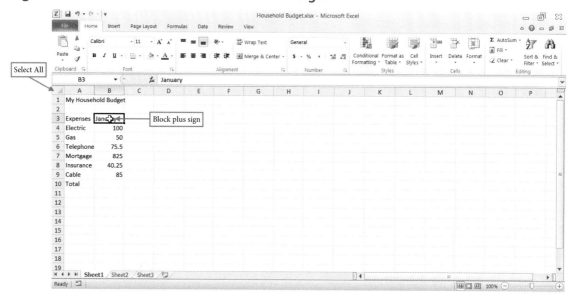

Figure 6.11 Range Selected

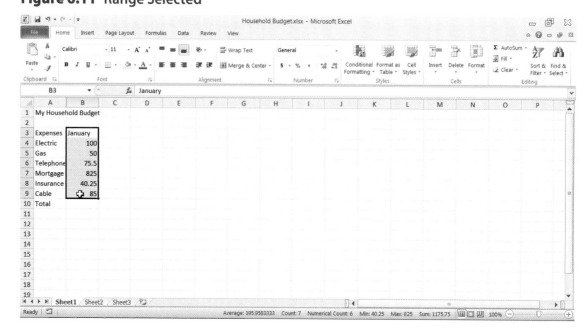

Figure 6.12 Enter Range in Name Box

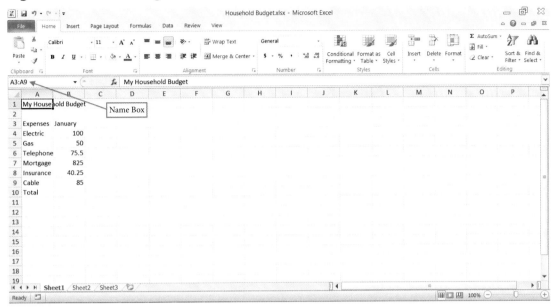

Copy, Cut, Paste, and Move Cell Contents

You can easily cut, copy, and paste cells in the workbook. These commands are available in the Clipboard group on the Home tab. These commands can also be accessed by right-clicking a cell and selecting the commands from the shortcut menu. When you cut or copy cells, they are stored on the **Clipboard**. The Clipboard holds up to 24 items that have been cut or copied. The Clipboard can be accessed by clicking the Clipboard dialog box launcher on the Home tab. You can also move cells to a different location in the workbook. **Table 6.4** describes how to move, copy, cut, and paste cells.

Clipboard: Holds up to 24 items that have been cut or copied

Table 6.4 Move, Cut, Copy, and Paste Commands	
Task	**Steps**
Move cell contents by dragging	• Click the cell you want to move.
	• Point to a cell border and a four-headed arrow displays.
	• Drag the cell to a new cell location.
	If you move the cell to a cell that contains data, a dialog box displays and asks if you want to replace the contents of the destination cells.
Move cell contents by using the Cut command	• Click the cell you want to move.
	• Click the **Cut** button in the Clipboard group on the Home tab (**Figure 6.13**). A blinking dashed border displays around the cell.
	• Click the new cell location.
	• Click the **Paste** button in the Clipboard group on the Home tab.
Copy/paste cell contents	• Click the cell you want to copy.
	• Click the **Copy** button in the Clipboard group on the Home tab (Figure 6.13). A blinking dashed border displays around the cell.
	• Click the cell where you want to paste the information.
	• Click the **Paste** button in the Clipboard group on the Home tab (Figure 6.13).

Table 6.4 *continued*	
Task	Steps
Paste cells using the Clipboard	• Click the **Clipboard dialog box launcher** (Figure 6.13) and the Clipboard displays on the left side of the application window. • Click the cell where you want to paste the information. • Click the item that you want to paste in the Clipboard, and it is inserted into the cell.

Table 6.5 displays the shortcut keys to access these commands.

Table 6.5 Keyboard Shortcuts	
Command	Keyboard Shortcuts
Cut	Ctrl + X
Copy	Ctrl + C
Paste	Ctrl + V

When you paste cells, the Paste Options button displays to provide you with special options for pasting cells (**Figure 6.14**). Some of the common paste options are listed in **Table 6.6**.

Table 6.6 Paste Options	
Paste Option	Description
Paste	Pastes both the cell contents and format of the cell.
Values	Pastes the value in the cell only. The format of the cell is not copied.
Formatting	Pastes the cell formatting only; the cell contents are not copied.

Hands-On Exercise: Move, Copy, and Paste Cells

1. Click cell B8 . You will move the contents of the cell to cell C8.
2. Point to the cell border, and a four-headed arrow displays.
3. Drag the cell to C8 , and the cell content moves to cell C8.
4. You will copy cell C8 to cell B8. Click the Copy button in the Clipboard group on the Home tab (Figure 6.13). Cell C8 contains a blinking dashed line around its cell border, indicating the cell is selected for copying.
5. Click cell B8 .
6. Click the Paste button in the Clipboard group on the Home tab (Figure 6.13). Do not press the Paste arrow. Click directly on the Paste button. The Paste Options button automatically displays below the cell that was copied (Figure 6.14). The Paste Options button

displays options on how to paste the information into the cell. The available options that display depend on the type and format of the content you are pasting.

(7) Press the Esc key on the keyboard to remove the highlight from cell C8 and to remove the Paste Options button.

(8) Click cell C8 and press Delete . The worksheet should resemble **Figure 6.15**.

(9) Click Save on the Quick Access Toolbar.

Figure 6.13 Clipboard Commands

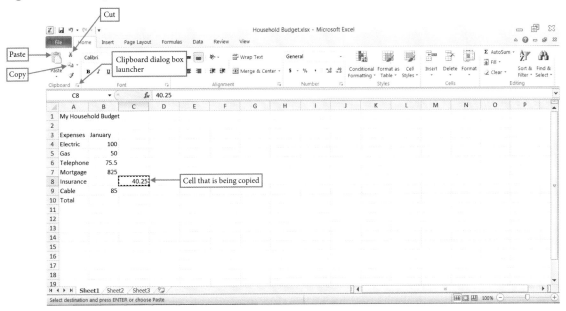

Figure 6.14 Paste Options Button

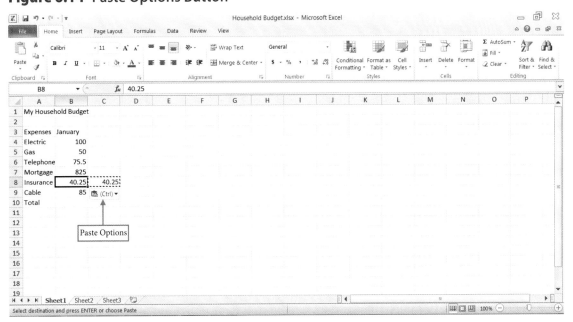

Figure 6.15 Delete Contents of Cell C8

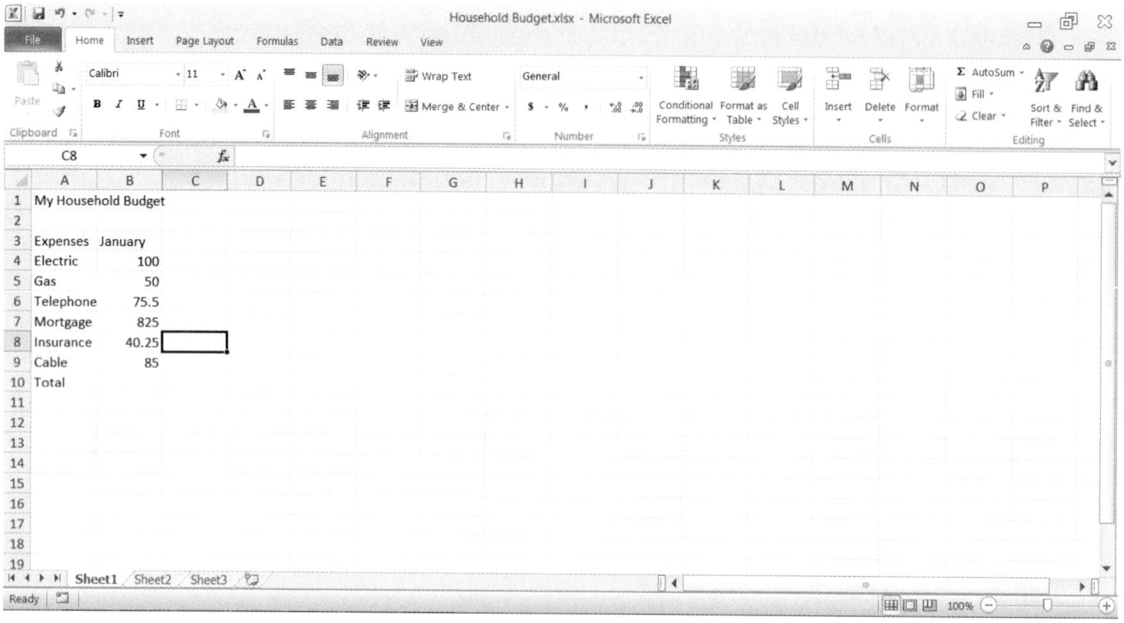

Fill Handle

Fill handle: Used to copy or fill data to other cells. The fill handle is located at the lower-right corner of a cell and resembles a small black square.

The **fill handle** is used to copy or fill data to other cells. The fill handle is located at the lower-right corner of a cell and resembles a small black square (**Figure 6.16**). When you point to the fill handle, the mouse pointer changes to a black plus sign (**Figure 6.17**).

Use these steps to copy or fill data to other cells using the fill handle:

- Select the cell or range of cells that you want to copy.
- Point to the fill handle (Figure 6.16), which is located at the lower-right corner of the cell, and the mouse pointer changes to a black plus sign (Figure 6.17). If you selected a range of cells to copy, point to the fill handle of the last cell in the range.
- Drag the fill handle across the cells that you want to fill.

Series: A list of text, values, dates, or times that contain a pattern such as the months of the year, days of the week, or numbers in a sequence.

A **series** is a list of text, values, dates, or times that contain a pattern such as the months of the year, days of the week, or numbers in a sequence. Once Microsoft Excel 2010 recognizes a pattern, the fill handle can be used to automatically fill the rest of the series.

Use these steps to create a series:

- Type the starting value(s) for the series in the worksheet.
- Select the cell(s) that contain the starting values.
- Point to the fill handle (Figure 6.16), which is located at the lower-right corner of the cell, and the mouse pointer changes to a black plus sign (Figure 6.17).
- Drag the fill handle across the cells to fill the series. The AutoFill Options button displays next to the series and contains options to change how the selection is filled or copied.

If you want to create a list of the months, you need to enter the first month in a cell. Next, drag the fill handle to complete the rest of the months. To create a series that lists the numbers 1 through 10, you enter the two starting values in adjacent cells. Then select both cells and drag the fill handle to complete the series.

Microsoft Excel 2010 recognizes the following series:

- Months
- Days
- Quarters (for example, quarter 1, quarter 2)
- Numbers in a pattern (you must enter the first two numbers in the series and select both numbers to complete the series)
  - Example: 1, 2, 3, 4, 5
  - Example: 10, 20, 30 40, 50
  - Example: 100, 90, 80, 70, 60, 50

Hands-On Exercise: Use the Fill Handle to Create a Series and to Copy Cells

You will enter the next two months in the worksheet. Instead of typing the months, you will use the fill handle to complete the series.

① Click cell B3 .

② Point to the fill handle (Figure 6.16) located at the lower-right corner of the cell. The mouse pointer changes to a black plus sign (Figure 6.17).

③ Drag the fill handle through cell D3 and release the mouse. The series is created. Cell C3 contains the month *February* and cell D3 contains the month *March* (**Figure 6.18**).

④ The Auto Fill Options button displays next to the series (Figure 6.18). The Auto Fill Options button allows you to change how the selection is filled or copied. Point to the Auto Fill Options button and a arrow displays.

⑤ Click the Auto Fill Options arrow (**Figure 6.19**).

⑥ Click Copy Cells . The contents of cell B3, which is *January*, is copied to the rest of the selection instead of the series of months.

⑦ Point to the Auto Fill Options button, and a arrow displays.

⑧ Click the Auto Fill Options arrow.

⑨ Click Fill Series . The selection displays the series of months: *January, February, and March*.

⑩ Next you will copy the expenses from January to the months of February and March. Position the mouse pointer in the middle of cell B4.

⑪ When the block plus sign appears, drag the mouse through cell B9 to select the cells. The selected cells have a border around them.

⑫ Drag the fill handle from cell B9 through cell D9. The expenses are copied to February and March (**Figure 6.20**).

Figure 6.16 Fill Handle

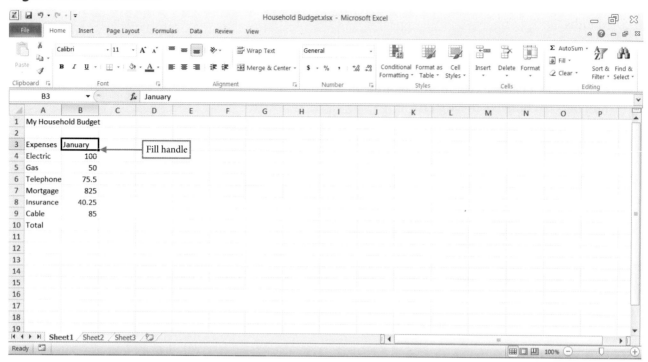

Figure 6.17 Mouse Pointer Changes

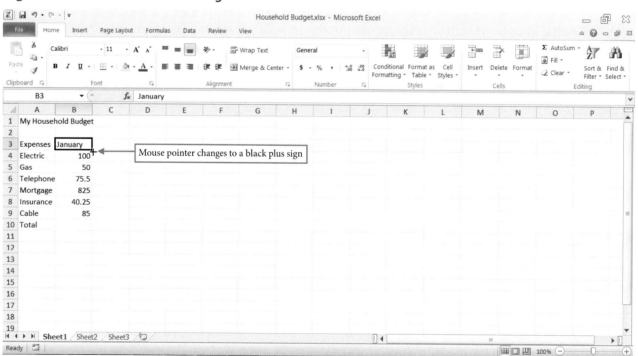

Figure 6.18 Series Created

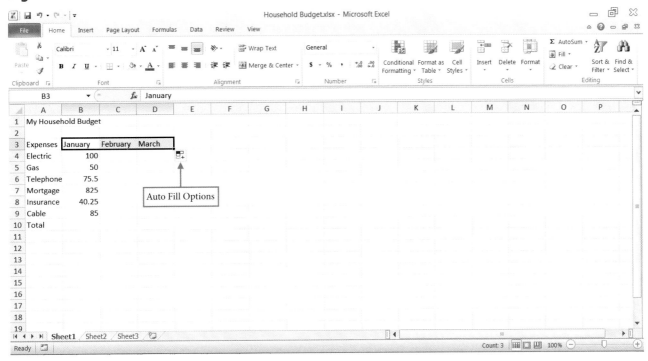

Figure 6.19 Auto Fill Options

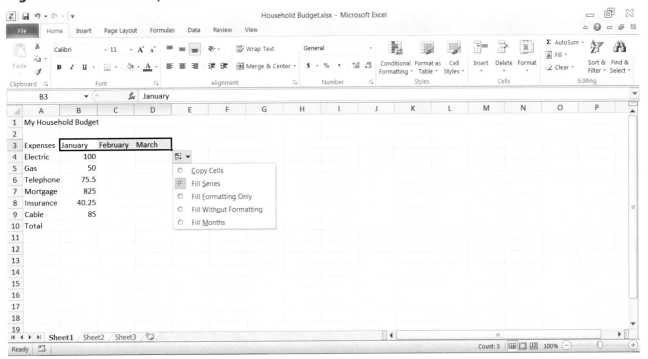

Figure 6.20 Expense Amounts Copied

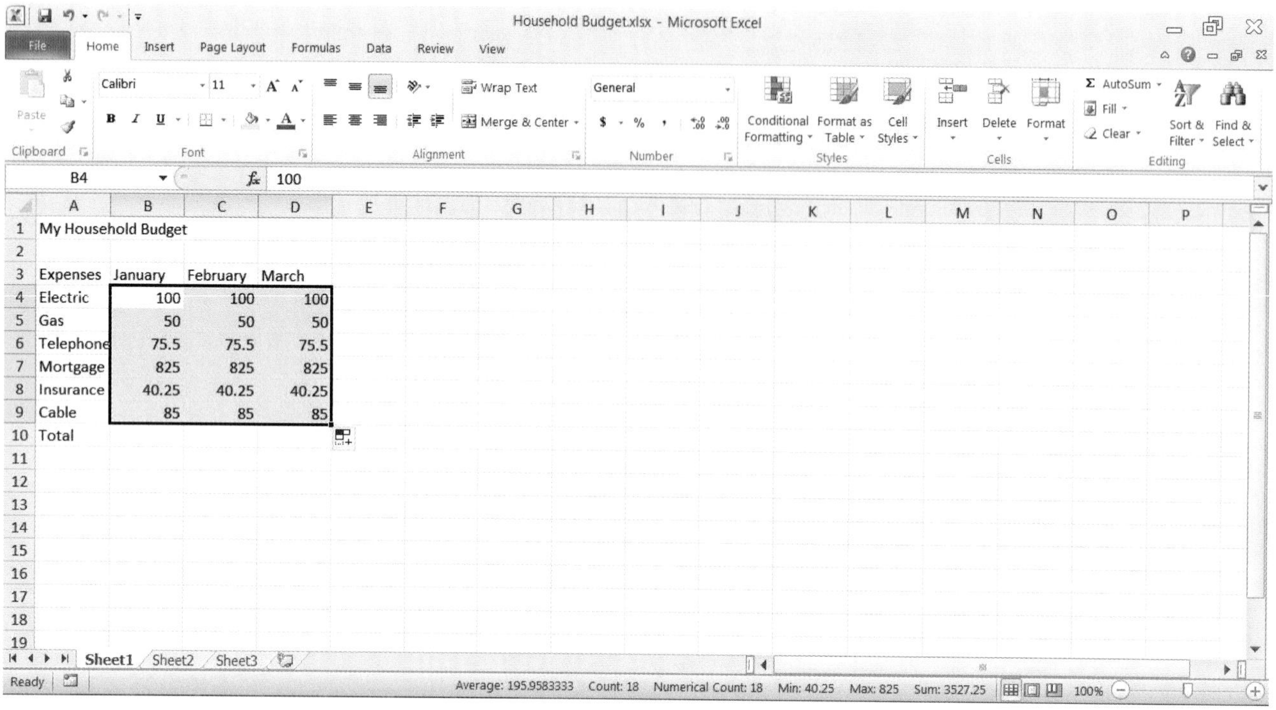

Insert and Delete Rows and Columns

Rows and columns can be inserted or deleted in a worksheet. A row is inserted above the active row and a column is inserted to the left of the active column. **Table 6.7** describes how to insert and delete rows and columns.

Table 6.7 Commands to Insert/Delete Columns and Rows

Task	Steps
Insert row	• Select the row heading(s) where you want the new row(s) to be inserted. • Right-click the row heading(s). • Click **Insert** on the shortcut menu. or • Select the row heading(s) where you want the new row(s) to be inserted. • Click the **Insert** button in the Cells group on the Home tab, or click the **Insert arrow** and click **Insert Sheet Rows (Figure 6.21)**.
Insert column	• Select the column heading(s) where you want the new column(s) to be inserted. • Right-click the column heading(s). • Click **Insert** on the shortcut menu. or • Select the column heading(s) where you want the new column(s) to be inserted. • Click the **Insert** button in the Cells group on the Home tab, or click the **Insert arrow** and click **Insert Sheet Columns** (Figure 6.21).

Table 6.7 *continued*	
Delete row/column	• Select the row or column heading(s) that you want to delete. • Right-click the row or column heading(s). • Click **Delete** on the shortcut menu. or • Select the row or column heading(s) you want to delete. • Click the **Delete** button in the Cells group on the Home tab, or click the **Delete arrow** and click **Delete Sheet Rows** or **Delete Sheet Columns** (Figure 6.21).

Hands-On Exercise: Insert and Delete Rows and Columns

1. You will insert a new row above the Mortgage expense row. Right-click row heading 7 .

2. Click Insert on the shortcut menu. A new blank row appears in row 7.

3. In cell A7, type **Water** and press the right arrow key to move to cell B7.

4. Type **0** in cell B7.

5. Type **100** in cell C7.

6. Type **0** in cell D7.

7. Because the gas expenses are higher in the winter, you need to budget additional money. Make the following changes to the worksheet:

   a. Type **200** in cell B5.

   b. Type **150** in cell C5.

8. The insurance expense needs to be adjusted because it is billed semiannually in January and July.

   a. Type **240** in cell B9.

   b. Type **0** in cell C9.

   c. Type **0** in cell D9.

9. Insert a new column between columns A and B.

   a. Click column heading B to select the column.

   b. Click the Insert arrow in the Cells group on the Home tab (Figure 6.21).

   c. Click Insert Sheet Columns and the new column is inserted in column B. The previous column B becomes column C.

10. Delete column B.

    a. Click column heading B if not already selected.

    b. Click the Delete arrow in the Cells group on the Home tab (Figure 6.21).

    c. Click Delete Sheet Columns and the column is deleted.

11. Press Ctrl + Home to navigate to cell A1.

12. Click Save on the Quick Access Toolbar. The worksheet should resemble Figure 6.21.

Figure 6.21 Insert and Delete Rows and Columns

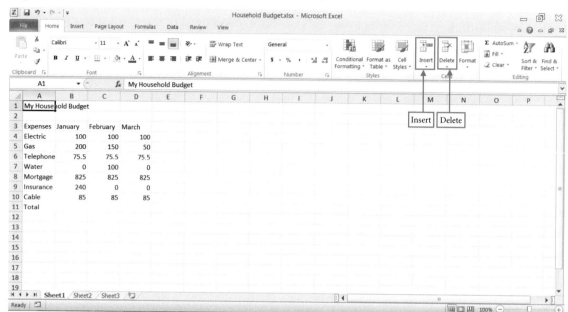

Calculate Totals Using the Sum Button

A powerful feature of Microsoft Excel is its calculation ability. Microsoft Excel can total numbers and perform mathematical calculations accurately and instantly.

The **Sum command**, also referred to as the **AutoSum command**, is used to quickly calculate the total of selected cells. The Sum command can also calculate averages, count values, and calculate the maximum and minimum values in a range of cells. Once you calculate a total using the Sum command, you can copy it to other cells so you do not have to recreate the same calculation again. The Sum button is located in the Editing group on the Home tab (**Figure 6.22**). The command is also available in the Formulas tab. The Sum button may display differently on your computer due to differences in monitor size and settings. Please note that the buttons on the Ribbon may be compressed or rearranged to accommodate smaller monitor sizes. The Sum button on your computer may display with or without the word *AutoSum* next to the graphic.

$$\Sigma \text{ AutoSum } \cdot \quad or \quad \Sigma \cdot$$

When you click the Sum command, it creates a formula that is displayed in the Formula bar and in the cell. A **formula** is an equation that performs a calculation on values. The syntax of the Sum formula is *=SUM(cell range, cell references, or values)*.

All formulas start with an equal sign. The function name displays after the equal sign. A **function** is a predefined formula that can perform mathematical, financial, statistical, and other types of calculations. SUM is the function used to total a range of cells. After the function name, the range of cells , cell references, or values display in parentheses. If the Sum command is used to total cells B4 through B10, the formula would be written as *=SUM(B4:B10)*.

Use one of the following methods to calculate totals:

Method 1:

- Click the cell where you want the total to display.

Sum (AutoSum) command: A command that quickly calculates the total of selected cells. The command can also calculate averages, count values, and calculate the maximum and minimum values in a range of cells. The Sum command is located in the Editing group on the Home tab.

AutoSum (Sum) command: A command that quickly calculates the total of selected cells. The command can also calculate averages, count values, and calculate the maximum and minimum values in a range of cells. The AutoSum command is located in the Editing group on the Home tab.

Formula: An equation that performs a calculation on values.

Function: A predefined formula that can perform mathematical, financial, statistical, and other types of calculations.

- Click the **Sum** button, and it automatically calculates the total of all the cells directly above the cell. If no values exist in the cells above, it will calculate the total of the cells to the left of the cell.
- Press **Enter** *or* click the **Enter** button in the Formula Bar to accept the range of cells to total.
  - If the range of cells selected is not correct, select the correct cells you want to total; then press **Enter** *or* click the **Enter** button in the Formula Bar.
- The total will display in the cell.

Method 2:
- Select the range of values you want to total.
- Click the **Sum** button. The total displays in the cell below the selected range. Make sure the cell below the selected range is blank before performing these steps.

Method 3 (Calculate total of adjacent cells):
- Click the cell where you want the total to display.
- Type =**SUM(**
- Select the cells you want to total.
- Press **Enter**.

Method 4 (Calculate total of non-adjacent cells):
- Click the cell where you want the total to display.
- Type =**SUM(**
- Type the cell reference or click the cell you want to total.
- If you want to add another cell to the total, insert a comma and repeat the previous step.
- Press **Enter** after you selected all the cells that you want to total.

Hands-On Exercise: Calculate Totals Using the Sum Button

1. You will calculate the January expense total. Click cell B11 .

2. Click the Sum button in the Editing group on the Home tab and it automatically selects all the cells above it, from B4 through B10 (Figure 6.22).

3. A formula is created to total the numbers. The formula displays in cell B11 and in the Formula Bar. The formula is =SUM(B4:B10) (Figure 6.22).

4. Press Enter and the total for January, *1525.5*, displays in cell B11.

5. You will copy the formula in cell B11 to columns C and D to calculate the totals for February and March. Click cell B11 .

6. Drag the fill handle through cells D11. The February and March expense totals are calculated (**Figure 6.23**).

7. Click cell C11 . The formula displayed in the Formula Bar is =SUM(C4:C10), which indicates that it will total the range of numbers from C4 through C10.

8. Click cell D11 . The formula displayed in the Formula Bar is =SUM(D4:D10), which indicates that it will total the range of numbers from D4 through D10.

Figure 6.22 Sum Command

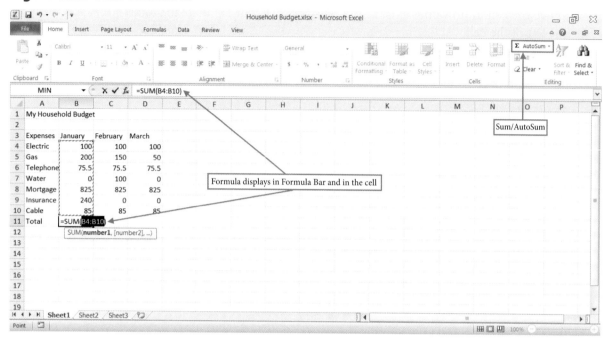

Figure 6.23 February and March Totals Calculated

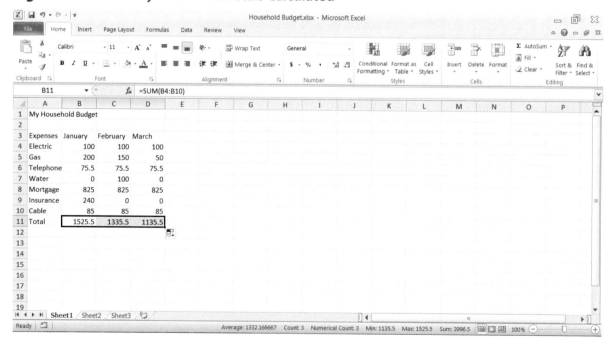

In the previous Hands-On Exercise, you calculated the totals for the monthly expenses. The formulas are shown in **Table 6.8**.

Table 6.8 Expense Formulas	
Expense Totals	Formula
January expenses formula (cell B11)	=SUM(B4:B10)
February expenses formula (cell C11)	=SUM(C4:C10)
March expenses formula (cell D11)	=SUM(D4:D10)

When you copied the January expenses total (B11) to February (C11), the formula was copied with one change. The column letter in the formula changed from B to C because the expenses for February are located in column C. The row number stayed the same because the formula was copied to a cell in the same row.

When you copy a formula from one column to another in the same row, it will change only the column letter in the formula. If you copy a formula from one row to another row and stay in the same column, it will change only the row number in the formula. Here is an example. If the formula =SUM(B6:E6) is in cell F6 and you copy that formula to cell F7, the only change to the formula will be to the row number because the formula is copied to the same column in a different row. The formula in cell F7 will be =SUM(B7:E7).

Hands-On Exercise: Calculate Totals

You will total the expenses for each expense category (electric, gas, etc.) using different techniques.

1. Type **Total** in cell E3 and press Enter . The total for each expense will be calculated in column E, which is currently blank.

2. Select cells E4:E11 .

3. Click the Sum button. The totals display for each expense (**Figure 6.24**).

4. Click cell E4 . The Formula Bar displays =SUM(B4:D4). The formula totaled the cells B4, C4, and D4, which are the electric expenses for the three months. If you review the other formulas in column E, they are similar. The only difference in the formula is the row numbers.

5. Double-click cell E5 . The formula is displayed in the Formula Bar and in the cell. The values used in the formula contain a blue border around them (**Figure 6.25**). This is a way to validate the calculations. If the wrong cells were used in the formula, you could select the correct values and then press Enter to recalculate the totals.

6. Press the Esc key to exit the cell.

7. You will practice totaling cells using another method. Select cells E4:E11 .

8. Press the Delete key to remove the totals from column E.

9. You will calculate the total electric expenses. Select cells B4:D4 .

10. Click the Sum button, and the total displays in the next empty cell, which is E4.

Figure 6.24 Expenses Totaled for Each Row

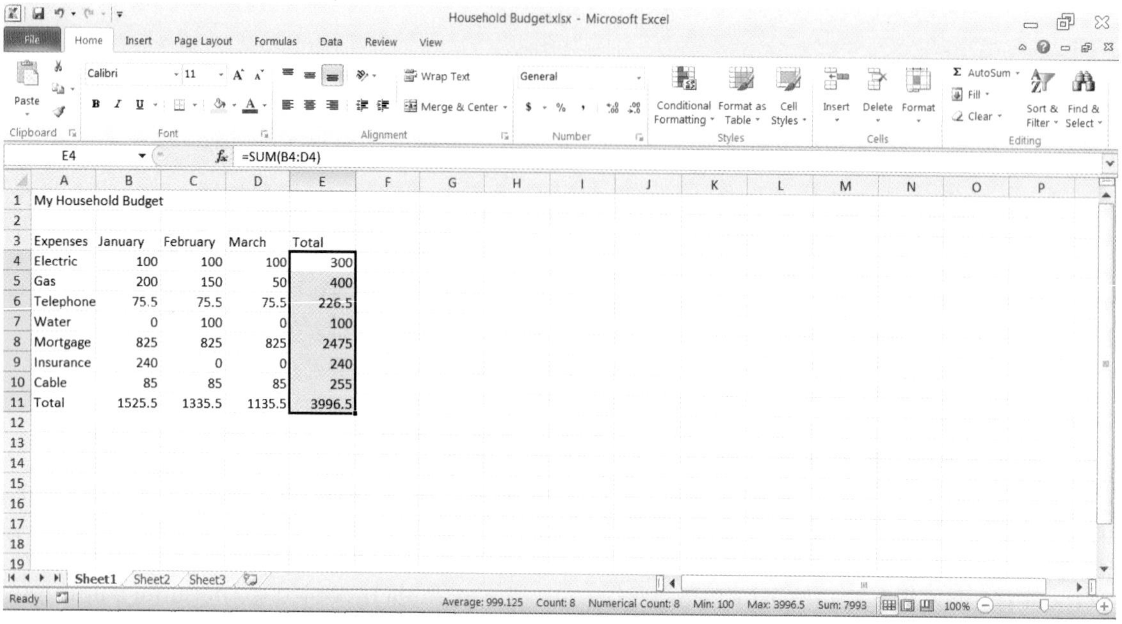

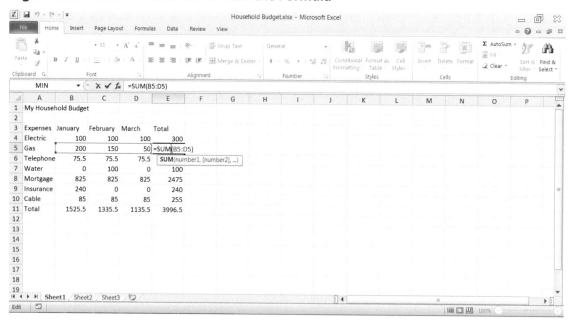

Figure 6.25 Double-Click Cell to View the Formula

Trace Error Button

If you create a formula and a green triangle displays in the top-left corner of the cell, this indicates a potential error in the formula (**Figure 6.26**). If this occurs, review the formula to ensure that it is correct. If you click the cell that contains the green triangle, the Trace Error button displays (**Figure 6.27**). Point to the **Trace Error** button and a ToolTip displays with the error message. Click the **Trace Error** arrow for a list of options. If the formula is correct, click **Ignore Error**.

Hands-On Exercise: Correct Error in Formula Using the Trace Error Button

1. Click cell E5 .

2. You will calculate the total gas expenses, but only for the months of February and March. Click the Sum button. Notice that it automatically highlights the cells to the left of E5, which are cells B5, C5, and D5.

3. Drag over cells C5 and D5. The formula states =SUM(C5:D5).

4. Press Enter and the total for the two months displays. A green triangle displays in the top-left corner of the cell (Figure 6.26). This indicates that there is a potential error in the formula of the cell. The reason it is flagged as a potential error is because the January expenses are not included in the total of the formula.

5. Click cell E5 , which contains the green triangle. The Trace Error button displays.

6. Point to the Trace Error button, and a ToolTip displays with the error message. (Figure 6.27).

7. Click the Trace Error button to view the list of options.

8. Click Update Formula to Include Cells . The green triangle no longer displays in the cell because the error is corrected.

9. Select cells E4:E5 .

10. Press Delete .

11. Select cells E4:E11 .

12. Click the Sum button. The totals display for each expense (**Figure 6.28**).

Figure 6.26 Green Triangle Displays Indicating Potential Error

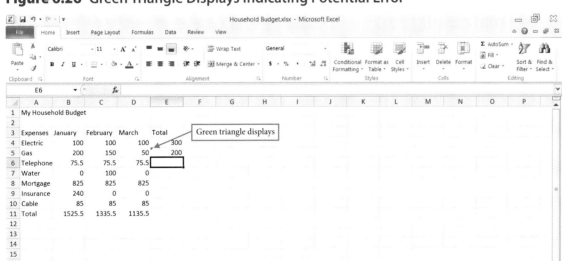

Figure 6.27 Trace Error Button Displays ToolTip of Error Message

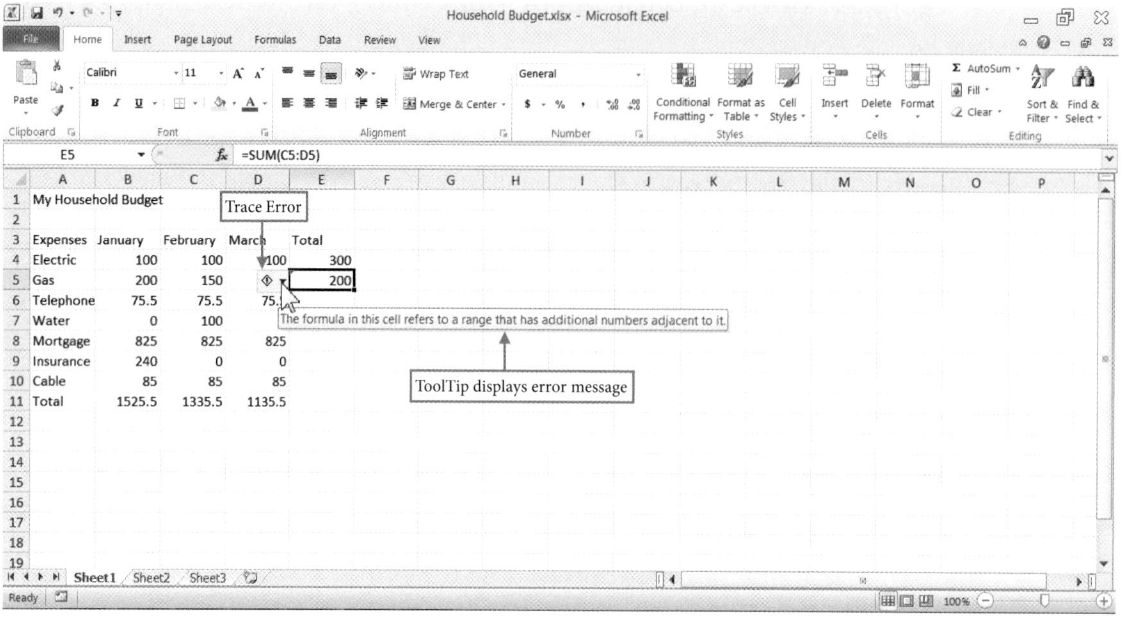

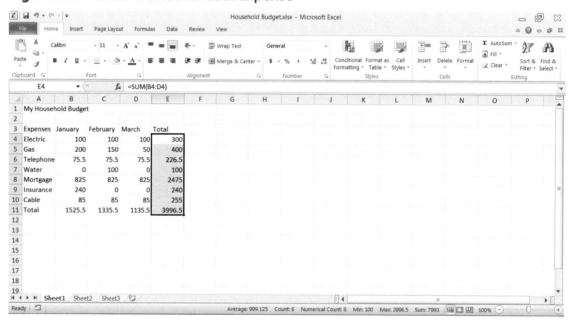

Figure 6.28 Totals Created for Each Expense

Apply Cell Formatting

You can apply cell formatting to give your worksheet a professional appearance. Select the cell(s) you want to format; then select the formatting feature you want to apply by clicking the format command from the Font and Alignment groups on the Home tab. If the command contains an arrow, that means that there are several options from which to choose. View the options and then make your selection. Some of the formatting commands, such as the Bold,

Italic, and Underline, are toggle buttons that turn on and off when clicked. If you click the command, it applies the format to the cell. Click the command again, and it removes the format from the cell.

You can choose from the many formatting features located in the Font and Alignment groups on the Home Ribbon. You can apply these commands to a cell, a range of cells, or the entire worksheet. **Table 6.9** contains a list of some of the cell formatting commands.

Table 6.9 Cell Formatting Commands

Command	Button	Description
Font	Calibri	Changes the font face.
Font Size	11	Changes the font size.
Bold	B	Bolds the selected text.
Italic	I	Italicizes the selected text.
Underline	U	Underlines the selected text.
Borders		Applies a border to the selected text.
Fill Color		Changes the color of the background of the cell.
Font Color	A	Changes the font color.
Align Text Left		Aligns text to the left.
Center		Centers text.
Align Text Right		Aligns text to the right.
Increase Indent		Increases the margin between the border and the text in the cell.
Decrease Indent		Decreases the margin between the border and the text in the cell.
Merge & Center	Merge & Center	Joins the selected cells into one larger cell and centers the content in the new cell.

Hands-On Exercise: Format Cells

1. Select cells A1:E1 .

2. Click the Merge & Center button (**Figure 6.29**). Cells A1:E1 are joined into one larger cell and the text is centered in the new cell.

3. Click the Bold button (Figure 6.29).

4. Click the Font Color arrow (Figure 6.29).

5. Click Light Blue in the Standard Colors group. It is the seventh option in the Standard Colors group.

⑥ Click the Font Size arrow (Figure 6.29).

⑦ Click 18 .

⑧ Select cells A3:E3 .

⑨ Click the Bold button.

⑩ Select cell A11 .

⑪ Click the Bold button.

⑫ Select cells A4:A10 .

⑬ Click the Increase Indent button (Figure 6.29).

⑭ Click the Italic button (Figure 6.29).

⑮ Select cells A11:E11 .

⑯ Click the Borders arrow (Figure 6.29).

⑰ Click Top and Double Bottom Border .

⑱ Click cell A1 .

⑲ Click Save on the Quick Access Toolbar. The worksheet should resemble Figure 6.29.

Figure 6.29 Formatted Worksheet

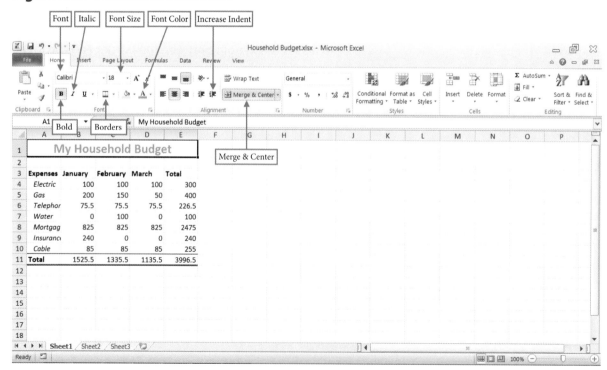

Format Numbers

Microsoft Excel 2010 provides many options to format numbers. These commands are located in the Number group on the Home tab. Select the cell(s) you want to format and click the formatting button to apply the format.

Table 6.10 Commands to Format Numbers

Command	Button	Description
Accounting Number Format	$ ▾	Displays the value as currency. It applies a dollar sign, commas, and two decimal places to the value.
		Example: $ 1,000.50
Percent Style	%	Displays the value as a percentage.
		Example: 0.45 displays as 45%
Comma Style	ﾞ	Displays the value with commas and two decimal places.
		Example: 1,000.50
Increase Decimal	⁺⁰₀₀	Increases the decimal place of the value by one digit.
Decrease Decimal	₀₀⁺₀	Decreases the decimal place of the value by one digit.
Number Format	General ▾	Click the arrow, and select a number format from the list.

Hands-On Exercise: Format Numbers

① Select cells B4:E4 .

② Click the Accounting Number Format button (**Figure 6.30**). The selected cells contain a dollar sign and two decimal places. There is a space between the dollar sign and the values. Commas do not display in the cells because the values are not greater than or equal to 1,000.

③ Select cells B11:E11 .

④ Click the Number Format arrow (Figure 6.30) and a list displays.

⑤ Click the Accounting option. This format does not contain a space between the dollar sign and the value.

⑥ Select cells B5:E10 .

⑦ Click the Comma Style button (Figure 6.30). The values in the cells include two decimal places. Commas do not display because the values are not greater than or equal to 1,000. Cells B7, D7, C9, and D9 display as a dash. When applying the comma format, cells with a value of zero display as a dash in the cell.

⑧ Click cell B5 .

→

⑨ Click the Increase Decimal button (Figure 6.30). The value in the cell displays with three decimal places.

⑩ Click the Decrease Decimal button (Figure 6.30) and a decimal place is removed from the value. The value now contains two decimal places.

⑪ Click Save on the Quick Access Toolbar. The worksheet should resemble Figure 6.30.

Figure 6.30 Format Values

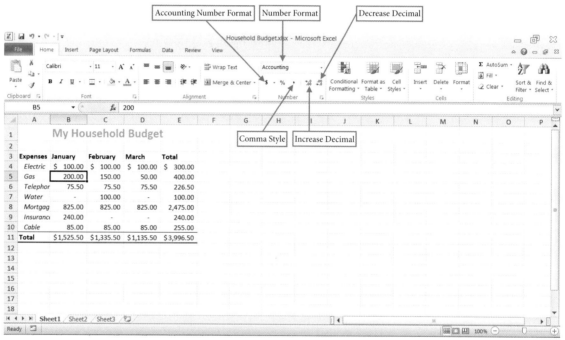

Clear Command

The Clear command is used to delete the contents of a cell, delete the formatting of a cell, or both. It can also be used to clear comments and hyperlinks from a worksheet. The Clear button is located in the Editing group on the Home tab (**Figure 6.31**).

Use these steps to clear the contents or formatting of a cell:

- Click the cell that you want to clear.
- Click the **Clear** button in the Editing group on the Home tab.
- Click an option from the list.

Hands-On Exercise: Clear Formats and Contents of Cells

① Click cell A1 .

② Click the Clear button in the Editing group on the Home tab (Figure 6.31). A list of options display.

③ Click Clear All . The cell contents is deleted as well as the formatting. The cell is no longer merged.

④ Click Undo on the Quick Access Toolbar.

⑤ Click the Clear button.

⑥ Click Clear Formats . The formatting of the cell is removed, but the text remains in the cell.

⑦ Click Undo on the Quick Access Toolbar.

⑧ Click the Clear button.

⑨ Click Clear Contents . The contents of the cell are deleted.

⑩ Type **Budget** and press Enter . Notice that the formatting of the cell is still intact.

⑪ Click the Undo button twice to undo the last two steps. The worksheet should resemble Figure 6.31.

Figure 6.31 Clear Button

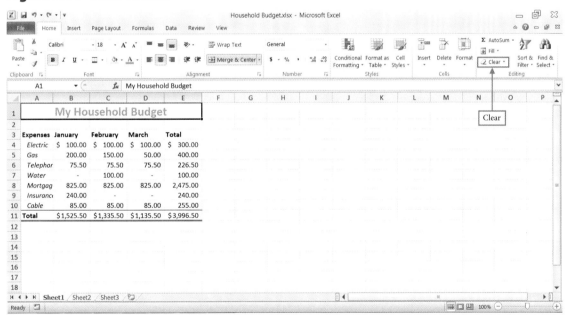

Modify Column and Row Size

Occasionally you will need to change the size of the columns or rows because the data is truncated (cut off) in the cell or because you want to improve the readability or appearance of the cell.

If pound signs (####) display in a cell, that indicates that the column width is too small to fit the contents of the cell. The column width can range from 0 to 255 characters. These values represent the number of characters that can be displayed in a cell that is formatted with the standard default font. The default font for Microsoft Excel 2010 is Calibri, and the default font size is 11 points. The default column width is set at 8.43 characters. The column will be hidden if the column width is set to 0 characters. You can modify multiple column widths simultaneously by selecting the columns before you modify the column size. The same holds true for modifying multiple row heights simultaneously.

Use any of these methods to modify the column width:

- Drag the right boundary of the column heading (**Figure 6.32**).
- Double-click the right boundary of the column heading to automatically adjust the column width to fit the contents of the cell.
- Right-click the column heading, and then click **Column Width**. The Column Width dialog box displays. Type the width in the Column width box and click **OK**.
- Click the column heading, click the **Format** button in the Cells group on the Home tab (Figure 6.32), and then click **Column Width**. The Column Width dialog box displays. Type the width in the Column width box and click **OK**.
- To automatically increase the column width to fit the contents of the cell, click the column heading, click the **Format** button in the Cells group on the Home tab, and then click **AutoFit Column Width**.

The default row height is 12.75 points. One point is approximately 1/72 inch. The row height can range from 0 to 409 points. If the row height is 0 points, the row will be hidden.

Use any of these methods to modify the row height:

- Drag the bottom boundary of the row heading (Figure 6.32).
- Double-click the bottom boundary of the row heading to automatically adjust the row height to fit the contents of the cell.
- Right-click the row heading and then click **Row Height**. The Row Height dialog box displays. Type the height in the Row height box and click **OK**.
- Click the row heading, click the **Format** button in the Cells group on the Home tab (Figure 6.32), and then click **Row Height**. The Row Height dialog box displays. Type the height in the Row height box and click **OK**.
- To automatically increase the row height to fit the cell contents, click the row heading, click the **Format** button in the Cells group of the Home tab, and then click **AutoFit Row Height**.

Hands-On Exercise: Modify Column and Row Size

Review the contents in column A. Notice that some of the text is not displaying. You will increase the size of the column in order to display all the cell contents.

1. Right-click column A .
2. Click Column Width . The Column Width dialog box displays.
3. Type **12** in the Column width box and click OK . All the text in the column now displays in the cells.

④ Next, you will increase the row height for row 1.

  a. Click row heading 1 to select the entire row.

  b. Click the Format button in the Cells group on the Home tab (Figure 6.32).

  c. Click Row Height . The Row Height dialog box displays.

  d. Type **40** in the Row height box and click OK . The row height increases.

⑤ Next you will decrease the column width for column C.

  a. Right-click column heading C .

  b. Click Column Width . The Column Width dialog box displays.

  c. Type **5** in the Column width box and click OK . Pound signs (####) display in the cells, which indicate that the column width is too small to fit the contents (Figure 6.32). Whenever pound signs display, make certain to increase the column width to display all the contents in the cells.

⑥ To automatically increase the column width to view all the contents in column C, double-click the right boundary of column heading C (Figure 6.32). The contents in column C are displayed.

⑦ Click cell A1 . The worksheet will resemble **Figure 6.33**.

Figure 6.32 Modify Column and Row Size

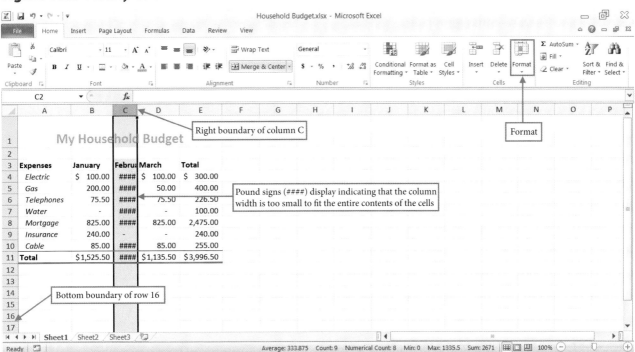

Figure 6.33 Autofit Contents of Column C

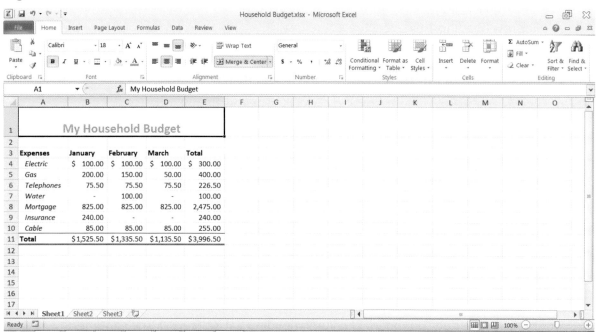

Display Formulas

Use one of the following methods to view the formulas entered in the worksheet:

- Press **Ctrl + `**. (The ` key is the key to the left of the number 1 on most keyboards.)
- Click the **Formulas** tab, and then click the **Show Formulas** button in the Formula Auditing group.

The formulas for the totals are displayed. To view the values again (the original default), press **Ctrl + `** again *or* click the **Show Formulas** button.

Hands-On Exercise: Display Formulas

1. Click the Formulas tab (**Figure 6.34**).
2. Click the Show Formulas button in the Formula Auditing group (Figure 6.34). The formulas display on the worksheet (Figure 6.34).
3. Click the Show Formulas button again. The values display on the worksheet.
4. Click Ctrl + ` to display the formulas. The formulas display on the worksheet.
5. Click Ctrl + ` to display the values.
6. Click the Home tab on the Ribbon to make it the active tab.

Figure 6.34 Display Formulas in Worksheet

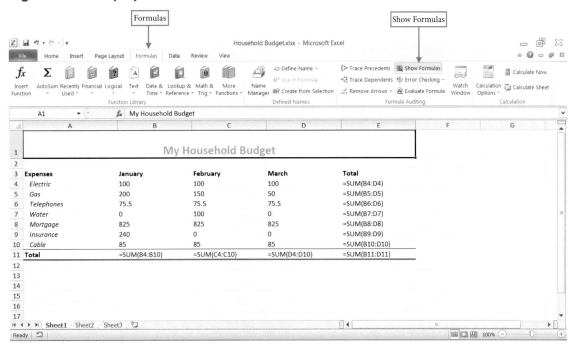

Check Spelling

Check a workbook for spelling errors before you print it. The Spelling button is located in the Proofing group on the Review tab (**Figure 6.35**). If you have multiple sheets in the workbook, you must check each worksheet. Before beginning the spell check, click the first cell of the worksheet so the spell check can begin at the beginning of the worksheet.

Use these steps to check and correct spelling errors:

- Click the **Review** tab.
- Click the **Spelling** button in the Proofing group, and the Spelling dialog box displays. This feature checks the worksheet for errors and displays the errors in the dialog box. Some proper names may not be included in the dictionary and may display as a potential spelling error. In this case, click **Ignore All** to indicate that the word is spelled correctly *or* click **Add to Dictionary** to store it in the dictionary.

Hands-On Exercise: Check Spelling

1. Click cell A1 .
2. Click the Review tab.
3. Click the Spelling button. The Spelling dialog box displays if spelling errors exist.
4. Correct all spelling errors. If there are no spelling errors or after you have corrected all spelling errors, a dialog box displays stating that the spelling check is complete (Figure 6.35). Click OK .
5. Click the Home tab to make it the active tab.
6. Click Save on the Quick Access Toolbar.

Figure 6.35 Spelling Button

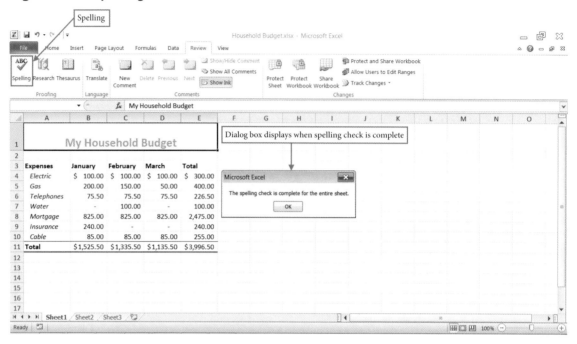

Print Workbook

You can print the contents of the workbook or print the formulas in a workbook. By default, the workbook prints in portrait orientation. **Portrait orientation** is a page orientation that prints on a vertical page, which means that the page is taller than it is wide. You can change the page orientation to landscape orientation. **Landscape orientation** is a page orientation that prints on a horizontal page, which means that the page is wider than it is tall.

You can print the workbook from the Backstage view. You can also press **Ctrl + P** to display the Print command in the Backstage view. You have many print options.

- Select the number of copies to print.
- Select a printer.
- Select the print area (active sheet, entire workbook, selection).
- Select the pages to print.
- Select paper size (letter, legal, etc.).
- Select page orientation (portrait or landscape).

Use these steps to print the workbook:

- Click the **File** tab.
- Click **Print**.
- Select **Print Active Sheets** in the Settings section to print the current active sheet in the workbook (**Figure 6.36**), *or* you can click the **Print Active Sheets** button and select **Print Entire Workbook** to print the entire workbook.
- To print in landscape orientation, click the **Portrait Orientation** button and select **Landscape Orientation** (Figure 6.36).
- A preview of the worksheet displays on the right side of the window (Figure 6.36).

- You can adjust the margins and other print settings as needed.
- Click **Print** after you have selected all the print settings (Figure 6.36).

Use this step to print the formulas in the workbook:

- Press **Ctrl + `** to view the formulas and then follow the same steps as listed above.

Hands-On Exercise: Print a Worksheet

① Click the File tab.

② Click Print . A preview of the printout displays on the right side of the window (Figure 6.36).

③ Select the printer you want to use (Figure 6.36).

④ Select Print Active Sheets in the Settings section (Figure 6.36).

⑤ Click the Print button (Figure 6.36).

Figure 6.36 Print Options

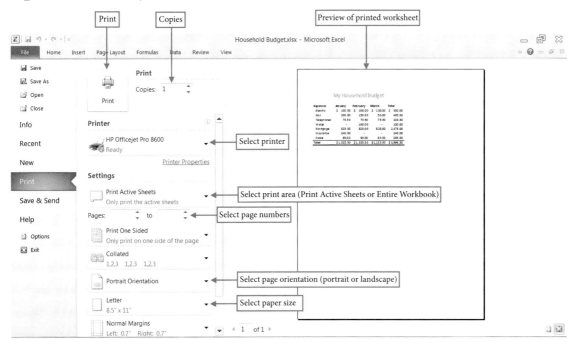

Page Breaks

A **page break** is a dashed vertical and/or horizontal line in the worksheet that indicates where the worksheet is divided into separate pages. The page breaks display after the Print command is accessed from the Backstage view. The page breaks are determined based on paper size, margins, scale options, and the position of manual page breaks.

A dashed vertical line displays after column I (**Figure 6.37**). This indicates a page break. You can hide the page breaks when in Normal view if you need to.

> **Page break:** A dashed vertical and/or horizontal line in the worksheet that indicates where the worksheet is divided into separate pages.

Use these steps to hide page breaks in Normal view:

- Click the **File** tab.
- Click **Options** and the Excel Options dialog box displays.
- Click **Advanced** (**Figure 6.38**).
- Click to remove the **Show page breaks** checkmark in the Display options for this worksheet category (Figure 6.38). You may need to scroll down to find this option.
- Click **OK**.

Figure 6.37 Page Break

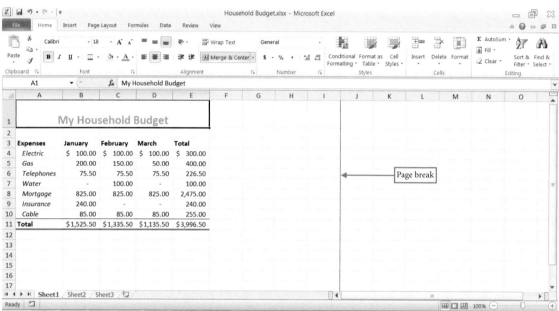

Figure 6.38 Remove Page Breaks

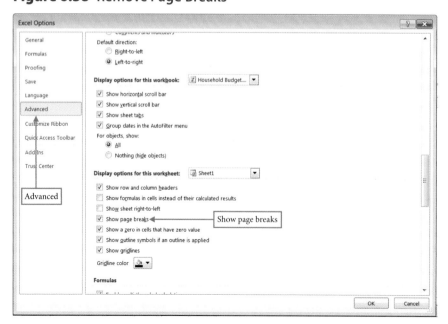

Help Button

You can use the Help feature if you need assistance with a task. The Help feature is accessed by clicking the Help button, which is located on the far-right corner of the Ribbon (**Figure 6.39**), *or* by pressing **F1** on the keyboard. You can also access the Help command from the File tab.

Hands-On Exercise: Use Help

① Click the Help button, and the Excel Help dialog box displays (Figure 6.39).

② Type **insert row** in the Search box (Figure 6.39) and press Enter .

③ Search results display in the Excel Help dialog box (Figure 6.39). Click on a hyperlink to view the information.

④ Click the Print button in the Excel Help dialog box to print the information (Figure 6.39).

⑤ Click the Close button on the Excel Help dialog box (Figure 6.39).

Figure 6.39 Help Command

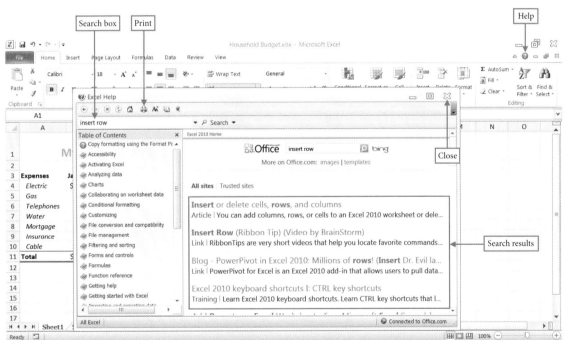

Close a Workbook

You should close the workbook when you are finished working with it. When you close a workbook, it will ask you to save if you have not done so already. This command does not close the application; it only closes the workbook.

To close a workbook:

- Click the **File** tab.
- Click **Close**.
- If the workbook has not been saved, it will prompt you to save the workbook at that time.

You can also close the workbook by clicking the **Close** button on the Ribbon (**Figure 6.40**). If only one workbook is open in Microsoft Excel 2010, you can close the workbook and exit the application at once by clicking the **Close** button on the title bar or double-clicking the **Microsoft Excel 2010 application icon** (Figure 6.40). If multiple workbooks are open, these commands would close only the active workbook.

Hands-On Exercise: Close a Workbook

① Click the Close button on the Ribbon (Figure 6.40).

② The workbook closes but the application remains open.

Figure 6.40 Close Commands

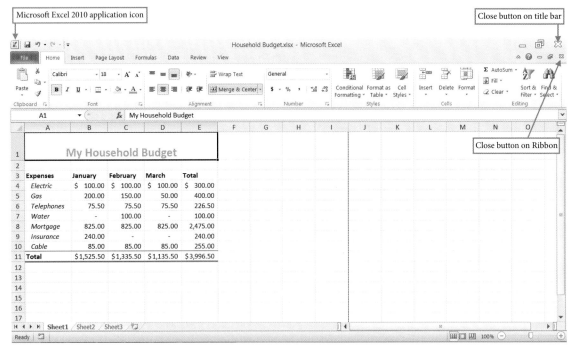

Exit Application

Use the Exit command to exit the application. The Exit command is located on the File tab, *or* it can be accessed by pressing **Alt + F4**. You can also close the application by clicking the **Close** button on the title bar if only one workbook is open.

Hands-On Exercise: Exit Application

① Click the File tab.

② Click Exit and the application closes.

Multiple-Choice Questions

1. Microsoft Excel 2010 is a _____ application.
   a. Presentation graphics
   b. Word processing
   c. Spreadsheet
   d. Database

2. Which of the following is true about the boundary of a row?
   a. Double-click the bottom boundary of a row to add a row.
   b. Click the bottom boundary of a row and press Delete on your keyboard to delete a row.
   c. Drag the bottom boundary of a row to change the height of the row.
   d. Double-click the bottom boundary of a row to delete a row.

3. Press _____ to edit the contents of a cell.
   a. F5
   b. F2
   c. Ctrl + Alt + Delete
   d. Esc

4. By default, a workbook contains _____ sheet(s).
   a. One
   b. Two
   c. Three
   d. Five

5. By dragging the fill handle, you can _____ cells.
   a. Move
   b. Delete
   c. Copy
   d. Edit

6. Which of the following is an invalid cell reference?
   a. 100A
   b. C55
   c. az1000
   d. za1

7. The _____ function is used to total numbers in a workbook.

   a. Total

   b. Sum

   c. Calculate

   d. Formula

8. If cell A3 contains the value 1050 and you change the format to comma style, how would the data display in the cell?

   a. 1,050

   b. 1,050.00

   c. $1,050

   d. $1,050.00

9. The file extension of a Microsoft Excel 2010 workbook is _____ .

   a. excel

   b. xlsx

   c. xls

   d. excel2010

10. Press _____ to view the formulas in the worksheet.

   a. Ctrl+Enter

   b. Alt+Enter

   c. F1

   d. Ctrl+`

Project #1: Create a Workbook Displaying the Costs of Vacation Packages

You work for a travel agency and need to prepare a listing of all the vacation packages for the summer. You will use Microsoft Excel 2010 to accomplish this task.

① Set the column width of column A to 20.

② Enter the data from **Figure** 6.41 in the worksheet.

Figure 6.41 Enter Data in Worksheet

	A	B
1	Paradise Travel	
2		
3	Vacation Package	Cost
4	Hawaii	2500
5	Caribbean Cruise	1500
6	Disney Package	1750
7	Las Vegas	999
8		

③ Merge and center cells A1 through B1.

④ Make the following changes to A1:

    a. Bold

    b. Font color = Blue

    c. Font size = 18

⑤ Make the following format changes:

    a. Bold cells A3 and B3.

    b. Increase indent of cells B4:B7.

    c. Format cells B4:B7 as Accounting Number Format.

⑥ Insert a row at row 6.

⑦ Add the following data to the cells:

    a. Type **European Cruise** in cell A6.

    b. Type **2000** in cell B6.

⑧ Spell-check the workbook and correct any mistakes.

⑨ Save the workbook as **Paradise Travel**. The worksheet should resemble
Figure 6.42.

⑩ Delete row 5.

⑪ Save the workbook as **Paradise Travel Revised**. The worksheet should resemble
Figure 6.43.

⑫ Print the workbook in landscape orientation.

⑬ Close the workbook.

Figure 6.42 Paradise Travel Workbook

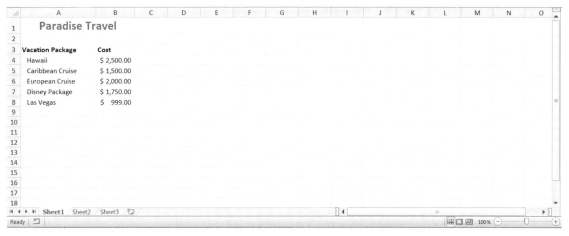

Figure 6.43 Paradise Travel Revised Workbook

	A	B	C	D	E	F	G	H	I	J	K	L	M	N	O
1	Paradise Travel														
2															
3	Vacation Package	Cost													
4	Hawaii	$ 2,500.00													
5	European Cruise	$ 2,000.00													
6	Disney Package	$ 1,750.00													
7	Las Vegas	$ 999.00													
8															
9															
10															
11															
12															
13															
14															
15															
16															
17															
18															

Sheet1 / Sheet2 / Sheet3

Ready   100%

Project #2: Create a Workbook for a Law Firm to Track Hours Worked Weekly for Each Client

Your boss needs to track the hours he spends weekly on each of his clients. This information is used to process the client invoices each month. You will use Microsoft Excel 2010 to keep track of his hours.

① Create the worksheet in **Figure 6.44**.

Figure 6.44 Enter Text in Worksheet

	A	B	C
1	Orland Law Firm		
2			
3	Client		
4	CK Sporting Goods		
5	Pete's Exports		
6	Global Accountants		
7	Total		

② Merge and center A1 through F1.

③ Type **Week 1** in cell B3.

④ Make the following changes to A1:

   a. Bold

   b. Font color = Blue, Accent 1

   c. Font size = 28

   d. Fill color = White, Background 1, Darker 15%

⑤ Change the column width of column A to 20.

⑥ Using the fill handle, copy cell B3 to cells C3 through E3 to complete the series. The text *Week 2, Week 3*, and *Week 4* will be displayed in the cells.

⑦ Add the following data to the cells:

   a. Type **20** in cell B4.

   b. Type **15** in cell C4.

   c. Type **10** in cell D4.

   d. Type **5** in cell E4.

   e. Type **14** in cell B5.

   f. Type **7** in cell C5.

   g. Type **20** in cell D5.

   h. Type **20** in cell E5.

   i. Type **12** in cell B6.

   j. Type **18** in cell C6.

   k. Type **10** in cell D6.

   l. Type **15** in cell E6.

   m. Type **Total** in cell F3.

⑧ Calculate the totals in cells F4:F6. The total should be the sum of the hours for each client.

⑨ Calculate the totals in cells B7:F7. The totals should be the sum of the hours for each week.

⑩ Apply the following formats:

   a. Bold the cells in A3:F3.

   b. Italicize cells A4:A6.

   c. Increase indent of cells A4:A6.

   d. Format cells B4:F7 as comma style.

   e. Add a top and double bottom border around cells A7:F7.

⑪ Insert a row below row 6 and add the following data:

   a. Type **Georgia's Hair Salon** in cell A7.

   b. Type **2** in cells B7, C7, D7, and E7.

   c. Calculate the total for Georgia's Hair Salon in cell F7.

⑫ Spell-check the worksheet and correct any mistakes.

⑬ Save the workbook as **Orland Law Firm**. The worksheet should resemble **Figure 6.45**.

⑭ Print the worksheet.

⑮ Print the worksheet with the formulas.

⑯ Change the client name in cell A4 to **JK Sporting Goods**.

⑰ Change the row height of row 8 to 24.

⑱ Delete row 6.

⑲ Save the workbook as **Orland Law Firm Revised**. The worksheet should resemble Figure 6.46.

⑳ Print the worksheet.

㉑ Close the workbook.

Figure 6.45 Orland Law Firm Workbook

Figure 6.46 Orland Law Firm Revised Workbook

Project #3: Create a Workbook to Calculate the Quarter Sales for a Company

You work for Pedro Electronics. You will use Microsoft Excel 2010 to keep track of the first quarter sales for the company.

① Create the worksheet in **Figure 6.47.**

Figure 6.47 Enter Text

	A	B	C
1	Pedro Electronics		
2	First Quarter Sales Report		
3			
4	Product	January	
5	Computers		
6	Printers		
7	Phones		
8	Music CD		
9	Games		
10			

② Merge and center cells A1 through E1.

③ Merge and center cells A2 through E2.

④ Make the following changes to cells A1 and A2:

  a. Bold

  b. Font color = Green

  c. Font size = 22

  d. Fill color = White, Background 1, Darker 15%

⑤ Change the column width of column A to 15.

⑥ Change the column widths of columns B, C, D, and E to 12.

⑦ Using the fill handle, copy cell B4 to C4:D4 to complete the series. The text *February* and *March* will be displayed in the cells.

⑧ Add the following data to cells B5:D9 (**Figure 6.48**):

Figure 6.48 Enter Values

	A	B	C	D	E	F
1		Pedro Electronics				
2		First Quarter Sales Report				
3						
4	Product	January	February	March		
5	Computers	10500	8500	7430		
6	Printers	3000	1800	2500		
7	Phones	8000	12000	9760		
8	Music CD	5000	5010	5080		
9	Games	8100	9500	6500		
10						

⑨ Type **Total** in cell E4.

⑩ Type **Total** in cell A10.

⑪ Calculate the totals in cells E5:E9. The totals are the sum of the monthly sales for each product.

⑫ Calculate the totals in cells B10:E10. The totals are the sum of the sales for each month.

⑬ Make the following format changes:

   a. Bold cells A4:E4.

   b. Bold cell A10.

   c. Right-align cells B4:E4.

   d. Italicize cells A5:A9.

   e. Indent cells A5:A9.

   f. Format cells B6:E9 as comma style. Decrease decimal places so that none are displayed.

   g. Format cells B5:E5 and B10:E10 as Accounting Number Format. Decrease decimal places so that no decimal places are displayed.

   h. Add a top and double bottom border around cells A10:E10.

⑭ Spell-check the worksheet and correct any mistakes.

⑮ Save the workbook as **Pedro Electronics**. The worksheet should resemble **Figure 6.49**.

⑯ Print the worksheet.

⑰ Print the worksheet with the formulas.

⑱ Close the workbook.

⑲ Exit Microsoft Excel 2010.

Figure 6.49 Pedro Electronics Workbook

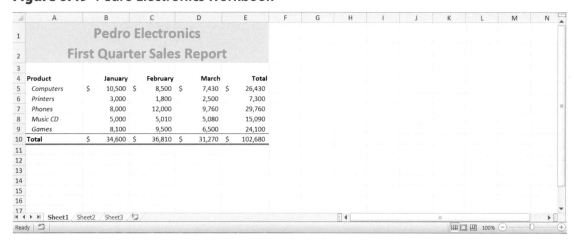

Create Formulas, Charts, and Tables

Chapter Objectives

After completing this chapter, you will be able to do the following:

- Create formulas.
- Insert functions.
- Create and modify charts.
- Manipulate worksheets.
- Format cells as a table.
- Sort and filter data.
- Apply conditional formatting.
- Insert headers and footers.

Now that you have learned the basics of Microsoft Excel 2010, you will learn how to create formulas to perform mathematical calculations quickly and accurately. If any of the values change in all or part of a formula in a workbook, Microsoft Excel 2010 automatically recalculates the formula and updates the result in the workbook.

In this chapter, you will learn how to create formulas, insert functions, create charts, and format cells as a table. Additionally, you will learn how to manipulate data in order to make effective business decisions.

Open a Workbook

DOWNLOAD

Before beginning this exercise, you need to download the student data files. You will open the *CK Appliances* workbook, which is one of the student data files provided with the textbook. The instructions for downloading the student data files are located in the preface.

Use these steps to open a workbook:

- Click the **File** tab.
- Click **Open**.
- Select the location in which the workbook is stored.
- Double-click the **workbook**, and the workbook opens.

Hands-On Exercise: Open a Workbook

① Click the Start button.

② Click All Programs .

③ Click Microsoft Office .

④ Click Microsoft Excel 2010 . A blank workbook displays. You will open the *CK Appliances* workbook.

⑤ Click the File tab to open the Backstage view.

⑥ Click Open .

⑦ Select the location and folder in which the workbook is stored such as the Documents library or USB Flash drive.

⑧ Double-click the workbook named *CK Appliances,* and the workbook opens. The workbook should resemble **Figure 7.1**.

There are two sheets in the workbook that contain data. You will begin working with Sheet1, which contains sales information for each employee.

Figure 7.1 CK Appliances Workbook

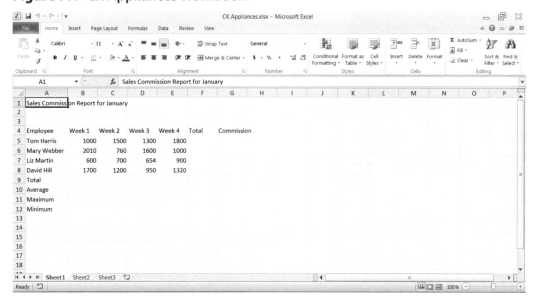

Wrap Text

The **Wrap Text** command displays text on multiple lines within a cell. The Wrap Text button is located in the Alignment group on the Home tab (**Figure 7.2**). There are two ways to wrap text in a cell (**Table 7.1**). The cell can be formatted so that the text wraps automatically, *or* you can enter a manual line break within a cell.

Wrap Text: A command that displays text on multiple lines within a cell.

Table 7.1 Wrap Text Commands	
Task	**Steps**
Wrap text automatically	• Select the cell(s) in which you want to wrap text. • Click the **Wrap Text** button in the Alignment group on the Home tab (Figure 7.2).
Enter a manual line break	• Position the insertion point at the location in the cell where you want to insert the line break. • Press **Alt + Enter**. • Press **Enter** or **Tab** to exit the cell.

Hands-On Exercise: Wrap Text

1. Double-click cell B4. You will insert a manual line break so that the week number displays on the next line within the cell.
2. Position the insertion point before the number *1*.
3. Press Alt + Enter .
4. Press Tab to navigate to cell C4.
5. Double-click cell C4 .
6. Position the insertion point before the number *2*.
7. Press Alt + Enter .
8. Press Tab to navigate to cell D4.
9. Double-click cell D4 .
10. Position the insertion point before the number *3*.
11. Press Alt + Enter .
12. Press Tab to navigate to cell E4.
13. Double-click cell E4 .
14. Position the insertion point before the number *4*.
15. Press Alt + Enter .
16. Press Tab to exit the cell. The worksheet should resemble Figure 7.2.

Figure 7.2 Wrap Text

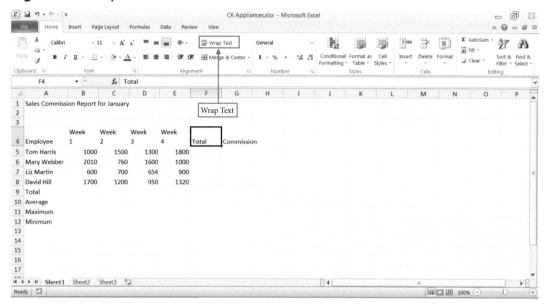

Hands-On Exercise: Calculate Totals

Next, you will calculate the total sales for each week and for each employee.

① Select cells F5:F8 .

② Click the Sum button in the Editing group on the Home tab (**Figure 7.3**). The totals for each employee are calculated and displayed in cells F5:F8.

③ Select cells B9:F9 .

④ Click the Sum button. The totals for each week are calculated and displayed in cells B9:F9. The worksheet should resemble Figure 7.3.

Figure 7.3 Totals Calculated

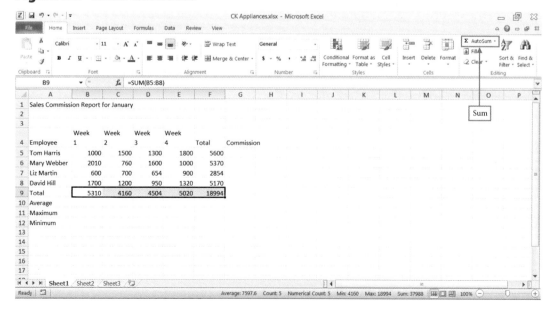

Display Calculations on the Status Bar

The status bar can be customized to perform simple calculations automatically on a group of values. The results of the calculations display on the status bar. The status bar can display the sum, average, numerical count, count, maximum, and minimum values of data that are selected.

- The **Sum function** calculates the total of the values in a range.
- The **Average function** calculates the average of the values in a range.
- The **Numerical Count** function counts the number of cells that contain values in a range.
- The **Count function** counts the total number of cells in a range, regardless of the type of data that is stored in the cells.
- The **Max function** calculates the largest value in a range.
- The **Min function** calculates the smallest value in a range.

Use the following steps to display the results of a calculation on the status bar:

- Select the data you want to calculate.
- Right-click the **status bar** and the Customize Status Bar menu displays (**Figure 7.4**).
- Enable the functions you want to display (Average, Count, Numerical Count, Minimum, Maximum, or Sum).
  - A feature is enabled if a checkmark displays before the option.
  - To deselect a feature that is enabled, click the option, and the checkmark disappears.
- Press Esc to close the Customize Status Bar menu.

Once the features are enabled, you can select data, and the results of the calculations display in the status bar.

Sum function: A function that calculates the total of the values in a range.

Average function: A function that calculates the average of the values in a range.

Numerical Count function: A function that counts the number of cells that contain values in a range.

Count function: A function that counts the total number of cells in a range, regardless of the type of data that is stored in the cells.

Max function: A function that calculates the largest value in a range.

Min function: A function that calculates the smallest value in a range.

Hands-On Exercise: Display Calculations on the Status Bar

1. Select cells A5:E5 .

2. Right-click the status bar and the Customize Status Bar menu displays (Figure 7.4).

3. Enable the Average, Count, Numerical Count, Minimum, Maximum, and Sum functions by clicking the functions that do not contain a checkmark (Figure 7.4).

4. Click Esc to close the Customize Status Bar menu.

5. The results of the calculations display on the status bar (**Figure 7.5**). The average is *1400*. The count is *5* because there are five cells selected. The numerical count is *4* because there are only four cells that contain numerical values. The minimum value is *1000*, which is the smallest value in the selected range. The maximum value is *1800*, which is the largest value in the selected range. The sum is *5600,* which matches the total in cell F5.

Figure 7.4 Customize Status Bar

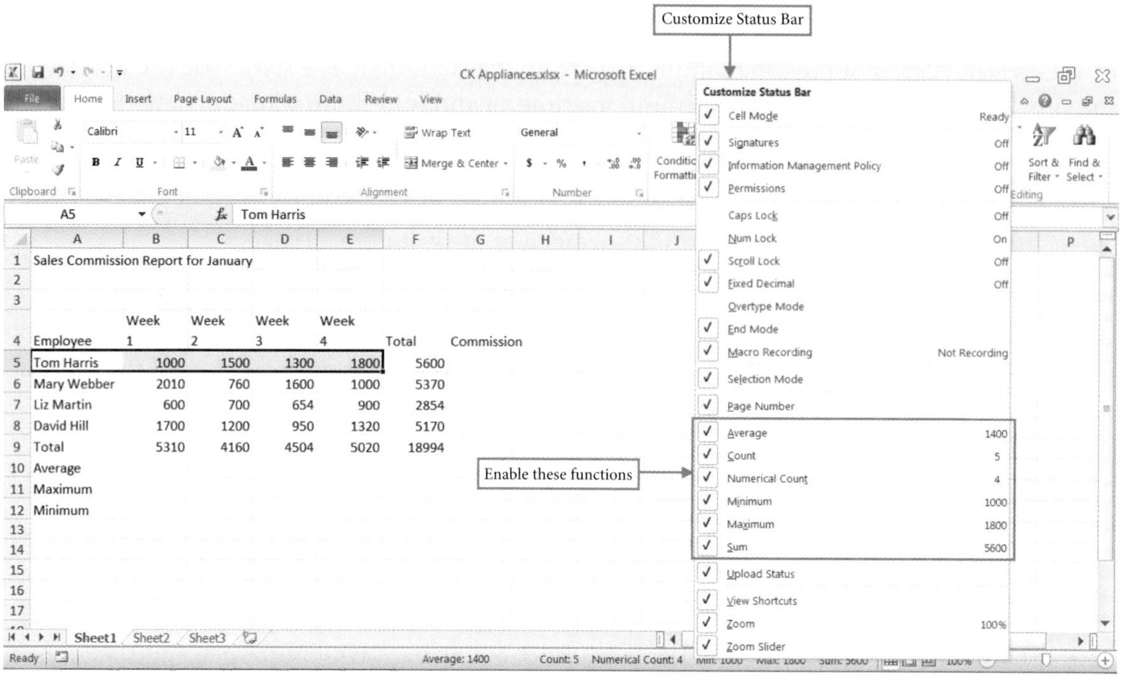

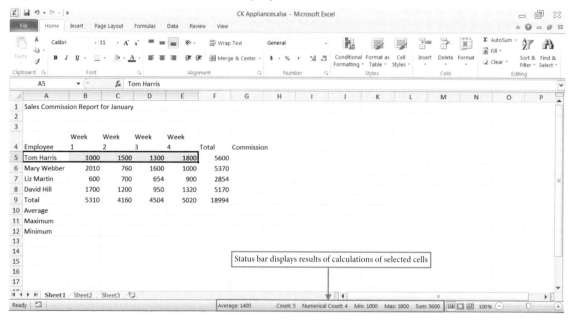

Figure 7.5 Results of Calculations Display in Status Bar

Create Formulas

Formula: An equation that performs calculations on data.

Microsoft Excel 2010 has the capability to create formulas. A **formula** is an equation that performs calculations on data. You can add, subtract, multiply, and divide values using formulas. All formulas must begin with an equal sign. **Table 7.2** contains a list of arithmetic operators that can be used in a formula.

Use the following steps to create a formula:

- Click the cell where you want the formula result to display.
- Type = (equal sign).
- Type the equation for the formula. The equation may contain numbers, operators, and cell addresses.

If you include a cell address in a formula, you can type the cell address, *or* click the cell and the cell address is automatically inserted into the formula. For example, if you want to add 5 to cell A1, the formula is written as =5 + A1. You could type the cell address A1 in the formula, *or* you could click cell A1 and the cell address is inserted into the formula.

Table 7.2 Arithmetic Operators

Arithmetic Operators	Operation
+	Addition
−	Subtraction
*	Multiplication
/	Division
^ (caret)	Exponentiation
%	Percent

Table 7.3 contains examples of formulas.

Table 7.3   Examples of Formulas

Example	Formula
Add 3 + 2	=3 + 2
Add 5 to cell A5	=5 + A5
Multiply cells A10 and A20	=A10 * A20
Subtract 3 from A10 and then add 10	=A10 − 3 + 10
Divide cell B2 by 2	=B2 / 2

Hands-On Exercise: Create a Formula

You are going to calculate the commission for each employee. The commission is calculated by multiplying the total sales for each employee by 10%.

① Click cell G5 . You will create a formula to calculate the commission amount for Tom Harris. The formula for the commission is the total sales multiplied by 10%.

→

② Type = and then click cell F5 , which contains the total sales for employee Tom Harris. Notice that cell F5 is now highlighted.

③ Press the * key.

④ Type **10%**. The formula displays as =F5*10% (**Figure 7.6**).

⑤ Press Enter and the result, 560, displays in cell G5.

⑥ You will create the commission amount for Mary Webber. Instead of clicking on the cell that contains the total sales for Mary, you will type the cell address in the formula. In cell G6, type **=F6*10%**. Notice that cell F6 is now highlighted. Press Enter and the result, 537, displays in cell G6.

⑦ You will copy the formula to cells G7:G8 to calculate the commission for the rest of the employees. Click cell G6 .

⑧ Drag the fill handle through cells G8 and then release the mouse. The commission has been calculated for the rest of the employees.

⑨ Click cell G9 . You will calculate the total commission for all employees.

⑩ Click the Sum button.

⑪ Verify that the cells G5:G8 are selected. If not, select cells G5:G8.

⑫ Press Enter . The worksheet should resemble **Figure 7.7**.

Figure 7.6 Commission Formula

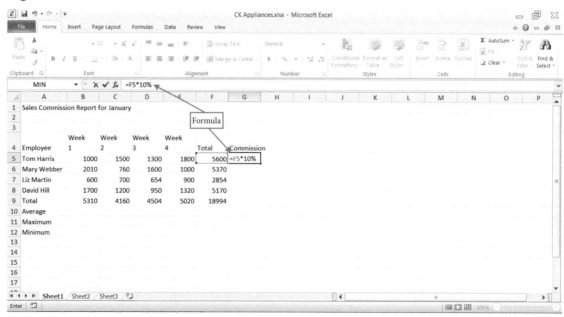

Figure 7.7 Commission Calculated for All Employees

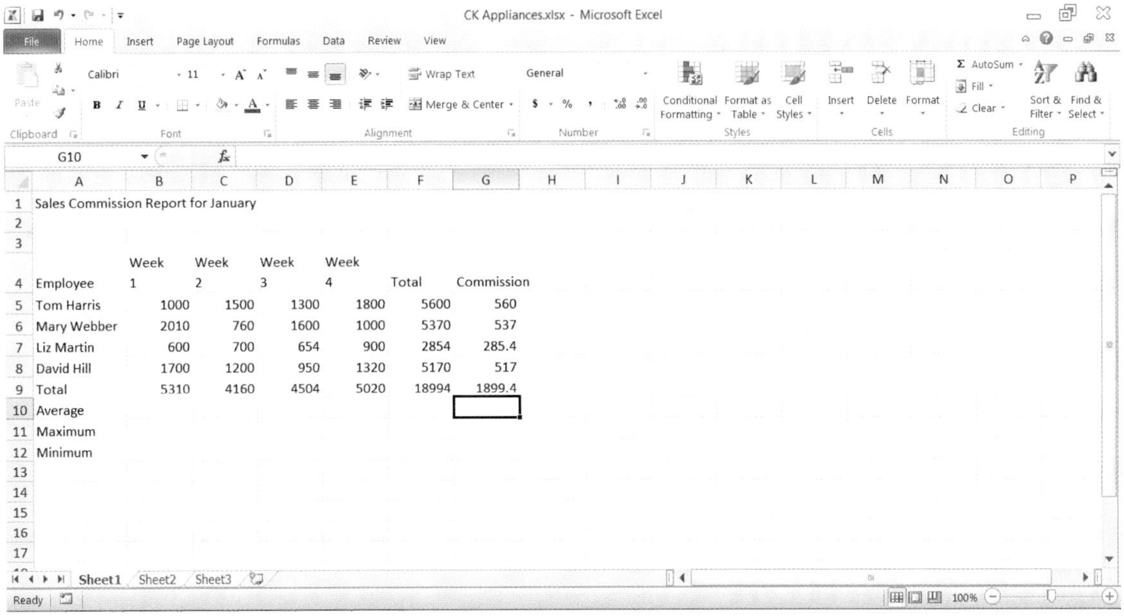

Insert Functions

A **function** is a prewritten formula that performs calculations on values. The most commonly used Microsoft Excel 2010 functions are:

- SUM, which calculates the total of a group of numbers.
- AVERAGE, which calculates the average of a group of numbers.
- MAX, which determines the largest value of a group of numbers.
- MIN, which determines the smallest value of a group of numbers.

A function contains an equal sign, function name, opening parenthesis, arguments, and closing parenthesis. The **arguments** are the values that a function uses to perform the calculations. The arguments may contain numbers or cell addresses. The function name can be written using uppercase or lowercase letters. **Table 7.4** contains examples of Microsoft Excel 2010 functions.

Function: Prewritten formula that performs calculations on values.

Arguments: The values that a function uses to perform the calculations.

Table 7.4 Functions	
Task	Function
Calculate the average of a group of numbers	=AVERAGE(*type cell range*) Example: **=AVERAGE(B4:B7)**
Calculate the sum of a group of numbers	=SUM(*type cell range*) Example: **=SUM(B4:B7)**
Determine the largest value of a group of numbers	=MAX(*type cell range*) Example: **=MAX(B4:B7)**
Determine the smallest value of a group of numbers	=MIN(*type cell range*) Example: **=MIN(B4:B7)**

Instead of typing the formula for a function, you can insert the function by clicking the Sum arrow in the Editing group on the Home tab and selecting the function from the list.

Use these steps to use the Sum button to insert a function:

- Click the cell where you want the result of the function to display.
- Click the **Sum arrow**.
- Select the function from the list.
- Select the arguments.
- Press **Enter** when completed.

Hands-On Exercise: Insert the Average Function

You will insert a function to average the weekly sales.

① Click cell B10 . You will calculate the average sales for week 1.

② Type **=average(**.

③ Select cells B5:B8 . Make certain not to select the total when calculating averages.

④ Type **)** to close the parentheses. The function displays as *=average(B5:B8)* in the Formula Bar and in the cell (**Figure 7.8**).

⑤ Press Enter and *1327.5* displays in cell B10.

⑥ Click cell B10 . The formula in the Formula Bar displays as *=AVERAGE(B5:B8)*. It automatically converted the function name to uppercase.

⑦ Press Delete . You will create the formula again using a different method.

⑧ Type **=av** and you will notice a list displays with function names that begin with the letters *av* (**Figure 7.9**).

⑨ Click AVERAGE from the list and press Tab . The function name and opening parenthesis is automatically inserted in the cell.

⑩ Select cells B5:B8 . Make certain not to select the total when calculating averages.

⑪ The function displays as *=AVERAGE(B5:B8* in the Formula Bar and in the cell.

⑫ Press Enter and *1327.5* displays in cell B10. You did not insert the closing parenthesis in the formula. When you pressed Enter, the formula automatically inserted the closing parenthesis.

⑬ You will copy the formula to cells C10:E10 to calculate the average sales for the rest of the weeks. Click cell B10 .

⑭ Drag the fill handle through cells E10 and then release the mouse. The average sales are calculated for the rest of the weeks (**Figure 7.10**).

Figure 7.8 Calculate the Average of Week 1

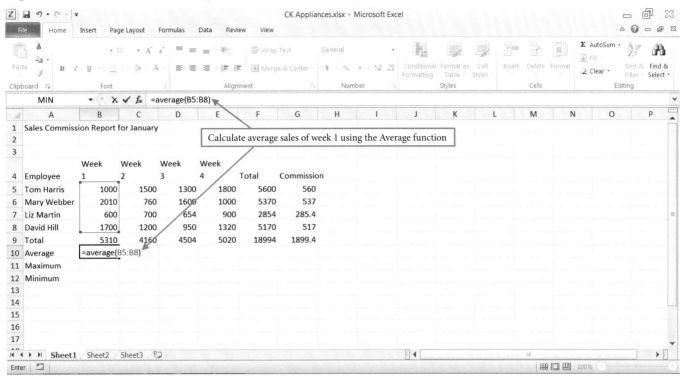

Figure 7.9 List of Functions

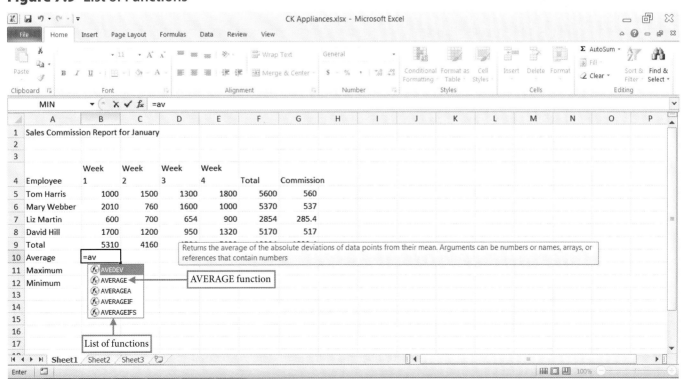

Figure 7.10 Averages Calculated

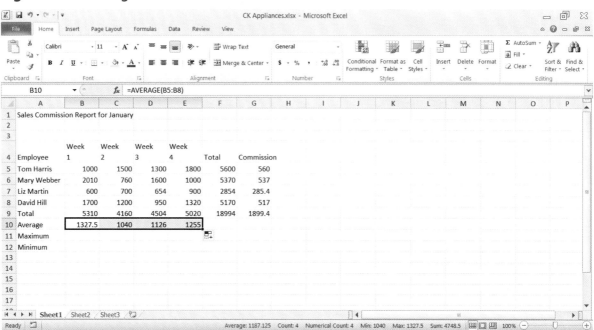

Hands-On Exercise: Insert the Max and Min Functions

You will insert a function to determine the largest and smallest weekly sales amount.

1. Click cell B11 .

2. You will determine the largest sales amount for week 1. Type **=max(**.

3. Select cells B5:B8 .

4. Type **)** to close the parentheses. The function displays as *=max(B5:B8)* in the Formula Bar and in the cell. Closing the parenthesis is not mandatory. When you press Enter, it will automatically close the parenthesis if it is missing.

5. Press Enter and 2010 displays in cell B11. You will copy the formula to cells C11:E11.

6. Click cell B11 .

7. Drag the fill handle through cell E11 and then release the mouse. The largest sales amounts have been calculated for each week.

8. You will insert a function to determine the smallest weekly sales amount using the Sum button. Click cell B12 .

9. Click the Sum arrow on the Editing group on the Home tab.

10. Click Min . Cells B5:B11 are selected. You need to find the minimum sales amount in cells B5:B8. However, cells B9:B11 are also selected. You need to highlight the correct cells.

11. Select cells B5:B8 . The function displays as *=MIN(B5:B8)* in the Formula Bar and in the cell.

⑫ Press Enter and *600* displays in cell B12. You will copy the formula to cells C12:E12.

⑬ Click cell B12 .

⑭ Drag the *fill handle* through cell E12 and then release the mouse. The smallest sales amounts have been calculated for each week. The worksheet should resemble **Figure 7.11**.

⑮ Click the File tab.

⑯ Click Save As and the Save As dialog box displays.

⑰ Type **CK Appliances Revised** in the File name box.

⑱ Click Save .

Figure 7.11 MAX and MIN Functions

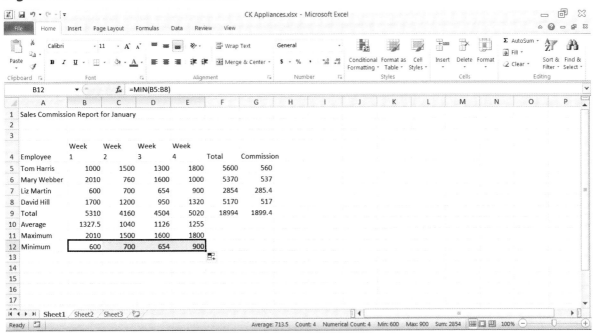

Insert Function Button

You can insert a function using the Insert Function button on the Formula Bar (**Figure 7.12**).

Use these steps to insert a function using the Insert Function button:

- Click in the cell where the function will be inserted.
- Click the **Insert Function** button on the Formula Bar (Figure 7.12), and the Insert Function dialog box displays (**Figure 7.13**).
- Click the **Or select a category** arrow and click **All**. A list of functions displays.
- Select the function you want to use and click **OK**.
- Answer the questions in the dialog box, and click **OK** when completed.

Hands-On Exercise: Insert the MIN Function Using the Insert Function Button

① Click cell B12 .

② Press Delete .

③ Click the Insert Function button (Figure 7.12) and the Insert Function dialog box displays (Figure 7.13).

④ If the MIN function does not display in the *Select a function* list, click the Or select a category arrow and select All (Figure 7.13).

⑤ Click MIN from the *Select a function* list (Figure 7.13).

⑥ Click OK and the Function Arguments dialog box displays.

⑦ Type **B5:B8** in the *Number 1* box (**Figure 7.14**), *or* you can select cells B5:B8 with the mouse.

⑧ Click OK and *600* displays in cell B12. The worksheet should resemble **Figure 7.15**.

⑨ Press Ctrl + ` to view the formulas that were created.

⑩ Press Ctrl + ` to view the values in the worksheet.

⑪ Click the Save button on the Quick Access Toolbar.

Figure 7.12 Insert Function Button

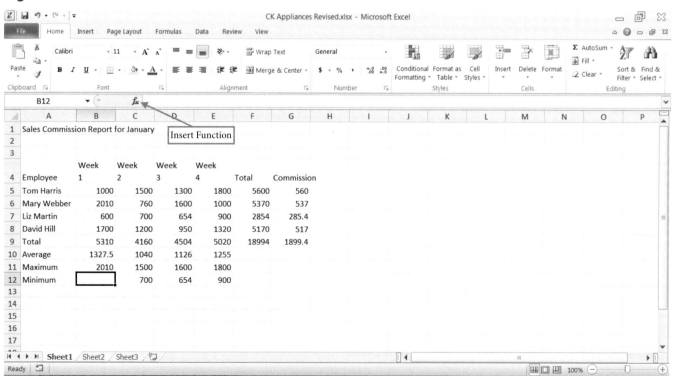

Figure 7.13 Insert Function Dialog Box

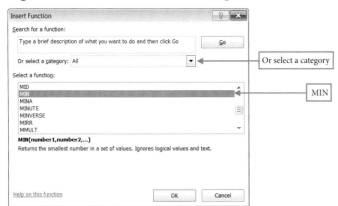

Figure 7.14 Function Arguments Dialog Box

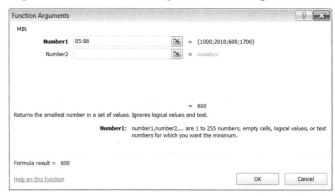

Figure 7.15 Insert Minimum Function to Cell B12

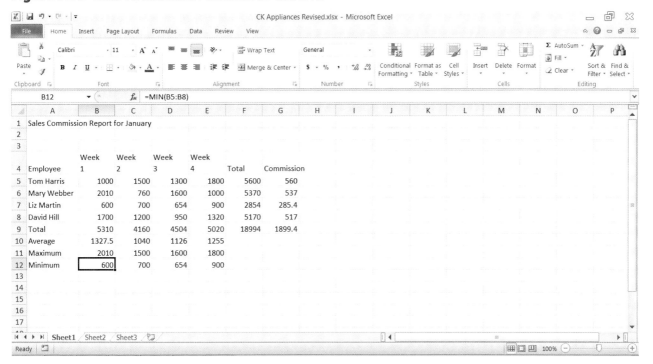

Create a Chart

You can create column, line, pie, bar, area, scatter, and other types of charts. Before creating a chart, you must select the data points you want to include in the chart. The **data points** are the cells in the worksheet that you want to chart. You should include the row and column titles when selecting the data points so that the titles display in the chart. If the data in a worksheet are revised and the data are part of a chart, the chart is automatically updated to reflect the revised data.

Use these steps to create a chart:

- Select the data points you want included in the chart. Include row and column titles if you want them included in the chart.

Data points: The cells in a worksheet that you want to chart.

Axis: The vertical or horizontal line that identifies the information in the chart.

Chart title: The title for the chart.

Data label: The actual value of an element on a chart.

Data points: The cells in a worksheet that you want to chart. The data points should include the row and column titles.

Data series: A group of related data points in a chart. Each data series contains a unique color or pattern that is displayed on the chart and in the legend.

Horizontal axis: An axis on a chart that contains the category labels that describe the information in the chart. In a bar chart, the horizontal axis displays the numeric values of the categories.

Legend: An area on a chart that defines the colors that are assigned to the data series in the chart.

Vertical axis: An axis on a chart that contains the numeric values that represent the categories. In a bar chart, the vertical axis displays the category labels.

- Click the **Insert** tab.
- Select the **chart type** in the Charts group and a gallery displays.
- Click a **chart** from the gallery and the chart displays in the middle of the worksheet.

When the chart is selected, it contains a double border around it. A chart can be moved, resized, or deleted when selected.

A chart contains many elements (**Figure 7.16**). **Table 7.5** describes the various elements of a chart.

Table 7.5 Chart Elements

Chart Element	Description
Axis	An axis is the vertical or horizontal line that identifies the information in the chart.
Chart title	A chart title is the title for the chart.
Data label	A data label is the actual value of an element on a chart.
Data points	The data points are the cells in a worksheet that you want to chart. The data points should include the row and column titles.
Data series	A data series is a group of related data points in a chart. Each data series contains a unique color or pattern that is displayed on the chart and in the legend.
Horizontal axis	In most charts, the horizontal axis contains the category labels that describe the information in the chart. In a bar chart, the horizontal axis displays the numeric values of the categories.
Legend	A legend is an area on a chart that defines the colors that are assigned to the data series in the chart.
Vertical axis	In most charts, the vertical axis contains the numeric values that represent the categories. In a bar chart, the vertical axis displays the category labels.

Figure 7.16 Chart Elements

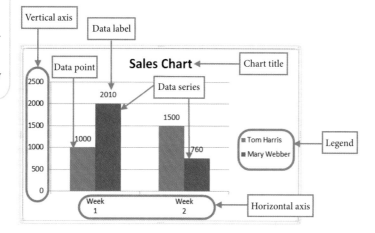

There are 11 types of charts that can be created in Microsoft Excel 2010. **Table 7.6** illustrates some popular chart types.

Table 7.6   Chart Types

Chart Type	Description
Column chart	A column chart illustrates how data change over a period of time. A column chart can also show comparisons among items. Column charts can be created when the data to be charted are arranged in columns and rows. Categories are usually displayed on the horizontal axis, and the values are displayed on the vertical axis.
Line chart	A line chart illustrates continuous data over a period of time, best suited for showing trends in the data. Line charts can be created when the data to be charted are arranged in columns and rows. Categories are usually displayed on the horizontal axis, and the values are displayed on the vertical axis.
Pie chart	A pie chart illustrates the relationship of items in a data series and compares the size of each item to the whole data series. Pie charts can be created when the data to be charted are arranged in one column or row.
Bar chart	A bar chart illustrates comparisons among individual items. Bar charts can be created when the data to be charted are arranged in columns and rows.

Column chart: A chart that illustrates how data change over a period of time.

Line chart: A chart that illustrates continuous data over a period of time, best suited for showing trends in the data.

Pie chart: A chart that illustrates the relationship of items in a data series and compares the size of each item to the whole data series.

Bar chart: A chart that illustrates comparisons among individual items.

Hands-On Exercise: Create a Chart

You will create a 3-D Column chart to display the weekly sales amounts for the employees. The totals, average, maximum, and minimum values will not be displayed on the chart.

(1) Select cells A4:E8 .

(2) Click the Insert tab.

(3) Click the Column button in the Charts group (**Figure 7.17**).

(4) Select the first option in the 3-D Column group named *3-D Clustered Column* (**Figure 7.17**).

(5) The chart is created and displays in the middle of the worksheet (**Figure 7.18**). The chart is surrounded by a double border, indicating that the chart is selected. The Chart Tools contextual tab displays on the Ribbon. The data points are outlined with a blue border. The labels on the horizontal axis are outlined with a purple border (week 1, week 2, etc.). The items in the legend are outlined with a green border (Tom Harris, Mary Webber, etc.).

Figure 7.17 Column Chart Options

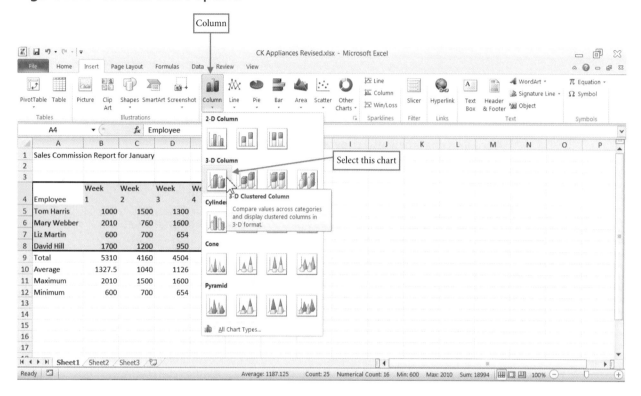

Figure 7.18 Column Chart Created

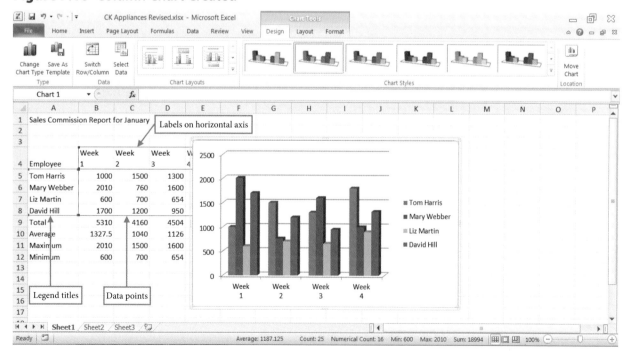

Resize, Move, and Delete a Chart

A chart can be resized, moved, or deleted once the chart is selected. Click the chart border to select the chart. **Table 7.7** describes how to resize, move, and delete a chart.

Table 7.7	Resize, Move, and Delete a Chart
Task	**Steps**
Resize a chart	• Click the **chart border** to select the chart. • Position the mouse pointer on a sizing handle, and a double arrow displays. A sizing handle displays as four dots in the middle of each chart border and as three dots on the corners of the chart border. • Drag the border to resize the chart.
Move a chart to another location on the current sheet	• Click the **chart border** to select the chart. • Position the mouse pointer on the chart border. A four-headed arrow displays. • Drag the chart to another location.
Delete a chart	• Click the **chart border** to select the chart. • Press **Delete** on the keyboard.

Hands-On Exercise: Move, Resize, and Delete a Chart

(1) If the chart is not selected, click the chart border to select it.

(2) You will move the chart below row 13. Position the mouse pointer on the chart border. A four-headed arrow displays.

(3) Drag the chart so that it is positioned in column A of row 14.

(4) Next, you will change the size of the chart so that is extends through the end of column I. Position the mouse pointer on the sizing handle on the right side of the chart border.

(5) When the double arrow displays, drag the border through column I. The chart should resemble **Figure 7.19**.

(6) Next you will delete the chart. Press Delete and the chart is deleted.

(7) Click the Undo button on the Quick Access Toolbar so that the chart reappears.

Figure 7.19 Chart Resized and Moved

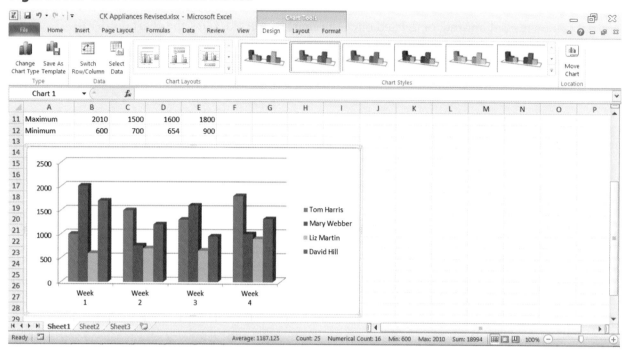

Insert a Chart Title

A chart title can be inserted onto a chart. There are two types of chart titles: A Centered Overlay Title overlays and centers the chart title on the chart without resizing the chart. The Above Chart option displays the chart title at the top of the chart and resizes the chart. The Chart Title button is used to insert a chart title. The Chart Title button is located in the Labels group on the Layout tab of the Chart Tools contextual tab (**Figure 7.20**).

Hands-On Exercise: Insert a Chart Title

1. If the chart is not selected, click the chart border to select it.

2. Click the Layout tab on the Chart Tools contextual tab (Figure 7.20).

3. Click the Chart Title button in the Labels group (Figure 7.20).

4. Click Above Chart (Figure 7.20). A generic chart title called *Chart Title* displays at the top of the chart. You will select the text *Chart Title* and replace it with another chart title.

5. Select the text Chart Title by dragging the mouse across the text or by double-clicking on the text.

6. Type **Weekly Sales Chart**. The chart will resemble **Figure 7.21**.

7. Click the Save button on the Quick Access Toolbar.

Figure 7.20 Chart Title Options

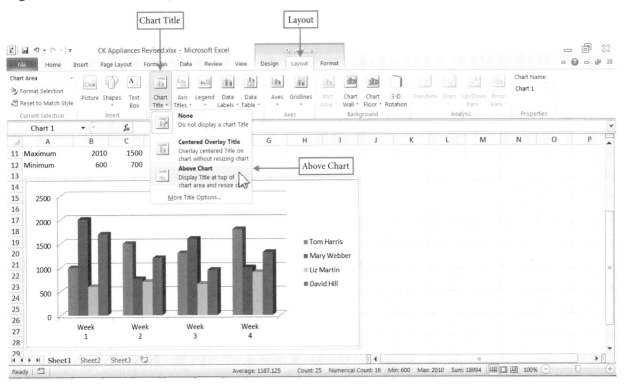

Figure 7.21 Chart Title Inserted

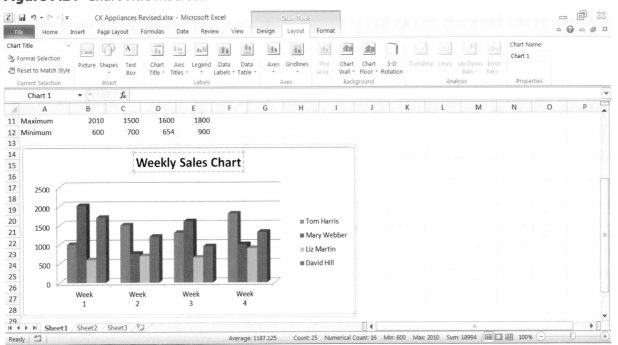

Modify the Data Range of a Chart

You can modify a data range used to create a chart by using the Select Data button. The Select Data button is located in the Data group on the Design tab of the Chart Tools contextual tab (**Figure 7.22**).

Hands-On Exercise: Modify the Data Range of the Chart

(1) Click the chart border to select the chart.

(2) Click the Design tab on the Chart Tools contextual tab (Figure 7.22).

(3) Click Select Data in the Data group (Figure 7.22) and the Select Data Source dialog box displays (**Figure 7.23**). The current data range is selected (Figure 7.23).

(4) You will select all employees but will display the sales for weeks 1 and 2 only. Select cells A4:C8 (**Figure 7.24**). If the Select Data Source dialog box displays on top of the cells that you need to select, you will need to move the Select Data Source dialog box to the right so you can select the data.

(5) Click OK in the Select Data Source dialog box. The chart should resemble **Figure 7.25**. You may need to scroll down the worksheet to display the entire chart.

Figure 7.22 Select Data Button

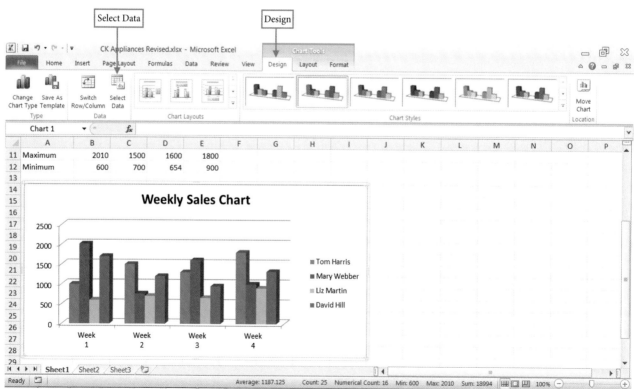

Figure 7.23 Select Data Source Dialog Box

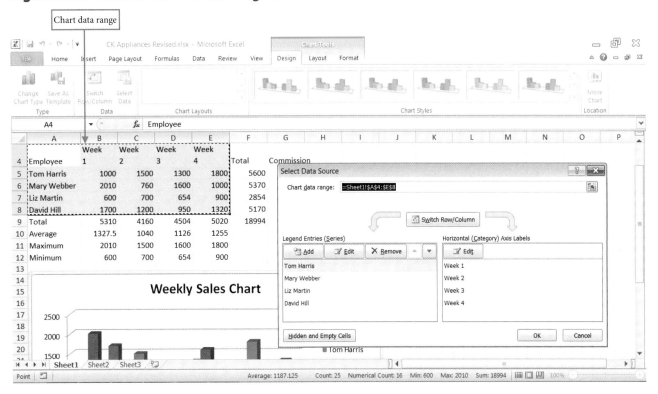

Figure 7.24 Select Chart Data Range

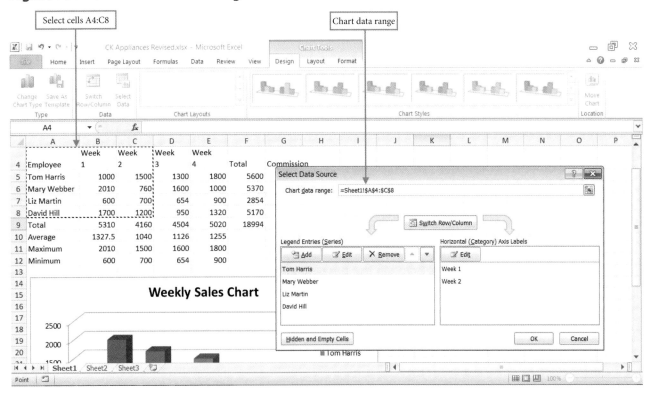

Figure 7.25 Chart Displaying Sales for Weeks 1 and 2

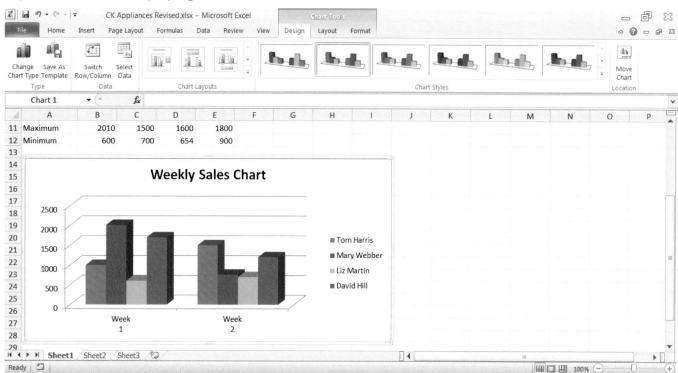

Change a Chart Type

A chart type can be modified after it has been created. The Change Chart Type button is used to change the chart type. The Change Chart Type button is located in the Type group on the Design tab of the Chart Tools contextual tab (**Figure 7.26**).

Hands-On Exercise: Change a Chart Type

1. If the chart is not selected, click the chart border to select it.

2. Click the Design tab on the Chart Tools tab.

3. Click Change Chart Type in the Type group (Figure 7.26) and the Change Chart Type dialog box displays (**Figure 7.27**).

4. Click the Bar category on the left side of the dialog box (Figure 7.27).

5. Click the first chart type in the Bar category on the right side of the dialog box, which is named *Clustered Bar* (Figure 7.27).

6. Click OK . The chart should resemble **Figure 7.28**.

Figure 7.26 Change Chart Type Button

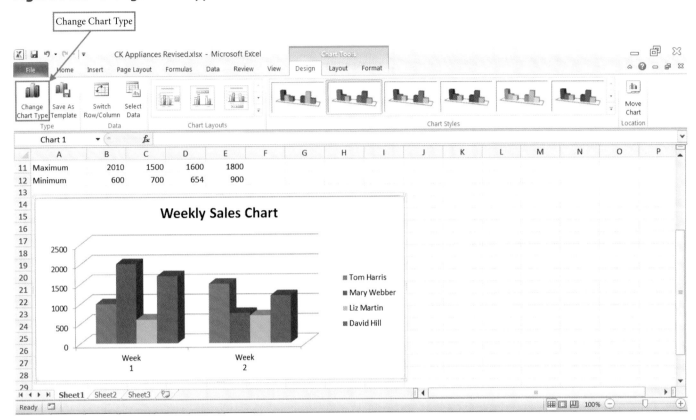

Figure 7.27 Change Chart Type Dialog Box

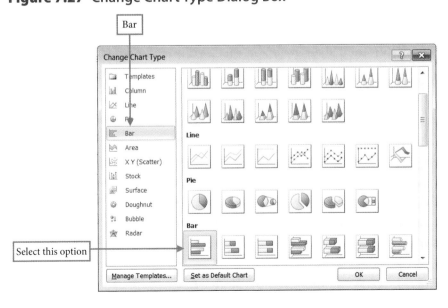

Figure 7.28 Bar Chart

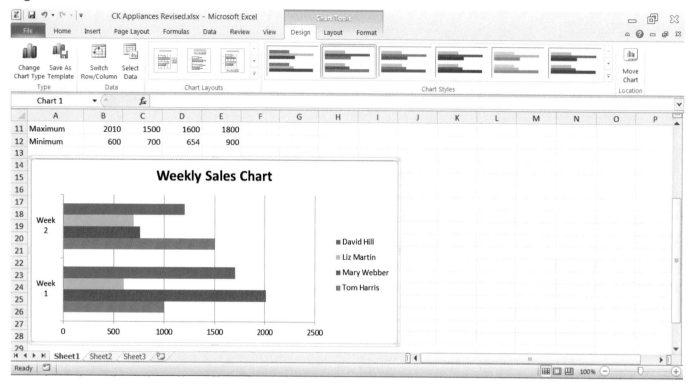

Display Data Labels

Data labels can be displayed on a chart. A data label is the actual value of an element in a chart. The data labels can be positioned in the center, inside end, inside base, or outside end of a data point. The Data Labels button is used to insert data labels on the chart. The Data Labels button is located in the Labels group on the Layout tab of the Chart Tools contextual tab.

Hands-On Exercise: Display Data Labels

① If the chart is not selected, click the chart border to select it.

② Click the Layout tab.

③ Click the Data Labels button in the Labels group (**Figure 7.29**).

④ Select Outside End . The chart should resemble Figure 7.29.

Figure 7.29 Data Labels

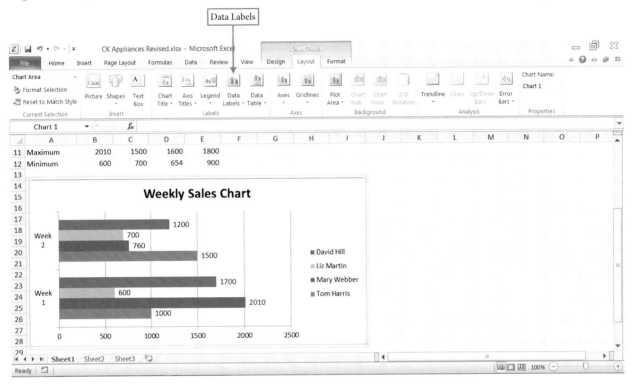

Move a Chart to a New Sheet

A chart can be moved to a new sheet in the workbook. The Move Chart button is used to move a chart. The Move Chart button is located in the Location group on the Design tab of the Chart Tools contextual tab (**Figure 7.30**).

Hands-On Exercise: Move a Chart to a New Sheet

① If the chart is not selected, click the chart border to select it.

② Click the Design tab.

③ Click the Move Chart button in the Location group (Figure 7.30), and the Move Chart dialog box displays.

④ Click the New Sheet option (**Figure 7.31**).

⑤ Type **Sales Chart** in the New sheet box (Figure 7.31).

⑥ Click OK . The chart is moved to a new sheet called Sales Chart (**Figure 7.32**).

⑦ Click the Save button on the Quick Access Toolbar.

Figure 7.30 Move Chart Button

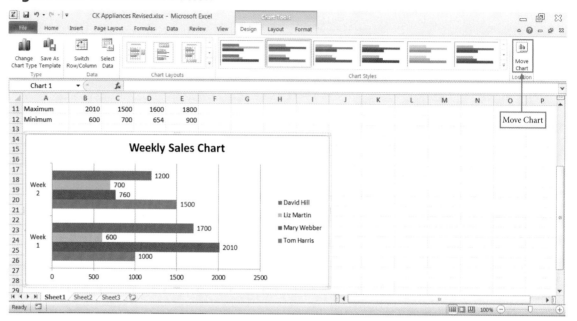

Figure 7.31 Move Chart Dialog Box

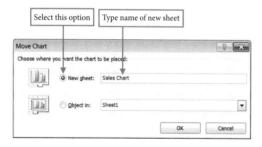

Figure 7.32 Chart Moved to New Sheet

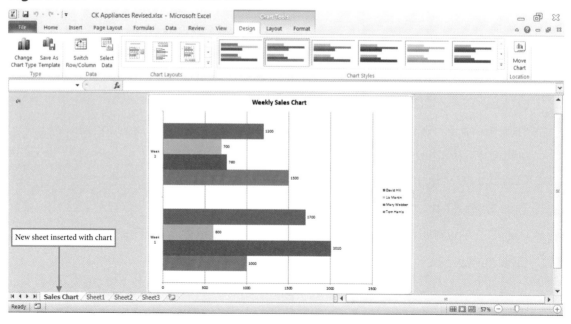

Modify a Chart Legend

A legend is an area on the chart defines the colors assigned to the data series in the chart. The legend automatically displays once a chart is created. However, the legend can be deleted or moved to another location. The Legend button is used to insert the legend on a chart. The Legend button is located in the Labels group on the Layout tab of the Chart Tools contextual tab (**Figure 7.33**).

Hands-On Exercise: Modify a Chart Legend

1. If the chart is not selected, click the chart border to select it.

2. Click the Layout tab.

3. Click the Legend button in the Labels group (Figure 7.33).

4. Click None to turn off the legend. The chart is updated, and the legend is removed.

5. Click the Legend button.

6. Click Show Legend at Bottom . The chart is updated, and the legend displays at the bottom of the chart (**Figure 7.34**).

7. Click the Save button on the Quick Access Toolbar.

Figure 7.33 Legend Button

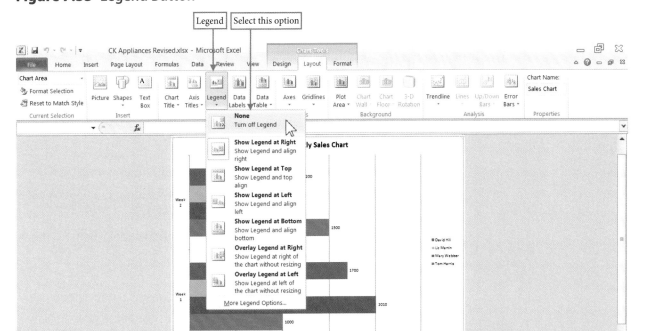

Figure 7.34 Show Legend at Bottom of Chart

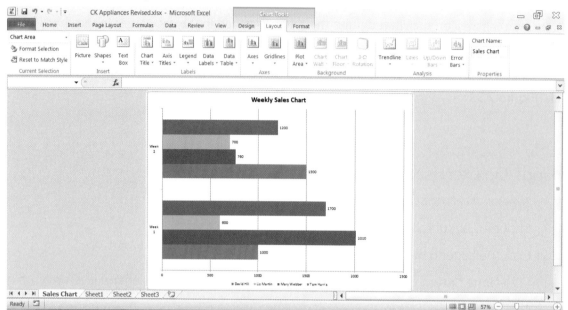

Manipulate Worksheets

When you create a Microsoft Excel 2010 workbook, three worksheets (or sheets) display by default. The names of the worksheets are Sheet1, Sheet2, and Sheet3. The names of the worksheets display on the Sheet tab bar located at the bottom of the window (**Figure 7.35**). You can insert, delete, and rename worksheets. A worksheet name can contain up to 31 characters. Additionally, you can change the order of the worksheets and change the tab color of the worksheets. **Table 7.8** describes how to manipulate worksheets.

Table 7.8 Sheet Commands

Task	Steps
Insert a worksheet at end of existing worksheets	• Click the **Insert Worksheet** button on the Sheet tab bar (**Figure 7.36**).
Insert a worksheet in front of an existing worksheet	• Click the **sheet tab** where you want to insert a new sheet. • Click the **Insert arrow** in the Cells group on the Home tab (Figure 7.35). • Click **Insert Sheet** and the new sheet is inserted. ○ Example: If you click Sheet1 and then insert a sheet, the new sheet will be inserted before Sheet1. *Or,* use the shortcut menu: • Right-click the **sheet tab** where you want to insert a new sheet. • Click **Insert** on the shortcut menu and the Insert dialog box displays. • The Worksheet icon on the General tab should be automatically selected. If it is not, select the **Worksheet** icon. • Click **OK**.

Table 7.8 *continued*

Delete a worksheet	• Click the **sheet tab** you want to delete. • Click the **Delete arrow** in the Cells group on the Home tab (Figure 7.35). • Click **Delete Sheet** and the sheet is deleted. *Or,* use the shortcut menu: • Right-click the **sheet tab** you want to delete. • Click **Delete** on the shortcut menu.
Rename a worksheet	• Right-click the **sheet tab** you want to rename. • Click **Rename** on the shortcut menu and type the new sheet name. • Press **Enter**. *Or:* • Double-click the **sheet tab** and type the new sheet name. • Press **Enter**.
Change the order of worksheets	• Drag the sheet to new location on the Sheet tab bar.
Activate a sheet	• Click the **sheet tab**. *Or:* • Right-click a **tab scroll button** on the Sheet tab bar (Figure 7.36). A list of sheets displays on the shortcut menu. • Click the **sheet** to activate. *Or:* • Press **Ctrl + Page Down** to navigate to the next sheet. • Press **Ctrl + Page Up** to navigate to the previous sheet.
View more or less sheet tabs on the sheet tab bar	• Drag the **tab split bar** to the right or left (Figure 7.36). • Double-click the **tab split bar** to return the tab split bar to its original position.
Display sheet tabs on sheet tab bar	If all the sheet tabs are not displayed in the Sheet tab bar, use the tab scroll buttons to display the sheet tabs (Figure 7.36). Four tab scroll buttons are displayed at the beginning of the Sheet tab bar. ◄ ◄ ► ► • The first button brings the first sheet tab into view. • The second button brings the previous sheet tab into view. • The third button brings the next sheet tab into view. • The last button brings the last sheet tab into view.
Change tab color	You can modify the color of the sheet tab so you can visually locate a specific sheet. • Right-click the **sheet tab**. • Point to **Tab Color** and a gallery of colors displays. • Select the **color** from the gallery.

Hands-On Exercise: Rename, Insert, Delete, and Change Tab Colors of Sheets

(1) Click Sheet1 on the Sheet tab bar to navigate to Sheet1.

(2) Double-click Sheet1 , and the sheet name is selected.

(3) Type **Sales Commission** and press Enter . *Sales Commission* is the new name of the sheet.

(4) You will insert a new worksheet before Sheet3. Click Sheet3 on the Sheet tab bar.

(5) Click the Insert arrow in the Cells group on the Home tab (Figure 7.35).

(6) Click Insert Sheet , and the new sheet displays before Sheet3. The name of the new sheet is *Sheet1*.

(7) You will delete *Sheet1*. Right-click Sheet1 , and the shortcut menu displays.

(8) Click Delete .

(9) You will delete *Sheet3*. Right-click Sheet 3 , and the shortcut menu displays.

(10) Click Delete .

(11) Right-click the Sheet2 sheet tab.

(12) Click Rename .

(13) Type **Employee Data** and press Enter . Sheet2 is now named *Employee Data*.

(14) You will change the order of the sheets. You will move the Sales Commission sheet so that it is the first sheet in the workbook. Drag the *Sales Commission* sheet tab before the *Sales Chart* sheet.

(15) Press Ctrl + Home to navigate to cell A1.

(16) Next you will change the tab colors of the sheets. Right-click the Sales Chart sheet tab.

(17) Point to Tab Color .

(18) Click the Yellow color from the Standard Colors group.

(19) Right-click the Employee Data sheet tab.

(20) Point to Tab Color .

(21) Click the Blue color from the Standard Colors group.

(22) Right-click the Sales Commission sheet tab.

(23) Point to Tab Color .

(24) Click the Green color from the Standard Colors group.

(25) Click the Save button on the Quick Access Toolbar. The worksheet should resemble Figure 7.36.

Figure 7.35 Sheet Tab Bar and Insert and Delete Buttons

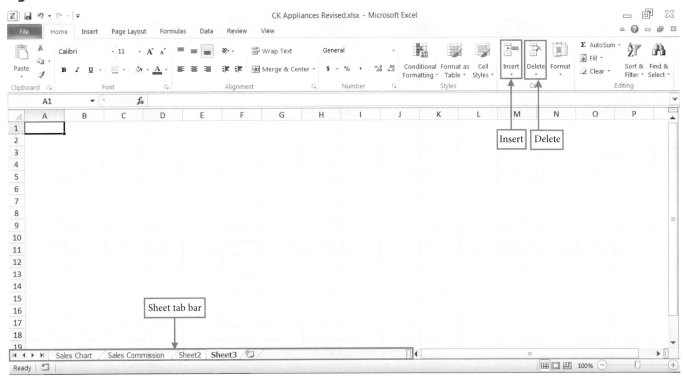

Figure 7.36 Revised Sheet Tab Bar

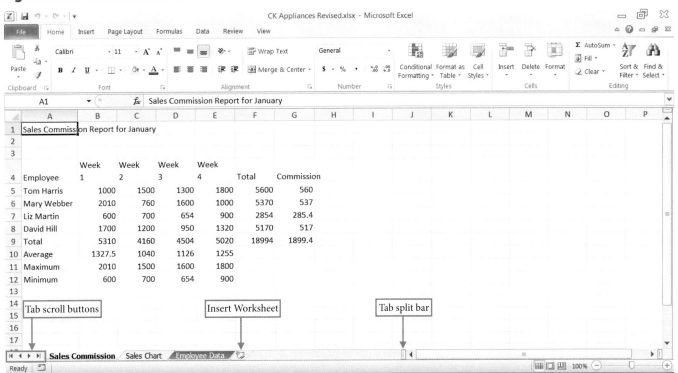

Cell Styles

Cell Styles: A command that quickly formats a cell by selecting one of the predefined styles in the gallery.

The **Cell Styles** command allows you to format a cell quickly by selecting one of the predefined styles in the gallery. Cell styles are used to emphasize data in a worksheet. The styles are organized in the gallery by category. As you point to various items in the gallery, a preview of the effect displays in the cell. The Cell Styles command is located in the Styles group on the Home tab (**Figure 7.37**).

Use these steps to apply a cell style:

- Select the **cell** you want to format with a cell style.
- Click the **Cell Styles** button in the Styles group on the Home tab.
- Select a **cell style** from the gallery.

Use these steps to remove a cell style:

- Select the **cell** that contains the cell style you want to remove.
- Click the **Cell Styles** button.
- Click **Normal** from the gallery.

Hands-On Exercise: Format Cells Using Cell Styles

1. Click cell A1 .

2. Click the Cell Styles button in the Styles group on the Home tab and the gallery displays (Figure 7.37).

3. Click Title from the Titles and Headings group, and the style is applied to cell A1 (Figure 7.37).

4. Select cells A9:G9 .

5. Click the Cell Styles button.

6. Click Total from the Titles and Headings group. A top and double bottom border is inserted around the selected cells and the text is bold.

7. Select cells A4:G4 .

8. Click the Cell Styles button.

9. Click Heading 3 from the Titles and Headings group.

10. Click cell A1 , and cells A4:G4 are deselected.

11. The word *Commission* in cell G4 overlaps to column H. Double-click the right boundary of the column heading G to automatically adjust the column width to fit the contents of the cells. The worksheet should resemble **Figure 7.38**.

Figure 7.37 Cell Styles

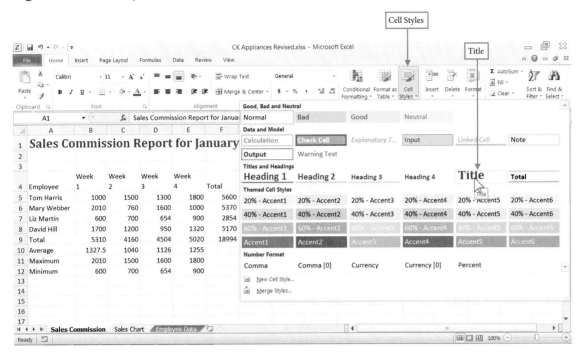

Figure 7.38 Cell Styles Applied to Worksheet

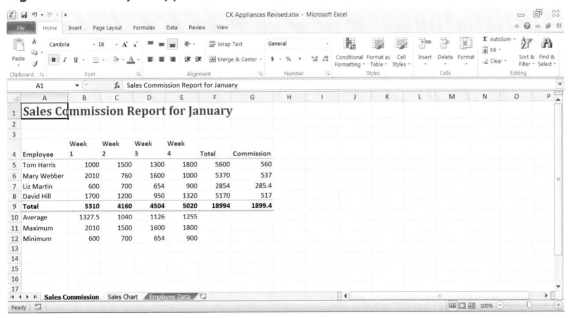

Format Cells Using the Format Cells Dialog Box

The Format Cells dialog box can be used to format cells. You can select number formats, alignment, font, border, and other formatting options. The Format Cells dialog box allows you to select multiple formatting options instead of selecting each option individually from the Ribbon. The Format Cells dialog box can be accessed by clicking the Format button in the Cells group on the Home tab and selecting Format Cells (**Figure 7.39**). The Format Cells dialog box can also be accessed by clicking the dialog box launcher next to the Font, Alignment, or Number groups on the Home tab (Figure 7.39).

Hands-On Exercise: Format Cells Using the Format Cells Dialog Box

1. Select cells B5:G5 .

2. Hold the Ctrl key and select cells B9:G9 . Pressing the Ctrl key allows you to select multiple nonadjacent cells. You will format these cells with the currency format.

3. Click the Format button (Figure 7.39).

4. Click Format Cells .

5. Click Currency in the Category list (Figure 7.39). The currency format is used to display monetary values.

6. Click the third option in the Negative numbers list (Figure 7.39). This option displays negative numbers in parentheses.

7. Click OK .

8. Select cells B6:G8 . You will format these cells with the comma format.

9. Hold the Ctrl key and select cells B10:E12 .

10. Click the Comma Style button in the Number group on the Home tab.

11. Select cells B4:G4 . You will center the text horizontally in the cells.

12. Click the dialog box launcher next to the Alignment group. The Format Cells dialog box displays. The Alignment tab is active because you launched the dialog box from the Alignment group (**Figure 7.40**). You can click the tabs to view the options that are available.

13. Click the Horizontal arrow (Figure 7.40).

14. Select Center from the list.

15. Click OK .

16. Right-click row heading 2 .

17. Click Delete to delete the row.

18. Click cell A1 . The worksheet should resemble **Figure 7.41**.

19. Click the Save button on the Quick Access Toolbar. The formatting changes you applied to the cells are automatically updated on the chart. Click the Sales Chart sheet tab. Notice that the values at the bottom of the chart are formatted as currency and the values for each data point are formatted with the comma style.

Figure 7.39 Format Cells Dialog Box

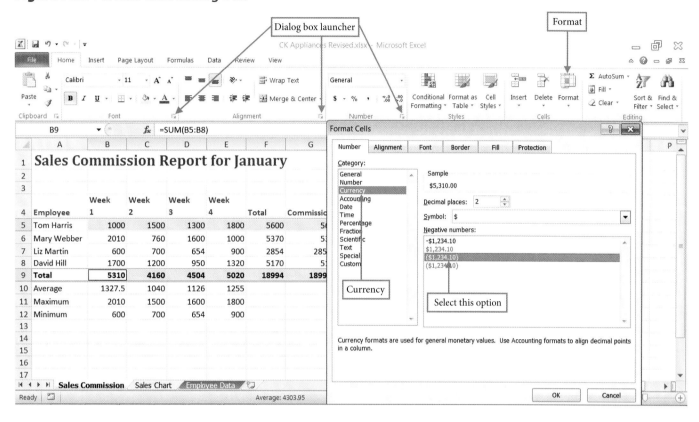

Figure 7.40 Alignment Tab on Format Cells Dialog Box

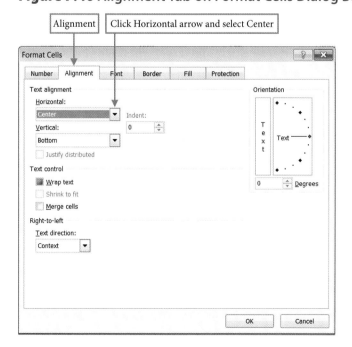

Figure 7.41 Worksheet Formatted

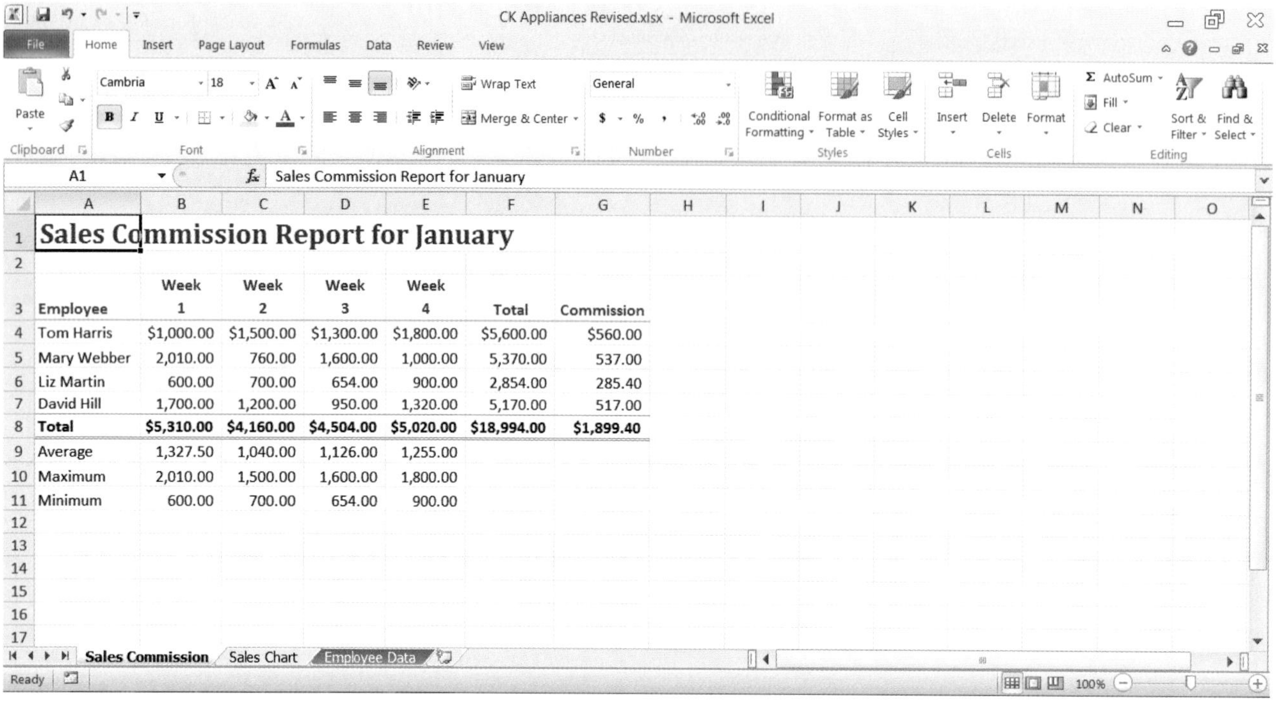

Absolute Reference

Relative reference: A cell address that changes the row or column in the formula based on the location in which the formula is being copied.

Absolute reference: A cell address that does not change when a formula is copied.

Mixed reference: A cell address where part of the cell address changes when the formula is copied.

All the formulas you created thus far have been using relative references. A **relative reference** is a cell address that changes the row or column in the formula based on the location in which the formula is being copied. For example, the commission formula in cell G4 is *=F4*10%*. When the formula was copied to cell G5, the formula changed the row number to 5 to reflect the row number where the formula was copied. The formula in G5 is *=F5*10%*.

An **absolute reference** is a cell address that does not change when the formula is copied. The dollar sign ($) symbol is used to make a cell address an absolute reference. A dollar sign must be inserted before the column letter and row number of a cell that is an absolute reference. For example, to make the commission formula is cell G4 an absolute reference, the formula must be *=$F$4*10%*. You can press **F4** after the cell address in the formula and it will change the cell address to an absolute reference and insert the dollar signs. If you were to copy the formula *=$F$4*10%* to another cell, the formula would not change.

A **mixed reference** is a cell address where part of the cell address changes when the formula is copied. A mixed cell reference contains one dollar sign which is placed before the column letter or row number that will not change when copied. For example, a formula of *=$A10*5* is a mixed reference because it contains one dollar sign in the cell address. When the formula is copied to other rows, the cell address referencing column A does not change because it is an absolute reference to column A. The row number would change relative to the row in which the formula is being copied. When the formula is copied to row 11, the formula would display as *=$A11*5*.

Hands-On Exercise: Use Absolute Reference in a Formula

Assume the company is offering a 5% bonus based on the total sales of the employee for the month of January. You will create a formula using an absolute reference to calculate the bonus amounts in Column H.

1. Click the Sales Commission sheet tab.

2. Click cell A13 .

3. Type **Bonus Percent** and press the right arrow . The active cell is B13.

4. Type **5%** and press Enter .

5. Click cell H3 .

6. Type **Bonus Amount** and press Enter . Cell H3 is automatically formatted the same as cells A3:G3 because Microsoft Excel 2010 noticed that a pattern existed and applied it to the next cell. The only format it does not apply is borders. The active cell is H4.

7. You will calculate the bonus amount for the employee. The bonus amount is calculated by multiplying the total sales amount in cell F4 by the bonus percent in cell B13.

   a. Type **=F4*B13** and press Enter . The bonus is $280.00.

8. You will copy the formula to cells H5:H7.

   a. Click cell H4 .

   b. Drag the fill handle through cells H7. All the bonus amounts for the rest of the employees are zero because when the formula was copied, it used relative addresses. Click cell H5 . The formula is =F5*B14. There are no data in cell B14. The formula needs to include cell B13 instead of B14. You need to make B13 an absolute reference so when the formula is copied, the cell address (B13) does not change.

9. Select cells H4:H7 .

10. Press Delete .

11. Click cell H4 .

12. Type **=F4*B13**.

13. Press F4 , on the keyboard and the dollar signs display before the column letter and row number of cell address B13. The formula displays as =F4*$B$13 in the cell and Formula Bar, as shown in **Figure 7.42**.

14. Press Enter . $280.00 displays in cell H4.

15. Click cell H4 .

16. Drag the fill handle through cells H7 to copy the formula.

Figure 7.42 Absolute Reference in Formula

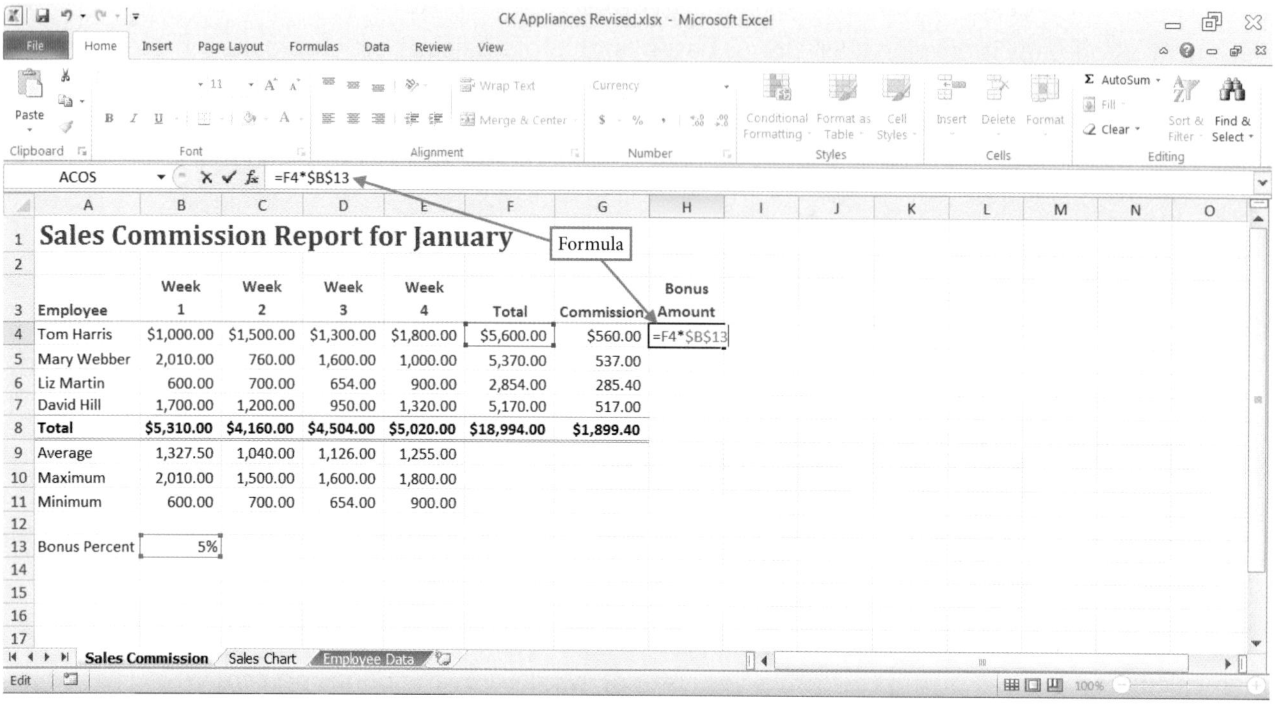

Format Painter Button

The Format Painter button copies the formatting of a selected cell and applies that formatting to other cells in a workbook.

Use these steps to copy formatting:

- Click in the cell that has the formatting that you want to copy.
- Click the **Format Painter** button in the Clipboard group on the Home tab if you want to copy the format to one selection or range (**Figure 7.43**).
- Drag the mouse pointer, which has changed to a brush, over the cells to which you want to copy the format.

If you want to use the Format Painter to format cells throughout a workbook multiple times, double-click the Format Painter button. It will remain active until you click it again or press the Esc key.

Hands-On Exercise: Use the Format Painter Button to Copy Formats

① You will copy the format of cells G3:G8 to cells H3:H8. Select cells G3:G8 .

② Click the Format Painter button in the Clipboard group on the Home tab (Figure 7.43).

③ Drag the mouse pointer over cells H3:H8 .

④ Double-click cell H3 . You will wrap the text in the cell. Position the insertion point before the word *Amount*.

⑤ Press Alt + Enter , and the word *Amount* wraps to the next line.

⑥ Press Enter to exit the cell.

Figure 7.43 Format Painter Button

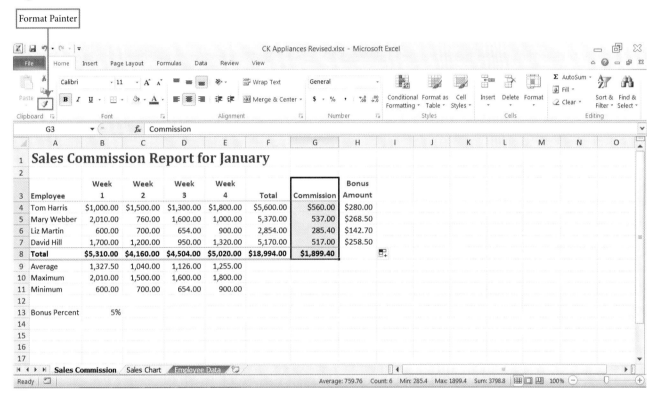

Hands-On Exercise: Calculate Total of Bonus Amounts

① You will calculate the total of the bonus amounts. Click cell H8 .

② Click the Sum button.

③ Verify that cells H4:H7 are selected. If not, select the cells. Press Enter . The total is $949.70.

④ Click cell B13 . If you change the bonus percent, the values in column H will change as it calculates the new bonus amounts.

⑤ Type **2%** and press Enter . The bonus amounts in Column H change.

⑥ Click the Undo button on the Quick Access Toolbar.

⑦ Click the Save button on the Quick Access Toolbar. The worksheet should resemble **Figure 7.44**.

Figure 7.44 Total of Bonus Amounts Calculated

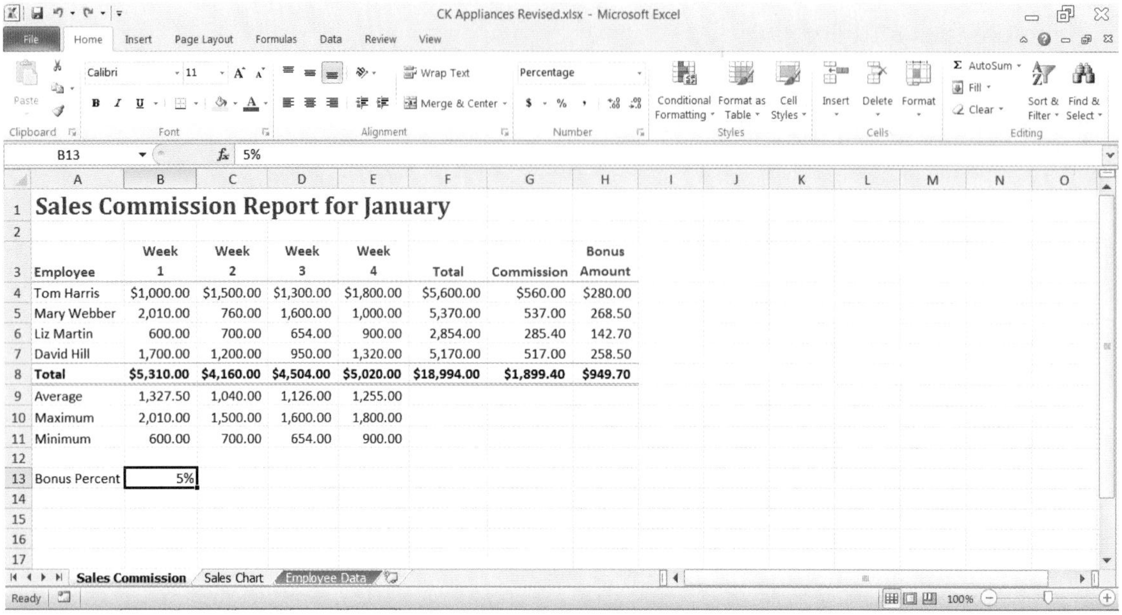

Freeze Panes

Freeze Panes: A command that allows certain rows and/or columns of a worksheet to be visible even while scrolling to other parts of a worksheet.

The **Freeze Panes** command allows certain rows and/or columns of a worksheet to be visible even while scrolling to other parts of a worksheet. This is especially handy when you want to keep the column and row titles visible at all times while navigating a worksheet. The Freeze Panes button is located in the Window group on the View tab. When the Freeze Panes button is clicked, a list displays with three choices:

- Freeze Panes

  —The Freeze Panes option freezes both rows and columns at the same time.
- Freeze Top Row

  —The Freeze Top Row option freezes only the top row of the worksheet.
- Freeze First Column

  —The Freeze First Column option freezes only the first column of the worksheet.

A solid vertical line displays under the rows that are frozen. A solid horizontal line displays to the right of the columns that are frozen. **Table 7.9** describes the various Freeze Panes commands.

Table 7.9 Freeze Panes Command

Task	Steps
Freeze rows only	• Click the **row heading** below the row(s) you want to keep visible. • Click the **View** tab. • Click the **Freeze Panes** button in the Window group (**Figure 7.45**). • Click **Freeze Panes.**

Table 7.9 *continued*

Freeze columns only	• Click the **column heading** to the right of the column(s) you wish to keep visible. • Click the **View** tab. • Click the **Freeze Panes** button in the Window group (Figure 7.45). • Click **Freeze Panes**.
Freeze rows and columns	• Click the **cell** below and to the right of the row(s) and column(s) you want to keep visible. • Click the **View** tab. • Click the **Freeze Panes** button in the Window group (Figure 7.45). • Click **Freeze Panes**.
Freeze top row	• Click the **View** tab. • Click the **Freeze Panes** button in the Window group (Figure 7.45). • Click **Freeze Top Row**.
Freeze first column	• Click the **View** tab. • Click the **Freeze Panes** button in the Window group (Figure 7.45). • Click **Freeze First Column**.
Unfreeze rows or columns	• Click the **View** tab. • Click the **Freeze Panes** button in the Window group (Figure 7.45). • Click **Unfreeze Panes**.

Hands-On Exercise: Freeze Panes

(1) Click the Employee Data sheet tab. This worksheet contains information about each employee.

(2) Press the Page Down key a few times. Row 1 is no longer visible. You will freeze row 1 so that the column titles in row 1 are always displayed, even when scrolling through the sheet.

(3) Press Ctrl + Home to navigate to the beginning of the worksheet.

(4) Click the View tab.

(5) Click the Freeze Panes button in the Window group (Figure 7.45).

(6) Click Freeze Top Row . A solid vertical line displays below the first row indicating that the row is frozen (Figure 7.45).

(7) Press the Page Down key a few times and you will notice that Row 1 is visible at all times, even when scrolling.

(8) Press Ctrl + Home to navigate to the top of the worksheet. Next, you will unfreeze the panes.

(9) Click the Freeze Panes button.

(10) Click Unfreeze Panes .

Figure 7.45 Freeze Panes

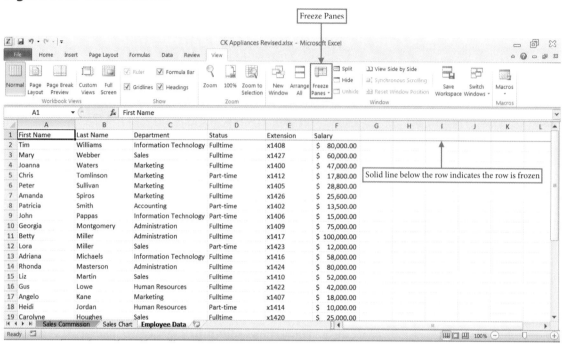

Format Cells as a Table

You can organize and manipulate data easily by formatting the cells in a table format. The **Format as Table** command converts a range of cells to a table and allows you to select a predefined table format. By formatting the data as a table, you can easily sort and filter the data based on specific criteria.

Use these steps to format data as a table:

- Select the data that you want to format as a table. Include the column headings if you want them included in the table.
- Click the **Format as Table** button in the Styles group on the Home tab (**Figure 7.46**).
- Select a **table style** from the gallery and the Format As Table dialog box displays.
- Click the **My table has headers checkbox** if the selected data contains column headings. The column headings are also referred to as column headers.
- Click **OK**.

Use these steps to remove a table format:

- Select the cells that are part of the table.
- Click the **Clear** button in the Editing group on the Home tab.
- Click the **Design** tab in the Table Tools contextual tab.
- Click the **Convert to Range** button in the Tools group.
- A dialog box displays asking you if you want to convert the table to a normal range. Click **Yes**.
- Click **Clear Formats** and the formatting is removed from the table.

Use these steps to remove the sort and filter feature from the table:

- Click in the table.
- Click the **Sort & Filter** button in the Editing group on the Home tab (Figure 7.46).
- Click **Filter**.

Hands-On Exercise: Format Cells as a Table

1. Select cells A1:F29 .

2. Click the Home tab.

3. Click the Format as Table button in the Styles group (Figure 7.46).

4. Select Table Style Medium 2 , which is the second option in the Medium category in the gallery (Figure 7.46). The Format As Table dialog box displays.

5. The My table has headers checkbox should be selected to indicate that the table contains headers (**Figure 7.47**).

6. Click OK .

7. Press Ctrl + Home . The worksheet should resemble **Figure 7.48**. The table is formatted. An arrow displays next to the column headers in Row 1, which contain options for sorting and filtering the data in the table. The arrows will not display when the worksheet is printed. The table contains banded rows, which means that the even rows are formatted with different shading than the odd rows to make the table easier to read.

Figure 7.46 Format Cells as a Table

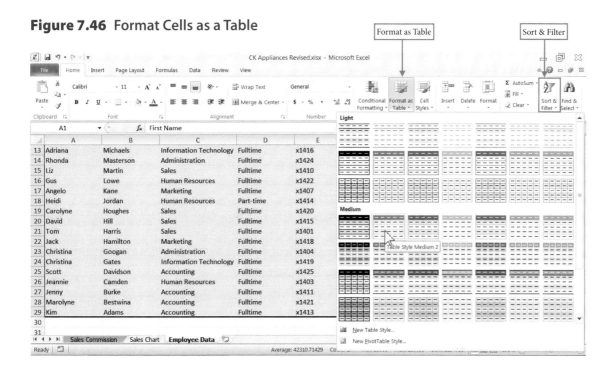

Figure 7.47 Format As Table Dialog Box

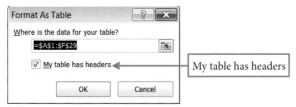

Figure 7.48 Table Style Applied to Cells

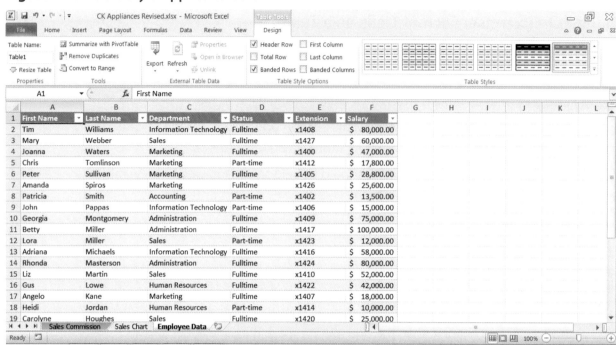

Sort and Filter Data

Sorting: Rearranges data in a certain order.

Filtering: A quick method for locating specific data or data based on specific criteria.

Once the data are formatted as a table, you can sort and filter the data. **Sorting** rearranges data in a certain order. The data can be sorted in ascending or descending order. Sorting and filtering can be performed on one or more columns in a worksheet. **Filtering** data is a quick method for locating specific data or data based on specific criteria. **Table 7.10** describes the sort and filter commands.

Table 7.10	Sort and Filter Commands
Task	**Steps**
Sort data	• Click the arrow next to the column header you want to sort, and a variety of sorting options displays. 　○ For numeric fields, you can select **Sort Smallest to Largest** or **Sort Largest to Smallest**. 　○ For text fields, you can select **Sort A to Z** or **Sort Z to A**.
Filter data	• Click the arrow next to each column header you want to filter and a variety of filtering options display. By default, all values in the column appear in the list and are displayed in the table. The Select All checkbox and the checkbox next to each value is automatically selected. 　○ To filter for specific data, click the **Select All** checkbox to deselect all checkboxes in the list and then click the checkbox for the data you want to filter. 　○ To filter for certain criteria, point to **Text Filters** or **Number Filters** and then select a filter from the list.
Clear filter	• Click the arrow next to the column header and click **Clear Filter**. *Or:* • Click the **Sort & Filter** button in the Editing group on the Home tab, and then click **Clear**.

Hands-On Exercise: Sort and Filter Data

1. You will sort the data in ascending order by last name. Click the arrow next to the *Last Name* column header in Row 1 (**Figure 7.49**).

2. Click Sort A to Z . The last names are sorted in ascending order. *Kim Adams* is the first employee listed.

3. You will filter the data to display all employees who work in the Marketing department. Click the arrow next to the *Department* column header in Row 1.

4. Click the Select All checkbox to deselect all departments.

5. Click the Marketing checkbox to filter for the Marketing department (**Figure 7.50**).

6. Click OK . Six employees who work in the Marketing department are displayed. Notice that the arrow next to the Department column changes to a Filter button, indicating that a filter was applied (**Figure 7.51**). The arrow also changed in the Department column when the sorting was applied to the column (Figure 7.51). The status bar indicates the number of records that match the filter. The status bar states *6 of 28 records found* (Figure 7.51).

7. You will remove the filter. Click the Filter button (Figure 7.51) next to the Department column header and click Clear Filter from "Department" .

8. You will filter the data to locate the employees whose salary is greater than $50,000. Click the arrow next to the Salary column header.

9. Point to Number Filters (**Figure 7.52**).

10. Click Greater Than (Figure 7.52), and the Custom AutoFilter dialog box displays.

11. Enter **50000** in the box to the right of the Salary is greater than box, and click OK (**Figure 7.53**).

12. Ten employees match the criteria. The other employees are not shown, but they are not deleted from the worksheet. Once the data are unfiltered, all the data reappear.

13. Next you will unfilter the data. Click the Filter button next to the Salary column header.

14. Click Clear Filter from "Salary" and all the data reappears.

15. Click the Save button on the Quick Access Toolbar.

Figure 7.49 Sort Last Name Column

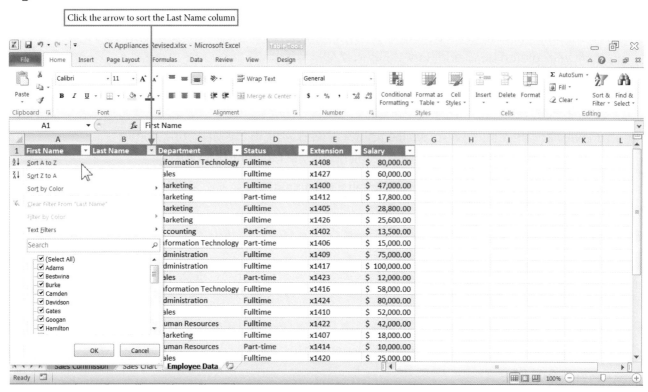

Figure 7.50 Filter on the Marketing Department

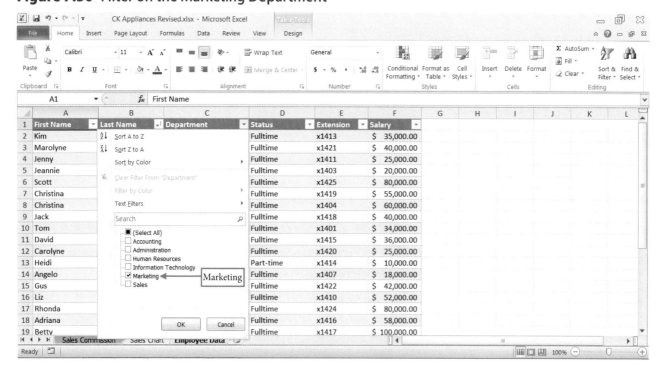

Figure 7.51 Filter Applied to Department

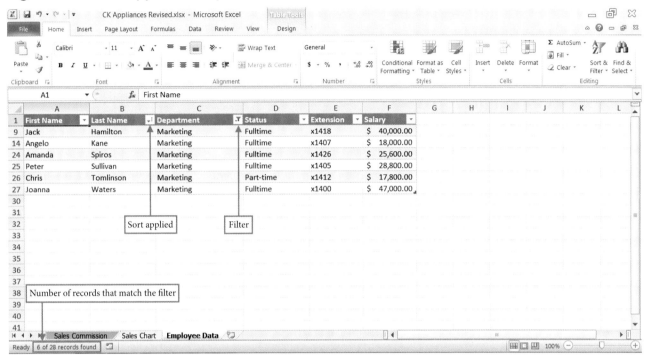

Figure 7.52 Number Filters

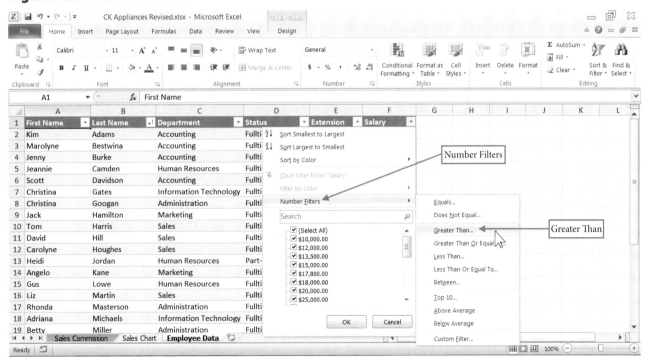

Figure 7.53 Custom AutoFilter Dialog Box

Conditional Formatting

Conditional formatting is a command that changes the formatting of a cell range when a specified condition is true. This helps the user visualize the answers to specific questions about the data. Conditional formatting can be applied on any cell range or table in a worksheet. For example, you may want to locate the employees who had sales over $5,000 in a month. Conditional formatting locates the employees and formats the cells differently to draw attention to the data.

> **Conditional formatting:** A command that changes the formatting of a cell range when a specified condition is true.

Use these steps to apply conditional formatting:

- Select the cells in which to apply conditional formatting.
- Click the **Conditional Formatting** button in the Styles group on the Home tab (**Figure 7.54**) and select an option from the list.

Use these steps to remove conditional formatting:

- Select the cell(s), sheet, or table that contains the conditional formatting that you want to remove.
- Click the **Conditional Formatting** button in the Styles group on the Home tab (Figure 7.54).
- Click **Clear Rules** and select an option from the list:
  - Clear Rules from Selected Cells
  - Clear Rules from Entire Sheet
  - Clear Rules from This Table

Hands-On Exercise: Apply Conditional Formatting to Cells

1. Click the Sales Commission sheet tab.
2. You will apply conditional formatting to employees who had sales over $5,000 for the month. Select F4:F7 .
3. Click the Conditional Formatting button in the Styles group on the Home tab (Figure 7.54).
4. Point to Click Highlight Cells Rules (Figure 7.54).
5. Click Greater Than (Figure 7.54), and the Greater Than dialog box displays.
6. Type **5000** in the Format cells that are GREATER THAN box (**Figure 7.55**).
7. Click the arrow in the *with* box and select Green Fill with Dark Green Text (Figure 7.55).
8. Click OK .
9. Click cell A1 to deselect the cells. Three of the cells are highlighted in green fill and dark green text, indicating that the sales amounts are greater than $5,000. The worksheet should resemble **Figure 7.56**.

Figure 7.54 Conditional Formatting

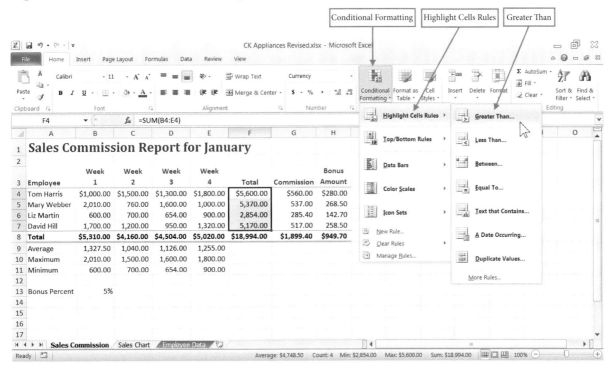

Figure 7.55 Greater Than Dialog Box

Figure 7.56 Conditional Formatting Applied to Worksheet

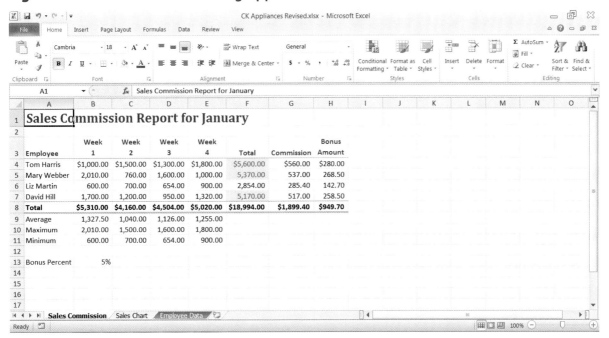

Insert Headers and Footers

Header: Text that displays at the top margin of each page in a workbook.

Footer: Text that displays at the bottom margin of each page in a workbook.

Headers and footers can be inserted into a workbook. A **header** is text that displays at the top margin of each page in a workbook. A **footer** is text that displays at the bottom margin of each page in a workbook. The header and footer are divided into three sections (left, center, and right). You can insert the date and time, page number, and the file name to the header or footer. The header and footer do not display on the worksheet in Normal view. It displays only in Page Layout view and when the workbook is printed.

Use these steps to insert a header or footer:

- Click the **Insert** tab.
- Click the **Header & Footer** button in the Text group (**Figure 7.57**). The Page Layout view displays. The Header & Footer Tools contextual tab, which contains a Design tab, displays on the Ribbon.
- Click the section where you want to display the header, and type the header information. You can click an element you want to insert, such as the page number, current date, current time, or file name from the Header & Footer Elements group on the Design tab of the Header Tools tab. A code displays for each element that is inserted. For example, when you insert the current date element in the header, *&[Date]* displays in the header. Once you navigate to another section of the header, the date displays.
- Click **Go to Footer** in the Navigation group to navigate to the footer section.
- Click the section where you want to display the footer (left, center, right), and type the footer information.
- Click a cell in the worksheet.
- Click the **Normal view** button on the status bar to exit.

Hands-On Exercise: Insert Header and Footer

1. Click the Insert tab.
2. Click the Header & Footer button in the Text group (Figure 7.57). The Page Layout view displays. The insertion point is located in the middle section of the header.
3. Click the left section in the header.
4. Click the Current Date button in the Header & Footer Elements group (**Figure 7.58**). The code *&[Date]* displays in the header. When you click another section of the header, the date displays.
5. Click the right section in the header. The date now displays in the left section of the header.
6. Type **Prepared by: Matt Smith**. The header should resemble **Figure 7.59**.
7. Click the Go to Footer button in the Navigation group (Figure 7.59).
8. Click the left section of the footer.
9. Click the File Name button in the Header & Footer Elements group.
10. Click the right section of the footer.

(11) Click Page Number in the Header & Footer Elements group.

(12) Click the middle section of the footer. The footer will resemble (**Figure 7.60**).

(13) Click in cell A45 or any cell in the worksheet to exit the footer section.

(14) Click the Normal view button on the status bar (Figure 7.60).

(15) Press Ctrl + Home to move to cell A1.

(16) Click the Save button on the Quick Access Toolbar.

Figure 7.57 Header & Footer Button

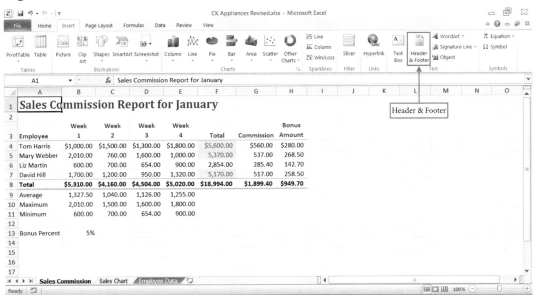

Figure 7.58 Current Date Inserted Into Header

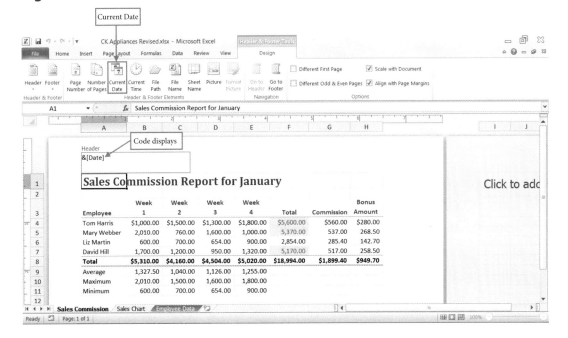

Figure 7.59 Header Created

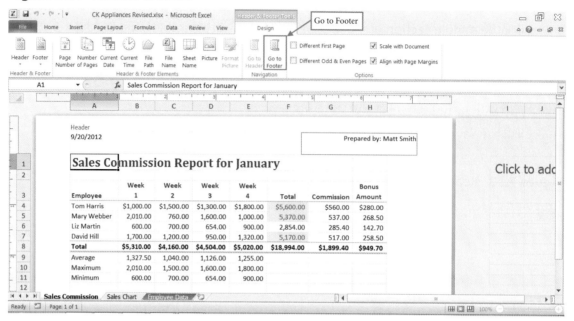

Figure 7.60 Footer Created

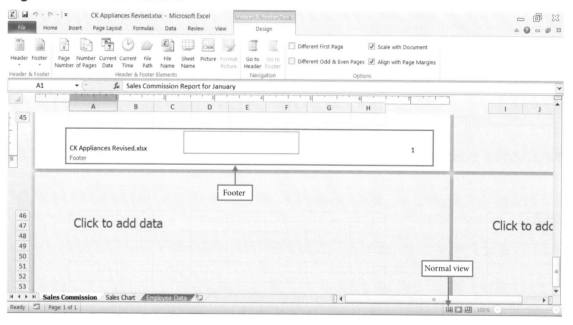

Hands-On Exercise: Print the Workbook

The workbook is completed. You will print the workbook.

① Click the File tab to open the Backstage view.

② Click Print . A preview of the worksheet displays on the right side of the window. The header and footer display in the preview.

③ Click the Print Active Sheets button and select Print Entire Workbook to print all the sheets in the workbook (**Figure 7.61**). At the bottom of the window *1 of 4* displays, which indicates that four pages will print.

④ The Employee Data sheet displays on two pages, pages 3 and 4. You will change page 3 to landscape orientation so that all the data displays on one page. Type **3** in the Current Page box (Figure 7.61) and press Enter to navigate to page 3.

⑤ Click the Portrait Orientation button and select Landscape Orientation . The worksheet now displays on one page. At the bottom of the window, it states *1 of 3*, indicating that three pages will print.

⑥ Click Print .

Figure 7.61 Print Workbook

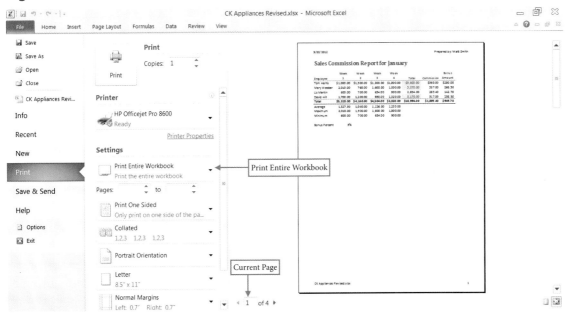

Hands-On Exercise: Exit Application

① Click the Save button on the Quick Access Toolbar.

② Click the File tab.

③ Click Exit to exit Microsoft Excel 2010.

Multiple-Choice Questions

1. The _____ command allows text to display on multiple lines within a cell.

    a. Freeze Panes

    b. Wrap Text

   c. Format as Table

   d. Filter

2. Which of the following formulas will average the data in cells A2 through A5?

   a. AVG(A2,A5)

   b. =AVERAGE(A2, A5)

   c. AVERAGE(A2:A5)

   d. =AVERAGE(A2:A5)

3. All formulas must _____.

   a. Be enclosed in parenthesis

   b. Begin with an equal sign

   c. Contain three or more operands

   d. Begin with the word SUM

4. A chart can be created by clicking the chart type in the _____ tab on the Ribbon.

   a. Insert

   b. Chart

   c. Home

   d. Data

5. The _____ function will count the number of cells that contain values in a range.

   a. Count

   b. Max

   c. Numerical Count

   d. Min

6. The _____ command changes the formatting of a cell range when a specified condition is true.

   a. Conditional Formatting

   b. Format as Table

   c. Tab Color

   d. Filter

7. The _____ function is used determine the largest value in a range.

   a. Min

   b. Max

   c. Low

   d. High

8. Which of the following formulas contains an absolute reference?

   a. =a1+b2

   b. =b1*10%

    c. =c5*d10

    d. =$d5+a10

9. A _____ is a prewritten formula that performs calculations on values.

    a. Chart

    b. Legend

    c. Filter

    d. Function

10. Which of the following elements can you modify on a chart?

    a. Legend

    b. Chart title

    c. Both A and B

    d. You cannot modify a chart once it has been created.

Project #1: Sort and Filter Patient Data

You work in a physician's office. The office manager wants you to sort and filter patient data.

① Open the Chicago Physician Group workbook.

② Rename Sheet1 to **Patient Data**.

③ Change the tab color of the Patient Data sheet to Blue.

④ Delete Sheet2 and Sheet3.

⑤ Format the data in cells A1:G9 of the Patient Data sheet as a table using Table Style Light 2 in the Light group.

⑥ Sort the data by ascending order by Patient Last Name. Print the results in landscape orientation.

⑦ Filter the data to show all patients who have a deductible greater than 0. Print the results.

⑧ Clear the filter.

⑨ Filter the data to show all patients who have Dr. Hill as their physician. Print the results.

⑩ Clear the filter.

⑪ Sort the data by policy number in descending order. Print the results.

⑫ Save the workbook as **Chicago Physician Group Revised**. The workbook should resemble **Figure 7.62**.

⑬ Close the workbook.

Figure 7.62 Chicago Physician Group Workbook

	A	B	C	D	E	F	G
1	Patient First Name	Patient Last Name	Patient ID	Insurance	Policy #	Deductible	Physician
2	Lisa	Perry	A1005	AC Health Premium Group	R59384	20	Dr. Hill
3	Melissa	Smith	A1004	NA Health Group	P39042	100	Dr. Meyers
4	Andrew	Romney	A1003	AC Health Premium Group	H73084	10	Dr. Meyers
5	David	Jones	A1006	AC Health Premium Group	G57394	20	Dr. Hill
6	Morgan	Brown	A1008	CK Insurance	F50384	0	Dr. Meyers
7	Jonathan	Rose	A1002	NA Health Group	C30212	0	Dr. Meyers
8	Jacquelyn	Chung	A1007	CK Insurance	B22147	25	Dr. Meyers
9	Cathleen	McCain	A1001	CK Insurance	B20332	0	Dr. Hill

Patient Data

Project #2: Create a Workbook to Calculate and Chart the Quarterly Sales for a Company

You work for Music Galaxy. Your supervisor has asked you to create a workbook to calculate and chart the total quarterly sales.

① Change the column width of Columns A through F to 12.

② Create the worksheet in (**Figure 7.63**). Be certain to wrap the text in cells B3:E3.

Figure 7.63 Create Music Galaxy Workbook

	A	B	C	D	E	F
1	Music Galaxy Sales Report					
2						
3		First Quarter	Second Quarter	Third Quarter	Fourth Quarter	Total
4	North Region	50003	40000	48000	60000	
5	South Region	30201	23003	28009	35600	
6	East Region	55344	44098	36594	54300	
7	West Region	10090	12000	7900	15000	
8	Total					
9	Average					
10	Highest					
11	Lowest					

③ Save the workbook as **Music Galaxy**.

④ Merge and center cells A1:G1.

⑤ Make the following changes to cell A1:

    a. Change the font size to 18.

    b. Change the font color to Light Blue.

    c. Bold the text.

⑥ Change the row height of Row 1 to 30.

⑦ Bold cells B3:F3.

⑧ Right-align cells B3:F3.

⑨ Italicize cells A4:A7.

⑩ Create the totals for each region in cells F4:F7.

⑪ Calculate the totals for each quarter in cells B8:F8.

⑫ Calculate the average sales for each quarter in cells B9:E9.

⑬ Calculate the highest sales for each quarter in cells B10:E10.

⑭ Calculate the lowest sales for each quarter in cells B11:E11.

⑮ Format cells B4:F11 as comma style.

⑯ Change the cell styles for cells A8:F8 to Total.

⑰ Rename Sheet1 as **Sales Report**.

⑱ Change the tab color of the Sales Report sheet to green.

⑲ Create a 3-D Clustered Column chart (first option in the 3-D Column category) of the sales for all quarters for all regions. Use A3:E7 as the data range for the chart.

⑳ Move the chart to a new sheet, and name the sheet **Sales Chart**.

㉑ Change the tab color of the Sales Chart sheet to Yellow.

㉒ Move the legend so that it displays at the bottom of the chart.

㉓ Insert an Above Chart title. Type **Music Galaxy Yearly Sales** as the chart title.

㉔ Move the Sales Report sheet so it is the first sheet on the sheet tab bar.

㉕ The company assumes they will have a 10% increase in sales next year. You will calculate the projected increase in column G of the Sales Report sheet.

㉖ Type **Projected Increase** in cell G3. Wrap the text so that the word *Increase* is displayed on the second line within the cell.

㉗ Bold cell G3.

㉘ Right-align cell G3.

㉙ Type **% Increase** in cell A13.

㉚ Type **10%** in cell B13.

㉛ Calculate the projected increase in cell G4, which is calculated by multiplying cell F4 by cell B13. Make certain to use an absolute cell reference for cell B13.

㉜ Copy the formula in cell G4 to cells G5:G7.

㉝ Calculate the total in cell G8.

㉞ Use the Format Painter command to copy the formatting of cell F8 to cell G8.

㉟ Create a header that contains your name in the right section.

㊱ Create a footer that contains the page number in the center section.

㊲ Save the workbook. The workbook should resemble **Figures 7.64** and **7.65**.

㊳ Print the entire workbook in portrait orientation.

㊴ Print the Sales Report worksheet with the formulas in landscape orientation.

㊵ Close the workbook.

Figure 7.64 Sales Report Worksheet

	A	B	C	D	E	F	G
1			Music Galaxy Sales Report				
2							
3		First Quarter	Second Quarter	Third Quarter	Fourth Quarter	Total	Projected Increase
4	North Region	50,003.00	40,000.00	48,000.00	60,000.00	198,003.00	19,800.30
5	South Region	30,201.00	23,003.00	28,009.00	35,600.00	116,813.00	11,681.30
6	East Region	55,344.00	44,098.00	36,594.00	54,300.00	190,336.00	19,033.60
7	West Region	10,090.00	12,000.00	7,900.00	15,000.00	44,990.00	4,499.00
8	Total	145,638.00	119,101.00	120,503.00	164,900.00	550,142.00	55,014.20
9	Average	36,409.50	29,775.25	30,125.75	41,225.00		
10	Highest	55,344.00	44,098.00	48,000.00	60,000.00		
11	Lowest	10,090.00	12,000.00	7,900.00	15,000.00		
12							
13	% Increase	10%					
14							
15							
16							

Sales Report Sales Chart Sheet2 Sheet3

Figure 7.65 Sales Chart Worksheet

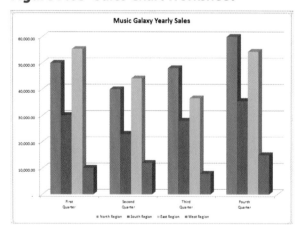

Project #3: Create a Workbook to Trace Ticket Sales for a Theater

You work for Kolston Theater. You will create a worksheet to keep track of the ticket sales for the theater.

① Create the worksheet in **Figure 7.66**. Be certain to wrap the text in cells B3:D3.

② Save the workbook as **Kolston Theater**.

Figure 7.66 Kolston Theater Workbook

(3) Merge and center cells A1:D1.

(4) Make the following changes to cell A1:

   a. Change the font size to 14.

   b. Bold the text.

   c. Change the font color to Purple.

   d. Change the fill color to White, Background 1, Darker 15%.

(5) Change the row height for Row 1 to 30 and the column widths for columns A through D to 12.

(6) Change the font for the entire worksheet to Times New Roman.

(7) Create the totals sales in cells D4:D6. The total sales are calculated by multiplying the tickets sold by the ticket price.

(8) Calculate the totals in cells B7:D7.

(9) Calculate the averages in cells B8:D8.

(10) Bold cells B3:D3 and cells A7:A8.

(11) Italicize cells A4:A6.

(12) Format cells B4:D8 as comma style.

(13) Remove the decimal places from cells B4:B7.

(14) Add a top and double bottom border to cells A7:D7.

(15) Apply conditional formatting to cells D4:D6 for all total sales that are greater than $1,000. Apply the Light Red Fill with Dark Red Text.

(16) Rename Sheet1 to **Ticket Sales**.

(17) Change the tab color of the Ticket Sales sheet to Purple.

(18) Create a 3-D pie chart of the tickets sold. Select the first option in the 3-D pie chart category. Use cells A3:B6 as the data range for the chart.

⑲ Move the chart to a new sheet, and name the sheet **Sales Chart**.

⑳ Move the legend to the bottom of the chart.

㉑ Insert data labels on the outside end of the pie chart.

㉒ Change the chart title to **Kolston Ticket Sales**.

㉓ Change the tab color of the Sales Chart sheet to Yellow.

㉔ Move Ticket Sales so that it is the first sheet in the workbook.

㉕ Delete Sheet2 and Sheet3.

㉖ Save the workbook. The worksheet should resemble **Figures 7.67** and **7.68**.

㉗ Print the workbook.

㉘ Print the Ticket Sales worksheet with the formulas in landscape orientation.

㉙ Close the workbook.

㉚ Exit Microsoft Excel 2010.

Figure 7.67 Ticket Sales Worksheet

	A	B	C	D	E	F	G	H	I	J	K	L	M	N	O
1		Kolston Theater Sales Report													
2															
3		Tickets Sold	Ticket Price	Total Sales											
4	Adult	250	10.50	2,625.00											
5	Child	105	7.25	761.25											
6	Senior	60	5.50	330.00											
7	Total	415	23.25	3,716.25											
8	Average	138.33	7.75	1,238.75											
9															
10															
11															
12															
13															
14															
15															
16															
17															

Ticket Sales / Sales Chart

Figure 7.68 Sales Chart Worksheet

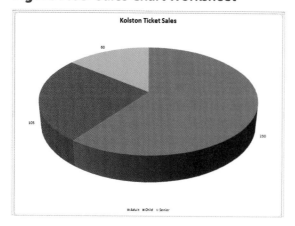

Create Databases Using Microsoft Access 2010

Chapter Objectives

After completing this chapter, you will be able to do the following:

- Understand database design.
- Identify Microsoft Access 2010 components.
- Create a database.
- Create tables using Datasheet and Design view.
- Add records using Datasheet view.
- Navigate records.
- Print a datasheet.
- Compact and repair a database.
- Close a database.

Microsoft Access 2010 is a database management system (DBMS) used to store and maintain large amounts of data. It has the ability to locate and retrieve data in a matter of seconds. Databases are used in many organizations, such as educational institutions, airlines, hotels, medical facilities, credit card companies, manufacturing firms, and retail establishments to store company and customer information.

There are many reasons why individuals use Microsoft Access 2010. Speed, accuracy, and security are among some of the reasons.

In this chapter, you will become acquainted with various features and elements of Microsoft Access 2010. You will learn how to create a database, create a table, add records to a table, and navigate among records.

Database Design

Microsoft Access 2010: A database management system (DBMS) used to store and maintain large amounts of data.

Have you ever booked your hotel and flight online? Or, have you ever ordered products online? If so, you have used databases. A **database** is a collection of related information about people, items, places, or events.

The best way to explain the concept of databases is with an example. Assume a new medical center is opening and you are hired to create a system to maintain the patient and physician information. Microsoft Access 2010 can store the information about the patients and physicians in one database.

Database: A collection of related information about people, items, places, or events.

Table: A database object that is used to store data about a particular subject such as customers, employees, or products.

A database contains one or more related tables. A **table** is a database object that is used to store data about a particular subject such as customers, employees, or products. A table contains fields and records. A **field** is a single characteristic of a table, such as the first name, last name, or birthdate of an employee. A field is also commonly referred to as an **attribute**. A table contains one or more fields. A **record** is a collection of field values in a table.

Field (attribute): A single characteristic of a table.

Attribute (field): A single characteristic of a table.

In the medical center database, there are two tables. One table stores information about the patients. The other table stores information about the physicians. The Patients table includes fields such as the first name, last name, and date of birth of the patients. Every patient in the table is a single record. If the table contains 50 patients, then it contains 50 records.

Record: A collection of field values in a table.

Primary key: A unique field or groups of fields that identify a particular record.

A **primary key** is a unique field or groups of fields that identify a particular record. It is unique in that no other record contains the same value in the primary key field in the table. A Social Security number and a credit card number are examples of primary key fields. There cannot be two individuals with the same Social Security number or credit card number. The system will alert you if you enter a value in a primary key field that already exists in the table. Although a primary key field is not required in a table, it is highly recommended to prevent duplicate records from being entered.

Table 8.1 illustrates the Patients table. The table contains rows and columns. It resembles a Microsoft Excel 2010 worksheet. The columns represent the fields, and the rows contain the records. There are eight fields in the Patients table: the Patient ID, First Name, Last Name, Home Phone, Date of Birth, Insurance, Policy #, and Physician ID fields. There are seven records in the table, which means there are seven patients listed in the table. The Patient ID is the primary key field for this table because each patient has a unique Patient ID that identifies the individual patient. No two patients can have the same Patient ID.

Table 8.2 illustrates the Physicians table. There are five fields in this table: the Physician ID, First Name, Last Name, Specialty, and Office Phone fields. There are three records in this table, which means there are three physicians listed in this table. The Physician ID is the

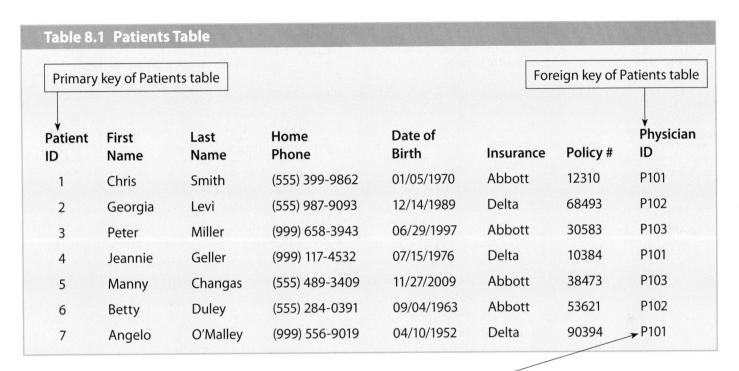

Table 8.1 Patients Table

Primary key of Patients table

Foreign key of Patients table

Patient ID	First Name	Last Name	Home Phone	Date of Birth	Insurance	Policy #	Physician ID
1	Chris	Smith	(555) 399-9862	01/05/1970	Abbott	12310	P101
2	Georgia	Levi	(555) 987-9093	12/14/1989	Delta	68493	P102
3	Peter	Miller	(999) 658-3943	06/29/1997	Abbott	30583	P103
4	Jeannie	Geller	(999) 117-4532	07/15/1976	Delta	10384	P101
5	Manny	Changas	(555) 489-3409	11/27/2009	Abbott	38473	P103
6	Betty	Duley	(555) 284-0391	09/04/1963	Abbott	53621	P102
7	Angelo	O'Malley	(999) 556-9019	04/10/1952	Delta	90394	P101

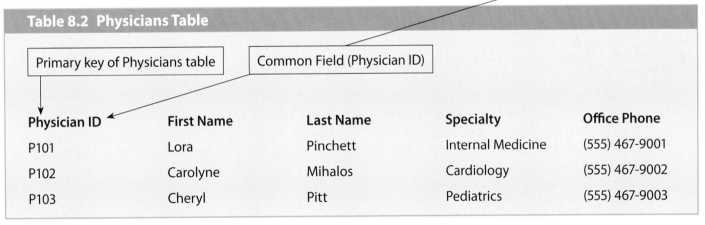

Table 8.2 Physicians Table

Primary key of Physicians table

Common Field (Physician ID)

Physician ID	First Name	Last Name	Specialty	Office Phone
P101	Lora	Pinchett	Internal Medicine	(555) 467-9001
P102	Carolyne	Mihalos	Cardiology	(555) 467-9002
P103	Cheryl	Pitt	Pediatrics	(555) 467-9003

primary key field for this table because each physician has a unique Physician ID that identifies the individual physician.

Notice that the two tables have a **common field**, which is a field that appears in both tables and contains the same data. The common field is the Physician ID field. When tables have a common field, they are said to be *related*. A **foreign key** is a field that links to a primary key field in a related table. The foreign key in the Patients table is the Physician ID field because it links to the primary key field in the Physicians table.

When tables are related, you can join the tables and view all the data in both tables that pertain to each record. For example, if you were viewing the record of Chris Smith in the Patients table, you would be able to locate the physician's name, specialty, and office phone, even though that information is not actually contained in the Patients table, because the tables are joined.

A **one-to-many relationship** is a relationship between two tables in which one record in one table is related to many records in another table. The Physicians table has a one-to-many

Common field: A field that appears in two tables and contains the same data.

Foreign key: A field that links to a primary key field in a related table.

One-to-many relationship: A relationship between two tables in which one record in one table is related to many records in another table.

relationship to the Patients table. One record in the Physicians table has many related records in the Patients table. This indicates that one physician in the Physicians table is related to multiple patients in the Patients table.

A **many-to-one relationship** is a relationship between two tables in which many records in one table are related to one record in another table. The Patients table has a many-to-one relationship to the Physicians table. Many records in the Patients table are related to one record in the Physicians table. This indicates that many patients in the Patients table are related to one physician in the Physicians table.

> **Many-to-one relationship:** A relationship between two tables in which many records in one table are related to one record in another table.

You may wonder why there are two separate tables. Could the data be combined in one table? A table should be created in a way that reduces data redundancy and prevents data-entry errors. Assume that all the data were located in one table, such as **Table 8.3**, and the table contained 5,000 records. Fifteen hundred of the patients have Dr. Mihalos for a physician. Assume Dr. Mihalos changed her phone number. You would need to update 1,500 records to correct the phone number. That is not an efficient process. If you have the data in two separate tables, the phone number would need to be updated only once in the Physicians table. This would minimize the potential data-entry errors that could occur when updating all the records.

Many people question why a database is used instead of a Microsoft Excel 2010 workbook. A workbook can be used to save the information in these tables. However, Microsoft Excel 2010 is not able to relate or join tables. This is a benefit of using Microsoft Access 2010. The database may contain thousands of records that need to be organized and maintained. Microsoft Access 2010 can maintain the data efficiently.

Create a Database

When you create a database, it creates a new file with a file extension of *accdb*. By default, the database file name is *Database1*, and it is stored in the *Documents* library. The location of the database and the name of the database can be modified.

You will create a database for a medical center. First you need to open Microsoft Access 2010.

Hands-On Exercise: Launch Microsoft Access 2010

(1) Click the Start button.

(2) Click All Programs .

(3) Click Microsoft Office . You may need to scroll through the Start menu to locate the folder.

(4) Click Microsoft Access 2010 .

(5) The Backstage view displays, which will allow you to create or open an existing database (**Figure 8.1**).

Table 8.3 Data Combined in One Table

Patient ID	First Name	Last Name	Home Phone	Date of Birth	Insurance	Policy #	Physician ID	First Name	Last Name	Specialty	Office Phone
1	Chris	Smith	(555) 399-9862	1/5/1970	Abbott	12310	P101	Lora	Pinchett	Internal Medicine	(555) 467-9001
2	Georgia	Levi	(555) 987-9093	12/14/1989	Delta	68493	P102	Carolyne	Mihalos	Cardiology	(555) 467-9002
3	Peter	Miller	(999) 658-3943	6/29/1997	Abbott	30583	P103	Cheryl	Pitt	Pediatrics	(555) 467-9003
4	Jeannie	Geller	(999) 117-4532	7/15/1976	Delta	10384	P101	Lora	Pinchett	Internal Medicine	(555) 467-9001
5	Manny	Changas	(555) 489-3409	11/27/2009	Abbott	38473	P103	Cheryl	Pitt	Pediatrics	(555) 467-9003
6	Betty	Duley	(555) 284-0391	9/4/1963	Abbott	53621	P102	Carolyne	Mihalos	Cardiology	(555) 467-9002
7	Angelo	O'Malley	(999) 556-9019	4/10/1952	Delta	90394	P101	Lora	Pinchett	Internal Medicine	(555) 467-9001

Figure 8.1 Backstage View

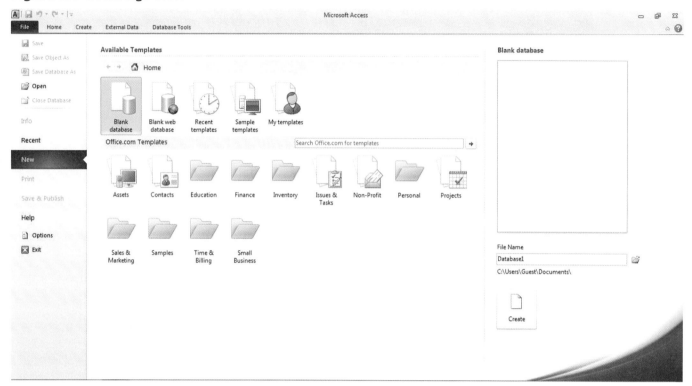

Hands-On Exercise: Create a Database

You will create a new database and name it Orland Medical Center.

① Click Blank database if it is not selected (**Figure 8.2**).

② Type **Orland Medical Center** in the File Name box (Figure 8.2). By default, new data-bases are stored in the Documents library.

- If you want to store the database in another location such as the Student Data Files folder or to the USB Flash drive, click the Browse button (Figure 8.2) next to the File Name box and the File New Database dialog box displays (**Figure 8.3**).

- Select the location and folder to save the database. Click OK when you are done.

③ Click Create (Figure 8.2), and the database is created. Depending on your monitor settings, you may need to scroll down to locate the Create button. Your screen should resemble **Figure 8.4**.

Figure 8.2 Create a New Database

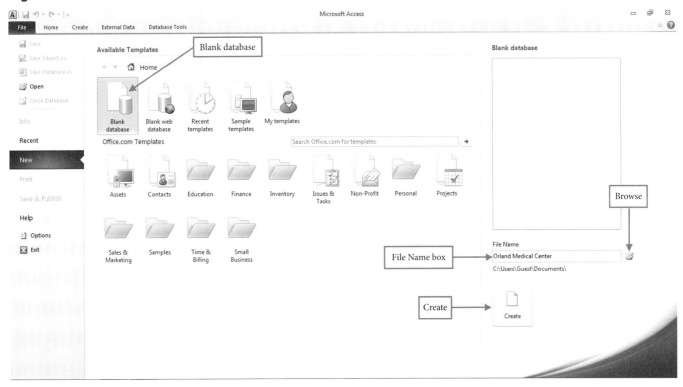

Figure 8.3 File New Database Dialog Box

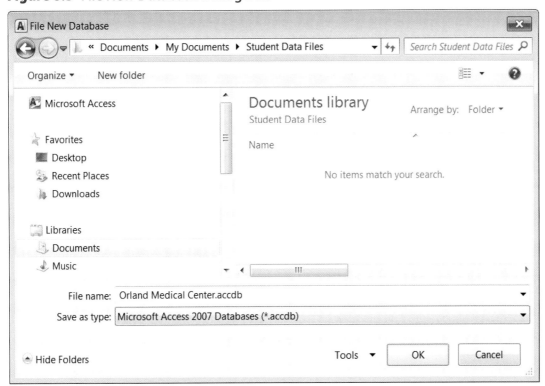

Figure 8.4 Database Created

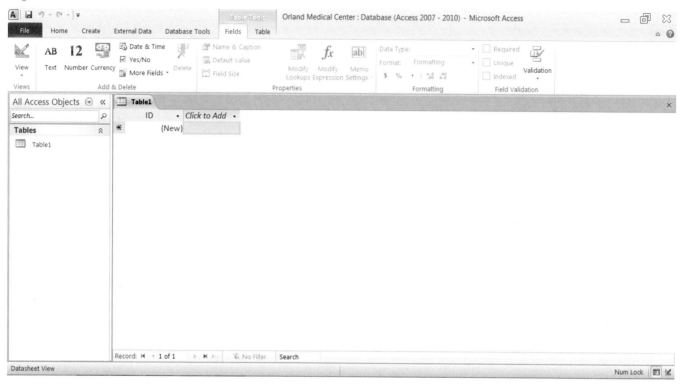

Identify Microsoft Access 2010 Components

A database contains various objects, such as tables, forms, queries, and reports.

- A table is a database object that can store data about a particular subject or entities such as events, items, customers, employees, people, products, and places.
- A **form** is a database object used to add or modify records in a table. A form displays one record at a time.
- A **query** is a database object that can answer a question about the data and displays the results in a worksheet format.
- A **report** is a database object that can list information from tables and queries. A report can be viewed on the screen or can be printed.

In summary, Microsoft Access 2010 provides users with the ability to do the following:

- Create databases containing tables.
- Create relationships between tables that have a common field.
- Maintain data (add, update, and delete records) using forms or datasheets.
- Create queries to display answers to specific questions about the data.
- Create reports.

Table 8.4 illustrates the common elements and key terms used in the Microsoft Office 2010 applications.

Form: A database object used to add or modify records in a table. A form displays one record at a time.

Query: A database object that can answer a question about the data and displays the results in a worksheet format.

Report: A database object that can list information from tables and queries. A report can be viewed on the screen or can be printed.

Table 8.4 Common Microsoft Office 2010 Elements and Key Terms

Common Element/ Key Terms	Description
Backstage view	The Backstage view contains commands to manage your database, such as creating, opening, saving, and printing. Click the **File tab** to open the Backstage view.
Command	A command is a button or text that performs an action or task.
Dialog box	A dialog box is a window that allows a user to perform commands or apply settings. A dialog box displays when the dialog box launcher is clicked. A dialog box launcher is a button that resembles a diagonal arrow, which displays to the right of a group name on the Ribbon.
Quick Access Toolbar	The Quick Access Toolbar provides access to the most frequently used commands. By default, the Quick Access Toolbar is located at the left corner of the title bar (**Figure 8.5**).
Ribbon	The Ribbon contains all the commands you need to create and modify the database objects (Figure 8.5). The Ribbon is located below the title bar and contains tabs that are organized by groups of related commands (Figure 8.5). Four tabs display by default at the top of the Ribbon, starting with the Home tab. The File tab is not considered part of the Ribbon.
Scroll bar	A scroll bar allows you to navigate either up and down or left and right to view the information in the application window.
Shortcut menu	A shortcut menu displays when you right-click an object or area of the window. It contains a list of commands related to the object.
Status bar	The status bar provides information about the status of the database. The status bar is located at the bottom of the application window (Figure 8.5).
Title bar	The title bar displays the name of the database that is currently open and the name of the application. The title bar is the top bar on the application window (Figure 8.5).
ToolTip (ScreenTip)	A ToolTip (ScreenTip) lists the name of the command and sometimes includes a brief description of the command. A ToolTip displays when the mouse hovers, or points to, a command. It may also display keyboard shortcuts that can be used to initiate the command using the keyboard.
View buttons	The View buttons provide options for viewing the database objects. The View buttons are located on the right side of the status bar (Figure 8.5). By default, the database opens in Datasheet view.

Backstage view: Contains commands to manage your database, such as creating, opening, saving, and printing. Click the File tab to open the Backstage view.

Command: A button or text that performs an action or task.

Dialog box: A window that allows a user to perform commands or apply settings. A dialog box displays when the dialog box launcher is clicked.

Dialog box launcher: A button that resembles a diagonal arrow, which displays to the right of a group name on the Ribbon.

Quick Access Toolbar: Provides access to the most frequently used commands. By default, the Quick Access Toolbar is located at the left corner of the title bar.

Ribbon: Contains all the commands you need to create the database objects. The Ribbon is located under the title bar and contains tabs that are organized by groups of related commands.

Scroll bar: A tool that allows you to navigate either up and down or left and right to view the information in the application window.

Shortcut menu: Displays when you right-click an object or area of the window. It contains a list of commands related to the object.

Status bar: Provides information about the status of the database. The status bar is located at the bottom of the application window.

Title bar: Displays the name of the database that is currently open and the name of the application. The title bar is the top bar on the application window.

ToolTip (ScreenTip): Lists the name of the command and sometimes includes a brief description of the command. A ToolTip displays when the mouse hovers, or points to, a command.

View buttons: Provide options for viewing the database objects. The View buttons are located on the right side of the status bar.

The name of the database displays in the title bar (Figure 8.5). The Navigation Pane (Figure 8.5) is located on the left side of the application window below the Ribbon. The **Navigation Pane** organizes the database objects by category. Tables, queries, forms, and reports are considered database objects. You can use the Navigation Pane to browse the database objects in the database. Double-click an object in the Navigation Pane, and the object will open, *or* right-click an object and select Open from the shortcut menu.

Use this step to open or close the Navigation Pane:

- Press **F11** or click the **Shutter Bar Open/Close** button in the Navigation Pane (Figure 8.5).

A database object, when opened, is displayed as a tabbed document in a single pane to the right of the Navigation Pane. The tabbed document has an orange background that contains the name of the database object (Figure 8.5). A table named *Table1* is automatically created when you create a database. The table is displayed in the pane to the right of the Navigation Pane and contains a tab labeled *Table1,* which is the default name of the table (Figure 8.5).

The Table Tools contextual tab displays in the Ribbon (Figure 8.5). A **contextual tab** is a tab that displays on the Ribbon when you create or select a particular object, such as a table. A contextual tab contains commands that pertain to the object that is selected. In this case, the Table Tools contextual tab displays commands to create and modify a table.

Navigation Pane: A pane that organizes the database objects by category. The Navigation Pane is located on the left side of the application window below the Ribbon.

Contextual tab: A tab that displays on the Ribbon when you create or select a particular object, such as a table.

Figure 8.5 Microsoft Access 2010 Components

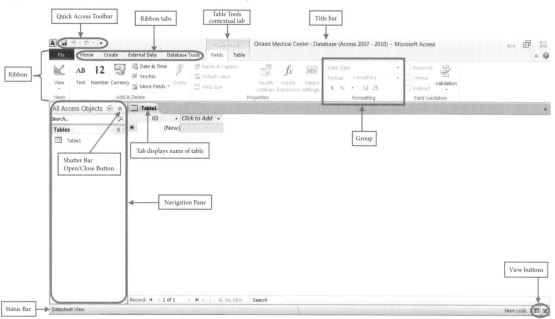

Define Table Structure

Microsoft Access 2010 automatically created a table named *Table1* and is ready for you to input the field names. There are two views that can be used to create tables, the Datasheet view and Design view. The current view is Datasheet view, which resembles a worksheet that contains rows and columns. The view name displays on the left side of the status bar. *Datasheet View* is currently displayed on the status bar, indicating that the Datasheet view is the current view.

Before you create the table, you must define the table structure:

- Identify the fields in the table.
- Identify the primary key of the table.
- Identify the data type of each field.
- Identify the field size of each field.

You can insert a caption and description for each field. A **caption** is the label that displays for the field by default in the forms, reports, tables, and queries. If the caption is blank, the field name displays as the label for the field. A **description** is used to describe the field. The description displays in the left corner of the status bar when the field is active. The description is optional and can be left blank.

> **Caption:** The label that displays for the field by default in the forms, reports, tables, and queries.
>
> **Description:** Used to describe the field.

Field Names

Try to be as descriptive as possible when naming the fields in the table.

- Field names can consist of a maximum of 64 characters.
- Field names must not begin with a space.
- Field names may not contain periods, exclamation points, accent graves (`), or square brackets.

Data Types

The **data type** of a field specifies the type of data that can be stored in a field. **Table 8.5** describes some of the basic data types that are used in Microsoft Access 2010.

> **Data type:** Specifies the type of data that can be stored in a field.

Table 8.5 Data Types	
Data Type	**Description**
Text	Text is the most common data type. This data type may store text or numerical characters. Text data fields are not used to perform mathematical calculations.
Number	The Number data type stores only numeric data. A number field should be used only if mathematical calculations will be performed on the field. For example, a zip code field contains numbers but is not used for mathematic calculations. Therefore, the zip code field should be assigned a data type of text.
Currency	Currency stores monetary values. A dollar sign and two decimal places automatically display for a Currency field.
Date & Time	This field stores date and time values.
Yes/No	Only yes and no values are allowed in this field.
Memo	This field is used to store large amounts of text. It can hold up to 65,536 alphanumeric characters.
AutoNumber	This data type automatically increments the value in the field each time a new record is added to the table. This data type is often assigned to the primary key field of a table because it creates unique values. The value of the field in the first record is assigned the number 1, and it increments by 1 each time a new record is added.

Field Size

You can specify the field size for each field so that it adjusts the amount of space needed for each record in the table. A text field can hold a maximum of 255 characters. The common field size options for Number data types include byte, integer, long integer, single, and double. **Table 8.6** lists the common field sizes for Number data types.

Table 8.6 Field Sizes for Number Data Types	
Field Size	**Description**
Byte	Integers (whole numbers) ranging from 0 to 255.
Integer	Integers (whole numbers) ranging from −32,768 to +32,767.
Long Integer	Integers (whole numbers) ranging from −2,147,483,648 to +2,147,483,647.
Single	Numeric values with decimals that contain up to 7 significant digits, including whole numbers and decimal places. Examples: • 123.45 contains 5 significant digits • 20045.367 contains 8 significant digits. Because the system can only hold seven significant digits, Microsoft Access 2010 rounds the decimal places and displays the value as *20045.37.*
Double	Numeric values with decimals that contain up to 15 significant digits.

Create Fields in the Datasheet View

Datasheet view:
Resembles a grid
that contains rows
and columns.

You will create the Patients table using the Datasheet view. **Datasheet view** resembles a grid that contains rows and columns. The columns represent the fields, and the rows represent the records.

Use these steps to create the fields in Datasheet view:

- Select the data type and name the field:
  - Click the **Click to Add** column, and a list of data types displays.
  - Select the **data type**.
  - Enter the *name* of the field.
  - Repeat these steps until all fields in the table have been created.
- Once the fields are created, enter the field sizes for each field:
  - Click in the column of the field you want to modify.
  - Type the field size in the **Field Size** box in the Properties group on the Fields tab.
- Enter a caption or description for a field:
  - Click in the column of the field you want to modify.
  - Click the **Name & Caption** button in the Properties group in the Fields tab (**Figure 8.6**). The Enter Field Properties dialog box displays.
  - Enter the *field name* in the Name box.
  - Enter the *caption* in the Caption box.
  - Enter the *description* in the Description box.
  - Click **OK** when completed.

- Select the primary key of the table:
  - Click in the column that contains the primary key.
  - Click the **Unique** checkbox in the Field Validation group in the Fields tab.
- Change the data type of a field:
  - Click in the column of the field you want to modify.
  - Click the **Data Type arrow** in the Formatting group in the Fields tab (Figure 8.6) and select the appropriate data type.
- Change the name of a field:
  - Double-click the field name.
  - Type in the *new field name* and press **Enter**.

Table 8.7 lists the Patients table structure that you will create. The first step is to enter the fields that will be part of the Patients table. Microsoft Access automatically created an ID field that is the primary key for the table. The ID field has a data type of AutoNumber. You will modify the field and name it *Patient ID*.

As you enter the information, you are creating the table structure. Each column in the table is a field in the table. Do not worry about making mistakes. You can add, modify, or delete fields at any time.

Table 8.7 Patients Table Structure

Field	Data Type	Field Size	Primary Key
Patient ID	AutoNumber		Yes
First Name	Text	10	
Last Name	Text	15	
Home Phone	Text	10	
Date of Birth	Date		
Insurance	Text	10	
Policy #	Text	5	
Physician ID	Text	4	

Hands-On Exercise: Create Fields in Datasheet View

1. The first field, called ID, was created automatically when the table was created. The ID field has an AutoNumber data type. You will make changes to that field and call it Patient ID:

   a. Click the ID column.

   b. Click the Name & Caption button in the Properties group on the Fields tab, and the Enter Field Properties dialog box displays (Figure 8.6).

   c. Type **Patient ID** in the Name box (Figure 8.6).

   d. Type **Patient Identification Number** in the Description box (Figure 8.6).

   e. Click OK .

   f. The AutoNumber data type is assigned to the first field of the table. The data type is displayed in the Data Type list in the Formatting group on the Fields tab (Figure 8.6).

   g. This field is the primary key. Click the Unique checkbox in the Field Validation group on the Fields tab if it is not selected (Figure 8.6). The field is created.

(2) Next, you will create the fields for the rest of the table:

   a. Click the Click to Add column, and a list of data types displays (**Figure 8.7**).

   b. Click Text . *Field1* displays in the column heading.

   c. Type **First Name**.

   d. Click the Click to Add column.

   e. Click Text . *Field1* displays in the column heading.

   f. Type **Last Name**.

   g. Click the Click to Add column.

   h. Click Text . *Field1* displays in the column heading.

   i. Type **Home Phone**.

   j. Click the Click to Add column.

   k. Click Date & Time . *Field1* displays in the column heading.

   l. Type **Date of Birth**.

   m. Click the Click to Add column.

   n. Click Text . *Field1* displays in the column heading.

   o. Type **Insurance**.

   p. Click the Click to Add column.

   q. Click Text . *Field1* displays in the column heading.

   r. Type **Policy #**.

   s. Click the Click to Add column.

   t. Click Text . *Field1* displays in the column heading.

   u. Type **Physician ID**.

(3) Next, you will enter the field sizes for the fields.

   a. Click the First Name column.

   b. Type **20** in the Field Size box in the Properties group on the Fields tab (**Figure 8.8**).

   c. Click the Last Name column.

   d. Type **15** in the Field Size box.

   e. Click the Home Phone column.

f. Type **10** in the Field Size box.

- You may be wondering why the field size is 10 when a home phone contains 13 characters, including the parentheses and hyphen. The field size is determined by the number of digits in the phone number. Although the home phone contains 13 characters, only 10 of the characters are stored in the field. The parentheses and hyphen are part of the format and are not counted toward the field size.

g. Click the Date of Birth column.

- You will format this field using the Format property. The Format property allows you to select a layout for the field. Click the Format arrow in the Formatting group of the Fields tab (**Figure 8.9**). Click Short Date (Figure 8.9).

h. Click the Insurance column.

- Type **10** in the Field Size box.

i. Click the Policy # column.

- Type **5** in the Field Size box.

j. Click the Physician ID field.

- Type **5** in the Field Size box.

- Click the Name & Caption button.

- Type **Foreign key related to Physician ID in Physicians table** in the Description box.

k. Click OK . The table should resemble **Figure 8.10**.

Figure 8.6 Enter Field Properties Dialog Box

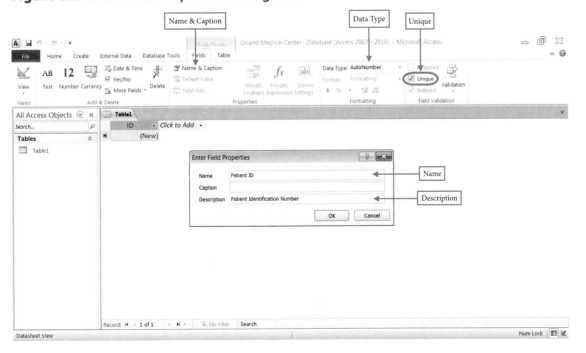

Figure 8.7 Add New Field

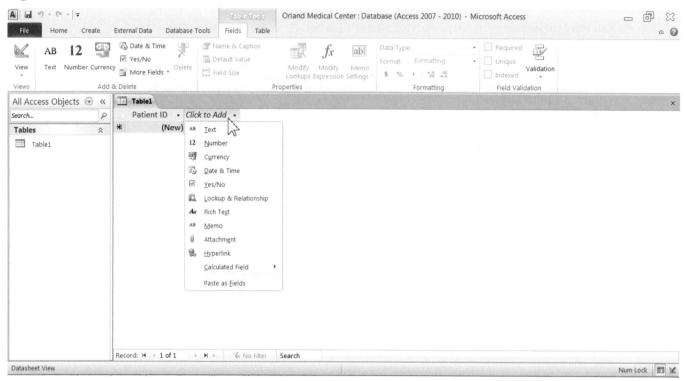

Figure 8.8 Modify Field Size

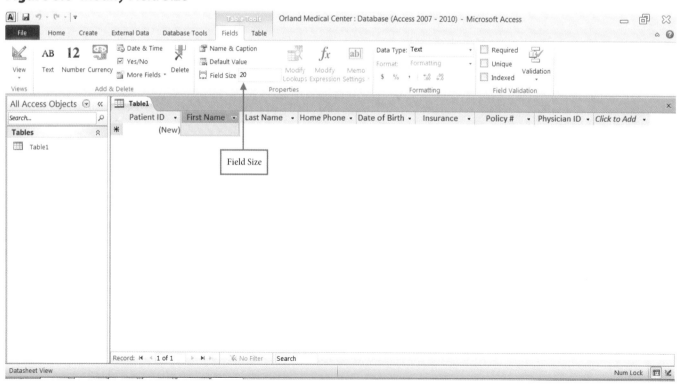

Figure 8.9 Modify Format of Field

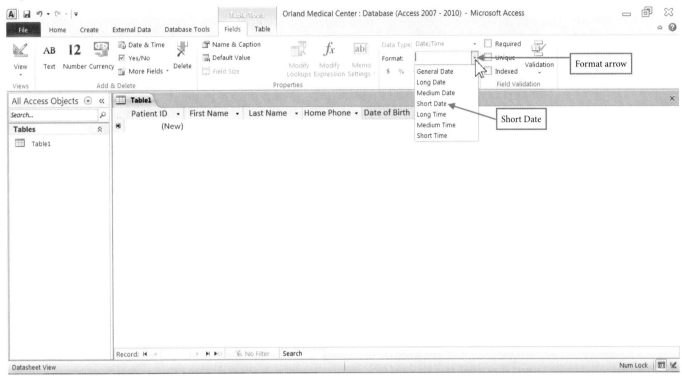

Figure 8.10 Table Created

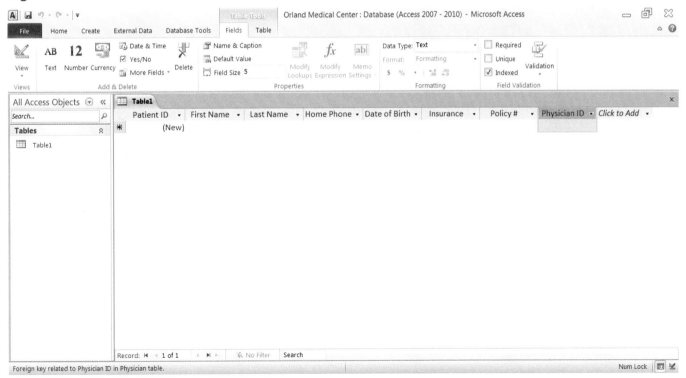

Modify Table Design

You can modify or delete fields from Datasheet View.

Use either of the following methods to delete a field from a table:

- Right-click the field name and click **Delete Field**.
- Click in the column and then click the **Delete** button in the Add & Delete group on the Fields tab.

Use these steps to modify a field:

- Click the field name to select the field.
- Make the changes using the commands in the Fields tab of the Table Tools tab.

Hands-On Exercise: Modify and Delete Fields

① You will change the field size for the Physician ID field:

    a. Click the Physician ID column if it is not selected.

    b. Type **4** in the Field Size box.

② Next, you will add a new field in the table:

    a. Click the Click to Add column in the last column of the table.

    b. Click Text . *Field1* displays in the column heading.

    c. Type **Address** and press the down arrow to exit the field.

③ Finally, you will delete the Address field from the table:

    a. Right-click the Address column.

    b. Click Delete Field . The screen will resemble **Figure 8.11**.

Figure 8.11 Modified Table

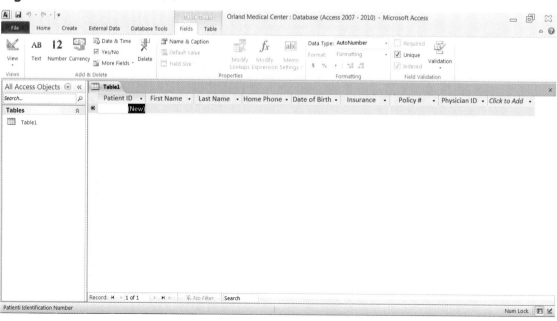

Save a Table

Once you finished creating a table, you need to save it with an appropriate name. The table is automatically stored in the database that is open. The table cannot be saved to another database.

Use either of these methods to save a table:

- Click the **Save** button on the Quick Access toolbar.
- Right-click the **Table** tab, which contains an orange background (**Figure 8.12**). Click **Save** on the shortcut menu.

Hands-On Exercise: Save a Table

(1) Right-click the Table1 tab, which contains an orange background (Figure 8.12). A shortcut menu displays.

(2) Click Save .

(3) Type **Patients** in the Table Name box (Figure 8.12).

(4) Click OK . The table name *Patients* displays in the Table tab and in the Tables group in the Navigation pane (**Figure 8.13**).

Figure 8.12 Save As Dialog Box

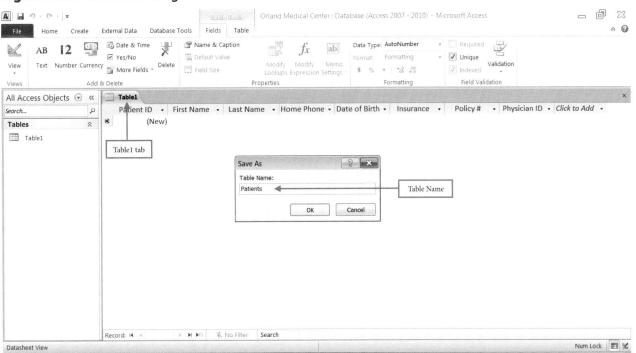

Figure 8.13 Patients Table Saved

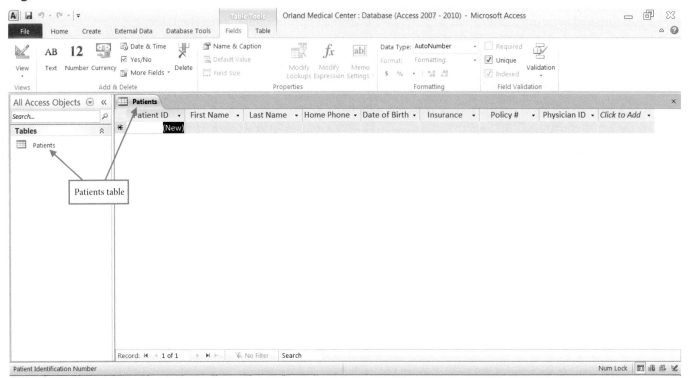

Close a Table

You should close the table when you are done working with it. When a table is closed, it displays in the Tables group in the Navigation Pane.

Use either of these methods to close a table:

- Right-click the **Table** tab and click **Close** on the shortcut menu.
- Click the **Close** button, which is located at the far right of the Table tab (**Figure 8.14**).

Hands-On Exercise: Close a Table

① Click the Close button to the far right of the Table tab (Figure 8.14). The screen will resemble **Figure 8.15**.

Figure 8.14 Close Button

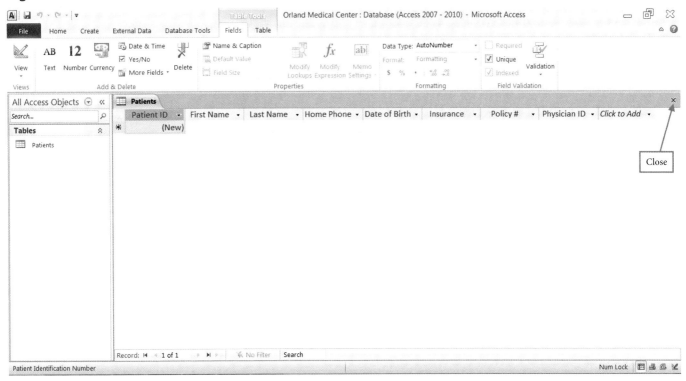

Figure 8.15 Table Closed

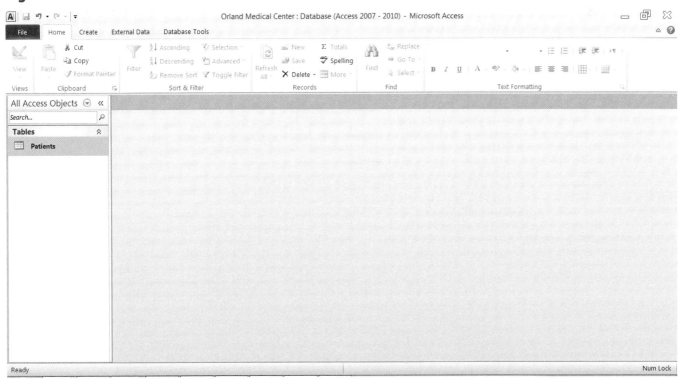

Create a Table Using Design View

Design view: A detailed view where the structure of the database object is defined and various settings are applied.

You will create the Physicians table using Design view instead of Datasheet view. **Design view** is a detailed view where the structure of the database object is defined and various settings are applied. When creating a table using Design view, you have the option of applying various field properties to the fields in the table. Many of these field settings are unavailable in Datasheet view. Only the fields are defined in Design view. Records cannot be added in this view.

Use these steps to create a table:

- Click the **Create** tab.
- Click the **Table Design** button in the Tables group (**Figure 8.16**).

Hands-On Exercise: Create a Table Using Design View

① Click the Create tab (Figure 8.16).

② Click Table Design (Figure 8.16), and the screen in **Figure 8.17** displays.

Figure 8.16 Table Design Button

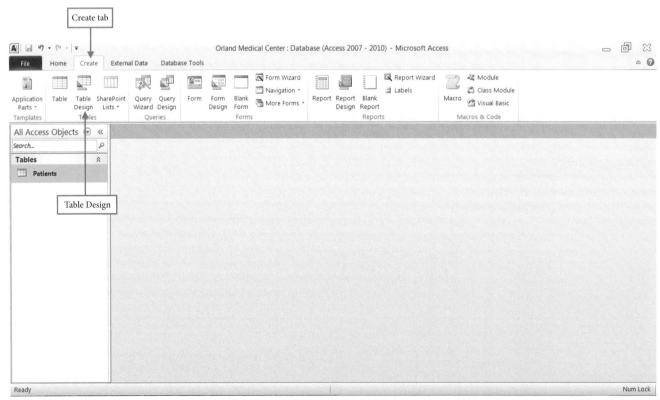

Figure 8.17 Design View

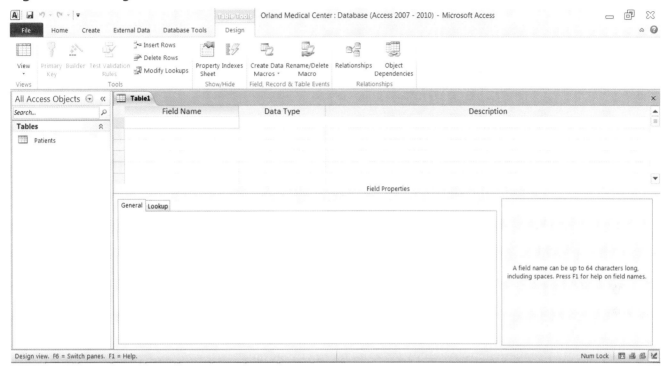

Create Fields in Design View

A table is created and contains the default name of *Table1*, which displays in the Table tab (**Figure 8.18**). The Table Tools contextual tab displays on the Ribbon and contains the Design tab. *Design view* displays on the left side of the status bar (Figure 8.18). The top part of the window is called the design grid (Figure 8.18). The fields are defined in each row of the design grid. You will enter the field name, data type, and description of each field. Press **Tab** or **Enter** or use the arrow keys to navigate between the columns and rows in the design grid. You can apply field properties, such as the field size, format, and caption properties, from the Field Properties pane located at the bottom of the window (Figure 8.18). You can press **F6** to navigate between the panes in the window.

Use these steps to create a field:

- Type the *field name* in the Field Name box.
- Click the **Data Type** arrow, and select the data type from the list.
- Type the *description* of the field. The description field is optional and can be left blank.
- Select the field settings in the Field Properties pane at the bottom of the window. The field settings are different, depending on the data type of the field you are creating.
- Type the *field size* in the Field Size box in the Field Properties pane. If the field is a Number data type, click the **Field Size arrow** and select the field size, such as byte, integer, long integer, etc., from the list.
- Type the *caption* in the Caption box in the Field Properties pane.
- Select a format by clicking the **Format arrow** in the Field Properties pane and selecting a format from the list.
- Save the table when you are finished.

Figure 8.18 Design View Elements

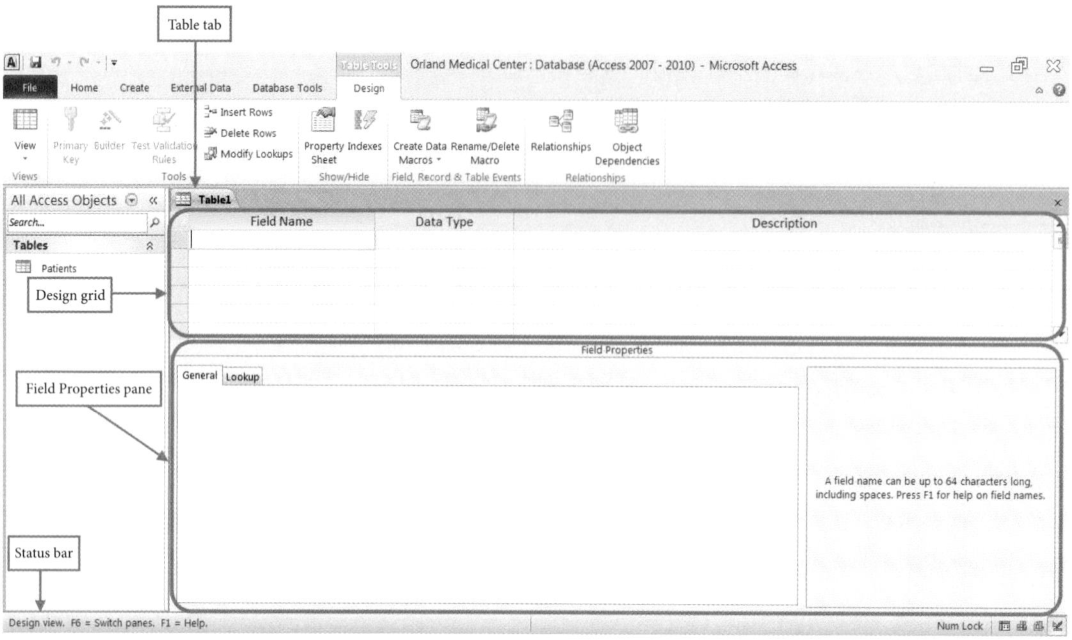

Use these steps to specify the primary key of the table:

- Click in the row that contains the field that is the primary key of the table.
- Click the **Primary Key** button in the Tools group on the Design tab (**Figure 8.19**). A key displays in the row selector for the field (Figure 8.19).

You will create the Physicians table using the field settings in **Table 8.8**.

Table 8.8 Fields in the Physicians Table					
Field	**Data Type**	**Field Size**	**Primary Key**	**Caption**	**Description**
Physician ID	Text	4	Yes		Primary key for the Physicians table
First Name	Text	10		Physician First Name	
Last Name	Text	15		Physician Last Name	
Specialty	Text	20			
Office Phone	Text	10		Physician Office Phone	

Hands-On Exercise: Create Fields in Design View

① The insertion point is positioned in the Field Name column. You will create the Physician ID field.

    a. Type **Physician ID** and press Tab . The Field Properties pane changes, and the various field properties display.

    b. The insertion point moves to the Data Type column. By default, Text displays as the data type. The Physician ID is a Text field, so you do not need to modify the data type.

c. The field size of the Physician ID is 4. Press F6 to navigate to the Field Properties pane, or click in the Field Size box in the Field Properties pane.

d. Type **4** in the Field Size box (Figure 8.19).

e. Click the Description box in the design grid, and type **Primary key for the Physicians table**.

f. You need to specify that this field is the primary key. Click the Primary Key button in the Tools group on the Design tab (Figure 8.19). A key displays on the row selector, indicating this field contains the primary key. The screen should resemble Figure 8.19.

g. Press Tab to move to the second row and to enter the next field.

② Next, you will create the First Name field.

a. Type **First Name** in the Field Name box and press Tab .

b. You are in the Data Type column. The data type defaults to Text. Press F6 to navigate to the Field Properties pane.

c. Type **10** in the Field Size box.

d. Type **Physician First Name** in the Caption box.

③ Next, you will create the Last Name field.

a. Click the Field Name box of the next row to enter the next field.

b. Type **Last Name** in the Field Name box and press Tab .

c. You are in the Data Type column. The data type defaults to Text. Press F6 to navigate to the Field Properties pane.

d. Type **15** in the Field Size box.

e. Type **Physician Last Name** in the Caption box.

④ Next, you will create the Specialty field.

a. Click the Field Name box in the next row to enter the next field.

b. Type **Specialty** in the Field Name box and press Tab .

c. You are in the Data Type column. The data type defaults to Text. Press F6 to navigate to the Field Properties pane.

d. Type **20** in the Field Size box.

⑤ Next, you will create the Office Phone field.

a. Click the Field Name box in the next row to enter the next field.

b. Type **Office Phone** in the Field Name box and press Tab .

c. You are in the Data Type column. The data type defaults to Text.

d. Type **10** in the Field Size box.

⑥ Now, you will save the table as *Physicians*. Click the Save button in the Quick Access Toolbar and the Save As dialog box displays.

⑦ Type **Physicians** in the Table Name box and click OK . The table name, *Physicians*, displays in the Table tab. The table displays under the Tables group in the Navigation Pane. The screen should resemble **Figure 8.20**.

Figure 8.19 Physician ID Field

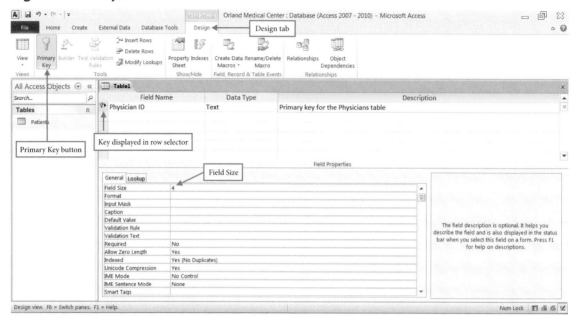

Figure 8.20 Physicians Table Created

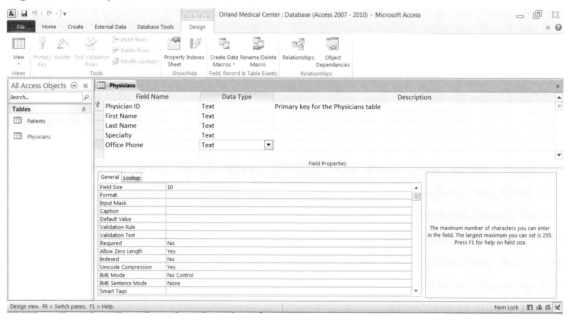

Create an Input Mask

Input mask: A pattern that controls how data are entered in the field.

An **input mask** is a pattern that controls how data are entered in the field. For example, you can apply an input mask to a phone number field, which will automatically create a pattern in which data are entered in the format *(555) 999-9999*. The pattern contains the parentheses and the dash. The pattern is not actually stored in the table; only the numbers are stored.

Use the following steps to create an input mask:

- Click the **Input Mask** box in the Field Properties Pane (**Figure 8.21**). The Build button displays to the right of the box.
- Click the **Build** button (Figure 8.21) and the Input Mask Wizard displays.
- Select an *Input Mask* and click **Finish**.

Before you create an input mask for a field, the table must be saved.

Hands-On Exercise: Create an Input Mask

In this exercise, you will apply an input mask to the Phone Number field.

(1) The insertion point should be located in the Office Phone field. If not, click in the Office Phone row in the design grid.

(2) Click the Input Mask box in the Field Properties pane (Figure 8.21). The Build button displays once you click the Input Mask box.

(3) Click the Build button (Figure 8.21) and the Input Mask Wizard dialog box displays (**Figure 8.22**).

(4) Click Phone Number .

(5) Click Finish .

(6) The Input Mask box displays the pattern for the Phone Number, which is !\(999") "000\-0000;;_ .

(7) Click the Save button on the Quick Access Toolbar. The screen should resemble Figure 8.23.

Figure 8.21 Input Mask and Build Button

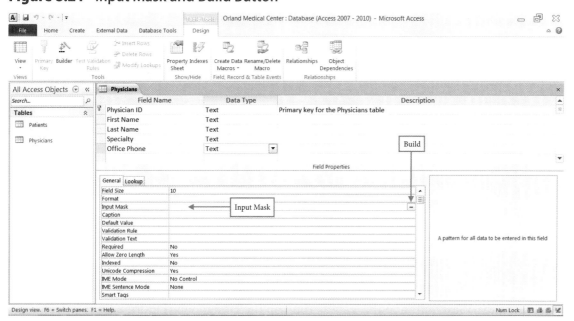

Figure 8.22 Input Mask Wizard

Figure 8.23 Input Mask Inserted

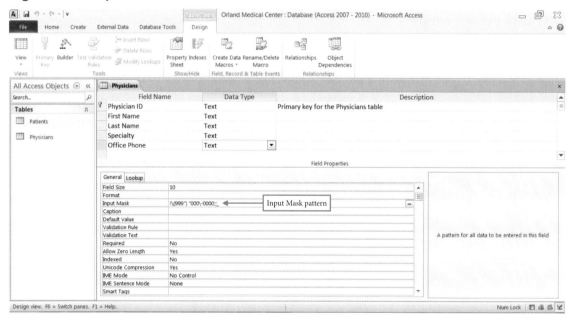

Switching Views

You can switch between Design view and Datasheet view at any time.

Use any of these methods to switch views:

- Click the **View buttons** on the right side of the status bar.
- Click the **View** button in the Views group on the Design tab (**Figure 8.24**).

Hands-On Exercise: Switch Views and Close Table

① Click the View button on the Design tab (Figure 8.24), *or* click the View arrow and select Datasheet View. The Datasheet view displays.

② Click the Design View button on the status bar and the Design View displays (Figure 8.24).

③ Click the Close button on the far right of the Physicians tab (**Figure 8.25**) or right-click the Physicians tab , and click Close from the shortcut menu (Figure 8.25).

Figure 8.24 Switching Views

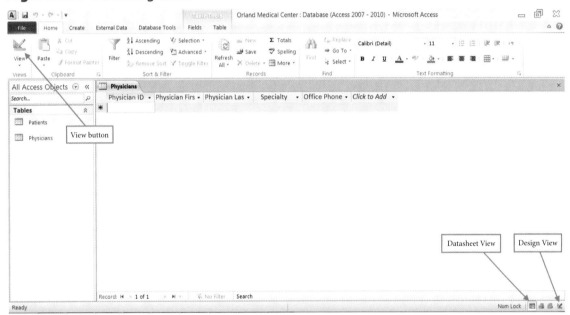

Figure 8.25 Close Physicians Table

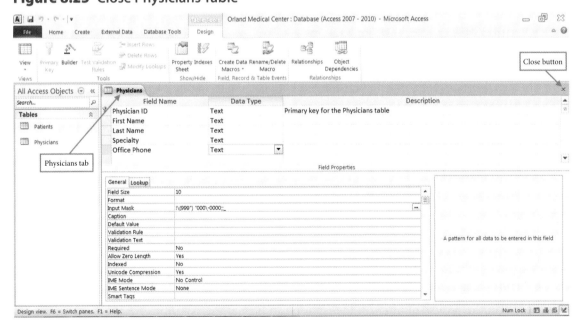

Open a Table in Datasheet View

After a table is created, the next step is to add records to the table. The Datasheet view can be used to enter records.

Use either of these steps to open a table in Datasheet view:

- Double-click the table in the Navigation Pane.
- Right-click the table in the Navigation Pane and then click **Open** from the shortcut menu.

Hands-On Exercise: Open a Table in Datasheet View

① Double-click the Physicians table in the Navigation Pane, and the Datasheet view displays (**Figure 8.26**).

Figure 8.26 Open Physicians Table in Datasheet View

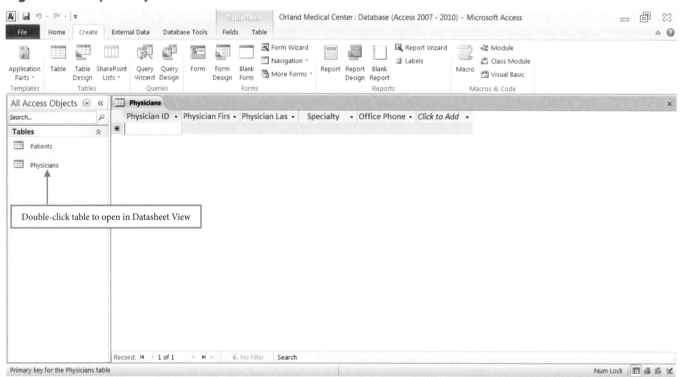

Modify Column or Row Size

If you are unable to view the entire field name or data in the fields, you can increase the width of the column in the datasheet. Additionally, you can change the height of a row.

Use these steps to resize the column width:

- Position the mouse pointer on the right boundary of the column.

- Double-click when the mouse pointer becomes a double-sided arrow, which is called the resize pointer (**Figure 8.27**), and the column size automatically adjusts to fit the contents of the column. *Or*, drag the right boundary of the column.

Use these steps to resize the row height:

- Position the mouse pointer on the bottom boundary of the row.
- When the resize pointer displays, drag the bottom boundary of the row.

Hands-On Exercise: Modify Column Size

(1) Position the mouse pointer on the right boundary of the Physician First Name column (Figure 8.27).

(2) Double-click when the mouse pointer becomes a double-sided arrow (Figure 8.27). The Physician First Name column increases to fit the field name.

(3) Position the mouse pointer on the right boundary of the Physician Last Name column.

(4) Double-click when the mouse pointer becomes a double-sided arrow. The Physician Last Name column increases to fit the field name. The screen will resemble **Figure 8.28**.

Figure 8.27 Resize Pointer Displays

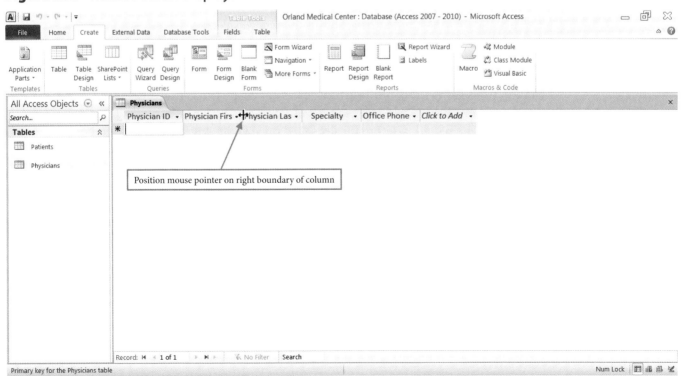

Figure 8.28 Columns Resized

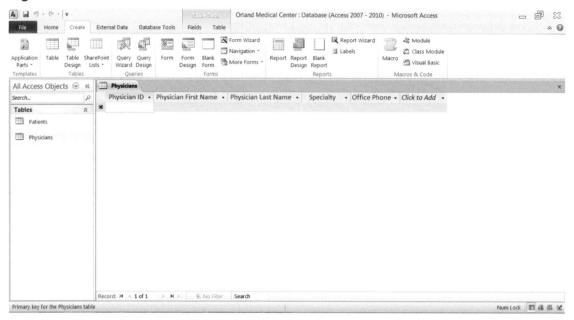

Add Records in a Table Using the Datasheet View

The Datasheet view resembles a Microsoft Excel 2010 workbook, which contains rows and columns. By default, new records are inserted at the end of the table. A star displays in the record selector of the last row, indicating where the new record will be inserted. The **record selector** is the small box to the left of a record (**Figure 8.29**).

> **Record selector:** The small box to the left of a record in a datasheet.

Use any of the following methods to insert a new record:

- Click the row that contains the star in the record selector.
- Click the **New (blank) Record** button at the bottom of the window (**Figure 8.30**).
- Click the **New** button in the Records group on the Home tab.

You can press **Enter**, **Tab**, or the arrow keys to navigate through the fields in the table. When you are on the last field of a record, you can press **Enter** or **Tab** to automatically create a new record. The record is automatically saved once you navigate to another record. When you are entering data into a field, a pencil displays in the record selector.

You will enter the records for the Physicians table using the information in **Table 8.9**.

Table 8.9 Records in Physicians Table				
Physician ID	**First Name**	**Last Name**	**Specialty**	**Office Phone**
P101	Lora	Pinchett	Internal Medicine	(555) 467-9001
P102	Carolyne	Mihalos	Cardiology	(555) 467-9002
P103	Cheryl	Pitt	Pediatrics	(555) 467-9003

Hands-On Exercise: Add Records in a Table Using the Datasheet View

1. The star displays in the record selector of the first row. The insertion point is in the Physician ID field. Type **P101**. The status bar states *Primary key for the Physicians table*, which is the description that was entered for the field (Figure 8.30). The record selector changes to a pencil, indicating that you are entering the contents of a record (Figure 8.30).

2. Press Tab to navigate to the Physician First Name field.

3. Type **Lora** in the Physician First Name field and press Tab .

4. Type **Pinchett** in the Physician Last Name field and press Tab .

5. Type **Internal Medicine** in the Specialty field.

6. The Specialty column is not wide enough to display the contents of the field. Position the mouse pointer on the right boundary of the Specialty column.

7. Double-click when the mouse pointer becomes a double-sided arrow. The Specialty column increases to fit the contents of the field.

8. Press Tab to navigate to the Office Phone field.

9. Type **5554679001** in the Office Phone field. The input mask displays with the parentheses and hyphen for the phone number.

10. Press Tab . The record is automatically saved and moves to the next record. The insertion point is placed in the second row, ready for you to enter the second record.

11. Type **P102** in the Physician ID field and press Tab .

12. Type **Carolyne** in the Physician First Name field and press Tab .

13. Type **Mihalos** in the Physician Last Name field and press Tab .

14. Type **Cardiology** in the Specialty field and press Tab .

15. Type **5554679002** in the Office Phone field and press Tab . The insertion point moves to the third row.

16. Type **P103** in the Physician ID field and press Tab .

17. Type **Cheryl** in the Physician First Name field and press Tab .

18. Type **Pitt** in the Physician Last Name field and press Tab .

19. Type **Pediatrics** in the Specialty field and press Tab .

20. Type **5554679003** in the Office Phone field and press Tab . Your screen should resemble **Figure 8.31**.

㉑ The records you entered are automatically saved in the table. The only time you need to save the table is if you make changes to the format of the table and you want to save it, such as if you increased the column size of the Specialty field. If you save the table, the column size will be saved. You will not need to resize the column the next time you open the datasheet. Click the Save button on the Quick Access Toolbar to save the format of the table.

Figure 8.29 Record Selector

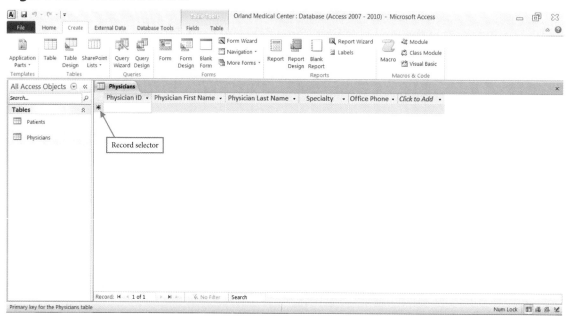

Figure 8.30 First Record Being Entered

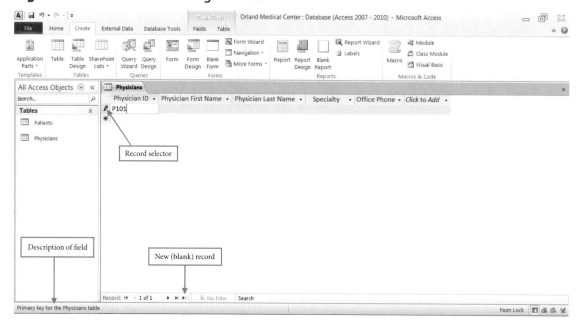

Figure 8.31 Records Added to Physicians Table

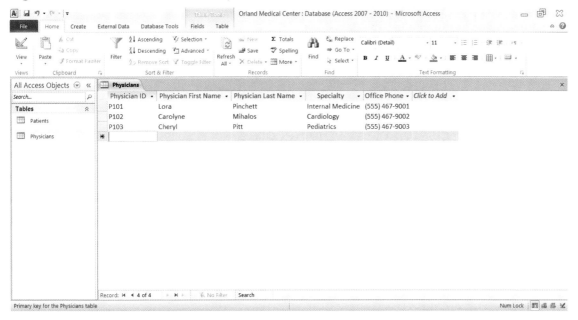

Navigating Records

The Record Navigation buttons display at the bottom of the window in the Record Navigation bar (**Figure 8.32**). These buttons allow a user to navigate through the records in the table. **Table 8.10** defines the buttons on the Record Navigation bar.

Table 8.10 Record Navigation Buttons

Name	Button	Description
First record	⏮	Navigates to the first record in the table.
Previous record	◀	Navigates to the previous record in the table.
Current Record	4 of 4	Displays current record position and the total number of records in the table.
Next record	▶	Navigates to the next record in the table.
Last record	⏭	Navigates to the last record in the table.
New (blank) record	▶*	Adds a new blank record to the table.
Search	Search	Type the data to search for in the Search box.

To navigate to a specific record in a table, enter the record number in the Current Record box and press **Enter**. To find a value in a field, type the data in the Search box. The first matching value will be highlighted in the datasheet.

Hands-On Exercise: Navigate the Records

① Click the First record button, and the first record displays. The Current Record box displays *1 of 3* (**Figure 8.33**).

② Click the Last record button, and the last record displays.

③ Click the Previous record button, and the second record displays.

④ Click the Next record button, and the third record displays.

⑤ Type **2** in the Current Record box and press Enter . The second record is selected. This is a quick way to navigate to a specific record in the table.

⑥ Type **Cardiology** in the Search box. The first matching value is highlighted in the datasheet (**Figure 8.34**).

Figure 8.32 Record Navigation Bar

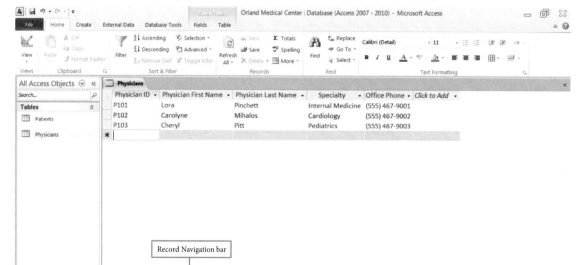

Figure 8.33 Current Record Box

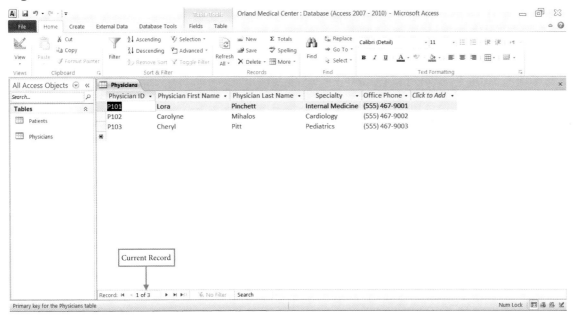

Figure 8.34 Search Box

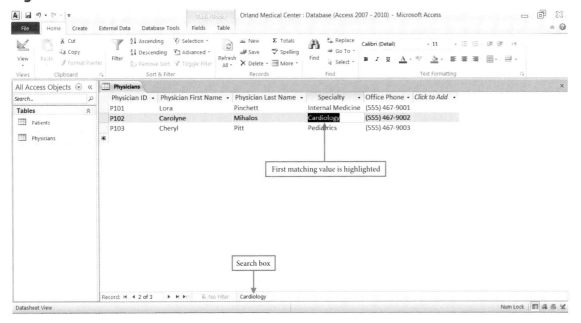

Print a Datasheet

You can print a datasheet, which contains all the records in a table. Before printing it, you may want to preview the datasheet to ensure it fits properly on the page. If you have many fields in a table, it may be best to change the page orientation to landscape orientation. The print command is located on the File tab.

Use the following steps to print a datasheet:

- Open the datasheet if not already opened.
- Click the **File** tab.
- Click **Print**.
- Click **Print Preview** to preview the datasheet.
- Adjust any print settings from the Print Preview tab.
- Click the **Print** button in the Print group.

Hands-On Exercise: Print a Datasheet

(1) Click the File tab to open the Backstage view.

(2) Click Print (**Figure 8.35**).

(3) Click Print Preview (Figure 8.35) and a preview of the datasheet displays (**Figure 8.36**).

(4) If you want to print the datasheet in landscape orientation, click the Landscape button in the Page Layout group on the Print Preview tab. Click the Print button in the Print group on the Print Preview tab to print the datasheet (Figure 8.36).

(5) Click Close Print Preview (Figure 8.36).

(6) Click the Close button on the far right of the Physicians tab.

(7) Click Yes if a dialog box displays asking you to save the changes to the layout of the table.

Figure 8.35 Print Preview Button

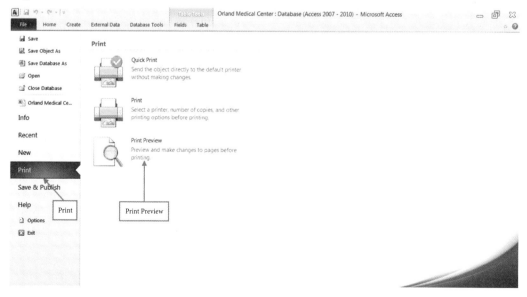

Figure 8.36 Print Preview Options

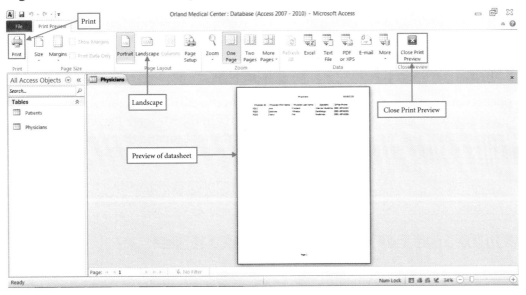

Help Button

You can use the Help feature if you need assistance with a task. The Help feature is accessed by clicking the Help button, which is located on the far-right corner of the Ribbon (**Figure 8.37**), or by pressing **F1** on the keyboard. You can also access the Help command from the File tab.

Hands-On Exercise: Use Help

① Click the Help button, and the Access Help dialog box displays (Figure 8.37).

② Type **create tables** in the Search box (Figure 8.37) and press Enter .

③ Search results display in the Access Help dialog box. Click a hyperlink to view the information.

④ Click the Close button on the Access Help dialog box (Figure 8.37).

Figure 8.37 Access Help Dialog Box

Compact and Repair a Database

Databases can become damaged or corrupted. The Compact & Repair Database command can be used to fix or prevent damages and corruption to a database. The Compact & Repair Database command is located on the Info tab in the Backstage View (**Figure 8.38**).

If you open a database and it is corrupted, Microsoft Access 2010 will automatically prompt you to repair the file. If a security warning displays in the Message Bar, click **Enable Content** (**Figure 8.39**). The Message Bar displays under the Ribbon and displays in a yellow background.

Hands-On Exercise: Compact and Repair a Database

1. Click the File tab.

2. Click Info .

3. Click Compact & Repair Database .

4. If a security warning displays on the Message Bar (Figure 8.39), click Enable Content .

Figure 8.38 Compact & Repair Database

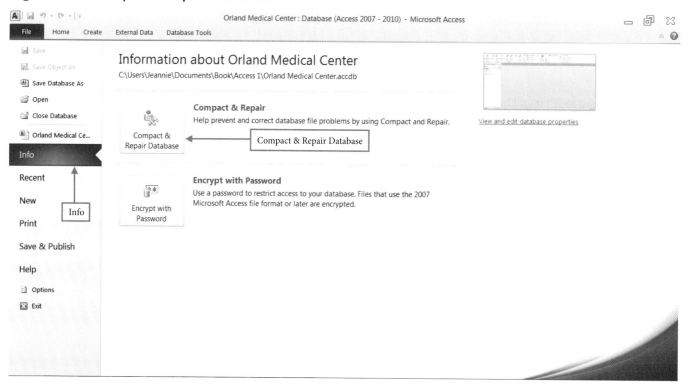

Figure 8.39 Security Warning on Message Bar

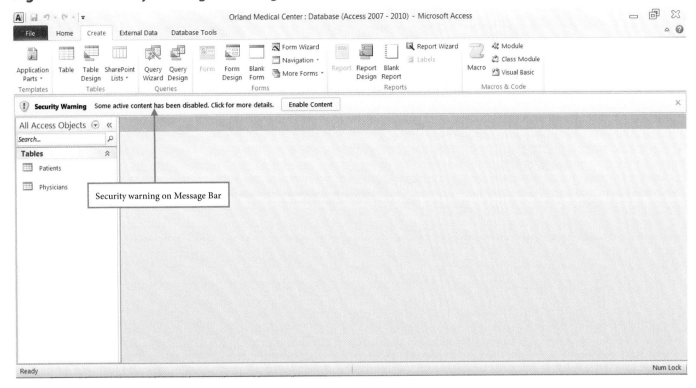

Security warning on Message Bar

Close a Database

You should close the database when you are finished working with it. The Close Database command is located on the File tab (**Figure 8.40**). This command does not close the application; it only closes the database.

Use the following steps to close a database:

- Click the **File** tab.
- Click **Close Database**.

If only one database is open in Microsoft Access 2010, you can close the database and exit the application at once by clicking the **Close** button on the title bar, pressing **Alt+F4**, or double-clicking the **Microsoft Access 2010 application icon** (Figure 8.40). The Microsoft Access 2010 application icon is located at the upper-left corner of the window, to the left of the Quick Access Toolbar. If multiple databases are open, these commands would only close the active database.

Hands-On Exercise: Close a Database

① Click the File tab.

② Click Close Database (Figure 8.40). The database closes but the application remains open.

Figure 8.40 Close Database

Exit Application

Use the Exit command to exit the application. The Exit command is located on the File tab.

Hands-On Exercise: Exit Application

① Click the File tab.

② Click Exit and the application closes.

Multiple-Choice Questions

1. Microsoft Access 2010 is a _____.
   a. Presentation graphics program
   b. Word processing program
   c. Spreadsheet program
   d. Database management system

2. A _____ is a database object that is used to store data about a particular subject.
   a. Field
   b. Datasheet

   c. Table

   d. Record

3. A _____ is a single characteristic of a table.

   a. Field

   b. Database

   c. Table

   d. Record

4. A _____ is a unique field or groups of fields that identifies the particular record.

   a. Common field

   b. Primary key

   c. Foreign key

   d. Related field

   Use **Table 8.11** to answer Questions 5–7.

Table 8.11 Customer Table		
Name	**Credit Card Number**	**Balance**
John Doe	1002391837	$100.00
Mary Smith	3984930293	$1050.00
Kim Milter	9038492738	$0.00
Tom Jeffrey	8371928379	$750.00

5. How many fields are in the Customer table?

   a. 2

   b. 3

   c. 4

   d. 5

6. How many records are in the Customer table?

   a. 2

   b. 3

   c. 4

   d. 5

7. Which data type should be used for the Credit Card Number field?

   a. Number

   b. Text

   c. Currency

   d. Yes/No

8. A Text field can contain a maximum of _____ characters.

   a. 10
   b. 25
   c. 64
   d. 255

9. The file extension of a Microsoft Access 2010 database is _____.

   a. access
   b. acc
   c. accdb
   d. accdx

10. To navigate through the fields in the table using Datasheet view, you can use all the following keys except _____.

    a. Tab
    b. Enter
    c. F5
    d. Arrow keys

Project #1: Create an Alumni Database

You are planning an alumni golf outing for the high schools in the Summit High School District. You will create a database to store information about the schools in the district and their alumni.

① Create a database called **Summit High School**.

② Create a table named **Schools** using the information in **Table 8.12**. Use an input mask for the Phone field.

Table 8.12 Schools Table				
Field	**Data Type**	**Field Size**	**Primary Key**	**Caption**
School ID	AutoNumber		Yes	
School Name	Text	25		
Address	Text	20		School Address
City	Text	20		School City
State	Text	2		School State
Phone	Text	10		School Phone
Principal	Text	20		

③ Enter the following records in **Table 8.13** into the Schools table. Adjust all column sizes to fit the contents of the data in the columns. The datasheet should resemble **Figure 8.41**.

Table 8.13 Records for the Schools Table

School ID	School Name	Address	City	State	Phone	Principal
1	Tanty High School	850 West Sacramento	Los Angeles	CA	(555) 467-9014	Tom Mullen
2	Washington High School	1056 North Central	Santa Anna	CA	(999) 678-9031	Gina Williamson
3	Los Angeles High School	943 South Lake Shore	Los Angeles	CA	(555) 841-3112	Rita Pochinski
4	Carmel High School	367 East Jackson	Burbank	CA	(999) 665-3456	Ahmed Musa

④ Print the datasheet in landscape orientation.

⑤ Save the table.

⑥ Close the table.

⑦ Create a table called **Alumni** using the information in **Table 8.14**. Use an input mask for the Phone field.

Table 8.14 Alumni Table

Field	Data Type	Field Size	Primary Key	Caption
Alumni ID	AutoNumber		Yes	
School ID	Number	Long Integer		Foreign key related to School ID in Schools table
First Name	Text	15		Alumni First Name
Last Name	Text	20		Alumni Last Name
Address	Text	20		Alumni Address
City	Text	20		Alumni City
State	Text	2		Alumni State
Zip Code	Text	5		Alumni Zip Code
Phone	Text	10		Alumni Phone
Graduation Year	Text	4		

⑧ Close the table.

⑨ Compact and repair the database.

⑩ Close the database.

⑪ Exit Microsoft Access 2010.

Figure 8.41 Schools Datasheet

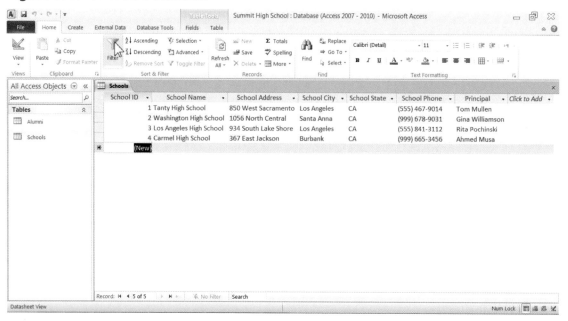

Project #2: Create a Database for a Retail Book Store

You work for a retail book store named Morgan Books. You will create a database to store information about the books they sell.

① Create a database called **Morgan Books**.

② Create a table named **Publisher** using the information in **Table 8.15**. Use an input mask for the Publisher Zip Code field.

Table 8.15 Publisher Table			
Field Name	**Data Type**	**Field Size**	**Primary Key**
Publisher ID	Text	4	Yes
Publisher Name	Text	25	
Publisher City	Text	20	
Publisher State	Text	2	
Publisher Zip Code	Text	9	

③ Enter the records in **Table 8.16** into the Publisher table. Adjust all column sizes to fit the contents of the data in the columns. The datasheet should resemble **Figure 8.42**.

Table 8.16 Add Records to the Publisher Table

Publisher ID	Publisher Name	Publisher City	Publisher State	Publisher Zip Code
B101	Breeze Publishing	Austin	TX	76700-5621
J101	Jefferson Publishing	Boston	MA	33315-1040
P101	P&G Publishing	Chicago	IL	60609-3304

Figure 8.42 Publisher Datasheet

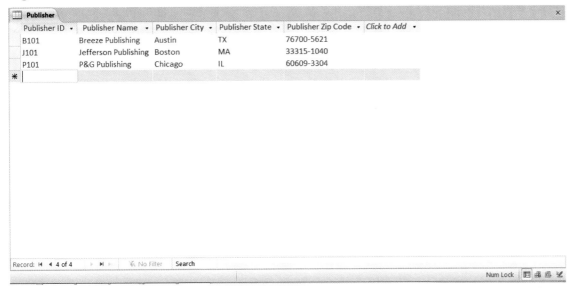

④ Print the datasheet in landscape orientation.

⑤ Save the table.

⑥ Close the table.

⑦ Create a table named **Books** using the information in **Table 8.17**.

Table 8.17 Books Table

Field	Data Type	Field Size	Primary Key	Caption	Description
ISBN	Text	13	Yes		
Book Title	Text	20			
Author	Text	20			
Publisher ID	Text	4			Foreign key related to Publisher ID in Publisher table
Quantity	Number	Long Integer		Quantity In Stock	
Price	Currency				

⑧ Close the table.

⑨ Close the database.

⑩ Exit Microsoft Access 2010.

Project #3: Create a Database for a Park District

You work for Calumet West Park District and need to create a database to store the special events that will be offered for the year.

① Create a database called **Calumet West Park District**.

② Create a table called **Special Events** using the information in **Table 8.18**.

Table 8.18 Special Events Table

Field	Data Type	Field Size	Primary Key	Format
Event ID	AutoNumber		Yes	
Event Description	Text	30		
Event Date	Date/Time			Short Date
Event Time	Date/Time			Medium Time
Price	Currency			

③ Enter the records in **Table 8.19** into the Special Events table. Adjust all column sizes to fit the contents of the data in the columns. The datasheet should resemble **Figure 8.43**.

Table 8.19 Records for Special Events Table

Event ID	Event Description	Event Date	Event Time	Price
1	Line Dancing	1/10/2014	7:00 PM	$25.00
2	Valentine's Dance	2/14/2014	7:00 PM	$25.00
3	Field Museum Trip	3/25/2014	8:00 AM	$30.00
4	Easter Egg Hunt	4/3/2014	9:00 AM	$0.00
5	Movie Day	5/15/2014	5:00 PM	$10.00
6	Zumba Dancing	6/20/2014	8:00 AM	$5.00
7	Back to School Dance	7/31/2014	6:00 PM	$10.00

Figure 8.43 Special Events Datasheet

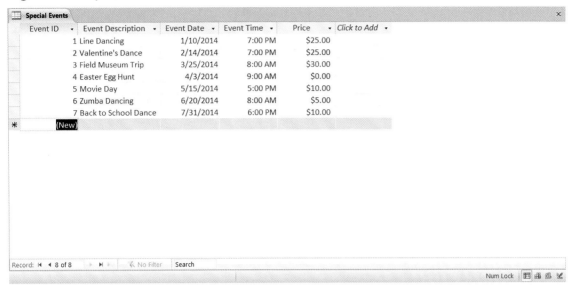

④ Print the datasheet in landscape orientation.

⑤ Save the table.

⑥ Close the table.

⑦ Create a table called **Participants** using the information in Table 8.20. Use an input mask for the Home Phone field.

Field	Data Type	Field Size	Primary Key	Description
Table 8.20 Participants Table				
Participant ID	AutoNumber		Yes	
Event ID	Number	Long Integer		Foreign key related to Event ID in Special Events table
First Name	Text	15		
Last Name	Text	20		
Home Phone	Text	10		
Payment	Currency			

⑧ Close the table.

⑨ Close the database.

⑩ Exit Microsoft Access 2010.

Create Forms, Queries, and Reports

9

Chapter Objectives

After completing this chapter, you will be able to do the following:

- Modify table design.
- Create table relationships.
- Maintain records using a form.
- Use a subdatasheet.
- Sort and filter data in a datasheet.
- Create and modify a query.
- Create a report using the report wizard.

Now that you know the basics of Microsoft Access 2010, you are going to learn how to create forms, queries, and reports. A wizard can be used to guide you through the process of creating database objects quickly. A wizard asks a few questions about the database object, and then it creates the object based on the responses.

You will also learn how to create relationships between tables. Additionally, you will learn how to manipulate data in tables using sorting and filtering commands.

Wizard: Asks a few questions about the database object, and then it creates the object based on the responses.

Open a Database

You will open the Orland Medical Center database that you created in the previous chapter. The Open command is located in the Backstage view.

Hands-On Exercise: Open a Database

1. Click the Start button.

2. Click All Programs .

3. Click Microsoft Office . You may need to scroll through the Start menu to locate the folder.

4. Click Microsoft Access 2010 . The Backstage view displays.

5. Click Open (**Figure 9.1**) and the Open dialog box displays.

6. Select the location and folder in which the database is stored (Documents library or USB Flash drive).

7. Double-click the Orland Medical Center database (**Figure 9.2**), *or* click the Orland Medical Center database and click Open . The database opens (**Figure 9.3**). If a security warning displays in the Message Bar, click Enable Content .

Figure 9.1 Backstage View

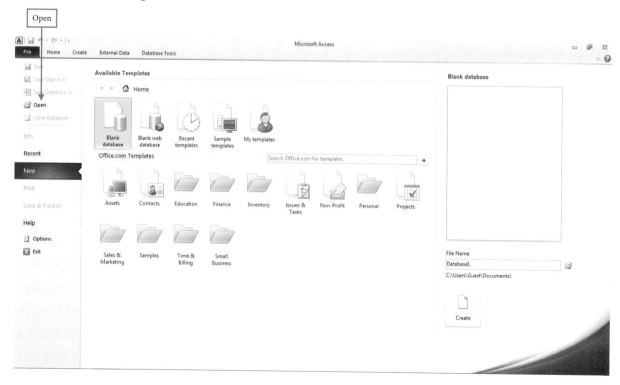

Figure 9.2 Open Dialog Box

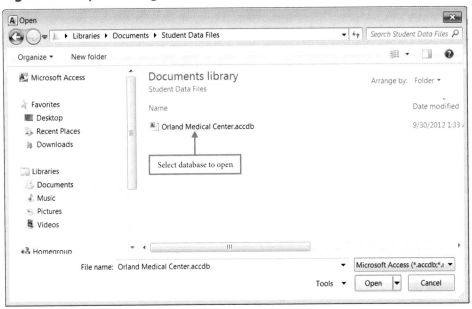

Figure 9.3 Database Opened

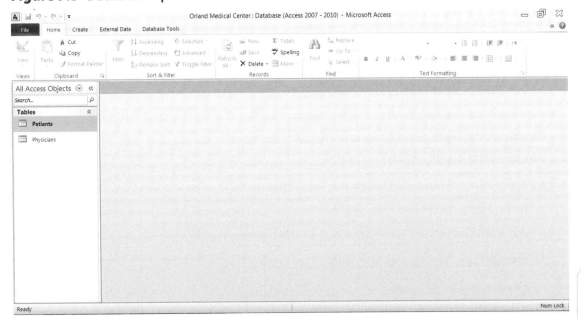

Modify Table Design

You can add, modify, or delete fields in a table. Additionally, you can apply field properties to a field. The Decimal Places property is used to specify the number of decimal places to display for the number in the field. The Input Mask property is used to select a pattern for the field that controls how the data are to be entered.

Decimal Places property: A property used to specify the number of decimal places to display for the number in the field.

Input Mask property: A property used to select a pattern for a field that controls how the data are to be entered.

Use these steps to modify table properties:

- Right-click the **table** in the Tables objects in the Navigation Pane.
- Click **Design View** on the shortcut menu (**Figure 9.4**).
- The Table Tools contextual tab displays; it contains the Design tab. The Design tab contains commands to modify the table. Make the changes to the table and save the table when completed.

Use these steps to insert a field:

- Click the **row selector** of the row where you want to insert the field (**Figure 9.5**). The row selector is located to the left of the Field Name box.
- Click the **Insert Rows** button in the Tools group on the Design tab (Figure 9.5).

Use these steps to delete a field:

- Click the **row selector** of the field you want to delete.
- Click the **Delete Rows** button in the Tools group on the Design tab (Figure 9.5).

Use this step to move a field:

- Drag the **row selector** to another location in the design grid.

Hands-On Exercise: Modify Table Design

You will open the Patients table and add a new field called *Balance*.

1. Right-click the Patients table in the Tables objects in the Navigation Pane.

2. Click Design View on the shortcut menu (Figure 9.4).

3. You will insert a field before the Physician ID field. The Physician ID field is the last field in the design grid. Scroll through the fields in the design grid and click the row selector for the Physician ID field (Figure 9.5).

4. Click the Insert Rows button in the Tools group on the Design tab (Figure 9.5). A blank row displays above the Physician ID row.

5. Type **Balance** in the Field Name box in the new row and press Tab .

6. Click the Data Type arrow and select Currency .

7. Type **2** in the Decimal Places box in the Field Properties pane, *or* you can click the Decimal Places arrow and select 2 from the list (**Figure 9.6**). This will ensure that two decimal places are displayed in the field.

8. You will move the Policy # field above the Insurance field. Click the row selector of the Policy # field.

9. Drag the row selector of the Policy # field up one row. When you click the row selector to start dragging, a line displays above the Policy # row. Drag the row selector up until the line displays above the Insurance row (**Figure 9.7**).

⑩ The Policy # field displays in the row above the Insurance field. Click the Save button on the Quick Access Toolbar. The screen should resemble **Figure 9.8**.

⑪ You will apply an input mask to the Home Phone field. Click the row selector of the Home Phone field. You may need to scroll up to find the field.

⑫ Click the Input Mask box in the Field Properties pane (**Figure 9.9**).

⑬ Click the Build button (Figure 9.9) and the Input Mask Wizard dialog box displays (**Figure 9.10**).

⑭ Click Phone Number .

⑮ Click Finish . The Input Mask box automatically inserts the pattern for the Home Phone field, which is !\(999") "000\-0000;;_. The character *9* in the input mask pattern indicates that a space or a digit from 0 to 9 is allowed. The character *0* in the input mask pattern indicates that a digit from 0 to 9 is required.

⑯ Click the Save button on the Quick Access Toolbar.

⑰ Click the Close button to the right of the Patients tab (Figure 9.9).

Figure 9.4 Design View on the Shortcut Menu

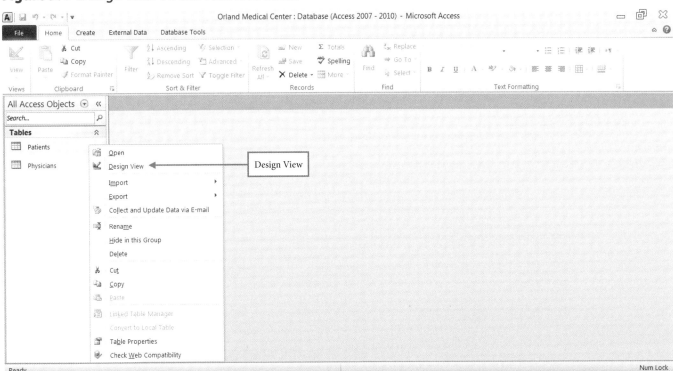

Figure 9.5 Row Selector and Insert Rows and Delete Rows Buttons

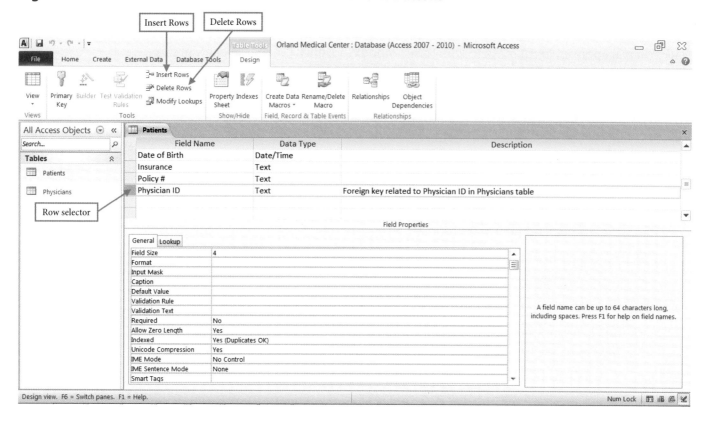

Figure 9.6 Decimal Places Property

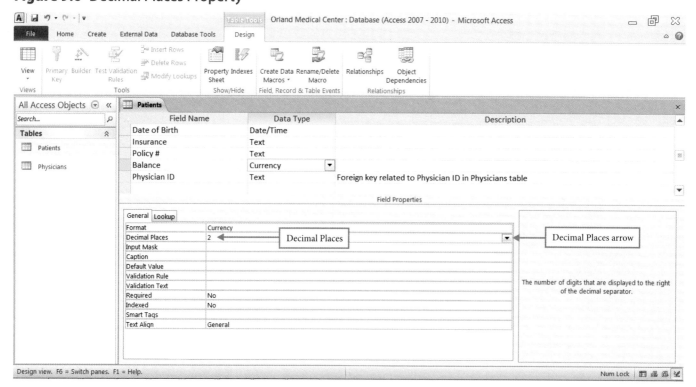

Figure 9.7 Move a Field

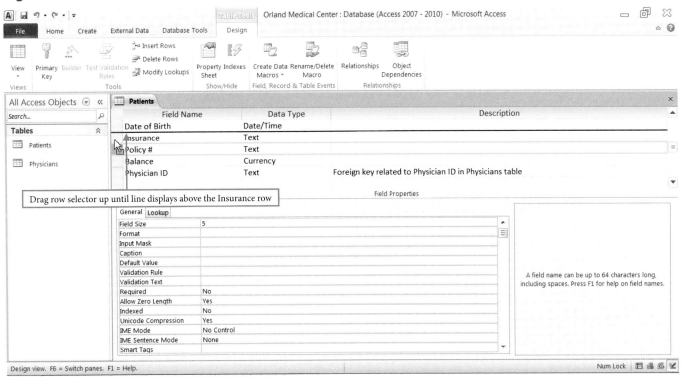

Figure 9.8 Policy # Field Moved

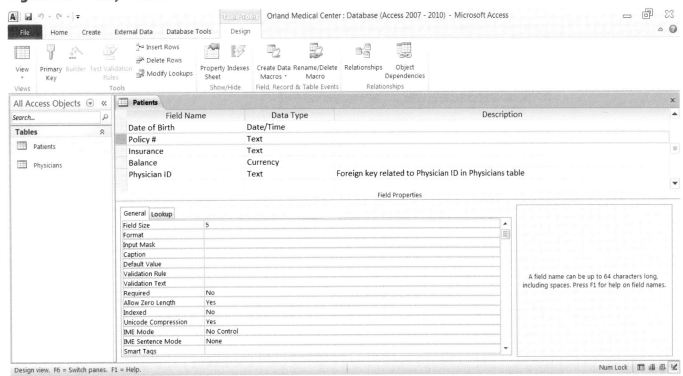

Figure 9.9 Input Mask

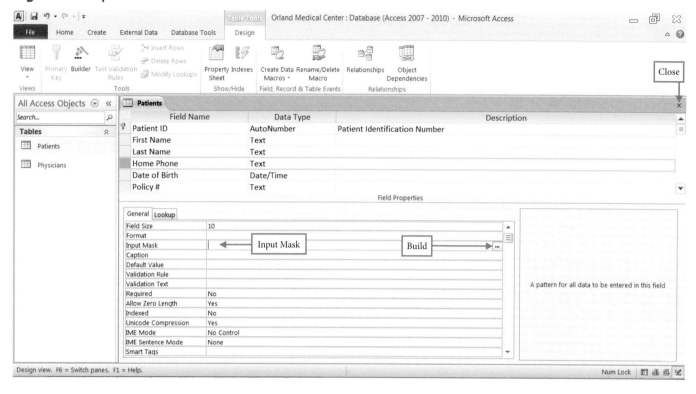

Figure 9.10 Input Mask Wizard

Create a Table Relationship

Relationship:
Combines data from
two tables that have
a common field.

Microsoft Access 2010 is a relational database system. One of the benefits of using Microsoft
Access 2010 is the ability to create relationships between tables. Creating a relationship helps
reduce data redundancy in the database. A **relationship** combines data from two tables that

have a common field. A common field is a field that exists in both tables and contains the same data.

> Common field: A field that exists in two tables and contains the same data.

You can create a relationship between tables if the following are true:

- The tables contain a common field. The common field must contain the same data type and field size. The only exception is when a primary key field in one table is an AutoNumber data type: In this case, the foreign key of the related table can be a Number data type as long as the field size of both fields are identical. It is not required that the field names of the common fields be identical.

- The common field in the one table is the primary key of that table.

- The common field in the other table is the foreign key. The foreign key field links to the primary key of the other table.

A one-to-many relationship is a relationship between two tables in which one record in one table is related to many records in another table. The Physicians table has a one-to-many relationship between the Patients table. One record in the Physicians table is related to many records in the Patients table. This indicates that one physician in the Physicians table can have multiple patients in the Patients table. The common field is Physician ID. Physician ID is the primary key of the Physicians table and is the foreign key in the Patients table.

> One-to-many relationship: A relationship between two tables in which one record in one table is related to many records in another table.

Use these steps to create a relationship:

- Click the **Database Tools** tab on the Ribbon (**Figure 9.11**).

- Click the **Relationships** button in the Relationships group (Figure 9.11). The Show Table dialog box displays, which lists all the tables and queries in the database.

- Select the tables that will be joined and click **Add** (**Figure 9.12**).

- Click **Close** to close the Show Table dialog box.

- To join the tables, drag the common field (primary key) from the table to the common field (foreign key) in the other table.

- The Edit Relationships dialog box displays. It lists the tables that are joined and the common field of the tables. Click the **Enforce Referential Integrity** checkbox if needed. Enforce Referential Integrity are rules that are enforced when creating relationships to ensure that valid field values are entered into the table that contains the foreign key. It will also ensure that a value in the common field that is the primary key of the table is not deleted if the value exists in the common field in the other table.

  - For example, you will not be allowed to enter a Physician ID in the Patients table if the Physician ID does not exist in the Physicians table. Additionally, you will not be able to delete a record in the Physicians table if that Physician ID exists in the Patients table.

- Click **Create** and the relationship is created. A relationship line, also called a join line, displays between the tables indicating that there is a relationship between the two tables.

> Enforce Referential Integrity: Rules that are enforced when creating relationship to ensure that valid field values are entered into the table that contains the foreign key.

> Relationship line: A line that displays between the tables indicating that there is a relationship between the two tables.

Use these steps to remove a relationship:

- Click the **relationship line.**

- Press **Delete**.

> Join line: A line that displays between the tables indicating that there is a relationship between the two tables.

Hands-On Exercise: Create a Relationship

You will create a relationship between the Physicians and Patients table.

① Click the Database Tools tab on the Ribbon (Figure 9.11).

② Click the Relationships button in the Relationships group (Figure 9.11). The Show Table dialog box displays (Figure 9.12).

③ You need to select the tables that will be joined. Click the Physicians table.

④ Click Add (Figure 9.12).

⑤ Click the Patients table.

⑥ Click Add .

⑦ Click Close to close the Show Table dialog box. Both tables are displayed in the Relationships window (**Figure 9.13**).

⑧ Drag the bottom border of the Patients table to enlarge the table so that all the fields display in the window (Figure 9.13). A key displays to the left of the fields that contain a primary key (Figure 9.13).

⑨ To join the tables, drag the common field (primary key) from the table to the common field (foreign key) in the other table. Drag the Physician ID field from the Physicians table to the Physician ID field in the Patients table.

⑩ The Edit Relationships dialog box displays (**Figure 9.14**). It lists the tables that are joined and the common field of the tables. The Relationship Type states *One-To-Many,* which indicates that one record in the Physicians table can be related to multiple records in the Patients table (Figure 9.14).

⑪ Click the Enforce Referential Integrity checkbox. When a value is entered in the Physician ID field in the Patients table, it will verify that the Physician ID exists in the Physicians table. If the Physician ID does not exist, the value cannot be added to the Patients table. This helps prevent data-entry errors because only valid Physician ID values can be added to the Patients table.

⑫ Click Create , and the relationship is created. A relationship line displays that links the common fields (**Figure 9.15**). The number *1* displays to the right of the Physician ID field in the Physicians table, and the infinity symbol (∞) displays to the left of the Physician ID field in the Patients table. This denotes a one-to-many relationship. These notations will display only if referential integrity is enforced. If you create a relationship by mistake, you can click the relationship line and press Delete to remove the relationship.

⑬ Click the Save button on the Quick Access Toolbar to save the relationship.

⑭ Click the Relationship Report button in the Tools group on the Design tab to print the relationship report (Figure 9.15).

⑮ A preview of the report displays (**Figure 9.16**).

⑯ Click Print to print the report (Figure 9.16).

⑰ Click the Close button to the right of the Relationships for Orland Medical Center tab (Figure 9.16).

⑱ A dialog box displays asking if you want to save changes to the design of the report. Click No .

⑲ Click the Close button in the Relationships group on the Design tab (Figure 9.15).

Figure 9.11 Relationships Button

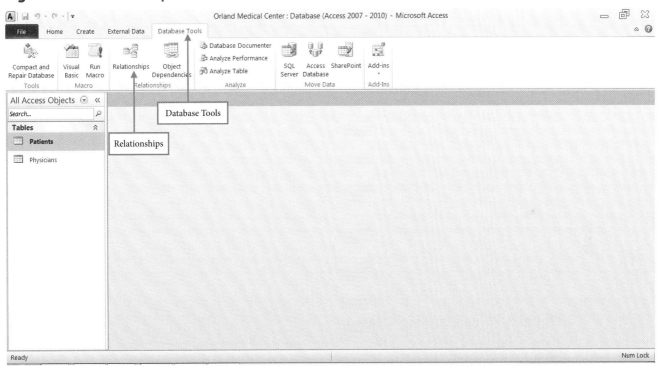

Figure 9.12 Show Table Dialog Box

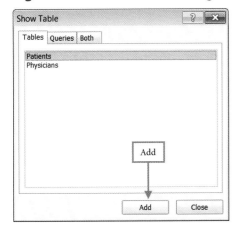

Figure 9.13 Relationships Window

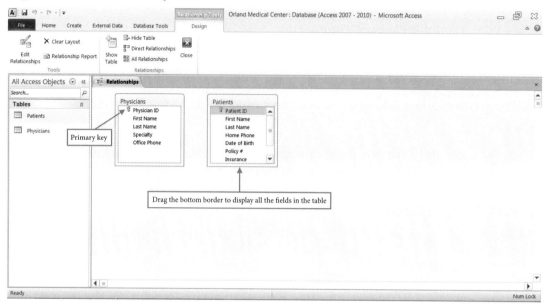

Figure 9.14 Edit Relationships Dialog Box

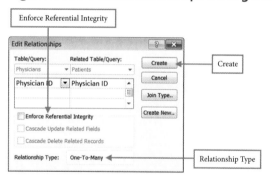

Figure 9.15 Relationship Created

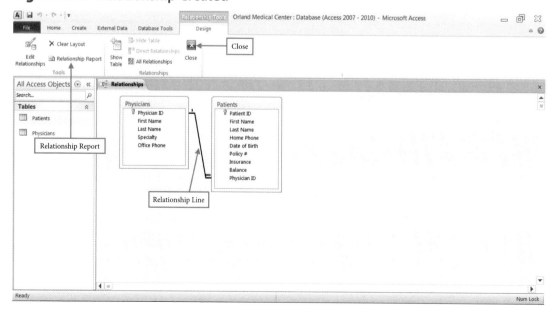

Figure 9.16 Print Relationship Report

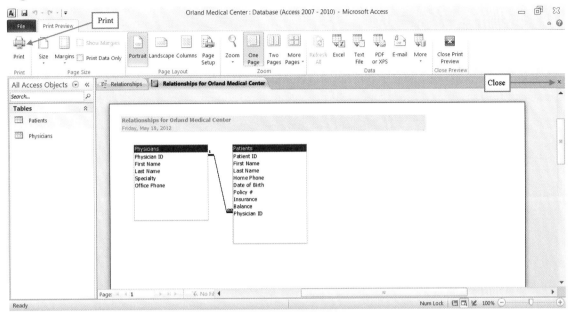

Create a Form to Add Records

In the previous chapter you added new records using a datasheet. You can also add records to a table using a form. A **form** is a database object used to add or modify records in a table. A form displays one record at a time, whereas the datasheet displays many records at a time.

> **Form:** A database object used to add or modify records in a table.

When you enter data in a form or table, it verifies that the correct data type is entered in the field. For example, the Balance field is a Currency data type. If you entered text in that field, a dialog box would display, stating that the value you entered was not valid for the field. You would need to retype the correct information in the field. When entering data in a form or table, the referential integrity rules that were set up when you created the relationship is enforced. For example, the foreign field in a table must contain a matching value in the related table. When entering a Physician ID in the Patients table, the system will check to ensure that the Physician ID exists in the Physicians table. If the Physician ID does not exist in the Physicians table, it will not store the value in the field.

Use these steps to create a form:

- Click the **table** in the Tables object in the Navigation Pane.
- Click the **Create** tab on the Ribbon (**Figure 9.17**).
- Click the **Form** button in the Forms group (Figure 9.17). The Form Layout Tools contextual tab displays, which contain the Design, Arrange, and Format tabs.
- Click the **View arrow** in the Views group on the Design tab and click **Form View** (**Figure 9.18**).

The form is created and includes all the fields in the table. The Form View is a view that is used to add, modify, and delete records in a table. Press the **Tab**, **Enter**, or **arrow keys** to navigate the fields on the form. Use the **Delete** or **Backspace** keys to correct any mistakes

> **Form View:** A view that is used to add, modify, and delete records in a table.

while entering data. The Record Navigation bar displays at the bottom of the Form window (Figure 9.18). You can navigate the records using the buttons on the Record Navigation bar.

Hands-On Exercise: Create a Form and Add Records

1. Click the Patients table in the Tables object in the Navigation Pane.

2. Click the Create tab on the Ribbon (Figure 9.17).

3. Click the Form button in the Forms group (Figure 9.17). The form opens in Layout view and displays the first record of the Patients table, which is blank (Figure 9.18). Layout view is used to format the contents and the layout of the form. You will switch the view to Form view.

4. Click the View arrow in the Views group on the Design tab (Figure 9.18) and click Form View. The screen resembles **Figure 9.19**.

5. You will enter the record for the first patient. After you enter the contents of each field, you can press **Enter**, **Tab**, or the **arrow keys** to navigate to the next field. The insertion point is in the Patient ID field. This field is the primary key and is set as an AutoNumber data type, which means that the program will automatically assign a value to it. The current value is *(New)*. Once you add data to the record, the Patient ID field is updated with a value.

6. Press Tab to navigate to the First Name field.

7. Type **Chris** in the First Name field and press Tab . Notice that the Patient ID field was updated with a value of *1*.

8. Type **Smith** in the Last Name field and press Tab .

9. Type **5553999862** in the Home Phone field and press Tab . The input mask displays the parentheses and hyphen for the phone number.

10. A calendar icon displays to the right of the Date of Birth field (**Figure 9.20**). You can select a date from the calendar or type the date in the field. Type **1/5/1970** in the Date of Birth field and press Tab .

11. Type **12310** in the Policy # field and press Tab .

12. Type **Abbott** in the Insurance field and press Tab .

13. Type **50** in the Balance field. You do not need to type in the dollar sign. That will be added automatically, as will the two decimal places, once you exit the field.

14. Press Tab and *$50.00* displays in the Balance field.

15. Type **P106** in the Physician ID field and press Tab .

16. A Microsoft Access dialog box displays a message stating *You cannot add or change a record because a related record is required in table 'Physicians'* (**Figure 9.21**). This means that Physician ID P106 does not exist in the Physicians table. You must reenter a valid Physician ID to proceed. Click OK .

⑰ Type **P101** in the Physician ID field. The screen should resemble **Figure 9.22**. Notice that the description of the field is displayed at the left corner of the status bar.

⑱ Press Tab , and a new blank record displays. Enter the rest of the records in the form using the data in **Table 9.1**.

Table 9.1 Patients Table

Patient ID	First Name	Last Name	Home Phone	Date of Birth	Policy #	Insurance	Balance	Physician ID
2	Georgia	Levi	(555) 987-9093	12/14/1989	68493	Delta	350	P102
3	Peter	Miller	(999) 658-3843	6/29/1997	30583	Abbott	20	P103
4	Jeannie	Geller	(999) 117-4532	7/15/1976	10384	Delta	100	P101
5	Manny	Changas	(555) 489-4209	11/27/2009	38473	Abbott	20	P103
6	Betty	Duley	(555) 284-0391	9/4/1963	53621	Abbott	0	P102
7	Angelo	O'Malley	(999) 556-9019	4/10/1952	90394	Delta	180	P101

⑲ Do not press Tab after entering the last record. You should have seven records entered in the table. The Current Record button in the Record Navigation bar displays *7 of 7* (**Figure 9.23**).

⑳ Next you will save the form. Click the Save button on the Quick Access Toolbar.

㉑ The Save As dialog box displays. *Patients* displays as the default form name, which is also the name of the table. Click OK to accept the default name. The Patients form displays in the Forms objects in the Navigation Pane. The screen should resemble Figure 9.23.

Figure 9.17 Form Button

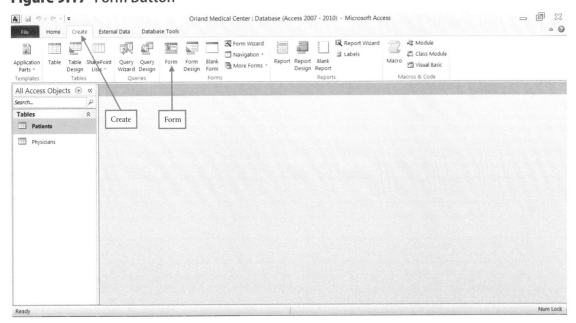

Figure 9.18 View Arrow and Record Navigation Bar

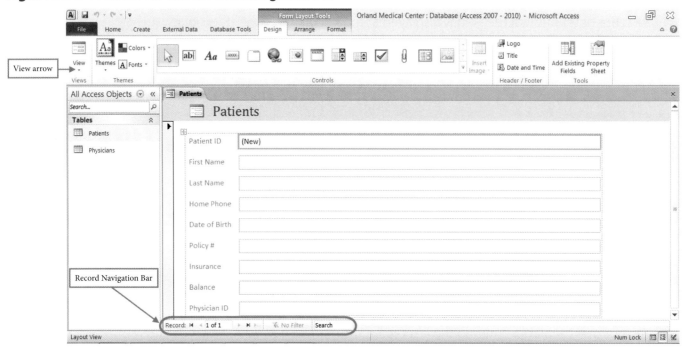

Figure 9.19 Form View

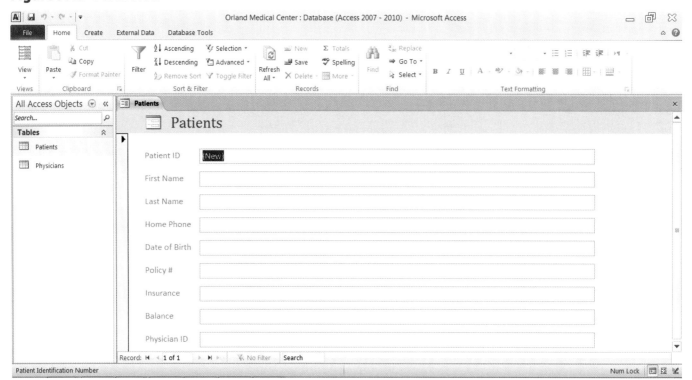

Figure 9.20 Calendar Icon

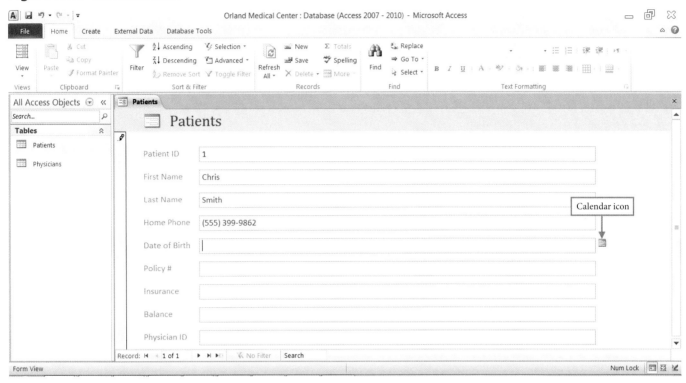

Figure 9.21 Invalid Physician ID

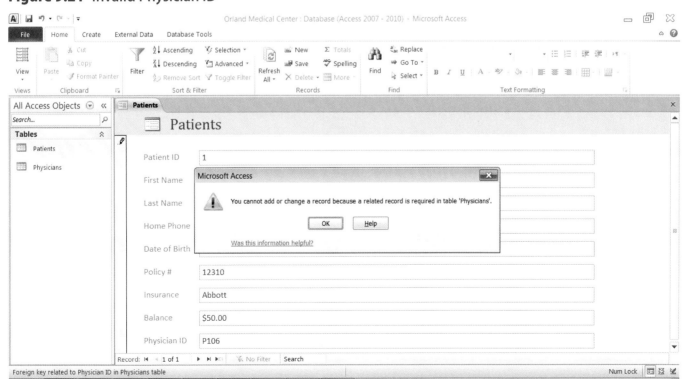

Figure 9.22 First Record Entered

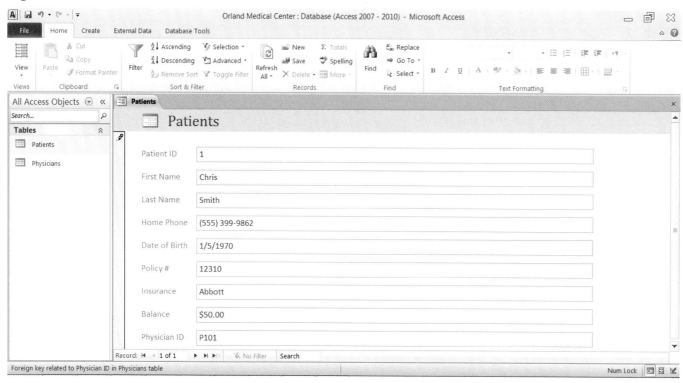

Figure 9.23 Patients Form Saved

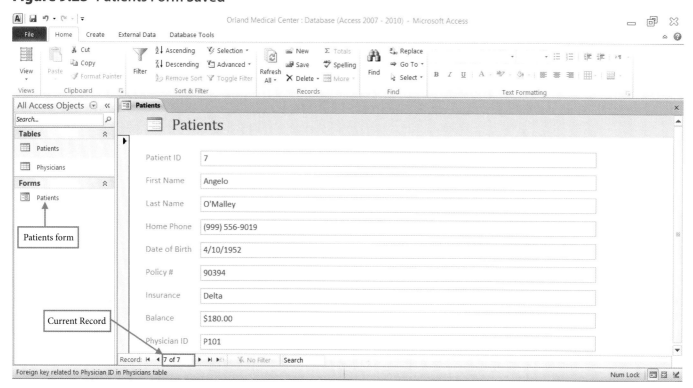

Navigate Records on a Form

The **Record Navigation buttons** display at the bottom of a form in the Record Navigation bar (**Figure 9.24**) and allow a user to navigate through the records in a form. **Table 9.2** defines the buttons on the Record Navigation bar.

Record Navigation buttons: Buttons that are used to navigate through the records in a table or form.

Table 9.2 Record Navigation Buttons

Name	Button	Description
First record	⏮	Navigates to the first record.
Previous record	◀	Navigates to the previous record.
Current Record	7 of 7	Displays the current record position and the total number of records.
Next record	▶	Navigates to the next record.
Last record	⏭	Navigates to the last record.
New (blank) record	▶✱	Adds a new blank record.
Search	Search	Searches the records for data entered in the Search box.

To navigate to a specific record in a form, enter the record number in the Current Record box. To find a value in a field, enter the data in the Search box. The first matching value will be highlighted on the form.

Hands-On Exercise: Navigate Records on a Form

① Click the First record button, and the first record displays. The Current Record box displays *1 of 7.*

② Click the Last record button, and the last record displays.

③ Click the Previous record button, and the sixth record displays.

④ Click the Next record button, and the seventh record displays.

⑤ Type **2** in the Current Record box and press Enter . The second record displays.

⑥ Type **Miller** in the Search box. The first matching value is highlighted on the form (Figure 9.24).

Figure 9.24 Record Navigation Bar

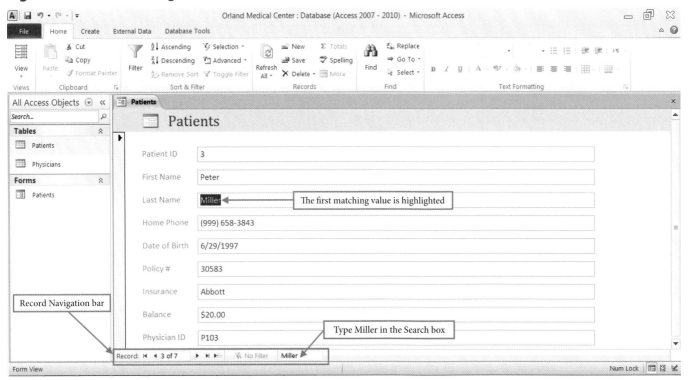

Delete a Record Using a Form

You can delete records on a form. Once you delete a record, you cannot use the Undo button to undo the deletion. It is permanently deleted.

Use the following steps to delete a record:

- Click the **record selector** of the record you want to delete (**Figure 9.25**). The record selector is the bar located to the left of the fields on the form.
- Press **Delete** *or* click the **Delete** button in the Records group on the Home tab (Figure 9.25).
- A message will display asking you if you are sure you want to delete the record. Click **Yes** and the record is deleted.

Hands-On Exercise: Delete a Record Using a Form

① Click the New (blank) record button on the Record Navigation bar to add a new record (Figure 9.25).

② Type **Henry** in the First Name field and press Tab .

③ Next you will delete the record. Click the record selector to select the record (Figure 9.25). The record selector becomes black.

④ Click the Delete button in the Records group on the Home tab (Figure 9.25).

⑤ A message displays asking if you are sure that you want to delete the record. Click Yes and the record is deleted.

Figure 9.25 Delete Record

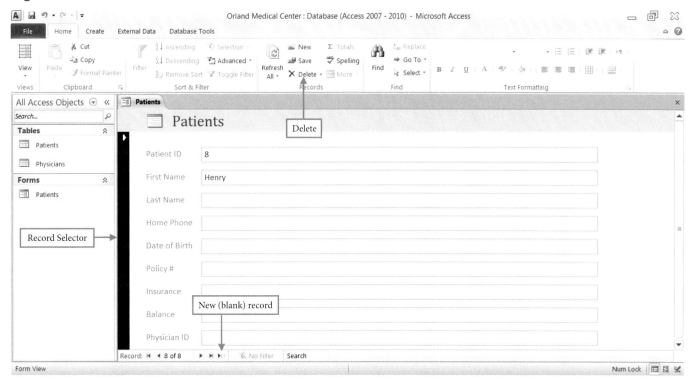

Print a Form

You can print a form that contains selected records or all the records in a table.

Use these steps to print a specific record:

- Navigate to the record you want to print.
- Click the **File** tab.
- Click **Print**.
- Click the **Print** button in the Print options. The Print dialog box displays.
- Click the **Selected Record(s)** option in the Print Range section (**Figure 9.26**).
- Click **OK**.

Use these steps to print all records:

- Click the **File** tab.
- Click **Print**.
- Click the **Print** button in the Print options. The Print dialog box displays.
- Click the **All** option in the Print Range section.
- Click **OK**.

Use these steps to print in landscape orientation:

- Click the **File** tab.
- Click **Print**.
- Click the **Print Preview** button in the Print options.

- Click the **Landscape** button in the Page Layout group.
- Click the **Print** button in the Print group.
- Click **OK**.
- Click the **Close Print Preview** button in the Close Preview group.

Hands-On Exercise: Print a Form

You will print record number 5.

1. Type **5** in the Current Record box in the Record Navigation bar and press Enter . The fifth record displays.

2. Click the File tab.

3. Click Print .

4. Click the Print button in the Print Options section. The Print dialog box displays.

5. Click the Selected Record(s) option in the Print Range section (Figure 9.26).

6. Click OK .

7. Click the Close button to the right of the Patients form tab. The Patients form displays in the Forms object in the Navigation Pane.

Figure 9.26 Print Selected Records on a Form

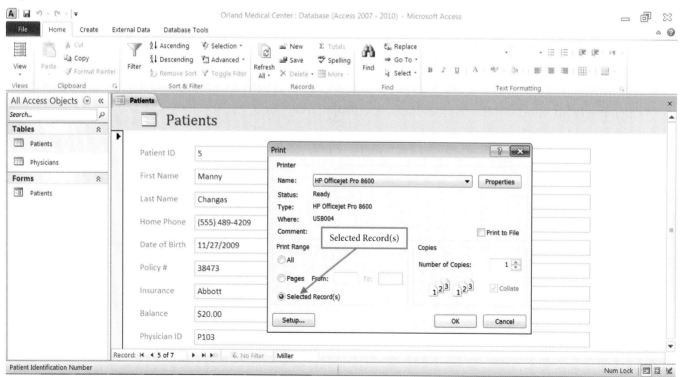

Rename or Delete Database Objects

The Navigation Pane displays all the objects in a database grouped by category. An icon displays before the object name that represents the object type. A table icon displays before the name of the tables, and the form icon displays before the name of the form (**Figure 9.27**).

Use these steps to change the name of the object or delete the object from the Navigation Pane:

You will change the name of the form from *Patients* to *Patients Form*.

- Right-click the **object** in the Navigation Pane.
- Click **Rename** or **Delete** from the shortcut menu.

Hands-On Exercise: Rename Form

1. Right-click the Patients form in the Forms object in the Navigation Pane.

2. Click Rename on the shortcut menu.

3. The name of the form is selected. Type **Patients Form** and press Enter . The screen should resemble Figure 9.27.

Figure 9.27 Rename Form

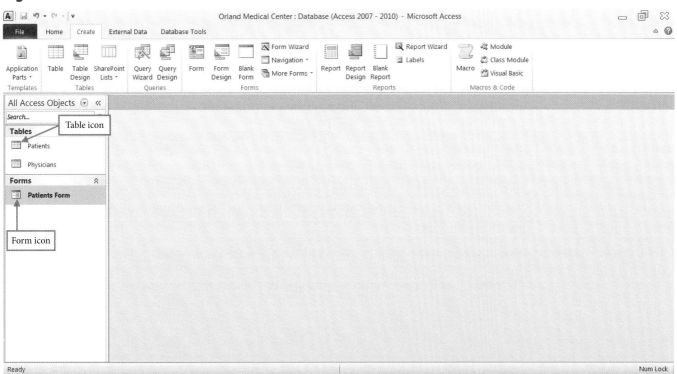

Use a Subdatasheet

Subdatasheet: An embedded datasheet that displays data from tables that are related.

A **subdatasheet** is an embedded datasheet that displays data from tables that are related. A subdatasheet is automatically created for tables that meet one of the following conditions:

- The table is in a one-to-one relationship.
- The table is the "one" side of a one-to-many relationship.

The subdatasheet displays all the records from the related table. When you open a table in Datasheet view, the Expand indicator displays when a subdatasheet exists. The Expand indicator displays as a plus sign (**Figure 9.28**). When the plus sign is clicked, the records from the related table display (**Figure 9.29**). The Expand indicator changes to a minus sign. Click the minus sign to collapse the subdatasheet.

The Physicians table contains a subdatasheet because this table is the "one" side of the one-to-many relationship between the Patients table. When you click the Expand indicator (plus sign) for a record in the Physicians table, all the patients in the Patients table for that physician will display.

Hands-On Exercise: Use a Subdatasheet

1. Double-click the Physicians table in the Tables object in the Navigation Pane to open the datasheet. The Expand indicator displays a plus sign, indicating that a subdatasheet exists (Figure 9.28).

2. Click the Expand Indicator (+) for the first record, which contains Physician ID P101, and the subdatasheet displays the records from the related Patients table (Figure 9.29). The Expand indicator changes to a minus sign, indicating that the records from the related table are displayed. Dr. Lora Pinchett has three patients, and the patient information displays below the physician information.

3. Click the Expand Indicator (–) for Physician P101, and the subdatasheet collapses (closes).

4. Next you will view the patients for Physician ID P103. Click the Expand Indicator (+) for Physician ID P103, and the subdatasheet displays (**Figure 9.30**). Dr. Cheryl Pitt has two patients.

5. Click the Expand Indicator (–) for Physician ID P103, and the subdatasheet collapses.

6. Click the Close button to the right of the Physicians tab to close the table.

Figure 9.28 Expand Indicator

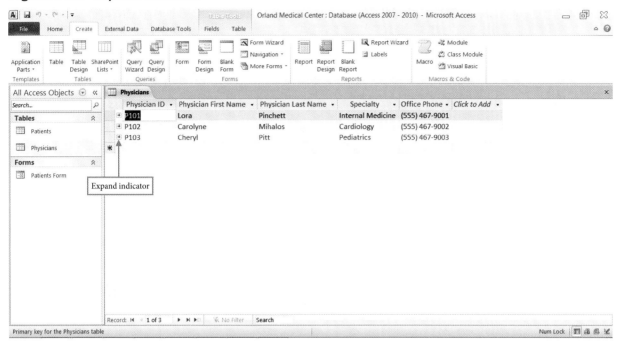

Figure 9.29 Subdatasheet Displays

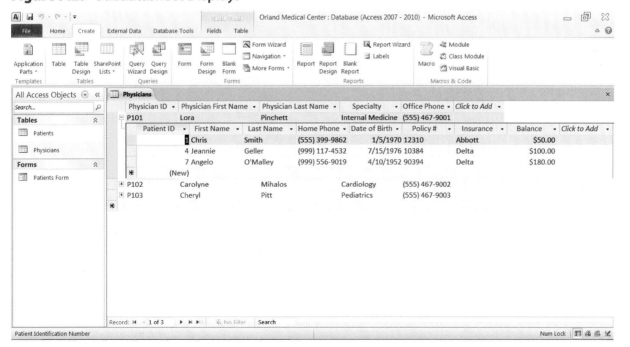

Figure 9.30 Subdatasheet Displays for Physician ID P103

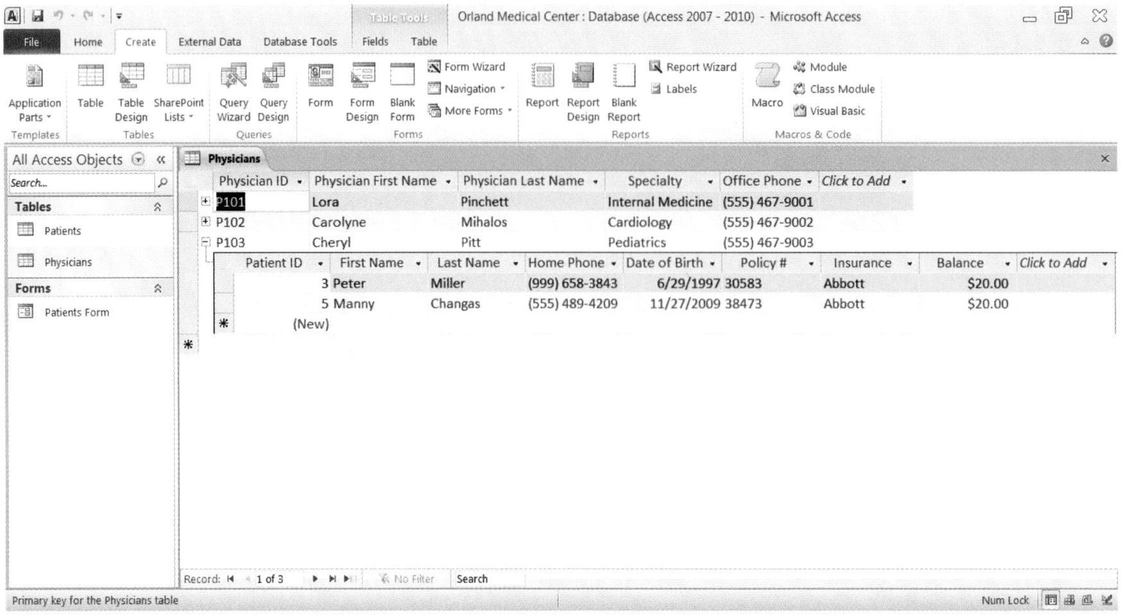

Sort Data

Sorting: Rearranges the records in the table based on the field that is being sorted.

Microsoft Access 2010 has the capability to sort fields in a datasheet. **Sorting** rearranges the records in the table based on the field that is being sorted. The data can be sorted in ascending or descending order. You can sort one or more fields in a table. **Table 9.3** illustrates how to sort data in a table.

Table 9.3 Sort Commands

Task	Steps

Sort data	First Method
	• Open the **datasheet** for the table you want to sort.
	• Click the **arrow** next to the column (field name) in the datasheet that you want to sort. The sorting option displays.
	  ◦ For text fields, select **Sort A to Z** to sort the field in ascending order or **Sort Z to A** to sort in descending order.
	  ◦ For numeric fields, select **Sort Smallest to Largest** to sort in ascending order or **Sort Largest to Smallest** to sort in descending order.
	Second Method
	• Open the **datasheet** for the table you want to sort.
	• Position the insertion point in the field you want to sort.
	• Click the **Home** tab.
	• Click the **Ascending** or **Descending** button in the Sort & Filter group.

Remove Sort	• Position the insertion point in the field from which you want to remove the sort. • Click the **Home** tab. • Click the **Remove Sort** button in the Sort & Filter group.

Hands-On Exercise: Sort Data

1. Double-click the Patients table in the Tables objects in the Navigation Pane.

2. You will sort the data in descending order by the Last Name field. Click the arrow next to the Last Name column (**Figure 9.31**).

3. Click Sort Z to A . The Last Name field is sorted in descending order (**Figure 9.32**). The arrow next to the Last Name column changes to a sort icon (⊣), indicating that a sort was performed on the column (Figure 9.32).

4. You will remove the sort. Click the Home tab if not selected.

5. Click the Remove Sort button in the Sort & Filter group (Figure 9.32).

6. You will sort the data by the Balance field in order from smallest to largest. Position the insertion point in the Balance field in any of the records in the table.

7. Click the Ascending button in the Sort & Filter group on the Home tab (**Figure 9.33**). The records are sorted. The first record is Betty Duley, who has a balance of $0.00.

8. Click the Remove Sort button to remove the sort from the table.

Figure 9.31 Sort Options

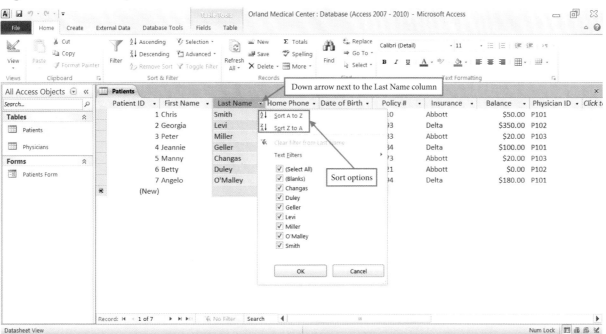

Figure 9.32 Remove Sort

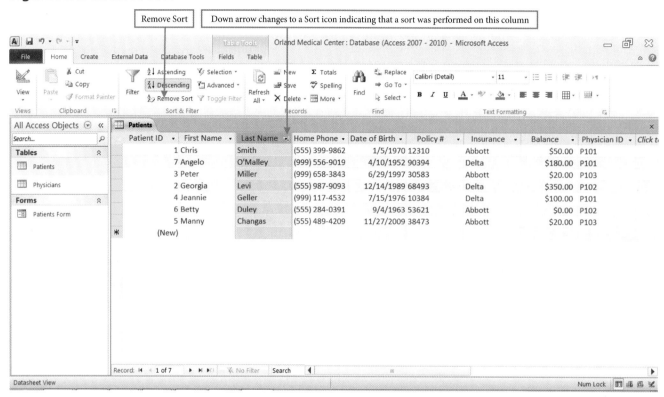

Figure 9.33 Sort Balance Field in Ascending Order

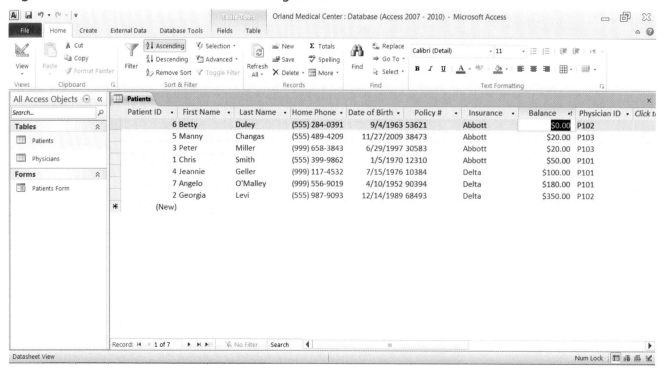

Filter Data

Microsoft Access 2010 has the capability to apply filters to the data. A **filter** locates specific data based on the criteria that are entered. Once the filter is applied, only records that meet the filter criteria are displayed. The rest of the records are hidden until you remove the filter.

> **Filter:** Locates specific data based on the criteria that are entered.

When a table is filtered, the word *Filtered* displays in the Record Navigator bar. When the table is not filtered, the word *No Filter* displays in the Record Navigator bar. **Table 9.4** illustrates how to filter data in a datasheet.

Table 9.4 Filter Commands	
Task	Steps
Filter data	• Open the **datasheet** for the table you want to filter. • Click the **arrow** next to the column (field) you wish to filter. A listing of all the unique values in the field displays. By default, the Select All checkbox is selected, which means that all the unique values in the datasheet are currently displayed. • Use these steps to filter for specific data in the field: ○ Click the **Select All** option to clear all the checkboxes (**Figure 9.34**). ○ Click the **checkbox** for the value you wish to filter. ○ Click **OK**. • To filter for certain criteria: ○ Select **Text Filters** or **Number Filters** and then select an option.
Clear filter	• Use one of these methods to clear the filter: ○ Click the **arrow** next to the column (field) you want to unfilter, and click **Clear Filter**. ○ Click the **Toggle Filter** button in the Sort & Filter group on the Home tab (**Figure 9.35**).

Hands-On Exercise: Filter Data

① You will filter the data to display all patients who have Abbott insurance. Click the arrow next to the Insurance column.

② Click the Select All option to uncheck (deselect) all the insurance types (Figure 9.34).

③ Click the Abbott checkbox to filter for patients who have Abbott insurance (Figure 9.34).

④ Click OK . Four patient records that have Abbott insurance display (Figure 9.35). The word *Filtered* displays in the Record Navigation bar indicating that the datasheet is filtered (Figure 9.35). The arrow next to the Insurance column changes to a Filter icon ( ), indicating that a filter was applied on the column (Figure 9.35).

→

⑤ Next you will remove the filter. Click the Toggle Filter button in the Sort & Filter group on the Home tab (Figure 9.35).

⑥ Next you will filter the data to locate all patients whose balance is greater than or equal to $100.00. Click the arrow next to the Balance column.

⑦ Point to Number Filters (**Figure 9.36**).

⑧ Click Greater Than (Figure 9.36), and the Custom Filter dialog box displays (**Figure 9.37**).

⑨ Type **100** in the Balance is greater than or equal to box (Figure 9.37).

⑩ Click OK .

⑪ Three patients match the criteria. The other patients are not shown, but they are not deleted from the table. Once you unfilter the data, the data will reappear.

⑫ Next you will unfilter the data. Click the arrow next to the Balance column.

⑬ Click Clear filter from Balance (**Figure 9.38**).

⑭ Click the Close button to the right of the Patients tab to close the table.

   a. If a message displays asking you to save the changes to the design of the Patients table, click No .

Figure 9.34 Select Filter Options

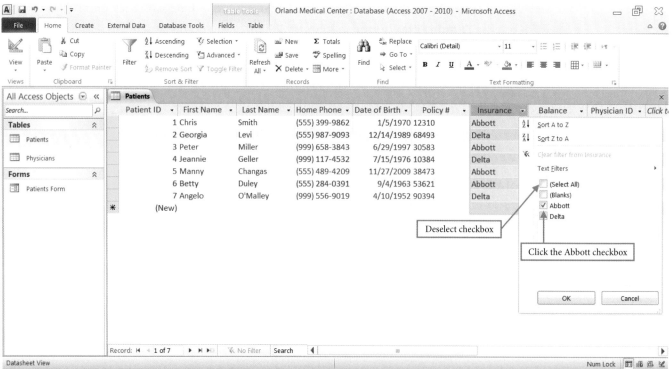

Figure 9.35 Filtered Applied to Insurance Field

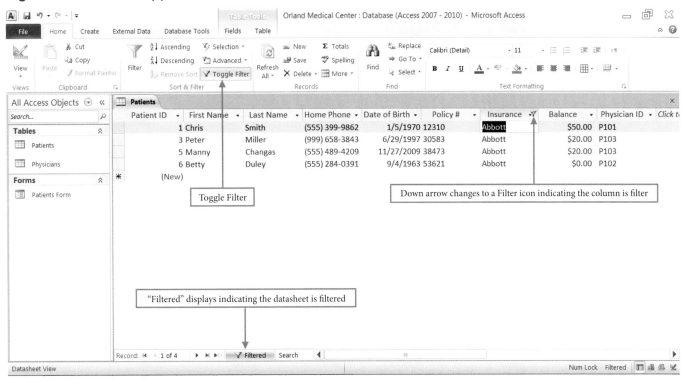

Figure 9.36 Number Filters

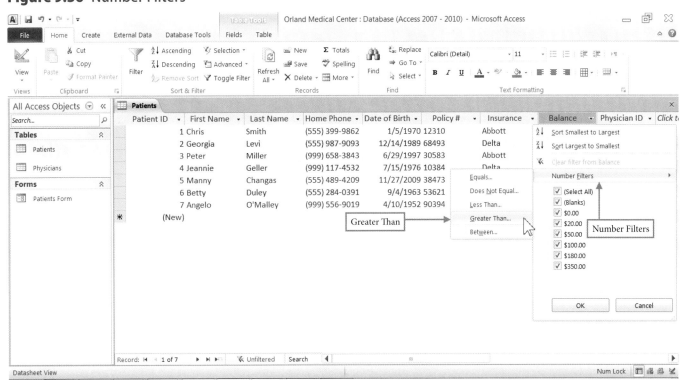

Figure 9.37 Apply Filter to the Balance Field

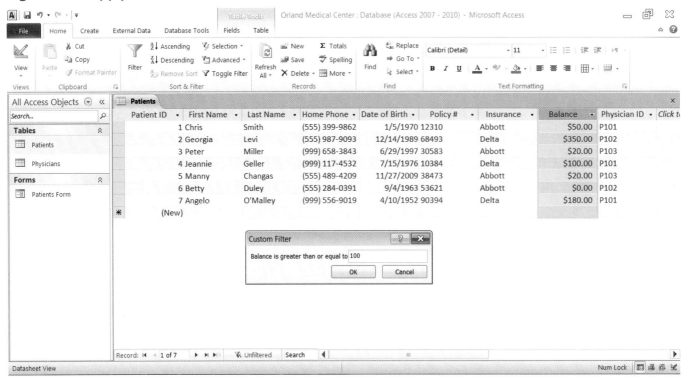

Figure 9.38 Clear Filter

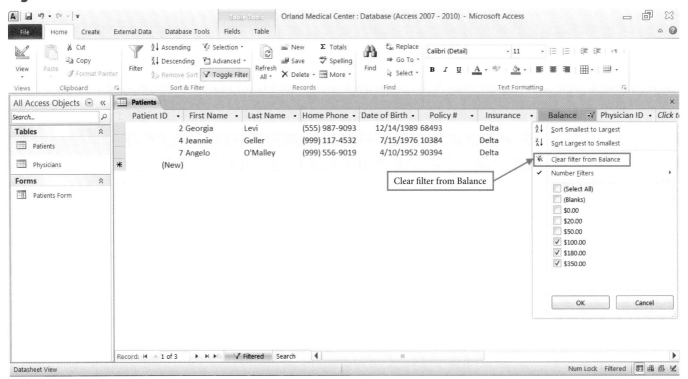

Create a Query Using the Query Wizard

A **query** is a database object that can answer a question about the data and displays the results in a datasheet. A query can be saved so that you can run the query again at a later time. Additionally, a query can display data from one or more related tables or from other queries.

With a query you can do the following:

- Combine data from multiple tables or other queries.
- Select the fields you want to display.
- Select records that meet certain criteria.

A **select query** is a query that is created to retrieve data from tables. The quickest way to create a select query is to use the Query Wizard. The **query wizard** is a wizard that guides the user in creating a query. It asks a few questions about the query to be created and then it creates the query based on the responses.

Use these steps to create a query using the query wizard:

- Click the **Create** tab (**Figure 9.39**).
- Click the **Query Wizard** button in the Queries group (Figure 9.39). The New Query dialog box displays.
- Click **Simple Query Wizard** if it is not already selected (**Figure 9.40**). This wizard creates a select query based on the fields you select.
- Click **OK**. The Simple Query Wizard displays. Answer the questions in the wizard, and the query is created.
  - Choose the table or query you want as the source of the data.
  - Specify the fields you want to include in the results.
  - If the query contains numeric fields, you will specify if you want a detail or summary report. A detail report displays every field you selected for every record. A summary report can calculate the summary values (sum, average, maximum, minimum) of numeric fields.
  - Name the query.

> **Query:** A database object that can answer a question about the data and displays the results in a datasheet.
>
> **Select query:** A query that is created to retrieve data from tables.
>
> **Query Wizard:** A wizard that guides the user in creating a query. The query wizard asks a few questions about the query to be created and then it creates the query based on the responses.

Hands-On Exercise: Create a Query Using the Query Wizard

You will create a query that displays the Patient ID, First Name, Last Name, and Balance fields for all patients in the Patients table.

1. Click the Create tab (Figure 9.39).
2. Click Query Wizard in the Queries group (Figure 9.39). The New Query dialog box displays.
3. Click Simple Query Wizard if it is not selected (Figure 9.40).

→

④ Click OK . The Simple Query Wizard displays.

⑤ Click the arrow in the Tables/Queries list, and select Table: Patients if it is not selected (**Figure 9.41**).

⑥ A list of the fields in the Patients table displays in the Available Fields list. You will select the fields you want to display in the query. Click the field in the Available Fields list and click the greater than button, ⊡, to add the field to the query. Or, double-click the field in the Available Fields list, and it moves to the Selected Fields list. If you click the button with two greater than signs, ⊡, all the fields in the Available Fields list move to the Selected Fields list.

⑦ Click the Patient ID field in the Available Fields list.

⑧ Click the greater than button, ⊡ (**Figure 9.41**). The field moves to the Selected Fields list.

⑨ Double-click the First Name field in the Available Fields list. The field moves to the Selected Fields list.

⑩ Double-click the Last Name field in the Available Fields list. The field moves to the Selected Fields list.

⑪ Double-click the Balance field in the Available Fields list. The field moves to the Selected Fields list. The screen should resemble Figure 9.41.

⑫ Double-click the Insurance field in the Available Fields list.

⑬ If you make a mistake and added the wrong field, you can remove it easily. You will remove the Insurance field. Click the Insurance field in the Selected Fields list.

⑭ Click the less than button, ⊡, to remove the field from the Selected Fields list. The field moves back to the Available Fields list. The button with two less than signs, ⊡, removes all fields from the Selected Fields list.

⑮ Click Next .

⑯ The Simple Query Wizard asks if you want a detail or summary query. Click Detail . A detail query displays every field that you selected for every record in the table (**Figure 9.42**).

⑰ Click Next .

⑱ The Simple Query Wizard asks for the title of the query. Type **Patients Balance Query** (**Figure 9.43**).

⑲ At the bottom of the Simple Query Wizard, you are asked if you want to open the query or modify the design. Click Open the query to view information (Figure 9.43).

⑳ Click Finish , and the query results display in a datasheet (**Figure 9.44**).

㉑ Right-click the Patients Balance Query tab and click Close .

Figure 9.39 Query Wizard Button

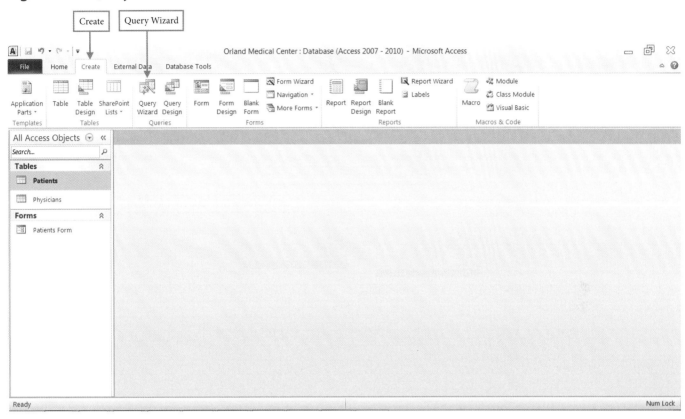

Figure 9.40 New Query Dialog Box

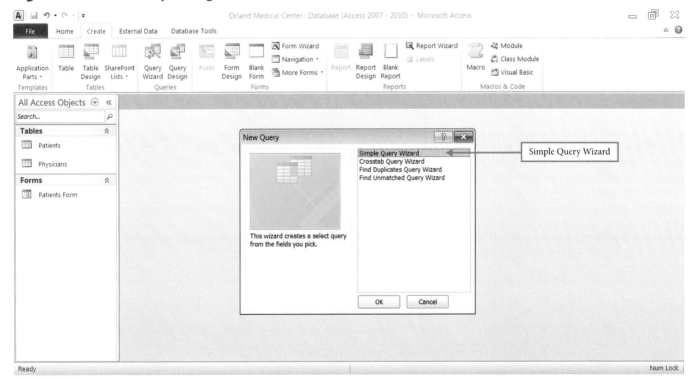

Figure 9.41 Select Fields

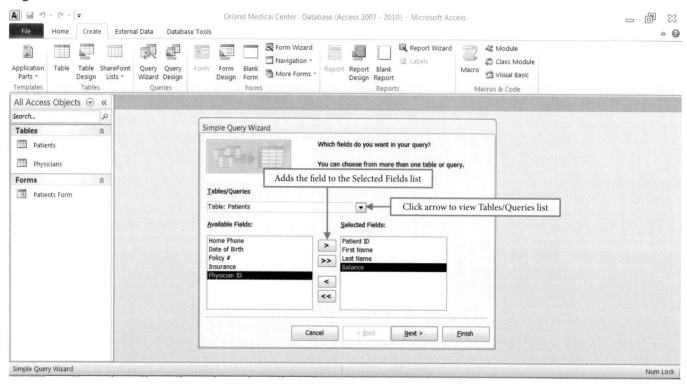

Figure 9.42 Detail or Summary Query

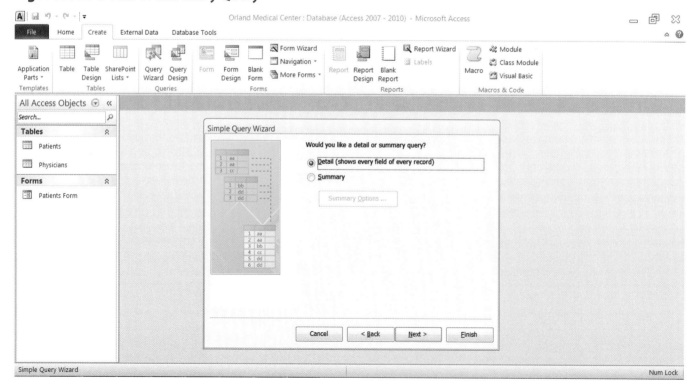

Figure 9.43 Title of Query

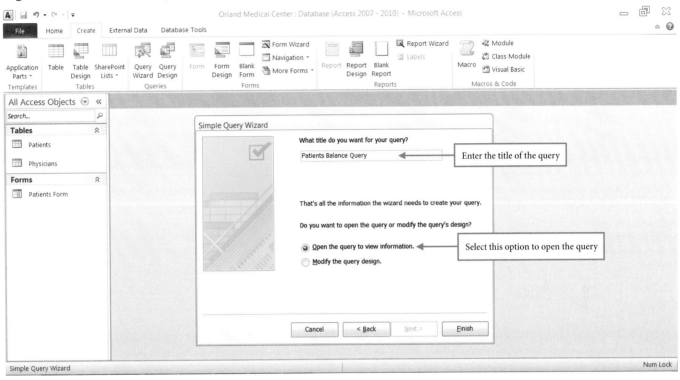

Figure 9.44 Query Results Display in Datasheet

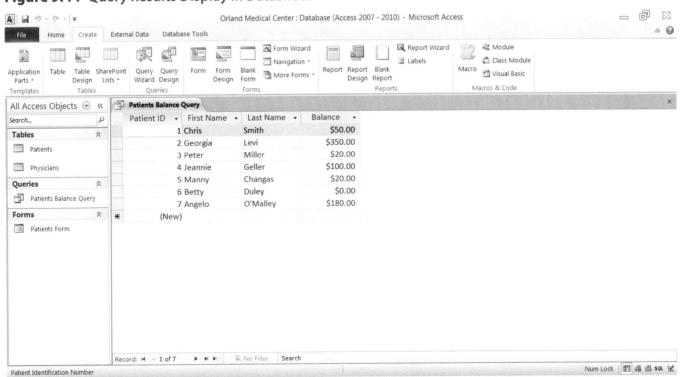

Modify a Query

You can modify the query using Design view. You can add additional fields, remove fields, sort fields, or filter data for specific criteria. When a query is open in Design view, the Query Tools contextual tab displays; it contains the Design tab that contains commands to modify the query.

Query designer: The top pane of the query window that contains the table(s) used in the query.

Query design grid: The bottom pane of the query window that contains the fields that will display in the query along with the sorting and criteria options.

The **query designer** is the top pane of the query window that contains the table(s) used in the query. Each table contains the list of fields included in the table (**Figure 9.45**). The **query design grid** is the bottom pane of the query window that contains the fields that will display in the query, along with the sorting and criteria options (Figure 9.45).

- The Field row displays the field name of all the fields that are in the query.
- The Table row specifies the name of the table where the fields are located.
- The Sort row is used to select the sorting options for the fields.
- The Show row indicates whether the field will show (or display) in the query. If the Show checkbox is selected, the field will display in the query results.
- The Criteria row specifies the criteria for which you are searching.

Table 9.5 describes how to modify a query.

Table 9.5 Query Commands

Task	Steps
Insert a field	Use any of these methods to insert a field in the query: • Double-click the **field** you want to insert from the Table window in the query designer (Figure 9.45). • Drag a **field** from the Table window in the query designer to a column in the query design grid. • Click an **empty column** in the Field row in the query design grid. Click the **Field arrow**, and select the field from the list. • Double-click the **asterisk** (*) in the Table window to insert all the fields in the query.
Delete a field	• Click in the **column** in the query design grid that contains the field to delete. • Click **Delete Columns** from the Query Setup group on the Design tab (Figure 9.45).
Sort fields	• Click in the **column** that contains the field to sort. • Click the **Sort** arrow and select the sort option.
Filter criteria	• Type the criteria for which you are looking in the Criteria row for the field.
Run the query	• Click the **Run** button in the Results group on the Design tab (**Figure 9.46**).
Navigate to Design or Datasheet View	Use any of these methods to navigate to Design or Datasheet View: • Click the **Design View** button or **Datasheet View** button from the status bar (Figure 9.46). • Click the **View arrow** in the Results group on the Design tab, and select **Design View** or **Datasheet View** (Figure 9.46). • Click the **View arrow** in the Results group on the Home tab, and select **Design View** or **Datasheet View**.

Hands-On Exercise: Modify a Query

You will modify the query and display only the patients who have an outstanding balance. You will sort the query by the patient's last name.

1. Double-click the Patients Balance Query in the Queries object in the Navigation Pane.

2. Click the View button in the Views group on the Home tab or click the View arrow and select Design View. The screen should resemble Figure 9.45. The Select button in the Query Type group is active and contains an orange background, which indicates a Select query.

3. You want to find all patients who have an outstanding balance. Click in the Criteria row for the Balance field.

4. Type >0 in the Criteria row for the Balance field (Figure 9.46).

5. You will sort the query by the patient's last name. Click in the Sort row for the Last Name field.

6. Click the Sort arrow in the Last Name field.

7. Click Ascending (Figure 9.46).

8. Click the Run button in the Results group on the Design tab to run the query (Figure 9.46). Six records display in the query results (**Figure 9.47**). All the patients shown have an outstanding balance and are sorted in ascending order by last name.

9. Use any of these methods to navigate back to Design view:

    a. Click the Design View button on the status bar (Figure 9.47).

    b. Click the View button in the Views group on the Home tab (Figure 9.47).

    c. Click the View arrow in the Views group on the Home tab, and select Design View.

10. You will add the Insurance field to the query. Drag the bottom border of the Patients table in the query designer to make the table larger to display all the fields.

11. Double-click the Insurance field, and it is added to the query design grid (**Figure 9.48**).

12. Next you will run the query using a different method. Click the Datasheet View button in the status bar to run the query (Figure 9.48). The Insurance field is displayed in the datasheet.

13. Click the View button to return to Design View.

14. You will delete the Insurance field from the query. Click in the Insurance field column.

→

⑮ Click the Delete Columns button from the Query Setup group on the Design tab (Figure 9.48).

⑯ You want to display the patients who have a balance but you don't want to display their balance. Click the Show checkbox in the Balance field to deselect the option (**Figure 9.49**).

⑰ Click the Run button. The Balance field no longer displays in the query results (**Figure 9.50**).

⑱ Click the View button to return to Design view.

⑲ Click the Show checkbox in the Balance field to select the option.

⑳ Click the Save button on the Quick Access Toolbar to save the query.

㉑ Click the Close button to the right of the Patients Balance Query tab. The query displays in the Queries object in the Navigation Pane.

Figure 9.45 Query Design View

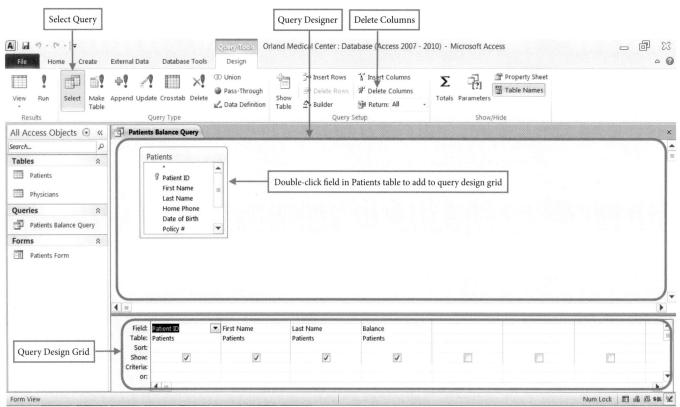

Figure 9.46 Sort and Criteria Options

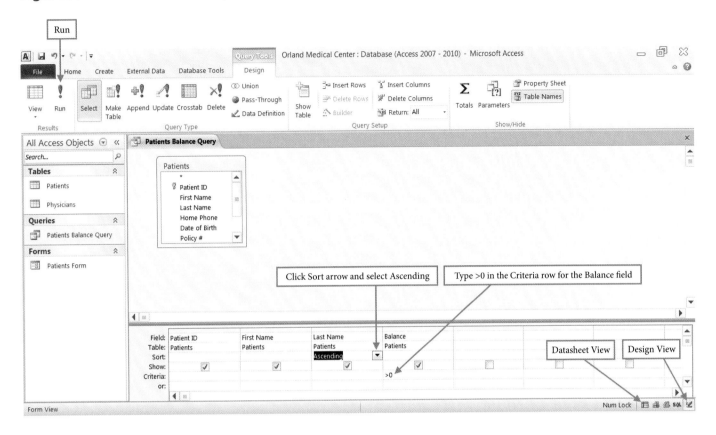

Figure 9.47 Query Results Displayed

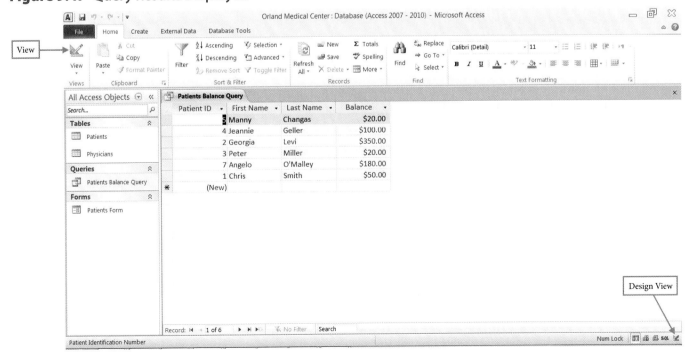

Figure 9.48 Add and Delete Insurance Field

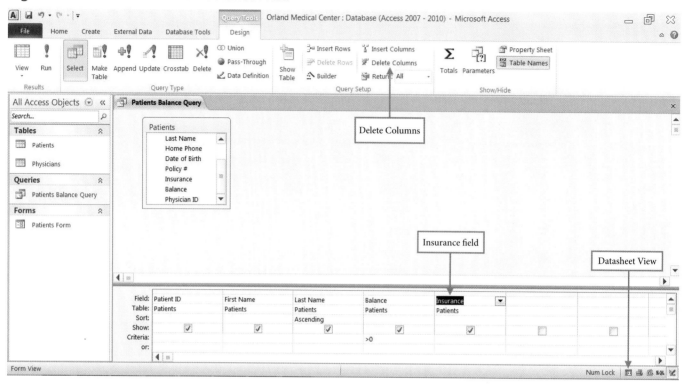

Figure 9.49 Show Checkbox

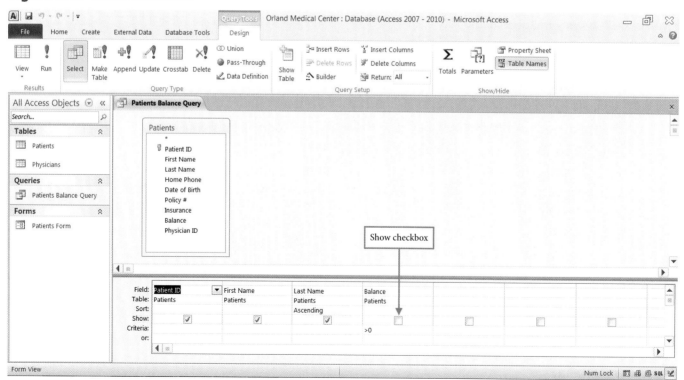

Figure 9.50 Balance Field Not Displayed in Query Results

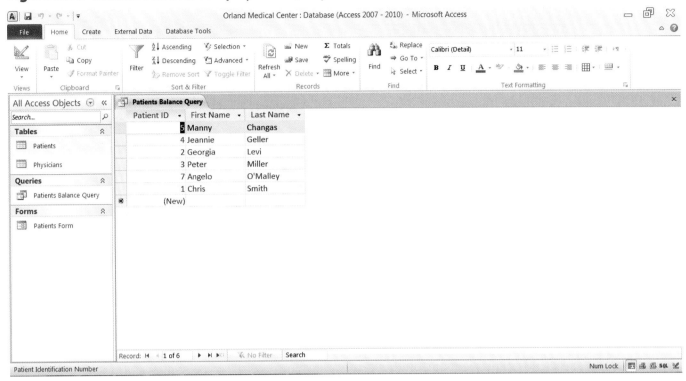

Create a Query Using Design View

You can create a query using Design view instead of a wizard. You can create queries using data from multiple tables that are related. When you run the query, the results display in Datasheet view. You can print the query results by clicking the Print command on the File tab.

Use these steps to create a query:

- Click the **Create** tab on the Ribbon.
- Click **Query Design,** and the Show Table dialog box displays (**Figure 9.51**).
- Select the **tables** you want to include in the query and click **Add** (Figure 9.51).
- Click the **Close** button after you select the tables in your query.
- Double-click the **fields** you want in the query, and they display in the query design grid. Double-click the **asterisk** (*) in the Table window to display all fields in the query. This automatically displays the fields in the order in which they are entered in the table.
- Enter the sort and criteria options.
- Click the **Run** button in the Results group on the Design tab to run the query.

Use this step to add a table to the query:

- Click the **Show Table** button in the Query Setup group and select the table you want to add (**Figure 9.52**).

Use this step to remove a table from the query:

- Click in the table in the query designer and press **Delete**.

Hands-On Exercise: Create a Query with Two Tables Using Design View

① Click the Create tab.

② Click the Query Design button in the Queries group (Figure 9.51). The Show Table dialog box displays (Figure 9.51). You will select the tables or queries you want to use in this query.

③ Click the Physicians table (Figure 9.51).

④ Click Add (Figure 9.51).

⑤ Click Close to close the Show Table dialog box. The Physicians table displays in the query designer in the top pane.

⑥ Double-click the asterisk (*) in the Physicians table to include all the fields in the table in the query (Figure 9.52).

⑦ Click the Run button in the Results group. All the fields display in the datasheet (**Figure 9.53**).

⑧ Click the View button to return to Design view.

⑨ You will delete the first column in the query design grid. Click in the first column in the query design grid.

⑩ Click Delete Columns from the Query Setup group on the Design tab.

⑪ You want to display data from the Patients table in the query. You need to add the Patients table to the query designer. Click the Show Table button in the Query Setup group to redisplay the Show Table dialog box (**Figure 9.54**).

⑫ Click the Patients table.

⑬ Click Add .

⑭ Click Close to close the Show Table dialog box. The Physicians and Patients tables display in the query designer in the top pane.

⑮ Drag the bottom border of the Patients table to increase the size of the table so that all fields display in the window. A relationship line (or join line) displays between the tables, indicating that there is a relationship between the two tables (**Figure 9.55**). The tables are related by the Physician ID field. The number *1* displays to the right of the Physician ID field in the Physicians table, and an infinity symbol (∞) displays to the left of the Physician ID field in the Patients table. This indicates that there is a one-to-many relationship between the tables.

(16) You will add the fields to the query from the Patients table. Double-click the First Name field from the Patients table, and the field is inserted into the query design grid.

(17) Double-click the Last Name field from the Patients table.

(18) You will add another field to the query using a different method. Click in the Field row of the third column in the query design grid, which is an empty column. Click the Field arrow and select Patients.Insurance from the list (**Figure 9.56**).

(19) Double-click the Balance field from the Patients table.

(20) Double-click the Physician ID field from the Patients table.

(21) Next you will select the fields from the Physicians table. Double-click the First Name field from the Physicians table.

(22) Double-click the Last Name field from the Physicians table. The screen should resemble **Figure 9.57**. There are two First Name fields and two Last Name fields in the query design grid. The First Name and Last Name fields from the Patients and Physicians table will display in the query results. When the query is run, the query displays the caption of the field in the datasheet. However, if a caption does not exist and the same field name exists in a query, the query results will display the field name as the table name, followed by a period, followed by the field name. *Patients.First Name* will display as the column heading for the First Name field of the Patients table.

(23) Click the Run button.

(24) The first two columns in the datasheet are too small to view the entire field names. Double-click the right boundary of the first column Patients.First Name, to increase the column size.

(25) Double-click the right boundary of the second column Patients.Last Name to increase the column size. The datasheet should resemble **Figure 9.58**.

(26) Click the View button to return to Design view.

(27) You will display only the patients who have Abbott insurance. Type Abbott in the Criteria row in the Insurance column (**Figure 9.59**).

(28) Click Run . Four patient records display (**Figure 9.60**).

(29) Click the View button to return to Design view.

(30) Click the Save button on the Quick Access Toolbar. The Save As dialog box displays.

(31) Type **Patients with Abbott Insurance Query** in the Query Name box.

(32) Click OK .

Figure 9.51 Show Table Dialog Box

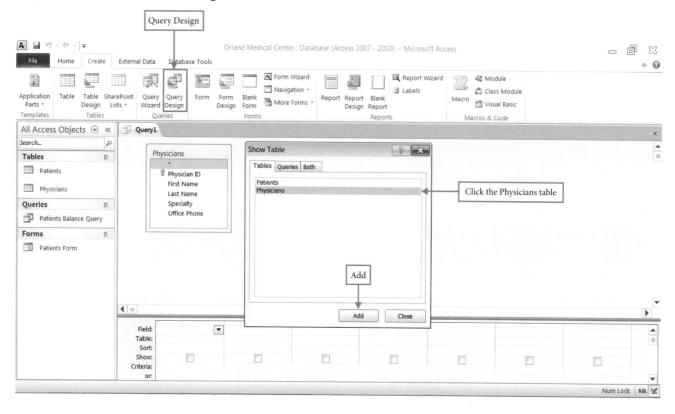

Figure 9.52 Asterisk Includes All Fields in Query

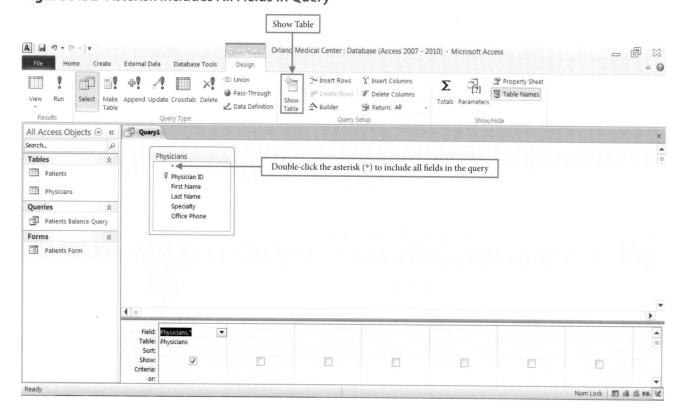

Figure 9.53 Datasheet Displays All Fields In the Physicians Table

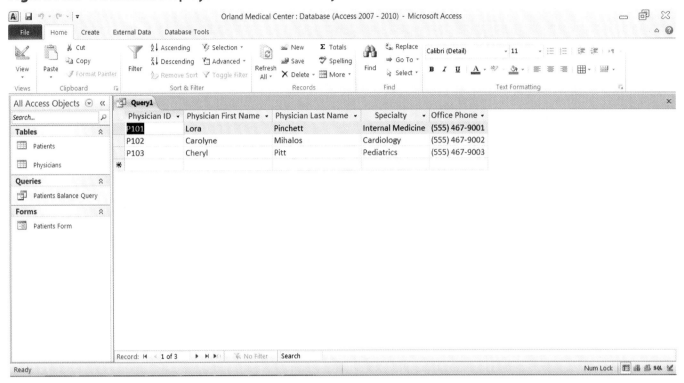

Figure 9.54 Show Table

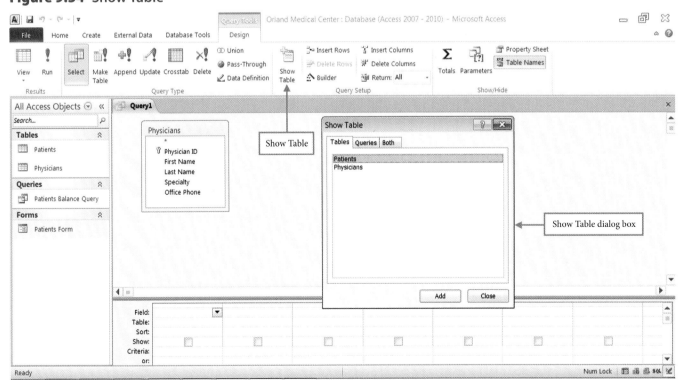

Figure 9.55 Join Line

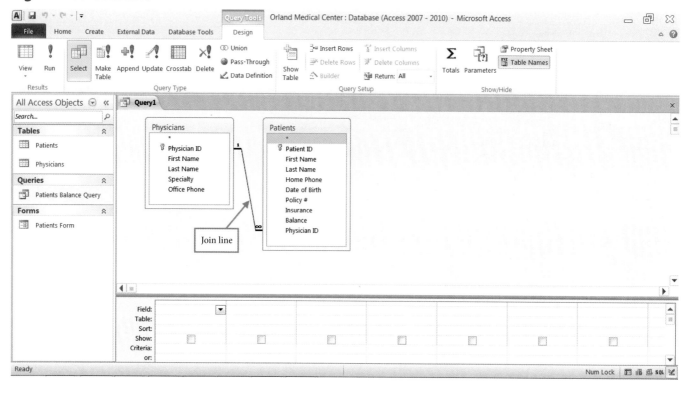

Figure 9.56 Select the Insurance Field

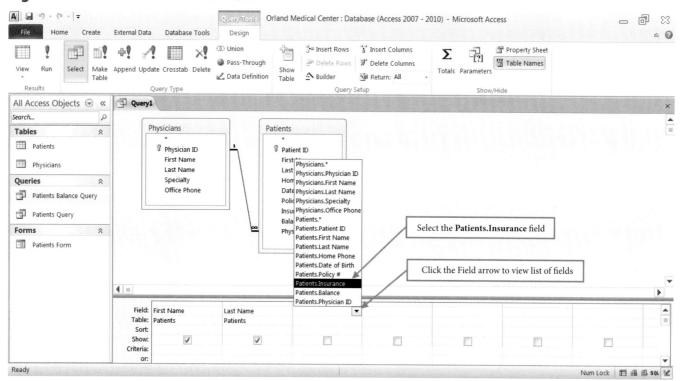

Figure 9.57 Fields Selected

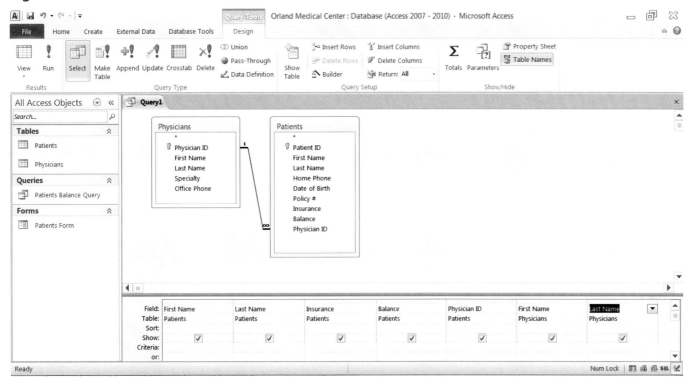

Figure 9.58 Query Displays with Data from Two Tables

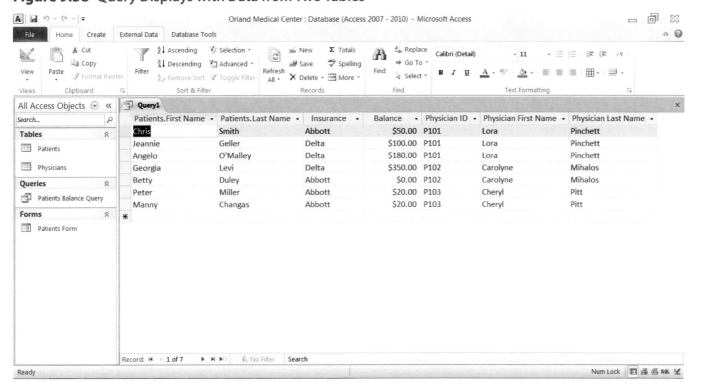

Figure 9.59 Enter Criteria in Insurance Column

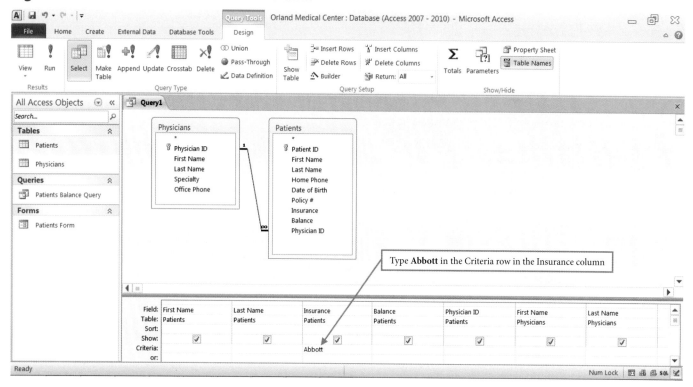

Figure 9.60 Query of Patients with Abbott Insurance

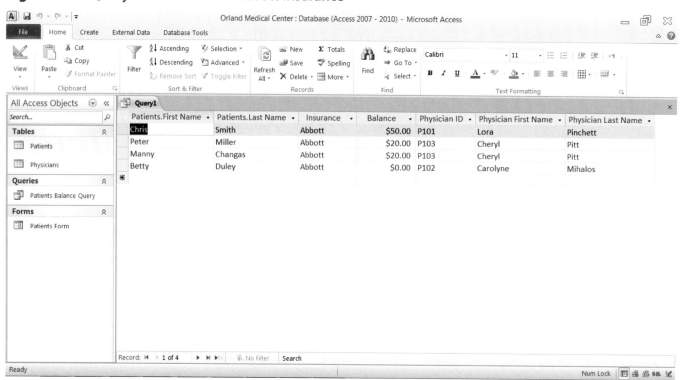

Save a Query with a New Name

In this next exercise, you will modify the query and save it with a different query name.

Use these steps to save a query with a different name:

- Click the **File** tab.
- Click **Save Object As**, and the Save As dialog box displays.
- Enter the new *name* of the query and click **OK**.
- Click the **Design** tab on the Query Tools contextual tab to return to Design view, *or* click the **Home** tab on the Ribbon.

Hands-On Exercise: Save a Query with a New Name

1. Click the File tab.
2. Click Save Object As , and the Save As dialog box displays (Figure 9.61).
3. Type Physician ID P103 Query in the Save box (Figure 9.61).
4. Click OK .
5. Click the Design tab on the Query Tools tab to return to Design view (Figure 9.61).

Figure 9.61 Save Object As

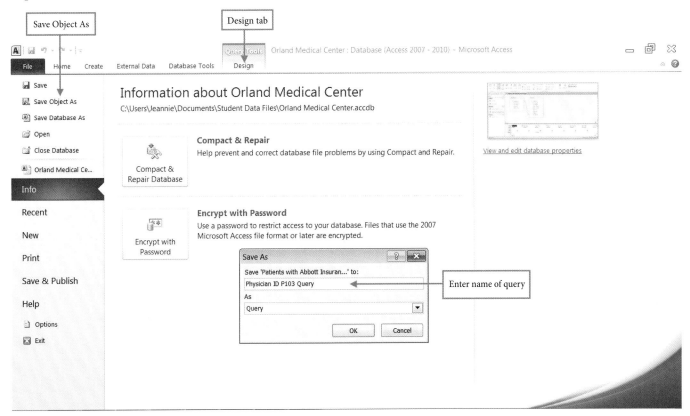

Hands-On Exercise: Modify a Query

You will modify the query to display all the patients of Dr. Pitt. The Physician ID for Dr. Pitt is P103.

① You will delete the Insurance field from the query. Click in the Insurance column.

② Click Delete Columns in the Query Setup group on the Design tab.

③ Type **P103** in the Criteria row of the Physician ID column.

④ Next, you will sort the query by the Last Name field of the Patients table. Click in the Sort row for the Last Name column of the Patients table.

⑤ Click the Sort arrow in the Last Name column of the Patients table. (Make certain not to sort the Last Name column of the Physicians table.

⑥ Click Descending . The screen should resemble **Figure 9.62**. Quotes display around the text *P103* in the Criteria row of the Physician ID column. The query automatically puts quotes around text in the Criteria row.

⑦ Click Run . Two patients display that have Dr. Pitt for a physician (**Figure 9.63**).

⑧ Click the View button to return to Design view.

⑨ Click the Save button on the Quick Access Toolbar.

⑩ Click the Close button to the right of the Physician ID P103 Query tab.

Figure 9.62 Sort and Criteria Options Entered

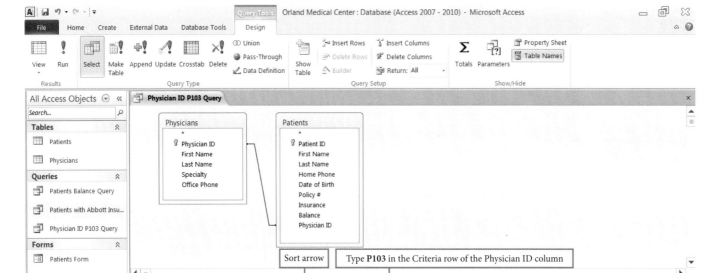

Figure 9.63 Physician ID P103 Query Results

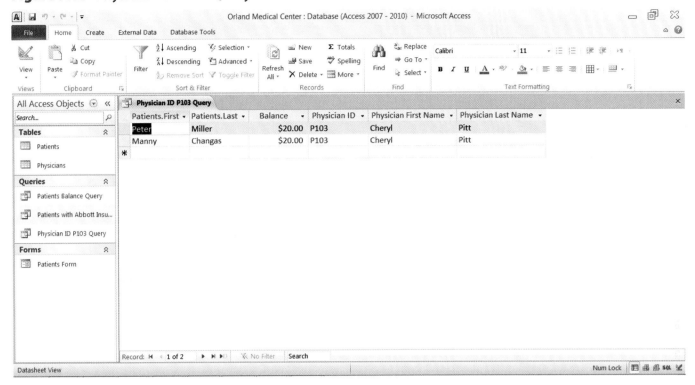

Enter Criteria for a Date Field

You will create a query to select all patients who were born on or after January 1, 2000. When you enter criteria in a date field, a pound sign displays before and after the date.

Hands-On Exercise: Create a Query that Contains Criteria in a Date Field

① Click the Create tab.

② Click Query Design . The Show Table dialog box displays.

③ Click the Patients table.

④ Click Add .

⑤ Click Close to close the Show Table dialog box. The Patients table displays in the query designer.

⑥ You will add the fields to the query. Double-click the First Name field from the Patients table.

⑦ Double-click the Last Name field from the Patients table.

⑧ Double-click the Date of Birth field from the Patients table.

⑨ Type **>=1/1/2000** in the Criteria row of the Date of Birth column.

Move a Field in the Query Design Grid

Use the following steps to move a field in the query design grid:

- Point to the **column (field) selector**, which is the gray bar at the top of the column (**Figure 9.64**). An arrow displays. Click the **column selector**, and the entire column is selected.
- Drag the **column selector** to a new location in the query design grid.

Hands-On Exercise: Move a Field in the Query Design Grid

1. You will move the First Name field so it displays after the Last Name field. Click the column selector of the First Name field (Figure 9.64).

2. Drag the column selector so it is located to the right of the Last Name field. Click in an empty area in the query designer to deselect the column. The criteria in the Date of Birth column displays as >=#1/1/2000#. Pound signs are automatically inserted before and after the date. The screen should resemble Figure 9.64.

3. Click Run . Only one patient displays (**Figure 9.65**).

4. Click the View button to return to Design view.

5. Click the Save button on the Quick Access Toolbar, and the Save As dialog box displays.

6. Type **Birthdate >= 01/01/2000 Query** in the Query Name box.

7. Click OK .

8. Click the Close button to the right of the Birthdate >=01/01/2000 Query tab.

Figure 9.64 Criteria in the Date of Birth Column

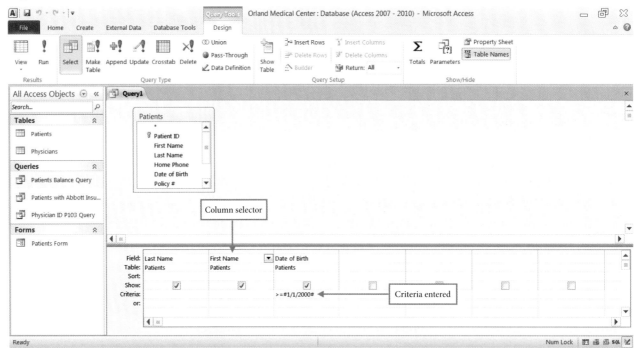

Figure 9.65 Query Displayed for Date of Birth >=01/01/2000

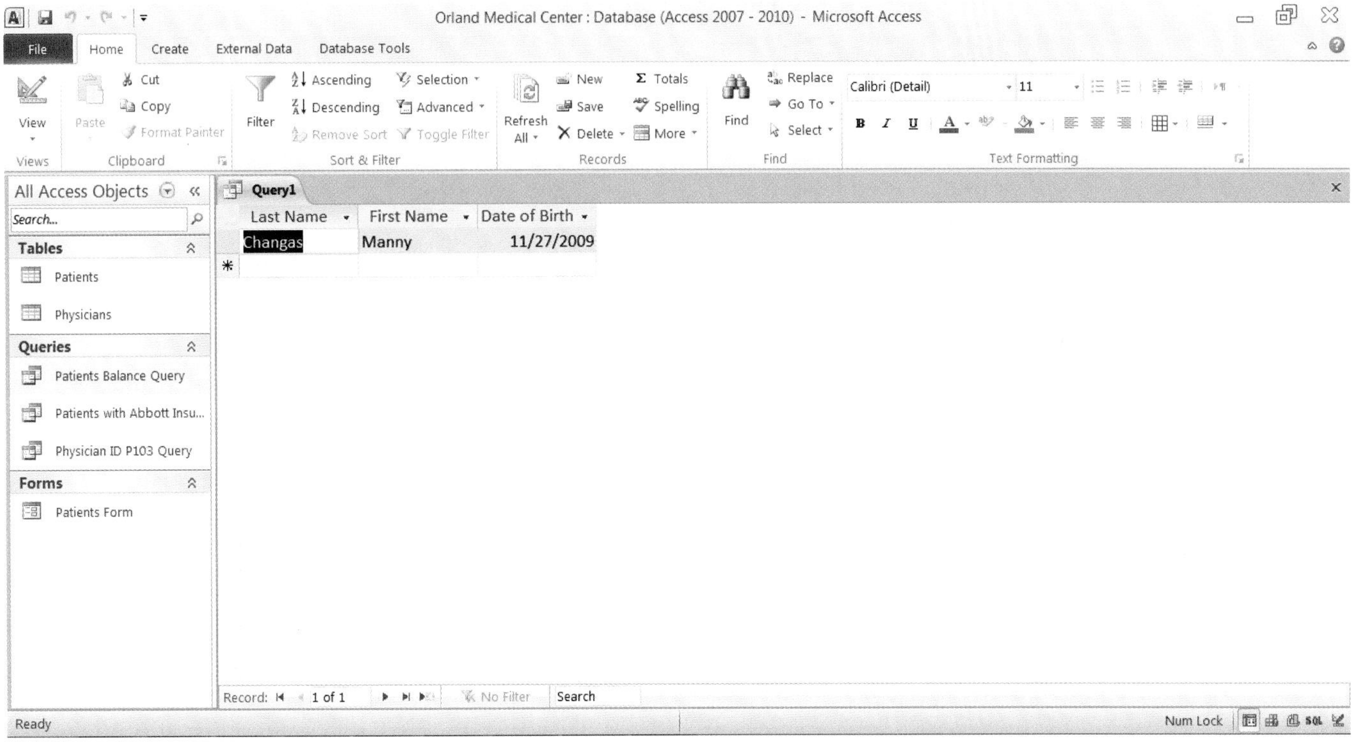

Use Wildcards in a Query

A wildcard is a character that is used in queries to represent a character or group of characters. An asterisk (*) is a wildcard that represents any number of characters. A question mark (?) represents one character.

> **Wildcard:** A character that is used in queries to represent a character or groups of characters.

Here are some examples:

- To find all patients who have a last name starting with the letter P, type **P*** in the criteria. This indicates that the last name starts with the letter P and any character or characters can follow it.

- To find a patient whose last name contains exactly five characters and begins with a P, type **P????** in the criteria. This indicates that the first name begins with the letter P, and there are four more characters after it.

- To find a last name that ends with the letter s, type ***s** in the criteria.

- To find a last name that contains four characters and ends with the letter s, type **???s** in the criteria.

Hands-On Exercise: Create a Query that Contains a Wildcard in the Criteria

In this exercise, you will create a query to select all patients who have a last name that begins with the letter O.

① Click the Create tab.

② Click Query Design . The Show Table dialog box displays.

③ Click the Patients table.

④ Click Add .

⑤ Click Close to close the Show Table dialog box. The Patients table displays in the query designer.

⑥ You will add the fields to the query. Double-click the First Name field from the Patients table.

⑦ Double-click the Last Name field from the Patients table.

⑧ Type **O*** in the Criteria row of the Last Name column. The screen should resemble **Figure 9.66**. The query will locate the patients who have a last name beginning with the letter O. The query is not case sensitive, so you can enter an uppercase or lowercase O in the criteria.

⑨ Press Enter to navigate to the next column. The system automatically inserts quotes around the criteria that was entered and inserts the word *Like* before the criteria. It will display as *Like "O*"*.

⑩ Click Run . Only one patient displays (**Figure 9.67**).

⑪ Click the Save button on the Quick Access Toolbar, and the Save As dialog box displays.

⑫ Type **Last Name Begins with O Query** in the Query Name box.

⑬ Click OK .

⑭ Click the View button to return to Design view.

⑮ Delete the contents in the Criteria row of the Last Name column.

⑯ Type ***r** in the Criteria row of the Last Name column to locate patients who have a last name ending with the letter *r*.

⑰ Click Run . The records for Peter Miller and Jeannie Geller display.

⑱ Click the Close button to the right of the Last Name Begins with O Query tab.

⑲ If the system prompts you to save the query, click No .

Figure 9.66 Enter Wildcard in Criteria

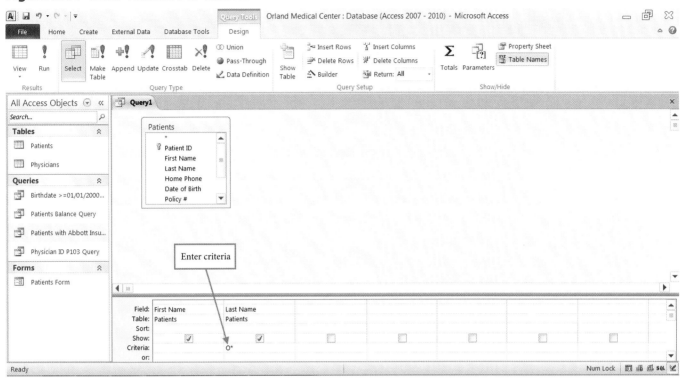

Figure 9.67 Query Results for Last Names Beginning with O

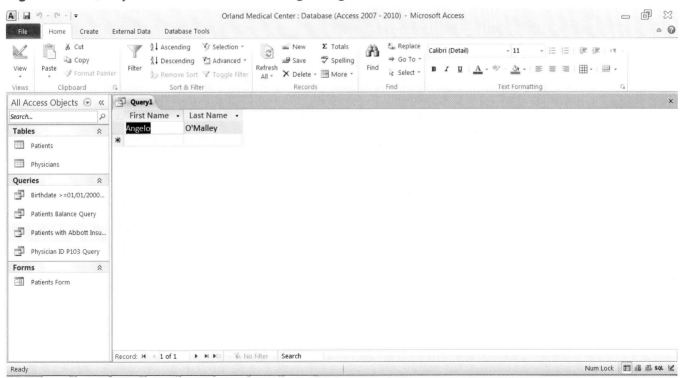

Print a Query

You can print the query results from Datasheet view or Design view. It is best to preview the document before you print. If the query contains several fields, the fields may not all display on one page. You can change the orientation to landscape to increase the number of fields that display on the page. You can use the shortcut key **Ctrl + P** to print a query.

Use these steps to print the query:

- Open the query.
- Click the **File** tab to open the Backstage view.
- Click the **Print** button below the File tab (**Figure 9.68**).
- Click the **Print Preview** button in the Print options (Figure 9.68). The Print Preview tab displays (**Figure 9.69**).
- Select the print settings.
- Click **Print** (Figure 9.69), and the Print dialog box displays.
- Click **OK** to print.
- Click the **Close Print Preview** button in the Close Preview group (Figure 9.69).

Hands-On Exercise: Print a Query

1. Double-click the Physician ID P103 Query in the Queries object in the Navigation pane.

2. Click the File tab to open the Backstage view.

3. Click the Print button below the File tab (Figure 9.68).

4. Click the Print Preview button in the Print options (Figure 9.68). The Print Preview tab, which contains commands to modify the print settings, is active. All the fields in the query results do not display on the first page.

5. Click the Next Page button to view the next page (Figure 9.69).

6. You want all the fields to display on one page, so you will print in landscape orientation. Click the Landscape button in the Page Layout group (Figure 9.69). All the fields now display on the page.

7. Click the Print button in the Print group (Figure 9.69), and the Print dialog box displays.

8. Click OK to print.

9. Click the Close Print Preview button in the Close Preview group (Figure 9.69).

10. Click the Close button to the right of the Physician ID P103 Query tab.

Figure 9.68 Print Commands

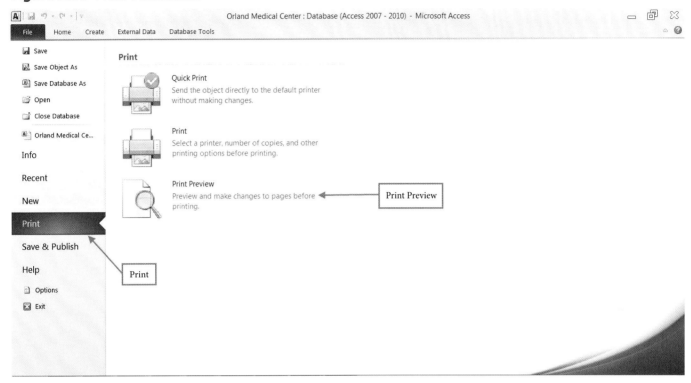

Figure 9.69 Print Preview Tab

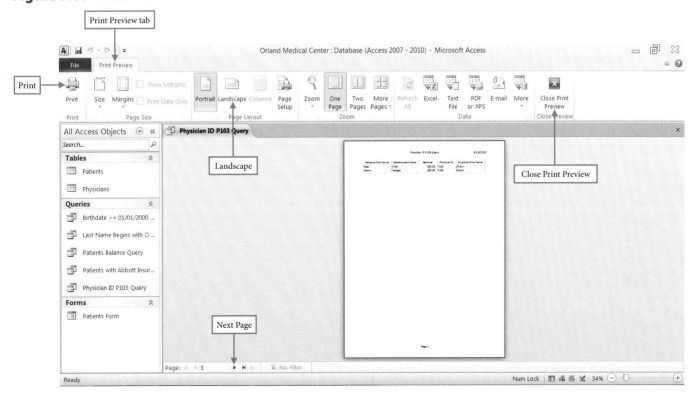

Modify the Navigation Pane

The entire names of the queries might not display in the Navigation Pane. You can resize the Navigation Pane to display the entire object names. Drag the right border of the Navigation Bar to the right to increase the size of the pane (**Figure 9.70**).

You can expand and collapse the database objects on the Navigation Pane. Click the **Collapse** button, ⌃, to hide the objects in a category (Figure 9.70). Click the **Expand** button, ⌄, to display all the objects in a category (**Figure 9.71**).

Hands-On Exercise: Modify the Navigation Pane

① Position the mouse pointer on the right border of the Navigation pane (Figure 9.70).

② Drag the right border of the Navigation pane to the right to make the width of the pane larger.

③ Click the Collapse button on the Queries group to hide the queries (Figure 9.70). The Collapse button changes to the Expand button.

④ Click the Expand button on the Queries group to display the queries (Figure 9.71).

Figure 9.70 Resize Navigation Pane and Collapse Button

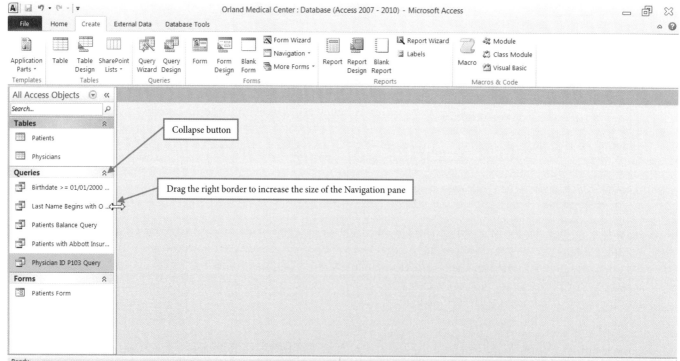

Figure 9.71 Expand Button

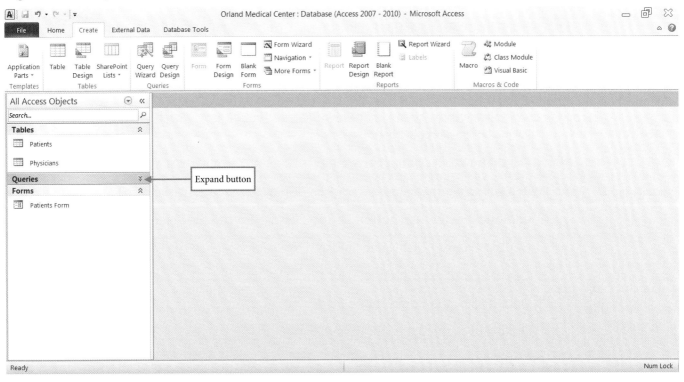

Create a Report Using the Report Wizard

A **report** is a database object that can list information from the tables and queries in a professional-looking format. A report can be viewed on the screen or can be printed.

Use these steps to create a report using the Report Wizard:

- Click the **Create** tab.
- Click the **Report Wizard** button in the Reports group (**Figure 9.72**), and the Report Wizard dialog box displays.
- Select the **table or query** that contains the data for the report from the Tables/Queries list.
- Select the **fields** you want to display in the report. You can click the **field** in the Available Fields list and click the **greater than** button, $\boxed{>}$, to add the field to the report. Or, you can double-click the **field** in the Available Fields list and it will move the field to the Selected Fields list. If you click the button with two greater than signs, $\boxed{>>}$, that will move all fields to the Selected Fields list.
- Click **Next**.
- Answer the remaining questions in the Report Wizard dialog box, and the report will be created.

Report: A database object that can list information from the tables and queries in a professional-looking format.

Hands-On Exercise: Create a Report Using the Report Wizard

You will create a report of the Patients table using the Report Wizard.

1. Click the Patients table in the Tables objects in the Navigation Pane.

2. Click the Create tab.

3. Click the Report Wizard button in the Reports group (Figure 9.72) and the Report Wizard dialog box displays.

4. Select the Table: Patients in the Tables/Queries list, if it is not selected.

5. You will select the fields you want to display in the report. Click the Patient ID field.

6. Click the greater than button, ⊡. The field moves to the Selected Fields list.

7. Double-click the First Name field and the field moves to the Selected Fields list.

8. Double-click the Last Name field.

9. Double-click the Home Phone field.

10. Double-click the Date of Birth field.

11. Double-click the Balance field. The screen should resemble **Figure 9.73**.

12. Click Next .

13. The next screen asks if you want to add any grouping levels. You are not adding grouping at this time. Click the Next button.

14. The next screen asks if you want to sort the records. You will sort the records by the Last Name field. Click the arrow in the first text box, and select Last Name (**Figure 9.74**). The Ascending button displays indicating that the field will be sorted in ascending order (Figure 9.74). If you click the Ascending button, it toggles to the Descending button. Click the Descending button, and it toggles to the Ascending button. Make certain to sort this field in ascending order.

15. Click Next .

16. The next screen asks you to select the layout of the report. Keep the defaults and click Next .

17. The next screen asks you to enter a title for the report. Type **Patients Report** for the report title (**Figure 9.75**).

18. Click Finish . A preview of the report displays (**Figure 9.76**). The report displays in the Reports object in the Navigation Pane.

19. Click the Print button in the Print group on the Print Preview tab to print the report.

20. The Print dialog box displays. Click OK to print the report.

21. Click the Close button to the right of the Patients Report tab to close the report.

Figure 9.72 Report Wizard Button

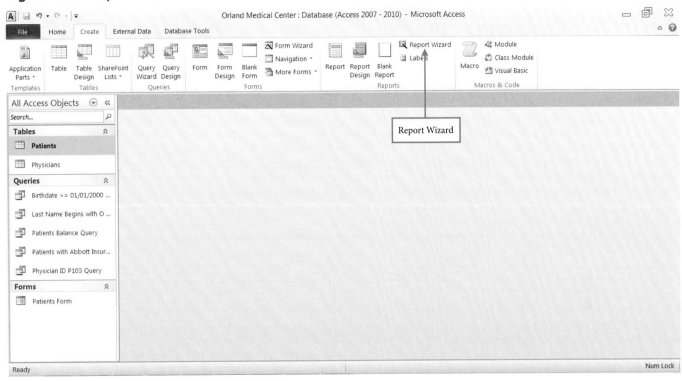

Figure 9.73 Select Fields for Report

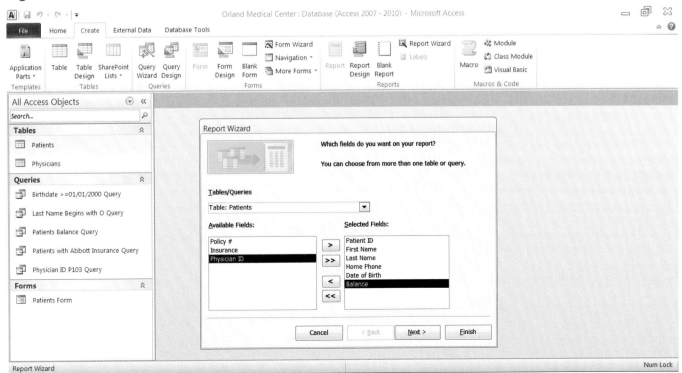

Figure 9.74 Sort Options

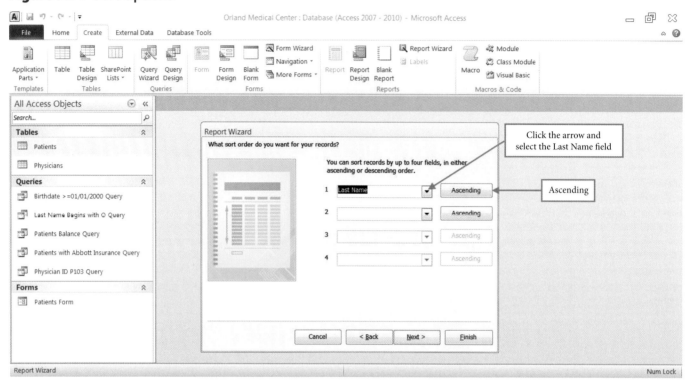

Figure 9.75 Report Title

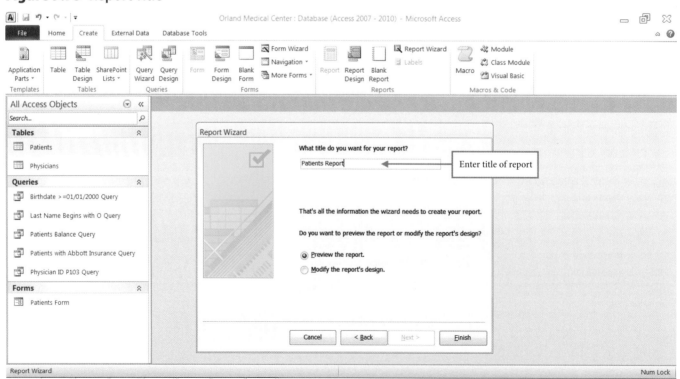

Figure 9.76 Patients Report Created

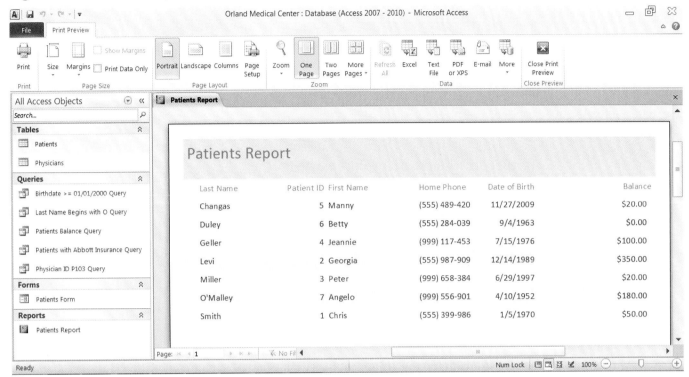

Print a Report

You can print a report from the Navigation Pane.

Use these steps to print a report:

- Right-click the **report** you want to print.
- Click **Print** from the shortcut menu, and it automatically prints to the default printer in portrait orientation. *Or*, click **Print Preview** to apply print settings.

Hands-On Exercise: Print a Report

You will print the Patients Report from the Navigation Pane.

(1) Right-click the Patients Report in the Reports objects in the Navigation Pane.

(2) Click Print from the shortcut menu and the report is printed.

Hands-On Exercise: Close the Database and Exit Application

(1) Click the File tab.

(2) Click Close Database .

(3) Click Exit .

Multiple-Choice Questions

1. To find all customers whose first name begins with the letter J, type _____ in the Criteria row for the field.
   a. J
   b. J?
   c. J*
   d. J????

2. The Report Wizard button is located on the _____ tab.
   a. Home
   b. Design
   c. Database Tools
   d. Create

3. When creating a query with two related tables, a _____ displays between the tables.
   a. Primary key icon
   b. Wildcard
   c. Collapse button
   d. Join line

4. When you run a simple query, the results displays in a _____.
   a. Form
   b. Datasheet
   c. Report
   d. Workbook

5. A(n) _____ combines data from two tables that have a common field.
   a. Relationship
   b. Input mask
   c. Build
   d. Foreign key

6. A _____ is an embedded datasheet that displays data from tables that are related.
   a. Table
   b. Relationship report
   c. Subdatasheet
   d. Foreign key

7. A _____ is a field that exists in two tables and contains the same data.
   a. Common field
   b. Relationship

    c. Foreign Key

    d. Primary Key

8. A _____ guides you through the process of creating database objects quickly.

    a. Query

    b. Navigation pane

    c. Relationship report

    d. Wizard

9. When a table is filtered, the word *Filtered* displays in the _____.

    a. Status bar

    b. Record Navigation bar

    c. Navigation Pane

    d. Record selector

10. A _____ is a database object used to add or modify records one record at a time.

    a. Form

    b. Datasheet

    c. Query

    d. Report

Project #1: Create Relationship, Forms, Queries, and Reports in the Summit High School Database

You will open the Summit High School database you created in the last chapter and create forms, queries, and reports.

1. Open the database called Summit High School.

2. Add an input mask to the Phone field in the Alumni table.

3. Create a relationship between the Alumni and Schools table using the School ID field. Enforce Referential Integrity.

4. Print the Relationship Report.

5. Create a form called **Alumni Form** to enter data into the Alumni table. Enter the records shown in **Table 9.6** into the form.

6. Print all the records on the form in landscape orientation.

7. Create a query called **Alumni Query** that displays the First Name, Last Name, Phone, and Graduation Year fields of all the alumni in the Alumni table. Increase the size of the columns, if necessary, to ensure that all the data display in the columns of the datasheet. Print the results.

Table 9.6 Records for Alumni Table

Alumni ID	School ID	Alumni First Name	Alumni Last Name	Alumni Address	Alumni City	Alumni State	Alumni Zip Code	Alumni Phone	Graduation Year
1	2	Harry	Costello	1620 S. Cicero	Los Angeles	CA	55555	(555) 334-1016	1994
2	1	Mohamed	Abi	9053 W. 22nd Street	Burbank	CA	55555	(555) 422-1057	1982
3	4	Yolanda	Hacker	19800 S. Harlem	Sacramento	CA	55555	(555) 257-6775	2005
4	3	Joseph	Culver	55 W. Adams	Burbank	CA	55555	(555) 578-1084	1985
5	3	Mary	Reynolds	6751 S. Kingsley	Santa Anna	CA	55555	(555) 217-1135	2006
6	2	Connie	Stevenson	14 E. Lake Street	Chicago	IL	99999	(999) 780-5060	1995
7	1	Pedro	Martinez	6514 S. Harlem	Los Angeles	CA	55555	(555) 248-1799	2000

⑧ Create a query called **Graduates of Year 2000 and After Query**. Include the First Name, Last Name, Address, City, State, Zip Code, and Graduation Year fields from the Alumni table for all alumni who graduated in or after 2000. Sort the query in ascending order by the Last Name field. Increase the size of the columns, if necessary, to ensure that all the data display in the columns of the datasheet. Print the results in landscape orientation.

⑨ Create a query called **Alumni Living in CA**. Include the First Name, Last Name, City, State, Zip Code, and Phone fields from the Alumni table. Include the School Name field from the Schools table. Find the alumni who live in California. Sort the query in ascending order by the City field. Increase the size of the columns, if necessary, to ensure that all the data display in the columns of the datasheet. Print the results in landscape orientation.

⑩ Create a report called **Alumni Report** using the Alumni table. Include the Last Name, First Name, Phone, and Graduation Year fields. Sort the report in ascending order by the Last Name field. Print the report.

⑪ Close the database.

⑫ Exit Microsoft Access 2010.

Project #2: Create Relationships, Forms, Queries, and Reports in the Morgan Books Database

You will open the Morgan Books database you created in the last chapter and create relationships, forms, queries, and reports.

① Open the Morgan Books database.

② Create a one-to-many relationship between the Books and Publisher table using the Publisher ID field. Enforce Referential Integrity.

③ Print the Relationship Report.

④ Create a form called **Book Form** to enter data into the Books table. Enter the records in Table 9.7 into the form.

Table 9.7 Records for Book Table

ISBN	Book Title	Author	Publisher ID	Quantity In Stock	Price
1429309948156	Southern Cooking	Paul Mitchell	B101	100	$10.00
1750294833543	A Day in the Sun	Cindy Morrison	J101	100	$25.00
3045009293333	Islands in Europe	Fernando Villa	B101	75	$62.00
5734729091100	Baby Dinosaurs	Tom Wilkes	J101	500	$60.00
6782019283945	Dinner in 30 Minutes	Alissa Chung	P101	200	$35.00
8850394411930	Business Management	Justin Redmond	P101	10	$150.00
9303493839234	Computer Are Fun	Mary Hansen	P101	55	$40.00

⑤ Print record 6 of the form.

⑥ Print the datasheet of the Books table in landscape orientation. Increase the size of the columns, if necessary, to ensure that all the data display in the columns of the datasheet.

⑦ Create a query called **Books Query** that displays the ISBN, Book Title, Author, Quantity, and Price fields of all the books in the table. Sort the results in alphabetical order by Book Title. Increase the size of the columns, if necessary, to ensure that all the data display in the columns of the datasheet. Print the results.

⑧ Create a query called **Price Query**. Include the ISBN, Book Title, and Price fields for all books that have a price less than $100. Sort the query by price in descending order. Increase the size of the columns, if necessary, to ensure that all the data display in the columns of the datasheet. Print the results.

⑨ Create a query called **Publisher Query** that combines data from the Books and Publisher table. Include the ISBN, Book Title, Author, Quantity, and Price fields from the Books table. Include the Publisher Name field from the Publisher table. Sort the results in ascending order by Publisher Name. Increase the size of the columns, if necessary, to ensure that all the data display in the columns of the datasheet. Print the results in landscape orientation.

⑩ Create a query called **Publisher Books J101 Query** that combines data from the Books and Publisher table. Include the ISBN, Book Title, Author, and Publisher ID fields from the Books table. Include the Publisher Name and Publisher City fields from the Publisher table. The query should display all books that are from the Publisher ID J101. Sort the results in ascending order by ISBN. Increase the size of the columns, if necessary, to ensure that all the data display in the columns of the datasheet. Print the results in landscape orientation.

⑪ Create a report called **Report of All Books** using the Books table. Include the Book Title, ISBN, Author, Quantity, and Price fields. Sort the results in alphabetical order by Book Title. Print the report in landscape orientation.

⑫ Close the database.

⑬ Exit Microsoft Access 2010.

Project #3: Create Relationships, Forms, Queries, and Reports in the Calumet West Park District Database

You will open the Calumet West Park District database you created in the last chapter. You will create relationships, forms, queries, and reports.

① Open the database called Calumet West Park District.

② Create a one-to-many relationship between the Participants and Special Events table using the Event ID field. Enforce Referential Integrity.

③ Print the Relationship Report.

④ Create a form called **Participant Form** to enter data into the Participants table. Enter the records in Table 9.8 into the form.

⑤ Print all the records in the form in landscape orientation.

⑥ Create a query called **Events Query** that displays the Event ID, Event Description, Event Date, Event Time, and Price fields for all the records in the Special Events table. Sort the results in alphabetical order by Event Description. Print the results.

⑦ Create a query called **Events in Summer Query**. Include the Event Description, Event Date, and Event Time fields of all the records in the Special Events table that take place after June 1, 2014. Sort the results in descending order by Event Date. Print the results.

Table 9.8 Records for Participants Table

Participant ID	Event ID	First Name	Last Name	Home Phone	Payment
1	1	Leah	Huange	(555) 039-8334	$25.00
2	4	Tamika	Harris	(555) 383-2732	$0.00
3	6	Jesse	Morales	(555) 983-9401	$0.00
4	7	Patricia	Salerno	(555) 203-9839	$10.00
5	2	Candace	Garza	(555) 450-0593	$0.00
6	5	Sam	Montana	(555) 092-8321	$0.00
7	2	Sylvia	Jackson	(555) 398-4893	$25.00
8	6	Jenny	Palmero	(555) 650-4932	$5.00
9	1	Alex	Bestwina	(555) 309-8493	$25.00
10	4	Timothy	West	(555) 490-3039	$0.00
11	3	Mary	Fulton	(555) 930-9831	$10.00
12	7	Dorothy	Kaminski	(555) 909-3231	$5.00

8 Create a query that combines data from the Special Events and Participants table. Name the query **Participants in Events Query**. Include the Event Description and Price fields from the Special Events table. Include the First Name, Last Name, and Payment fields from the Participants table. Sort the results in alphabetical order by the Event Description field. Print the results.

9 Create a query that combines data from the Special Events and Participants table. Name the query **Participants in Dancing Query**. Include the First Name, Last Name, and Payment fields from the Participants table. Include the Event Description field from the Special Events table. Display records in which the Event Description field ends with the word *dancing*. Sort the results in ascending order by the Event Description field. Print the results.

10 Create a report called **Special Events Report**. Include the Event Description, Event Date, Event Time, and Price fields for all the events in the Special Events table. Sort the results in ascending order by Event Description. Print the report.

11 Close the database.

12 Exit Microsoft Access 2010.

Integrate Projects Using Microsoft Office 2010 Applications

10

Chapter Objectives

After completing this chapter, you will be able to do the following:

- Embed data and objects between applications.
- Link data and objects between applications.

A benefit of using the Microsoft Office 2010 applications is that the data from one application can be used in other applications. The Microsoft Office 2010 applications use Object Linking and Embedding (OLE) technology to share data between applications. In this chapter, you will learn how to embed and link data from one application to another.

Embed an Object

Embed: Copy an object from one application to another.

Source file: The file that contains the object to be embedded.

Destination file: The file in which you are embedding the object.

An object can be embedded, or copied, from one application to another. An object is any element in an application such as text, clip art, pictures, tables, charts, and other content. You can embed objects using the Copy and Paste commands in the Clipboard group on the Home tab. The file that contains the object to be embedded is called the source file. The file in which you are embedding the object is called the destination file. If you change the data in the source file, the data in the destination file do not change.

Use the following steps to embed an object:

- Select the **object** you want to embed.
- Click the **Copy** button in the Clipboard group on the Home tab (**Figure 10.1**).
- Navigate to the location in the destination file where you want to embed the object.
- Click the **Paste** button in the Clipboard group on the Home tab (**Figure 10.2**).
  - If you click the Paste arrow, more options for pasting the object appear.
- The Paste Options button displays next to the pasted object and provides you with special options that you can select (**Figure 10.3**). Click the **Paste Options** button to select additional options. The most common Paste Options are listed in **Table 10.1**.

You can also use the shortcut keys or shortcut menu to access the Copy and Paste commands as shown in **Table 10.2**.

Table 10.1 Paste Options

Paste Option	Description
Keep Source Formatting	Pastes the object and retains the formatting of the copied object.
Match Destination Formatting	Pastes the object but uses the formatting of the destination file.
Keep Text Only	Pastes the text only. Removes all formatting and nontext elements from the copied object.

Table 10.2 Keyboard Shortcuts for Copy and Paste Commands

Command	Keyboard Shortcuts
Copy	Ctrl + C
Paste	Ctrl + V

Hands-On Exercise: Embed Objects from Microsoft PowerPoint 2010 to Microsoft Word 2010

You will open the Microsoft PowerPoint 2010 presentation named *Tripoli Distributions Logo*. You will also open the Microsoft Word 2010 document named *Memo VP Sales*. You will embed the logo and the organization chart from the presentation in Microsoft PowerPoint 2010 to the document in Microsoft Word 2010. Both of these files are student data files provided with the textbook. Before beginning this exercise, you need to download the data files. The instructions for downloading the student data files are given in the preface.

1. Open the Memo VP Sales document in Microsoft Word 2010.

2. Open the Tripoli Distributions Logo presentation in Microsoft PowerPoint 2010. The Microsoft Word 2010 and Microsoft PowerPoint 2010 icons display on the taskbar (Figure 10.1).

3. Click the logo at the top of Slide 1 of the presentation to select it (Figure 10.1).

4. Click the Copy button in the Clipboard group on the Home tab (Figure 10.1).

5. Click the Microsoft Word icon in the taskbar to navigate to the Memo VP Sales document (Figure 10.1).

6. The insertion point should be located at the top of the document. If not, press Ctrl + Home to navigate to the top of the document.

7. Click the Paste button in the Clipboard group on the Home tab (Figure 10.2).

8. The logo is embedded into the document. The Paste Option button displays to the right of the pasted logo (Figure 10.3). Click the logo to select it.

9. Click the Align Text Right button (Figure 10.3).

10. You will insert the organization chart on Slide 2 of the presentation at the end of the document. Click the Microsoft PowerPoint icon in the taskbar to navigate to the Tripoli Distributions Logo presentation.

11. Navigate to Slide 2.

12. Click the organization chart to select it (**Figure 10.4**). Be certain to select the entire organization chart. A double border displays around the organization chart when selected.

13. Click the Copy button.

14. Click the Microsoft Word icon in the taskbar to navigate to the Memo VP Sales document.

15. Press Ctrl + End to navigate to the end of the document.

16. Click the Paste button. The document should resemble **Figure 10.5**.

17. You will insert the CEO's information on Slide 1 of the presentation at the end of the document. Click the Microsoft PowerPoint icon in the taskbar to navigate to the Tripoli Distributions Logo presentation.

18. Navigate to Slide 1.

19. Select the three bullets (**Figure 10.6**).

→

20. Click the Copy button.

21. Click the Microsoft Word icon in the taskbar to navigate to the Memo VP Sales document.

22. Press Enter to navigate to the next line in the document below the organization chart.

23. Click the Paste arrow (**Figure 10.7**).

24. Click Keep Text Only (Figure 10.7).

25. The document should resemble **Figure 10.8**. The Paste Options button displays to the right of the pasted text (Figure 10.8). Click the Paste Options button. Point to the various options to preview the effects to the pasted text. If you point to the first option called *Use Destination Theme*, it formats the text as it is formatted in Microsoft PowerPoint 2010. After previewing all the options, click the Keep Text Only option.

26. Click the File tab.

27. Click Save As .

28. Save the document as **Memo VP Sales Revised**.

29. Close both documents.

30. Exit Microsoft PowerPoint 2010. Microsoft Word 2010 should remain open.

Figure 10.1 Select Logo in the Presentation

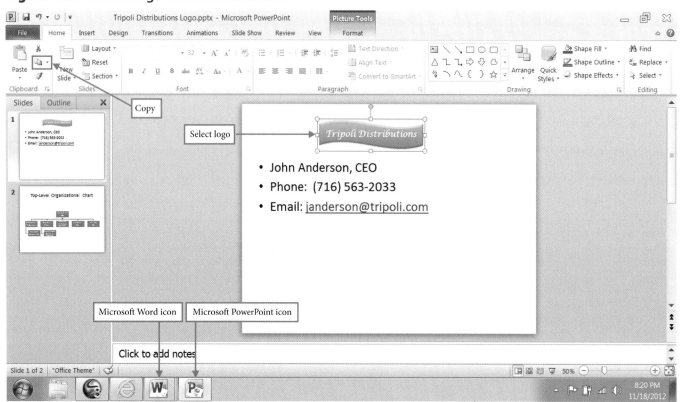

Figure 10.2 Paste Button

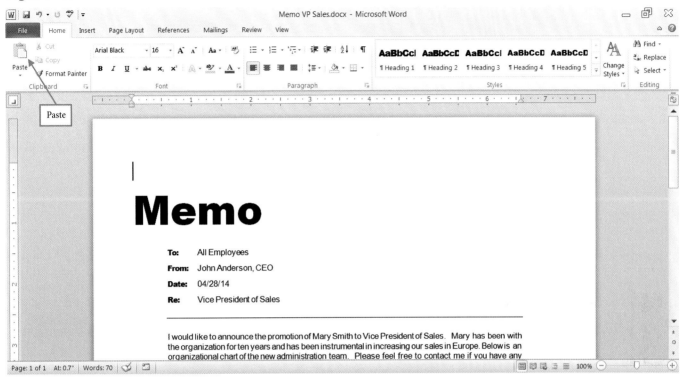

Figure 10.3 Logo Embedded into the Document

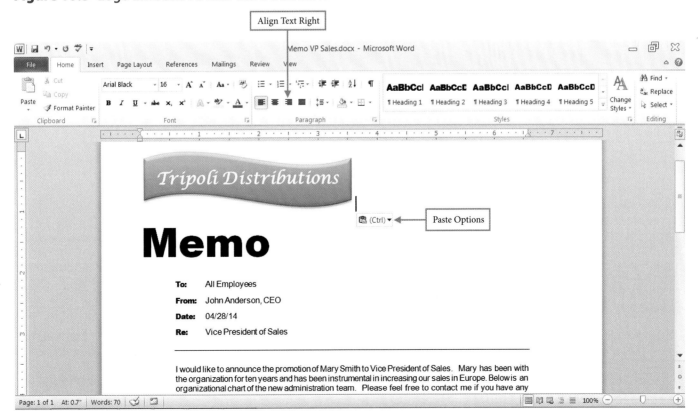

Figure 10.4 Organization Chart Selected

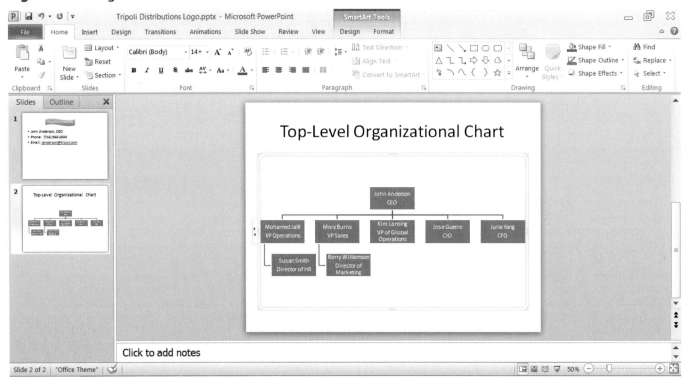

Figure 10.5 Organization Chart Embedded into the Document

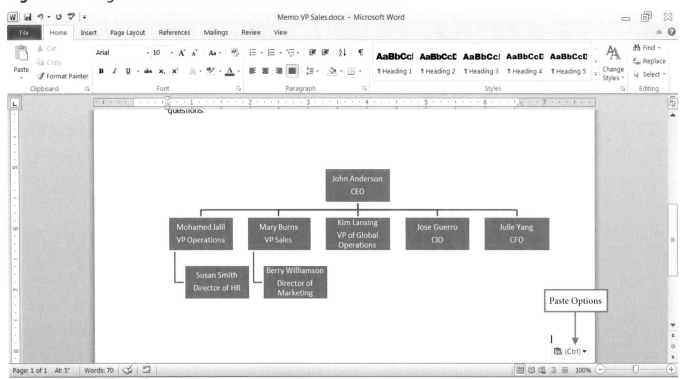

Figure 10.6 Select Bulleted List

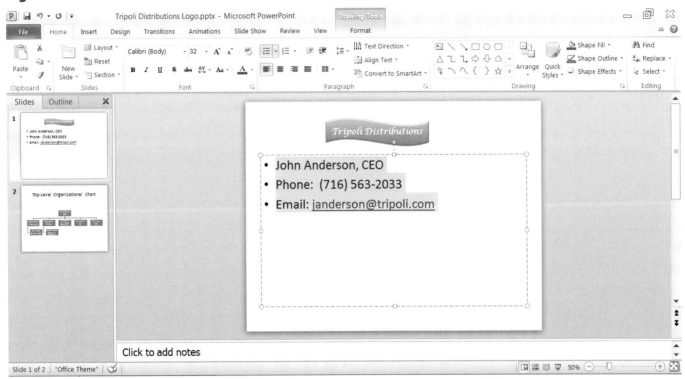

Figure 10.7 Keep Text Only Option

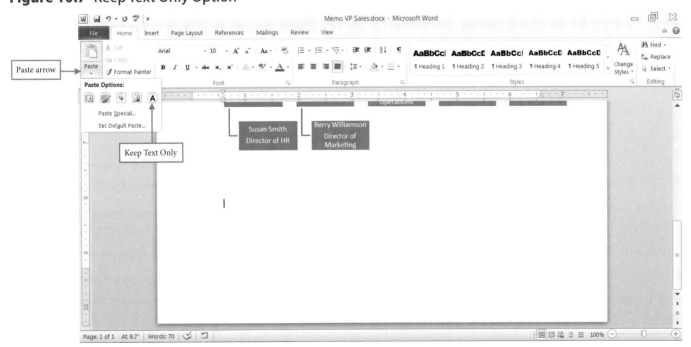

Figure 10.8 Text Embedded into the Document

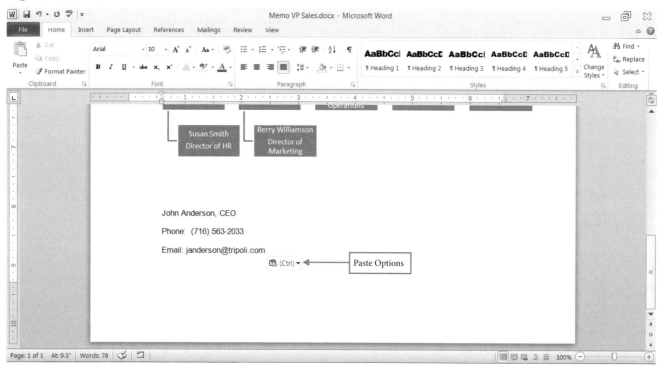

Link an Object

A Microsoft Excel 2010 worksheet can be embedded or linked to a Microsoft Word 2010 document. When you embed an object, you copy an object from one application (source file) to another (destination file). If you change the data in the source file, the data in the destination file do not change. Alternatively, when you link an object, you copy an object from one application (source file) to another (destination file) where the connection remains between the source and destination files. If the data change in the source file, the data also change in the destination file, as long as a connection exists between the two files. For example, if both the source and destination files are on the same computer or same network, a connection exists.

> **Link:** Copy an object from one application (source file) to another (destination file) where the connection remains between the source and destination files.

Hands-On Exercise: Open Files

DOWNLOAD ⬇

In the following exercise, you will link a Microsoft Excel 2010 worksheet with a Microsoft Word 2010 document. Before beginning this exercise, you need to download the student data files provided with the textbook. The instructions for downloading the student data files are given in the preface.

1. Open the Tripoli Distributors Memo document in Microsoft Word 2010. The document resembles **Figure 10.9**.

2. Open the Tripoli Distributors Sales Report workbook in Microsoft Excel 2010. The workbook contains two sheets. The first sheet is named *Sales Report* (**Figure 10.10**). The second sheet is named *Third Quarter Sales Chart* (**Figure 10.11**).

Figure 10.9 Tripoli Distributors Memo

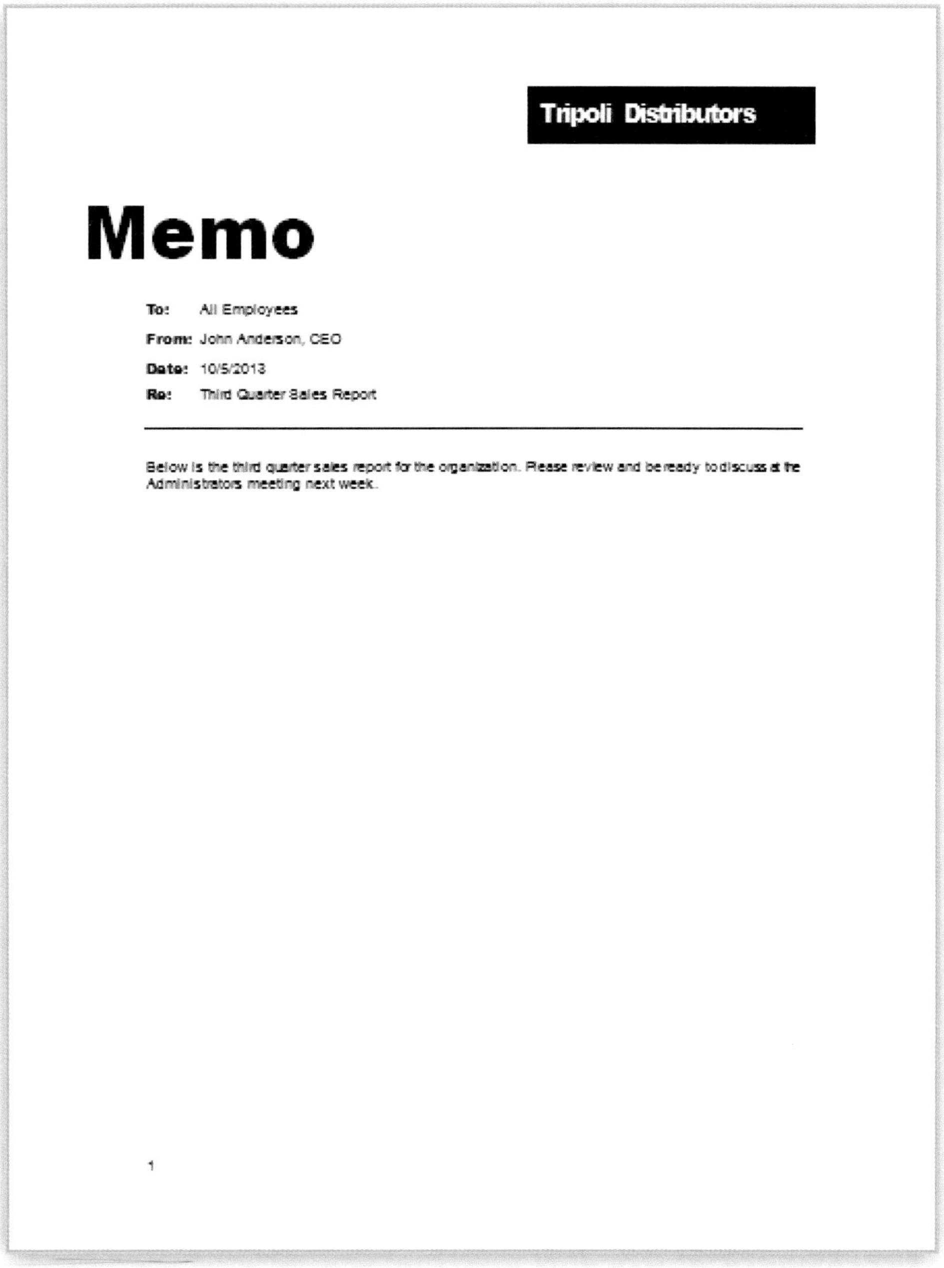

Tripoli Distributors

Memo

To: All Employees

From: John Anderson, CEO

Date: 10/5/2013

Re: Third Quarter Sales Report

Below is the third quarter sales report for the organization. Please review and be ready to discuss at the Administrators meeting next week.

1

Figure 10.10 Sales Report Sheet

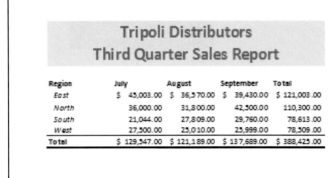

Figure 10.11 Third Quarter Sales Chart Sheet

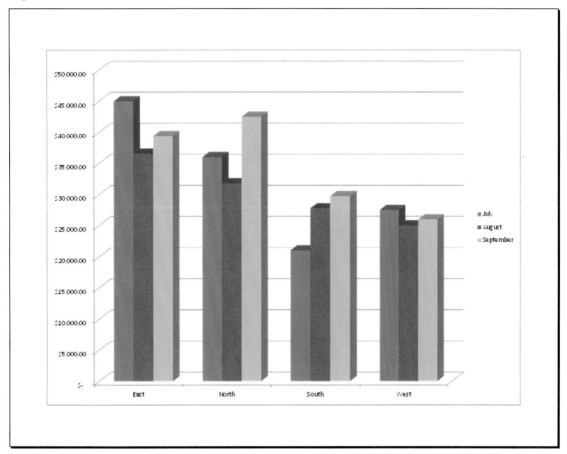

Link a Microsoft Excel 2010 Worksheet to a Microsoft Word 2010 Document

Use these steps to link data from a Microsoft Excel 2010 worksheet to a Microsoft Word 2010 document:

- Select the **data** that are to be linked in the source file (Microsoft Excel 2010).
- Click the **Copy** button in the Clipboard group on the Home tab (**Figure 10.12**).
- Click in the **location** in the destination file (Microsoft Word 2010) to which you want to link the data.
- Click the **Paste** arrow in the Clipboard group on the Home tab (**Figure 10.13**).
- Click **Paste Special** (Figure 10.13), and the Paste Special dialog box displays (**Figure 10.14**).
- Click the **Paste link** option (Figure 10.14).
- Click **Microsoft Excel Worksheet Object** in the As box (Figure 10.14).
- Click **OK**.

Hands-On Exercise: Link a Microsoft Excel 2010 Worksheet to a Microsoft Word 2010 Document

1. Select cells A1:E9 from the Sales Report sheet in the Tripoli Distributors Sales Report workbook.

2. Click the Copy button in the Clipboard group on the Home tab (Figure 10.12).

3. Navigate to the Tripoli Distributors Memo document.

4. Press Ctrl + End to navigate to the end of the document.

5. Click the Paste arrow in the Clipboard group on the Home tab (Figure 10.13).

6. Click Paste Special (Figure 10.13) and the Paste Special dialog box displays.

7. Click the Paste link option (Figure 10.14).

8. Click Microsoft Excel Worksheet Object in the As box (Figure 10.14).

9. Click OK . The worksheet displays in the document and is linked to the worksheet in Microsoft Excel 2010.

10. Click the File tab.

11. Click the Save As button.

12. Save the document as **Tripoli Distributors Memo Revised**. The Tripoli Distributors Memo should resemble **Figure 10.15**.

Figure 10.12 Select Data to Link

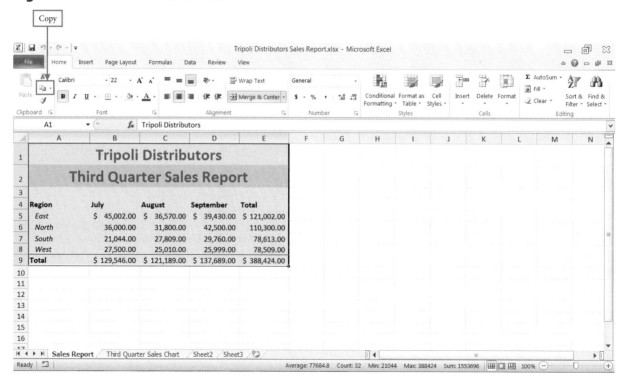

Figure 10.13 Paste Special Option

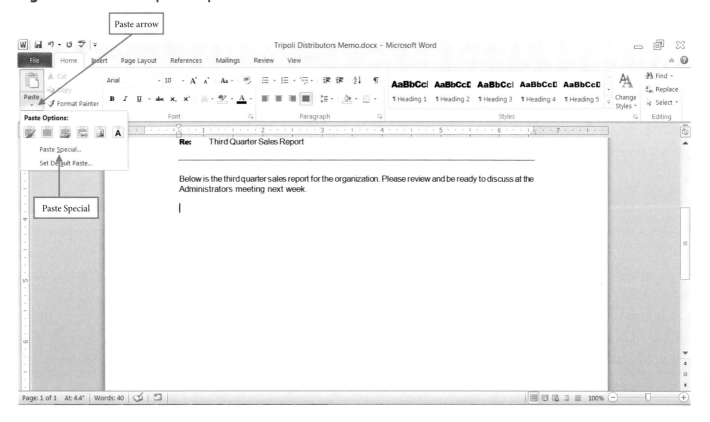

Figure 10.14 Paste Special Dialog Box

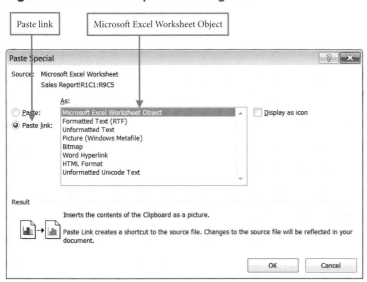

Figure 10.15 Tripoli Distributors Memo Revised

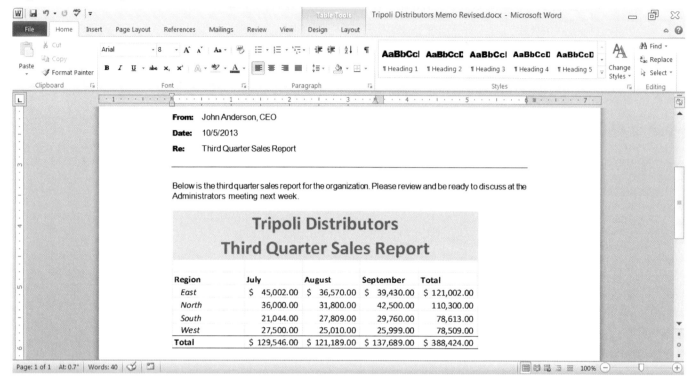

Update Data in the Source Document

When you update data in a source file, the data in the linked file are updated as long as there is a connection between the source and destination files.

Use the following steps to update data in the linked document:

- Make the changes to the source file.
- Navigate to the destination file.
- Right-click the **linked object**.
- Click **Update Link** (**Figure 10.16**).

Hands-On Exercise: Update Data in the Source Document

You will update a value in the Sales Report sheet and update the link in the Tripoli Distributors Memo Revised document.

1. Navigate to the Sales Report sheet in the Tripoli Distributors Sales Report workbook.

2. Press Esc to remove the blinking lines around the data that was copied.

3. Type **41003** in cell B5 and press Enter .

④ Click the Save button on the Quick Access Toolbar to save the workbook.

⑤ Navigate to the Tripoli Distributors Memo Revised document.

⑥ Right-click the linked worksheet .

⑦ Click Update Link on the shortcut menu (Figure 10.16). The sales amount for the East region for July changes to 41003.

⑧ Click the Save button on the Quick Access Toolbar. The document should resemble **Figure 10.17**.

⑨ Click the File tab.

⑩ Click Exit .

⑪ Navigate to the Tripoli Distributors Sales Report workbook.

⑫ Click the File tab.

⑬ Click Exit .

Figure 10.16 Update Link Command

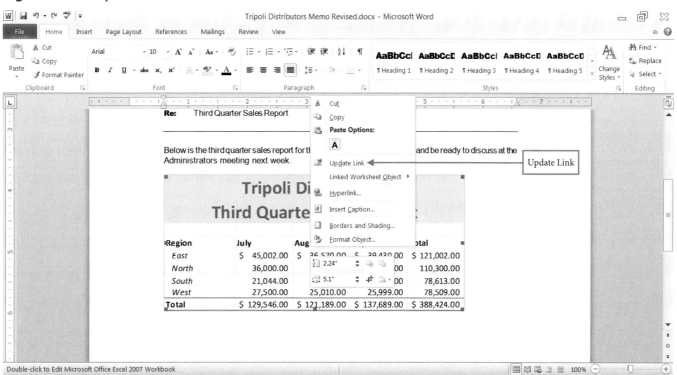

Figure 10.17 Data in the Linked Document Are Updated

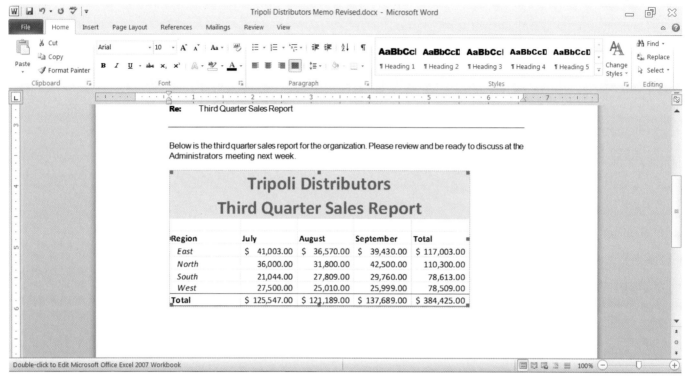

Export Data from Microsoft Access 2010 to Microsoft Excel 2010

Export feature: A feature in Microsoft Access 2010 that copies data from a table in Microsoft Access 2010 to another format, such as a workbook in Microsoft Excel 2010.

You can use the **export feature** in Microsoft Access 2010 to copy data from a table in Microsoft Access 2010 to another format, such as a workbook in Microsoft Excel 2010. When you export data from Microsoft Access 2010 to Microsoft Excel 2010, Microsoft Access 2010 creates a copy of the data and pastes it into a Microsoft Excel 2010 workbook.

Use these steps to export data from Microsoft Access 2010 to Microsoft Excel 2010:

- Click the **External Data** tab on the Ribbon in Microsoft Access 2010 (**Figure 10.18**).

- Click the **table** you want to export in the Navigation Pane.

- Click the **Excel** button in the Export group (**Figure 10.19**). The Export—Excel Spreadsheet dialog box displays (**Figure 10.20**).

- Answer the questions in the dialog box, and the export is completed.

Hands-On Exercise: Export Data from Microsoft Access 2010 to Microsoft Excel 2010

You will export the Customers table from the MK Consulting database into a workbook in Microsoft Excel 2010. The MK Consulting database is a student data file provided with the textbook. Before beginning this exercise, you need to download the data files. The instructions for downloading the student data files are given in the preface.

 DOWNLOAD

(1) Open the MK Consulting database in Microsoft Access 2010.

(2) Click Enable Content in the Message Bar if a Security Warning message displays on the screen (Figure 10.18).

(3) Click the External Data tab (Figure 10.18).

(4) Click the Customers table in the Navigation Pane (Figure 10.19).

(5) Click the Excel button in the Export group (Figure 10.19). The Export—Excel Spreadsheet dialog box displays.

(6) The File name box displays the name of the file that will be created in Microsoft Excel 2010 (Figure 10.20). By default it is named the same as the table name, which is *Customers*. It is automatically saved in the Documents library. You can change the location of the workbook by clicking the Browse button and selecting the location to save the workbook (Figure 10.20). *Excel Workbook* displays in the File format box, indicating that the file will be exported to a Microsoft Excel workbook.

(7) Click the Export data with formatting and layout checkbox (Figure 10.20). This option will export the formatting of the data as well as the actual data in the table.

(8) Click the Open the destination file after the export operation is complete checkbox (Figure 10.20). This will open the Microsoft Excel 2010 workbook when the export is completed.

(9) Click OK . The export is completed. The Customers workbook is created and contains the information from the Customers table (**Figure 10.21**).

(10) Click the File tab.

(11) Click the Exit button to exit the application.

(12) Navigate back to Microsoft Access 2010.

(13) The Export—Excel Spreadsheet dialog box asks if you want to save the export steps (**Figure 10.22**). You will not save the steps. Click Close .

(14) Click the File tab.

(15) Click Close Database .

Figure 10.18 External Data Tab

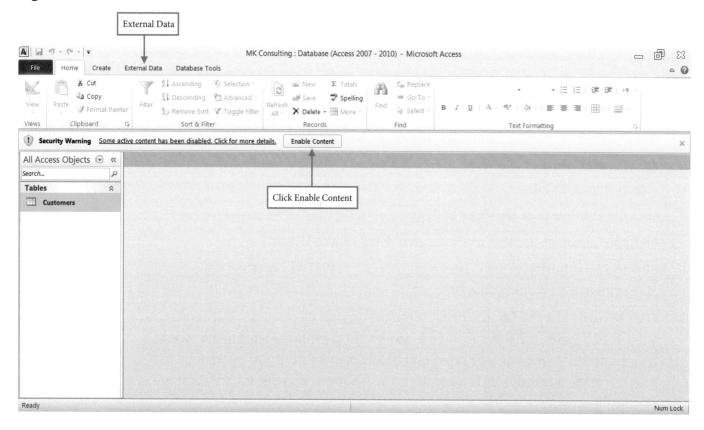

Figure 10.19 Export Customers Table to Microsoft Excel 2010

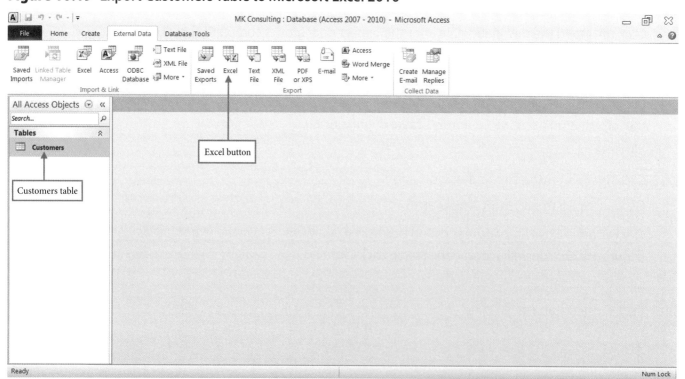

Figure 10.20 Export—Excel Spreadsheet Dialog Box

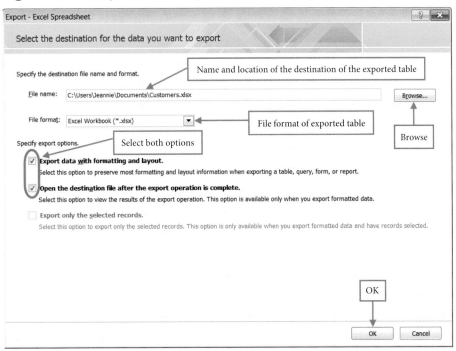

Figure 10.21 Customers Workbook Exported from Microsoft Access 2010

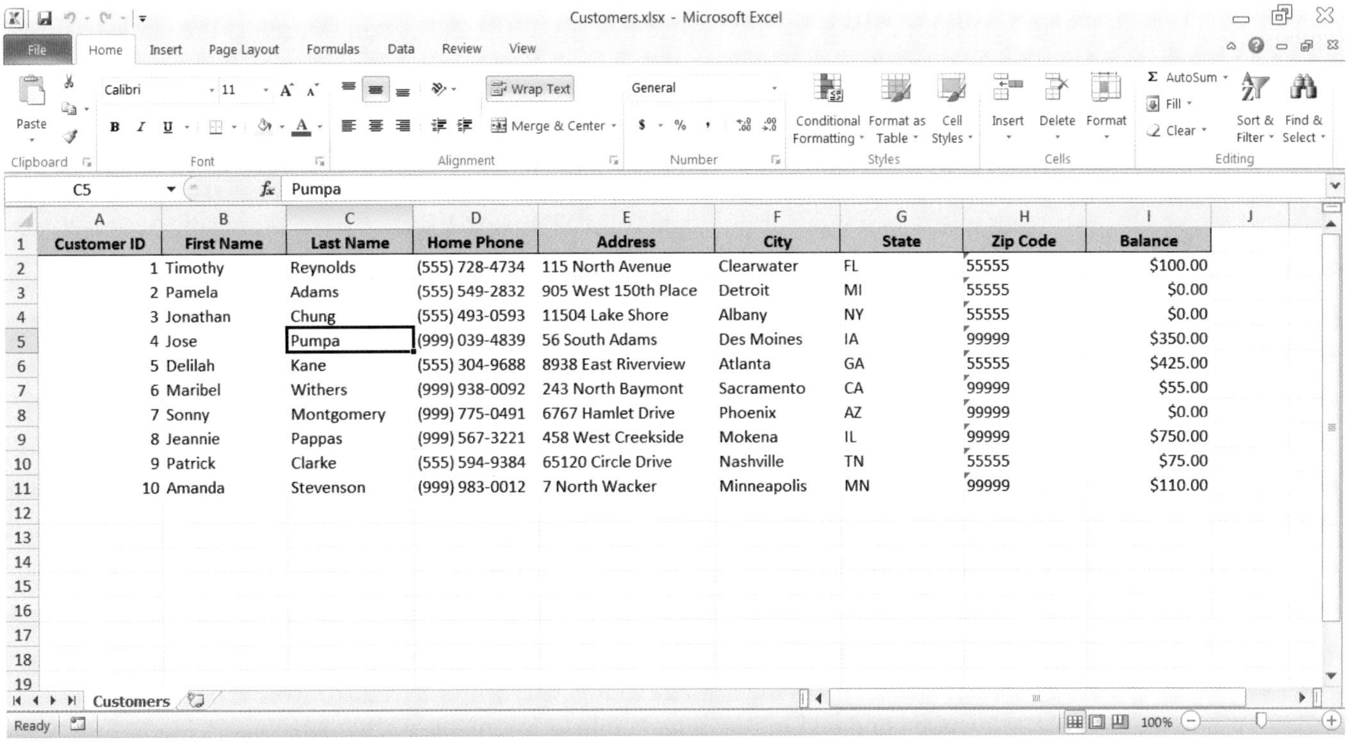

	Customer ID	First Name	Last Name	Home Phone	Address	City	State	Zip Code	Balance
2	1 Timothy		Reynolds	(555) 728-4734	115 North Avenue	Clearwater	FL	55555	$100.00
3	2 Pamela		Adams	(555) 549-2832	905 West 150th Place	Detroit	MI	55555	$0.00
4	3 Jonathan		Chung	(555) 493-0593	11504 Lake Shore	Albany	NY	55555	$0.00
5	4 Jose		Pumpa	(999) 039-4839	56 South Adams	Des Moines	IA	99999	$350.00
6	5 Delilah		Kane	(555) 304-9688	8938 East Riverview	Atlanta	GA	55555	$425.00
7	6 Maribel		Withers	(999) 938-0092	243 North Baymont	Sacramento	CA	99999	$55.00
8	7 Sonny		Montgomery	(999) 775-0491	6767 Hamlet Drive	Phoenix	AZ	99999	$0.00
9	8 Jeannie		Pappas	(999) 567-3221	458 West Creekside	Mokena	IL	99999	$750.00
10	9 Patrick		Clarke	(555) 594-9384	65120 Circle Drive	Nashville	TN	55555	$75.00
11	10 Amanda		Stevenson	(999) 983-0012	7 North Wacker	Minneapolis	MN	99999	$110.00

Figure 10.22 Save Export Steps

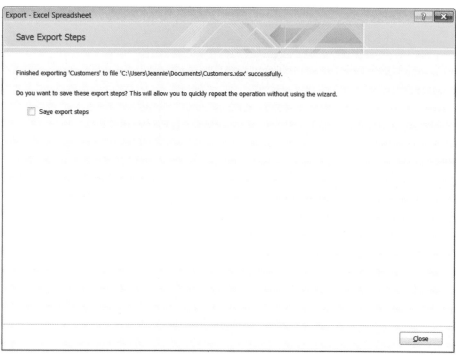

Import or Link Data from Microsoft Excel 2010 to Microsoft Access 2010

Import feature: A feature in Microsoft Access 2010 that copies data from an application to Microsoft Access 2010.

Microsoft Access 2010 has an **import feature** that copies data from an application to Microsoft Access 2010. You can import data from a worksheet in Microsoft Excel 2010 to a table in Microsoft Access 2010. Microsoft Access 2010 allows you to import the worksheet or link to the worksheet. If you import the worksheet to Microsoft Access 2010 and you update the worksheet in Microsoft Excel 2010, the changes will not be updated in the table in Microsoft Access 2010. However, if you link the worksheet, changes made to the Microsoft Excel 2010 worksheet will also be updated in the table in Microsoft Access 2010.

Use these steps to import or link data from Microsoft Excel 2010 to Microsoft Access 2010:

- Click the **External Data** tab on the Ribbon in Microsoft Access 2010 (**Figure 10.23**).
- Click the **Excel** button in the Import & Link group (Figure 10.23), and the Get External Data—Excel Spreadsheet dialog box displays.
- Click the **Browse** button to locate the source file in Microsoft Excel 2010 (**Figure 10.24**).
- You have two options (Figure 10.24):
  - Click the **Import the source data into a new table in current database** option.
    - This option will embed (copy) the data from Microsoft Excel 2010 to a table in Microsoft Access 2010.
  - Click the **Link to the data source by creating a linked table** option.
    - This option will link the data from Microsoft Excel 2010 to a table in Microsoft Access 2010. Changes made to the Microsoft Excel 2010 worksheet (source file) will be updated in the linked table in Microsoft Access 2010.

- Click **OK**. The Import Spreadsheet Wizard displays.
- Select the **worksheet** you want to import (**Figure 10.25**). The data display at the bottom of the dialog box. Click **Next**.
- The next screen asks if the first row contains column headings (**Figure 10.26**). If yes, click the **First Row Contains Column Headings** so that a checkmark displays. Click **Next**.
- The next screen asks if you want to change field options, such as the field name and data type (**Figure 10.27**). Click the **column heading**, and adjust the field options as needed. You can also modify the field settings from Microsoft Access 2010 once the table is created. Click **Next**.
- The next screen allows you to select the primary key of the table (**Figure 10.28**). Make your selection and click **Next**.
- The next screen asks you to name the table. The table name defaults to the sheet name of the Microsoft Excel 2010 workbook (**Figure 10.29**). Type the *table name* and click **Finish**.
- The next screen asks if you want to save the import steps (**Figure 10.30**). Click **Close**, and the table is created.

Hands-On Exercise: Import Data from Microsoft Excel 2010 to Microsoft Access 2010

You will import the data in the Student Grades workbook to a table in the Madison High School database. Both files are student data files provided with the textbook. Before beginning this exercise, you need to download the data files. The instructions for downloading the student data files are given in the preface.

1. Open the Madison High School database in Microsoft Access 2010.

2. Click Enable Content in the Message Bar if a Security Warning message displays on the screen.

3. Click the External Data tab on the Ribbon (Figure 10.23).

4. Click the Excel button in the Import & Link group (Figure 10.23), and the Get External Data—Excel Spreadsheet dialog box displays.

5. You will locate the source file in Microsoft Excel 2010. Click the Browse button and select the Student Grades workbook (Figure 10.24).

6. Click the Import the source data into a new table in current database option (Figure 10.24).

7. Click OK . The *Import Spreadsheet Wizard* displays.

8. You will select the worksheet you want to import. Click the BUS101 Student Grades sheet (Figure 10.25). The data in the worksheet display at the bottom of the dialog box. Click Next .

9. The next screen asks if the first row contains column headings (Figure 10.26). The worksheet contains column headings, so First Row Contains Column Headings should contain a check mark. If a check mark does not display, click the First Row Contains Column Headings checkbox. Click Next .

→

⑩ The next screen asks if you want to change field options, such as the field name and data type (Figure 10.27). You will not make any changes to the field properties. Click Next .

⑪ The next screen allows you to select the primary key of the table. Click the Choose my own primary key option.

⑫ Click the arrow and select Student ID from the list (Figure 10.28).

⑬ Click Next .

⑭ The next screen asks you to name the table. The table name defaults to the sheet name of the Microsoft Excel 2010 workbook (Figure 10.29). You will keep the default table name. Click Finish .

⑮ The next screen asks if you want to save the import steps (Figure 10.30). You will not be saving the steps. Click Close and the table is created.

⑯ Double-click the BUS101 Student Grades table in the Tables object in the Navigation pane to open the datasheet (**Figure 10.31**).

⑰ Click the Close button to the right of the BUS101 Student Grades table to close the datasheet.

Figure 10.23 **External Data Tab**

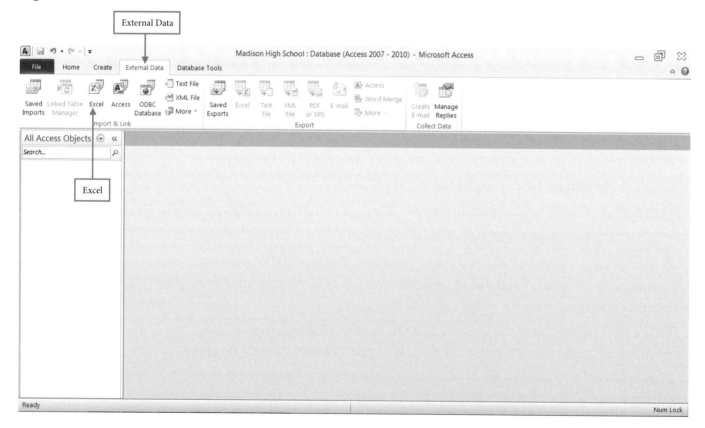

Figure 10.24 Select File to Import

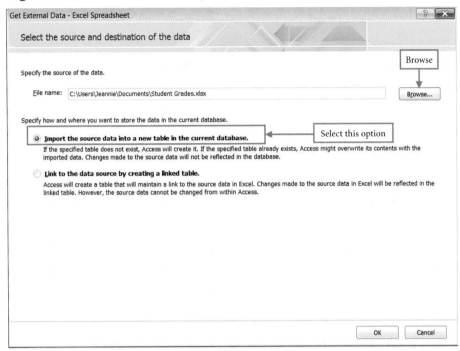

Figure 10.25 Select Worksheet to Import

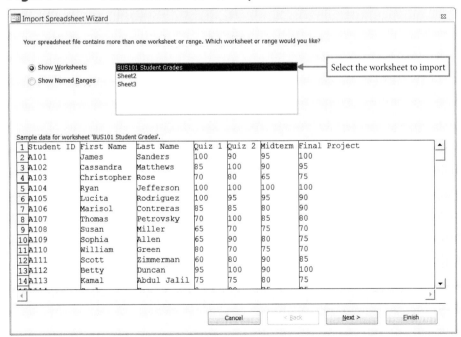

Figure 10.26 First Row Contains Column Headings Checkbox

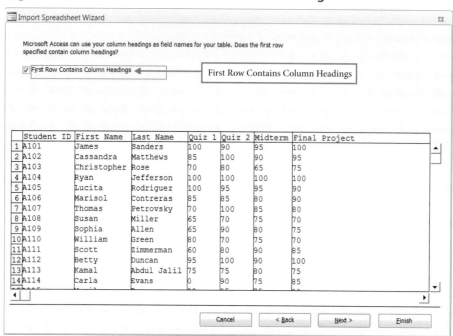

Figure 10.27 Set Field Options

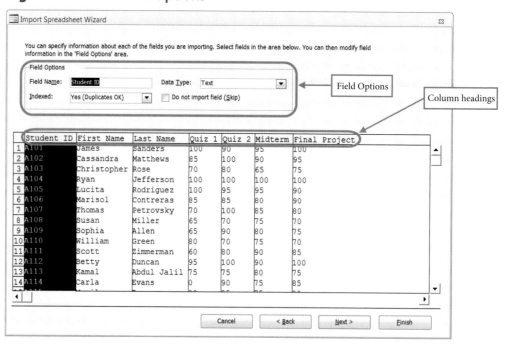

Figure 10.28 Select Primary Key Field

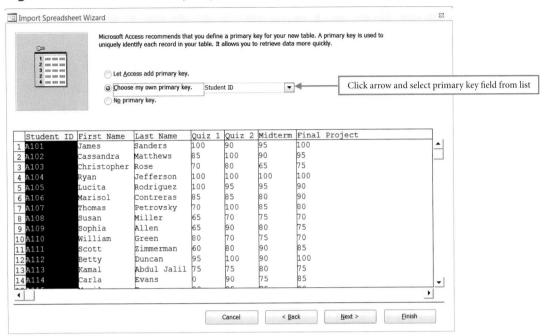

Figure 10.29 Name the Table

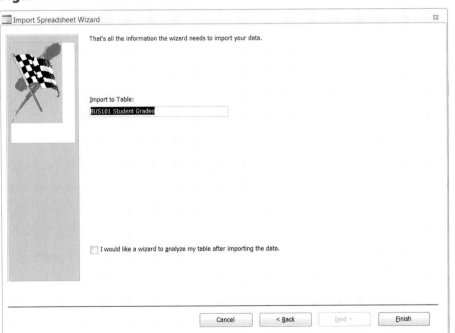

Figure 10.30 Save Import Steps

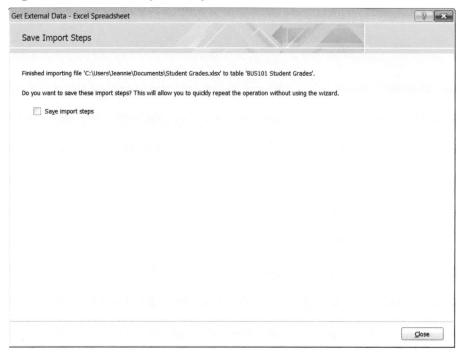

Figure 10.31 BUS101 Student Grades Table

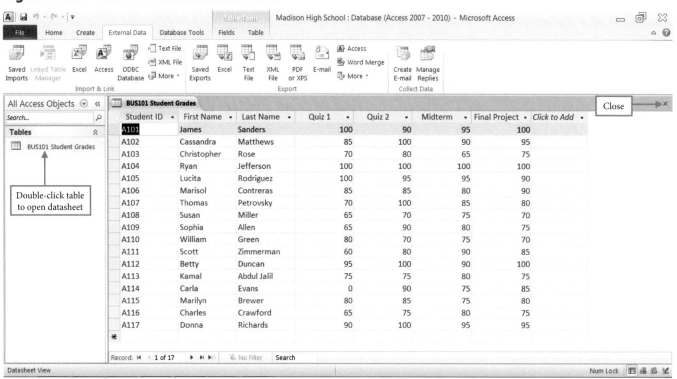

Copy Data from Microsoft Access 2010 to Microsoft Word 2010

You can copy data from a table in Microsoft Access 2010 to a document in Microsoft Word 2010.

Use these steps to copy data from Microsoft Access 2010 to Microsoft Word 2010:

- Select the **data** you want to copy from the table in Microsoft Access 2010.
- Click the **Copy** button in the Clipboard group on the Home tab.
- Navigate to Microsoft Word 2010.
- Click at the **location** where you want to embed the table.
- Click the **Paste** button in the Clipboard group on the Home tab.

This same process can be used to copy (embed) a table from Microsoft Access 2010 to the other Microsoft Office 2010 applications.

Hands-On Exercise: Copy Data from Microsoft Access 2010 to Microsoft Word 2010

You will copy the BU101 Student Grades table in the Madison High School database into a blank document in Microsoft Word 2010.

1. Open Microsoft Word 2010.
2. Navigate to the Madison High School database in Microsoft Access 2010.
3. Double-click the BU101 Student Grades table in the Tables object in the Navigation Pane to open the datasheet.
4. Click the Select All button to select all the data in the table (**Figure 10.32**).
5. Click the Copy button in the Clipboard group on the Home tab.
6. Navigate to Microsoft Word 2010.
7. Click at the top of the document.
8. Click the Paste button in the Clipboard group on the Home tab.
9. Click the Save button in the Quick Access Toolbar. Name the file **BUS101 Student Grades**. The document should resemble **Figure 10.33**.
10. Click the File tab.
11. Click Exit .
12. Navigate to the Madison High School database in Microsoft Access 2010.
13. Click the File tab.
14. Click Close Database . Click No if a dialog box displays asking you to save the data on the Clipboard.
15. Click Exit .

Figure 10.32 Select Table Data

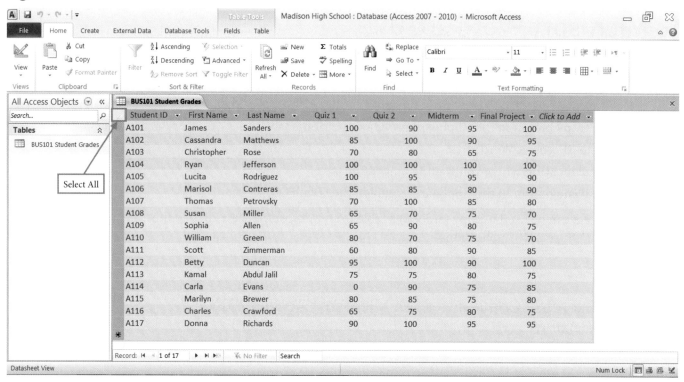

Figure 10.33 Microsoft Access 2010 Table Copied to a Microsoft Word 2010 Document

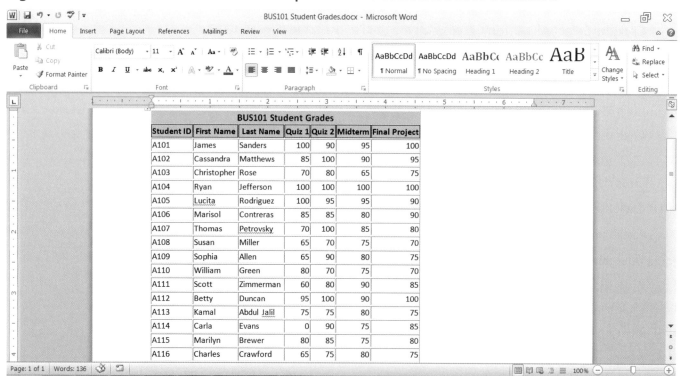

Multiple-Choice Questions

1. _____ technology can be used to share data between applications.
   a. Source file
   b. OLE
   c. Destination file
   d. External data

2. Which Paste Option will paste the object using the formatting of the destination file?
   a. Keep Source Formatting
   b. Match Destination Formatting
   c. Keep Text Only
   d. Merge Formatting

3. Press _____ to copy data.
   a. F5
   b. Ctrl + V
   c. Ctrl + C
   d. Alt + C

4. The Copy and Paste commands are located on the _____ tab.
   a. Create
   b. Insert
   c. View
   d. Home

5. To export data from Microsoft Access 2010 to Microsoft Excel 2010, use the _____ tab in Microsoft Access 2010.
   a. External Data
   b. Create
   c. Insert
   d. View

6. Press _____ to paste selected data.
   a. F5
   b. Ctrl + V
   c. Ctrl + C
   d. Alt + V

7. The file that contains the object to be embedded is called the _____.
   a. Destination file
   b. OLE
   c. Linked file
   d. Source file

8. The file where the object is being embedded to is called the _____.

   a. Destination file

   b. OLE

   c. Linked file

   d. Source file

9. If you _____ an object, it copies the object from one application to another. If a change is made to the data in the source file, the data in the destination file do not change.

   a. Link

   b. Select

   c. Embed

   d. Highlight

10. If you _____ an object, a connection remains between the source and destination files. If the data change in the source file, the data also change in the destination file.

   a. Link

   b. Select

   c. Embed

   d. Highlight

Project #1: Copy Objects from a Presentation in Microsoft PowerPoint 2010 to a Document in Microsoft Word 2010

You will copy a logo and table from a presentation and insert it into a document.

  Before beginning these projects, you need to download the data files. The instructions for downloading the student data files are given in the preface.

① Open the Electronics Galaxy Memo document in Microsoft Word 2010.

② Open the Electronics Galaxy Summer Specials presentation in Microsoft PowerPoint 2010.

③ Copy the Electronics Galaxy logo from Slide 1 of the presentation to the top of the Electronics Galaxy Memo document.

④ Copy the table from Slide 2 of the presentation to the bottom of the Electronics Galaxy Memo document.

⑤ Make the following changes to the table you embedded in the Electronics Galaxy Memo document.

   a. Apply the Light List—Accent 3 table style to the table.

   b. Center the table.

⑥ Embed the clip art image of a computer from Slide 1 of the Electronics Galaxy Summer Specials presentation at the bottom of the Electronics Galaxy Memo document.

⑦ Make the following changes to the clip art you embedded in the Electronics Galaxy Memo document:

   a. Set the Shape Height to 1.67.

   b. Set the Shape Width to 1.2.

   c. Apply the Relaxed Perspective, White picture style to the clip art image.

   d. Set the position of the clip art to Position in Bottom Center with Square Text Wrapping. The clip art image should be centered at the bottom of the first page.

⑧ Save the document as **Electronics Galaxy Memo Revised**.

⑨ Print the document. The document should resemble **Figure 10.34**.

⑩ Exit both applications.

Figure 10.34 Electronics Galaxy Memo Revised

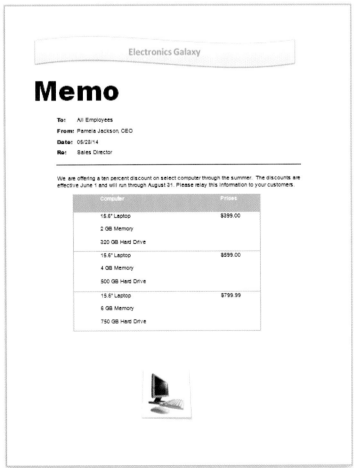

Project #2: Import a Worksheet from Microsoft Excel 2010 to a Table in Microsoft Access 2010

① Create a database called **Brighton University**.

② Import the Course Information workbook from Microsoft Excel 2010. The workbook resembles **Figure 10.35**.

    a. Import the Course Information sheet.

    b. The first row contains column headings.

    c. The primary key is the Course Number field.

③ Name the table **Course Information**.

④ Open the Course Information table.

⑤ Increase the size of the columns so all data and column headings display (**Figure 10.36**).

⑥ Print the datasheet.

⑦ Close the database.

⑧ Exit Microsoft Access 2010.

Figure 10.35 Course Information Workbook

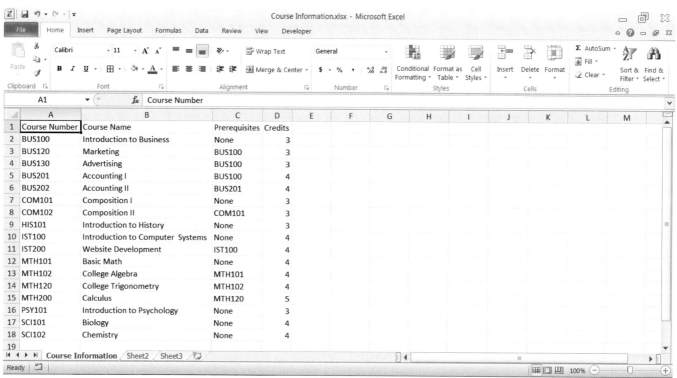

Figure 10.36 Course Information Table

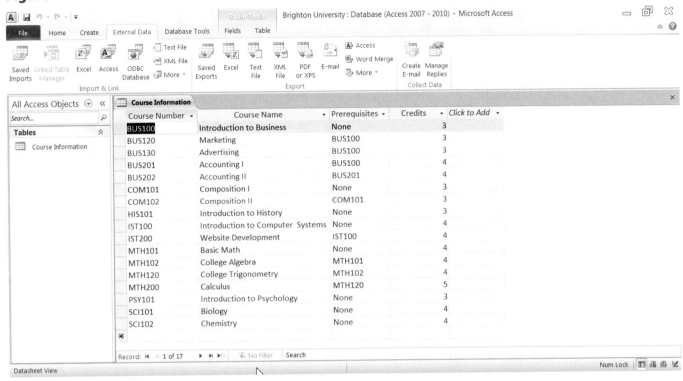

Project #3: Link a Microsoft Excel 2010 Worksheet to a Document in Microsoft Word 2010

① Open the Lemont University Course Information workbook (**Figure 10.37**).

② Create a new blank Microsoft Word document. Save the document as **Course Information for Lemont University**.

③ Type **Course Information for Lemont University** at the top of the document and press **Enter** twice.

④ Link cells **A2:D17** of the Course Information sheet of the Lemont University Course Information workbook to the Course Information for Lemont University document.

⑤ Center the embedded worksheet in the document.

⑥ Make the following changes to the heading at the top of the Course Information for Lemont University document:

   a. Center the text.

   b. Bold the text.

   c. Underline the text.

   d. Change the font to Times New Roman.

e. Change the font size to 18.

f. Change the font color to Light Blue.

⑦ Save the document.

⑧ Print the document. It should resemble **Figure 10.38**.

⑨ You will make changes to the Course Information sheet of the Lemont University Course Information workbook.

a. Change cell C12 to **MTH101**.

b. Change cell D11 to **5**.

c. Change cell D12 to **5**.

⑩ Save the workbook.

⑪ Navigate to the Course Information for Lemont University document.

⑫ Update the link in the document.

⑬ Insert a header with the text **Revised document** in the left section of the header.

⑭ Save the document as **Course Information for Lemont University Revised**.

⑮ Print the document. The document should resemble **Figure 10.39**.

⑯ Exit both applications.

Figure 10.37 Lemont University Course Information Workbook

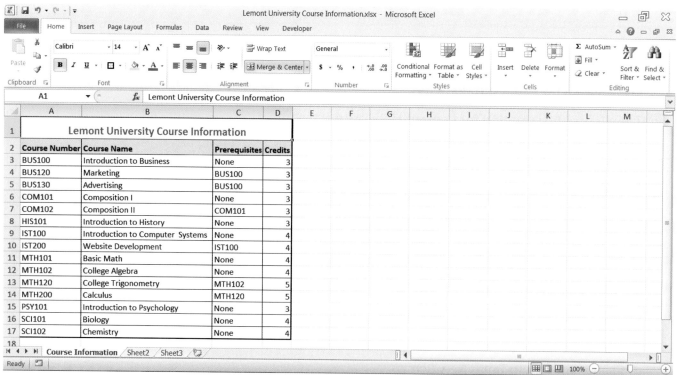

Figure 10.38 Course Information for Lemont University Document

Course Information for Lemont University

Course Number	Course Name	Prerequisites	Credits
BUS100	Introduction to Business	None	3
BUS120	Marketing	BUS100	3
BUS130	Advertising	BUS100	3
COM101	Composition I	None	3
COM102	Composition II	COM101	3
HIS101	Introduction to History	None	3
IST100	Introduction to Computer Systems	None	4
IST200	Website Development	IST100	4
MTH101	Basic Math	None	4
MTH102	College Algebra	None	4
MTH120	College Trigonometry	MTH102	5
MTH200	Calculus	MTH120	5
PSY101	Introduction to Psychology	None	3
SCI101	Biology	None	4
SCI102	Chemistry	None	4

Figure 10.39 Course Information for Lemont University Revised Document

Revised document

Course Information for Lemont University

Course Number	Course Name	Prerequisites	Credits
BUS100	Introduction to Business	None	3
BUS120	Marketing	BUS100	3
BUS130	Advertising	BUS100	3
COM101	Composition I	None	3
COM102	Composition II	COM101	3
HIS101	Introduction to History	None	3
IST100	Introduction to Computer Systems	None	4
IST200	Website Development	IST100	4
MTH101	Basic Math	None	5
MTH102	College Algebra	MTH101	5
MTH120	College Trigonometry	MTH102	5
MTH200	Calculus	MTH120	5
PSY101	Introduction to Psychology	None	3
SCI101	Biology	None	4
SCI102	Chemistry	None	4

Glossary

A

Absolute reference   A cell address that does not change when a formula is copied.

Active cell   The cell that has a black border around it. When you enter data in the worksheet, the data is placed in the active cell.

Animation effect   The movement of objects on a slide, which displays during a slide show.

Antonym   Words with opposite meanings.

Applications   Software programs that help users perform specific tasks.

Arguments   The values that a function uses to perform the calculations.

Attribute (field)   A single characteristic of a table.

AutoComplete   This feature automatically completes words that you are typing such as the days of the week and the months. Type the first four characters of the word and a ToolTip displays asking you if you want to insert the completed word.

AutoCorrect   This feature automatically checks commonly misspelled or mistyped words and corrects the word with a word from the main dictionary.

AutoFit Contents   A command that automatically adjusts the column widths in a table to fit the contents of the text in the cells.

AutoSum (Sum) command   A command that quickly calculates the total of selected cells. The command can also calculate averages, count values, and calculate the maximum and minimum values in a range of cells. The AutoSum command is located in the Editing group on the Home tab.

Average function   A function that calculates the average of the values in a range.

Axis   The vertical or horizontal line that identifies the information in the chart.

B

Backstage view   A view that displays when the File tab is selected. It contains commands to manage your files such as creating, opening, saving, and printing a file.

Bar chart   A chart that illustrates comparisons among individual items.

C

Cancel button   Clears the contents from the cell. The button is located on the Formula Bar and is available only if data is being entered or modified in a cell.

Caption   The label that displays for the field by default in the forms, reports, tables, and queries.

Cell   The intersection of a row and column.

Cell address (cell reference)   Indicates the location of the cell in the worksheet. The cell address is the column letter followed by the row number of the cell.

Cell Styles   A command that quickly formats a cell by selecting one of the predefined styles in the gallery.

Chart title   The title for the chart.

Clip art   A multimedia item such as an illustration, photograph, video, or audio clip that can be inserted into a file.

Clipboard   Holds up to 24 items that have been cut or copied.

Close button   Closes a document.

Column boundary   The vertical line that separates the columns in a table.

Column chart   A chart that illustrates how data change over a period of time.

Column headings   Identify the columns in the worksheet.

Command   A button or text that performs an action or task.

Common field   A field that appears in two tables and contains the same data.

Conditional formatting   A command that changes the formatting of a cell range when a specified condition is true.

Contextual tab   A tab that displays on the Ribbon when you create or select a particular object, such as a table. It contains commands that pertain to that object.

Copy   A command that copies selected text and objects and places it on the Clipboard.

Count function   A function that counts the total number of cells in a range, regardless of the type of data that is stored in the cells.

Crop   A command that is used to delete part of the image you do not want or need.

Customize Quick Access Toolbar   The last button on the Quick Access Toolbar, which allows you to customize the toolbar.

Cut   A command that removes selected text and objects from the document and places them on the Clipboard.

D

Database   A collection of related information about people, items, places, or events.

Data label   The actual value of an element on a chart.

Data points   The cells in a worksheet that you want to chart. The data points should include the row and column titles.

Data series   A group of related data points in a chart. Each data series contains a unique color or pattern that is displayed on the chart and in the legend.

Datasheet view   Resembles a grid that contains rows and columns.

Data type   Specifies the type of data that can be stored in a field.

Decimal Places property   A property used to specify the number of decimal places to display for the number in the field.

Decrease List Level button   A button that decreases the indent level of a paragraph.

Default A setting that is automatically set by the application.

Description Used to describe the field.

Design view A detailed view where the structure of the database object is defined and various settings are applied.

Destination file The file in which you are embedding the object.

Dialog box A window that allows a user to perform commands or apply settings.

Dialog box launcher A button that resembles a diagonal arrow, which appears to the right of the group names on the Ribbon.

Document window An area in the application in which you create and edit a document. The document window is located below the Ribbon.

Draft view A view used to edit and format text quickly. Some elements, such as headers and footers, page breaks, backgrounds, and some pictures, do not display in Draft view.

Duplicate Slide A command that makes a copy of a slide.

E

Embed Copy an object from one application to another.

Enforce Referential Integrity Rules that are enforced when creating relationship to ensure that valid field values are entered into the table that contains the foreign key.

Enter button Stores the data in a cell. The button is located on the Formula Bar and is available only if data is being entered or modified in a cell.

Exit command Exits (or quits) the application.

Export feature A feature in Microsoft Access 2010 that copies data from a table in Microsoft Access 2010 to another format, such as a workbook in Microsoft Excel 2010.

F

Field (attribute) A single characteristic of a table.

File-name extension A three- to five-letter suffix that identifies the application used to create the file. The file-name extension follows the file name and a dot.

Fill handle Used to copy or fill data to other cells. The fill handle is located at the lower-right corner of a cell and resembles a small black square.

Filter Locates specific data based on the criteria that are entered.

Filtering A quick method for locating specific data or data based on specific criteria.

Floating object An object that keeps its position relative to the page.

Font A character set of a single size and style of a typeface.

Footer Text that displays in the bottom margin of each page in a file.

Foreign key A field that links to a primary key field in a related table.

Form A database object used to add or modify records in a table. A form displays one record at a time.

Format as Table command A command that converts a range of cells to a table and allows you to select a pre-defined table format.

Format Painter A command that copies the formatting of selected text and applies that formatting to other text in the document.

Formula An equation that performs calculations on data.

Formula Bar A horizontal bar located below the Ribbon. It displays the contents of the active cell.

Form View A view that is used to add, modify, and delete records in a table.

Freeze Panes A command that allows certain rows and/or columns of a worksheet to be visible even while scrolling to other parts of a worksheet.

Function A predefined formula that can perform mathematical, financial, statistical, and other types of calculations.

G

Gallery A collection of visual options that display when the More button is clicked.

Graphical user interface (GUI) Allows the user to communicate and interact with the application through the use of graphical elements such as icons, buttons, and menus.

Grayscale A series of shades of black and white used to display the text and graphics in the presentation.

Group Buttons arranged by related tasks on the Ribbon. Group name displays at the bottom of the Ribbon.

H

Header Text that displays in the top margin of each page in a file.

Horizontal axis An axis on a chart that contains the category labels that describe the information in the chart. In a bar chart, the horizontal axis displays the numeric values of the categories.

Hover Refers to positioning the mouse on an object.

Hyperlink (link) An object that, when clicked, navigates to another location.

I

Import feature A feature in Microsoft Access 2010 that copies data from an application to Microsoft Access 2010.

Increase List Level button A button that increases the indent level of a paragraph.

Inline object An object that is inserted like text in a document and moves along with the text around it.

Input mask A pattern that controls how data are entered in the field.

Input Mask property A property used to select a pattern for a field that controls how the data are to be entered.

Insertion point The vertical blinking line in the application, which indicates where text is inserted when you type.

J

Join line   A line that displays between the tables indicating that there is a relationship between the two tables.

K

Keyboard shortcut   Keys you can use to access a command.

Key Tip   A shortcut for accessing the commands on the Ribbon and Quick Access Toolbar. The Key Tips are displayed when the Alt key is pressed.

L

Landscape orientation   A page orientation that prints on a horizontal page, which means that the page is wider than it is tall.

Layout view   A view used to format the contents and the layout of the form.

Legend   An area on a chart that defines the colors that are assigned to the data series in the chart.

Line chart   A chart that illustrates continuous data over a period of time, best suited for showing trends in the data.

Link   Copy an object from one application (source file) to another (destination file) where the connection remains between the source and destination files.

M

Many-to-one relationship   A relationship between two tables in which many records in one table are related to one record in another table.

Max function   A function that calculates the largest value in a range.

Maximize button   Enlarges a window to fill up the entire screen.

Merge cells   A command that combines two or more cells in a table into one cell.

Microsoft Access 2010   Application used to create databases to track and report information.

Microsoft Excel 2010   Application used to create spreadsheets that consist primarily of numbers that can be manipulated to help make decisions. Charts can be created based on the data in the spreadsheet.

Microsoft PowerPoint 2010   An application used to create presentations that are shared with an audience in the form of a slide show.

Microsoft Word 2010   Application used to create professional-looking documents that consist primarily of text and graphics.

Min function   A function that calculates the smallest value in a range.

Minimize button   Collapses a window to an icon on the taskbar.

Mini Toolbar   Contains formatting commands that can be applied to the selected text. The Mini Toolbar displays at the top right of the selected text and appears faded or dimmed.

Mixed reference   A cell address where part of the cell address changes when the formula is copied.

N

Name Box   The area on the Formula Bar that contains the cell address of the active cell.

Navigation Pane   A pane that organizes the database objects by category. The Navigation Pane is located on the left side of the application window below the Ribbon.

Normal view   A view that allows the user to enter text and graphics directly on the slide. Normal view has four working areas: Slide pane, Notes pane, Slides tab, and Outline tab.

Notes pane   An area in Normal view used to add speaker notes for each slide. The Notes pane is located under the Slide pane.

Numerical Count function   A function that counts the number of cells that contain values in a range.

O

Object   An item that can be inserted into a presentation such as a table, image (clip art, picture), illustration, WordArt, text box, placeholder, and media elements.

One-to-many relationship   A relationship between two tables in which one record in one table is related to many records in another table.

Outline tab   A tab in Normal view that displays the text on each slide in an outline format. Graphics and multimedia elements are not displayed in the Outline tab.

P

Page break   A command that inserts a new page at the location of the insertion point.

Page margins   The blank spaces at the top, bottom, and left and right sides of the document between the text and the edge of the paper.

Paste   A command that allows you to paste items from the Clipboard.

Pie chart   A chart that illustrates the relationship of items in a data series and compares the size of each item to the whole data series.

Placeholder (Microsoft PowerPoint)   A box with a dotted border that allows you to insert text or objects such as charts, tables, and pictures.

Placeholders (Microsoft Word)   Indicate where you need to supply information. Commonly found in templates and display in brackets or appear as bold text.

Portrait orientation   A page orientation that prints on a vertical page, which means that the page is taller than it is wide.

Primary key   A unique field or groups of fields that identify a particular record.

Print Layout view   A view that depicts how the document will look when the document is printed.

Programs   Software applications that help users perform specific tasks.

Q

Query   A database object that can answer a question about the data and displays the results in a datasheet.

Query designer   The top pane of the query window that contains the table(s) used in the query.

Query design grid   The bottom pane of the query window that contains the fields that will display in the query along with the sorting and criteria options.

Query Wizard   A wizard that guides the user in creating a query. The query wizard asks a few questions about the query to be created and then it creates the query based on the responses.

Quick Access Toolbar   A toolbar that provides quick access to the most frequently used commands. By default, it is located in the left-hand corner of the title bar.

R

Range   Two or more adjacent cells in a worksheet. A range is identified by the starting cell, followed by a colon, followed by the ending cell.

Record   A collection of field values in a table.

Record Navigation buttons   Buttons that are used to navigate through the records in a table or form.

Record selector   The small box to the left of a record in a datasheet.

Redo button   Redoes an action that was undone.

Relationship   Combines data from two tables that have a common field.

Relationship line   A line that displays between the tables indicating that there is a relationship between the two tables.

Relative reference   A cell address that changes the row or column in the formula based on the location in which the formula is being copied.

Reorder slides   Move a slide from one location in the presentation to another.

Repeat button   Repeats the last action performed.

Report   A database object that can list information from tables and queries. A report can be viewed on the screen or can be printed.

Restore Down button   Changes a window to its original size.

Ribbon   Contains all the commands a user needs to create and edit a file. The Ribbon is located below the title bar and contains tabs that are organized by groups of related commands.

Row boundary   The horizontal line that separates the rows in a table.

Row headings   Identify the rows in the worksheet. The row headings are numbered sequentially and start with row 1.

Ruler   Used to align objects in a presentation.

Ruler bar   Used to align text, graphics, and other elements in a document. The *horizontal ruler* displays below the Ribbon, and the *vertical ruler* displays to the left of the document window.

S

Save As command   Saves the file with a new file name, type, or location.

Save command   Saves the file with the current settings.

Screenshot   A command used to capture a snapshot (take a picture) of an open window.

Scroll bar   A tool that allows you to navigate either up and down or left and right to view the information in the application window.

Select   A command that is used to select a table, row, or column.

Select query   A query that is created to retrieve data from tables.

Series   A list of text, values, dates, or times that contain a pattern such as the months of the year, days of the week, or numbers in a sequence.

Shading   A command that colors the background of selected text.

Sheet   A page in a workbook.

Shortcut menu   A menu that displays when the user right-clicks an object or area of the window. It contains a list of commands related to the object.

Show/Hide button   A command that displays paragraph marks and other hidden formatting symbols in the document.

Slide layout   A layout that contains a variety of formatting, positioning, and placeholder options for the content that displays on a slide.

Slide pane   An area in Normal view where the presentation is created and edited. The Slide pane displays one slide at a time.

Slide show   A display of the entire presentation to the audience, one slide at a time.

Slides tab   A tab in Normal view that displays a thumbnail (miniature picture) of the slides.

Slide transition   A motion effect that is applied when you navigate to another slide in a presentation.

SmartArt   A graphic that enables you to visually display and communicate information. SmartArt graphics can display graphical lists, processes, and various diagrams.

Sorting   Rearranges data in a certain order.

Source file   The file that contains the object to be embedded.

Spelling & Grammar   A command that checks the entire document at once for errors and displays the errors in a dialog box.

Split cells   A command that splits the selected cells into multiple new cells.

Start button   A button located at the bottom-left corner of the desktop that opens the Start menu.

Start menu   Displays a list of commonly used programs installed on the computer.

Status bar   Provides information about the status of a file. The status bar is located at the bottom of the application window.

Style   A set of formatting characteristics, such as font, size, color, paragraph spacing, and alignment.

Subdatasheet   An embedded datasheet that displays data from tables that are related.

Sum (AutoSum) command   A command that quickly calculates the total of selected cells. The command can also calculate averages, count values, and calculate the maximum and minimum values in a range of cells. The Sum command is located in the Editing group on the Home tab.

Sum function   A function that calculates the total of the values in a range.

Symbol   A special character that does not appear on the keyboard.

Synonym   Words with the same meaning.

T

Tab   Located on the Ribbon and contains a set of commands related to specific tasks.

Table   Displays information that is organized by rows and columns.

Table (Microsoft Access)   A database object that is used to store data about a particular subject such as customers, employees, or products.

Table move handle   Displays at the top left corner of the table and is used to select and/or move the table.

Tabs   Align text to a specific place in the document.

Tab Selector   Located to the far left of the horizontal ruler and used to select various tabs.

Taskbar   A bar, usually located at the bottom of the desktop, which displays the icons of open applications.

Template   A prebuilt document that contains formatting and standard text that can be modified to fit your specifications.

Text Box   A command that inserts a box on a slide, in which you can add text.

Theme   A set of predefined colors, fonts, and backgrounds that help create professional-looking presentations.

Thesaurus   Used to find synonyms and antonyms of words.

Thumbnail   A miniature picture.

Title and content layout   A layout that allows the user to enter a title for the slide and insert content such as text or a table, chart, SmartArt graphic, picture, clip art, or media clip.

Title bar   Displays the name of the file that is currently open and the name of the application. The title bar is the top bar on the application window.

Title Slide   A slide that contains the title and subtitle for the presentation and is by default the first slide of a new presentation.

Toggle button   A button that switches back and forth to a different state when clicked.

ToolTip (ScreenTip)   Lists the name of the command and sometimes includes a brief description of the command. A ToolTip displays when the mouse points, or hovers, over a command. It may also display keyboard shortcuts that can be used to initiate the command using the keyboard.

U

Undo button   A command that will undo (or remove) the last action performed as well as previous actions. The Undo button is located on the Quick Access Toolbar and can be accessed by using the shortcut keys Ctrl + Z.

V

Vertical axis   An axis on a chart that contains the numeric values that represent the categories. In a bar chart, the vertical axis displays the category labels.

View buttons   Provide options for viewing a file. The View buttons are located on the right side of the status bar.

W

Wildcard   A character that is used in queries to represent a character or groups of characters.

Wizard   Asks a few questions about the database object, and then it creates the object based on the responses.

WordArt   Decorative text, such as shadowed or mirrored text, that can be inserted into a file.

Word wrap   As the user types a line of text and reaches the end of the line, the insertion point and text automatically wrap to the next line.

Workbook   Contains a collection of worksheets used to organize information.

Worksheet   A page in a workbook.

Wrap Text (Microsoft Excel)   A command that displays text on multiple lines within a cell.

Wrap Text (Microsoft Word)   A command that changes the way the text wraps around an object, such as a picture or clip art.

Z

Zoom controls   Allow the user to zoom in and out of specific areas in the file. This feature controls the magnification of the file. The Zoom controls are displayed on the right side of the status bar.

Index

Figures and tables are indicated by *f* and *t* following the page number.